MW01265465

Annotated Teacher's Edition

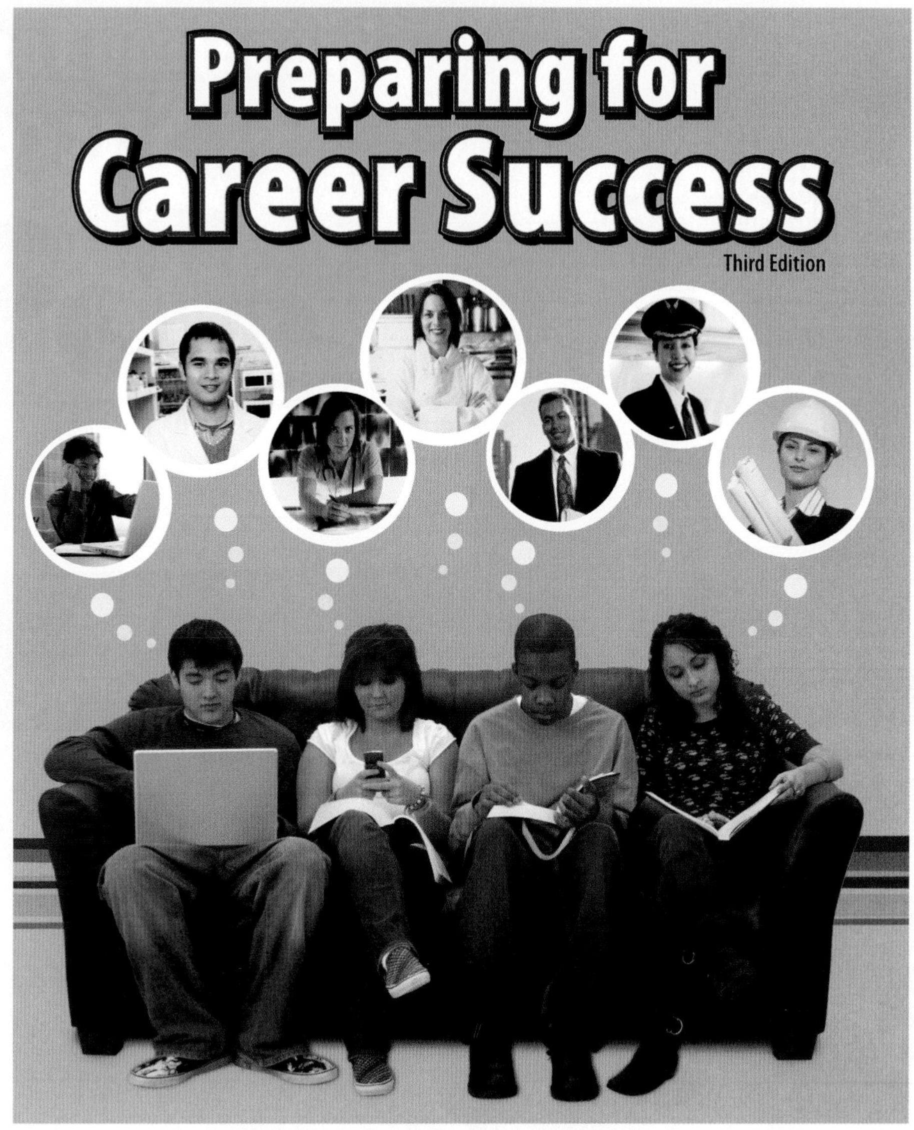

Preparing for Career Success

Third Edition

Jerry Ryan
Roberta Ryan

ADDITIONAL COMPONENTS IN THIS PACKAGE

Preparing for Career Success Student Interest Inventory helps students correlate their interests with career clusters.

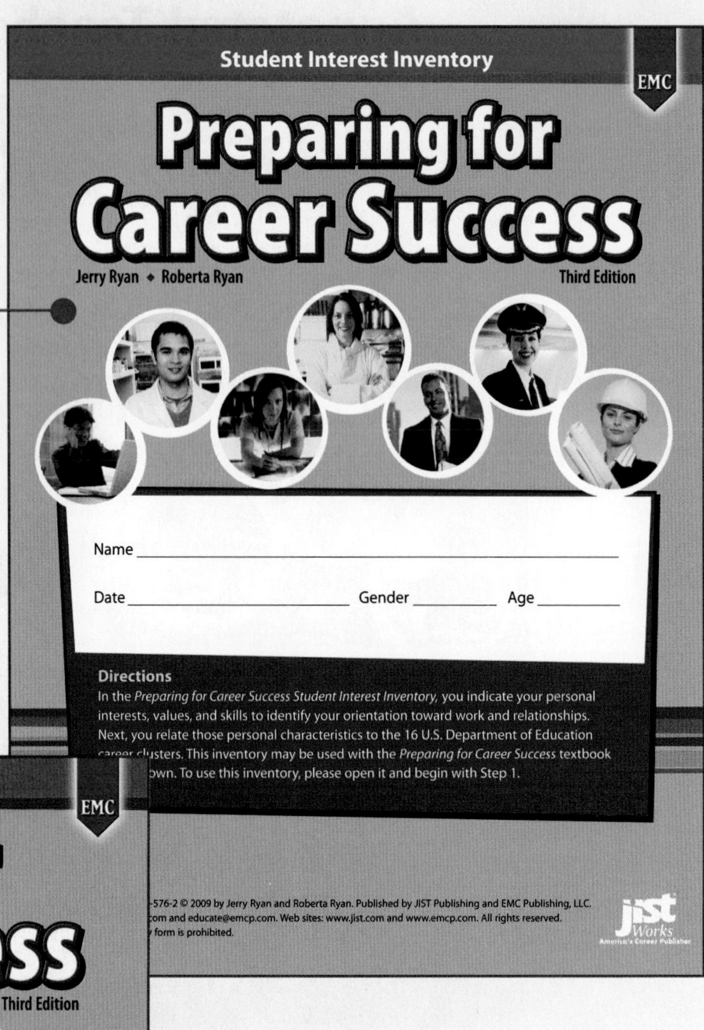

Student Activity Book
EMC
Preparing for Career Success
Jerry Ryan ◆ Roberta Ryan
Third Edition
jist Works
America's Career Publisher

Preparing for Career Success Student Activity Book, Third Edition, contains a set of true/false questions and unique supplementary worksheets for each chapter of the textbook.

Preparing for Career Success Interactive Lesson Planner Plus Instructor's Resources on CD-ROM contains PowerPoint presentations, extra activities, and software to help you create customized lesson plans.

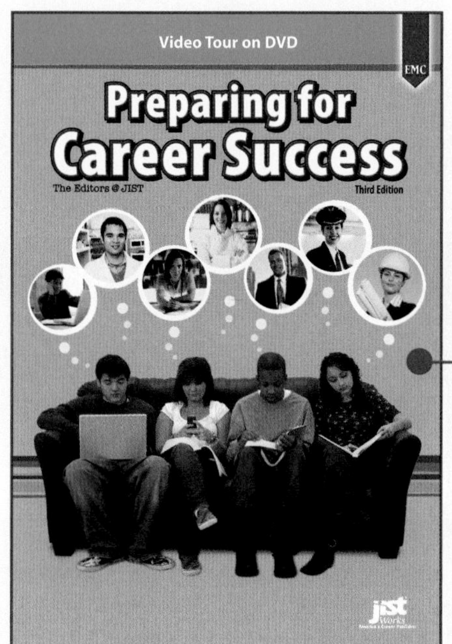

Preparing for Career Success Video Tour on DVD includes a short, engaging video introduction for each chapter in the textbook.

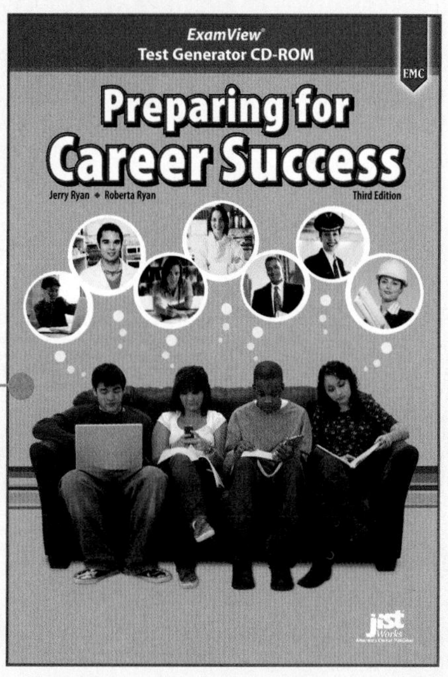

Preparing for Career Success ExamView© Test Generator CD-ROM, Third Edition, contains multiple-choice, fill-in-the-blank, matching, completion, short answer, essay, and case study questions. You can customize each chapter assessment to meet your criteria.

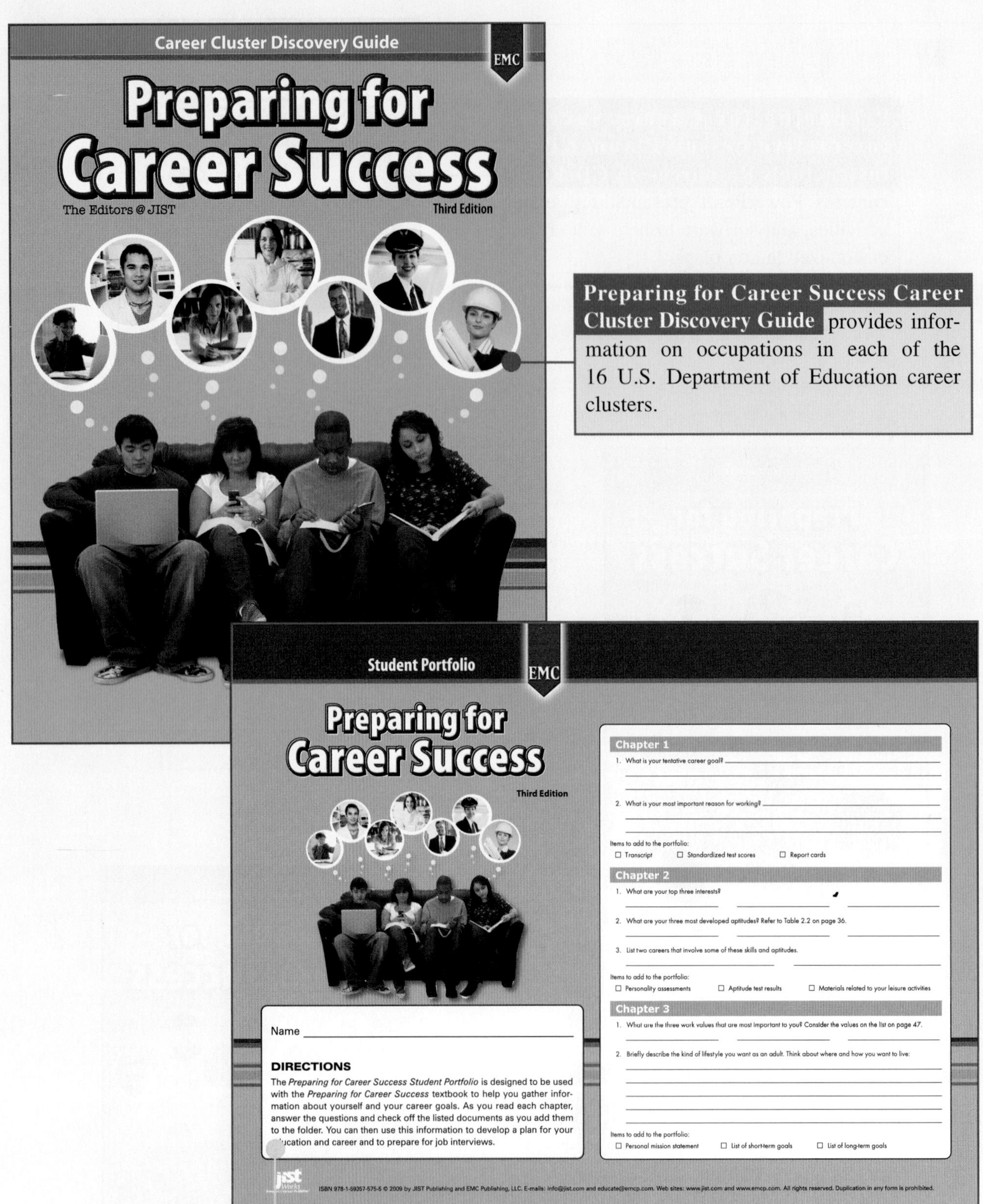

Career Cluster Discovery Guide
EMC
Preparing for Career Success
The Editors @ JIST
Third Edition
Student Portfolio
EMC
Preparing for Career Success
Third Edition
Name
DIRECTIONS
The Preparing for Career Success Student Portfolio is designed to be used with the Preparing for Career Success textbook to help you gather information about yourself and your career goals. As you read each chapter, answer the questions and check off the listed documents as you add them to the folder. You can then use this information to develop a plan for your education and career and to prepare for job interviews.
Chapter 1
1. What is your tentative career goal?
2. What is your most important reason for working?
Items to add to the portfolio:
☐ Transcript ☐ Standardized test scores ☐ Report cards
Chapter 2
1. What are your top three interests?
2. What are your three most developed aptitudes? Refer to Table 2.2 on page 36.
3. List two careers that involve some of these skills and aptitudes.
Items to add to the portfolio:
☐ Personality assessments ☐ Aptitude test results ☐ Materials related to your leisure activities
Chapter 3
1. What are the three work values that are most important to you? Consider the values on the list on page 47.
2. Briefly describe the kind of lifestyle you want as an adult. Think about where and how you want to live:
Items to add to the portfolio:
☐ Personal mission statement ☐ List of short-term goals ☐ List of long-term goals
jist Works
ISBN 978-1-59357-575-6 © 2009 by JIST Publishing and EMC Publishing, LLC. E-mails: info@jist.com and educate@emcp.com. Web sites: www.jist.com and www.emcp.com. All rights reserved. Duplication in any form is prohibited.

Preparing for Career Success Career Cluster Discovery Guide provides information on occupations in each of the 16 U.S. Department of Education career clusters.

Preparing for Career Success Student Portfolio follows the textbook chapter by chapter to help students create a career plan and keep track of portfolio documents.

 © JIST Works

Introduction to *Preparing for Career Success Annotated Teacher's Edition*

The student edition of *Preparing for Career Success, Third Edition,* was written to help students prepare for employment that makes use of their aptitudes, career interests, and skills and as a result become productive members of society and achieve personal fulfillment. This fully updated edition features

- Current information regarding employment trends, federal laws, and social issues affecting the workplace
- Thorough coverage of major career education topics, including assessing aptitudes, finding and applying for jobs, resolving workplace conflicts, and setting goals
- An interior design with high student appeal that includes engaging, updated color photographs, interesting sidebars, and informative tables and charts based on the latest government statistics

Whether you teach cooperative education, work experience, tech-prep, an abbreviated overview of career-oriented high-school course options, or a year-long career planning course, your students have similar career development needs. The *Preparing for Career Success* package helps you meet those needs with easy-to-access information. The teacher annotations in the margins of the *Preparing for Career Success Annotated Teacher's Edition* provide

- Background information to enhance the text content
- Questions to promote classroom discussion
- Activity suggestions
- Answers to the review questions at the end of each chapter
- References to materials on the *Instructor's CD-ROM* and *Student Activity Book* to make it easy to connect the textbook to the other components in the *Preparing for Career Success* package

Career courses offered throughout the nation vary greatly in length and purpose. The *Preparing for Career Success* package satisfies the curriculum needs for a full-year (36-week) course, but teachers of career-related courses with a specific focus or shorter time span can easily extract lesson plans, information, and student activities that correlate with their course objectives.

A Look Inside *Preparing for Career Success*

The Learning Objectives on the first page of each chapter are a list of expected learner outcomes.

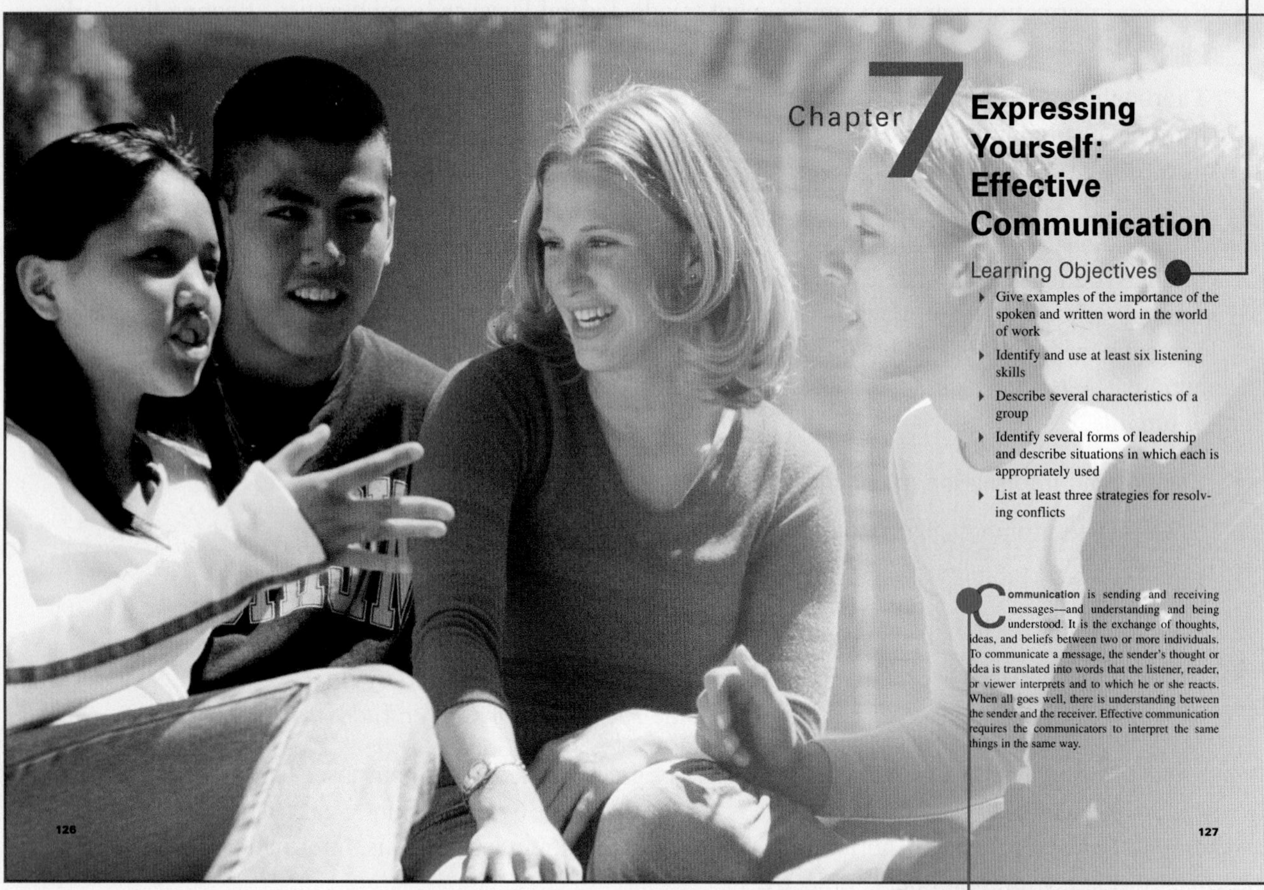

Chapter 7
Expressing Yourself: Effective Communication
Learning Objectives
Give examples of the importance of the spoken and written word in the world of work
Identify and use at least six listening skills
Describe several characteristics of a group
Identify several forms of leadership and describe situations in which each is appropriately used
List at least three strategies for resolving conflicts
Communication is sending and receiving messages—and understanding and being understood. It is the exchange of thoughts, ideas, and beliefs between two or more individuals. To communicate a message, the sender's thought or idea is translated into words that the listener, reader, or viewer interprets and to which he or she reacts. When all goes well, there is understanding between the sender and the receiver. Effective communication requires the communicators to interpret the same things in the same way.
126
127

Vocabulary words are highlighted in red where the word is first defined. These words are also defined in the glossary at the back of the book.

© JIST Works

The colorful design and clear format of *Preparing for Career Success* invites students to explore important career information and emphasizes the key ideas in each chapter.

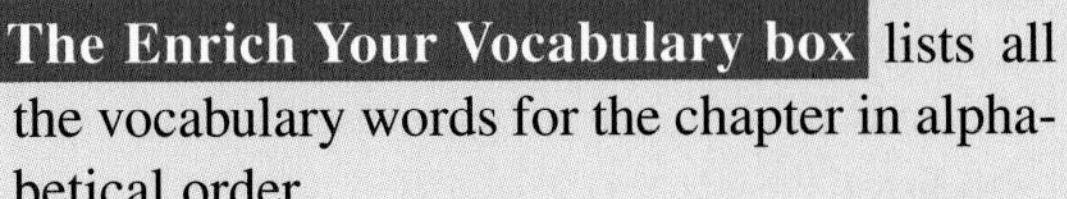

The Enrich Your Vocabulary box lists all the vocabulary words for the chapter in alphabetical order.

Enrichment activities encourage students to expand upon what they have learned in the chapter.

Enrich Your Vocabulary

In reading this chapter and doing the exercises, you will learn the following important terms:

Americans with Disabilities Act (ADA)	flextime	pension plans
antitrust laws	fraud	price fixing
Civil Rights Act of 1964	fringe benefits	Social Security Act
contingent worker	insider abuse	whistle-blowing
credit unions	merit rating	workers' compensation laws
Equal Pay Act of 1963	monopolies	workshops
ethics	parenting leave	

Vocabulary
You can use the "Developing Your Vocabulary" worksheet in Chapter 12 of the *Preparing for Career Success Instructor's CD-ROM, Third Edition* as a pretest for chapter concepts or as a reteaching worksheet.

Do you plan to be a leader in the world of work? What philosophy will you use to make important management decisions? How will you manage a large organization? Would society be better off to stop relying on politicians and return to the management methods used by employers in "the good old days"?

You have probably listened to adults discussing these issues at home. Perhaps you have raised them yourself. As you read and discuss the information in this chapter, consider all of the different points of view.

School-to-Work Transition
Explain the relationship between school evaluations and employer evaluations (Teacher = Supervisor; School = Employer; Report Card = Performance Appraisal; Employer's Production Goals = Teacher's Learning Goals; School's Permanent Record = Employer's Permanent Record).

Section 1: Performance Appraisals

Employers have the right to evaluate the work performance of their employees. Most employers use performance appraisals to measure and evaluate a worker's accomplishments over a specific time. The appraisal is based on the job description and the employer's goals. During your career, you can expect your immediate supervisor to conduct an annual performance appraisal. As a new employee, you can expect the supervisor to evaluate you more often. Information contained in your performance appraisal will become part of your employer's permanent records.

We judge ourselves by what we feel capable of doing, while others judge us by what we have already done.

—Henry Wadsworth Longfellow

Measurement and evaluation of performance are a part of an employee's permanent record just as evaluation of academic performance is part of a student's permanent record. How high would an employer rate your student performance?

266 Unit 3 Understanding the World of Work © JIST Works

Performance appraisals are not new. As far back as the third century A.D., Chinese emperors employed an "imperial rater" to evaluate the performance of official family members. In the early 1800s, Robert Wen, owner of cotton mills in Scotland, established the first performance appraisals in industry by hanging a cube of colored wood over each employee's workstation. The color of the wood represented each worker's performance level. In the United States, General Lewis Cass of the U.S. Army used performance appraisals as early as 1813. He submitted to the War Department an evaluation of each man under his command. General Cass described his men in such colorful terms as "a good-natured man" or "a knave despised by all."

The Civil Rights Act of 1964 and the Equal Employment Opportunity Commission (EEOC), formed in 1966, established guidelines for the regulation of employment selection procedures. The act and the EEOC placed strong legal pressure on employers to use performance appraisal systems that are fair to all employees.

Key to Success

Good job performance appraisals are important. If you leave your current job for any reason, potential employers will usually check with your past employers to find out about the quality of your work.

Video Tour on DVD
Show students the Chapter 12 segment to introduce them to the content.

Purpose of Evaluation

Using one method or another, your employer will measure the degree of your career success. In a large organization, your supervisor might use a standard evaluation form and established procedures to evaluate your work performance. In a small organization, your evaluation might be your manager's personal observations and informal discussions with you. In both cases, evaluation judgments will influence decisions regarding your

- Promotion to a better job
- Salary increase
- Possible *discharge* (firing)
- Transfer to a different job or department
- Admission into a training program

Enrichment
Have students fill out the "Self-Evaluation" worksheet in Chapter 12 of the *Preparing for Career Success Student Activity Book, Third Edition.*

The amount of your annual pay usually depends on your measured *output* (the quantity of work you produce) or on your **merit rating** (a formal, periodic written evaluation of your job performance). How the employer uses the information in your performance appraisal will be determined by the employer or, in the case of a union shop, by a contract between workers and the employer.

Evaluators must be *objective* (not allow personal feelings to interfere) if they are to evaluate employees accurately. If you are rated against others, as in the case of measured output, your rating must be in numerical terms.

Graham Matthews's employer is very concerned that assemblers put together high-quality control boxes. The sale of defective products could result in the loss of important contracts with the aerospace industry or could be the cause of a major accident. Graham's employer uses the rating sheet shown in Figure 12.1 to determine each assembler's accuracy. The rating is based on the amount of work that passes inspection the first time and does not require rebuilding.

Take Note

The Electronic Communications Privacy Act of 1986 permits an employer to listen to business-related phone calls, but the employer is to hang up the instant the conversation turns personal. By the time the employer realizes the conversation is personal, however, you may have said things you would have preferred to keep private.

© JIST Works Chapter 12 Defining Roles, Rights, and Responsibilities 267

Quotes placed throughout the text engage students' interest.

The Take Note boxes are interesting asides that provide information on related topics or highlight important points related to the chapter.

Case Studies relate to the chapter's topic and feature young adults facing problems in their lives. Each case study focuses on one of several key themes, including personal and career planning, personal responsibility, problem-solving techniques, character, and life skills.

Vocabulary Builder notes present additional terms that are related the chapter's subject matter that you can introduce to your class. They also provide language activities for the vocabulary in the chapter.

Critical Thinking questions and activities lead students to think about how to handle the real-life situations described in the case studies.

Vocabulary Builder/
Cooperative Learning

Write the following terms on the chalkboard: *layoff, pink slip, severance pay,* and *outplacement program.* Divide the class into learning pairs. Pass a sheet of paper to each pair, and explain the following rules:

1. Each pair must write three grammatically correct sentences.
2. Each sentence must contain at least one of the four terms on the chalkboard.
3. Do not use a term more than once.

Explain that the first team to finish wins if all three sentences are correct. Then start the students as you would a race.

Comprehension Check

Instruct your students to close their books. Then ask them: In your own words, what is the purpose of giving unemployment insurance payments to unemployed workers? Do you think this is a good idea? Why or why not?

CAREER FACT

Trade Adjustment Assistance (TAA) is available to workers who lose their jobs or whose hours of work and wages are reduced by increased imports. Under the Trade Act of 1974, workers who lose their jobs or whose hours of work are reduced by increased imports may apply for TAA benefits and reemployment services. TAA provides job training, a job search allowance, a relocation allowance, and weekly trade adjustment allowances. For more information, use your search engine to contact the U.S. Department of Labor, Employment and Training Administration Program.

reasonably suited in terms of training, past experience, and past wages. Cash benefits are paid. Federal law establishes certain minimum requirements, but each state determines who is eligible, how much money each person receives, and how long benefits are paid. To be eligible, a person must be unemployed, able to work, available for employment, and seeking work. All employers are required to pay premiums for this insurance.

Building Character: Persistence Pays

As Ken Schaum cast his line into the still waters around the boat, he glanced at his grandfather. He hated to tell him that he was out of work and could not find a job. Grandpa had always had a good job, and Ken did not want to seem like a failure. Ken was thinking about how proud Grandpa had been two years ago when Ken started working at DRS Bearings, the same firm that Grandpa had retired from after 42 years of service. Now Ken had to tell him that DRS had laid him off.

Ken started talking, and the story poured out. DRS planned to close the plant. Ken's interviews with six other employers had all ended in rejection. He was so embarrassed that he almost hated to have another employer interview him for fear that the employer would reject him.

Grandpa listened quietly, and then he reminded Ken about the vegetable garden they had planted when Ken was in the fifth grade. They worked an entire day preparing the soil and planting the seeds. Ken checked the garden every day, but nothing seemed to be growing. He became discouraged. Then one morning, Ken and Grandpa went out to look at the garden and saw the first green sprouts coming through the ground.

They were both quiet for a while, and then Grandpa said, "I was proud of you then, and I'm proud of you now. You're not a quitter, Ken."

That evening at home, Ken thought a lot about being laid off, searching for a new job, and the garden he had helped to plant years ago. He sorted through several employment ads he had cut out of the newspaper but had not answered. He would send his resume to those employers in the morning, and this time he would be proud of himself.

308 Unit 3 Understanding the World of Work © JIST Works

Critical Thinking

On a separate sheet of paper, describe something you have accomplished that makes you feel proud. List any failures you experienced before you succeeded. How did you overcome your failures? What advice would you give to someone who wanted to accomplish what you have done?

Ken overcame his feeling of depression and increased his sense of personal confidence. Using events in the story, list as many reasons as you can for Ken's change of attitude. Can you use any of these reasons to increase your sense of confidence? If so, how? If not, why not?

Termination by Discharge

Discharge of an employee means dismissal from employment. The term implies discipline for unsatisfactory performance. Virtually all courts have supported the employer's right to discharge an employee who is demonstrably unacceptable, incompetent, lazy, uncooperative, or abusive to other employees.

There is no general law that prohibits private employers from discharging employees without good cause. Employers have historically had the right to fire employees at will unless a written contract protected against this type of dismissal. This broad right has been limited by federal laws that prohibit discrimination based on gender, race, color, religion, national origin, age, physical or mental disability, union activity, wage garnishment, and filing complaints or assisting in procedures related to enforcing these laws.

In addition to federal laws, some states and municipalities have passed laws prohibiting employers from discharging employees who serve on jury duty, file workers' compensation claims, or refuse lie detector tests or from discriminating against employees based on marital status or sexual orientation. Employee complaint procedures and collective bargaining agreements between employers and unions also place limitations on an employer's absolute right to fire workers.

Some employees who have challenged their discharges in court have succeeded in placing additional limitations on the employer's right to discharge. For example, an employer cannot discharge an employee

- For refusing to commit *perjury* (swearing that something is true when you know it is false)
- For refusing to approve market testing of a potentially harmful drug when it is not based on good faith and fair dealing
- For refusing to date a supervisor
- To save the employer from paying a large commission

In some organizations, employers give a series of progressively more serious warnings to hourly employees before termination. The supervisor gives the employee formal notification of the need for improvement in

CLUSTER LINK

Although production occupations are experiencing job losses to foreign competition, they are projected to add 164,184 new jobs between 2006 and 2016. If you are interested in the occupations of welder, machinist, or food processing worker, review the Manufacturing career cluster. See the appendix for more information.

Cooperative Learning

Divide your class into small groups. Assign each group to write about a work situation in which one employee is obviously unacceptable, incompetent, lazy, uncooperative, or abusive to other employees. Allow time for each group to present their work to the class.

CAREER FACT

In most firings, the released employee has an idea that termination is coming because he or she has received a bad performance rating or a warning from the supervisor. Alternatively, the boss may avoid talking to the employee, may give fewer assignments without any explanation, or may increase the number of reviews of the employee's work performance.

© JIST Works Chapter 13 Managing Career Change and Growth 309

Career Fact boxes provide numbers from government data and surveys and other information to illustrate key points in the chapter.

Cluster Links connect chapter material to one of the U.S Department of Education's career clusters and refer students to the appendix for more information.

The Get Involved questions and activities reinforce the content of each major section by having students think and write about what they have learned.

Comprehension Check exercises present ways to review and teach understanding of the material presented.

Find Out More boxes direct students to established organizations, reliable Web sites, and comprehensive reference materials to start exploring a topic in depth.

Section 3: Get Involved

Interview a student who is presently attending a postsecondary school you are considering, and find out the answers to the following questions. Write down the answers on a separate sheet of paper, and be prepared to discuss your responses in class.

1. How much time does the student spend in the library?
2. How much time does he or she spend on daily studies?
3. What type of homework is assigned?
4. Where does the student usually study or complete writing assignments?
5. What is the most difficult adjustment the student found going from high school to a postsecondary school?
6. What special advice does he or she have for you?

Comprehension Check

What advantages would an apprentice have over a young worker taking an entry-level job in the same industry?

Community Resources

Assign a committee of volunteer students to contact local craft unions and construction contractors. Also, have them locate a professional who works with apprenticeship programs. Provide the committee with a list of possible dates and times, and ask them to schedule their contacts to speak to the class about apprenticeship programs.

Section 4: Apprenticeship Programs

Benjamin Franklin was an apprentice printer under his older brother. From this beginning, he became the wealthiest man in the New World. Apprenticeship is a relationship between an employer and an employee during which the beginning worker, or apprentice, learns a trade. Apprentices train for occupations that require a wide range of skills and knowledge as well as maturity and independent judgment. Apprenticeship programs combine daily, supervised, on-the-job work experience with technical classroom instruction.

Apprenticeship is a centuries-old method of on-the-job training under the watchful eye of a master craftsman. The twelfth-century **guilds** (unions of craftsmen) of England were widespread in the skilled trades. Today's apprenticeship programs usually require about four years of training but range from one to six years. The apprentice receives wages during this learning period. A beginning apprentice earns about half the pay of a skilled craftsperson, with periodic raises throughout the apprenticeship.

In addition to on-the-job work experience, an apprentice receives classroom instruction from skilled craftspeople and specialists in related occupations. Trade manuals and other educational materials are required reading. Classes cover techniques of the trade, theory, and safety precautions.

An experienced worker who is known as a journey worker supervises the apprentice on the job. The **journey worker** is a certified, experienced, skilled craftsperson who has successfully completed an apprenticeship. Under the journey worker's guidance, the apprentice gradually learns the skills of the trade and performs the work under less and less supervision.

Apprenticeship programs are sponsored and operated by employers or employer associations or by management and labor on a voluntary basis. The sponsors plan, administer, and pay for the program. The government's role is to provide support services to these program sponsors.

108 Unit 1 Getting Ready for the World of Work © JIST Works

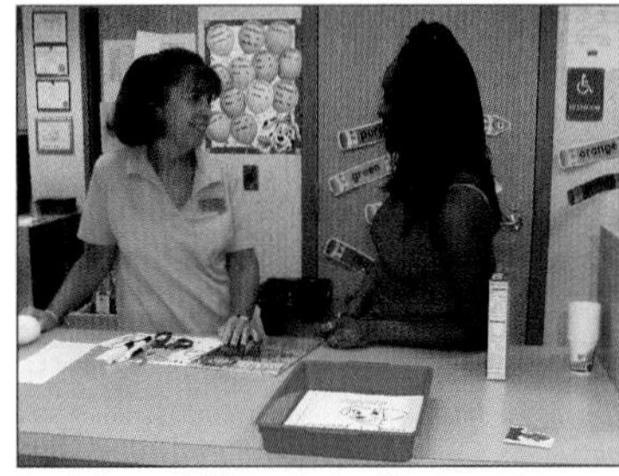

Apprenticeships are available for occupations from child care to construction. An apprentice is paid to learn a trade while under the watchful eye of a journey worker. Do you have the academic skills necessary to enter an apprenticeship program?

Find Out More

The Employment and Training Administration of the U.S. Department of Labor offers a CD-ROM and several brochures describing apprenticeship. For a copy of these materials, call 1-866-487-2365, or for more detailed information, go online at www.doleta.gov/atels_bat/. Additionally, America's Workforce Network toll-free help line is 1-877-872-5672. Operators can provide information about career counselors and apprenticeship programs in a caller's ZIP code.

Most programs require applicants to have a high school diploma or its equivalent. In some cases, college graduates are sought. All apprentices must be proficient in reading, writing, and mathematics. Courses in shop, math, algebra, geometry, drafting, physics, and other subjects related to the technical and mechanical trades are also highly recommended.

After the application is approved, the Joint Apprenticeship Committee or another administrative body representing the sponsor will interview each applicant. Once accepted, the applicant must wait for a place in the program. The length of the wait depends on the number of qualified applicants and the number of apprenticeship openings.

When an apprentice is accepted into a program, he or she and the sponsor sign an apprenticeship agreement. The apprentice agrees to perform the work faithfully and to complete the related course of study. The sponsor agrees to make every effort to keep the apprentice employed and to comply with the standards established for the program.

Upon successful completion of a registered program, the apprentice receives a certificate of completion from the U.S. Department of Labor or from a federally approved state apprenticeship agency. What similarities do you see between the twelfth-century guilds and today's apprenticeship programs?

More than 850 occupations may be entered through apprenticeship programs (see Table 6.3). However, apprenticeships related to construction and manufacturing are most common. Possibilities range from telecommunications, environmental protection, and pastry making to health care, child

The earning potential and skills required in apprenticeship programs are the same for men and women.

© JIST Works Chapter 6 Looking Ahead: Education and Training 109

Community Resources suggest people and organizations to contact who can provide a real-world perspective to the topic being studied.

Discussion Starter statements and questions stimulate thought and sometimes controversy among your students.

Cross-References refer you to a previous source of the subject in the book to help you connect the current chapter to earlier lessons.

Comprehension Check

Instruct your students to close their books. Ask several students: Describe an example of how technology has increased the production of workers in a specific occupation.

As new technology creates changes at a dizzying pace, the skill requirements for jobs become more sophisticated. To produce the maximum number of high-quality products or services, employees will need to maintain and develop the skills necessary to use these new technologies.

Investing in advanced technology; improving current products, processes, and services; and creating entirely new ones are essential for the United States to improve its productivity and competitiveness. Newly automated businesses must deal with worker issues that result from the use of new technology. These issues include employment security, training for new skills, changes in work organization, and a need for teamwork.

Increased Productivity

Discussion Starter

What is another area of production in which advanced technology has increased the quality and quantity of a product or service?

Productivity is the amount of goods or services that a worker produces in a certain time (usually an hour). Improving the technology of tools and machines increases worker productivity. A hundred years ago, thousands of American farmers produced corn. A farmer with a good team of horses could plow about two acres of land each day. Using horses to pull metal plows, disks, and seeders, each farmer could prepare, plant, cultivate, and harvest about 30 acres of land each year, producing about 50 bushels of corn per acre. A single farmer produced far more corn per year than was produced by all of the workers in the earlier Indian village.

Farmers, ranchers, and agricultural managers held about 258,000 jobs in 2006. Most manage crop production activities, while others manage livestock production. The trend continues toward fewer and larger farms.

Today, a much smaller workforce of farmers, equipped with giant air-conditioned tractors, not only produces a much larger harvest of corn than their counterparts of 100 years ago, but in one hour can harvest 900 bushels. The difference in these three periods of corn production results from the technology available to the workers. Which farmer worked the hardest? Which had the least product to show for his or her labor?

Just as consumers expect high-quality goods or services for the dollars they spend, employers expect high-quality production for the dollars they spend on wages. As workers have produced more goods or services per day, employers have reduced the number of hours in the workweek. For example, a 60-hour workweek was common in 1850, but since 1950, a 40-hour week is typical. Still, the average American worker's standard of living, measured in purchasing power, has increased dramatically.

Education and Training/Cooperative Learning

Divide your class into learning pairs. Allow five minutes for each pair to research changes in the education and training requirements for one specific occupation during the past 100 or more years. Allow time for each pair to report their answer to the class

352 Unit 3 Understanding the World of Work © JIST Works

Occupational Specialization

One hundred and fifty years ago, more than 90 percent of the workforce was involved in agriculture. At that time, families were largely independent, producing most of their own food and clothing and frequently building their own homes. There were few specialists in the workforce. Today, less than 2 percent of the workforce is involved in agriculture, and more than 99 percent of U.S. families are interdependent: They produce goods or provide services for others, and they use their earnings to purchase necessities and luxuries. With few exceptions, today's workers are specialists.

Cross-Reference

See the vocabulary term *interdependence* in "Section 1: Having a Positive Attitude," in Chapter 10.

Occupational specialization occurs when a worker focuses on producing one particular item of goods or providing one particular service. It is the foundation of all modern economic systems.

Through specialization, our nation is able to produce a higher volume of goods or services at a lower cost than would otherwise be possible. In turn, specialists use their wages to purchase goods and services from other specialists at a lower cost. The efficiency that results from specialization enables all members of the workforce to have a higher standard of living. Figure 15.5 demonstrates the high degree of interdependence among workers and businesses in the U.S. economy. Notice how money flows in a cycle through our economic system.

Figure 15.5 The interdependence of workers in a specialized economy.

Specialization may be regional. Regional specialization occurs when producers use specific natural resources in a geographic region. Potatoes from Idaho, wine from California, peaches from Georgia, and cheese from Wisconsin are examples of regional specialization. What specialization takes place in your region of the country? What natural resources or other factors have influenced specialization? What occupations are in demand because of this specialization?

When certain geographic regions or nations are able to produce more of a certain product or provide more of a certain service at a better price than others because of the efficiency they gain from specialization, they have a comparative advantage over competing regions or nations. A **comparative advantage** is the ability of a producer to provide a good or service at a lower opportunity cost than other producers. For example, the nations of Southeast Asia have a comparative advantage over most of the world in their ability to produce natural rubber, largely due to the region's climate. By specializing in a product in which they have a comparative advantage, the nations of Southeast Asia are able to sell natural rubber on the world market. They use the money they receive to purchase other goods and services from other nations.

Cluster Link

Communications and media technology are an important part of every American business. If you are interested in writing articles, designing print materials, or making commercials, you should explore the Arts, A/V Technology, and Communications career cluster. See the appendix for more information.

© JIST Works Chapter 15 Connecting Economics and Work 353

Education and Training activities link education to careers and to the preparation needed after high school.

Updated illustrations capture the attention of visual learners while conveying main ideas.

Self-Understanding exercises help students increase their level of understanding of personal interests, aptitudes, values, attitudes, and competence.

Sidebars highlight useful information throughout the book for easy reference.

Developing your interpersonal skills and learning to work in groups are valuable in preparing for your future career.

interpersonal aspects of life. Unpleasant relationships are frequently caused by poor communication.

Interpersonal relationships are built on the understanding that grows between two or more people. Each of us tends to like people whose behavior satisfies or rewards us in someway, someone with whom we have similarities. It is easy for us to dislike people who are very different from us.

Mutual trust occurs when two people become convinced that the other person is reliable and honest. It takes several experiences with the other person over a period of time to develop trust. Think about a person that you trust, perhaps a friend, relative, or teacher. What experiences convinced you that this person is trustworthy? How much time did this take?

Self-Understanding

Instruct your students to write the name of a close friend on the top of a sheet of paper. They should then list the similarities and differences they have with their friend. Ask your students: What similarities pull you and your friend together? What differences push you apart?

Cooperative Learning

Have students complete the "Belonging to a Group" worksheet in Chapter 7 of the *Preparing for Career Success Instructor's CD-ROM, Third Edition.*

Key to Success

Recognizing your personal style of communication and understanding the style of other workers is important.

Belonging to a Group

Whether it is a family, clique, school class, social club, athletic team, church, musical group, employee union, political party, work team, or professional association, you will be a member of various groups throughout your life.

A group is made up of a number of people interacting with a common purpose in mind. Some groups have many rules and are highly organized; others are informal and have very few rules and little organization. However, all groups have some form of organization, rules for establishing leadership, and expectations regarding member behavior.

Effective groups have an atmosphere of equality among members. Each member has a sense of belonging, importance, and purpose. Members usually know one another on a first-name basis. Depending on the situation, leadership is frequently shared by different members of the group. Every member is a leader, and every member is a follower. Members are sensitive to the roles that other members perform and how they relate to their own particular role in the group.

Group meetings are related to the needs of members. Problems are expressed, alternatives are discussed, and solutions are arrived at through joint effort. Groups are more effective when tasks are divided among the members. Members are more likely to follow the established rules of the group and to identify with the group's goal when they are personally involved in the process of group communication and problem solving.

Tips for Effective Group Relationships

Which four of the following tips do you practice most often? Which four tips do you practice the least?

1. Treat others with respect.
2. Be willing to listen attentively.
3. Stick to the task.
4. Don't dominate the group.
5. Think before you speak.
6. Don't be afraid to speak up.
7. Avoid making cynical remarks.
8. Apologize if you offend someone.
9. Recognize and correct your mistakes.
10. Take the initiative to participate.
11. Provide feedback to other speakers.
12. Don't prejudge other people.
13. Keep an open mind.
14. Don't be a know-it-all.
15. Cooperate with others.
16. Be open to suggestions.
17. Make suggestions to the group.
18. Evaluate all suggestions sincerely.
19. Criticize in a constructive way.
20. Tolerate differences in others.
21. Speak for yourself (say "I believe...").
22. Allow speakers time to pause and think.

Changes in the behavior of an individual frequently reflect membership in a particular group. Groups can exert considerable pressure on individual members to conform. Can you think of a group you belong to that expects you to behave in a certain way? Do you ever behave in a certain manner to please the group when you personally disapprove of the behavior?

As you will learn in Chapter 11, workers are often organized into teams so that appropriate talents and skills can be directed through group effort to accomplish important tasks and achieve goals. When the group achieves its goals, the members are more cohesive, feel more secure about their jobs, communicate more openly, and work more cooperatively.

School-to-Work Transition

Explain that learning to get along with others in group situations is important preparation for career success. Ask individual students to respond to the following questions: What's the name of a group in which you are a member? What attitudes and behaviors have you learned that cause other members of the group to accept and respect you? Will these same attitudes and behaviors influence your career success? If so, how? If not, why?

What makes a group successful?

Technology

Businesses use instant messaging software to help employees in different locations share information easily. Keep in mind that sending instant messages to coworkers is different than sending instant messages to friends. To be professional, you should avoid using abbreviations such as LOL or smileys such as :).

Technology Tips provide relevant information about issues concerning the connection between technology and careers.

School-to-Work Transitions are exercises aimed at relating school subjects and experiences to the world of work.

Cooperative Learning activities promote interest and dialog among students and encourage them to learn more about concepts taught in the textbook by working in small groups.

Cooperative Learning

Divide your class into groups. Assig[illegible] one of the features of the futur[illegible] workforce to each group. Inst[illegible] each group to tell how their assig[illegible] feature will affect their future paychecks, education and training, family life, and overall lifestyle. Have them report their conclusions and the reasons for their conclusions to the class.

TAKE NOTE

Demand is rising for workers with skills related to the design, development, and maintenance of Web sites and the servers that house them. Occupations frequently specified include Webmaster, Web developer, network systems administrator, programmer, and customer service representative.

Enrichment

Have students complete "The Past—The Future" worksheet in Chapter 14 of the *Preparing for Career Success Student Activity Book, Third Ed[illegible]*

- **Consumer spending:** Of all goods components, consumer spending on computers and software is projected to have the largest and fastest growth at 8.2 percent or $469 billion. The overall annual growth rate for goods will be 0.4 percent.
- **New ways of working:** The line between work life and private life will continue to blend. Workers' job requirements will spill over into the rest of their lives.
- **Increasing levels of education and training:** Among the causes of gains in labor quality will be higher levels of educational attainment among workers, improving worker skills and productivity. An associate's or bachelor's degree is the most significant source of postsecondary education or training for 5 of the 10 fastest-growing occupations. Short-term on-the-job training is the most significant source of postsecondary education or training for 9 of the 10 occupations with the largest job growth.

Table 14.1 illustrates the projected increase in numbers of workers in various occupational groups. Can you think of an occupational group that will benefit or suffer because of a major event that took place in the past five years?

Table 14.1 Numeric Growth in Employment by Major Occupational Groups (2006–2016)

Occupational Group	Increased Number of Workers
Food preparation and serving	1,436,191
Healthcare practitioners, technologists, and technicians	1,422,626
Education, training, and library	1,264,510
Personal care and service	1,094,051
Business and financial operations	1,062,764
Healthcare support	997,094
Building and grounds cleaning and maintenance	850,134
Computer an[illegible]hematical science	821,809
Community an[illegible]ocial services	541,221
Management	533,052

Source: U.S. Department of Labor

The Effect of Technology

Improved technology, new inventions, and discovery have a long-term influence on occupations. Entire industries come into existence, creating new occupations.

- **New technology changes the way people work.** It is a driving force in determining the job tasks and numbers of workers in a specific occupation. For example, business offices have increased their use of computers and other communications technologies at a rapid pace. Consequently, the growth of clerical and managerial jobs has declined, but the demand for workers with knowledge of computers, office technology (systems analysts), and office machine repair has increased.
- **Superior technology is an important source of competitive advantage.** It eliminates jobs that are no longer efficient and creates new jobs to replace them. One change that has had an impact on employment is the shift in importance from producing computer hardware to producing computer software and providing technical services. This shift has caused a decrease in computer manufacturing employment, whereas the number of jobs related to software production and technical services has continued to grow.
- **New technology creates business opportunities and jobs.** Emerging opportunities and occupations may be entirely new, created by changes in technology, society, markets, or government regulations. For example, Webmasters or coordinators write the computer code necessary to publish or update text and images on Internet Web sites. As more organizations establish a presence on the Internet, more Web-related businesses and occupations emerge.

Cooperative Learning

Divide your class into groups of three. Ask each group to write a brief paragraph detailing how technology has both increased and decreased their career opportunities. Allow time for each group to report to the class.

Enrichment

Have students complete the "A Change of Pace" worksheet found in Chapter 14 of the *Preparing for Career Success Instructor's CD-ROM, Third Edition.*

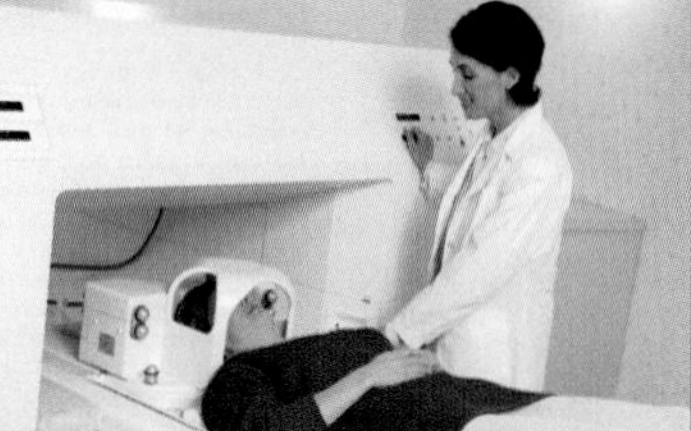

Learning to use new technology is an important factor in career success.

Many workers believe that they cannot keep up with these changes and that they are a very unimportant part of the economy. Nothing could be further from the truth, however. Labor is one of the most important factors of production. Therefore, a quality workforce is the foundation for our nation's economic strength and international competitiveness.

Management and labor are increasingly involved in teamwork decision making for matters related to product quality, operating procedures, and job responsibilities. In today's global market, competition requires continual improvement by U.S. companies. They must place the most up-to-date communication and production technology in the hands of their employees. In turn, employees must maintain and develop the skills necessary to use this technology to produce the maximum number of high-quality products or services.

KEY TO SUCCESS

When you consider an occupation, find out how many jobs exist in that occupation. Are the number of j[illegible]owing or declining?

Global Competition

Competition in the global marketplace continually tests the quality and cost of U.S. products. Countries in Europe, Asia, and other parts of the world have emerged as strong challengers in international commerce. As a

Updated tables based on the latest government data help students develop important information skills.

Key to Success tips help students avoid common pitfalls and reach their potential.

Reteaching notes include a variety of exercises intended to strengthen important concepts in the chapter. Often these notes point you to relevant materials in the *Student Activity Book.*

The Check Your Knowledge questions require the student to search and review the chapter in order to provide accurate answers.

Reteaching
Have students complete the "Finding the Right Words" and "Checking Your Location" worksheets in Chapter 9 of the *Preparing for Career Success Student Activity Book, Third Edition.*

Chapter 9 Review

Enrich Your Vocabulary

On a separate sheet of paper, number from 1 to 21. (Do not write in your textbook.) Match each of the following statements with the most appropriate term from the "Enrich Your Vocabulary" list at the beginning of the chapter by writing that term next to the number of the correct statement.

1. A document containing information that employers require before hiring new employees
2. A law that protects all workers, including minors
3. A document stating that you don't have an infectious disease or that you're free of certain drugs
4. A document stating that a person is eligible to work in the United States
5. Insurance that pays financial losses if an employee fails to perform his or her duty or is guilty of theft
6. A serious crime
7. Preemployment tests for government jobs
8. True and supported by facts
9. Readiness and ability to take the first steps in any undertaking
10. The people responsible for recruiting and hiring new employees
11. A program in which employers actively seek to hire minorities
12. An employer's formal proposal of employment
13. A job that provides you with an opportunity to assume adult responsibilities
14. A contribution of free labor
15. An agency that "rents" employees to employers
16. A document that is necessary for employees under 18 in most non-farm jobs
17. An investigation of a job applicant's former employers, schools, and references
18. A test to determine how well an applicant is likely to perform in a certain area of work
19. An opportunity to personally present yourself to an employer
20. The lowest amount an employer may pay for certain types of work
21. Organizations not intending or intended to earn a profit

Enrich Your Vocabulary Answers
1. job application form
2. Fair Labor Standards Act
3. health certificate
4. employment eligibility verification form
5. bond
6. felony
7. civil service examinations
8. valid
9. initiative
10. human resources department
11. fair employment program
12. job offer
13. full-time job
14. volunteer work
15. temporary employment service
16. work permit
17. background check
18. preemployment test
19. job interview
20. minimum wage
21. nonprofits

212 Unit 2 Finding a Job and Achieving Success © JIST Works

Check Your Knowledge

On a separate sheet of paper, complete the following activities. (Do not write in your textbook.)

1. List four kinds of information requested on most job applications.
2. When do job applications become legal documents?
3. How can you prove your date of birth to an employer?
4. At what age do you no longer need a work permit?
5. List five occupations permitted for 14- and 15-year-olds.
6. List three types of preemployment tests.
7. Name five resources that you can use to find information about a company or an organization.
8. How much time does a job interview usually take?
9. What determines the success of most job interviews?
10. What act of Congress contains the Equal Employment Opportunity Law?
11. Why do some companies like to use temporary help?
12. Approximately how many job changes will most of your generation make during their career?
13. What sector of the job market has had the greatest decline as a result of automation?

Develop SCANS Competencies

This activity will give you practice in developing the technology competencies needed to be a successful worker.

Choose four to five careers in which you have an interest. They could be part-time jobs you will look for in the near future, or they could be jobs that will require more education on your part.

Make a list of the technology you will need to be familiar with to be successful in each of these jobs. The technology might include different types of equipment, such as cash registers or computers. List technology with which you are already familiar. How can this knowledge help in your search for a job?

Check Your Knowledge Answers
1. Personal, education, references, employment desired, previous employment, hobbies and interests, and job skills.
2. When they are signed and dated.
3. By presenting your birth certificate.
4. 18.
5. Office and clerical work; cashiering; sales; art work; window trimming; price marking; packing and stocking shelves; bagging and carrying out customer orders; delivery work by foot, bicycle, or public transportation; and dispensing gasoline and oil and washing and polishing cars.
6. Aptitude, intelligence, proficiency, and psychological tests.
7. Employees who currently work for the company, the Internet, annual reports, brochures, advertisements, the Better Business Bureau, friends or relatives, the company itself, business periodicals and reference books, the local chamber of commerce, and the operation of similar companies.
8. 30 minutes to 1 hour.
9. The applicant's skill in communicating answers to specific questions.
10. The Civil Rights Act of 1964.
11. It saves them the expense of hiring full-time employees that they will need for only a short amount of time.
12. Six or more.
13. The manufacturing sector.

Enrichment
Have students complete the Chapter 9 section of the *Preparing for Career Success Student Portfolio, Third Edition.*

© JIST Works Chapter 9 Applying and Interviewing for a Job 213

The Enrich Your Vocabulary activity at the end of every chapter provides a list of statements or definitions the student will match with the appropriate term listed at the beginning of the chapter.

The Develop SCANS Competencies activities are based on the transferable skills identified by the Department of Labor's SCANS (Secretary's Commission on Achieving Necessary Skills) report as being important to performing well on the job and effectively adapting to change.

Also included in this book is a section that highlights the U.S. Department of Education career clusters. A bonus section contains information that expands on the topics presented throughout this book.

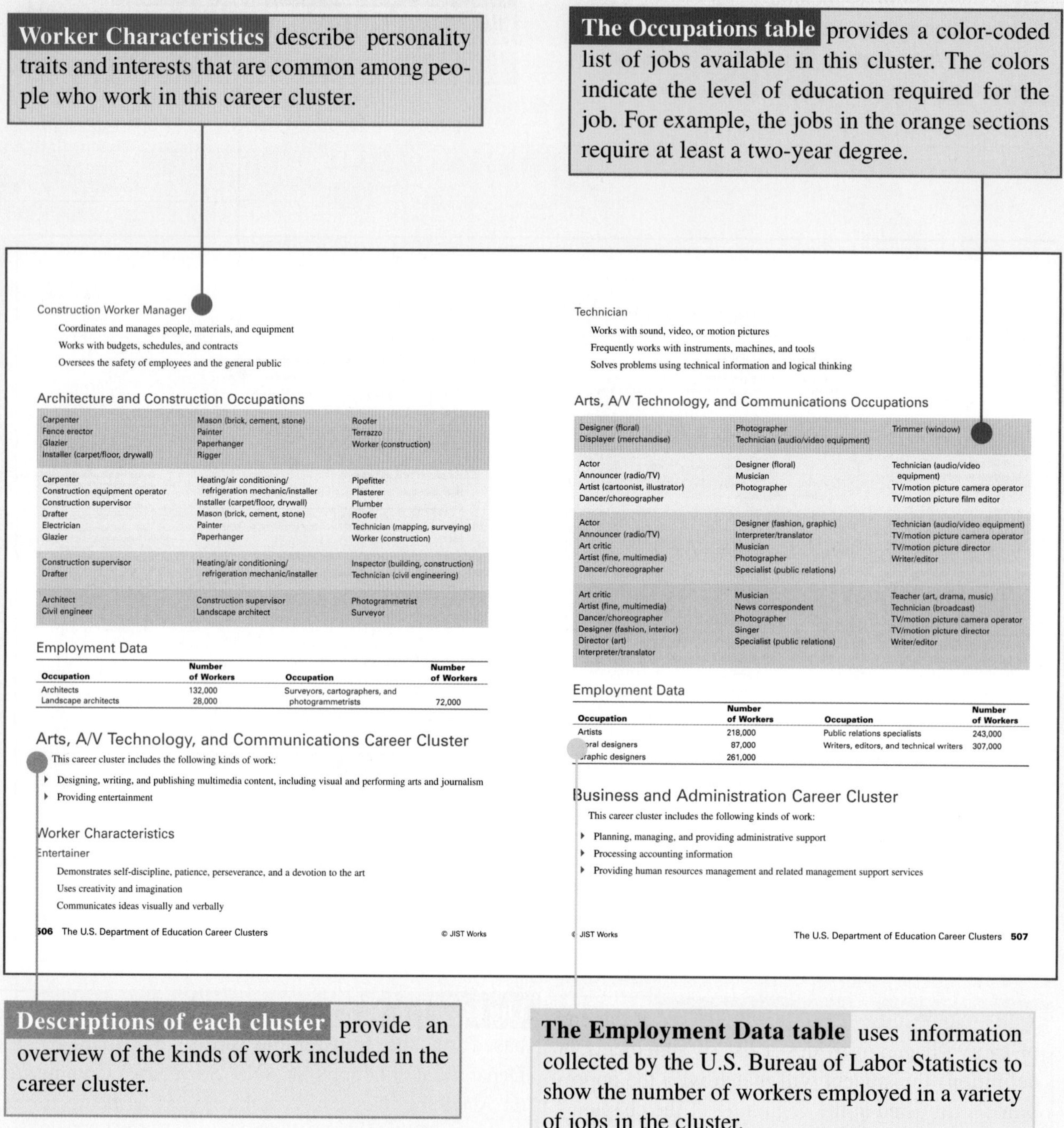

Worker Characteristics describe personality traits and interests that are common among people who work in this career cluster.

The Occupations table provides a color-coded list of jobs available in this cluster. The colors indicate the level of education required for the job. For example, the jobs in the orange sections require at least a two-year degree.

Construction Worker Manager

Coordinates and manages people, materials, and equipment
Works with budgets, schedules, and contracts
Oversees the safety of employees and the general public

Architecture and Construction Occupations

Carpenter Fence erector Glazier Installer (carpet/floor, drywall)	Mason (brick, cement, stone) Painter Paperhanger Rigger	Roofer Terrazzo Worker (construction)
Carpenter Construction equipment operator Construction supervisor Drafter Electrician Glazier	Heating/air conditioning/ refrigeration mechanic/installer Installer (carpet/floor, drywall) Mason (brick, cement, stone) Painter Paperhanger	Pipefitter Plasterer Plumber Roofer Technician (mapping, surveying) Worker (construction)
Construction supervisor Drafter	Heating/air conditioning/ refrigeration mechanic/installer	Inspector (building, construction) Technician (civil engineering)
Architect Civil engineer	Construction supervisor Landscape architect	Photogrammetrist Surveyor

Employment Data

Occupation	Number of Workers	Occupation	Number of Workers
Architects	132,000	Surveyors, cartographers, and photogrammetrists	72,000
Landscape architects	28,000		

Arts, A/V Technology, and Communications Career Cluster

This career cluster includes the following kinds of work:

- Designing, writing, and publishing multimedia content, including visual and performing arts and journalism
- Providing entertainment

Worker Characteristics

Entertainer

Demonstrates self-discipline, patience, perseverance, and a devotion to the art
Uses creativity and imagination
Communicates ideas visually and verbally

506 The U.S. Department of Education Career Clusters © JIST Works

Technician

Works with sound, video, or motion pictures
Frequently works with instruments, machines, and tools
Solves problems using technical information and logical thinking

Arts, A/V Technology, and Communications Occupations

Designer (floral) Displayer (merchandise)	Photographer Technician (audio/video equipment)	Trimmer (window)
Actor Announcer (radio/TV) Artist (cartoonist, illustrator) Dancer/choreographer	Designer (floral) Musician Photographer	Technician (audio/video equipment) TV/motion picture camera operator TV/motion picture film editor
Actor Announcer (radio/TV) Art critic Artist (fine, multimedia) Dancer/choreographer	Designer (fashion, graphic) Interpreter/translator Musician Photographer Specialist (public relations)	Technician (audio/video equipment) TV/motion picture camera operator TV/motion picture director Writer/editor
Art critic Artist (fine, multimedia) Dancer/choreographer Designer (fashion, interior) Director (art) Interpreter/translator	Musician News correspondent Photographer Singer Specialist (public relations)	Teacher (art, drama, music) Technician (broadcast) TV/motion picture camera operator TV/motion picture director Writer/editor

Employment Data

Occupation	Number of Workers	Occupation	Number of Workers
Artists	218,000	Public relations specialists	243,000
...oral designers	87,000	Writers, editors, and technical writers	307,000
...raphic designers	261,000		

Business and Administration Career Cluster

This career cluster includes the following kinds of work:

- Planning, managing, and providing administrative support
- Processing accounting information
- Providing human resources management and related management support services

© JIST Works The U.S. Department of Education Career Clusters 507

Descriptions of each cluster provide an overview of the kinds of work included in the career cluster.

The Employment Data table uses information collected by the U.S. Bureau of Labor Statistics to show the number of workers employed in a variety of jobs in the cluster.

Career Education and Community Collaboration

A basic concept of career education is collaboration among the formal education system; the home-family structure; and all parts of the working community: business, labor, industry, government, professions, service organizations, and others. The purpose of such collaboration is to help students see the relevance of their schoolwork and to meet their individual career goals within the realistic framework of employment opportunities in the local, national, and world economies.

Involving the Community

In many cases, the time commitment career educators are seeking from the community is significant, and in the world of work, time is money. In some cases, employers may allow certain employees to be involved while they are on the clock. In other cases, workers will need to alter their schedules or lose hours of income in order to participate in your program.

When you make contact with potential community participants, present the purpose of your program and the basic concepts involved. The potential participants will need to be convinced that your program is important to encourage the career success of the students and, in some cases, to improve the quality of local job seekers.

Expect potential participants to question why employers and the community at large should collaborate with schools in helping students relate education to work. After all, educating youth is the responsibility of the schools. You will need to explain that the whole society benefits when workers have the preparation to become well-adjusted, knowledgeable, and productive members of a community.

Schools alone cannot prepare students for the workplace. If career education is to be realistic and practical, students will need those in the workaday world outside the school to provide the benefit of their experience and knowledge. Up-to-date answers to the following questions can best come from those who are in the work sector:

- How does work relate to lifestyle?
- What are the advantages and disadvantages of various types of work?
- What is a day on a certain job really like?
- How does one prepare for a certain occupation or career track?
- What is the outlook for certain occupations in terms of local, national, and global opportunities?
- What education and training is required for specific occupations and career tracks?

Beginning Steps

Keeping community leaders who can make decisions about participation in your career education program informed is important. Try using these methods:

- Personally invite them to attend a special program where they will hear presentations on career education. Be sure to include school board members.
- Representatives of the school system can ask to speak about career education at meetings of community organizations to which they belong, as well as to others whose support is needed.
- Listen attentively to the suggestions and criticisms from community leaders and implement their suggestions wherever possible. If schools are serious about community input and feel that collaboration is necessary, the school system must be prepared to share decision-making power with community leaders in areas of the latter's expertise.

© JIST Works

After obtaining the commitment of key employers and community organizations, have them select the people in their respective organizations who will work with the schools in implementing the career education program. After this step, collaboration on specific informational and program activities can begin.

Career Education for All Students

Teachers, students, parents, and community participants should know that career education is not a program of study. Instead, it is a developmental process involving the life of every student in the educational system. This process of development begins in the home, magnifies during the school years, and continues throughout the life of the individual worker.

The impact that rapidly changing technology, social and economic systems, the natural environment, and numerous other factors will have on future work and workers is unknown. However, what is well-documented is the fact that significant change will be rapid, new work will evolve, and workers will need to acquire new skills.

Career education includes all of the studies and experiences through which the individual learns about work as part of living. It is a way of fusing facts, concepts, and skills relating to career choice and career preparation with existing school subjects and programs.

One of the basic objectives of career education is to assure that every student who leaves secondary school is prepared either to enter productive employment or to undertake additional education at the postsecondary level. Every high school student needs to view his or her course of study as important preparation for work, regardless of whether he or she

- Pursues a technical course of study as preparation for entry-level work, advanced technical education and training, or college entrance.
- Pursues a college preparatory curriculum that may include advanced placement courses.
- Is a special-needs student who is limited in his or her ability to pursue academic courses and some technical courses.

© JIST Works

Index of Special Features

Career Fact

(continued)

Career Fact *(continued)*

Case Studies

Cluster Link

Find Out More

© JIST Works

Key to Success

(continued)

Key to Success *(continued)*

Sidebars

 © JIST Works

Take Note

Technology Tip

Preparing for Career Success

Third Edition

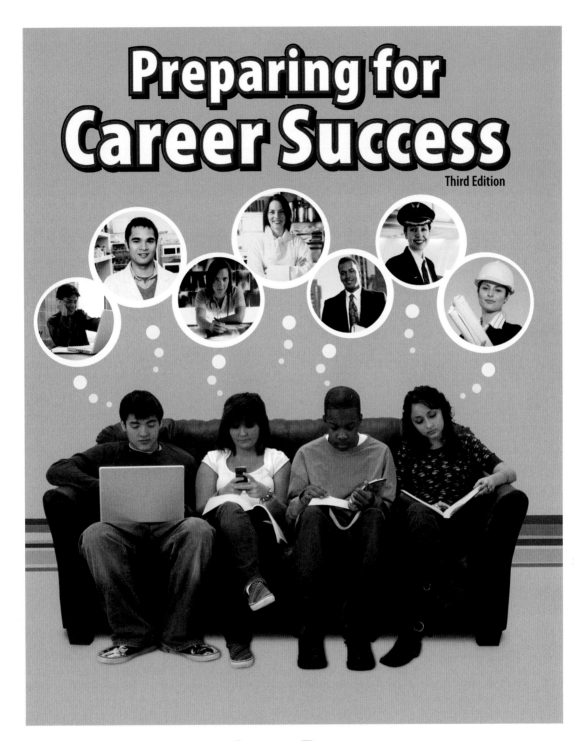

Jerry Ryan
Roberta Ryan

Preparing for Career Success, Third Edition

© 2009 by Jerry Ryan and Roberta Ryan and JIST Publishing

Published by JIST Publishing and EMC Publishing, LLC
E-mails: info@jist.com and educate@emcp.com
Web sites: www.jist.com and www.emcp.com

Note to Instructors

Support materials are available for *Preparing for Career Success, Third Edition. Preparing for Career Success Annotated Teacher's Edition* (978-1-59357-546-5) contains enrichment ideas, discussion topics, and answers to the chapter review questions. *Preparing for Career Success Interactive Lesson Planner Plus Instructor's Resources on CD-ROM* (ISBN 978-1-59357-573-1) has a multitude of tools and resource materials in electronic form. *Preparing for Career Success Student Activity Book* (ISBN 978-1-59357-577-9) features chapter review worksheets and activities that correspond to sections in each chapter of the textbook. *Preparing for Career Success Student Interest Inventory* (ISBN 978-1-59357-576-2) helps students correlate their interests with career clusters. *Preparing for Career Success Student Portfolio* (ISBN 978-1-59357-575-5) provides a folder for students to track their career plans and portfolio documents. *Preparing for Career Success Career Cluster Discovery Guide* (ISBN 978-1-59357-587-8) describes sample occupations in each career cluster. *Preparing for Career Success Video Tour on DVD* (ISBN 978-1-59357-574-8) gives a short, engaging video introduction to each chapter. *Preparing for Career Success ExamView® Test Generator CD-ROM* (ISBN 978-1-59357-588-5) offers a variety of types of test questions to assess student performance.

Visit www.jist.com for more information on JIST, free job search information, tables of contents and sample pages, and ordering instructions on our many products.

Quantity discounts are available for JIST books. Have future editions of JIST books automatically delivered to you on publication through our convenient standing order program. Please call our Sales Department at 800-648-5478 for a free catalog and more information.

Acquisitions Editor: Barb Terry Howe
Development Editor: Heather Stith
Copy Editors: Chuck Hutchinson, Jill Mazurczyk, Stephanie Koutek, Melissa Zabel
Researcher: Laurence Shatkin, Ph.D.
Cover Designer: Honeymoon Image & Design Inc.
Interior Designer and Page Layout: Marie Kristine Parial-Leonardo
Additional Compositors: Carolyn Newland, Aleata Howard
Art Directors: Lynn Miller, Trudy Coler
Illustrator: Katherine Knutson
Proofreaders: Jeanne Clark, Linda Quigley
Indexer: Cheryl Lenser

Printed in the United States of America

9 8 7 6 5 4 3 2 1 13 12 11 10 09 08

All rights reserved. No part of this book may be reproduced in any form or by any means, or stored in a database or retrieval system, without prior written permission of the publisher except in the case of brief quotations embodied in articles or reviews. Making copies of any part of this book for any purpose other than your own personal use is a violation of United States copyright laws. For permission requests, please contact the Copyright Clearance Center at www.copyright.com or (978) 750-8400.

We have been careful to provide accurate information in this book, but it is possible that errors and omissions have been introduced. Please consider this in making any career plans or other important decisions. Trust your own judgment above all else and in all things.

Trademarks: All brand names and product names used in this book are trade names, service marks, trademarks, or registered trademarks of their respective owners.

ISBN 978-1-59357-545-8 Hardcover Student Edition

ISBN 978-1-59357-546-5 Annotated Teacher's Edition

About the Authors

Jerry M. Ryan, M.Ed., has been an advocate of career education for more than 30 years. As project coordinator and liaison between the Akron Public Schools (Akron, Ohio) and the Akron Regional Development Board, he organized collaborative career education programs with business, industry, and labor organizations. As a developer/demonstrator for the U.S. Office of Education, he provided career education and career guidance training to thousands of teachers and counselors nationwide.

Roberta M. Ryan, M.Ed., has spent 30 years teaching, training, counseling, and developing curriculum materials for career education, career guidance, and the private sector. She has been a Coordinator of Career Education for the Akron Public Schools (Akron, Ohio); a trainer for the National Diffusion network of the U.S. Office of Education; a lecturer for the University of Akron; a field evaluator for the American Institute of Research; a curriculum reviewer for the U.S. Department of Education; and the owner and manager of Career Direction Services, Inc., a technical placement service. She has been a major contributor to numerous career education and career guidance curriculum guides at the local, state, and national levels.

During the past 10 years, Jerry and Roberta Ryan have devoted their full attention to writing career-related books, workbooks, and self-assessment materials for high school, college, and adult learners.

Dedication

To our family: To our parents for nurturing us during the first stages of life and for their continuous love and encouragement; to our daughters, Bonnie and Linda, for giving us a sense of purpose, returning our love, and becoming our reliable, understanding, and supportive friends as well as daughters; to our sons-in-law for the love and commitment they provide to our extended family; and to our grandchildren for helping us remember the joy of laughter and play, the magic of dreams, and the importance of preparing for career success.

Photography Credits

Trudy Coler; Judy Pierson; Robin Reuter; Christopher Stith; Brand X Pictures; Comstock, Inc.; Digital Stock; Digital Vision; iStockphoto® Images; Eric Louks of Andy Mohr Ford; Photodisc, Inc.; pages 49 and 147 © Andy Barrand, Chief Photographer, *Herald-Republican;* page 148 © Bob Daemmrich, PhotoEdit; page 167 © Spencer Grant, PhotoEdit; page 134 © Robin Nelson, PhotoEdit; pages 180 and 468 © Michael Newman, PhotoEdit; page 259 © Steve Skjold, PhotoEdit; page 271 © Mark Richards, PhotoEdit; page 427 © Jeff Greenberg, PhotoEdit; and page 485 © Stephen Rudd.

Table of Contents

© JIST Works

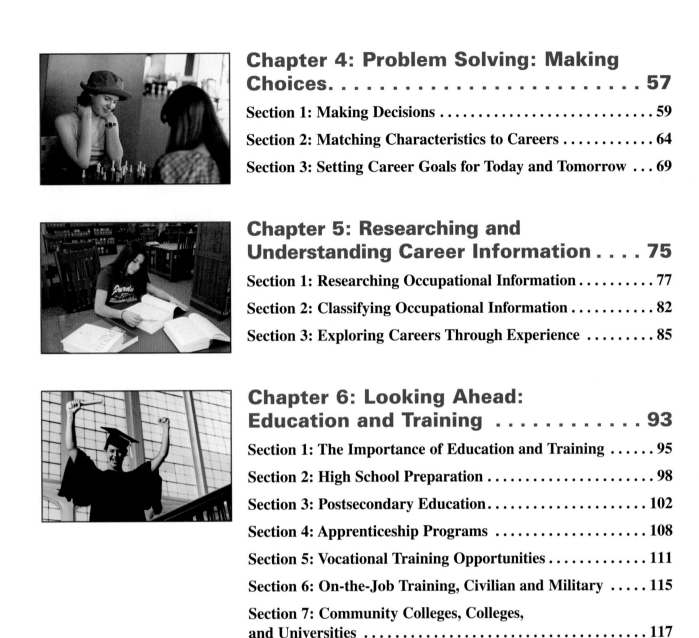

© JIST Works

Unit 3: Understanding the World of Work 262

© JIST Works

BANK
NO CARDBOARD

Introduction

Are you looking forward to being independent and making your own decisions? Are you concerned about planning your career, finding employment, and enjoying a lifetime of career growth when you complete your education and training? If you answered yes to these questions, then *Preparing for Career Success* was written with you in mind.

Career decisions influence most aspects of an individual's life, including

- Your family and social relationships
- The amount of money you spend for essentials, such as food, clothing, shelter, and transportation
- The amount of time and money you have to spend for nonessentials, such as travel and leisure activities
- Where you will live and the hours you will work
- Your social, economic, and political viewpoints
- Your feeling of social success and self-worth
- Your attitude toward work and working

The world of work you enter will offer numerous career possibilities and opportunities. Acquiring additional education and training beyond high school will increase your number of occupational choices as well as the income you will earn during your working years.

Higher-paying occupations are requiring more complex and technical job skills. In response to concerns about the education and training of the nation's future work force, many high schools offer career guidance courses. Some are limited to a few weeks or a semester; others last an entire school year. If your career course will last a semester or less, your class will probably not have enough time to cover the wide range of material in *Preparing for Career Success, Third Edition*. The following overview will help you to identify which sections deal with your most important career concerns. In addition, you may want to do independent work in certain chapters.

Unit 1: Getting Ready for the World of Work

Self-understanding is the foundation of a planned career choice. Unit 1 helps you explore your personal characteristics and shows how your major interests, aptitudes, and values relate to various occupations. You will also examine your attitudes and your career and lifestyle goals. This unit also explains where to find career information and how to determine the kind of education and training you will need for the career path you are considering.

Unit 2: Finding a Job and Achieving Success

Effective communication skills are the key to getting and keeping a job. Information in this section will help you improve your interpersonal skills and resolve conflicts. Once you decide to seek a job, you will need to develop and implement a job search. This unit covers everything from finding job leads to interviewing for positions. You will also learn how to be successful once you get the job. As you become familiar with a particular job and master the required skills, you can begin to look at ways to grow and achieve your next highest career goal.

Unit 3: Understanding the World of Work

What are the roles, rights, and responsibilities of workers and employers? In this unit, you will explore topics such as ethics in the workplace, federal rules and regulations, fringe benefits, and employee compensation.

This unit also provides guidance on how to handle change. Learning how to adjust to changing job situations is an important part of career success. Understanding the impact of cultural diversity, technology, and an expanding and competitive global economy will help you meet the challenges of a continuously changing job market, whether you decide to look for a new job, train for a different career, or start your own business.

Unit 4: Living on Your Own

Deciding which occupation you would like and getting the necessary education and training is only a part of life. When you begin living on your own, you will need to know as much as possible about finding a home, managing your income, using bank services and credit, and maintaining budgets. Learning the difference between necessities and frills and understanding your legal rights as a consumer will help you make mature financial decisions.

Life is about more than working and managing your money—it's about taking care of yourself, being a responsible citizen, caring for the world you live in, living as part of a family, and enjoying the rewards of your work. Learning how to balance your personal concerns with your work will help you to achieve success in your career and your life.

The U.S. Department of Education Career Clusters

The 16 career clusters follow a system developed by the U.S. Department of Education. The career clusters divide occupations according to their relationship to one another and sectors within the economy and society and include most occupations from entry through professional levels.

Exploring the clusters of occupations will help you to identify those that relate to your personal characteristics and to the level of education and training you plan to achieve. The appendix lists some occupations at more than one level of education and training because you can enter most occupations from more than one level. Note that workers who take lifelong education and training seriously are most likely to survive layoffs and receive promotions.

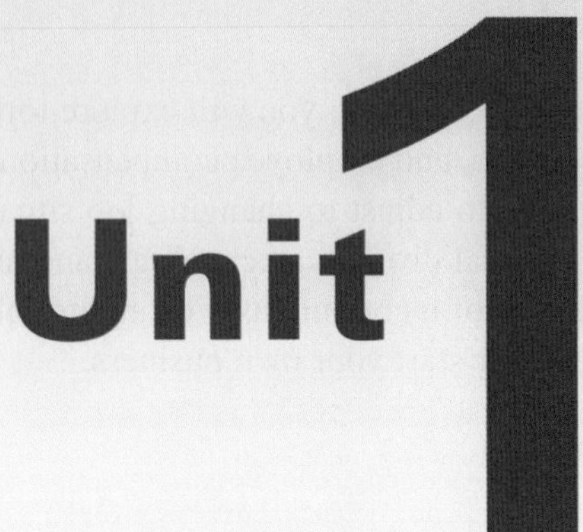

Unit 1 Getting Ready for the World of Work

Chapter 1: Preparing for Life's Many Tasks

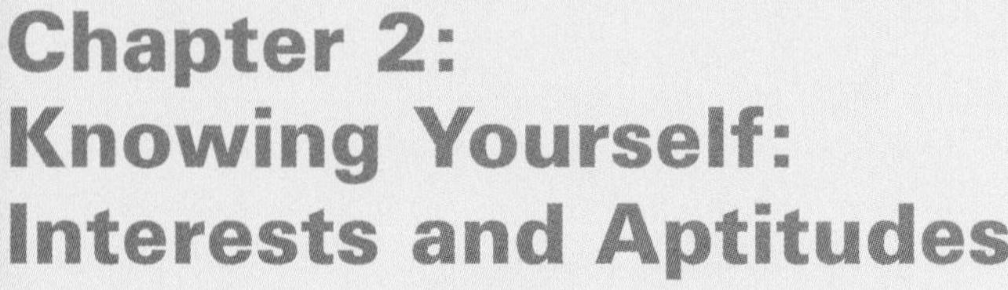

Chapter 2: Knowing Yourself: Interests and Aptitudes

Chapter 3: Knowing Yourself: Values and Goals

Chapter 4: Problem Solving: Making Choices

Chapter 5: Researching and Understanding Career Information

Chapter 6: Looking Ahead: Education and Training

Chapter 1 Resources

Lesson Plans and Preparation

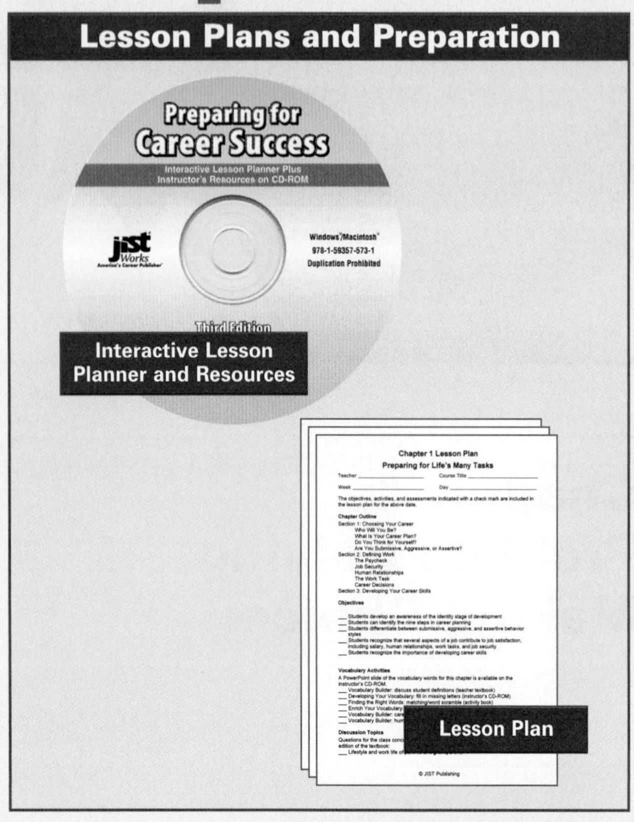

Interactive Lesson Planner and Resources

Lesson Plan

Multimedia

Chapter 1 Video Tour

PowerPoint Presentation

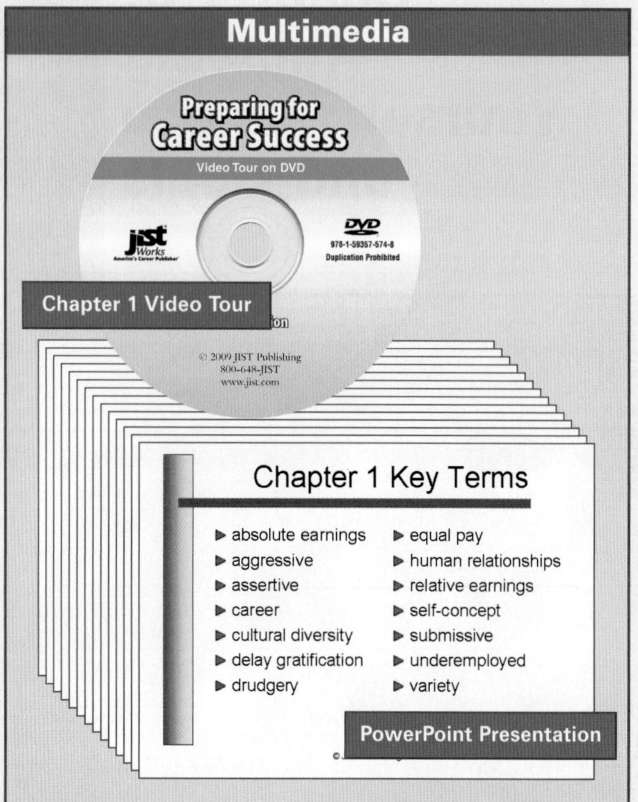

Activities

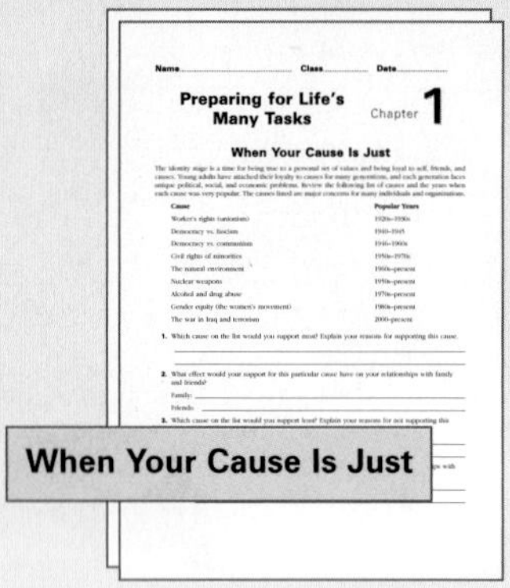

When Your Cause Is Just

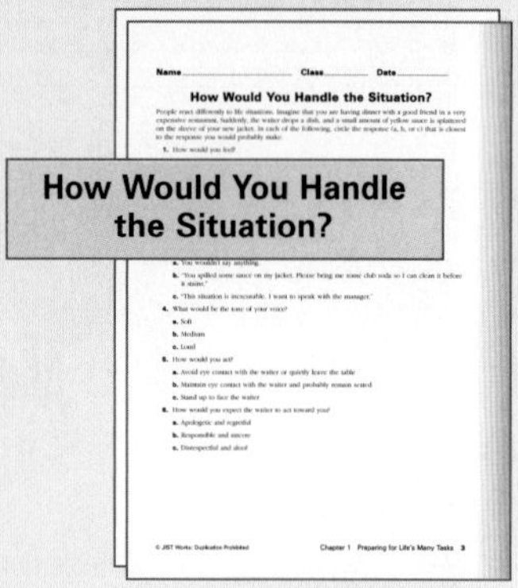

How Would You Handle the Situation?

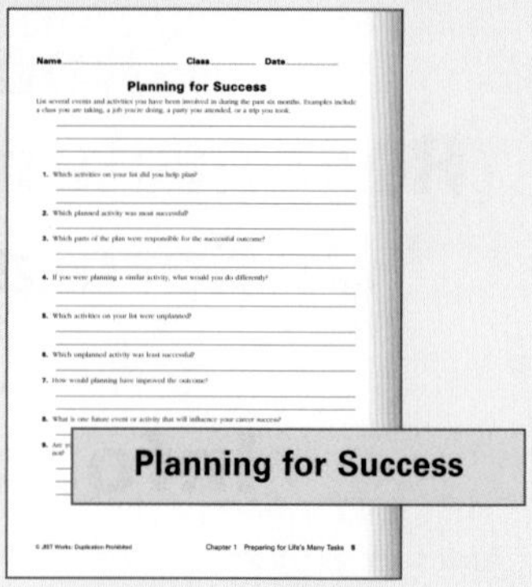

Planning for Success

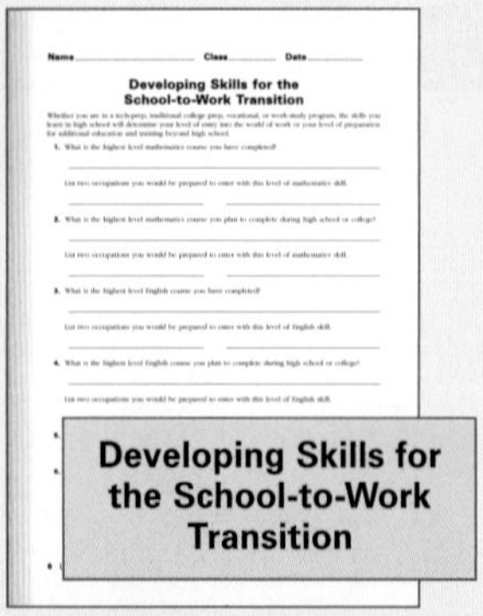

Developing Skills for the School-to-Work Transition

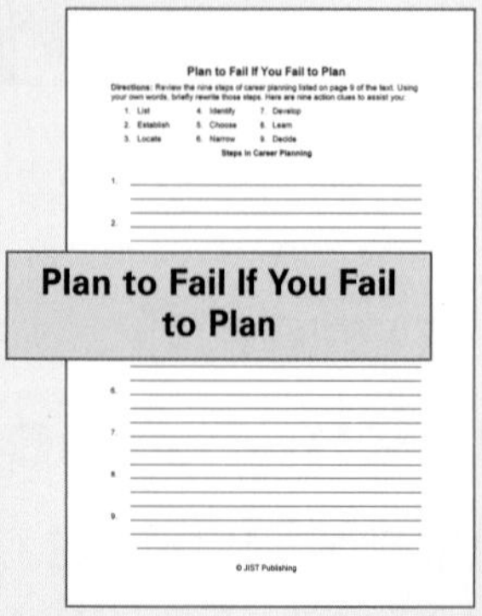

Plan to Fail If You Fail to Plan

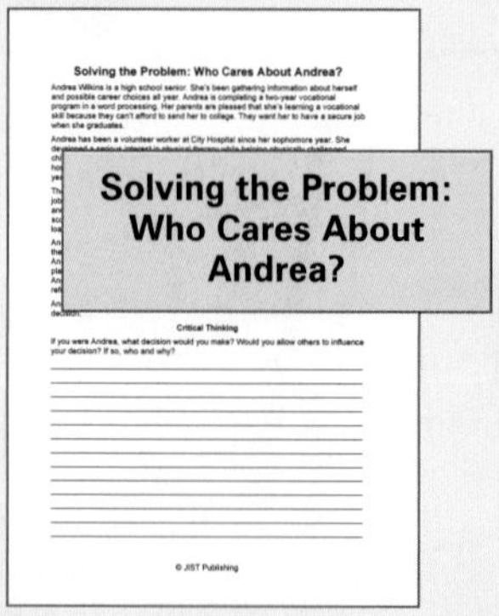

Solving the Problem: Who Cares About Andrea?

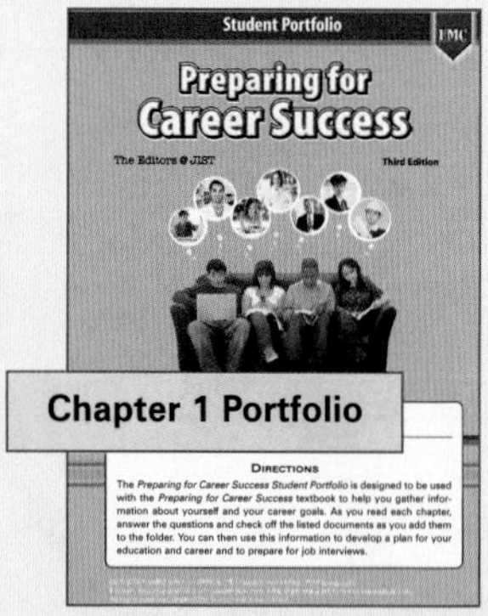

Chapter 1 Portfolio

 © JIST Works

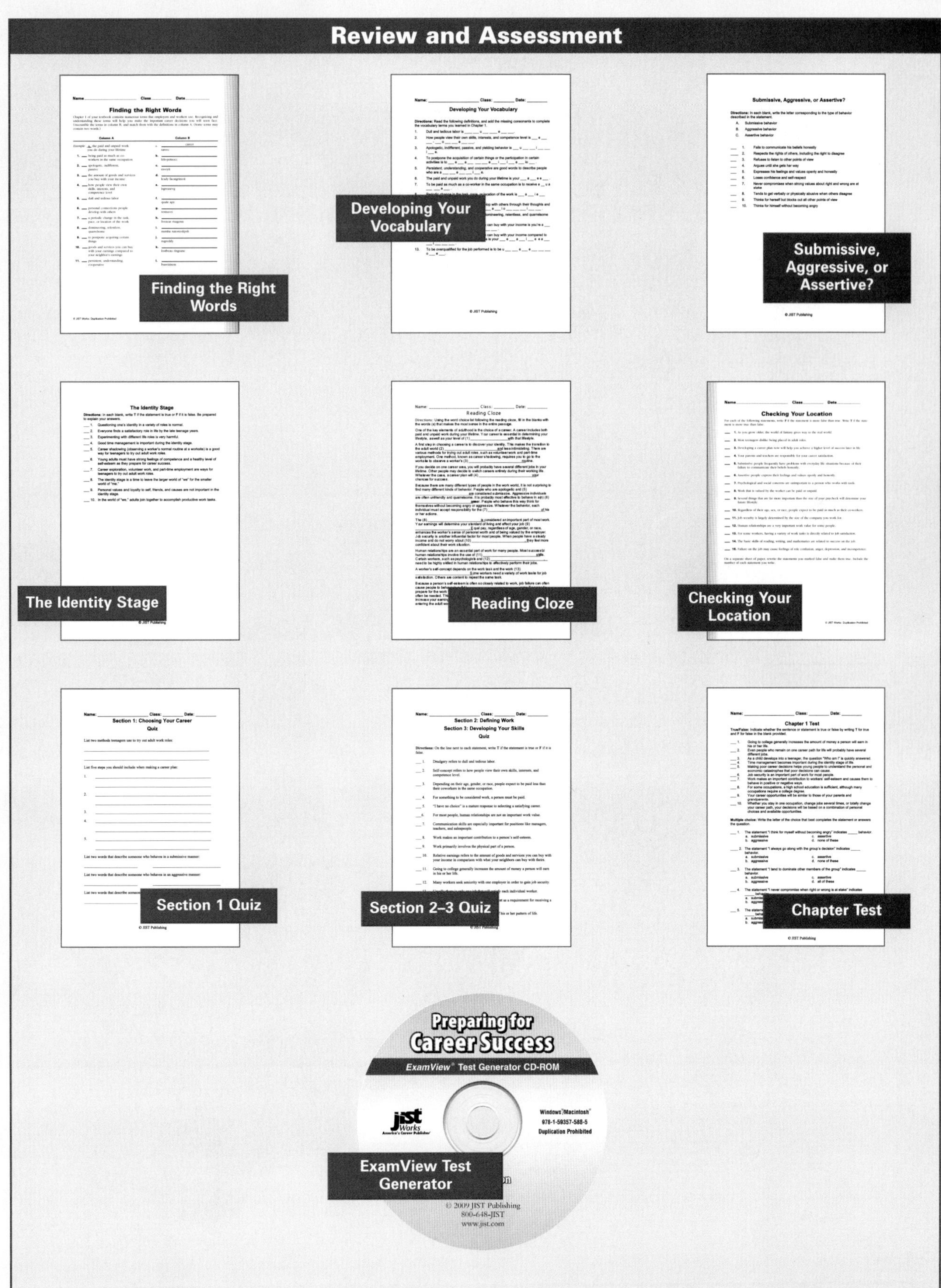
Review and Assessment
Finding the Right Words
Developing Your Vocabulary
Submissive, Aggressive, or Assertive?
The Identity Stage
Reading Cloze
Checking Your Location
Section 1 Quiz
Section 2–3 Quiz
Chapter Test
Preparing for Career Success
ExamView Test Generator CD-ROM
Windows/Macintosh
978-1-59357-588-5
Duplication Prohibited
© 2009 JIST Publishing
800-648-JIST
www.jist.com
ExamView Test Generator

Chapter 1 Preparing for Life's Many Tasks

Learning Objectives

- List specific personal characteristics related to the identity stage of development
- Appreciate the opinions of others but accept full responsibility for your decisions
- Describe how a worker's paycheck, job security, human relationships, and work tasks contribute to his or her level of job satisfaction
- Identify nine steps in a career plan and describe how each step relates to your life goals

During the twentieth century, the generations of your parents and grandparents entered the American workforce. Their work provided the food, clothing, shelter, and education needed to prepare your generation for life in the twenty-first century. In addition, they developed new technologies to expand the economy and create new jobs.

Enrich Your Vocabulary

In reading this chapter and doing the exercises, you will learn the following important terms:

absolute earnings	delay gratification	self-concept
aggressive	drudgery	submissive
assertive	equal pay	underemployed
career	human relationships	variety
cultural diversity	relative earnings	

Vocabulary Builder

The "Enrich Your Vocabulary" terms are highlighted and defined throughout the chapter. Discuss the "Enrich Your Vocabulary" terms before you assign the chapter. Ask students to write their own definitions, and then discuss their definitions in class.

Vocabulary

You can use the "Developing Your Vocabulary" worksheet for Chapter 1 on the *Preparing for Career Success Instructor's CD-ROM, Third Edition* as a pretest or as a reteaching worksheet.

TECHNOLOGY

As teenagers, your parents' generation used cassette players and VCRs. As adults, they've adapted to using cell phones and laptops. Consider the development of technology such as the BlackBerry and iPod during your lifetime. How might this technology affect the type and quantity of available jobs, the methods people use to search for jobs, and the way people perform daily work tasks? Being able to adapt to new technology is an important skill to have because technology is always changing.

Comprehension Check

Ask your students: What is and has been the work and lifestyle of your parents or grandparents? What do you already know about each of the changes listed for the twenty-first century?

During the twenty-first century, new changes will continue to reshape the American labor force and their workplace. New situations in the economy, the world, and shifting population tendencies will characterize the workforce and workplace of your future. Your career opportunities and lifestyle will be unlike those of your parents or grandparents in many ways:

- Inevitable changes in technology will continue to modify and transform the way people work as well as the type of work they do.
- The demands of an expanding and competitive global economy will give birth to new-fashioned business practices and situations for employers and employees.
- The composition of American families and companies will become more diverse due to an increase in the percentage of working women.
- **Cultural diversity** (a society with ethnic, religious, racial, and political differences) in the workplace will pay off in an expanded selection of career opportunities for Hispanics, African Americans, and disabled workers and will obligate employers to adopt diversity management systems to benefit and embrace different backgrounds and talents.
- The increased threat of terrorism in the workplace and throughout the nation will affect security procedures in the workplace.
- A frequently changing job market will make it necessary for individuals to plan for repeated job changes and to accept responsibility for their own career preparation and training throughout their working years.

These and other changes will be presented throughout the book.

As you begin to build your career and help provide for the next generation of workers, you will face important decisions and responsibilities. To handle them effectively, you will need a great deal of information—information about yourself and about the world around you. You will also need many skills, including skills for decision making, planning, and communication.

A key part of adulthood—a part that will have a major impact on all the other parts of your adult life—is your career. Your **career** (the paid and unpaid work you do during your lifetime) will determine

© JIST Works

- How much money you have to spend
- Whom you interact with every day
- How much free time you have
- How you feel about your activities and accomplishments

This chapter, like all the chapters in *Preparing for Career Success,* contains information that will help you make the important career decisions you will soon face. This chapter also helps you develop several life skills you will need to be successful and happy. After completing this chapter, you will be off to a fast start in your search for career and life success.

CAREER FACT

If you work 40 hours a week, you will have spent 2,080 hours on the job in one year. At that rate, if you retire after 40 years of working, you will have spent 83,200 hours of your life on the job. Use that time well by selecting a career path that you will enjoy.

Video Tour on DVD

Show students the Chapter 1 segment to introduce them to the content.

Section 1: Choosing Your Career

What do you want to be when you grow up? As a young child, you were probably asked this question many times. What did you answer? Many children give the name of a famous entertainer, a sports figure, or a favorite relative. Others name a "glamorous" occupation, such as astronaut, police officer, or firefighter.

Self-Understanding

Ask your students*:* When you were a small child, what was your fantasy career choice? What is your present tentative career choice? How do you account for any differences in the two choices?

Young children like to pretend, and they enjoy living in a fantasy world. However, as you grow older, the world of fantasy gives way to the real world. As a teenager, you are looking through the window of reality and

During the teenage years, considering more than one occupation is helpful. What occupations have you considered?

Choose a job you love, and you will never have to work a day in your life.
—Confucius

Discussion Starter

Ask your students: What did Confucius mean by this statement? Would this statement be true in today's world of work? Why or why not?

TAKE NOTE

Psychologist Erik Erikson developed the idea that people pass through eight life stages. For example, babies learn to trust others, and middle school students feel competent as they learn how to do more things. The identity stage is the fifth stage. How well you handle your current life stage depends on how well you mastered the skills of the previous life stages.

School-to-Work Transition

Ask your students: Have you used one of these four methods to try out adult work roles? Which method did you use, and what did you learn?

Reteaching

Have students complete "The Identity Stage" worksheet in Chapter 1 of the *Preparing for Career Success Instructor's CD-ROM, Third Edition.*

examining your personal interests, values, resources, and opportunities. Selecting your future career path is no longer a childhood fantasy. Suddenly, it is a responsibility with many tough choices. In the real world, you will need to make some compromises.

It is important to realize that you can be in control as you prepare for career success. Whether you take control or allow others to make your decisions for you, the future will arrive, and you will have a career. Your career will determine your lifestyle and your level of satisfaction with that lifestyle.

Who Will You Be?

As a child develops into a teenager, the question "Who am I?" arises more and more frequently. This time in a person's life is known as the *identity stage.* Many people are prepared to answer this question by their early twenties. Others find the answer much later in life, and a few never find a satisfactory answer. The question "Who am I?" or "Who will I be?" can be answered in terms of numerous adult roles:

1. What career role will I have?
2. Will I have a role as a wife or husband?
3. Will I be a parent? If so, what kind of parent will I be?
4. How will my gender affect and be affected by the adult roles I am seeking?

Teenagers commonly seek out experiences in which they can try out adult roles. Like actors on a stage, they experiment with different life roles. Having these experiences enables young people to discover their unique identities. Can you think of adult roles you have tried? Did you discover that they should be part of your life as an adult, or did you decide that they were not for you?

Teenagers try out adult work roles by using these four methods:

1. Volunteer work
2. Part-time employment
3. *Career exploration* ("hands-on" activities at a worksite)
4. *Career shadowing* (observing a worker's normal routine at a worksite)

During the identity stage, efficient time management becomes an important factor. School schedules require you to complete certain long-range tasks. You might have to integrate a part-time work schedule with your school schedule. In addition, your family might expect you to assume more responsibility at home. When you were a child at play, you could frequently ignore time. Now, hours, days, weeks, and years have become the ruler by which your life's accomplishments are measured.

© JIST Works

During the identity stage, young people realize that they will soon be responsible for obtaining their own food, clothing, and shelter as well as the "good things" that they desire. Paying for these items will no longer be their parents' responsibility. At this point in life, young adults can no longer afford a lack of self-confidence. They need to have strong feelings of competence and a healthy level of self-esteem as they prepare for career success in the adult world.

For many teens, the identity stage is a time to leave the self-centered, small world of "me" and join the larger world of "we." It is a time for being true to a personal set of values and being loyal to self, friends, and causes. In the world of "we," adults join together to accomplish productive work tasks.

Why is managing time as important as managing money?

What Is Your Career Plan?

What will your life be like when you are 22 years old? Will you be working a job or going to school? Will you be responsible for children?

What will life be like when you are 30? Will you own a business or work for someone else? Will you drive a new car or own your own home?

Taking time to plan your future career is important. Think about how you will support yourself after high school or college. Think about the occupation you are preparing for and the lifestyle you want.

You may decide to work in one career cluster (see the appendix of this book for more information on career clusters) for life, but you will probably have several different jobs. Some people change to totally different career clusters during their working life. For example, someone might leave a job in chemical research to become a high school teacher. In this case, the worker has not only changed jobs, but has also moved from the career cluster of Scientific Research and Engineering to the career cluster of Education and Training. Whether you stay in one occupation, change jobs several times, or totally change your career path, your decisions will be based on a combination of personal choices and available opportunities.

Comprehension Check

Explain that it is normal for children to be self-centered. Ask your students: What self-centered behaviors have you noticed in small children? How do these behaviors affect their ability to cooperate with other children? Can you think of a time when an adult you know used a similar, self-centered behavior? How did the adult's behavior affect his or her ability to cooperate with other adults?

School to Work: Is Experience Always the Best Teacher?

Ted Johnson knew that he wanted to be a bricklayer since he was in the eighth grade. His Uncle Fred is a bricklayer, and together they built a brick barbecue for Ted's grandparents.

After Ted graduated from high school, he entered a bricklayer's apprenticeship program. He hated working that first winter. Sometimes his fingers were so cold he could hardly feel them. Summer wasn't much better. Working in the hot summer sun was a lot different from going to the beach or driving around in his car. Ted felt trapped. He had never considered an occupation other than bricklayer. Ted quit the apprenticeship program and decided that the best way to select a job was to get more experience. Since then, Ted has been employed in six different jobs in the past two years.

KEY TO SUCCESS

When planning your career, consider what skills you have or will have to offer an employer and what you expect in return.

Reteaching

Have students complete the "Plan to Fail If You Fail to Plan" worksheet found in Chapter 1 of the *Preparing for Career Success Instructor's CD-ROM, Third Edition.*

Stacey Adams began thinking about her career in the ninth grade. The school counselor gave Stacey's class a career interest inventory, explained where to find career information, and suggested ways to use it. Using her knowledge about herself and about possible occupations, Stacey narrowed her choices to the very broad area of construction work.

In tenth grade, Stacey took a carpentry course. She also joined the school's chapter of SkillsUSA where she met construction professionals. She was surprised to learn that algebra and geometry were important subjects for construction work.

Following her 16th birthday, Stacey applied to several small construction companies for employment. She was hired for a summer job doing cleanup work at a construction site. Stacey took every opportunity to ask different construction workers about their job tasks and responsibilities. Stacey also asked how she could get training for that type of work.

Stacey is currently taking a one-year course in construction technology at a local technical college. She is not certain whether she wants to work as a plumber or an electrician. Stacey plans to make her choice when she graduates and then enter an apprenticeship program.

FIND OUT MORE

The U.S. Department of Labor's Occupational Employment Statistics (OES) program produces employment and wage estimates for more than 800 occupations. Contact the OES at www.bls.gov/OES.

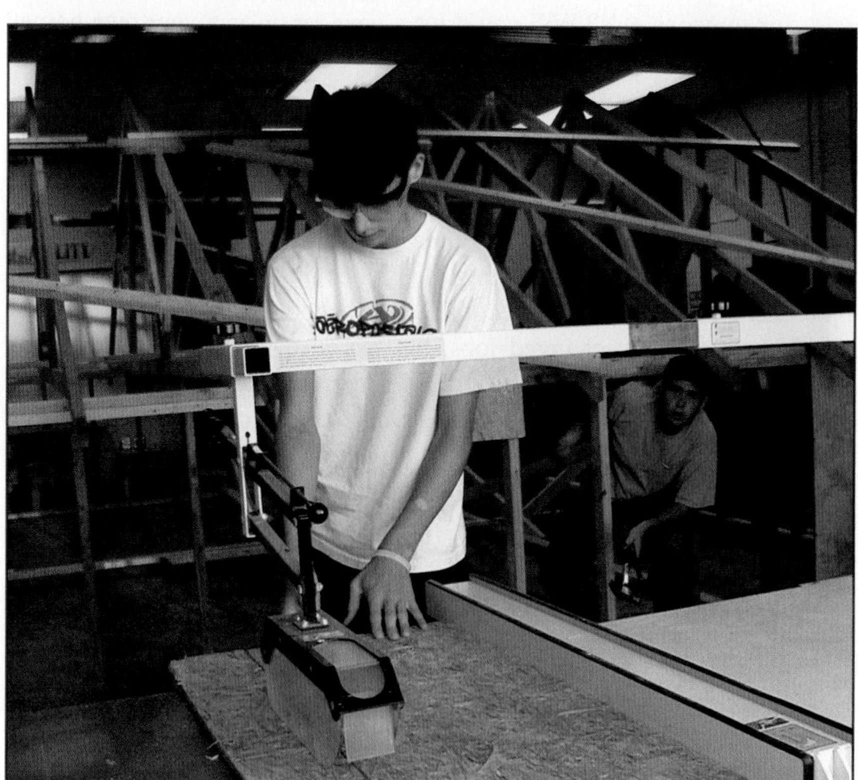

TAKE NOTE

SkillsUSA is a career and technical student organization with 13,000 school chapters. These chapters provide career education services to more than 280,000 students in order to develop their marketable skills in more than 60 occupations. These occupations range from architectural drafting and health science to Web design and welding. For more information, contact your local chapter or visit the Web site at www.skillsusa.org.

Critical Thinking

How would you describe Ted's career plan as he moved from school to work? How did career planning affect his career success? Give examples to support your opinion.

How would you describe Stacey's career as she moved from school to work? How did career planning affect her career success? Give examples to support your opinion.

© JIST Works

Can you imagine an NFL football team showing up for the Super Bowl without a game plan? If you are a football fan, you know that the team would probably lose. Making a career plan won't guarantee your future success any more than making a game plan ensures a football team of winning. However, not making a career plan will probably put your career success in the loss column, and you will have to live with the disappointment. Developing a career plan now will help you achieve a higher level of success later in life.

When making your career plan, include the following steps:

1. List your personal and career interests, natural abilities, job skills, academic achievements, and values.
2. Establish short- and long-term goals. It is important to establish dates for reaching your goals and to identify a method for evaluating your progress.
3. Locate and use occupational information.
4. Identify broad career areas that are related to your interests, talents, and important values.
5. Choose as many occupations as possible within your broad areas of career interest. Make certain that your selections are expected to offer future growth and stability and will provide experiences leading to higher-paying, more desirable occupations.
6. Narrow down your occupational choices to a few.
7. Develop a plan to acquire the education and training you will need to enter the occupations you have selected.
8. Learn job-seeking and job-keeping skills.
9. Decide what sacrifices you are willing to make to fulfill your career plan.

Each chapter in *Preparing for Career Success* provides information to help you to develop your unique career plan.

Cluster Link

If you are interested in helping students evaluate their interests, abilities, and disabilities and deal with personal, social, academic, and career problems, you might enjoy the career cluster of Education and Training. This cluster plans, manages, and provides education and training services and related learning support services. See the appendix for more information.

Key To Success

A portfolio is a collection of materials (either paper or electronic) that show your career interests, academic and technical preparation, skills, and accomplishments. It can include such items as test scores, a transcript, a resume, writing samples, photographs of completed projects, and letters of recommendation. You can use your portfolio to demonstrate your level of preparedness to a teacher or employer for acceptance into a class, program, internship, or job.

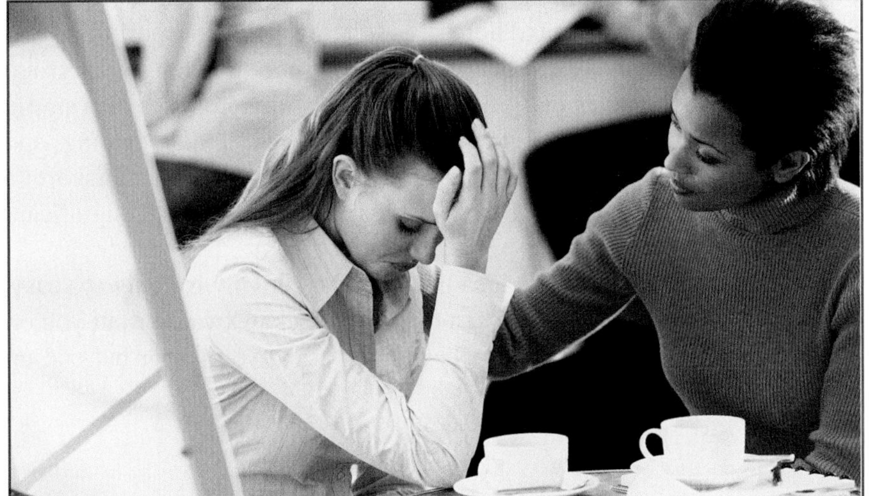

Why should a person have a workable plan before jumping into a career?

School-to-Work Transition

Explain that information concerning each of the nine steps will be covered in future chapters. Ask students to keep the nine steps in mind because they will be used later to write a personal career plan.

© JIST Works

Do You Think for Yourself?

Have you ever had doubts about your ability to make a wise career choice? Should you ask your friends or family what career to select? Choosing a specific occupation is very difficult because the career puzzle has so many parts. Therefore, getting as much information as possible about each piece is important.

Selecting a satisfactory career path is your responsibility. Wise decision makers ask others for their opinions and carefully consider the advice they receive. However, each individual must accept responsibility for the outcomes of his or her actions and should always make the final decision. If you make a poor career selection, you are likely to find yourself studying school subjects you dislike, paying for education and training that doesn't prepare you for the future, and going to work every day to a job that provides very little satisfaction.

Vocabulary Builder

Explain the meaning of the term *career path*. An example would be starting out in a restaurant washing dishes and advancing to kitchen helper, cook, chef, and ultimately restaurant manager. Ask the students for other examples of a career path.

Are You Submissive, Aggressive, or Assertive?

How do you behave with a group of friends? Do you go where they decide and do what they wish even when you disagree? If so, you are probably a submissive person. Submissive people frequently have problems with everyday life situations because of their failure to communicate their beliefs honestly. Their submissive behaviors cause them to lose confidence and self-respect. *Apologetic, indifferent, passive,* and *yielding* are good words to describe people who behave in a **submissive** manner.

KEY TO SUCCESS

An assertive individual confronts life's situations instead of ignoring them.

On the other hand, perhaps you refuse to listen to other points of view, argue until you get your way, and tend to become verbally or physically abusive when others disagree with you. If so, you would be considered an aggressive person. Aggressive people try to dominate others. They think for themselves but block out all other points of view. They send the message, "We'll do it my way, or we won't do it." *Unfriendly, insulting, domineering, relentless,* and *quarrelsome* are good words to describe people who behave in an **aggressive** manner.

Self-Understanding

Have students complete the "How Would You Handle the Situation?" worksheet in Chapter 1 of the *Preparing for Career Success Student Activity Book, Third Edition.*

A third type of behavior is assertiveness. Assertive people think for themselves without becoming angry or aggressive. They can express their feelings and values openly and honestly. Assertive people respect the rights of others, including the right to disagree. They may go along with group decisions even when they disagree, but they never compromise when strong values about right and wrong are at stake. *Persistent, understanding,* and *cooperative* are good words to describe people who behave in an **assertive** manner. Occupational research suggests that assertiveness is a significant factor in workplace success.

Cooperative Learning

Divide the class into groups of three. Assign a specific number of minutes for each group to think of a work situation involving the three types of people—submissive, aggressive, and assertive. Have various groups role-play their situations for the class. Have the class try to identify the behaviors of each role player as submissive, aggressive, or assertive.

Expressing a feeling or an idea that you value highly isn't always easy. Some people or some situations can make you feel awkward or put you on the defensive. You may want to behave in an assertive manner but end up

© JIST Works

being submissive or losing your cool and being aggressive. Has this ever happened to you? Did you think for yourself in this particular situation?

Submissive, aggressive, and assertive behaviors take place in the world of work every day. They affect a worker's performance evaluations, raises, promotions, and future recommendations.

Key To Success

You must first define success if you are to achieve it.

Solving the Problem: Who Gets the Promotion?

Jessica Young is a supervisor for the Mid-State Machinery Corporation. She is reviewing the employment files of three workers to determine who will be offered a promotion. All three have good attendance, four years of experience assembling specialized machinery, and all of the necessary technical skills.

The promotion will involve machine installation for customers. It will require a strong knowledge of machinery, the ability to diagnose and solve problems with newly installed machines, and good communication skills. The person selected must be an independent thinker. Help Jessica decide by reviewing the characteristics of the three workers being considered:

Case Study

Read the case study "Who Cares about Andrea?" found in Chapter 1 of the *Preparing for Career Success Instructor's CD-ROM, Third Edition* aloud and discuss the "Critical Thinking" questions with your students.

Self-Understanding

Ask your students whether they can share one of their characteristics that are similar to Ashley, Tony, or Sue. Ask how that characteristic might help or harm their career success.

Sue: Everyone in the plant considers Sue to be a very nice person. Sue was planning to go to college when she graduated from high school, but she decided to stay home, work, and help her parents with their living expenses. When any subject related to career success comes up, Sue talks about her plan to go to college—someday. During manufacturing team meetings, Sue always goes along with whatever the team wants to do. She doesn't like to rock the boat.

Tony: Most people think Tony is a little hard to take, but even those who dislike him personally agree that he knows more about manufacturing, installing, and troubleshooting machinery than anyone else in the plant. Tony always seems to notice when someone else is having a problem with a machine. He immediately drops what he is doing and gets involved in the other person's situation. His usual opening line is "Why don't you try doing it the right way for a change?" Tony gets on people's nerves, but he's usually right. Giving Tony suggestions isn't wise, though, because he will probably do just the opposite.

Ashley: Ashley always tries to do a good job and doesn't get upset about things she can't control. If Ashley doesn't understand something, she asks someone for advice. She doesn't proceed with a job until she is confident that she is doing it correctly. She has even asked Tony for advice, although she considers him to be a self-centered motormouth. Ashley takes pride in assembling quality machines. She tries to get along with everyone and is usually willing to compromise. However, when Ashley decides to do something a certain way, that's the way she does it.

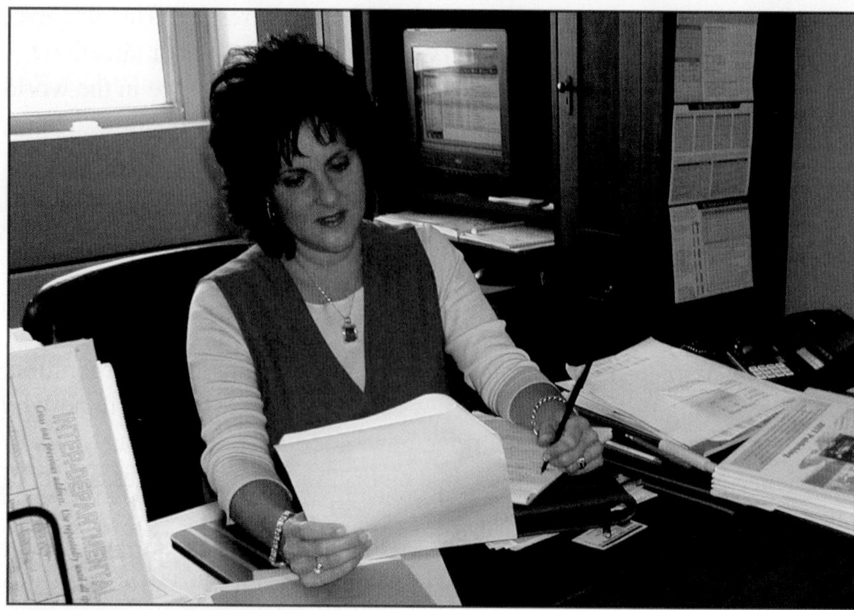

Critical Thinking

Which worker is best in situations that require independent thinking? Give examples to support your position.

If you were Jessica, which of the three workers would you select for the promotion? Why? How would you explain to the other workers why they were not selected?

Section 1: Get Involved

Answer the following on a separate sheet of paper, and be prepared to discuss your responses in class.

1. List the three people whom you admire and respect the most, in the order of their importance to you. They may be people you know well or people you have learned about from books or television. Have any of these people influenced your thinking about what career you should consider? Explain.
2. Have you done anything to discover more information about yourself, about occupations, or about the education and training needed for certain careers? If so, what have you done? If not, what could you do?
3. What decisions have you made using independent thinking skills? What decisions have you let others make for you?
4. Think of a situation in which you behaved in a passive or aggressive manner. If you could do it over again, what assertive behavior could you use?

Student Evaluation

To evaluate student mastery of concepts, you might want to use the Section 1 quiz found in the Chapter 1 file of the *Preparing for Career Success Instructor's CD-ROM, Third Edition.*

Section 2: Defining Work

Before you choose a career, you should have a good concept of what work is and why people do it. People have many reasons for working. Which of the following reasons are most important to you?

© JIST Works

1. “I have no choice. I must work.”
2. “I work to pay for my food, shelter, and clothing.”
3. “I work to buy the ‘good things’ of life—things I want but don’t need.”
4. “I work to provide my family with an acceptable lifestyle.”
5. “I work to feel productive, to make use of my skills and talents, and to gain rewards.”

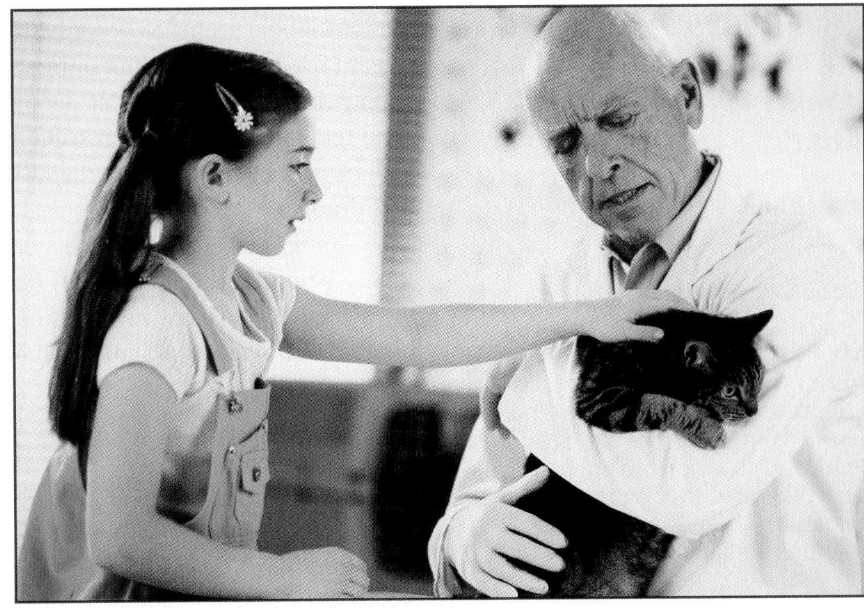

Some people enjoy caring for animals. What type of work would you enjoy?

The most mature response is number 5. It implies a desire to be a productive member of society. This response also demonstrates knowledge of personal interests and the way they relate to the work activities of certain occupations. In addition, it considers the personal and financial rewards of the occupation.

The least mature response is number 1. It implies a lack of personal control in the process of selecting a satisfying career. Taking responsibility for your career is an important part of preparing for career success.

Tim Watson is taking a career-planning class at Central High School. His assignment is to write a few paragraphs defining the word *work.* The assignment seemed easy before he started writing. The more Tim read about work, however, the more complicated the definition of the word became. Tim decided to interview several workers and ask them for their ideas about work. Here are their responses:

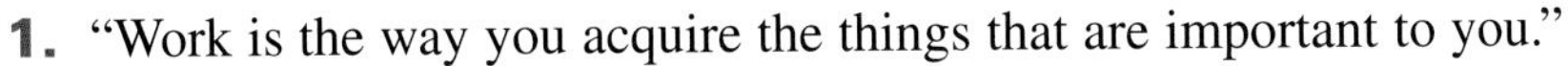

1. “Work is the way you acquire the things that are important to you.”
2. “Work is the only way you can survive in today’s world.”
3. “You only get as much out of your work as you put into it.”
4. “Work is doing what someone else wants and getting paid for it.”
5. “Being a volunteer or just doing something to help someone can be hard work, and you don’t get paid in money. It makes you feel good.”
6. “People respect a person who does good work.”
7. “I feel good inside when I know I’ve done a good job.”

Self-Understanding

Ask your students: Which of the seven responses is most important to you? Describe an experience during which you felt this way.

Tim realized that people were using their own words to tell him all of the things he had been reading about work. He decided that work involves all of the parts of a person—physical, social, and psychological. A worker’s attitudes, abilities, interests, values, personal satisfaction, and problems go to work with him or her every day. Whether the work involves tools,

It is essential that your job be as enjoyable and rewarding as possible. It would be a waste of a lifetime if it wasn't.

—Mihaly Csikszentmihalyi

Cooperative Learning

Assign a committee to investigate Mihaly Csikszentmihalyi (former professor of psychology at Chicago University) and his Flow Theory. Have them report to the class and lead a discussion about his ideas and the ways they relate to career success. Numerous books and Internet sites are available.

TAKE NOTE

In ancient Hindu text, flow is "the expression of acting and not being attached to the fruit of action." In today's world, flow is when your only thoughts are of doing the task well and enjoying the process.

people, or information, working indoors or out, or working alone or with others, the worker is involved as a total person.

Tim decided that there's more to work than a paycheck. After all, some people hate their jobs but want the paycheck. The word **drudgery** (dull and tedious labor) seems to describe their jobs better than the word *work.* They regard their work as being uninteresting and disagreeable rather than interesting and enjoyable. Other people volunteer to work for no pay, and they find their work to be interesting and rewarding. Tim concluded that work can be paid or nonpaid, but that if it isn't valued by the worker, it isn't work. It's drudgery.

Tim was eager to attend his career-planning class the next day. He was really beginning to understand the meaning of work. In class, the teacher presented a lot of new information, and Tim took careful notes. He realized that he also wanted to build paychecks and job security into his report.

The Paycheck

Although work can be paid or unpaid, the paycheck is an important part of most work. First of all, people must have money to pay for their food, clothing, and shelter. Whether you eat macaroni or steak for dinner, buy your clothes at a discount house or have them tailored, or live in public housing or a mansion, your lifestyle options are determined by the size of your paycheck.

Your level of absolute earnings will determine how well you live. **Absolute earnings** refers to the amount of goods and services you can buy with your income. **Relative earnings** refers to the amount of goods and services you can buy with your income compared with what your neighbors can buy with theirs. Your absolute earnings must be sufficient to maintain an adequate standard of living. However, your relative earnings are an important factor in determining your attitude toward your work and your job satisfaction.

Regardless of their age, sex, or race, people expect to be paid as much as their coworkers in the same occupation. **Equal pay** gives them a sense of personal worth and causes them to feel valued by their employer. People also expect to be paid as much as the employer can afford and as much as might be earned elsewhere.

Job Security

Job security is an important part of work for most people. *Job security* means that workers can be confident that their jobs will always be available to them. They know that they will have an income and that they need not worry about layoffs.

Job security is one reason many workers seek seniority with one employer. Others work in an occupation that is minimally affected by seasonal or periodic ups and downs in business. For some, job security is achieved through hard work and thrift. In today's rapidly changing world of

© JIST Works

work, job security increasingly depends on a worker's ability to adapt to new situations and to continually update employment skills.

That evening, Tim phoned his aunt Janet to discuss his report on work. Janet is a human relations specialist for a large corporation. She invited Tim to stop by her office the next day.

When Tim arrived at Janet's office, he showed her his report and asked if she could think of any additional information about work. Janet read the report and told Tim that it contained excellent information. In fact, she wanted a copy of the final draft for her office. Janet suggested that Tim might add some additional information about human relationships and the work task. She provided the information in the following section.

Comprehension Check

Present the following situation to your students: Imagine that you have worked for a company for three years and another company offers you a similar job with a 35 percent increase in pay. Would you take the offer? Imagine that, like most people, you accept the offer. Then imagine that your new boss is unfriendly and makes unreasonable demands on you. Your coworkers are constantly complaining, and your new job situation is very unpleasant. Would you look for another job? Why or why not?

Human Relationships

Human relationships are the personal connections people develop with others through their thoughts and behaviors. Human relationships are a very important work value for some people. The communication skills of reading, writing, speaking, and listening are involved in most successful relationships. In the workplace, human relationships exist between workers and their peers, superiors, subordinates, and customers. To establish and maintain effective two-way communication, all workers need the following:

- Recognition from other workers that they are different in some ways but are still understood and accepted
- A feeling of bcing important and appreciated
- A certain amount of independence to accomplish their job tasks (this could involve setting the pace of the work, being free from close supervision, or being able to openly express opinions about the work)
- Knowledge that evaluations and rewards are based on fair, clearly understood standards
- Knowledge that loyalty will be rewarded

Vocabulary Builder

Present the following example of a human relationship in the everyday world of work: A sales clerk uses a pleasant voice to offer assistance to a customer. Ask your students to provide other examples.

CAREER FACT

High pay is effective in attracting workers to new jobs, but it is less effective in holding them on the job.

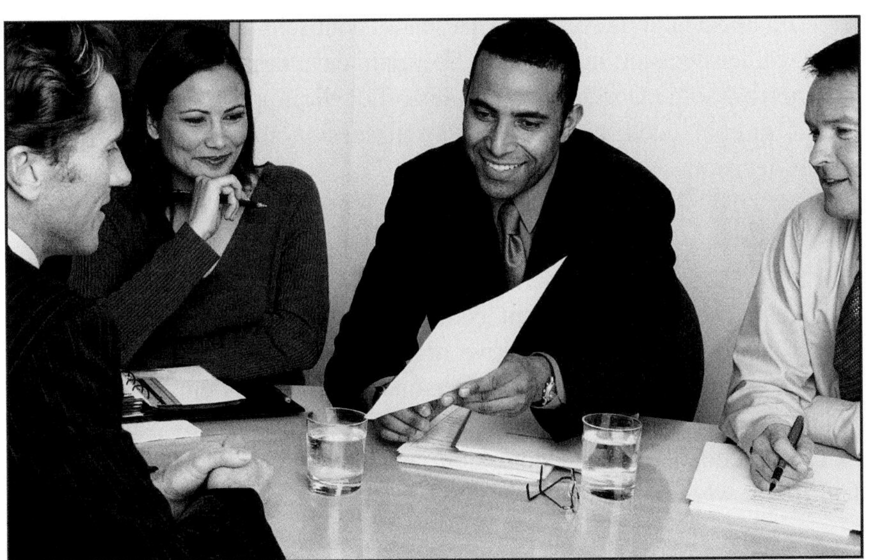

How can you develop your reading, writing, speaking, and listening skills so that you can solve the complex problems that often face groups?

© JIST Works

Although most workers must be able to communicate and get along with others, being highly skilled in human relationships is especially important for managers, personnel specialists, salespeople, teachers, and psychologists. What other occupations can you think of that require a high level of human relations skill? (See the appendix for more information.)

Tim thanked his Aunt Janet for the information and promised her a copy of his finished report. That evening, Tim reviewed all of the material he had collected on work and sat down at his computer to write the last section of the report. He wanted to include a little more information about the work tasks that people perform. He planned to end the report with a summary of the factors that provide job satisfaction to workers and the importance of making wise career choices.

Self-Understanding

Present the following situation to your students: Think about your own skills, interests, and competence level. Describe one work task that would fit with your self-concept and one that wouldn't.

The Work Task

The opportunity for self-expression exists in the performance of a work task if the task provides the worker with outlets for his or her abilities and interests. In other words, the work task and the work situation create a job role that is in keeping with the worker's **self-concept** (how a person views his or her own skills, interests, and competence level).

For some workers, having a variety of work tasks is directly related to job satisfaction. For others, it is unimportant. **Variety** entails a periodic change in the task, the pace, or the location of the work. The physical conditions in which the work task is performed, the way the job tasks are organized, and the availability of equipment and materials all contribute to a worker's job satisfaction.

KEY TO SUCCESS

Your effectiveness on the job will depend to a great degree on the match between yourself, the job task, and the workplace.

As he wrote his ideas on paper, Tim wondered why some people seem very satisfied with their work while others consider their jobs to be drudgery. He interviewed several workers and asked them to list the rewards they received from their jobs. Tim used their answers to demonstrate the wide range of job satisfaction, from the highest level to the lowest. See Table 1.1 for Tim's list. Of the job rewards listed in the table, which three would be most important to you? Which would be least important?

Tim decided to pay a visit to his school counselor to ask some questions about career decision making. Mr. Rotunda gave him a lot of ideas and let Tim borrow some workbooks from his office. Equipped with new information, Tim concluded his report with a discussion about the importance of career decisions.

Self-Understanding

Ask your students: Who can give an example of a time when completing a successful work task made you feel competent?

Career Decisions

Work makes an important contribution to workers' self-esteem and causes them to behave in positive or negative ways. Job success usually provides workers with a sense of personal identity, enjoyment, and a feeling of competence. On the other hand, failure on the job may cause feelings of role confusion, anger, depression, and incompetence. How would you feel if you were **underemployed** (overqualified for the job)?

© JIST Works

Table 1.1: Tim's List of Levels of Job Satisfaction

Levels of Job Satisfaction	Rewards of the Job
High	Paycheck satisfies realistic lifestyle desires. High level of skill provides security and job choices. Job provides prestige at work, home, and in the community. Coworkers are cooperative and supportive. Management has a high regard for the worker's performance. Work is interesting and requires the worker's full ability. The worker values the work tasks.
Average	Paycheck covers more than basic necessities. Seniority and job skills provide some security. Job provides respect at work, at home, and from peers. Coworkers are usually pleasant. Supervisor usually approves of worker's performance. Work is usually interesting. Tasks sometimes require full use of worker's skills.
Low	Paycheck covers basic food, shelter, and clothing. Security depends on the economy and approval of supervisor. Job is considered menial by others. Most coworkers are unpleasant or unconcerned. Supervisor is demanding and lacks understanding. Work is boring and repetitious.

Your work will affect the total pattern of your life—the place where you live, your personal relationships, the schedule you live by, your leisure activities, and your economic security.

There is more than one job that will satisfy each worker, and there is certainly more than one worker capable of satisfying each job. Take time to consider many possible careers, develop a plan, and prepare for your life's work with enthusiasm.

Section 2: Get Involved

Answer the following on a separate sheet of paper, and be prepared to discuss your answers in class.

1. List six characteristics of work. Which characteristic is most important to you? Which is least important? Why?
2. If you won a million dollars and could do anything you wanted with your time, what would you do?
3. Would the activity you select be work? Why or why not?
4. List 10 ways that our society would be different if nobody worked. What useful purpose does work serve?
5. Make a list of the feelings a person might have from being unemployed. Make another list of the feelings a person might have from being underemployed.

Career Fact

According to the U.S. Department of Labor, educational attainment alone does not determine an individual's earning potential over his or her lifetime. Other factors, including occupation, field of study, and work experience and continuity, also significantly affect a specific worker's income. However, over the course of their working lives, adults are likely to have higher earnings the more educated they are.

Section 3: Developing Your Career Skills

After you decide on a promising career area, you should begin preparing to acquire the necessary skills. For some occupations, a high school education is sufficient, though many occupations require a college degree. Other occupations require the completion of specialized course work or training. The difficulty, time, and cost of qualifying for an occupation vary widely and must be considered in your career planning. Depending on the occupation you select, preparation to begin work may last a few weeks, several months, or many years.

How many years do you plan to work? How much money will you earn during your working life? Some students in your graduating class will decide to increase their job skills before entering the world of work. Others will go directly into the job market. Those who enter the job market directly from high school will make less money during their working years.

If you begin a full-time job at age 20 and retire at age 60, you will spend 40 years earning money. Acquiring additional vocational or technical training, joining apprenticeship programs, and going on to college increase the amount of money you will earn during your working years. Participation in education and training programs requires the maturity necessary to **delay gratification** (postpone the acquisition of certain things or the participation in certain activities). Examine the information in Table 1.2 before making your education or training decision.

Many states have instituted competency tests for basic high school subjects as a requirement for receiving a high school diploma. The basic skills of reading, writing, and mathematics are strongly related to success on the job. What happens when workers don't have these skills?

Enrichment

Have students complete the "Developing Skills for the School-to-Work Transition" worksheet in Chapter 1 of the *Preparing for Career Success Student Activity Book, Third Edition.*

Discussion Starter

Ask your students: Is it fair to require high school students to pass competency tests as a requirement for receiving a high school diploma if they have passed all of their courses? Why or why not?

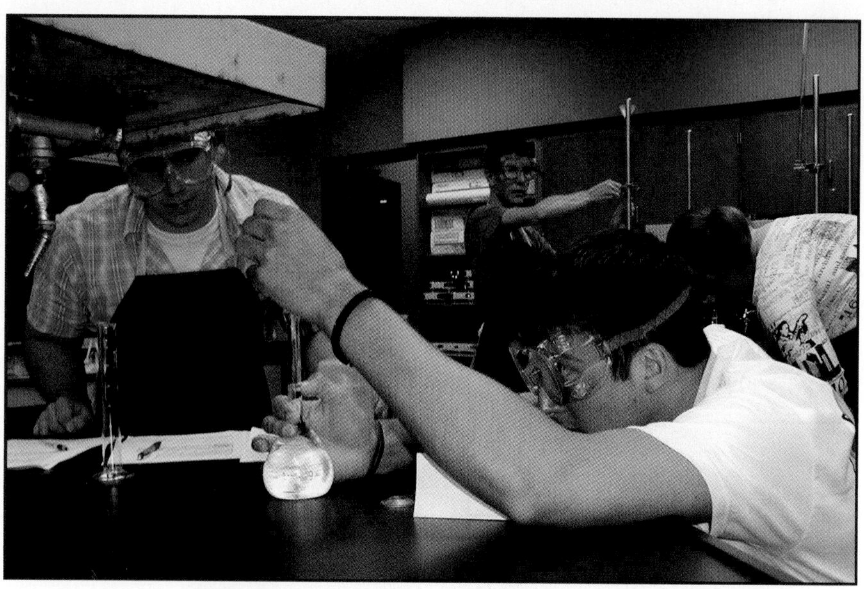

What job skills will you be able to offer your first full-time employer?

© JIST Works

In 1990, the U.S. Secretary of Labor appointed a *S*ecretary's *C*ommission on *A*chieving *N*ecessary *S*kills (**SCANS**) to examine the demands of the future workplace. One accomplishment of the commission was to develop a three-part foundation for building the career skills and personal qualities necessary for a successful career. Developing these foundation skills to a high level is crucial to your career success. Here are the three parts of the foundation skills:

- **Basic skills:** These skills form the core of basic education.

  Reading
  Writing
  Working with numbers
  Speaking
  Listening

- **Thinking skills:** Together these distinct skills form the process of thinking.

  Thinking creatively
  Making decisions
  Solving problems
  Visualizing
  Knowing how to learn
  Reasoning

- **Personal qualities:** These skills relate to a person's character.

  Being responsible
  Having self-esteem
  Being sociable
  Managing yourself
  Being honest

The commission also identified five workplace competencies that build on the foundation skills and are important for career success:

- **Resources skills**

  Managing money
  Managing time
  Managing materials and facilities
  Managing people

- **Interpersonal skills**

  Working with a team
  Teaching
  Serving customers
  Working with diversity
  Negotiating
  Leading

- **Technology skills**

  Selecting tools
  Applying technology
  Maintaining and troubleshooting equipment

- **Systems skills**

  Understanding systems
  Monitoring and correcting performance
  Improving and designing systems

School-to-Work Transition

Ask your students to name a basic skill learned in an English, social studies, mathematics, or science class that is also a job skill. Ask them to describe how the basic skill is used on the job.

Student Evaluation

To evaluate student mastery of concepts, you might want to use the Sections 2–3 quiz found in the Chapter 1 file of the *Preparing for Career Success Instructor's CD-ROM, Third Edition.* You can find a chapter test there as well.

© JIST Works

- **Information skills**

  Finding and evaluating information

  Organizing and maintaining information

  Interpreting and communicating information

  Using computers

Each chapter of this textbook ends with an activity titled "Develop SCANS Competencies." Completing these activities successfully will help you to build specific competencies for your career success.

Section 3: Get Involved

Answer the following on a separate sheet of paper, and be prepared to discuss your responses in class.

1. Whose responsibility is it to ensure that employees' skills are upgraded when job skill requirements change? Why?
2. Is your skill level in basic academic courses good enough for employment in the career field you are considering? List some examples to prove your point.

Chapter 1 Review

Enrich Your Vocabulary Answers

1. absolute earnings
2. human relationships
3. underemployed
4. submissive
5. aggressive
6. relative earnings
7. self-concept
8. assertive
9. delay gratification
10. variety
11. career
12. drudgery
13. equal pay
14. cultural diversity

Reteaching

Have students complete the "Finding the Right Words" and the "Checking Your Location" worksheets in Chapter 1 of the *Preparing for Career Success Student Activity Book, Third Edition.*

Enrich Your Vocabulary

On a separate sheet of paper, number from 1 to 14. Match each phrase with the most appropriate term from the "Enrich Your Vocabulary" list.

1. The amount of goods or services you can buy with your income
2. The personal connections people develop with others through their thoughts and behaviors
3. Overqualified for the job performed
4. Apologetic, indifferent, passive, and yielding
5. Unfriendly, insulting, domineering, relentless, and quarrelsome
6. The amount of goods or services you can buy with your income compared with what your neighbors can buy with theirs
7. How people view their own skills, interests, and competence level
8. Persistent, understanding, and cooperative
9. Postpone the acquisition of certain things or the participation in certain activities
10. Periodic change
11. The paid and unpaid work you do during your lifetime
12. Dull and tedious labor
13. To be paid as much as a coworker in the same occupation
14. A society with ethnic, religious, racial, and political differences

© JIST Works

Check Your Knowledge

On a separate sheet of paper, answer the following questions. (Do not write in your textbook.)

1. Why are many childhood thoughts about a career considered to be fantasy?
2. The identity stage comes just before adulthood. Why are independence, good time management, close relationships, a commitment to a cause, and a sense of "we" such important preparation for being an effective adult?
3. List five steps that your career plan should include.
4. If you make a poor career selection because you followed someone else's advice, who is to blame?
5. Would you prefer to be supervised by someone who is submissive, aggressive, or assertive? Explain your answer.
6. Providing one definition for the word *work* was difficult for Tim because he discovered that the word means different things to different people. What four main ideas did Tim use in his report to define the meaning of work?
7. List four of the ways that work affects the total pattern of your life.

Develop SCANS Competencies

This activity gives you practice in developing the information skills you need to be a successful worker. Develop a survey to find out what people feel is important about their jobs by using the "Rewards of the Job" column information in Table 1.1. List each reward, and then list a number scale after each reward. For example,

Paycheck satisfies realistic lifestyle desires.

Not Important				***Very Important***
1	2	3	4	5

People should circle the number that indicates how important that item is to them. Have at least 10 people respond to your survey.

Next, enter the responses into a spreadsheet and total the numbers circled for each item on the survey. For example, if in response to the item "Paycheck satisfies realistic lifestyle desires," four people marked 3, five people marked 5, and one person marked 2, the total for that item would be 39.

Finally, rank the items in order from the one with the highest total to the one with the lowest total. Those items with the highest totals are more important to people than items with lower totals. How did your results compare with those listed in Table 1.1? Were they very similar or very different?

Check Your Knowledge Answers

1. Answers will vary. Basically, such thoughts are not based on a realistic appraisal of personal abilities and available opportunities.
2. Answers will vary. Young people cannot become effective or well-adjusted adults until they master these responsible adult behaviors.
3. List personal and career interests, natural abilities, job skills, academic achievement, and values; establish short- and long-term goals; locate and use occupational information; identify broad career areas related to your interest, talents, and important values; chose as many occupations as possible within your broad areas of career interest; narrow down your occupational choices to a few; develop a plan to acquire the education or training needed to enter the occupations selected; learn job-seeking and job-keeping skills; and decide what sacrifices you are willing to make to fulfill your career plan.
4. Each person is responsible for his or her own career selection.
5. Answers will vary, but the most mature answer is *assertive*.
6. Paycheck or earnings, job security, human relationships, and the work task itself.
7. Work determines the place where you live, your personal relationships, the schedule you live by, your leisure activities, and your economic security.

Enrichment

Have students complete the Chapter 1 section of the *Preparing for Career Success Student Portfolio, Third Edition.*

© JIST Works

Chapter 2 Resources

Lesson Plans and Preparation

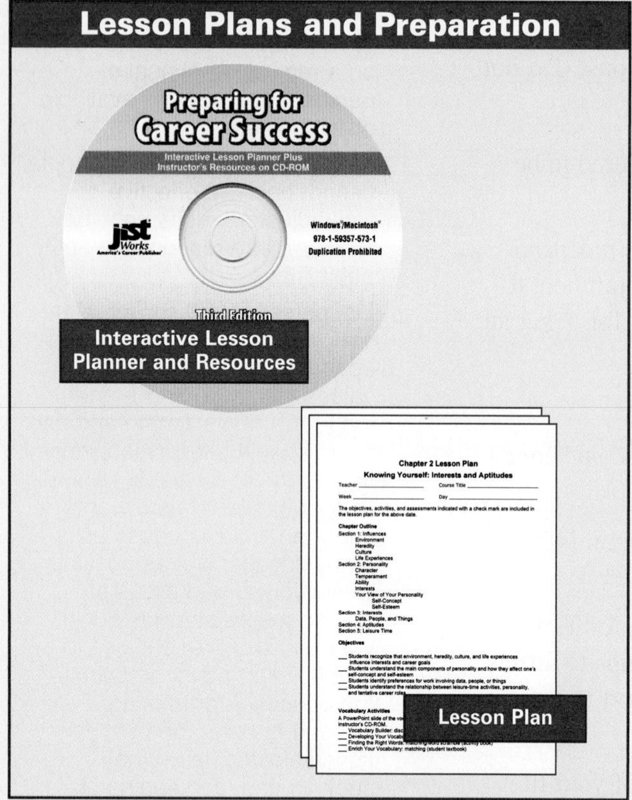

Multimedia

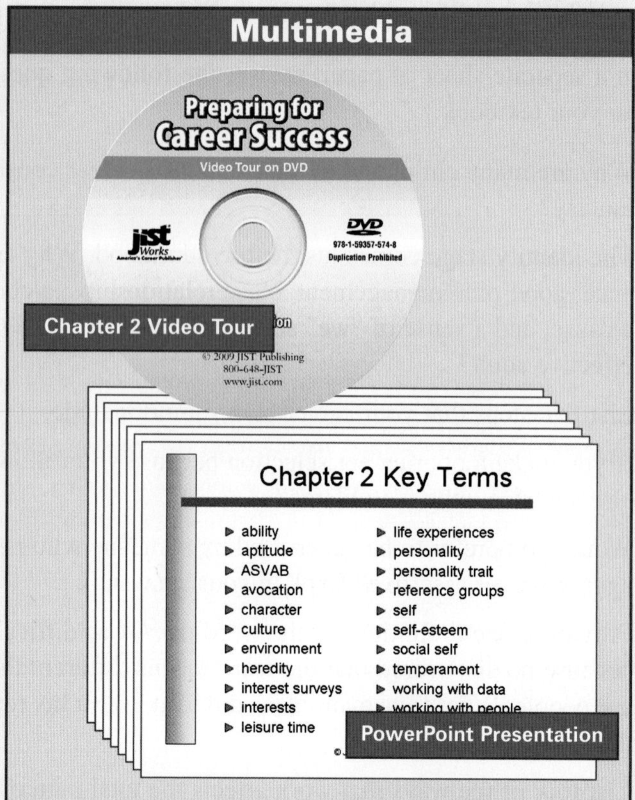

Activities

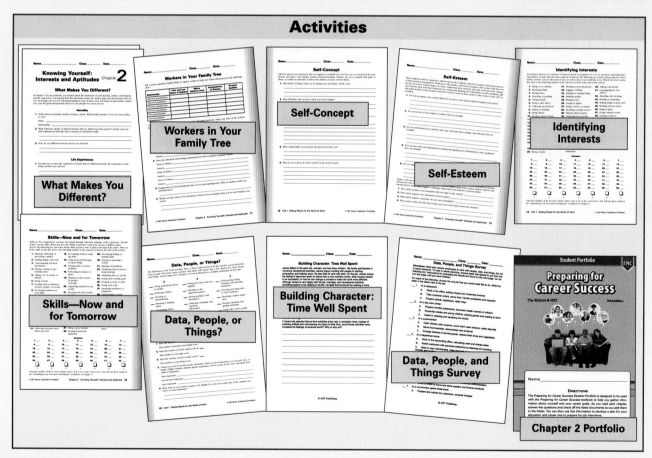

- What Makes You Different?
- Workers in Your Family Tree
- Self-Concept
- Self-Esteem
- Identifying Interests
- Skills—Now and for Tomorrow
- Data, People, or Things?
- Building Character: Time Well Spent
- Data, People, and Things Survey
- Chapter 2 Portfolio

© JIST Works

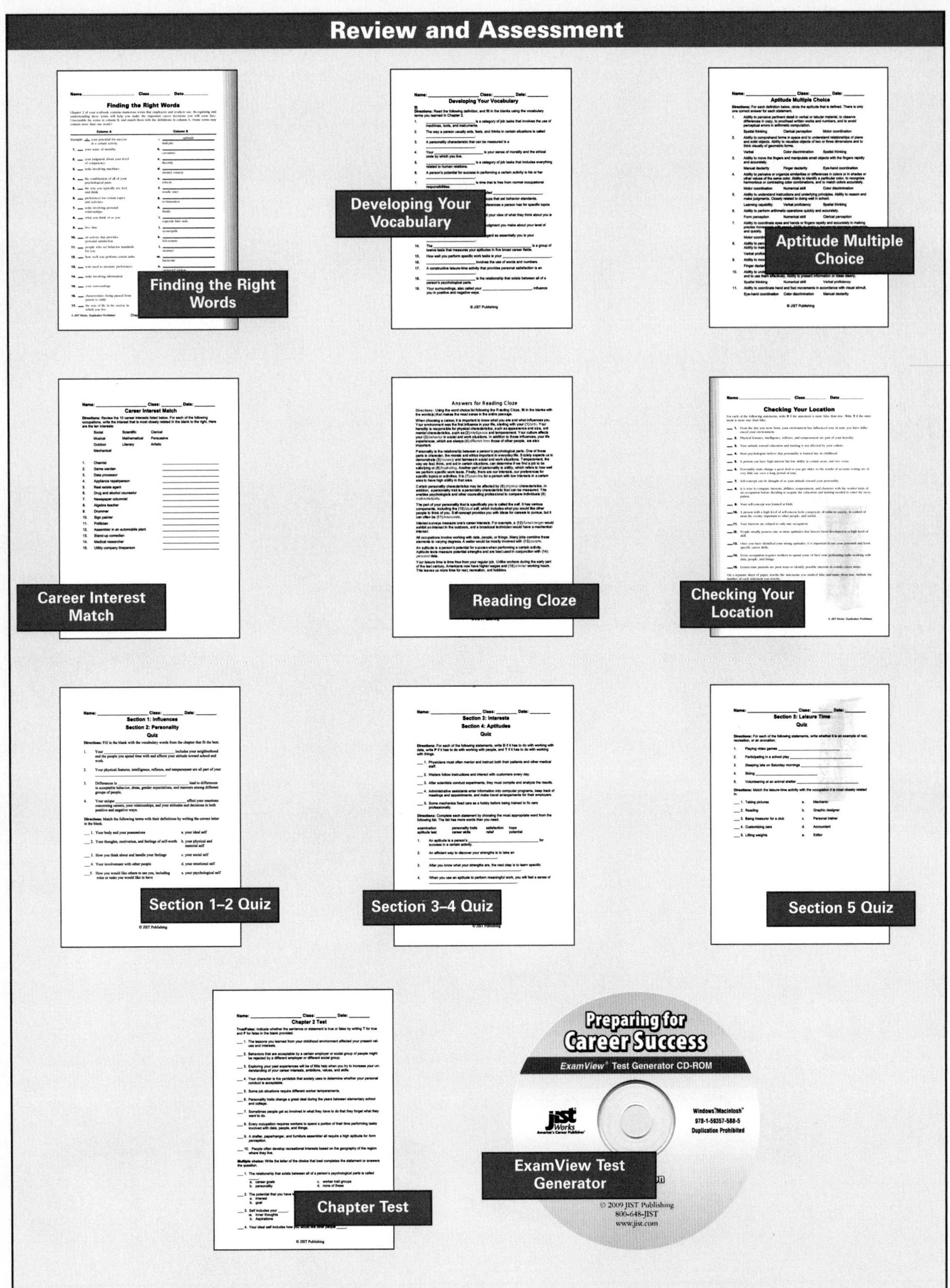
Review and Assessment
Finding the Right Words
Developing Your Vocabulary
Aptitude Multiple Choice
Career Interest Match
Reading Cloze
Checking Your Location
Section 1–2 Quiz
Section 3–4 Quiz
Section 5 Quiz
Chapter Test
ExamView Test Generator
Preparing for Career Success
ExamView® Test Generator CD-ROM
© 2009 JIST Publishing
800-648-JIST
www.jist.com

ART IN
LC BEARS
LAWRENCE CENTRAL
MEN'S SOCCER
2003 County Champs

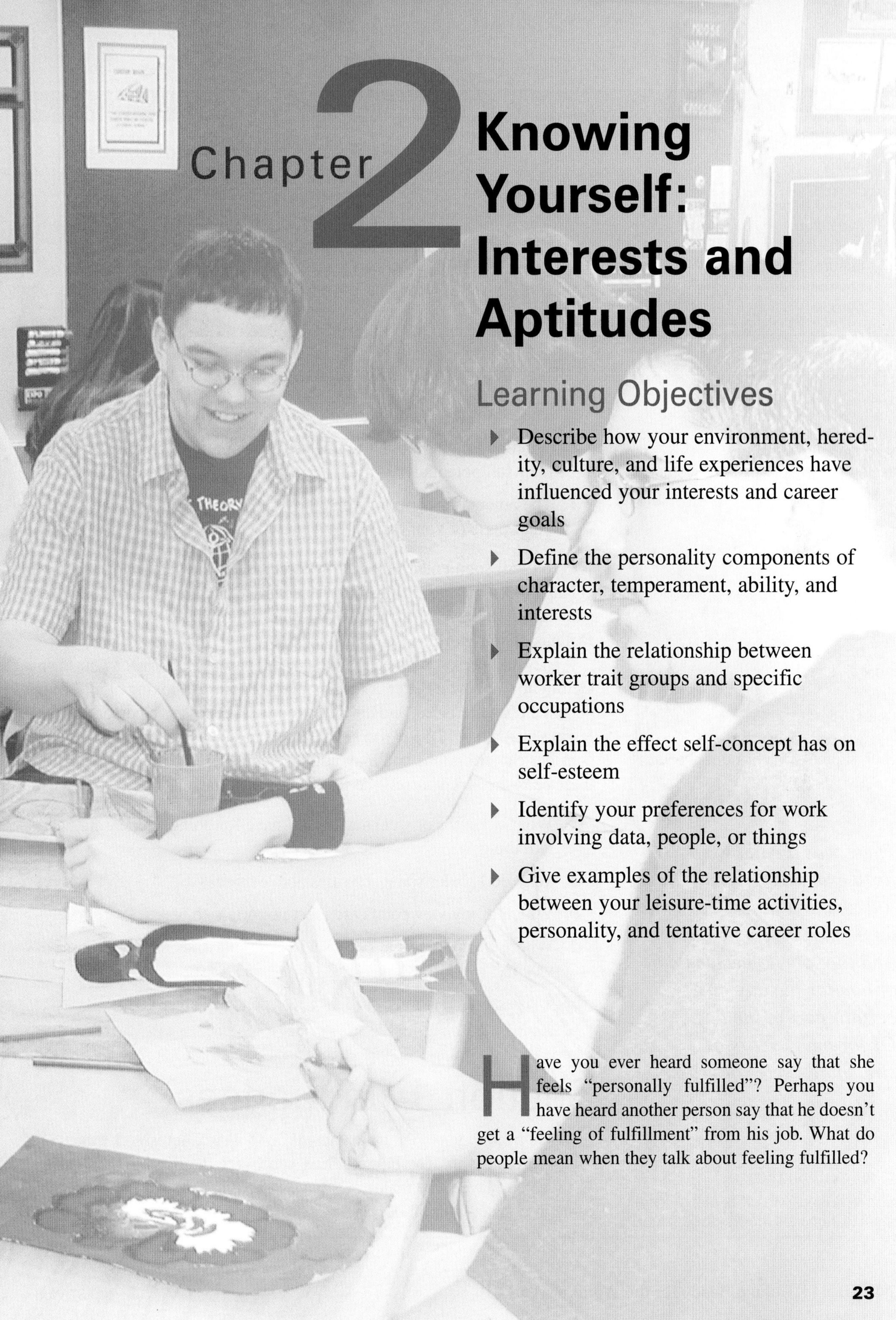

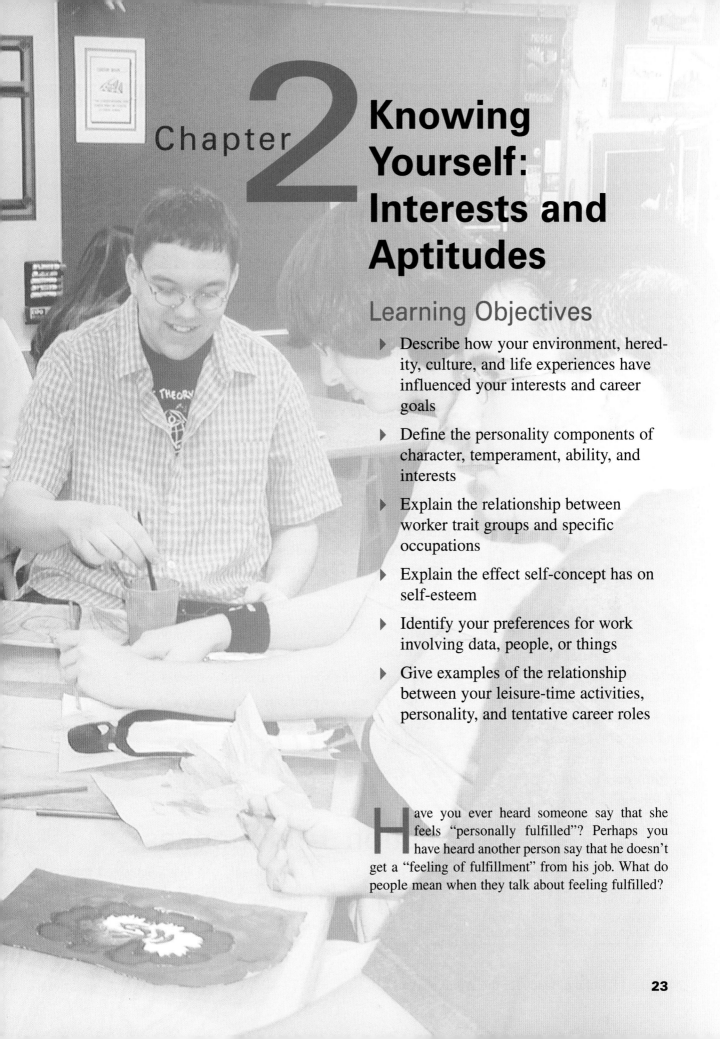

Chapter 2 Knowing Yourself: Interests and Aptitudes

Learning Objectives

- Describe how your environment, heredity, culture, and life experiences have influenced your interests and career goals
- Define the personality components of character, temperament, ability, and interests
- Explain the relationship between worker trait groups and specific occupations
- Explain the effect self-concept has on self-esteem
- Identify your preferences for work involving data, people, or things
- Give examples of the relationship between your leisure-time activities, personality, and tentative career roles

Have you ever heard someone say that she feels "personally fulfilled"? Perhaps you have heard another person say that he doesn't get a "feeling of fulfillment" from his job. What do people mean when they talk about feeling fulfilled?

Enrich Your Vocabulary

In reading this chapter and doing the exercises, you will learn the following important terms:

ability	interest surveys	self
aptitude	interests	self-esteem
Armed Services Vocational Aptitude Battery (ASVAB)	leisure time	social self
avocation	life experiences	temperament
character	personality	working with data
culture	personality trait	working with people
environment	reference groups	working with things
heredity		

Vocabulary Builder

The "Enrich Your Vocabulary" terms are highlighted and defined throughout the chapter. Discuss the "Enrich Your Vocabulary" terms before you assign the chapter. Ask students to write their own definitions, and then discuss their definitions in class.

Vocabulary

You can use the "Developing Your Vocabulary" worksheet in the Chapter 2 file of the *Preparing for Career Success Intructor's CD-ROM, Third Edition* as a pretest or as a reteaching worksheet.

Self-Understanding

Before reading the introduction, ask your students: What does the term *personal fulfillment* mean to you?

There was a child went forth every day,
And the first object he look'd upon, that object he became,
And that object became part of him for the day or a certain part of the day,
Or for many years or stretching cycles of years.

—Walt Whitman

Video Tour on DVD

Show students the Chapter 2 segment to introduce them to the content.

Three things can influence your sense of personal fulfillment:

1. The extent to which your daily tasks and relationships are interesting
2. Whether you have opportunities to use your skills and abilities to their full potential
3. The amount of harmony you enjoy between your personality and the other parts of your daily life

You will soon enter a long-term career role. The career you select can enhance your sense of fulfillment. This can be accomplished through self-expression, the respect of people who are important to you, and personal feelings of self-worth.

The only person who can make correct career choices for you is *you.* Getting to know *you* better is the first step. Begin by looking at all of your personal characteristics, and discover your uniqueness as a person. The following chapters will help you see yourself in new ways and will help you consider career options you may not have considered before. As you study these chapters, ask yourself the following questions:

1. What strengths or weaknesses do I have for doing and learning certain things?
2. Why do I prefer some activities above others?
3. Which of my viewpoints are most important to me?
4. Where do my personal beliefs and characteristics fit in the world of work?
5. What specific actions can I take to reach my career goals?

Section 1: Influences

As a child, you went forth each day and were impressed by the world around you. The home where you lived, the neighborhood where you played, the major events you experienced, and the people you came in contact with all became a part of you—and you became a part of them.

© JIST Works

Environment

From the day you were born, your **environment** (surroundings) has influenced you, and in turn your environment has been influenced by you. The lessons you learned from your childhood environment affected your present values and interests. They also affected your attitudes toward people, school, and work.

Discovering the positive and negative ways your environment has impressed you is important. Think for a minute about your present neighborhood and its influence on your daily life. Has the neighborhood influenced the way you think about work and workers? If so, how?

Heredity

Did you ever wish you would inherit a million dollars from a rich relative? Most of us would like that, but it's not something to count on. However, you can count on inheriting all the traits and characteristics that make up your physical features, intelligence, reflexes, and temperament. They are part of your **heredity** (the transmission of physical or mental characteristics from parent to offspring).

The next time you look into a mirror, try to identify your physical characteristics that are also recognizable in your close relatives. Do you resemble one family member more than others?

You have probably inherited certain talents for music, athletics, writing, leadership, art, mathematics, or working with tools. Can you think of occupations in which your special talents would be useful?

Culture

The **culture** (way of life in the society in which you live) also influences your attitude toward education and training. The United States is a nation of diverse (distinct or different) cultures. How has the accepted way of life in your community influenced the way you spend your time? Your hopes for the future? Your sense of right and wrong? Your career interests?

Behaviors that are acceptable by a certain employer or social group of people might be rejected by a different employer or different social group. Can you think of a time when you were in a cultural situation that was different from your own and you were embarrassed by your behavior or the behavior of another person?

As a small child, you probably learned that girls and boys were expected to behave in certain ways. You also learned acceptable table manners, language, personal hygiene, and what was expected of you in certain social situations. Now that you are a teenager, what is your standard of acceptable dress and behavior for going to school, church, or the mall? What level of education are you expected to complete? Are you expected to pursue a particular career because of your gender? How have you reacted to these cultural expectations?

FIND OUT MORE

Would you like to learn more about your family history? Enter the following site on your computer's Internet search engine: **Mormon Church Genealogy Search Engine.**

Discussion Starter

Ask your students: Which is most important in helping a child to become a successful adult—the people in the child's environment or the quality of the houses, school buildings, streets, and parks in the child's environment? Why?

How has the school you attend influenced your feelings about education?

Vocabulary Builder

Read the definition of the term *culture* aloud. Explain that all communities have unique cultural features. Provide the following examples: Some communities use buses for transportation and others use automobiles. In some communities people usually live in houses; in others they live in apartments. What are some features of your community's culture?

What have you learned from the students you associate with?

School-to-Work Transition

Ask your students to think about the accepted style of dress and use of language in their community's culture. Ask your students: Would this style of dress and use of language be acceptable or unacceptable by most employers outside your community if they were hiring a dishwasher? Restaurant host or hostess? Sales-person in a large appliance store? Long-distance truck driver? Manager? Why or why not?

Discussion Starter

Ask your students: Which of the four factors displayed in Figure 2.1 have the most influence on young children? Why? Which of the four factors have the least influence? Why?

KEY TO SUCCESS

Find an interesting route to your career goal, and you will enjoy the journey as much as the destination.

TAKE NOTE

Marco Polo, Cleopatra, Benjamin Franklin, and Anne Frank are just some of the famous individuals who kept diaries as a method to help them understand and keep track of their lives.

Life Experiences

In addition to your environment, heredity, and culture, your **life experiences** (significant events in a person's life that affect his or her actions and attitudes) have been different from those of other people. These experiences cause you to feel confident or fearful as you prepare for a career, develop friendships, or enter into a lifelong relationship. What positive or negative influence would you expect each of the following life experiences to have on a child's development?

1. The parents abuse alcohol or drugs.
2. The child participates in a statewide musical festival.
3. The child watches a loved one die a violent death.
4. The child enjoys a family vacation.
5. The child is abused at home.
6. The child is rewarded for having good grades with tickets to a major event.

What life experiences have influenced you? How have they affected your attitudes and decisions?

Exploring your past experiences will increase your understanding of your career interests, ambitions, values, and skills. Self-understanding will help you to gain more control over your life as you prepare for career success. The adult person you become will be a mixture of your environment, heredity, culture, and significant life experiences. Figure 2.1 demonstrates how these important factors influence your development.

© JIST Works

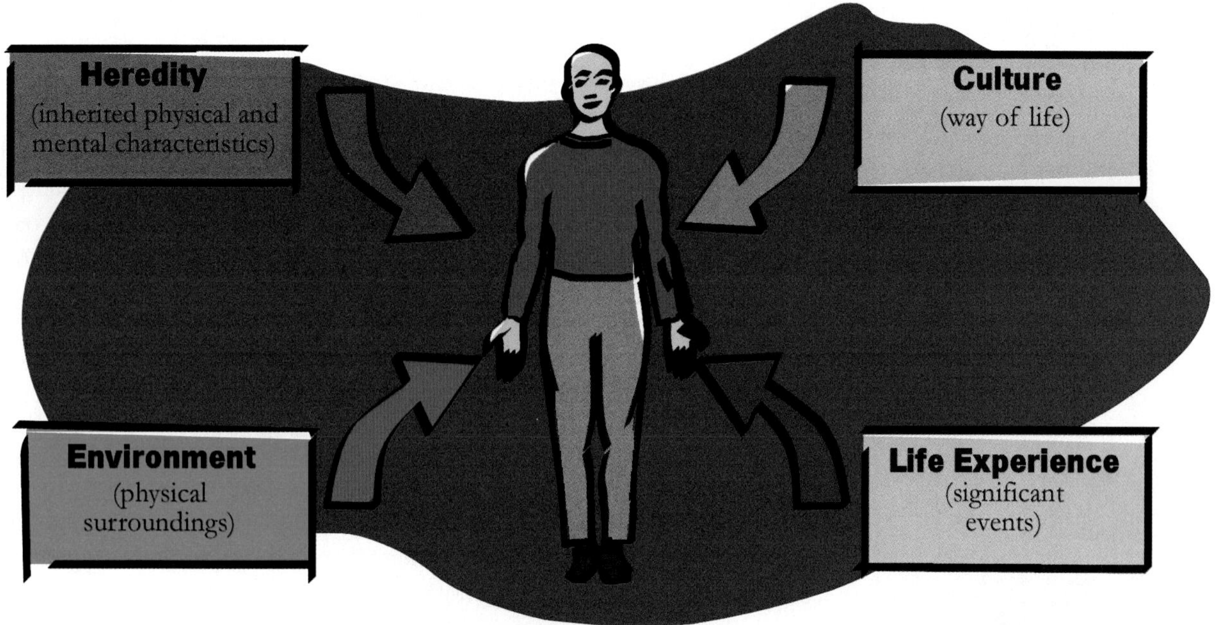

Figure 2.1 Factors that influence your development.

Section 1: Get Involved

Answer the following on a separate sheet of paper and be prepared to discuss your answers in class.

1. What cultural groups are represented in your classroom? African American? Hispanic? Asian? American Indian? Euro American? Do members of these groups stick together or mingle freely with other cultural groups? Can you think of a situation in which you have been rejected or accepted by other people because of your cultural background?
2. List one of your important childhood memories. Include who was involved, where, when, and why it is an important memory. Examples could include memories of family, school, places, friends, or major events. How did the events you have remembered influence you to become the person you are?

Section 2: Personality

How many times have you heard people say, "He has a nice personality," or "She doesn't have much personality"? What do they mean?

Personality is the relationship that exists between all of a person's psychological parts. These parts are *internal* (within the person) and cannot be observed easily by others. These inner parts are referred to as the *self.*

Personality determines the unique way that each person influences and responds to his or her surroundings, to new situations, and to other people. Most psychologists believe that personality is formed early in childhood. They also believe that major changes from early patterns of behavior are rare. However, gradual changes take place within everyone every day. Just as the wind slowly changes the face of a desert, gradual shifts in personal attitudes and beliefs change the way a maturing person adjusts to personal, interpersonal, and social situations.

Four terms are frequently used to describe the parts of personality: *character, temperament, ability,* and *interests.*

Self-Understanding

Explain that some people like changing situations, and others prefer that situations remain the same. However, all workers must deal with changing situations during their careers. Ask your students: Describe a desirable or undesirable change that happened in your life when you were a child. How did you react? Describe a desirable or undesirable change that happened in your life in recent months. How did you react?

CAREER FACT

Keep in mind that each of the four personality components (character, temperament, ability, and interests) relates to specific occupations. Understanding your personality and the way it relates to occupations will help you to make wise career decisions.

Character

Your **character** is your sense of morality and the ethical code by which you live. It is the yardstick that society uses to determine whether your personal conduct is acceptable. Behaviors and beliefs that demonstrate honesty, fairness, and trustworthiness are usually expected in social and work situations. How would you describe the behaviors and beliefs you find acceptable in the character of your friends? What behaviors and beliefs would you expect from coworkers and managers in the world of work?

Temperament

Temperament refers to the way you usually act, feel, and think in certain situations. How well you will be able to meet the demands of certain jobs will be influenced by your temperament. For example, one worker might enjoy a variety of duties, whereas another might prefer repeating the same tasks, with few changes in the daily routine. Can you think of jobs that would be satisfying or frustrating for workers with each of these temperaments? Some job situations require different worker temperaments. Here are some examples:

- Following detailed instructions, with little independent decision making
- Working in isolation from others
- Influencing other people
- Working under stressful conditions (deadlines and quotas)
- Using personal judgment or valid information to make decisions
- Interpreting ideas, feelings, or facts
- Setting standards to achieve goals

Which of these job situations match your temperament? Which don't?

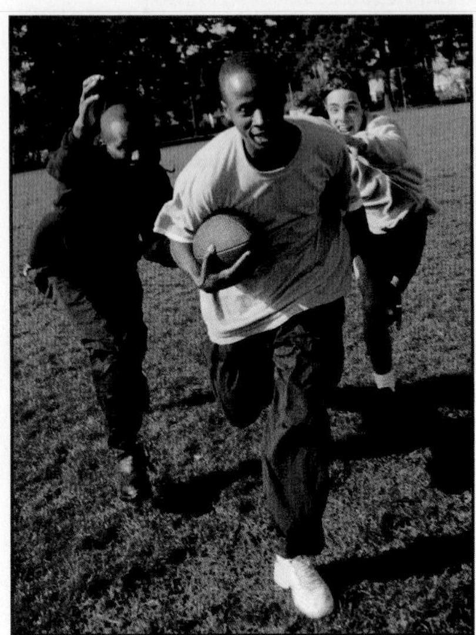

Using your abilities and skills successfully will give you feelings of joy and satisfaction and will motivate you to achieve at higher levels.

Discussion Starter

Ask your students: Which is most important for job success, the ability to perform specific work tasks or the potential to master a work skill? What are the reasons for your answer?

Self-Understanding

Read the list of career interests aloud and then ask your students: Which of the career interests rates highest for you? Which rates lowest? Have your interests changed in the past year? Do you expect them to change in the next year?

Ability

Ability refers to how well you perform specific work tasks. It also refers to the potential you have to master a job skill. Perhaps you have the ability to do well in auto mechanics. However, you will not be able to land a job as an automotive technician until you acquire the skills to do the job well.

Interests

Your **interests** are the preferences you have for specific topics or activities. Some examples of career interests are social, musical, outdoor, mechanical, scientific, mathematical, literary, clerical, persuasive, and artistic interests. It is possible to have high interest but low ability in a certain area, and vice versa.

© JIST Works

Your View of Your Personality

Take a moment to form an image of yourself. Start by closing your eyes and forming a mental description of your physical characteristics. If you gave this description of yourself to a stranger over the telephone, would he or she be able to find you in a room full of people?

Write a description of your interests, abilities, temperament, and character. Your list reflects your perception of yourself. Next, have a friend or close relative read your description and then agree with it or make any changes he or she wishes. The result is that person's perception of your personality.

Physical characteristics like appearance, physical strength or weakness, and general health may affect certain personality characteristics, such as temperament and ability. You are the total of all of your physical and psychological characteristics; they cannot be separated.

A **personality trait** is any personality characteristic that can be measured. The measurement of personality traits enables psychologists, counselors, social workers, and other helping professionals to make mathematical comparisons between individuals. Personality traits change very little, so the results of accurate testing are useful over a long period of time.

CAREER FACT

Employers have discovered that physically challenged workers frequently outperform other workers.

Self-Concept

You can think of *self-concept* as your attitude toward your personality. **Self** is that part of your experience that you regard as essentially you. It includes your inner thoughts, feelings, aspirations, fears, and fantasies. It is your perception (image) of what you were in the past, are in the present, and might become in the future. It is learned from your experiences and interactions with other people. The image you have developed about yourself includes these components:

- **Your physical and material self:** This self is made up of your physical body and the material possessions you own.
- **Your psychological self:** This self includes your inner thoughts and ideas, your feelings of self-worth, and your personal motivation to seek particular goals.
- **Your emotional self:** This self is the way you think and deal with your emotions when you are experiencing a situation. Experiences can have a positive or negative effect on a person's self-concept. For example, a frightening past experience may cause one person to fear water and refuse to learn to swim. Another person may decide to become a doctor because of a serious illness in childhood and a strong desire to help others in a similar situation.
- **Your social self:** This self is your involvement with other people and your view of what they think about you. Self-acceptance and self-respect are the result of being accepted and respected by others. On the other hand, being blamed, rejected, and belittled by others could lower your feelings of self-worth.

"There is a person inside of me."

Self-Understanding

Have students complete the "Self-Concept" worksheet in Chapter 2 of the *Preparing for Career Success Student Activity Book, Third Edition.*

© JIST Works

This above all—to thine own self be true; and it must follow, as the night the day, thou canst not then be false to any man.

—William Shakespeare

Education and Training

Ask your students to write on a sheet of paper the title of an adult career role that they would like. Next, ask your students: How are the classes you are taking and the grades you are earning preparing you for the career role you would like?

Key To Success

Be certain that your self-concept is accurate. An individual seeks a career that is consistent with his or her self-concept.

Technology

People who frequently use social networking sites such as Facebook and MySpace can quickly find themselves sharing personal information with hundreds of online friends. For your own safety, you need to be careful about what information you share online and with whom you share it. Make sure that you learn how to use the privacy controls on the networking site that you are using before you post anything.

- **Your ideal self:** This self includes the way you would like other people to think of you and react to you, tasks you would like to perform, and the social and career roles you would like to have.

Your self-concept provides you with an image of the types of occupations you should pursue. Unfortunately, a person's self-concept is not always accurate. One person might have a poor self-concept, consider himself to be inadequate, and eliminate from consideration careers that he is capable of achieving. Another person might overestimate her abilities and strive for a career goal that is beyond her reach. It is important to obtain an accurate understanding of your aptitudes, abilities, interests, and values and then acquire the skills and self-confidence you need to identify realistic career goals.

A young person's self-concept is shaped in large part by those around him or her. With encouragement from family, friends, and teachers, a young person can develop a positive self-concept. When this encouragement is missing, a negative self-concept might be the result. Consider the situation of Rhonda Benson and her twin brother, Roger, in the case study.

When people are members of a group, they feel similar to other members and strive to be like them. They compare themselves to the standards of other group members. The beliefs and feelings and the self-concept that grow out of these comparisons have a strong effect on the individual's career choices.

Building Character: Encouragement Makes a Difference

Rhonda enjoys her roles as student, basketball player, Sunday school teacher, and daughter. She feels as though she is a unique and capable person in each of her life roles. The people closest to Rhonda—her teachers, basketball coach and teammates, the members of her church, and her parents—have all provided encouragement and made her feel successful. Rhonda is exploring possible careers in teaching, nursing, and social work. She likes helping people and sees herself as being successful in life situations involving others.

Roger, on the other hand, gets passing grades but has never really enjoyed school. He hasn't been very involved with activities at school or at church. Roger's main source of enjoyment is his street bike. He likes to go to the park and perfect his tricks. He spends hours repairing or adjusting his bike, only to have his parents tell him he would be more successful if he spent the same amount of time on his schoolwork. Roger sometimes feels as though the whole world thinks he's a failure. Even Rhonda doesn't seem to understand him anymore. Roger plans to graduate in June and then travel the country to compete in contests. When he grows tired of riding and seeing things, Roger thinks he might go to college.

© JIST Works

> **KEY TO SUCCESS**
>
> A self-appraisal of your aptitudes as well as your interests, values, and goals will prepare you to make realistic career decisions.

Critical Thinking

People constantly measure their ideal self against their actual self. When their perceptions of who they ought to be are similar to who they actually are, then they have a positive, mature self-concept. Like most people, Rhonda and Roger have a strong desire to be unique. Is Rhonda's self-concept positive and mature? Is Roger's? How do you account for any differences?

Parents and other family members create a large part of your world. Young people measure their personal success and failure according to the judgments of that world. Labels such as hard working or lazy, bright or slow, friendly or mean, pretty or plain are attached to a young person's self-concept by the family and other social environments, such as school. Make a list of labels for Rhonda and Roger.

Many of the standards that people set for ideal behavior are learned as members of reference groups. Examples of reference groups include your family, classes at school, and clubs or organizations you have joined. Can you think of other reference groups to which you belong? Comparing yourself to other members of these groups affects your beliefs and values. What reference groups do Rhonda and Roger belong to? How did the standards of each reference group affect Rhonda's character? How did they affect Roger's character?

Think of what you have rather than of what you lack. Of the things you have, select the best and then reflect how eagerly you would have sought them if you did not have them.

—Marcus Aurelius

Self-Esteem

Everyone makes a judgment about his or her level of competence and adequacy as a person. This personal evaluation is called **self-esteem**. This evaluation is not always accurate, but the individual always views it as accurate. Self-esteem has a strong effect on how the individual perceives relationships with other people and situations such as school or work.

Comprehension Check

Tell students to close their books. Ask for a definition of *self-esteem* (a personal evaluation a person makes about his or her level of competence and adequacy as a person). Next, remind the students that a person with a high level of self-esteem has a feeling of competence. Ask the students to name four additional feelings (feeling of value to society, being in control of most life events, feeling important to other people, and feeling useful).

© JIST Works

Student Evaluation

To evaluate student mastery of concepts, you might want to use the Sections 1–2 quiz found in the Chapter 2 file of the *Preparing for Career Success Instructor's CD-ROM, Third Edition.*

A person with a high level of self-esteem feels competent, of value to society, in control of most life events, important to other people, and useful. On the other hand, a person with a low level of self-esteem feels incompetent, of little value to society, controlled by most life events, unimportant, and without purpose. Most people have areas of high and low self-esteem.

Strengthening your self-concept and raising your level of self-esteem are important steps in preparing for personal and career success. Exploring and understanding yourself and accepting the person you are will help you establish realistic career goals, make desired changes, and fulfill career objectives.

Section 2: Get Involved

Answer the following on a separate sheet of paper, and be prepared to discuss your responses in class.

1. Do you present the same image to everyone, or do you present a different image to your teachers, friends, and family? Describe the image you present to each.
2. Describe an experience that affected you in a positive way and one that affected you in a negative way. Perhaps it was a grade you received or something that was said to you about the way you look, talk, or act.
3. Which of the following best describes the image you project at school, at home, and with friends? Explain your answer by giving an example illustrating when you project this image.

A leader	Cooperative
A loner	Self-confident
A follower	Critical
Idealistic	Compassionate
Reliable	

Education and Training

Ask students to answer the following questions: Which school subject interests you most? Which interests you least? In which school subjects do you earn the highest grades? The lowest grades? Do many students earn the highest grades in the subjects they like most and the lowest grades in the subjects they like the least?

Comprehension Check

Ask your students to define the term *delayed gratification* in their own words. *(Delayed gratification:* Moving closer to a goal you are seeking by putting off an activity you enjoy more to perform an activity you enjoy less.) Ask your students to share an example of a time when they obtained a goal by delaying gratification. Ask what activity was delayed and what goal was obtained.

Section 3: Interests

Sometimes people get so involved in what they *have* to do that they forget what they *want* to do. If you first discover what your personal interests are, then you will be in a position to choose an interesting career.

Personal interests are those inner feelings that cause you to *want* to know something or *want* to perform a certain activity. If you were driving to a distant city, you would probably begin by identifying all of the possible routes and then selecting the one you prefer. If the route you select enables you to see things you like and do things you enjoy, it satisfies your interests.

Think for a moment about a school activity that you enjoy. Now, think about an activity that you do only because it is required. Have you ever noticed that when an activity arouses and holds your interest, you are less likely to quit and more likely to succeed?

© JIST Works

People sometimes participate in activities that they don't enjoy so that they can obtain something they want. The goal could be a certain grade, another person's approval, education or training for a certain occupation, or a job promotion. Sometimes you might need to delay gratification and perform activities you don't particularly enjoy to obtain a goal. Can you think of an activity you presently do or plan to do in the future that is not very interesting but has a payoff that will make it worthwhile?

Some people develop such a high interest in a certain activity that they become restless and bored when they are away from it. Have you ever started to read a book, watch a program on TV, build or repair something, or discuss a situation with another person and suddenly realized that several hours had passed without your noticing? What is the interest that kept you involved?

A specific interest may be related to many occupations. As an example, mechanical interest is related to the occupations of mechanic, mechanical engineer, appliance repairperson, broadcast technician, vocational teacher, aircraft mechanic, and machinist, to name only a few. What occupations can you think of that would be related to the following interests? (See the appendix for help answering this question.)

- Helping other people
- Being outdoors
- Doing science and mathematics
- Leading, persuading, and convincing other people

How are the occupations you selected related to these interests? Tests used to measure interests are frequently known as career or occupational **interest surveys** or interest inventories. They match your interests with the work activities or situations experienced in certain occupations. They also compare your interests with those of people who are successful and satisfied in certain occupations. There are no correct or incorrect responses to statements in an interest survey. Instead, you choose among numerous activities and situations, expressing your preference for one over another.

Data, People, and Things

If you could have the "perfect" job, what percentage of your time would you spend **working with data** (verbal or numerical information), **working with people**, and **working with things** (tools, instruments, or machines)?

A preference for working with data, people, or things is another method used to relate personal interests to various occupations. This method is effective because every occupation requires workers to spend some of their time performing tasks in each of these three categories.

Career Fact

Interests change very little between the ages of 25 and 55. They change much more between the ages of 15 and 25.

Enrichment

Have students complete the "Identifying Interests" worksheet in Chapter 2 of the *Preparing for Career Success Student Activity Book, Third Edition.*

Reteaching

Have students complete the "Career Interest Match" worksheet in Chapter 2 of the *Preparing for Career Success Instructor's CD-ROM, Third Edition.*

Cluster Link

According to a U.S. government Consumer Expenditure Survey, Americans have become a nation of travelers with pleasure trips and vacations a major expenditure for many consumers. The travel industry will add more than 250,000 new jobs to the economy between 2006 and 2016. This projected increase is good news for students interested in careers in the Hospitality and Tourism career cluster (see the appendix of this book), such as marketing and sales, management, security, human resources, and food preparation and service. To find out more about the hotel and lodging industry, key in **American Hotel & Lodging Association** on your Internet search engine.

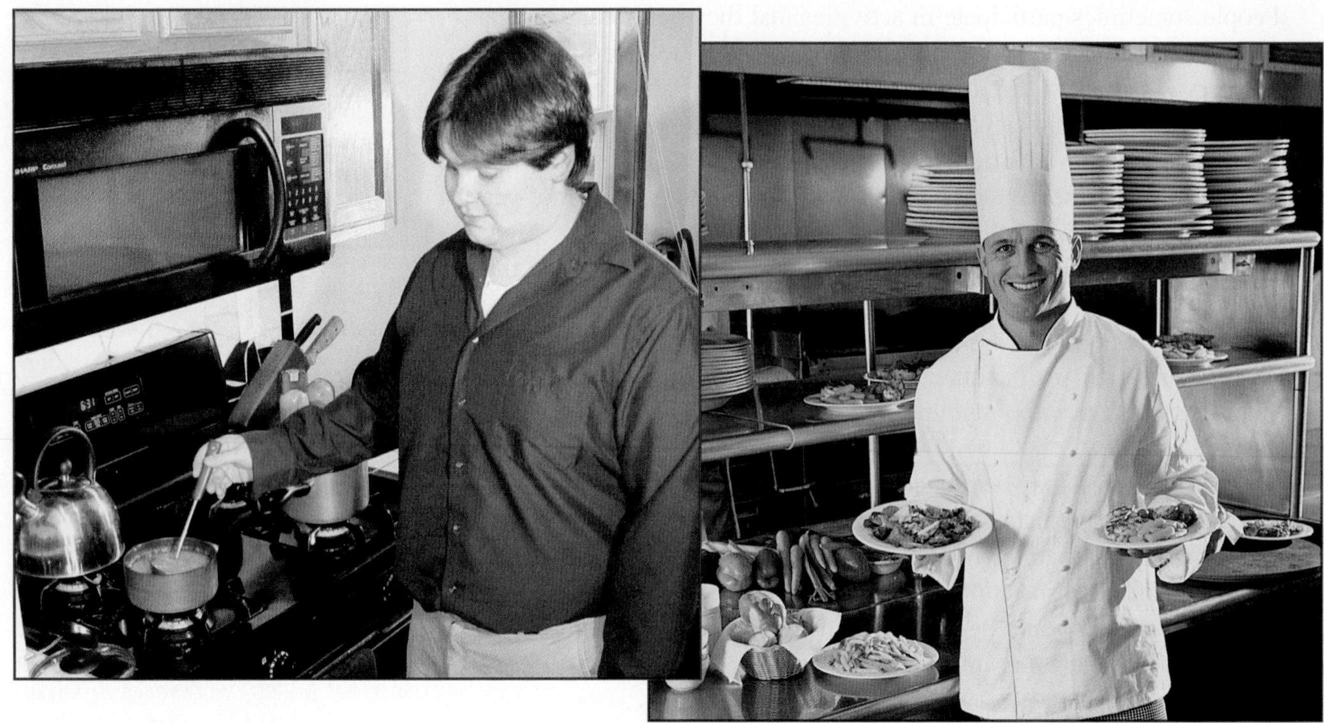

When Chris was a teenager, he enjoyed cooking at home. He never dreamed that he would become a highly skilled chef. What is your dream?

We must remember that knowledge of one's own deep nature is also simultaneously knowledge of human nature in general.

—Abraham Maslow

Enrichment

Have students complete the "Data, People, Things Survey" worksheet in Chapter 2 of the *Preparing for Career Success Instructor's CD-ROM, Third Edition.*

Vocabulary Builder

Divide the class into three groups. Assign one of the three categories of data, people, or things to each group. Give each group seven terms from Table 2.1 describing levels of working in those categories. Ask each group to write a dictionary definition for each assigned term. Next, have them write a sentence using each term in a work situation. Provide this example for the People category: *Negotiating* contracts and other agreements is an important job task for a lawyer.

Once again, think of an occupation you are considering for your future career. As you read the following descriptions, take into account how much of your time would be spent working with data, people, or things in that occupation. Is this consistent with your interest in the three categories of work?

- **Data:** This category includes job tasks using, identifying, or organizing information and knowledge. Numbers and words are the tools of the person who works with data.
- **People:** This category includes job tasks related to human relations. These work situations provide opportunities to lead, persuade, help, teach, or counsel others.
- **Things:** This category of job tasks includes everything related to the design, use, or repair of machines, tools, and instruments.

Each of the three categories may require the worker to use a complex level of responsibility and judgment or may be performed at a much less complicated level (see Table 2.1). For example, the occupations of waiter and physician are highly involved with people. However, the waiter works at the level of taking instructions, helping, serving, and speaking; whereas the physician must have higher-level skills in *mentoring* (serving as a trusted adviser), instructing, and persuading. Physicians must also work at a very high skill level with data and things. When you think of your future occupation, will you be required to work at a high, medium, or low level with data, people, and things?

© JIST Works

Table 2.1 Levels of Worker Involvement with Data, People, and Things

	Data	People	Things
High level	Synthesizing	Mentoring	Setting up
	Coordinating	Negotiating	Doing precision work
	Analyzing	Instructing	Operating, controlling
Medium level	Compiling	Supervising	Driving, operating
	Computing	Diverting	Manipulating
Low Level	Copying	Serving	Feeding, removing
	Comparing	Taking instructions, helping	Handling

Section 3: Get Involved

Answer the following on a separate sheet of paper, and be prepared to discuss your responses in class.

1. Make a list of activities you enjoy doing at home, at school, and with friends. Call this list **"Interests I Am Pursuing Now."**
2. Make a second list of activities you are not currently involved in but would enjoy trying at home, at school, and with friends. Call this list **"Interests I Hope to Pursue in the Future."**
3. Think about things going on in the world that concern you a great deal. Perhaps you have developed this awareness from conversations with friends or family; reading a newspaper, magazine, or book; watching TV; or participating in a class at school. Make a third list called **"Matters of Importance to Me."** Include your specific concerns for each of the following:
   - Events from the past
   - Events currently taking place
   - Future events
4. Just as seeds in a garden grow into plants and flowers, your inner needs and values grow into specific interests. Your "Matters of Importance" list comes from the concerns of your inner self. Compare your specific concerns to your interest lists. How are the two lists related? How have your inner concerns grown into interests? How have your interests caused you to be concerned about certain matters?
5. Once again, think of a specific occupation that you are considering. What levels of involvement would be required in the data, people, and things categories? Are these levels of involvement consistent with your present skills? What level of education or training would be required to achieve job skills at these levels of involvement? Where could you acquire the necessary training?

Section 4: Aptitudes

Have you ever overheard a teacher tell a student, "You are not working up to your potential"? An **aptitude** is a person's potential for success in performing a certain activity. This potential may be for acquiring certain knowledge or skills with education or training.

You probably possess one or more aptitudes that haven't been developed to a high level of skill. Look at the descriptions of 11 aptitudes that were identified by the U.S. Department of Labor in Table 2.2. After you read the descriptions, decide whether your potential for each aptitude is high, average, or low. As you can see, different occupations require higher or lower degrees of certain aptitudes. Which aptitudes have you developed the most? The least?

Comprehension Check

Tell students to close their books. Ask individual students to define the term *aptitude* in their own words.

Reteaching

Have students complete the "Aptitude Multiple Choice" worksheet in Chapter 2 of the *Preparing for Career Success Instructor's CD-ROM, Third Edition.*

Discussion Starter

Explain to the students that many unemployed youth have strong aptitudes but very few employment skills. Ask these questions: Who is responsible for developing a youth's aptitudes into career skills? Who should pay the living expenses for unemployed workers who have strong aptitudes but very low-level job skills?

Student Evaluation

To evaluate student mastery of concepts, you might want to use the Section 3–4 quiz found in the Chapter 2 file of the *Preparing for Career Success Instructor's CD-ROM, Third Edition.*

An efficient way to discover your potential strengths is to take an aptitude test. Ask your high school counselor if this type of testing is available at your school. Many schools have access to the **Armed Services Vocational Aptitude Battery (ASVAB).**

Aptitude tests are best used in conjunction with other personal data, such as interests, values, school grades, personality traits, and vocational preferences. Upon completion of your aptitude test, ask your high school counselor to review all of the personal data, academic information, and test results in your permanent records. He or she can explain the relationship of this information to your aptitude test results. After you identify your strong aptitudes, it is important to use your potential and learn specific career skills.

When you develop an aptitude to its full potential, you feel a sense of personal pride. When you begin using that aptitude to perform meaningful work, you will feel a sense of satisfaction. This cycle of pride and satisfaction is the cornerstone of career success.

Table 2.2 Aptitudes

Aptitude	Description
Learning capability, intelligence	Ability to understand instructions and underlying principles. Ability to reason and make judgments. Closely related to doing well in school. A physician requires a high degree of this aptitude, a registered nurse requires less, and an electrocardiogram technician requires even less.
Verbal proficiency	Ability to understand the meaning of words and the ideas associated with them and to use them effectively. Ability to comprehend language, to understand relationships between words, and to understand meanings of whole sentences and paragraphs. Ability to present information or ideas clearly. An editor requires a high degree of this aptitude, a teacher requires less, and a salesperson requires even less.
Numerical skill	Ability to perform arithmetic operations quickly and accurately. A mechanical engineer requires a high degree of this aptitude, a bookkeeper requires less, and a salesclerk requires even less.
Spatial thinking	Ability to comprehend forms in space and to understand relationships of plane and solid objects. Ability to visualize objects of two or three dimensions and to think visually of geometric forms. A dentist requires a high degree of this aptitude, a machinist requires less, and a carpenter requires even less.
Form perception	Ability to perceive pertinent details in objects or in pictorial or graphic material. Ability to make visual comparisons and discriminations and to see slight differences in shapes and shading of figures and widths and lengths of lines. A drafter requires a high degree of this aptitude, a paperhanger requires less, and a furniture assembler requires even less.
Clerical perception	Ability to perceive pertinent detail in verbal or tabular material. Ability to observe differences in copy, to proofread written works and numbers, and to avoid perceptual errors in arithmetic computation. A proofreader requires a high degree of this aptitude, a general office clerk requires less, and a cashier requires even less.

© JIST Works

Aptitude	Description
Motor coordination	Ability to coordinate eyes and hands or fingers rapidly and accurately in making precise movements with speed. Ability to make a movement response accurately and quickly. A word-processing operator requires a high degree of this aptitude, a machine tool operator requires less, and a butcher requires even less.
Finger dexterity	Ability to move the fingers and manipulate small objects with the fingers rapidly and accurately. A surgeon requires a high degree of this aptitude, an automobile mechanic requires less, and a cosmetologist requires even less.
Manual dexterity	Ability to move the hands easily and skillfully and to work with the hands in a placing and turning motion. An airplane engine specialist requires a high degree of this aptitude, a diesel mechanic requires less, and an upholsterer requires even less.
Eye-hand coordination	Ability to move the hand and foot coordinately with each other in accordance with visual stimuli. A baseball player requires a high degree of this aptitude, a truck driver requires less, and a forklift operator requires even less.
Color discrimination	Ability to perceive or recognize similarities or differences in colors or in shades or other values of the same color. An interior designer requires a high degree of this aptitude, a textile designer requires less, and a floral designer requires even less.

Section 4: Get Involved

Answer the following on a separate sheet of paper, and be prepared to discuss your responses in class.

1. List three occupations you have considered for your future career. For each occupation on your list, identify two or more aptitudes, and tell how they would be used in that particular occupation. Rate yourself high, average, or low for the aptitudes on your list. Which occupation is best suited to your aptitude strengths? Which is least suited?
2. Can you think of something you have repeatedly tried to do but cannot do very well, no matter how hard you try? Maturity and practice help to overcome some limitations, for example, when learning to ride a bike or to read. Sometimes, however, limitations are caused by physical handicaps you are born with or that occur because of an accident or illness.

   List the aptitudes that you read about in this chapter. Next to each aptitude, list any physical disabilities you can think of that would have a negative effect on a person's ability to use that aptitude in the world of work.

Section 5: Leisure Time

Leisure time is time free from your everyday job responsibilities. During leisure time, you may rest, be involved in recreation (fun and games), or pursue an **avocation** (a constructive activity that provides you with personal satisfaction).

The amount of time that Americans have available for leisure activities has changed dramatically during the past century. Most employers provide paid vacations, and some offer flexible work schedules, three- and four-day work weeks, and several legislated three-day holiday weekends. These

Comprehension Check

Tell students to close their books. Ask individual students to define the terms *recreation* and *avocation* in their own words. Next, ask individual students for an example of a recreational or avocational activity.

The time American workers have for leisure is increasing. What recreational or avocational activities do you enjoy?

policies have allowed time for workers to become involved in avocations as well as recreational activities.

Age and geographic location have an obvious effect on leisure. What is appropriate or even possible at one age may not be appropriate or possible at another. For example, someone who enjoyed riding a tricycle as a child will prefer driving an automobile as a teenager. At what age did you learn to ride a tricycle, a bicycle, or drive a car? How many people over 50 have you noticed riding skateboards? Although people change their leisure-time activities as they grow older, past or present skills and experience will influence their future selections.

What leisure-time activity would you expect Tony and Alice to enjoy when they are 50?

People also develop recreational interests based on the geography of the region. For example, lake country lends itself to fishing, coastal regions to beach activities, and the mountains to hiking and skiing.

As a student, you probably spend some of your leisure time on volunteer service, hobbies, part-time jobs, or involvement in organizations. All of these leisure-time pursuits are good ways to identify possible interests and abilities in certain career areas as well as to develop personal and employment skills. You can see the relationship between some common leisure-time activities, the personality characteristics associated with those activities, and related occupations in Table 2.3.

© JIST Works

Table 2.3 Relating Leisure Activities to Work

Leisure Activity	Personality Characteristics	Related Occupations
Being a club officer	Enjoys leading and persuading people	Politician, manager, supervisor
Collecting stamps or coins	Has good organizational skills	Accountant, bookkeeper, bank teller
Doing science projects	Likes working with information; enjoys solving problems	Chemist, oceanographer, astronomer
Baby-sitting	Likes helping people; enjoys children	Teacher, day-care worker, social worker
Making posters, working on sets for school plays	Likes creating things; likes using drawing skills; enjoys beautifying the environment	Designer, architect, commercial artist
Rebuilding cars, repairing bicycles	Enjoys using tools and machines; likes analyzing mechanical problems	Mechanic, machinist, engineer
Hunting, fishing, raising plants	Likes being outdoors; enjoys learning about nature	Fish and game warden, forester, farm operator

Section 5: Get Involved

Answer the following on a separate sheet of paper, and be prepared to discuss your responses in class.

1. List the leisure-time activities you have been involved in during the past month. Are these activities usually involved with data, people, or things? Are they done alone or with others? Are they done outdoors or indoors?
2. What is one leisure activity you would like to try that isn't on your list?
3. Name two occupations that are related to your list of leisure activities, and tell how they are related.

Chapter 2 Review

Enrich Your Vocabulary

On a separate sheet of paper, number from 1 to 22, and complete the following activity. (Do not write in your textbook.) Match each statement with the most appropriate term from the "Enrich Your Vocabulary" list at the beginning of the chapter by writing that term next to the number for the correct statement.

1. The sense of morality and the ethical code by which a person lives
2. The judgment you make about your level of competence and adequacy
3. A person's potential for success in performing a certain activity
4. A category of job tasks that involves the use of machines, tools, and instruments
5. The relationship that exists between all of a person's psychological parts
6. The way a person usually acts, feels, and thinks in certain situations

Student Evaluation

To evaluate student mastery of concepts, you might want to use the Section 5 quiz found in the Chapter 2 file of the *Preparing for Career Success Instructor's CD-ROM, Third Edition.* You can also find a chapter test in the Chapter 2 file.

School-to-Work Transition

Ask several students: What is one school activity in which you are involved this year? What skills have you acquired in this activity that you can use in the world of work? What future school activities do you hope to participate in? How might your experience in these activities be used in the world of work?

Enrich Your Vocabulary Answers

1. character
2. self-esteem
3. aptitude
4. working with things
5. personality
6. temperament

(continued)

Enrich Your Vocabulary Answers *(continued)*

7. interests
8. personality trait
9. ASVAB
10. working with people
11. self
12. leisure time
13. avocation
14. social self
15. reference groups
16. ability
17. interest surveys
18. working with data
19. environment
20. heredity
21. culture
22. life experiences

7. Preferences a person has for specific topics or activities
8. A personality characteristic that can be measured
9. Armed Services Vocational Aptitude Battery
10. A category of job tasks that includes everything related to human relations
11. The part of your experience that you consider to be you
12. Time that is free from normal occupational responsibilities
13. A constructive leisure-time activity that provides personal satisfaction
14. Your involvement with other people and your view of what they think about you
15. Groups that set behavior standards
16. How well you perform specific work tasks
17. Tests used to measure interests
18. A category of job tasks that involves the use of words and numbers
19. Your surroundings
20. The process of transmitting physical or mental characteristics from parent to child
21. The way of life in the society in which you live
22. Events that cause you to be confident or fearful as you prepare for a career

Check Your Knowledge

On a separate sheet of paper, answer the following questions. (Do not write in your textbook.)

1. What are the four major influences discussed in this chapter that shape the physical, psychological, and social characteristics of an individual?
2. Name three of the four terms used to describe the parts of personality.
3. List three of the components of self.

Check Your Knowledge Answers

1. Environment, heredity, culture, and life experiences.
2. Character, temperament, ability, and interests.
3. Physical and material self, psychological self, emotional self, social self, ideal self.

(continued)

© JIST Works

4. List three reference groups. Give an example of how each group might influence the beliefs of its members.
5. What can an individual do to reach a higher level of self-esteem?
6. What comparisons do career interest surveys make? Will interests match more than one occupation?
7. List six of the aptitudes described in the chapter.
8. Would a mechanic have a higher level of involvement with people and things, data and people, or things and data?
9. What are the three levels of leisure-time activities?
10. Would a person who enjoys collecting stamps be more likely to enjoy the occupation of bookkeeper or social worker? Why?

Develop SCANS Competencies

Government experts say that successful workers can productively use resources, interpersonal skills, information, systems, and technology. This activity will give you practice in developing interpersonal skills.

Work with someone who knows you well to determine whether he or she sees you as you see yourself. (Make sure you work with a person you can trust and who will help rather than hurt you.)

Use the five self components listed in Section 2 under the head "Self-Concept." Discuss with your partner how you see yourself in these areas and how he or she sees you in each of these areas.

Check Your Knowledge Answers *(continued)*

4. Reference groups include families, classes at school, and clubs or organizations. Answers will vary; the standards of the group affect the beliefs and feelings of the members.
5. Answers will vary. A person must participate in confidence-building activities. The individual must develop confidence in his or her personal sense of adequacy and competence to handle life events.
6. Career interest surveys match a person's interests with the work activities or situations involved in certain occupations. They compare the person's interests with those of people who are successful and satisfied in certain occupations. Several occupations relate to each person's interests.
7. Learning ability and intelligence, verbal proficiency, numerical skill, spatial thinking, form perception, clerical perception, motor coordination, finger dexterity, manual dexterity, eye-hand coordination, color discrimination.
8. Things and data.
9. Rest, recreation, and avocation.
10. Bookkeeper. Stamp collecting is a structured, individual activity. Bookkeepers spend most of their job time performing structured, individual activities and little time involved with people. Social workers are highly involved with people.

Reteaching

Have students complete the "Checking Your Location" worksheets in Chapter 2 of the *Preparing for Career Success Student Activity Book, Third Edition.*

Enrichment

Have students complete the Chapter 2 section of the *Preparing for Career Success Student Portfolio, Third Edition.*

© JIST Works

Chapter 3 Resources

Lesson Plans and Preparation

Preparing for Career Success
Interactive Lesson Planner Plus Instructor's Resources on CD-ROM
Third Edition
Interactive Lesson Planner and Resources
Chapter 3 Lesson Plan
Knowing Yourself: Values and Goals
Lesson Plan

Multimedia

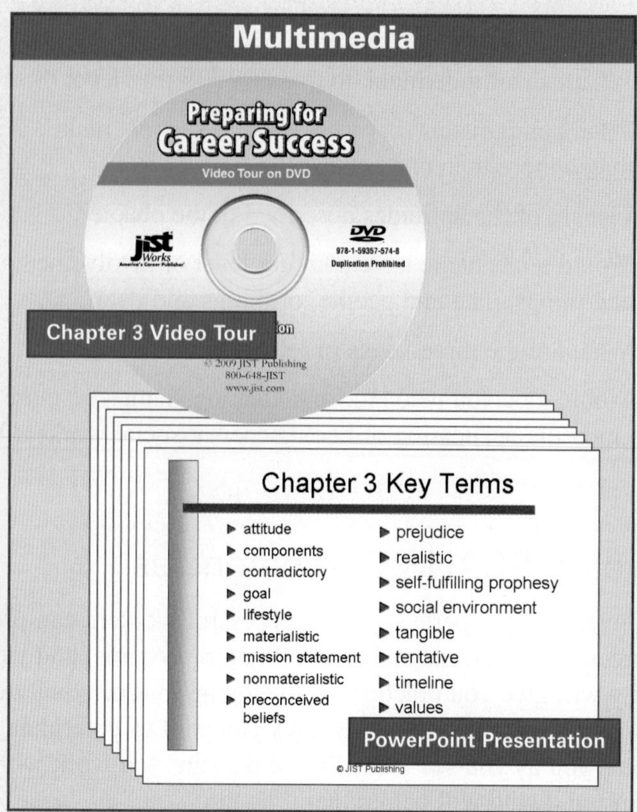

Preparing for Career Success
Video Tour on DVD
978-1-59357-574-8
Duplication Prohibited
Chapter 3 Video Tour
© 2009 JIST Publishing
800-648-JIST
www.jist.com
Chapter 3 Key Terms
attitude
components
contradictory
goal
lifestyle
materialistic
mission statement
nonmaterialistic
preconceived beliefs
prejudice
realistic
self-fulfilling prophesy
social environment
tangible
tentative
timeline
values
PowerPoint Presentation
© JIST Publishing

Activities

- Examining Your Work Values
- What's Most Important?
- The Time Is Now!
- Your Attitude Is Showing
- Lifestyle Options
- Being Responsible: When Values Conflict
- Goal Guidelines to Share
- Planning Makes a Difference: An Occupation That Works
- Chapter 3 Portfolio

© JIST Works

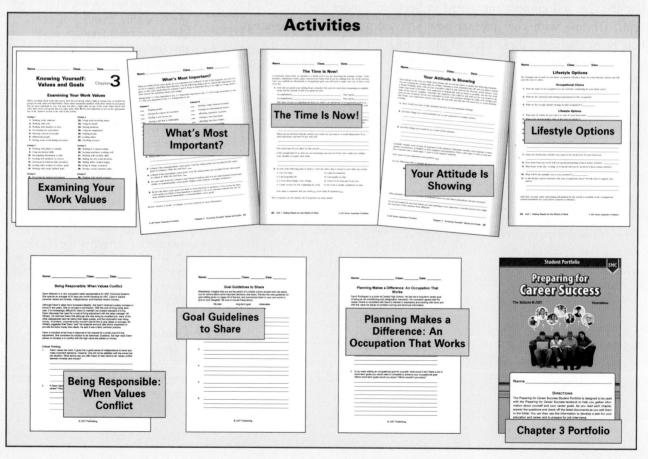

Review and Assessment

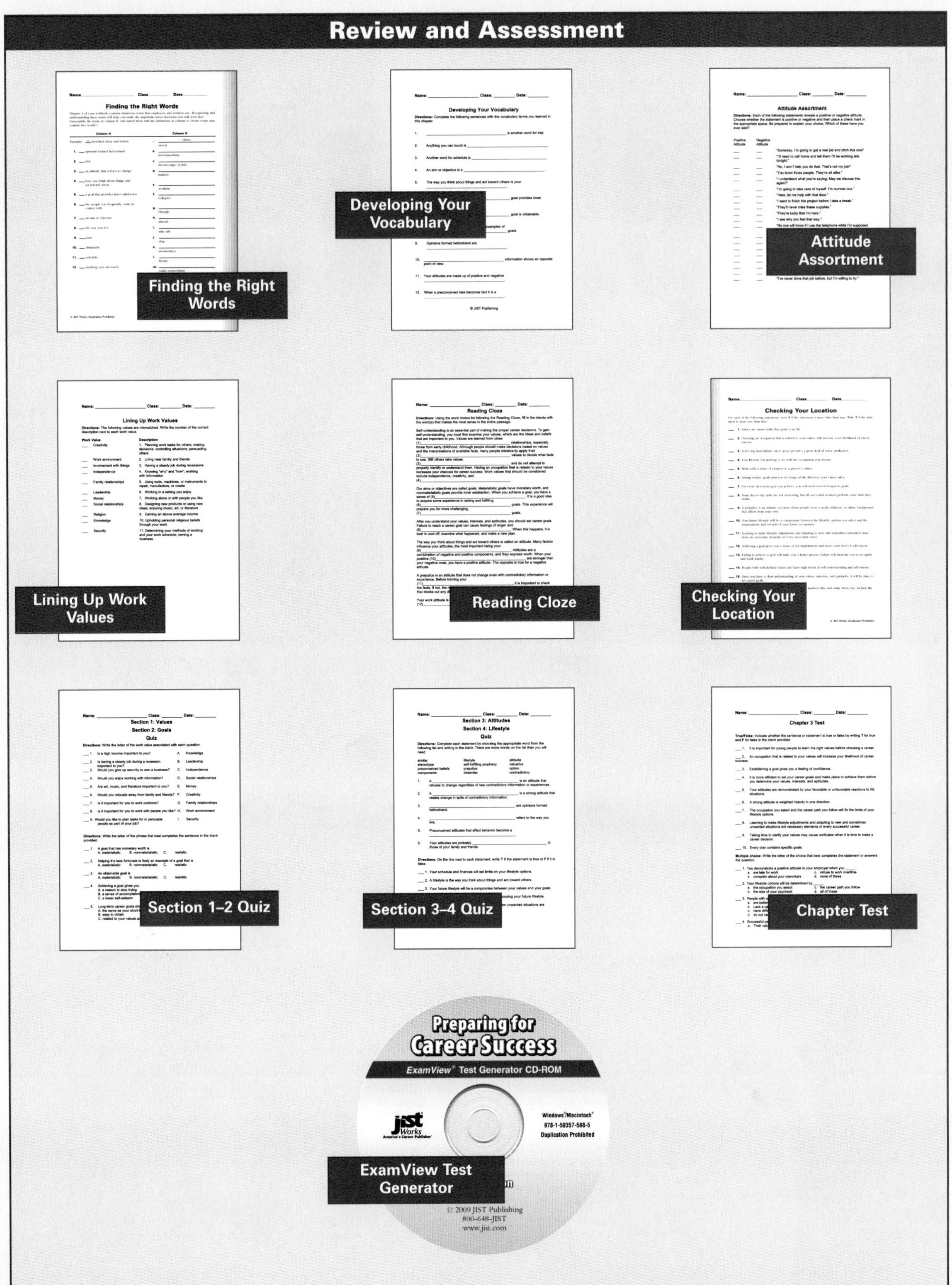

Chapter 3 Knowing Yourself: Values and Goals

Learning Objectives

- Explain the relationship between your personal values, goals, attitudes, career choices, and lifestyle options
- Describe your unique set of values and relate them to lifestyle and job satisfaction
- Set realistic short-term and long-term career goals
- Recognize your positive and negative attitudes toward yourself, others, and work

In the first two chapters of this text, you learned how differences in interests and aptitudes affect a worker's personal satisfaction with career choices. In this chapter, self-understanding will focus on values, goals, attitudes, and lifestyle choices. All of these factors are important in building your character.

By sorting and prioritizing your unique combination of values and goals, you can gain a better understanding of the factors that motivate you to be successful. In the process, you may discover potential talents and career choices that you had never considered. Self-understanding will help you set realistic goals, maintain a positive attitude, and begin making important decisions about your personal journey to career success.

Enrich Your Vocabulary

In reading this chapter and doing the exercises, you will learn the following important terms:

attitude	mission statement	social environment
components	nonmaterialistic	tangible
contradictory	preconceived beliefs	tentative
goal	prejudice	timeline
lifestyle	realistic	values
materialistic	self-fulfilling prophesy	

Vocabulary Builder

The "Enrich Your Vocabulary" terms are highlighted and defined throughout the chapter. Discuss the "Enrich Your Vocabulary" terms before you assign the chapter. Ask students to write their own definitions and then discuss their definitions in class.

Vocabulary

You can use the "Developing Your Vocabulary" worksheet in Chapter 3 of the *Preparing for Career Success Instructor's CD-ROM, Third Edition* as a pretest or a re-teaching worksheet.

Video Tour on DVD

Show students the Chapter 3 segment to introduce them to the content.

Employment is nature's physician, and is essential to human happiness.

—Galen

Discussion Starter

Review the four questions in terms of the strong personal beliefs the students have identified. Remind the students that values are personal; the discussion should not be judgmental. Ask for volunteers to list several strong values on the chalkboard. Ask the students which occupations would encourage or discourage certain values on the list.

Section 1: Values

How much importance do you place on owning a nice-looking car? How much of your time are you willing to volunteer to help others or improve the environment? Why is donating money to a particular charity important to you? Examining your **values** (cherished ideas and beliefs) will help you answer these questions. Likewise, understanding your values will help you determine the importance you place on particular material things, people, ideas, or situations.

Your values are not necessarily right or wrong. However, as long as you consider them to be true, you will use them to guide the direction of your life. Think about one of your strongest beliefs about people or ideas. Then use the following questions to determine whether your belief is strong enough to be considered a value:

1. Do I have strong feelings about this belief?
2. Have I carefully considered this belief and selected it to be important, without pressure from other people?
3. Do I cherish the belief I have selected?
4. Do I behave in such a way that other people are aware of my belief?

If you answered "yes" to three or four of these questions, your belief is a strong personal value. If you answered "no" to three or four questions, your belief isn't very strong and should not be considered a value. If you had two "yes" answers and two "no" answers, you might wish to reevaluate your belief. Can you think of an activity that might help you to examine this belief further?

People with well-defined values also have high levels of self-understanding and self-esteem. In addition, they are better prepared to make realistic career plans.

Your values are more than the way you see extremes of right and wrong, good and bad, or true and false. They are a driving force behind your willingness or reluctance to make commitments, accept changes, strive for high achievement, or develop new skills. Your values have already influenced the way you feel, think, and behave in your social life. In the future, they will influence the decisions you make about your career and lifestyle.

© JIST Works

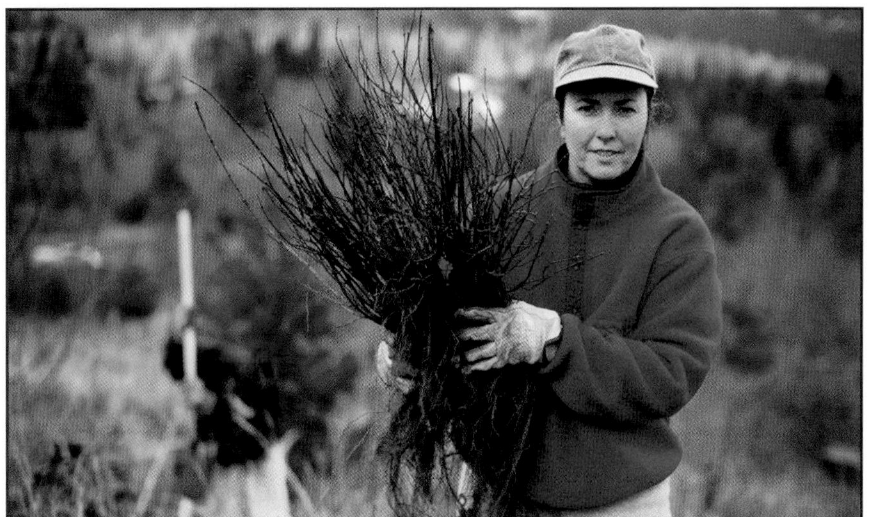

Clarifying your values before you make career decisions is important. Is working outdoors important to you?

Case Study

Have students read the case study "When Values Conflict" found in Chapter 3 of the *Preparing for Career Success Instructor's CD-ROM, Third Edition* and discuss the "Critical Thinking" questions.

Discussion Starter

Instruct the students to bring to class a newspaper or magazine article describing a business or political decision that affects workers. Ask the students what values and facts the decision makers used. Ask how the decision will affect workers. Ask the students what the decisions reveal about the character of the decision makers.

Successful people usually make decisions based on their values and their interpretation of the available facts. Sometimes, though, people decide which facts to use on the basis of their personal values, rather than on the accuracy of the facts. How do your values enter into your decisions?

Some people take their values for granted, without identifying or understanding them. Taking time to clarify your values will give you a more accurate understanding of yourself.

Values are learned from close social relationships, largely from early childhood home situations. Children constantly observe the choices made by parents, teachers, and other important adults. They are quick to understand the values being expressed by adult behaviors. They mimic the behavior of the adults around them and frequently accept the adults' values.

As children grow older and are exposed to a larger number of people and experiences, they may change the importance they place on certain values.

Take Note

People often express their values to others by making a statement. On July 4, 1776, the Continental Congress made some of the most famous values statements in history in the Declaration of Independence. The statement "all men are created equal" reflects the belief in equality. The phrase "certain unalienable rights, that among these are life, liberty, and the pursuit of happiness" demonstrates the value of freedom. The value of democracy is shown in this definition of government: "to secure these rights, governments are instituted among men, deriving their just powers from the consent of the governed."

Building Character: Role Models Are Important

Reggie Swanson's parents are alcohol abusers. They sometimes argue loudly and even hit each other. Each morning during his childhood, Reggie had to select his clothes, fix something to eat, and walk to school alone. Reggie was ashamed of his parents and avoided lasting friendships. His grades were usually very low, and his parents didn't seem to care.

When Reggie was 11, he started taking liquor from his parents' bottles while they were asleep. In the seventh grade, he was suspended from school for 10 days for being drunk during a school assembly program.

When Reggie was in the eighth grade, he became friends with Jack Anderson. Jack's parents make Reggie feel like one of the family. Reggie frequently eats meals and spends the night at Jack's house. The Andersons even took him along on their vacation last summer. Jack's parents don't approve of drinking, and neither does Jack. Reggie has decided to quit drinking because he respects the Anderson family and wants them to respect him.

Jack's parents have encouraged Reggie to acquire a good education. Reggie's grades have improved, and he has decided to attend the technical high school next year. He wants to study diesel engine repair.

Career Fact

Values give shape to your goals, and goals are the cornerstone of a successful career plan.

Technology

Writing a *blog* (an online journal) can be a great way to build your communication and computer skills and connect with friends and potential employers. However, it can have negative consequences, too. People have been sued, suspended from school, and fired from their jobs for material they have posted on their blogs.

To prevent this from happening to you, don't

- Post rumors. Writing untrue statements that harm someone's reputation is called defamation, and you can be sued for it.
- Share photos or other information about your family and friends without asking for permission first.
- Include illegal or obscene content.

Critical Thinking

In Reggie's case, expanding his social environment (the people he frequently comes in contact with) helped him discover new values and improve the quality of his life. Can you imagine a situation in which expanding a young person's social environment and experiences could have a negative effect on the quality of his or her life? Describe the situation.

Who is responsible for the values a child accepts? Is it the child's parents? friends? school? church? the government? the child? Be prepared to explain your answer in class.

Nonmaterialistic values are ones that have no monetary worth. What nonmaterialistic value(s) did Jack's parents express? What nonmaterialistic value(s) did Reggie express?

Based on Reggie's recent decisions, what are some words you could use to describe his character?

Enrichment

After students read the section "Work Values," have them complete the "Examining Your Work Values" worksheet in Chapter 3 of the *Preparing for Career Success Student Activity Book, Third Edition.*

Work Values

Everyone has work values, but many people don't clarify them in terms of their careers. An occupation that is related to your values will increase your likelihood of career success, financial rewards, and personal satisfaction.

© JIST Works

Your work values will be the standard of conduct and moral beliefs that determine what is important to you in your career. They will influence your work ethic and the way you conduct yourself with fellow workers. Selecting an occupation that rewards your personal values will allow you to live your values every day.

Determine the values that are important to you and relate them to **tentative** (trial) occupations. Do you place a high value on adding beauty to the world, protecting the environment, helping humanity, or discovering new ways of doing things? What values would your ideal occupation allow you to express? Here is a list of values you should consider:

- **Security:** Is it important for you to have a steady job during recessions? Are you willing to trade a higher paycheck for more security?
- **Knowledge:** Is it important for you to learn why certain events occur or how a certain device operates? Would you enjoy working with information?
- **Family relationships:** Would you relocate for a career opportunity if it meant being far away from family members or close friends?
- **Independence:** Is it important for you to determine your methods of working and your work schedule? Would you give up security to own a business?
- **Money:** Is it important for you to earn a great deal of money? Could you be satisfied with an average or somewhat above average income?
- **Religion:** Would you accept a job if the employer's product, service, or philosophy conflicted in any way with your religious beliefs?
- **Creativity:** Would you like to design new products or use new ideas? Is music, art, or literature important to you?
- **Leadership:** Would you like to plan work tasks for others? Do you enjoy making decisions, controlling a situation, and persuading others?
- **Work environment:** Is it important for you to work outdoors, in an office or factory, to have air-conditioning, or to work in a quiet setting?
- **Social relationships:** Is it important for you to work with people you like? Would you enjoy social relationships with some of your coworkers? On the other hand, would you prefer working alone?
- **Involvement with things:** Is it important for you to use tools, machines, or instruments to perform your work?

As you begin to consider more values in your career choice, fewer occupations will satisfy all of them. Review the examples in Table 3.1.

Self-Understanding

Ask the students if they know a person who enjoys his or her work. Does this person's work satisfaction carry over to his or her personal life? If so, how? Ask the students what they have accomplished in the past month that makes them feel proud. Tell them that *work* is another word for *accomplishment*.

CLUSTER LINK

If security is one of your high work values, you might enjoy working in the career cluster of Government and Public Administration. The federal government is the nation's largest employer and hires thousands of new workers in over 400 occupational specialties each year. See the appendix for more information.

Reteaching

Have students complete the "Lining Up Work Values" worksheet found in Chapter 3 of the *Preparing for Career Success Instructor's CD-ROM, Third Edition.*

Comprehension Check

Select one of the 11 work values listed and write it on the chalkboard. Ask the students to name occupations that satisfy the value you have listed. Ask why the value is important in this occupation. Write a second value on the board. Ask for occupations that satisfy both values. Repeat this process until several values and matching occupations are listed.

© JIST Works

Table 3.1 Relating Work Values to Occupations

Work Values Considered	Related Occupations
Working outdoors	Forester, bricklayer, construction equipment operator
Working outdoors and working with your hands	Bricklayer, construction equipment operator
Working outdoors, working with your hands, and working with machines	Construction equipment operator
Working outdoors, working with your hands, working with machines, and working with people	None of these three occupations satisfy all four of these work values.

Section 1: Get Involved

Answer the following on a separate sheet of paper, and be prepared to discuss your responses in class.

1. Rank the following with the item that has been most influential in forming your values as 1 and the item that has been least influential as 6. Be prepared to discuss your reasons in class.
   Family Church Media
   School Government Friends
2. If you knew the world would end in two days, what would you do during that time? What does your answer tell you about your values? About your character? What you cherish?
3. If you won a $10 million lottery, how would you spend the money? List the values expressed in your answer.
4. Cut out several help-wanted ads in the classified section of your Sunday newspaper. Based on the message in each ad, what work values do the different employers expect?

Comprehension Check

Ask the students to share a few of their short-term goals and list them on the chalkboard. Next, ask for long-term goals, and make a similar list. Ask the students to label each goal *materialistic* or *nonmaterialistic.*

"If you don't know where you're going, you'll probably end up somewhere else."

—David Campbell

Enrichment

Offer extra credit to students who read and report to class on David Campbell's small book, *If You Don't Know Where You're Going You'll Probably End Up Somewhere Else.*

Section 2: Goals

A **goal** is an aim or objective. In a football game, the goal is clear: It is marked with a crisp white line. Each team's objective is to carry the football across the opposing team's goal line. In life, there is a difference between short-term and long-term goals. In football, the short-term goal may be to move the ball 10 yards on four plays. The long-term goal could be to win the league championship.

The game of life is similar. Successful players have several goals; some are short-term goals, and others are long-term goals. However, the players in the game of life are responsible for choosing the location of their own goal line and determining the specific goals they are trying to achieve.

A **materialistic** goal (one that has monetary worth) would be the ownership of a **tangible** item (anything you can touch), such as a new coat, a bike, a computer, an automobile, or a house. A **nonmaterialistic** goal—such as helping less fortunate people, cleaning up the natural environment, or getting a good education—provides inner satisfaction.

Establishing a goal gives you a feeling of confidence. Achieving the goal gives you a sense of accomplishment and raises your self-esteem. On the other hand, people without goals often lack confidence, have no sense of accomplishment, and have a lower level of self-esteem. Deciding not to set goals allows others to make choices for you.

Most people will tell you that they want to improve their personal relationships, learn new skills, purchase a new car, or advance their career.

© JIST Works

However, many lack the plan and sense of commitment they need to achieve these goals. They substitute delays and excuses for deadlines. They prefer a flexible schedule, free from specific responsibilities, rather than a disciplined schedule aimed at a specific accomplishment. What does this tell you about their character?

Every plan contains specific goals. Learning to set **realistic** (obtainable) goals is an important part of planning for career success; it puts you in charge of the direction your career takes.

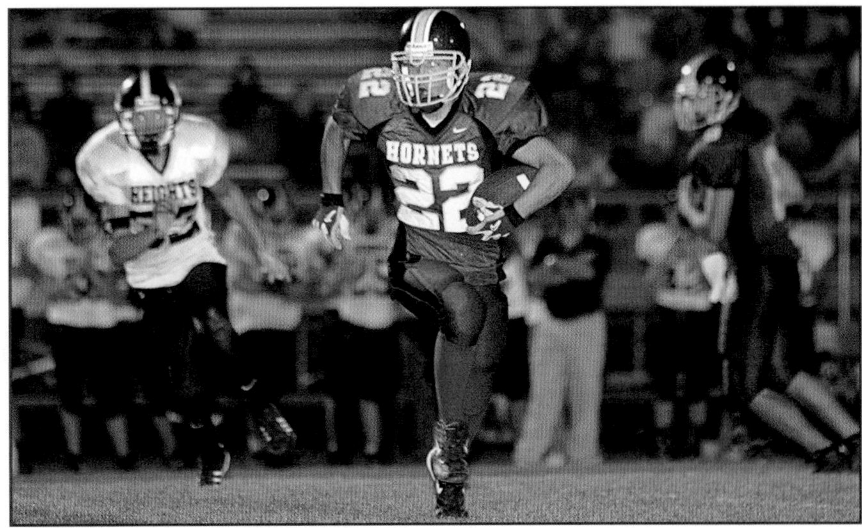

Determine the goal; then work to achieve it. What is your long-term career goal? What short-term goals must you reach first?

Goals are an important part of every successful life plan. They are like the route numbers on a road map. Can you imagine trying to drive across the country without having route numbers on your map or signs along the highways? Use the following guidelines to make a list of goals for your life plan:

1. Set your own goals. Listen to and learn from other people, but set goals that are important to you.
2. Base your goals on your important values. Otherwise, you will not consider them worthy enough to act on.
3. Make sure that the meaning of each goal is clear. Write your goals on a sheet of paper, or keep them in a small notebook.
4. Separate your general goals into easy-to-understand parts.
5. Be certain that each goal has a clear objective. This will help you measure your success in achieving it.
6. Make sure that each goal is possible. Consider any factors that could prevent you from achieving it.
7. Determine the amount of time and energy you are willing to invest in achieving each goal.
8. Develop a plan of action for reaching each goal. Be prepared to do what is necessary to make your plan succeed. Include a specific time to begin, as well as a time to reach each goal.
9. Review your written goals frequently.

Get into the habit of setting and achieving short-term goals. Be sure to have a **timeline** (schedule) for the completion of each goal. Some short-term goals you might wish to consider are improving your school attendance, obtaining a part-time job, cleaning or improving a part of your home, or establishing a friendship with a certain person.

Cooperative Learning

Assign students to groups of three. Allow five minutes for each group to write as many personal, career, and educational goals as possible. Allow each group to report their total number of goals. Allow each group time to identify one realistic and one unrealistic goal from their list. Have each group report to the class to confirm the accuracy of their choices.

Reteaching

Have students complete the "Goal Guidelines to Share" worksheet found in Chapter 3 of *Preparing for Career Success Instructor's CD-ROM, Third Edition.*

I never did anything worth doing by accident, nor did any of my inventions come by accident; they came by work.

—Thomas Alva Edison

Case Study

Have students read the case study "An Occupation That Works" found in Chapter 3 of the *Preparing for Career Success Instructor's CD-ROM, Third Edition* and discuss the "Critical Thinking" questions.

KEY TO SUCCESS

The attitude you have toward yourself influences your attitudes toward other people and toward work.

Self-Understanding

Have students write a mission statement to define where they are now in their career planning and their future career goals.

Discussion Starter

Ask the students to think about a goal they consider to be important. Which day-to-day tasks leading to the goal do they consider boring? Which tasks are interesting?

Student Evaluation

To evaluate student mastery of concepts, you might want to use the Section 1–2 quiz found in the Chapter 3 file of the *Preparing for Career Success Instructor's CD-ROM, Third Edition.*

After you acquire some experience setting and achieving short-term goals, begin working on long-term, more challenging goals. They might include acquiring and saving money for additional education or training, earning a scholarship, being accepted for an apprenticeship program, or purchasing an automobile.

Career Goals

Once you have a clear understanding of your values, interests, and aptitudes, your next step is to set career goals and make plans to achieve them. The term **mission statement** is a broad and specific statement used by many employers as a guideline to define the organization and inspire employees. It includes a planned sequence of *immediate* (short-term goals) and *long-range* (long-term goals) actions. You can use a mission statement to define where you are now in your career planning and your future career goals.

For every long-term career goal you achieve, you will need several short-term goals. Accomplishing short-term goals will help you realize that you can achieve long-term goals. Success will motivate you to achieve more success. The trick is sticking to your mission. Many people don't acquire their ideal job immediately. Instead, they perform some job tasks they dislike and interact with some supervisors they dislike. Sometimes they must get involved in unpleasant corporate politics. However, they need to focus on doing a good job, stay motivated, set realistic goals, and strive to meet them.

When setting your long-term career goals, be certain they are related to your values and personal interests. This will increase your likelihood of achieving career satisfaction.

You can easily become frustrated when you fail to reach a goal. Failure can cause feelings of anger and incompetence and can cause you to blame others. A wiser response to failure is to take a little time to cool off, determine the reasons for the failure, and define a new plan. When you are striving for goals, the old saying "Winners never quit, and quitters never win" is a good philosophy to follow.

Section 2: Get Involved

Answer the following on a separate sheet of paper, and be prepared to discuss your responses in class.

1. What are three materialistic goals you would like to achieve in the next year? The next 10 years? What is your plan to reach each of these goals? Be sure to include the necessary short-term goals in your plan.
2. What are three nonmaterialistic goals you would like to achieve in the next year? The next 10 years? Of the goals you have listed, which goal do you consider to be most important? Why?
3. What tentative career goals have you set? What are you presently accomplishing in school that will help you achieve your tentative career goals? How will your school accomplishments help?

© JIST Works

Section 3: Attitudes

An **attitude** is the way you think about things and act toward others. Attitudes are revealed through your positive or negative responses to another person's thoughts, feelings, and beliefs. They are demonstrated by your favorable or unfavorable reactions to life situations.

An attitude may be as simple as your evaluation of a certain breakfast cereal or as complex as your beliefs about free speech or gender equality. In either case, your attitude is an evaluation for or against a certain position.

Your attitudes are a combination of negative and positive **components** (parts), and they are *valuative* (express worth). Your attitudes will cause you to behave in a certain way toward the person, thing, or situation you are evaluating. When your positive feelings and emotions are stronger than your negative feelings and emotions, you have a positive attitude. When the reverse is true, your attitude is negative.

A strong attitude is weighted heavily in one direction. What strong positive or negative attitude do you have toward a certain person, thing, or situation? A weak attitude is slightly weighted in favor of its positive or negative component. Can you think of a certain person, thing, or situation that causes you to have a slightly positive or slightly negative attitude?

Attitudes toward people whose gender, skin color, language, religion, or customs are similar to or different from your own frequently bring out strong feelings and emotions leading to extreme positive or negative attitudes. A stereotype is a strong attitude that resists change in spite of **contradictory** (showing an opposite point of view) information. A **prejudice** is an attitude that refuses to change regardless of new contradictory information or experiences.

Although your family probably has the greatest influence on your attitudes, you also learn attitudes from newspapers and magazines, TV, personal experiences, and friends. As the old saying goes, "Birds of a feather flock together." If your attitudes were different from those of your closest *associates* (family or friends), you would be faced with continual criticism and correction.

Do you take time to question the accuracy of your personal beliefs and feelings before you take certain actions? Are you open to the fact that other people and situations change? Do you believe cultural diversity benefits America? If you can answer yes to these questions, you have probably reduced the role of prejudice and stereotypes in your personal relationships.

Evaluating all new information that you receive is important. Have you ever listened to a speaker and wondered whether the speaker really knew what he or she was talking about? If the subject were unfamiliar to you, finding out about the speaker's qualifications would be a good idea. Is he or she an expert on the topic? Does the speaker belong to a group with a special interest? Can the facts being presented be verified? Perhaps you can obtain a book by another expert to check the facts. Because speakers present their opinions, you would be wise to check the facts before forming yours.

Enrichment

Have students complete the "Your Attitude Is Showing" worksheet in Chapter 3 of the *Preparing for Career Success Student Activity Book, Third Edition.*

Self-Understanding

Ask students to describe school situations when others made positive or negative responses to their thoughts, feelings, or beliefs. Ask how they felt at that moment and how the responses helped or hindered the situation.

Showing an interest in assigned tasks demonstrates a positive working attitude. Do you demonstrate a positive working attitude when you are assigned a task at home or school?

© JIST Works

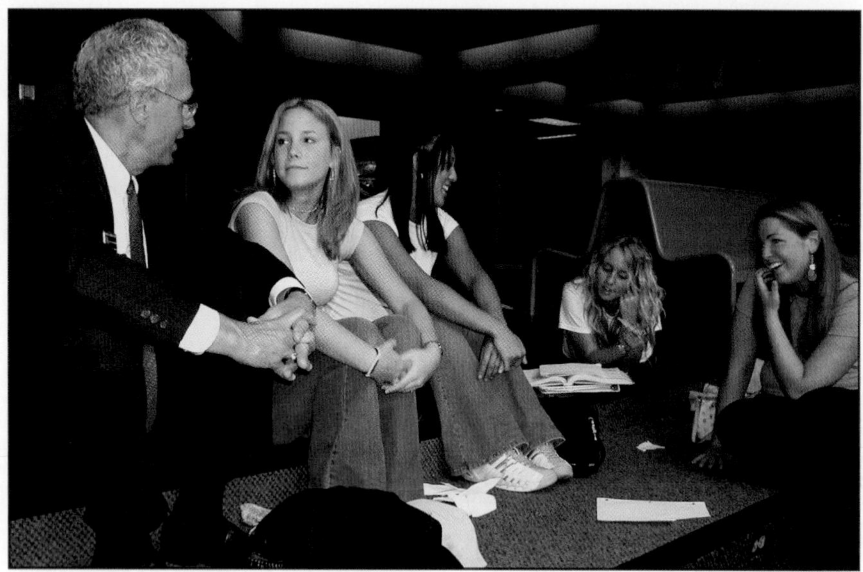

Attitudes are influenced by those you know, like, and trust.

Have you ever been in a conversation in which a certain topic came up and you knew your opinion immediately? Perhaps your **preconceived beliefs** (opinions formed beforehand) were so strong that they blocked out any information that didn't agree with your personal position. If your preconceived attitude insists that anything connected with a certain situation, thing, or person is absolutely right or wrong or that you can't accomplish a certain educational or occupational goal, you are likely to act or interpret events in a way that causes your beliefs to be reinforced. This is called a **self-fulfilling prophesy**.

Can you think of a time when you

- Refused to fly in an airplane?
- Stayed awake all night because the weather was bad?
- Were a guest at a meal and refused to eat the food?
- Had a teacher or employer you couldn't tolerate?

What was your strongest attitude in that situation? Try to determine the cause of your attitude, the purpose it served, and the effect it had on your life. What influenced your attitude most: emotions or facts? If the source of an attitude is a single personal experience, make certain your information is accurate and not too generalized.

Comprehension Check

Ask students for examples of their positive attitudes toward a nationally recognized person or situation. Next, ask for examples of their negative attitudes toward a nationally recognized person or situation.

Reteaching

Have students complete the "Attitude Assortment" worksheet found in Chapter 3 of *Preparing for Career Success Instructor's CD-ROM, Third Edition.*

Vocabulary Builder

Assign students to review newspaper or magazine articles for an example of a stereotype. Ask them to identify any contradictory information presented and determine whether a prejudice is being expressed.

School-to-Work Transition

Workers are more likely to be fired because of a negative attitude than weak job skills. Ask students who are part-time workers to share experiences involving coworkers with positive or negative attitudes.

A Working Attitude

Your attitude toward work is as important as your job performance. You demonstrate a positive work attitude to your employer when you show an interest in your assigned tasks, perform work beyond the required limits, and display approved behaviors on the job.

Your attitude affects your feelings about the future and, as a result, influences your career choices. If family and friends appreciate and encourage your aptitudes, skills, and accomplishments, you will be motivated toward future achievement and career success. On the other hand, if family and friends criticize your aptitudes and skills, overlook your accomplishments, and emphasize your failures, you will feel that future achievement and career success are unobtainable goals. You will become discouraged.

Many times, a person is motivated toward career success by the encouragement of one particular person. Who has encouraged you? Who has discouraged you? Who have you encouraged?

© JIST Works

Section 3: Get Involved

Answer the following on a separate sheet of paper, and be prepared to discuss your responses in class.

1. Identify three strong opinions that you have about a person, situation, or thing. Where did you learn these opinions? Have you ever had different opinions about these topics? If so, what caused you to change your mind?
2. What influenced the formation of your attitudes most? Was it personal experience, other people, or your emotions? Provide an example.
3. Describe a situation in which the media (TV, magazines, and newspapers) influenced you to believe in something or someone. Do you still feel the same? Why or why not?

Section 4: Lifestyle

The occupation you select and the career path you follow will fix the limits of your lifestyle options. The demands of your occupation will determine your daily and yearly schedules, the amount of money you have to spend, and the geographic region in which you live. In turn, your schedule and your finances will set limits on your lifestyle options. You will need to plan a lifestyle that balances your time, energies, capabilities, and needs with the demands and rewards of your work.

You are responsible for selecting your future **lifestyle** (the way you live). Use the information you have learned about yourself thus far to relate your personal values, interests, aptitudes, and experiences to your lifestyle choices. Review the following lifestyle options in terms of your personal characteristics.

- What region of the country do I prefer? North, East, West, South, Midwest?
- What geographic environment do I prefer? Mountains, coastal regions, forested areas, river areas, lake regions, farmland?
- What size community would I like to live in? City, suburb, small town, rural area?
- Which type of climate is best for me? Dry or rainy? Long cold winters or warm winters? (Be sure to consider special health problems in your decision.)
- What type of home do I prefer? Do I want to rent or own? (Be sure to include the distance to your place of employment, the method of transportation you will use, and the daily travel time in your decision.)
- What social surroundings do I prefer? Living close to family and friends? Single or married? Children? Being mobile to obtain career advancements?

Your future lifestyle will be a compromise between the lifestyle options you select and the requirements and rewards of your future occupation. For each occupation you consider, determine how many of your lifestyle options would be satisfied. Which options are your top priorities? Which options would you be willing to trade for career advancement?

Career Fact

Where you live and work influences your lifestyle spending patterns. Consider these findings from the Department of Labor:

- Southerners and Midwesterners have similar spending patterns; likewise, Northeasterners and Westerners are similar in their spending.
- Home ownership is most common in the Midwest and least common in the West.
- Income before taxes is greater in the Northeast and West than in the Midwest and South.

Vocabulary Builder

A *compromise* is a settling of matters by mutual adjustment, each side making some concessions. Ask the students to share a time when they resolved a situation by making a compromise.

Enrichment

Have students complete the "Lifestyle Options" worksheet in Chapter 3 of the *Preparing for Career Success Student Activity Book, Third Edition.*

Learning to make lifestyle adjustments and adapting to new and sometimes unwanted situations are necessary elements of every successful career. However, it is important to accept and be satisfied with each lifestyle compromise you make.

Section 4: Get Involved

Answer the following on a separate sheet of paper, and be prepared to discuss your responses in class.

1. Which of your preferred lifestyle options do you presently enjoy? Which of your preferred options are missing from your present lifestyle?
2. Among the occupations you are considering, which is most likely to provide you with your desired lifestyle? Why? Which is least likely? Why?
3. Locate a copy of the *Occupational Outlook Handbook* in your school or public library. Find the description of an occupation you are presently considering. What are the average earnings? What are the hours of work? What is the job outlook? What education or training will be required? How do these factors relate to your preferred lifestyle goals?

Reteaching

Have students complete the "Finding the Right Words" and "Checking Your Location" worksheets in Chapter 3 of the *Preparing for Career Success Student Activity Book, Third Edition.*

Chapter 3 Review

Enrich Your Vocabulary

On a separate sheet of paper, number from 1 to 17, and complete the following activity. Match each statement with the most appropriate term from the "Enrich Your Vocabulary" list at the beginning of the chapter by writing that term next to the number of the correct statement.

1. The way a person thinks about things and acts toward others
2. An aim or objective
3. The way you live
4. Having monetary worth
5. Having no monetary worth
6. People you frequently come in contact with
7. Opinions formed beforehand
8. An attitude that refuses to change regardless of new contradictory information or experiences
9. Obtainable
10. Important beliefs that you use to guide the direction of your life
11. A strong preconceived idea that becomes fact
12. Showing an opposite point of view
13. Trial
14. Parts

Enrich Your Vocabulary Answers

1. attitude
2. goal
3. lifestyle
4. materialistic
5. nonmaterialistic
6. social environment
7. preconceived beliefs
8. prejudice
9. realistic
10. values
11. self-fulfilling prophesy
12. contradictory
13. tentative
14. components

(continued)

 © JIST Works

15. Anything you can touch

16. Schedule

17. A broad and specific statement used to define the organization and inspire employees

Check Your Knowledge

On a separate sheet of paper, complete the following activity.

1. How does clarifying your values help you make plans that are more likely to be successful?
2. Which of the following occupations is most closely related to a high value of working outdoors?

   a. Bricklayer **b.** Teacher **c.** Computer programmer
3. Name six nonmaterialistic values.
4. Name six of the guidelines given in this chapter for developing a list of goals for your life plan.
5. Where are values learned?
6. Attitudes toward people of different racial or ethnic backgrounds frequently evoke strong feelings and emotions. When does an attitude become a prejudice?
7. What are two ways an occupation influences your lifestyle?

Develop SCANS Competencies

This activity will give you practice in developing the information and interpersonal skills that successful workers have.

Choose three careers to research. During your research, identify the values necessary for a worker to be successful in that career. Your list might include the following: enjoys precision work, works under pressure, works at a fast pace, works with others, enjoys contact with the public, has creative abilities, is physically able to do the work, is trustworthy, and so on.

After making your own list, talk with people who work in each of the careers you researched. Ask whether there are any values they would add to the list. After you complete your list of values, make a chart (see the following example) that shows which values are required in which careers. Notice the similarities and differences.

	Career 1	Career 2	Career 3
Enjoys change	X	X	
Works alone	X		
Is punctual	X	X	X

Enrich Your Vocabulary Answers *(continued)*

15. tangible

16. timeline

17. mission statement

Check Your Knowledge Answers

1. Answers will vary. When individuals understand what they value and strive for relevant goals, they will be motivated to achieve.
2. a. Bricklayer
3. Answers will vary. They could include honesty, courage, responsibility, perseverance, self-reliance, cooperation, and friendliness.
4. 1) Set your own goals. 2) Base your goals on your important values. 3) Make sure that the meaning of each goal is clear. 4) Separate your general goals into easy-to-understand parts. 5) Be certain that each goal has a clear objective. 6) Make sure that each goal is possible. 7) Determine the amount of time and energy you are willing to invest in achieving each goal. 8) Develop a plan of action for reaching each goal. 9) Review your written goals frequently.
5. Answers will vary but should include family, friends, newspapers, magazines, TV, and personal experiences.
6. An attitude becomes a prejudice when a person's thoughts, feelings, and behaviors become fixed and he or she refuses to accept new information and experiences.
7. Answers may vary but should include at least one of the following: It determines your daily and yearly schedule, the amount of money you have to spend on lifestyle wants, and the geographic location in which you live.

Enrichment

Have students complete the Chapter 3 section of the *Preparing for Career Success Student Portfolio, Third Edition.*

© JIST Works

Chapter 4 Resources

Lesson Plans and Preparation

Multimedia

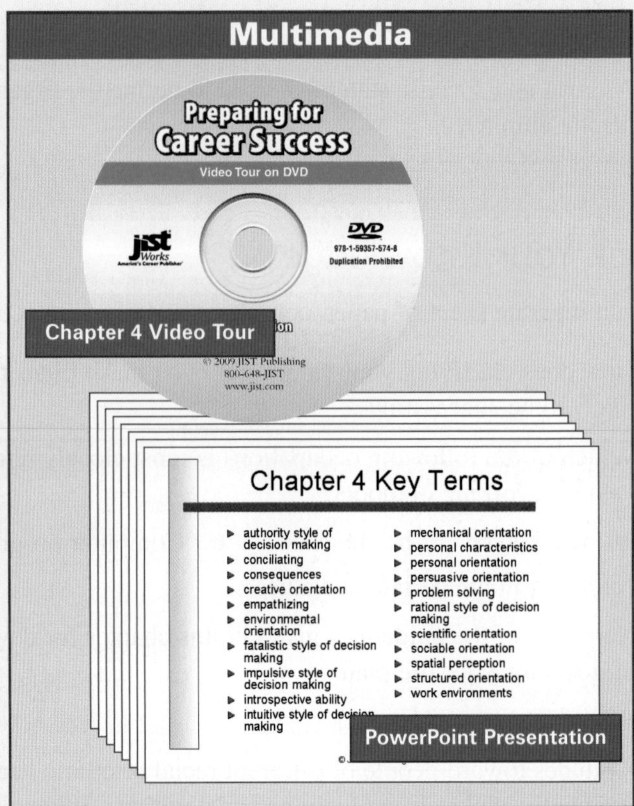

Activities

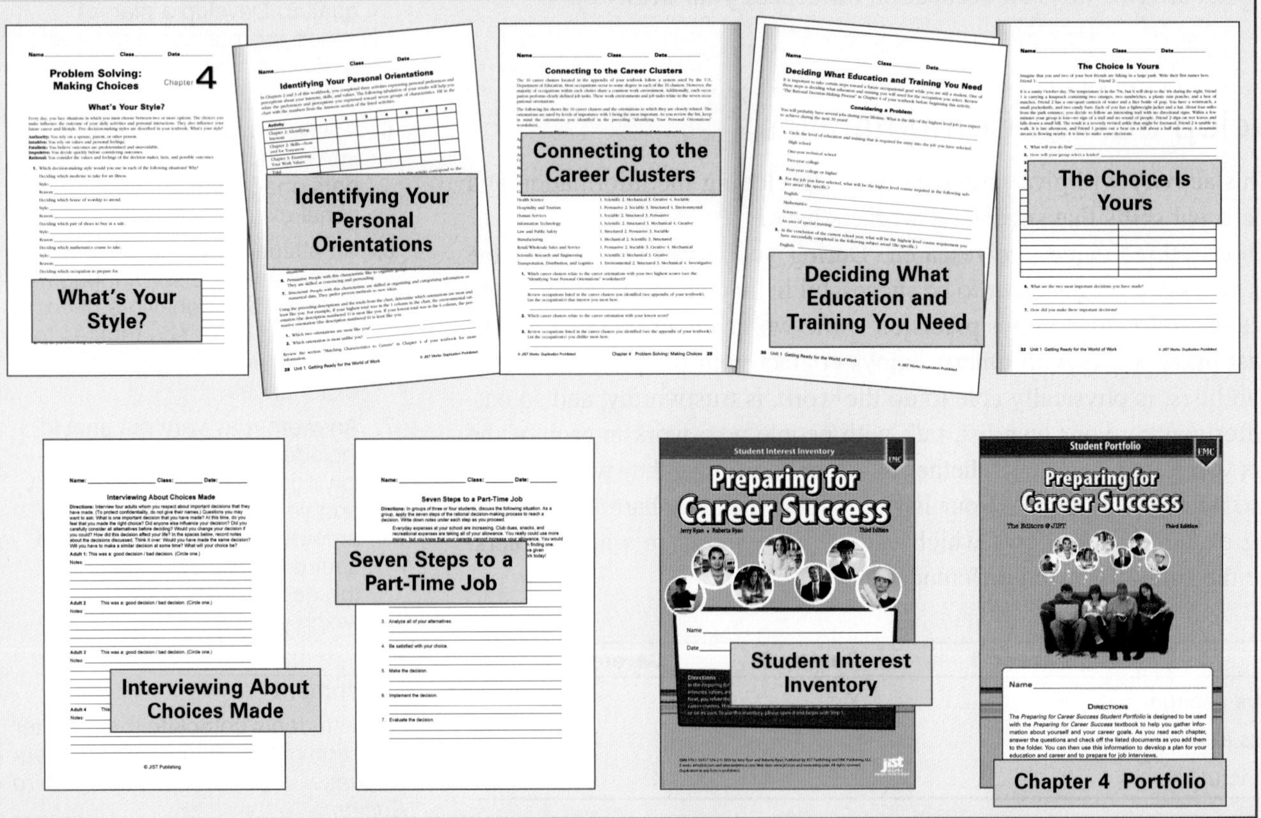

- What's Your Style?
- Identifying Your Personal Orientations
- Connecting to the Career Clusters
- Deciding What Education and Training You Need
- The Choice Is Yours
- Interviewing About Choices Made
- Seven Steps to a Part-Time Job
- Student Interest Inventory
- Chapter 4 Portfolio

© JIST Works

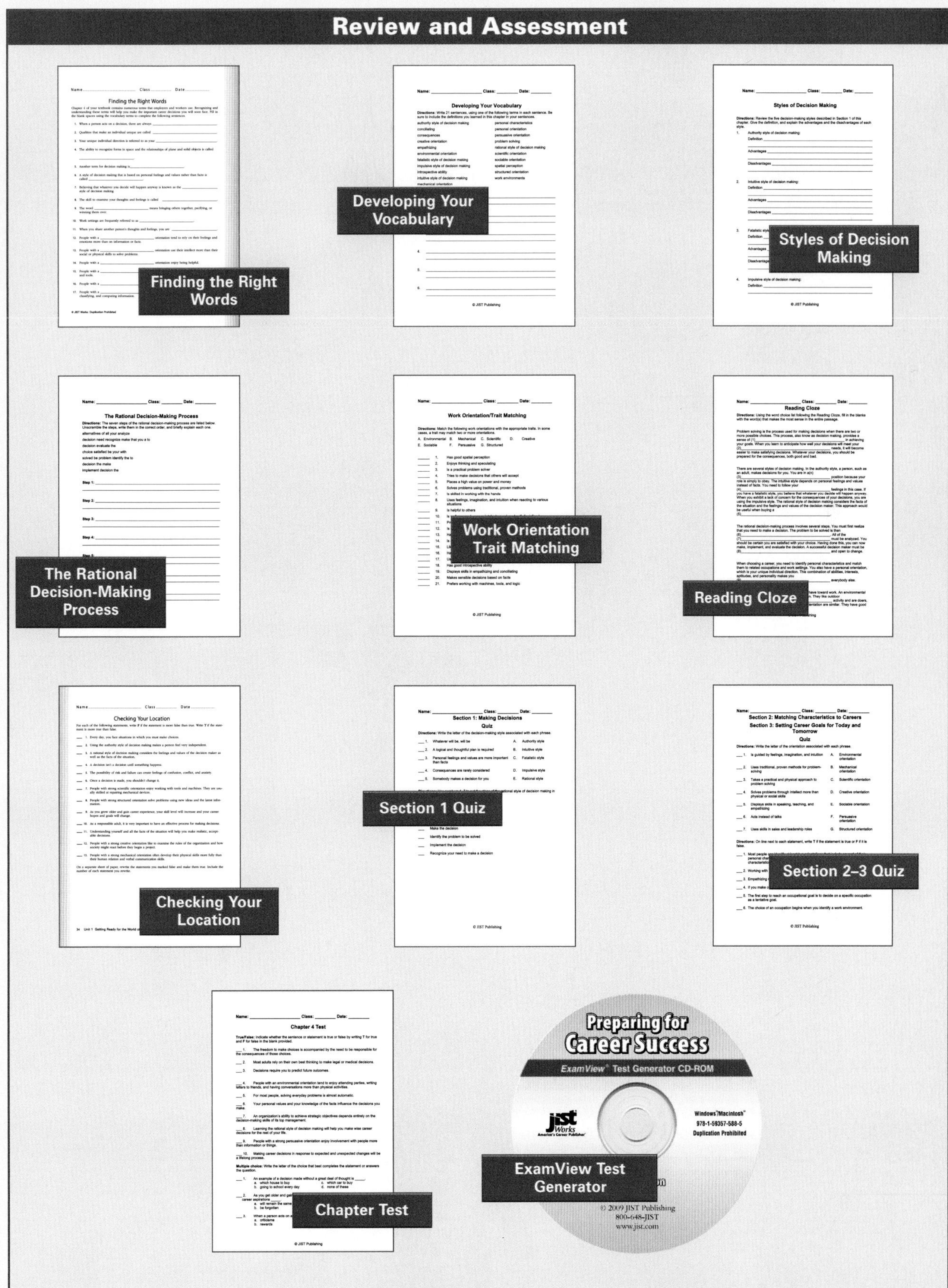
Review and Assessment
Finding the Right Words
Developing Your Vocabulary
Styles of Decision Making
The Rational Decision-Making Process
Work Orientation Trait Matching
Reading Cloze
Checking Your Location
Section 1 Quiz
Section 2–3 Quiz
Chapter Test
Preparing for Career Success
ExamView® Test Generator CD-ROM
ExamView Test Generator

Chapter 4 Problem Solving: Making Choices

Learning Objectives

- Discuss how decisions are made from a continual selection of choices with more than one solution
- Apply the rational style of decision making and increase your satisfaction with personal and career decisions
- Identify three satisfactory decisions that were influenced by your personal orientation
- Explain why satisfactory decisions depend on self-knowledge, reliable information, and clear thinking

Like the traveler in Robert Frost's poem "The Road Not Taken," you will arrive at points along the road of life where you must choose between two options. The choices you make will have different outcomes for your career, friendships, future lifestyle, and even selection of a spouse. You may wish to travel both roads, but reality will dictate that you make a choice.

Enrich Your Vocabulary

In reading this chapter and doing the exercises, you will learn the following important terms:

authority style of decision making	impulsive style of decision making	problem solving
conciliating	introspective ability	rational style of decision making
consequences	intuitive style of decision making	scientific orientation
creative orientation	mechanical orientation	sociable orientation
empathizing	personal characteristics	spatial perception
environmental orientation	personal orientation	structured orientation
fatalistic style of decision making	persuasive orientation	work environments

Vocabulary

You can use the "Developing Your Vocabulary" worksheet found in Chapter 4 of the *Preparing for Career Success Instructor's CD-ROM, Third Edition* as a pretest or used as a reteaching worksheet.

Two roads diverged in a yellow wood,
And sorry I could not travel both
And be one traveler; long I stood
And looked down one as far as I could
To where it bent in the undergrowth…

—Robert Frost, "The Road Not Taken"

Self-Understanding

Begin the chapter by reading aloud the passage from Robert Frost's poem "The Road Not Taken." Ask a student to read the first paragraph. Then ask the students for examples of choices they've made. Ask if they are satisfied with their choices.

Everyday, you face situations in which you must make choices. **Problem solving** (often called decision making) is the process used to make decisions when you select from two or more possible choices. Your personal values and your knowledge of the facts influence the decisions you make and your satisfaction with the outcomes.

When you woke up this morning, you had to make a decision. You had to decide whether to ignore the alarm or get out of bed. Then you had to decide what to wear to school and what to eat for breakfast. This afternoon you will make even more decisions. Will you go to the basketball game this evening or stay home and finish your schoolwork? Will you look for a part-time job or spend time with your family? Will you offer to help a friend who's in trouble, or will you mind your own business?

When a person acts on a decision, there are always **consequences** (resulting advantages and disadvantages). Can you think of a situation in which someone made a decision that resulted in a pleasant or unpleasant consequence for you? Can you think of a situation in which a decision you made had a pleasant or unpleasant consequence for another person? The freedom to make choices is accompanied by the need to be responsible for the consequences of those choices.

Your life requires making simple and complex decisions with multiple possibilities. You may already have the information needed to make these decisions, or it may be as handy as your Internet search engine. However, each decision has an alternative solution with different possible effects on your life. The ability to anticipate the possible outcomes of a choice depends on your knowledge of yourself and the facts, and on your ability to think logically. Learning and practicing the skills of an effective decision-making process will provide you with a sense of control in achieving daily and long-term goals and will increase the likelihood of satisfaction with your personal and career decisions.

As a responsible adult, you need to have an effective process for making decisions. In the world of work, an organization's ability to achieve its strategic objectives frequently depends on the problem-solving skills of its workforce.

© JIST Works

Section 1: Making Decisions

You make decisions when you are faced with new choices or problems. What problem do you have that needs a new decision? Schoolwork? Your best friend? Trouble at home? Your job? When you have many choices, facing problems and making new decisions can be especially difficult. You cannot be absolutely certain that the choice you make is best for the situation. Understanding yourself and all of the facts related to the problem will help you to make a realistic, acceptable decision.

Video Tour on DVD
Show students the Chapter 4 segment to introduce them to the content.

Imagination is more powerful than knowledge.
—Albert Einstein

Styles of Decision Making

When you were a small child, you had little or no control over life situations. Adults made decisions for you, and your only role in decision making was to obey. This is sometimes called the **authority style of decision making**. Some adults never outgrow this style and continue to rely on a spouse, parent, or other person to make decisions for them. The authority style of decision making places you in a dependent position.

Community Resources
Assign the students to interview a working adult and write a brief report on their findings. Suggest neighbors, parents, or local businesspeople. Ask the students to find examples of how a certain worker's problem-solving skills influence the success or failure of his or her employer's business. On the date you collect the assignment, allow time for a few brief individual reports and class discussion.

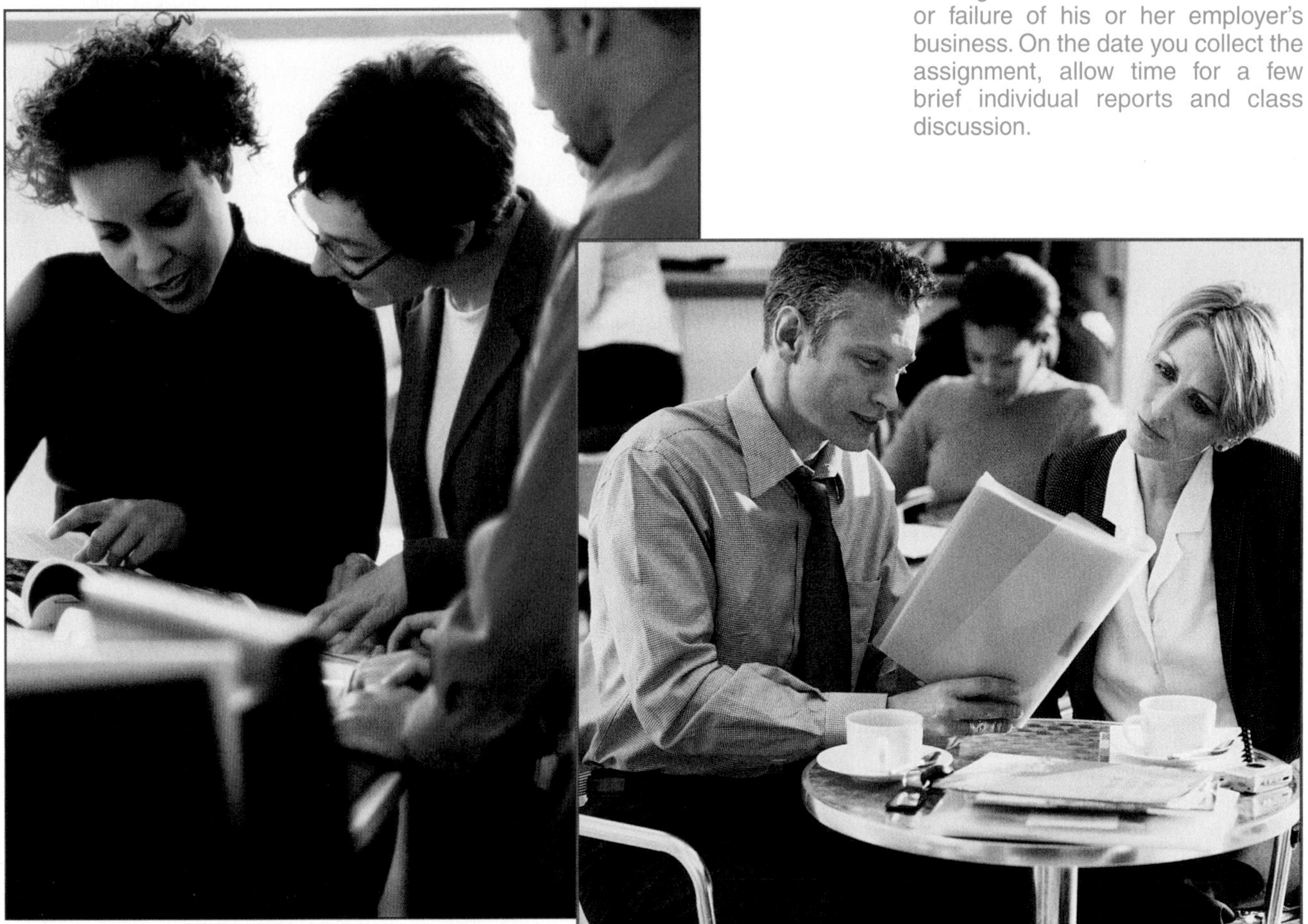

Successful workers are also successful problem solvers. What problems will you need to solve in your future career?

Enrichment

Have students complete the "What's Your Style?" worksheet in Chapter 4 of the *Preparing for Career Success Student Activity Book, Third Edition.*

Most adults rely on authorities to make legal or medical decisions. How is this different from a small child's decision-making situation? How is it the same? How can a person be reasonably certain that an authority is making the right decision?

Sean Ward is a self-employed sales representative. He buys used furniture at auctions and resells it. When Sean has a decision to make, he usually follows his "gut-level" feelings. Sean's philosophy of decision making is to make the choice that feels best and seems like the right thing to do. This method is sometimes called the **intuitive style of decision making**. Intuitive decision making is based on personal feelings and values rather than facts. Intuitive hunches could be nothing more than wishful thinking. Can you think of a situation in which intuitive decision making would be effective? Where would it be ineffective?

Cooperative Learning

Divide the class into five groups. Assign one of the five decision-making styles (authority, intuitive, fatalistic, impulsive, and rational) to each group. Ask each group to describe one successful and one unsuccessful decision that was made using this style. Who made the decision? Why does your group consider the decision successful or unsuccessful?

Some people believe that whatever will be, will be, and what a person decides doesn't make any difference. Believing that your decision doesn't change the consequences is known as the **fatalistic style of decision making.** Do you know anyone who uses this approach to decision making?

Vanessa Payne rarely considers the consequences of her decisions. She doesn't like to think ahead. She uses an **impulsive style of decision making.** Last week, she bought a new car. Vanessa liked her old car and didn't plan to buy a new one for two more years. When she saw the new car in the dealer's showroom, however, she became very excited about it and bought it. Now Vanessa is concerned about her monthly payments and may need to take a second job. Did you ever make an impulsive decision? How did it work out? Would you recommend this style of decision making?

Reteaching

Have students complete the "Styles of Decision Making" worksheet found in Chapter 4 of *Preparing for Career Success Instructor's CD-ROM, Third Edition.*

A **rational style of decision making** considers the feelings and values of the decision maker as well as the facts concerning the situation. This style requires the decision maker to be logical and thoughtful and to plan. Rational decisions balance the demands of a situation against the pros and

Key To Success

The rational style of decision making will help you make wise career decisions for the rest of your life.

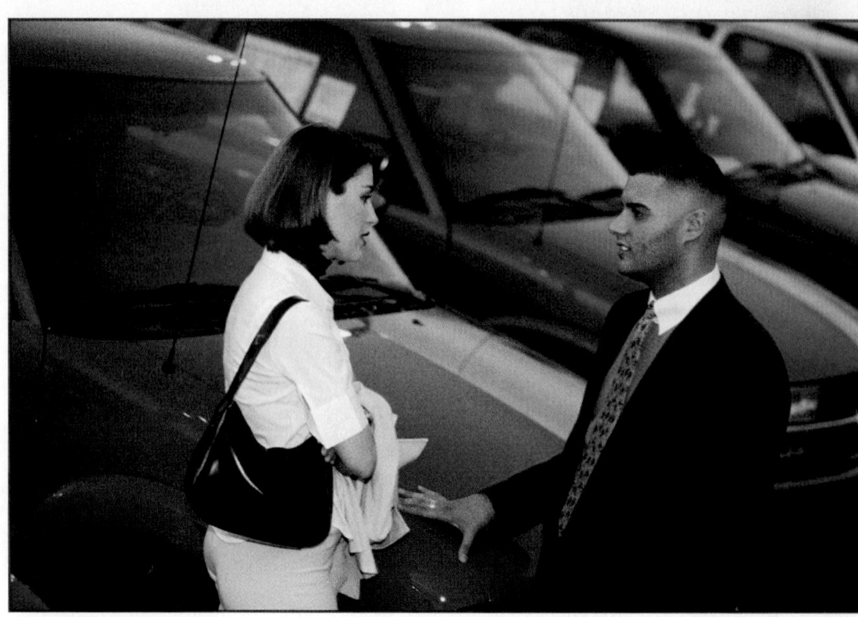

Buying a car requires a high level of decision-making skill. Which car do you want? Which one do you need? Which car can you afford?

© JIST Works

cons of the alternatives. They take into account the feelings and opinions of experts and of people close to the decision maker.

Using the rational decision-making process to select lunch in the school cafeteria, to buy a newspaper, or to determine which day you will bathe your pet would be a waste of time and energy. On the other hand, choosing to go steady, buy a new car, and enter a certain occupation are all complex decisions that require a higher-level method of decision making. Rational decision making will be more satisfactory in solving complex life situations than the other approaches mentioned.

The Rational Decision-Making Process

The rational decision-making process involves seven steps.

1. Recognize the Need for a Decision

Have you ever been frustrated, anxious, or uncomfortable with a life situation? Your feelings could have been coming from a conflict that was taking place between you and another person or between two people who were important to you. You will be faced with these situations in the world of work, just as you are in your personal life. You may have to choose between two or more job offers or decide on the purchase of an expensive item such as an automobile or a house. In each of these cases, you begin to realize a need for change. You become aware that you need to make a decision.

2. Identify the Problem to Be Solved

What is preventing you from reaching your goal? How does this situation make you feel? What is the cause of the problem? Why does this concern you? Who else is involved? What is preventing you from making a decision? Take time to consider these questions, and then write or state the answers to the "who, what, when, where, why, and how" of the situation.

3. Analyze Your Alternatives

Gather as much information as possible about the problem and each alternative for reaching an acceptable solution. Facts found on the Internet; in newspapers, magazines, books, and research articles; in advice from others; and from personal experience are all good sources of information. Make certain that your information is accurate and complete.

Make a list of your present alternatives, and try to find several new ones. Develop a "what-if" solution using each alternative. Include the satisfactory and unsatisfactory results of each alternative. List the consequences of each alternative in terms of time, cost, usefulness, and effect on other people. Eliminate the least acceptable alternatives, and then determine which of the remaining ones are most practical and attainable.

TECHNOLOGY

When you type keywords into an Internet search engine such as Google, you often get hundreds of links to Web sites as a result. How do you find the information you need? How do you determine the quality of the information? The following tips may help you:

- A current date on the Web site may indicate that the Web site is frequently updated and may therefore have reliable information.
- Government (.gov) and school (.edu) sites are usually good places for information.
- Reliable sites list sources for their information.

Reteaching

Have students complete the "Rational Decision-Making Process" worksheet found in Chapter 4 of *Preparing for Career Success Instructor's CD-ROM, Third Edition.*

KEY TO SUCCESS

As you make decisions, keep as many future options open as possible.

© JIST Works

Vocabulary Builder

Write the following words on the chalkboard: *evaluate, alternative, implement, commitment, solution, risk,* and *eliminate.* Next, divide the class into learning pairs. Allow 10 minutes for each pair to write as few correct sentences as possible using all seven words. The pair with the lowest score wins. Scoring: 1 point for each correct sentence; 1 point for each word used in a grammatically incorrect sentence; 1 point for each word not used.

Decisions require you to predict future outcomes. This element of uncertainty can create feelings of confusion, conflict, and anxiety. Can you think of a situation in which you took a chance by selecting one choice over another? How did you feel about the risk you were taking? Exploring and evaluating the alternatives when making a decision lessens negative feelings and gives you more confidence in the likelihood of a positive solution.

As an example, information is available for more than 20,000 occupations. When exploring the requirements and commitments for several occupations, you might feel anxious about the risks involved and the possibility of failure. However, by identifying the risks, advantages, and disadvantages of a particular occupation before making a decision to pursue it, you greatly reduce the probability of failure and increase the probability of career success.

4. Be Satisfied with Your Choices

Check each alternative solution against your personal attitudes, values, and culture. (Check your notes for the information that you learned about yourself in Chapters 2 and 3.) How personally desirable or undesirable do you find each alternative? Throw out the solutions that conflict most with your personal characteristics, and consider those that are most similar to your attitudes, values, and culture.

Remove from consideration any solutions that you lack the skill or information to accomplish. Avoid the temptation to pursue alternatives with high expectations for unrealistic goals.

CLUSTER LINK

If you are analytical and are interested in research and development, you might enjoy the career cluster of Scientific Research and Engineering. This cluster provides, plans, and manages scientific research and professional and technical services (including laboratory and testing services and research and development services) in the physical, social sciences, and engineering fields.

Rank your alternatives from most acceptable to least acceptable and then select one.

© JIST Works

5. Make the Decision

Review each acceptable alternative in terms of how it will affect you and the other people who are involved. Be certain that other people are satisfied with the solution. Rank the alternatives from most acceptable to least acceptable. It is important that you select one alternative at this point. No decision can be pursued to its most successful conclusion if the decision maker is emotionally divided and spending energy trying to make other alternatives workable. Choosing one alternative means eliminating others, at least temporarily and perhaps permanently.

All decisions involve a risk of failure. Successful decision makers have the courage to look at each decision honestly, reevaluate their decisions, and alter or abandon them if necessary. However, wise decision makers don't surrender to the pressure of personal conflicts, financial difficulty, fear of being considered unpopular, or fear of failure.

6. Implement the Decision

A decision isn't a decision until something happens. Do you know someone who talks a lot about the things that he or she is going to do, but rarely follows through? Take action to see that the alternative you have selected is carried to a successful conclusion. Perhaps your decision is to enter a training program in the fall, purchase a new car next spring, or raise your grades in a certain course. Whatever the situation, you will need to be firm, disciplined, and persistent in the course of action you follow.

KEY TO SUCCESS

Life usually grants us second chances. The majority of us succeed after experiencing failure at least once.

7. Evaluate the Decision

Implementing a decision could mean practicing new behaviors, following different procedures, or altering the life patterns of people who are involved. Situations change, mistakes can be made, revisions may be needed, and certain parts of the plan may have to be delayed. Evaluating all of the factors involved in a decision is important.

A successful decision maker remains flexible and open to the process of change. If the evaluation of a decision reveals that it's a failure, new information indicates a better solution, and the goal is still appropriate, a new alternative will be considered.

One of the most important points to remember when evaluating a decision is that changes will keep occurring in your social, physical, and economic environment. Your goals, beliefs, attitudes, values, and skills may be affected. Today's successful decision could be unacceptable tomorrow because of ever-changing factors.

© JIST Works

Section 1: Get Involved

Use the seven steps of the rational decision-making process to complete the following. Be prepared to discuss your responses in class.

1. Using step 1, identify a situation in your life that will require a decision on your part. What feelings do you have about this situation?
2. Using step 2, clearly define the problem of doing your homework assignments for the next two weeks.
3. Using step 3, make a list of at least three risks you will be taking if you choose to wait until after graduation from high school to make a tentative career decision.
4. Using step 4, describe a past decision that satisfied you. What factors gave you satisfaction? Describe a decision that you were not satisfied with. What factors caused you to be dissatisfied?
5. Using step 5, describe a situation in which you selected from two or more alternatives before making a decision. What factors influenced your choice?
6. Using step 6, list the decisions you have made and acted on today, this week, and this year.
7. Using step 7, consider a major decision you have made. How did it change your behavior, the procedures you followed, or the day-to-day pattern of your life?

Section 2: Matching Characteristics to Careers

What occupational roles will you have in the world of work? What career decisions should you make to ensure satisfaction and success? Not being certain of the answers to these questions bothers most high school and college students.

Your career choice may be the most important decision you will ever make because of the effect it will have on your other major life decisions. Some people hesitate to make career choices because they fear that a poor choice will keep them from succeeding in other areas of their life. But keep in mind that if you are not satisfied with one career choice, you can make another one. In fact, most people have several jobs and make numerous important career decisions before they settle on one career path.

The choice of an occupation begins when you identify **personal characteristics** (qualities that make an individual unique) and match them to related occupations and **work environments** (work settings). When this happens, career decisions tend to be both satisfying and meaningful. The more you know about occupations and your personal characteristics, the easier it will be to make satisfying career decisions.

You have a **personal orientation** (unique individual direction), which is the combination of your abilities, interests, aptitudes, and overall personality. This unique personal orientation makes you different from everyone else, and this uniqueness directs you toward the occupational roles and work environments that are most likely to provide personal satisfaction.

Reteaching

Have students complete the "Work Orientation/Trait Matching" worksheet found in Chapter 4 of the *Preparing for Career Success Instructor's CD-ROM, Third Edition.*

School-to-Work Transition

Explain to the students that clearly defined occupational roles exist in a business much as they do at school. For example, the leadership role at most schools belongs to a principal, and in business it belongs to a manager. Ask this question: What other occupational roles exist at school? in business?

Discussion Starter

Some people think high-school students should spend more time studying basic skills and less time considering future careers. Ask your students: Should career classes, career information, and career tests be eliminated from high schools? Why or why not?

© JIST Works

In general, personal characteristics can be divided into seven broad orientations. Most people can identify two or more orientations that include several of their personal characteristics and one or more orientations that are very different from their personal characteristics.

The following are descriptions of the seven orientations people have toward work. Which ones are most like you? Which are least like you?

School-to-Work Transition

Ask your students: What activities do you perform at school that require good spatial perception? What activities might a worker perform that require good spatial perception?

The Environmental Orientation

People with a strong **environmental orientation** tend to be frank, open, and natural. They are doers rather than talkers. These people like physical activity in the outdoor environment. They frequently enjoy fishing, camping, hiking, skiing, bicycle riding, backpacking, and other outdoor activities.

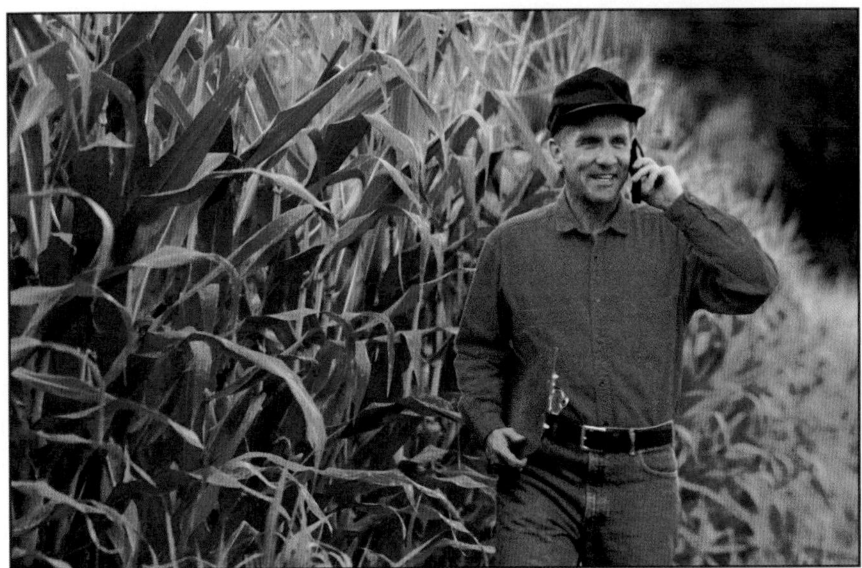

Do you enjoy the natural environment? Would you like to work outdoors?

People with this orientation are frequently skilled in working with their hands. They are practical problem solvers and able to use self-control in tense situations. They also tend to be more physical than verbal, and their physical skills are often developed to a higher level than their human relations, leadership, or verbal skills. In many ways, they are like people with a mechanical orientation.

The Mechanical Orientation

People with a strong **mechanical orientation** tend to prefer work involving machines, tools, and *logic* (reasoning, common sense) to work involving constant verbal communication. They are usually practical and physical in their approach to problem solving.

These people frequently enjoy working on bikes or cars, building things, making repairs, and being active participants in sports activities. They frequently demonstrate skills requiring practical thinking, working with hand tools, and good **spatial perception** (recognizing forms in space and the relationships of plane and solid objects).

People with a strong mechanical orientation often develop their physical and mechanical skills more fully than their human relations and verbal communication skills.

People with a strong mechanical orientation develop their physical and mechanical skills more fully than their verbal communication skills.

The Scientific Orientation

Do you enjoy working with information? Have you considered a scientific career?

People who have a strong **scientific orientation** frequently use their *intellect* (mind, mental power) more than their social or physical skills to solve problems. Ideas, words, and symbols are the tools of scientifically oriented people.

These people enjoy working with their thoughts and speculating about possible solutions to problems. They frequently enjoy playing chess, building models, reading mysteries, and using computers.

People with a strong scientific orientation usually prefer working with information to working with people. They occasionally prefer working alone to being in social situations or leadership roles. They also enjoy intellectual activities.

The Creative Orientation

People who have a strong **creative orientation** frequently react to social, school, and work situations by using their feelings, imaginations, and *intuition* (instincts, hunches). They may solve problems by nontraditional methods using unique ideas. In making decisions, they may rely on feelings and emotions more than practical information and facts.

Creative people frequently enjoy reading fiction, playing musical instruments, singing, writing, sketching, painting, theater, and photography.

People with this orientation frequently have good spatial perception, good eye-hand coordination, musical skills, writing skills, and **introspective ability** (skill to examine one's thoughts and feelings).

People with a strong creative orientation tend to dislike rigid rules of behavior, highly structured assignments, and other conventional social and economic values.

Self-Understanding

Ask students to raise their hand if they rely on feelings and emotions more than facts to make decisions. Explain to the students that people with a mechanical or scientific orientation rely more on facts.

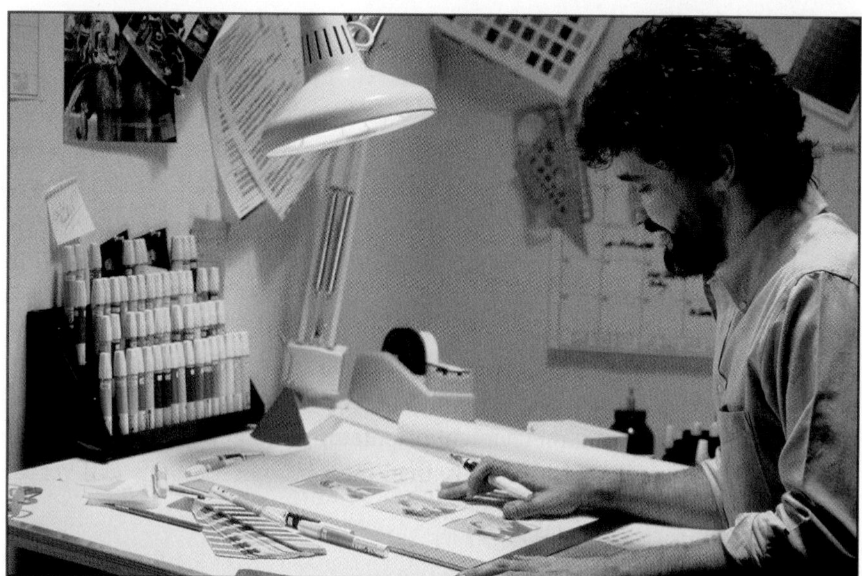
Creative aptitudes in music, writing, and sketching can be developed into career skills.

© JIST Works

The Sociable Orientation

People with a strong **sociable orientation** are usually helpful to others. They focus their caring nature on the poor, sick, aged, young, and those who need help or counseling.

When solving problems, these people rely more on their personal concern and emotion than on their intellectual ability. They discuss situations with other people and try to make decisions that others will accept.

Sociable people frequently enjoy attending parties, writing letters to friends, having conversations, and visiting with family and friends.

People with a strong sociable orientation frequently display skills in speaking, teaching, **empathizing** (sharing another's thoughts and feelings), listening, and **conciliating** (bringing others together, pacifying, winning over).

Vocabulary Builder

Ask your students: Can you think of a personal experience when you or another person used conciliating skills? What skill was used? Did it improve the situation?

Which sociable characteristics are similar to your characteristics? Would you enjoy this caregiver's job?

The Persuasive Orientation

Those who have a strong **persuasive orientation** enjoy involvement with people more than information or things. They like using their powers of persuasion in sales and leadership roles. They frequently place a high value on power and money.

When solving problems, persuasive people rely heavily on a small group of trusted associates for accurate information. They tend to make sensible decisions based on the facts provided and the goal they are trying to achieve.

Retail sales and management is a growing career field. What other occupations would satisfy a person with a strong persuasive orientation?

Comprehension Check

Ask your students: Who can name a famous person who has a strong persuasive orientation? Describe this person's persuasive characteristics and behaviors.

These people usually enjoy being class or club officers, speaking to groups, dressing well, and conversing with important people. People with this orientation have strong personal relations, persuasion, verbal communication, *organization* (structuring, arranging), and leadership skills.

Persuasive people frequently lack scientific skills and interests and tend to avoid activities that require information gathering and repeated observations. Confining activities restrict their adventurous spirit.

School-to-Work Transition

Ask your students: Who can name an occupation that fits well with the structured orientation. Are the students aware of any specific job tasks of this occupation that fit with specific structured characteristics?

The Structured Orientation

People with a strong **structured orientation** tend to select educational and career goals that are approved by society. They solve problems using traditional, proven methods.

These people are usually well-groomed, appropriately dressed, and self-disciplined. They frequently enjoy collecting coins or stamps, participating in church activities and club meetings, and keeping a diary.

Structurally oriented people are frequently skilled in coding, classifying, and computing information; retaining and following instructions; maintaining self-control; and managing a system or process.

People with this orientation usually dislike subjects or work tasks that require imagination and adjustment to changing situations. They also appreciate clearly defined tasks.

Enrichment

Have students complete the "Identifying Your Personal Orientations" and "Connecting to the Career Clusters" worksheets in Chapter 4 of the *Preparing for Career Success Student Activity Book, Third Edition.*

TAKE NOTE

If you have an environmental orientation, consider contacting your local chapter of the National FFA Organization (FFA) or visiting the Web site at www.ffa.org. FFA is a career and technical student organization that helps students develop skills in leadership and learn about agriculture and natural resources.

Coding, classifying, and computing information are very structured work tasks. Are you good at following directions and carrying out details?

© JIST Works

Section 2: Get Involved

Answer the following on a separate sheet of paper, and be prepared to discuss your responses in class.

1. Which two orientations are most like you? Describe the similarities. How is your decision-making style similar to or different from the style of people who have these two orientations?
2. Which two orientations are least like you? Describe the differences. How is your decision-making style similar to or different from the style of people who have these two orientations?

Section 3: Setting Career Goals for Today and Tomorrow

People make numerous decisions every day without thinking about the decision-making process. For most people, solving everyday problems is almost automatic. Think about your day up to this point. You selected clothes to wear, decided whether to bathe, made at least one decision concerning breakfast, and chose to come to school. Still, each decision had alternative solutions with different possible effects on your daily life. Decisions on this level include getting the car repaired, buying groceries, or going on a date.

Some decisions have consequences with a greater, long-term impact on your life. Decisions on this level include taking a position on drugs or alcohol, planning a lifestyle, selecting a marriage partner, or making a career choice.

As you grow older and gain career experience, your skill level will increase, and your career *aspirations* (hopes, goals) will change. Social and economic conditions and events, such as wars, terrorism, inflation, immigration, and natural disasters, might also affect your career opportunities. Do you know anyone who has had to change career plans due to circumstances such as these? Making career decisions in response to expected and unexpected changes will be a lifelong process.

Although you may have several jobs during your career, you can take certain steps toward a future occupational goal while you are still a student. If you change your occupational goal later, you can simply repeat the process. Like Dwayne Richards (see the following case study), you may make occupational changes based on personal career maturity and available opportunities. The following steps will help you reach each of your occupational goals:

1. Decide on a specific occupation as a tentative goal.
2. Gather as much information as possible about the tentative occupation. Be sure to include the day-to-day nature of the occupational role, working conditions, employment opportunities, potential earnings, and necessary education and training.

Enrichment

Have students complete the "Interviewing About Choices Made" worksheet located in Chapter 4 of the *Preparing for Career Success Instructor's CD-ROM, Third Edition.*

Comprehension Check

Have students close their books. Ask your students: Which of your future decisions will have the greatest long-term influence on your life? Give specific reasons for your answer.

Destiny is not a matter of chance; it is a matter of choice. It is not something to be waited for, but rather something to be achieved.

—William Jennings Bryan

Enrichment

Have students complete the "Deciding What Education and Training You Need" worksheet in Chapter 4 of the *Preparing for Career Success Student Activity Book, Third Edition.*

© JIST Works

3. Explore the occupation by interviewing a person employed in that occupation, visiting a worksite to observe the occupation, taking related course work in school, accepting related part-time employment, or doing volunteer work at a related worksite.
4. Decide whether to pursue entry into the occupation or to establish a new tentative occupational goal. Be certain to consider personal, educational, and financial barriers to your goal.
5. Take specific steps to acquire the necessary skills.
6. Seek employment in the occupation. See Unit 2 of this text, "Finding a Job and Achieving Success."

Planning Makes a Difference: Each Job Is a Learning Experience

Dwayne Richards graduated from high school last June. Within two weeks, he had a job interview at a car dealership. During the interview, Dwayne demonstrated a pleasant, positive attitude. In addition, the owner of the dealership was impressed with Dwayne's excellent high school attendance record.

Ten days later, Dwayne began his first full-time job at the car dealership. In the beginning, he performed custodial work and sometimes cleaned new cars. He occasionally took early-morning customers to their jobs while the agency worked on their cars. Six months later, Dwayne was promoted to cashier in the service department.

Dwayne has learned a lot about several jobs since he began working in the service department. One job in particular that fascinates him involves using a computer to maintain an inventory of several thousand parts and to identify the exact location of each part. Dwayne plans to attend night school to obtain the computer and business skills needed for an inventory-control job.

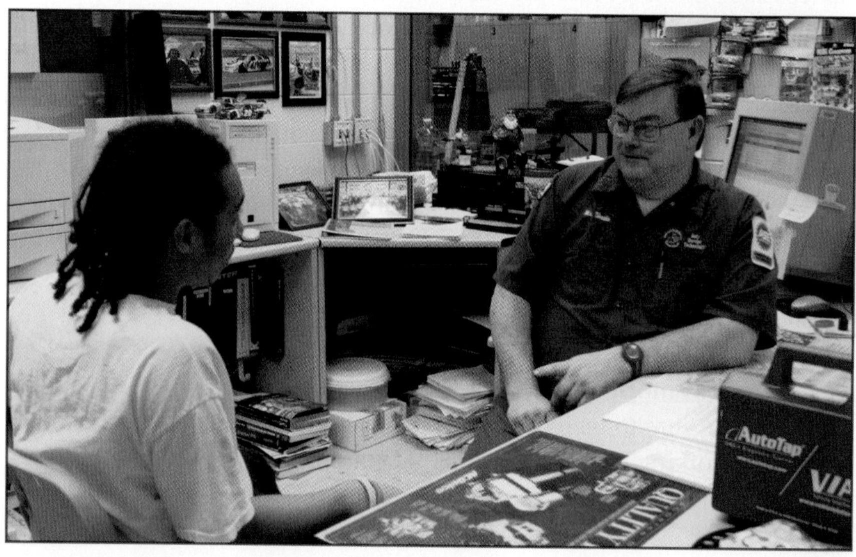

© JIST Works

Critical Thinking

If Dwayne follows his plan, do you think this will be his last major career decision? Explain your answer.

How are Dwayne's immediate behaviors related to his longer-term career goals? How are your immediate behaviors related to your longer-term career goals?

Section 3: Get Involved

Answer the following on a separate sheet of paper, and be prepared to discuss your responses in class.

1. What economic conditions in your community have helped or hindered your career opportunities during the past year? What about national economic conditions? Ask an adult friend this question, and be prepared to discuss your findings in class.
2. Name three changes during the past 10 years that have occurred in a career you have been considering.

Chapter 4 Review

Reteaching

Have students complete the "Finding the Right Words" and "Checking Your Location" worksheets in Chapter 4 of the *Preparing for Career Success Student Activity Book, Third Edition.*

Enrich Your Vocabulary

On a separate sheet of paper, number from 1 to 21 and complete the following activity. (Do not write in your textbook.) Match each statement with the most appropriate term from the "Enrich Your Vocabulary" list at the beginning of the chapter by writing that term next to the correct number.

1. A style of decision making in which decisions are made for you
2. Results
3. A personal orientation in which people frequently react to social, school, and work situations by using their feelings, imagination, and emotions
4. The process you use to make decisions
5. A style of decision making in which you believe that whatever you decide will happen anyway
6. A style of decision making in which you rarely consider the consequences of your decisions
7. A style of decision making based more on personal feelings than on facts
8. A personal orientation in which people tend to be frank, open, and natural
9. A style of decision making that requires logic, thoughtfulness, and planning and considers your feelings and values

Enrich Your Vocabulary Answers

1. authority style
2. consequences
3. creative orientation
4. problem solving
5. fatalistic style
6. impulsive style
7. intuitive style
8. environmental orientation
9. rational style

(continued)

© JIST Works

Enrich Your Vocabulary Answers *(continued)*

10. scientific orientation
11. personal characteristics
12. conciliating
13. work environments
14. empathizing
15. personal orientation
16. mechanical orientation
17. spatial perception
18. introspective ability
19. sociable orientation
20. persuasive orientation
21. structured orientation

10. A personal orientation in which people frequently use their intellect more than their social or physical skills to solve problems

11. The qualities that make an individual unique

12. Bringing together, pacifying

13. Work settings

14. Sharing in another's thoughts and emotions

15. A unique individual direction

16. A personal orientation in which people frequently develop physical and mechanical skills more than their human relations and verbal communication

17. Recognizing forms in space and the relationships of plane and solid objects

18. Skill to examine one's thoughts and feelings

19. A personal orientation in which people focus their caring nature on the poor, sick, and aged

20. A personal orientation in which people have strong personal relations, verbal communication, organizational, and leadership skills

21. A personal orientation in which people are frequently skilled in coding and classifying

Check Your Knowledge Answers

1. Knowledge of self and the facts and ability to think logically.
2. Authority, intuitive, fatalistic, impulsive, and rational.
3. (1) Recognize that you need to make a decision. (2) Identify the problem to be solved. (3) Analyze all of your alternatives. (4) Be satisfied with your choice. (5) Make the decision. (6) Implement the decision. (7) Evaluate the decision.
4. Today's successful decision could be unacceptable tomorrow because of these ever-changing factors.
5. Answers will vary. However, most everyday problems have numerous alternatives.

(continued)

Check Your Knowledge

On a separate sheet of paper, complete the following activity. (Do not write in your textbook.)

1. On what three things does your ability to anticipate the possible outcome of a choice depend?

2. What are the five styles of decision making discussed in this chapter?

3. What are the seven steps in the rational decision-making process?

4. One of the most important points to remember when evaluating a decision is the changing nature of the social, physical, and economic environments and your goals, beliefs, attitudes, values, and skills. Why are these things important?

5. People solve everyday problems almost automatically. Does this mean there are no alternatives to everyday problems? Explain your answer.

© JIST Works

6. What four areas of self make each person unique?
7. Personal characteristics are divided into seven broad orientations in this chapter. What are they?
8. Selecting a career may be the most important decision you will make. Why is a career choice so important?
9. Social and economic conditions make learning to adapt an important part of today's lifestyle. What steps will help you reach future occupational goals if you change your present goal?

Check Your Knowledge Answers *(continued)*

6. Abilities, interests, aptitudes, and overall personality.
7. Environmental, mechanical, scientific, creative, sociable, persuasive, and structured.
8. Career choice affects all other major life decisions.
9. (1) Decide on a specific occupation as a tentative goal. (2) Gather as much information as possible about the tentative occupation. (3) Explore the occupation. (4) Consider personal, educational, and financial barriers before deciding to enter the occupation. (5) Take specific steps to acquire the necessary skills. (6) Seek employment in the occupation.

Develop SCANS Competencies

Government experts say that successful workers are those who can productively use resources, interpersonal skills, information, systems, and technology. This activity will give you practice in developing systems skills.

Choose a career in which you have an interest. Use the rational decision-making process to determine the steps you would follow to become employed in this career. Draw a diagram similar to the one shown, which specifically details each step.

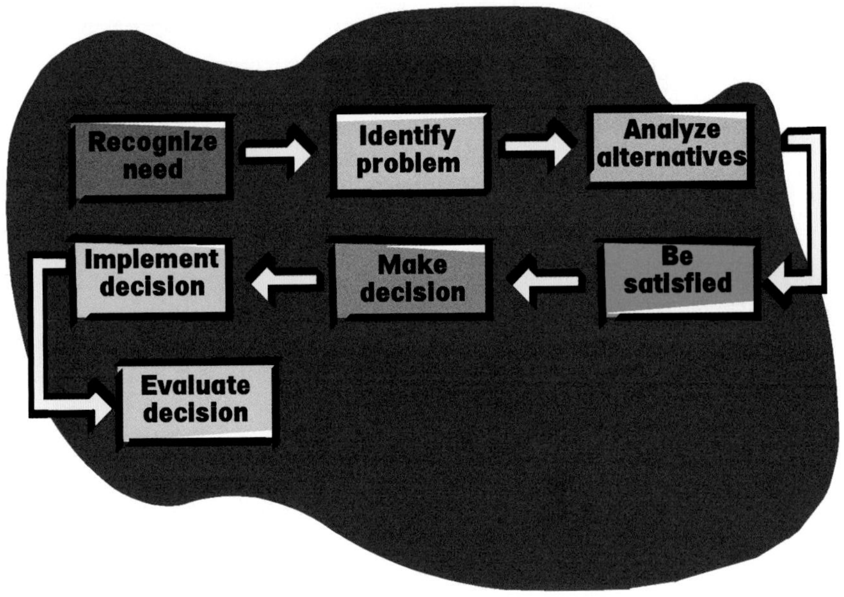

Enrichment

Have students complete the Chapter 4 section of the *Preparing for Career Success Student Portfolio, Third Edition.*

© JIST Works

Chapter 5 Resources

Lesson Plans and Preparation

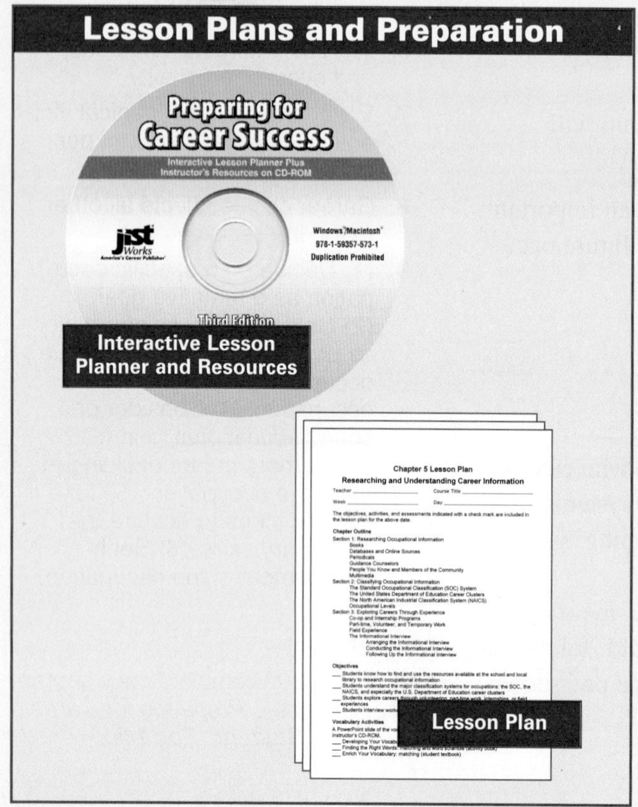

Preparing for Career Success
Interactive Lesson Planner Plus Instructor's Resources on CD-ROM
Windows/Macintosh
978-1-59357-573-1
Duplication Prohibited
Third Edition
Interactive Lesson Planner and Resources
Chapter 5 Lesson Plan
Researching and Understanding Career Information
Lesson Plan

Multimedia

Preparing for Career Success
Video Tour on DVD
DVD
978-1-59357-574-8
Duplication Prohibited
Chapter 5 Video Tour
© 2009 JIST Publishing
800-648-JIST
www.jist.com
Chapter 5 Key Terms
classification systems
computerized career information systems
employment outlook
Guide for Occupational Exploration (GOE)
InfoNet
informational interview
integrate
North American Industrial Classification System (NAICS)
Occupational Information Network (O*NET)
Occupational Outlook Handbook (OOH)
Standard Occupational Classification (SOC)
tech-prep program
transcript
U.S. Department of Education career clusters
PowerPoint Presentation

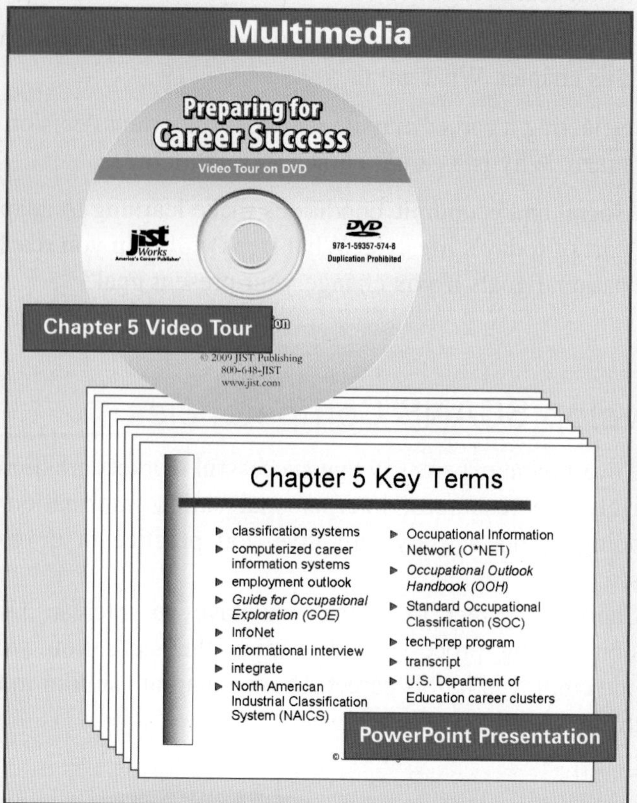

Activities

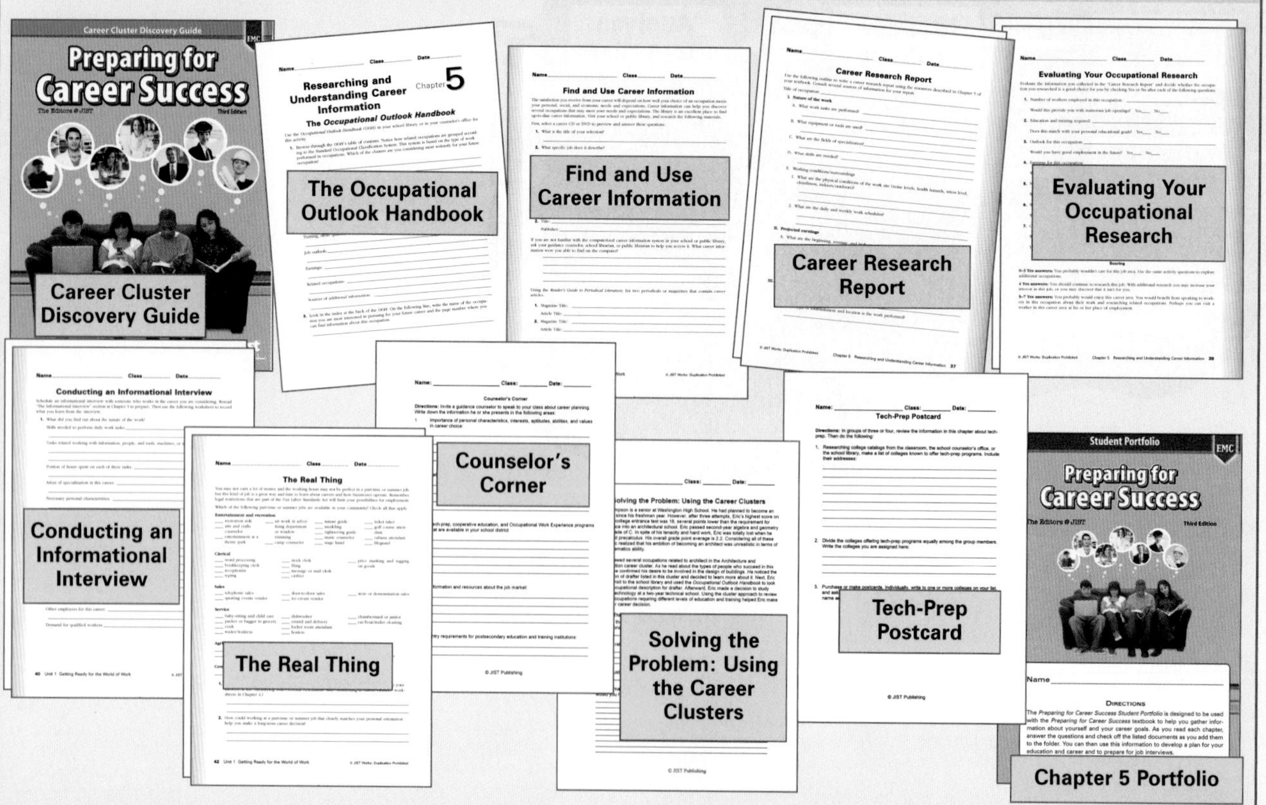

Career Cluster Discovery Guide
Preparing for Career Success
Career Cluster Discovery Guide
Researching and Understanding Career Information
The Occupational Outlook Handbook
Find and Use Career Information
Career Research Report
Evaluating Your Occupational Research
Conducting an Informational Interview
Counselor's Corner
The Real Thing
Solving the Problem: Using the Career Clusters
Tech-Prep Postcard
Student Portfolio
Preparing for Career Success
Chapter 5 Portfolio

© JIST Works

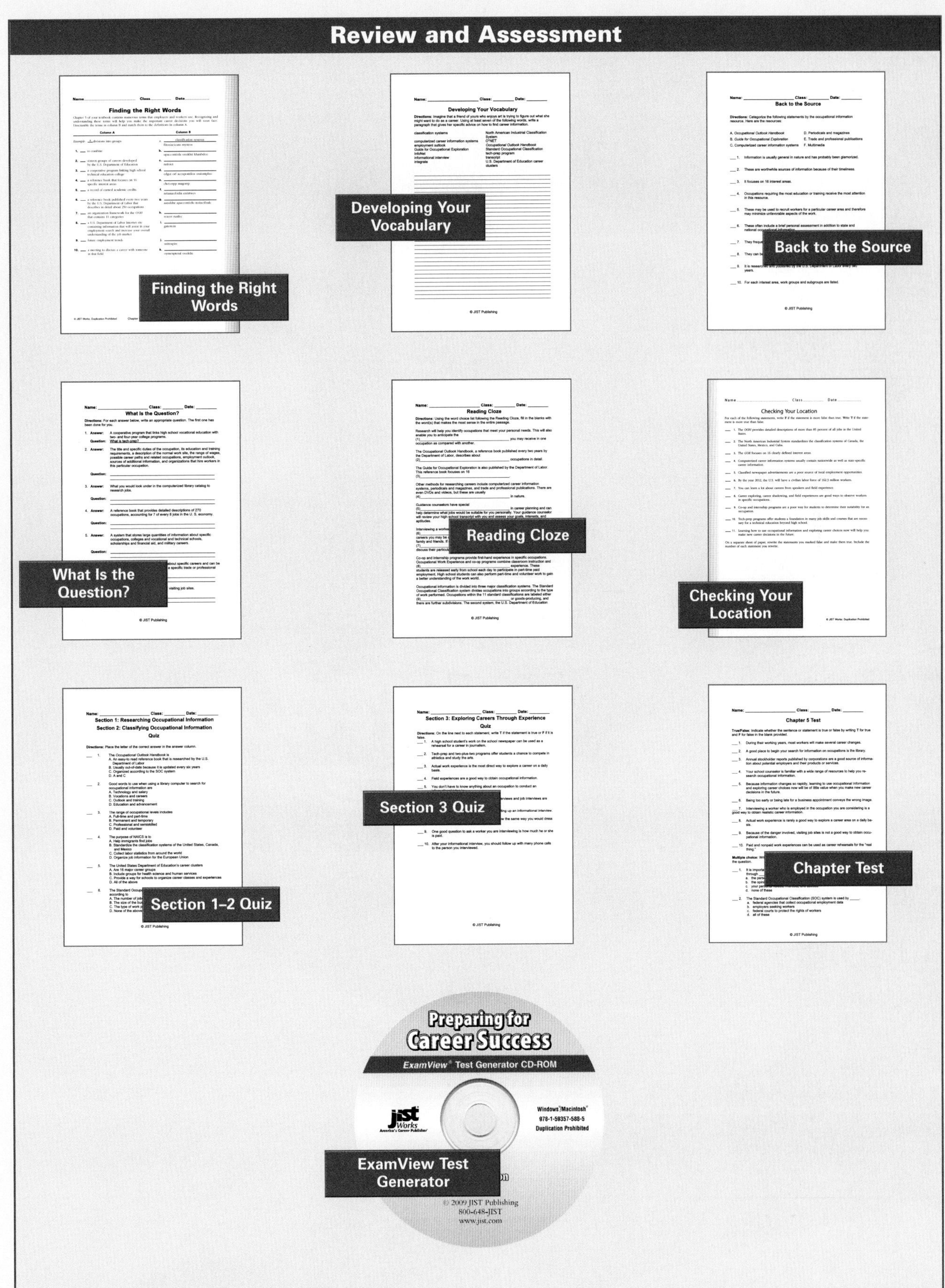
Review and Assessment
Finding the Right Words
Developing Your Vocabulary
Back to the Source
What Is the Question?
Reading Cloze
Checking Your Location
Section 1–2 Quiz
Section 3 Quiz
Chapter Test
Preparing for Career Success
ExamView® Test Generator CD-ROM
ExamView Test Generator
© 2009 JIST Publishing
800-648-JIST
www.jist.com

Est.
1869

Chapter 5 Researching and Understanding Career Information

Learning Objectives

- Identify and use several sources of occupational information
- Interview workers with questions that are related to your career concerns
- Use hands-on experience when you make career decisions
- Understand and use three standard methods of classifying occupational information
- Relate your personal characteristics to specific occupations and broad occupational groups

Students sometimes select an occupation without having enough information about it. A lack of career information can result in disappointment, dissatisfaction, and a feeling of failure. Satisfaction with your career choice depends on the extent to which it meets your personal, social, and economic needs and expectations. You therefore should investigate beyond your present knowledge of an occupation before making an occupational decision.

Enrich Your Vocabulary

In reading this chapter and doing the exercises, you will learn the following important terms:

classification systems
computerized career information systems
employment outlook
Guide for Occupational Exploration (GOE)
InfoNet
informational interview
integrate
North American Industrial Classification System (NAICS)
Occupational Information Network (O*NET)
Occupational Outlook Handbook (OOH)
Standard Occupational Classification (SOC)
tech-prep program
transcript
U.S. Department of Education career clusters

Vocabulary

You can use the "Developing Your Vocabulary" worksheet in Chapter 5 of the *Preparing for Career Success Instructor's CD-ROM, Third Edition* as a pretest for chapter concepts or as a reteaching worksheet.

Research will help you identify occupations that meet several of your personal needs. It will also help you anticipate the satisfaction that you may receive in one occupation as compared with another. Occupational information includes

- The title and specific duties of the occupation
- Its education and training requirements
- A description of the normal worksite
- The range of wages
- Possible career paths and related occupations
- The **employment outlook** (present and future employment trends)
- Sources of additional occupational information
- Organizations that hire workers in this particular occupation

Self-Understanding/ Cooperative Learning

Divide your class into learning pairs. Allow three minutes for one person in each pair to tell the other person the name of an occupation he or she is considering and the way it would meet his or her personal and economic needs. Next, allow three minutes for the second person to share the same information.

An increased knowledge of occupations and a thorough understanding of your personal characteristics will help you evaluate, match, and integrate information about yourself and various occupations into a satisfying career choice. Learning how to acquire and use occupational information and exploring career choices within the area of education and training you select will also prepare you to make future career decisions. During their working years, most workers will make several career changes.

In this chapter, you will become familiar with commonly used systems for organizing occupational information. Additionally, you will learn about sources of occupational information and methods for studying specific occupations.

Find Out More

Career Voyages is a collaboration between the U.S. Department of Labor and the U.S. Department of Education. It provides information on high-growth, high-demand occupations along with the required skills and education. Type **Career Voyages** in your search engine, or go online at www.careervoyages.gov.

Planning Makes a Difference: Everyday Job Tasks Are Important

Latoria Lambert's understanding of her personal characteristics was very complete when she decided to become a teacher. She was an outstanding math student and enjoyed helping her younger brothers and sisters with their schoolwork. She achieved a 3.6 grade point average in high school while taking the most difficult courses offered. Latoria's teachers, neighbors, and relatives considered her to be friendly and helpful.

© JIST Works

Latoria took summer classes every year and never gave a lot of thought to her future career. During her second year of college, Latoria was required to declare a major area of study. She selected the College of Education. Latoria had an image of a teacher's job, but she didn't have enough specific information about the occupation to understand the everyday tasks, problems, and rewards. For example, Latoria didn't realize that she would teach the same lessons over and over and spend most evenings preparing lessons and grading papers. Latoria also discovered that she would be required to complete additional college courses to maintain her state teaching certificate. Latoria has learned the importance of obtaining a complete understanding of an occupation before making a choice.

After two years of teaching mathematics at a local junior high school, Latoria has decided to leave teaching. She plans to spend her summer vacation looking for a different job.

Video Tour on DVD

Show students the Chapter 5 segment to introduce them to the content.

Key To Success

Make certain that the occupational information you use is accurate, up-to-date, and complete.

Career Fact

According to the U.S. Department of Labor, the United States will add 15.6 million workers to the economy between 2006 and 2016, bringing the civilian labor force up to 166.2 million workers. These new jobs will not be evenly distributed across major industrial and occupational groups. Changes in consumer demand, technology, and many other factors will contribute to the continually changing employment structure in the U.S. economy.

Critical Thinking

List Latoria's personal characteristics. How do the characteristics on this list relate to the job tasks of a teacher? How do they relate to the job tasks of three occupations other than teacher? Be specific.

What action could you take to help you avoid making the same mistakes and experiencing the same career disappointments as Latoria?

Section 1: Researching Occupational Information

Rita Levell plans to enter a **tech-prep program** (a cooperative program that links high school technical education with two- and four-year college programs) at Greenfield High next year. She is presently taking a career-planning course to help her select the tech-prep program that is right for her.

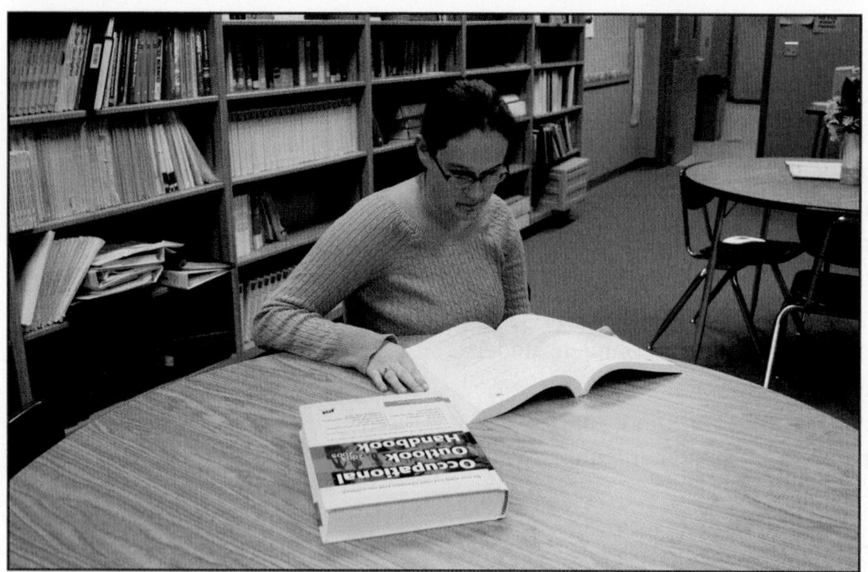

Rita uses the library because of its extensive occupational information resources. What should she be on the lookout for if she is to get an accurate picture of the occupation?

Rita has already found many occupational information resources in her guidance counselor's office and in the school and public libraries. She is careful to rely on recent information. Unfortunately, some of the information she finds is a few years old and of little value.

Occupational information concerning technology, economic conditions, demands for certain products and services, education and training requirements, and wages can change rapidly. To get an accurate picture of an occupation, Rita uses the resources described in this chapter.

Being able to locate various sources of occupational information and learning methods for studying specific occupations are useful lifelong skills. Becoming familiar with the sources and systems used to categorize and describe occupations and industries will help you make suitable matches between workplaces and occupations. A good place to begin your search for information is the library.

An increased knowledge of occupations and a thorough understanding of your personal characteristics will help you evaluate, match, and **integrate** (combine) information about yourself and various occupations into a satisfying career choice. Ask your teacher, counselor, or librarian to help you locate and use the following sources of occupational information, or begin your occupation search by looking in the library's computer listings under *occupations*, *vocations*, or *careers*.

Reteaching

Have students complete the "What Is the Question?" worksheet in Chapter 5 of the *Preparing for Career Success Instructor's CD-ROM, Third Edition.*

Education and Training

Make an appointment for your class to visit the school library. Ask the librarian to show the students how to use career information located in the library. Assign each student to locate, use, and write a brief (no more than one page) report about a specific piece of career information.

Books

The ***Occupational Outlook Handbook (OOH)*** is an easy-to-read reference book researched and published by the U.S. Department of Labor every two years. It provides detailed descriptions of about 270 occupations, accounting for 9 of every 10 jobs in the U.S. economy. In addition, summary information on 128 occupations, accounting for another 7 percent of all jobs, is presented for occupations that are not studied in detail.

KEY TO SUCCESS

Don't eliminate an occupation from consideration because of one characteristic. Various characteristics and possible work settings exist for every occupation. For example, most accountants work alone, but some spend a great deal of time with clients. Most work in an office, but some travel.

In this resource, occupations are grouped in categories according to the type of work performed and are also listed alphabetically in the index. Those requiring the most education or training provide the most information, including the nature of the work, working conditions, the education and training needed, advancement possibilities, earnings, job outlook, related occupations to consider, and sources for additional information.

Occupations described in the *OOH* are divided into the 11 categories listed under the heading "Standard Occupational Classification (SOC)

© JIST Works

System" in Section 2 of this chapter. In addition, the *OOH* further divides the 11 categories of occupations into 39 subcategories.

The ***Guide for Occupational Exploration (GOE)*** was developed originally by the U.S. Department of Labor. This occupational reference book divides occupations into 16 interest areas. For each interest area, work groups and subgroups are listed. Using these categories, you may select two or three interesting groups. You can then select occupations within each group, based on the amount of education or training you are willing to acquire.

CLUSTER LINK

Are you interested in designing, planning, managing, building, and maintaining physical structures including roads, bridges, and commercial or residential buildings? Whether you are operating heavy equipment, designing the project, or installing the heating and air conditioning system, you may find your future work in the Architecture and Construction career cluster. See the appendix for more information.

Databases and Online Sources

Computerized career information systems are available in many educational institutions. These systems allow you to explore occupations and educational preferences on a large database that is periodically updated. They may serve a single school, school district, or an entire state. In addition to nationwide information, each state system usually delivers information specific to the state.

You can use the computer's database to browse, explore, and clarify career and occupational information. A brief personal assessment or questionnaire is frequently included to match some of your personal characteristics to specific occupations or groups of occupations. Most systems contain information about

- Specific occupations
- Two- and four-year colleges and technical schools
- Scholarships and other forms of financial aid
- Military careers

Self-Understanding

If you know of a computerized career information system in your school, make arrangements for your students to observe a demonstration and use the system. Ask your school counselor, school librarian, or public librarian if you are not sure where students can access such a system.

The **Occupational Information Network (O*NET)** serves as an online library for career information. It provides a worldwide medium for exchanging information and data that is relevant to the U.S. job market. Using this database, you can acquire data about job characteristics and worker attributes for about 1,200 occupational titles. You can benefit by exploring career options and learning which skills employers seek for specific types of work. Employers benefit by increasing the efficiency of recruitment and training. To obtain more information online, simply type **O*NET** on your search engine, or go online at www.doleta.gov/programs/onet.

InfoNet is a U.S. Department of Labor Internet site containing occupational information that will assist in your employment search and increase your understanding of the job market. The Occupation Search option allows you to select information about employment outlook, earnings, and training for specific occupations. The Resources option accesses the Career Resource Library where you can explore your career interests, assess your skills, or explore other relevant career sites. Type **InfoNet** on your search engine, or go online at www.acinet.org/acinet.

CAREER FACT

Don't forget job opportunities in the U.S. Armed Forces when you conduct your occupational research. In 2007, more than 2.6 million people served in the U.S. Armed Forces. More than 1.4 million were on active duty. Another 1.2 million served in their Reserve components, and the Air and Army National Guard. In addition, another 40,000 served in the Coast Guard, which is now part of the U.S. Department of Homeland Security.

Enrichment

Have students complete the "Career Research Report" worksheet in Chapter 5 of the *Preparing for Career Success Student Activity Book, Third Edition.*

To locate more information, you can use e-mail to join a discussion group, a Usenet news group, or a listserv in a particular area of career interest. Subscribing to a discussion group will enable you to join conversations about issues and trends in your area of career interest. In addition, most companies, professional societies, academic institutions, and government agencies maintain Internet sites that highlight the organizations' latest information and activities. (You can enter keywords in your favorite Internet search engine to find these sites.) Additionally, you can scan professional journals for information about online services concerning your questions.

Enrichment

Assign a small group of students to prepare a career bulletin board. Assign students to look for used copies of the magazines listed in Table 5.1 or magazines with similar articles. Ask them to make copies of or clip the career articles (with permission, of course) and bring them to class. Allow students to make brief reports to the class about information in their articles and post them on the career bulletin board.

Periodicals

Periodicals and magazines also are worthwhile sources of career information because of their timeliness. In addition, they frequently provide information about little-known career opportunities. Table 5.1 lists examples of magazines that publish articles focusing on specific career information.

Many daily newspapers carry special business or financial pages that feature stories about employment opportunities in new or expanding businesses. Classified newspaper advertisements give you a general idea of the kinds of jobs that are available in your area. Annual stockholder reports published by corporations are another good source of information about potential employers and their products or services.

The Encyclopedia of Associations, located in the reference section of most libraries, lists names of thousands of trade and professional associations that can be contacted for information about specific careers. Descriptions of each association, Web site information, officers' names, and relevant phone numbers are included.

Additional sources of information include pamphlets and trade and professional publications, which are frequently published by organizations and kept in school libraries. You can obtain them by writing to a specific trade or professional group. Keep in mind that these publications are frequently used to recruit workers and present a good image of the organization to the public. As a result, they may minimize unfavorable aspects of the work and the organization.

CAREER FACT

Of the nearly 151 million jobs in the U.S. economy in 2006, wage and salary workers accounted for 138 million and self-employed workers accounted for 12.2 million. *Moonlighting* (people holding a second job) accounted for about 7 million jobs. Self-employed workers held about one-third of secondary jobs; wage and salary workers held most of the remainder.

Table 5.1 Magazines That Focus on Career Information

Types of Career Articles	Magazines
Career information for women	*Working Mother*
Business opportunities	*Changing Times* and *Kiplinger*
Business trends	*Business Week* and *Forbes*
Personnel problems and developments	*Fortune*

© JIST Works

Guidance Counselors

Guidance counselors receive special training in career planning and can help you understand the relationship between your personal characteristics and a particular occupation. Ask your guidance counselor to review your high school transcript with you. A **transcript** is a record of your academic credits earned, grades, attendance, standardized test scores, and extracurricular activities. In addition to relating your transcript information to occupations that you are considering, your counselor can guide you through an assessment of your goals, values, interests, and aptitudes. Armed with this information, you can begin to consider broad career areas and specific occupations within them.

Enrichment

Have students complete the "Counselor's Corner" worksheet in Chapter 5 of the *Preparing for Career Success Instructor's CD-ROM, Third Edition.*

Your school counselor is familiar with a wide range of resources to help you research occupational information. Ask him or her for information and resources concerning the job market, entry requirements for postsecondary education and training institutions, and financial aid.

In addition, contact counselors in the career planning and placement offices of colleges, private vocational or technical schools, vocational rehabilitation agencies, community service organizations, and the state *job service* (employment bureau).

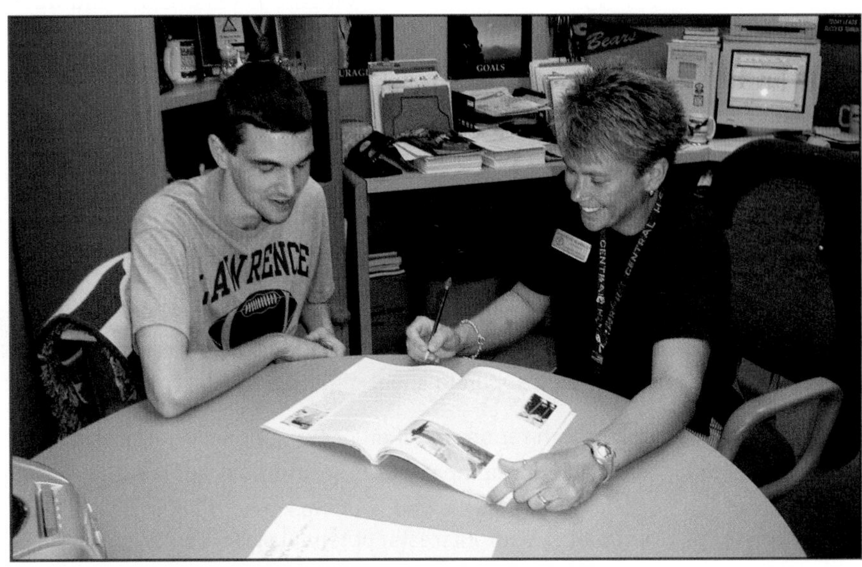

Your guidance counselor is familiar with a wide range of resources that will help you relate information about yourself to occupations. Have you taken the SAT or ACT and discussed the results with your counselor?

People You Know and Members of the Community

Family members, neighbors, and friends usually enjoy talking about their work and sharing their opinions and suggestions as well. Listening to them may help you clarify your own thinking. Don't overlook these personal contacts when you are seeking career information. They may be able to answer your questions directly or put you in touch with someone who can. This type of networking might lead to an interview with a worker who is able to answer your questions about a specific occupation. It might also give you a chance to visit an organization's worksite and acquire inside information about specific career areas.

If your school invites speakers to address students on a Career Day, take advantage of the opportunity to ask questions and discuss careers with visiting workers from different occupations. Organizations such as the American Chemical Society, the American Nurses' Association, the chamber of commerce, various trade associations, labor unions, and business

CAREER FACT

In George Washington's time, more than 8 out of 10 Americans worked in agriculture. By the time of the Civil War, 5 out of 10 workers were in agriculture. By World War II, that number declined to 1 out of 8. In the United States today, less than 1 worker in 80 earns a living in agriculture.

© JIST Works

Education and Training

Assign a committee of students to obtain a DVD or videotape that provides interesting career information. Ask them to limit the running time to less than 20 minutes. Have the committee preview the video or DVD, make arrangements to present it to the class, and be prepared to lead a brief discussion after the showing.

Reteaching

Have students complete the "Back to the Source" worksheet in Chapter 5 of the *Preparing for Career Success Instructor's CD-ROM, Third Edition.*

firms can usually put you in touch with someone who will come to your school and speak about a particular career area.

Many schools have advisory committees composed of local organizations. They usually meet after school. See your counselor or principal to find out whether your school has an advisory committee. If so, ask whether the committee would be willing to provide career speakers.

Multimedia

Videos, DVDs, CDs, and audiotapes also are available in most school and public libraries. When you view a DVD or video or listen to a CD or tape, keep in mind that what you observe or hear is usually general in nature and has probably been glamorized.

America's Career InfoNet video library offers online occupational videos. The video library describes careers of every type, from child care to physical therapy to working for the merchant marines. The videos are available online at www.acinet.org.

Section 1: Get Involved

Answer the following on a separate sheet of paper, and be prepared to discuss your responses in class.

1. Write a career research report about an occupation you are now considering most seriously.
2. Write to an association or company to request information about a career that interests you.
3. Read the biography of a person who is or was successful in an occupation that you are considering. Write a brief report comparing your interests, potential skills, career goals, and life goals to those of that person.

Enrichment

Have students complete the "Evaluating Your Occupational Research" worksheet in Chapter 5 of the *Preparing for Career Success Student Activity Book, Third Edition.*

Section 2: Classifying Occupational Information

Filtering the overwhelming amount of information available in books, the Internet, and various computerized occupational information systems through your personal values, interests, and abilities is important. Because remembering information about the 20,000 to 30,000 occupations in the world of work is impossible, **classification systems** (systematic divisions into groups) have been developed to simplify the relationship of occupations to one another. Each major occupational classification system has specific advantages for the audience it addresses.

TECHNOLOGY

To get an insider's view of a career or industry that interests you, subscribe to a related podcast or blog. Just type a job title and the word **podcast** or **blog** into a search engine, and you should receive many results from which to choose.

The Standard Occupational Classification (SOC) System

Federal agencies that collect occupational employment data use the **Standard Occupational Classification (SOC)** system. This system separates occupations into the following 11 categories, according to the type of work performed:

© JIST Works

1. Management, business, and financial operations occupations
2. Professional and related occupations
3. Service occupations
4. Sales and related occupations
5. Office and administrative support occupations
6. Farming, fishing, and forestry occupations
7. Construction trades and related workers
8. Installation, maintenance, and repair occupations
9. Production occupations
10. Transportation and material-moving occupations
11. Job opportunities in the Armed Forces

Within the 11 SOC categories, occupations are labeled either as part of service-producing organizations or goods-producing organizations. Service-producing organizations fall into these categories:

- Education and health services
- Professional and business services
- Information
- Leisure and hospitality
- Trade, transportation, and utilities
- Financial activities
- Government
- Other services except government

Goods-producing organizations fall into these categories:

- Construction
- Manufacturing
- Agriculture, forestry, and fishing
- Mining

The United States Department of Education Career Clusters

The **U.S. Department of Education career clusters** comprise the following 16 career groups, each of which has hundreds of job categories:

1. Agriculture and natural resources
2. Architecture and construction

TAKE NOTE

The American College Testing (ACT) Program has developed an online World-of-Work Map. Type **ACT World-of-Work Map** on your search engine, or go online at www.act.org/wwm. ACT has organized jobs into the following six clusters and referenced the educational preparation needed by clusters:

- Administration and sales
- Business operations
- Technical
- Science and technology
- Arts
- Social service

Cross-Reference

Assign specific SOC categories to your students (individually or in groups). Instruct them to compare their assigned SOC categories to the 16 U.S. Department of Education career clusters described in the appendix. Ask them: Which of the 16 clusters is most like your assigned SOC cluster? What are the similarities? Which cluster is most unlike your assigned SOC category? What are the differences?

Enrichment

Have students read the *Preparing for Career Success Career Cluster Discovery Guide* for more information about career clusters.

3. Arts, audiovisual technology, and communications
4. Business and administration
5. Education and training
6. Finance
7. Government and public administration
8. Health science
9. Hospitality and tourism
10. Human services
11. Information technology
12. Law and public safety
13. Manufacturing
14. Retail/wholesale sales and service
15. Scientific research and engineering
16. Transportation, distribution, and logistics

CAREER FACT

Once upon a time, the United States was the steel-producing king of the entire world! Today, the largest steel plant in the United States, U.S. Steel Corporation, is the sixth largest in the world. The high costs of energy, raw materials, and labor are considered to be major factors in the decline of job opportunities in the steel industry.

The career clusters provide a way for schools to organize instruction and student experience around 16 broad categories that encompass virtually all occupations from entry through professional levels. Related occupations that require different levels of education are described in each cluster. The appendix has additional information about each career cluster.

The North American Industrial Classification System (NAICS)

KEY TO SUCCESS

Identifying certain occupations, occupational classifications, and career clusters that you dislike will help you narrow your occupational choices.

The **North American Industrial Classification System (NAICS)** was approved in 1997 by Canada, Mexico, and the United States and began operating in 2004.

NAICS seeks to standardize the classification systems of the three partners to the North American Free Trade Agreement (NAFTA)—the United States, Canada, and Mexico. The new system makes it possible to compare economic statistics from the three NAFTA trading partners.

NAICS uses a six-digit classification system with 20 major sectors and 1,179 industries. Under the new system, industries are organized on the basis of their production activities alone.

NAICS recognizes new and emerging industries. It has an alphabetized list of more than 18,000 businesses and their corresponding NAICS codes. Being aware of the types of industries that are thriving and declining can help you to make wise career choices. For online information about NAICS, go to www.census.gov/epcd/www/naics.html.

© JIST Works

Occupational Levels

Occupations require varying levels of worker skills, education and training requirements, and job responsibilities. The following list displays a range of occupational levels, from professional to unskilled. Which occupational level do you hope to attain in your future career?

- Professional
- Managerial
- Semiprofessional
- Skilled
- Semiskilled
- Unskilled

The occupational level workers attain is directly related to the education and training level they achieve. What education and training level will you need to achieve for the occupational level you hope to attain?

- High school dropout
- GED
- High school graduate
- Some postsecondary training
- Apprenticeship training
- Technical trade school
- Two-year associate degree
- Four-year bachelor's degree
- Five-year (or more) college degree
- Graduate school degree

Cooperative Learning

Have students complete the "Tech Prep Postcard" worksheet in Chapter 5 of the *Preparing for Career Success Instructor's CD-ROM, Third Edition.*

Cross-Reference

Suggest that students scan the following: "Section 1: Influences" in Chapter 2 and "Work Values" in Section 1 of Chapter 3.

Section 2: Get Involved

Answer the following on a separate sheet of paper, and be prepared to discuss your responses in class.

1. Write down the title of a specific occupation you are considering for your future career. For the occupation you are considering, determine the Standard Occupational Classification and the career cluster.
2. Does the occupational level of the occupation you chose match your personal career goals? Does the education and training level match your personal education and training goals?
3. Would you be satisfied with the type of organization and work setting that is customary for this occupation?
4. Does this occupation seem to be a good match with your personal career goals? Why or why not?

Section 3: Exploring Careers Through Experience

Your paid and nonpaid work experiences can be used as career rehearsals for the "real thing." For example, being on the staff of your high school newspaper or yearbook provides experiences related to the occupations of reporter, editor, word processor, layout artist, and illustrator.

Some schools have career clubs for future teachers, farmers, and business leaders. Can you think of other high school career clubs and high school experiences that are related to the "real thing"?

Throughout the United States, employers and educators are working together to create educational programs that will prepare students for the world of work. Many high schools, postsecondary technical schools, and

Student Evaluation

Use the Section 1–2 quiz in the Chapter 5 file of the *Preparing for Career Success Instructor's CD-ROM, Third Edition.*

School-to-Work Transition

Use this activity before your class begins reading "Exploring Careers Through Experience." Send a writer to the chalkboard. Have the writer make two headings: "Paid Work" and "Nonpaid Work." Ask several students for examples of their personal paid or nonpaid work experiences. Instruct the writer to list the examples. Explain that many paid and nonpaid work experiences provide youthful workers with valuable work experience.

© JIST Works

two- and four-year colleges are cooperating with each other to prepare students with the skills needed to compete in a rapidly changing workplace.

Although the names of various high school programs and ways they are structured vary from one school district to another, the descriptions presented in this section will help you understand the basics of most career-exploring programs. Discuss the offerings at your high school with your teachers and guidance counselor.

TAKE NOTE

Learning where people in various occupations earn their living is as important as learning how they earn their living.

Co-op and Internship Programs

Co-op and internship programs provide firsthand work experience in specific occupations. These experiences help students determine their suitability for an occupation.

Many technical and skilled-trades high school programs also require practical work experience. Tech-prep and two-plus-two programs are increasingly being offered to high school students. This approach offers students a foundation in many of the job skills and academic courses that are necessary for a technical education beyond high school. Employers determine which workers need career skills and academic competencies, and schools determine how they will teach those skills and competencies.

Education and Training

Form a committee of students to invite their school counselor to visit your class. Have them ask the counselor to describe tech-prep, two-plus-two, cooperative education, and Occupational Work Experience programs that are available in your school district.

Occupational Work Experience (OWE) and co-op programs provide students with classroom instruction and on-the-job experience. In addition to the basic academic subjects of English, mathematics, science, and social studies, students receive classroom instruction in job-seeking and job-holding skills. Early release from school each day gives OWE and co-op students the time to acquire and participate in part-time, paid employment.

Part-time, Volunteer, and Temporary Work

Actual work experience is the most direct way to explore a career area on a daily basis. It provides an opportunity for you to observe a variety of occupations and job responsibilities, the types of people employed in a specific career area, and the work environment.

Obviously, a high school student can't acquire work experience as a nurse, physical therapist, physician, or other health-care professional. However, part-time employment or volunteer service in a hospital or nursing home will enable you to work in the same environment with these professionals, to observe them at work, and to ask questions. Can you think of other career areas where this is true?

CAREER FACT

There were almost 8.8 million private business establishments in the United States in 2006. Although large establishments are fewer in number, they hire more workers. In addition, they offer greater occupational mobility and advancement potential. On the other hand, small establishments offer greater interpersonal contact between workers, and they are found in almost every locality.

Field Experience

Visiting job sites is another good way to obtain occupational information. For example, if you are interested in learning to be a computer programmer, visit an office or plant where one is employed. Site visits may range from a few hours to a day or two.

© JIST Works

Field experiences (sometimes titled *career exploring* or *career shadowing*) can often be arranged by contacting the human resources office of an organization. People in that office have the authority to schedule an appointment to visit and observe workers in a specific occupation. A teacher, counselor, or a committee of students usually arranges field experiences for a group.

Chris is gaining experience editing films and can later decide whether he is suited for an occupation in this field. What programs offer such experience at your school?

Your school counselor may be able to provide information about programs that offer career field experience. Service organizations, such as the Boy Scouts and Girl Scouts of America, frequently sponsor career field experiences for students.

The Informational Interview

Interviewing a worker who is employed in the occupation you are considering is a good way to obtain realistic career information. However, researching the occupation before the interview is very important. The more information you have about the occupation before the interview, the more you will gain from the worker's answers to your questions.

An **informational interview** is a brief meeting between a person who wants to investigate a career and a person working in that career. The interviews usually last 20 to 30 minutes. Informational interviewing is a relatively new procedure for exploring specific career clusters and developing a network of established professionals for a future job search. Although much of the interviewing procedure is the same as job interviewing, the process and purpose are very different. Table 5.2 highlights a few of the similarities and differences.

Informational interviews are a very effective way to find out about specific jobs in the occupational cluster you are preparing to enter. This type of interview can help you obtain realistic career information and useful knowledge about specific occupations.

Key To Success

Learning to use occupational information and exploring career choices now will help you make new career decisions in the future. Your present career goals should include learning as much as possible about yourself and about occupations.

Table 5.2 Comparing an Informational Interview to a Job Interview

As an information seeker, you ...	As a job seeker, you ...
Request an interview with an established professional	Are requested to attend an interview with an established professional
Want to increase your knowledge about a specific career cluster and develop a contact for future networking	Want to fill an immediate or anticipated job opening in your specific area of career preparation
Prepare questions to ask the established professional	Prepare to answer questions you anticipate the established professional will ask

Key To Success

The contacts you develop through informational interviews provide immediate information about a specific career area and may be used later to network job leads and interviews.

Keep in mind that most successful professionals were once in your position. If you approach them in a positive manner, most of them are willing to share an insight, suggest a connection with another professional, or offer you some realistic advice. Be honest and sincere with your contacts; they likely receive many calls that are ploys to get unsolicited job interviews. Keep in mind that ethical behavior is an important part of career success, and people who play devious games usually lose.

The personal contacts you develop through this process can become a network of people who can provide you with current information about their specific careers and advice about your career direction. In addition, when you are ready to begin a job search, they may be able to inform you about possible job openings or provide you with contact information at other organizations.

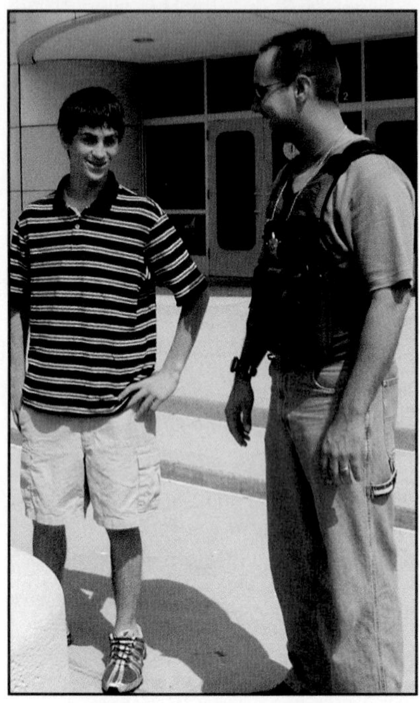

Sergeant Williams tells Josh that he chose this line of work because he enjoys working with people and that he believes maintaining law and order serves the public.

Arranging the Informational Interview

Finding appropriate organizations and making contacts for an informational interview will take some time. For local contacts, refer to the yellow pages of your area telephone book. The telephone will be the method you use most often to make initial contacts with an organization. In fact, the receptionist who answers your phone call may be the best source to obtain the name, title, and office address of the person with authority to conduct an informational interview.

People in the human resources office can usually arrange an interview or put you in touch with the manager of the department you wish to contact. Ask to speak with the manager, and when he or she answers, be prepared to

- Identify yourself, address the contact by name, and state the purpose of your call with enthusiasm.
- Request an appointment to interview the contact in person, at his or her place of business, for a specific amount of time.
- Establish the exact location, date, and time of your interview. Write it down and repeat aloud what you have written.

If you are unable to make the necessary phone contact to schedule an informational interview, another approach is to write a letter to a prospective contact. In any communication, be certain you have the correct spelling of the contact's name and title and that you include your telephone number, return mailing address, and e-mail address. If you don't receive a response to your letter within a week, make a follow-up telephone call. The contact is probably very busy and on a tight schedule.

School-to-Work Transition

Assign students to conduct an informational interview. After students conduct the informational interview, ask them to explain ways in which the interview was beneficial. After the informational interview, if they determine they do not want to work at the specific occupation, discuss the importance of identifying work they dislike as well as work they like.

Conducting the Informational Interview

If you are anxious about what questions to ask during the interview and the best way to ask them, you may want to develop a specific list and find

© JIST Works

a relative or friend to help you through a practice interview. Table 5.3 provides some examples.

If distance or traffic is a potential problem, arrive at the parking lot or building location a half hour early. Wait in your car before entering. Being too early or being late conveys the wrong image. The following tips will help you to learn and practice accepted business protocol:

- Arrive at the contact's office or designated location between 5 and 10 minutes early.
- Dress as you would if you were a professional in this occupation.
- Address each employee you meet with respect and enthusiasm.
- Remember, a firm handshake and direct eye contact convey a sense of poise and confidence.
- Carry a notebook or binder with a list of your interview questions and space to write answers.
- Wear a watch, and don't exceed the time your contact allotted for the interview.
- At the conclusion of the interview, thank your contact, and part with another handshake.

TAKE NOTE

The more information you gather about the occupation and the organization you are visiting before an informational interview, the more information you will acquire from the answers to your questions.

Table 5.3 Questions to Ask in an Informational Interview

Areas of Interest	Questions
The nature of the work	What skills are needed to perform your daily work tasks?
	What personal characteristics are needed to be successful in this career area?
The work environment	What are some characteristics of your coworkers?
	Where are some of the locations for employers in this career area?
Employment opportunities	What other organizations provide employment in this occupation?
	Is there a high demand for qualified workers in this career area?
Training, other qualifications, and advancement	What qualifications are employers seeking in entry-level and experienced employees?
	What additional training would I need to advance in this career area?
Financial rewards	What are the beginning earnings in this occupation?
	What future earnings and advancement opportunities should a successful worker anticipate?
Career mobility	What are the potential career paths in this career area?
Personal perspectives	Why did you choose this line of work?
	In what ways do you find your work satisfying?
	In what ways do you find your work unsatisfactory?
	What advice would you give a young person who is considering this line of work?
	Does this occupation affect your family life, leisure activities, or friendships? If so, how?

© JIST Works

Enrichment

Have students complete the Chapter 5 section of the *Preparing for Career Success Student Portfolio, Third Edition.*

Following Up the Informational Interview

After you complete the informational interview, evaluate what you have learned from the experience. Within 24 hours, write down how your personality, interests, and education match (or don't match) this career.

Follow up your informational interview with a thank-you note to your contact. Don't hesitate to send another note in a few weeks or months describing any progress or accomplishments that you experience and thanking him or her again for influencing your career. Maintaining communication with your contacts is a matter of sound business practice.

Section 3: Get Involved

Answer the following questions on a separate sheet of paper, and be prepared to discuss your responses and experiences in class.

1. List two or more occupations that you are considering for your future career. Then ask your school counselor whether your high school offers any type of tech-prep, co-op, or internship programs in the area of your career interest. What did you discover?
2. List the part-time or volunteer jobs held by students in your class. Then list additional occupations they observed while they were working. How did the part-time and volunteer work experiences of your classmates affect their present career plans?
3. Using your local telephone book and personal contacts, make a list of three businesses to contact for informational interviews. Follow the steps given in this chapter to set up and conduct an interview at one of these businesses. (Remember to thank the person you interviewed.) What did you learn in the informational interview?

Reteaching

Have students complete the "Finding the Right Words" and "Checking Your Location" worksheets in Chapter 5 of the *Preparing for Career Success Student Activity Book, Third Edition.*

Chapter 5 Review

Enrich Your Vocabulary

On a separate sheet of paper, number from 1 to 14. Write the most appropriate term from the "Enrich Your Vocabulary" list at the beginning of the chapter next to the number of the phrase it matches on your paper.

1. A U.S. Department of Labor publication that provides detailed descriptions of about 270 occupations
2. A method for exploring occupations on an extensive database
3. A cooperative program that links high school technical education with two- and four-year college programs
4. A publication that focuses on 16 specific career interest areas
5. A classification system, comprising 16 groups of careers, that was developed by the federal government
6. A classification system that seeks to standardize the industrial classification of the three partners to the North American Free Trade Agreement

Enrich Your Vocabulary Answers

1. *Occupational Outlook Handbook*
2. computerized career information systems
3. tech-prep program
4. *Guide for Occupational Exploration*
5. U.S. Department of Education career clusters
6. North American Industrial Classification System (NAICS)

(continued)

© JIST Works

7. Future job trends
8. An orderly division of groups
9. A record of academic credits earned
10. To combine
11. An automated database system for collecting, classifying, and disseminating data on jobs
12. A U.S. Department of Labor Internet site containing occupational information that will assist in your employment search
13. A system used by federal agencies that collect occupational employment data; this system separates occupations into groups according to the type of work performed.
14. A brief meeting between a person who wants to investigate a career and a person working in that career

Enrich Your Vocabulary Answers *(continued)*

7. employment outlook
8. classification systems
9. transcript
10. integrate
11. Occupational Information Network (O*NET)
12. InfoNet
13. Standard Occupational Classification (SOC)
14. informational interview

Check Your Knowledge

On a separate sheet of paper, answer the following questions.

1. When you use the library to research careers, what is the best way to begin?
2. What occupational classification system organizes jobs according to the type of work people perform?
3. What industrial classification system organizes jobs according to where people work?
4. Who should you contact to schedule an informational interview?
5. How can you acquire occupational experience as a student?
6. What are the six levels of employment in the world of work?
7. If you already know what career you will have, why should you research occupational information?

Check Your Knowledge Answers

1. Look in the computer listings under *Vocations* or *Careers* and then under specific occupations.
2. Standard Occupational Classification System (SOC)
3. North American Industrial System (NAICS)
4. People in the human resources office can usually arrange an interview or put you in touch with the manager of the department you wish to contact.
5. Through a tech-prep or co-op program, an internship, a part-time job, volunteer activities, or field experience (job shadowing).
6. 1) Professional 2) Managerial 3) Semiprofessional 4) Skilled 5) Semiskilled 6) Unskilled
7. Researching and evaluating additional occupations will increase your confidence in the career you have selected. Knowing how to use occupational information will be very helpful if you decide to make a career change later.

Develop SCANS Competencies

This activity will give you practice in developing the information and interpersonal skills that successful workers have. Form cooperative learning groups to research a specific occupation that your group decides on. As a group, develop an information sheet that includes the type of information each member will look for in his or her research. Assign each group member a different source of information to collect information from. Sources for research should include as many as are available from Section 1 of this chapter. After each member has completed his or her research, compare and contrast the information collected. Make a chart to display your information for the class.

Chapter 6 Resources

Lesson Plans and Preparation

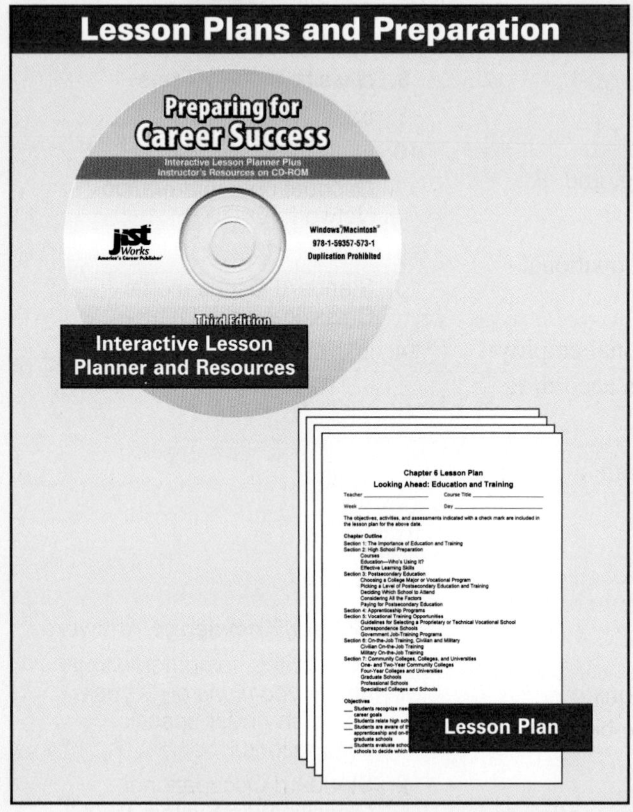

Preparing for Career Success
Interactive Lesson Planner Plus Instructor's Resources on CD-ROM
Interactive Lesson Planner and Resources
Chapter 6 Lesson Plan
Looking Ahead: Education and Training
Lesson Plan

Multimedia

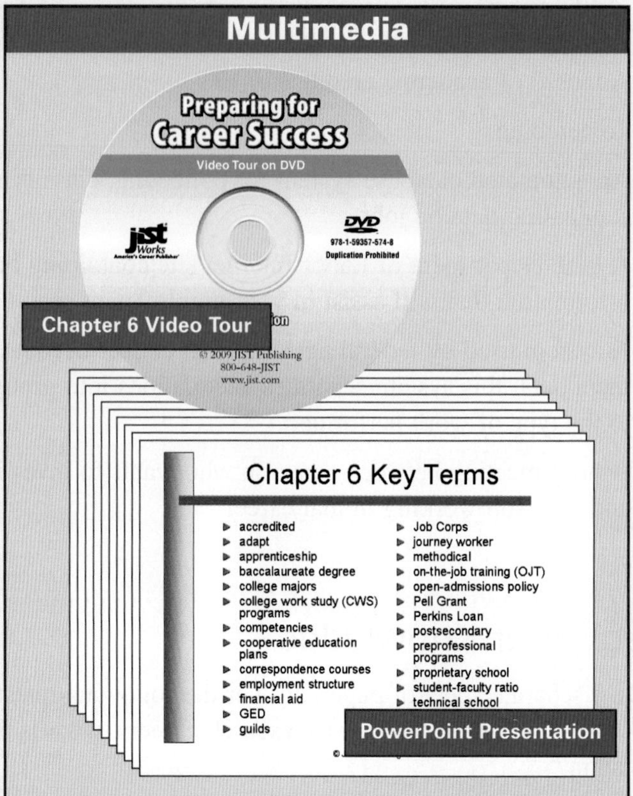

Preparing for Career Success
Video Tour on DVD
Chapter 6 Video Tour
© 2009 JIST Publishing
800-648-JIST
www.jist.com
Chapter 6 Key Terms
accredited
adapt
apprenticeship
baccalaureate degree
college majors
college work study (CWS) programs
competencies
cooperative education plans
correspondence courses
employment structure
financial aid
GED
guilds
Job Corps
journey worker
methodical
on-the-job training (OJT)
open-admissions policy
Pell Grant
Perkins Loan
postsecondary
preprofessional programs
proprietary school
student-faculty ratio
technical school
PowerPoint Presentation

Activities

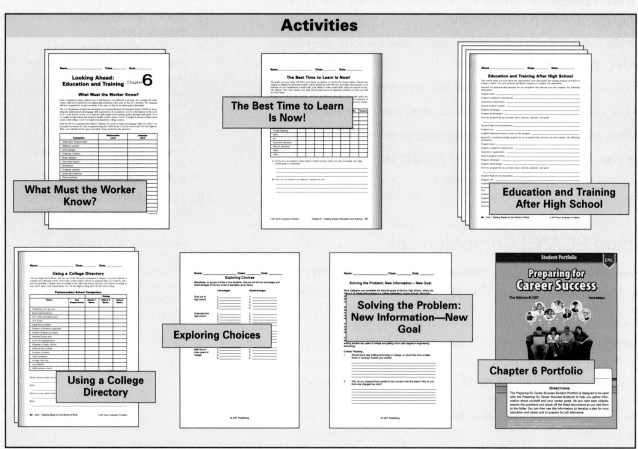

- What Must the Worker Know?
- The Best Time to Learn Is Now!
- Education and Training After High School
- Using a College Directory
- Exploring Choices
- Solving the Problem: New Information—New Goal
- Chapter 6 Portfolio

© JIST Works

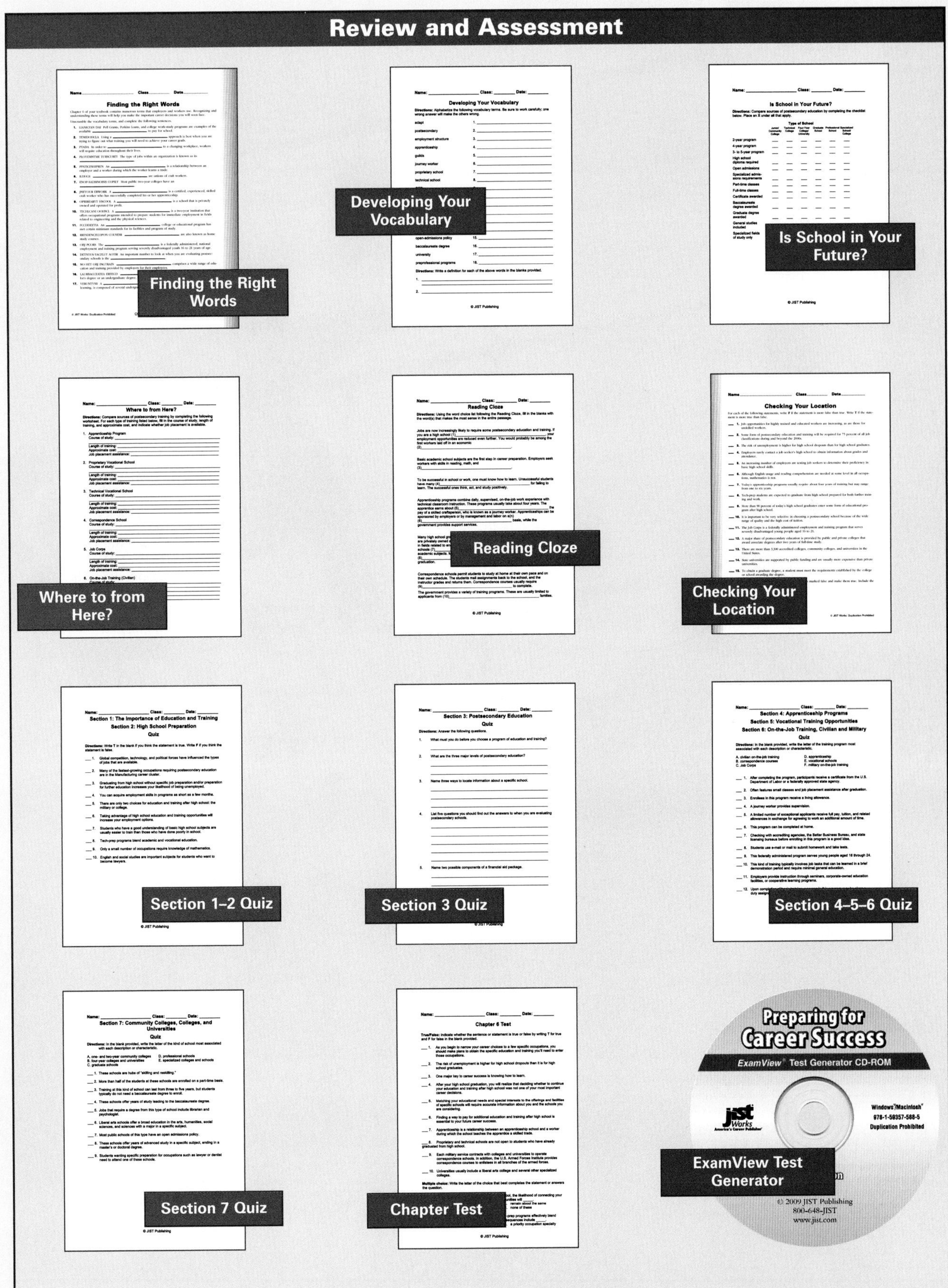
Review and Assessment
Finding the Right Words
Developing Your Vocabulary
Is School in Your Future?
Where to from Here?
Reading Cloze
Checking Your Location
Section 1–2 Quiz
Section 3 Quiz
Section 4–5–6 Quiz
Section 7 Quiz
Chapter Test
Preparing for Career Success
ExamView® Test Generator CD-ROM
Windows®/Macintosh®
978-1-59357-588-5
Duplication Prohibited
ExamView Test Generator
© 2009 JIST Publishing
800-648-JIST
www.jist.com

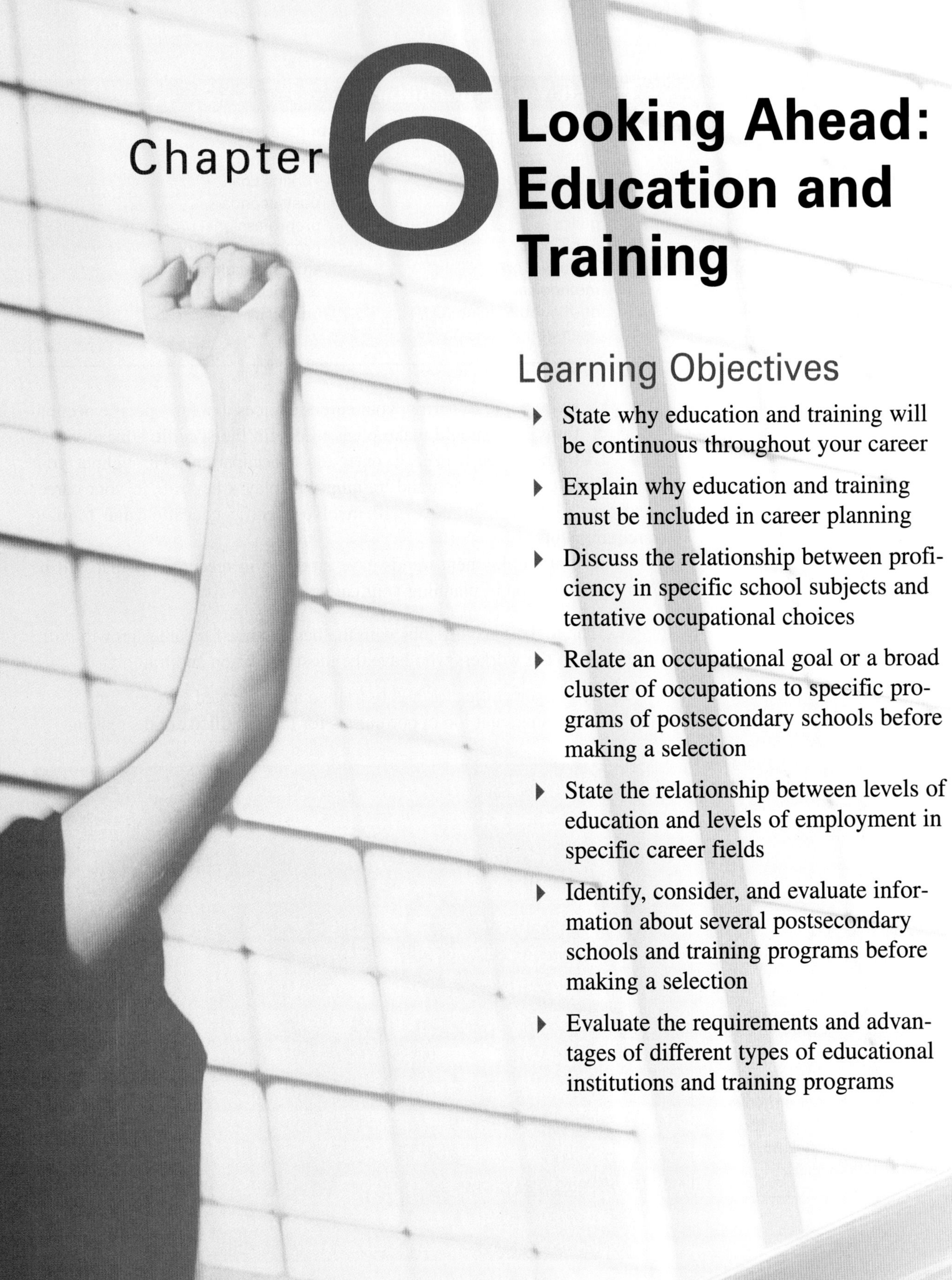

Chapter 6 Looking Ahead: Education and Training

Learning Objectives

- State why education and training will be continuous throughout your career
- Explain why education and training must be included in career planning
- Discuss the relationship between proficiency in specific school subjects and tentative occupational choices
- Relate an occupational goal or a broad cluster of occupations to specific programs of postsecondary schools before making a selection
- State the relationship between levels of education and levels of employment in specific career fields
- Identify, consider, and evaluate information about several postsecondary schools and training programs before making a selection
- Evaluate the requirements and advantages of different types of educational institutions and training programs

Enrich Your Vocabulary

In reading this chapter and doing the exercises, you will learn the following important terms:

accredited
adapt
apprenticeship
baccalaureate degree
college majors
college work study (CWS) programs
competencies
cooperative education plans
correspondence courses
employment structure
financial aid
GED
guilds
Job Corps
journey worker
methodical
on-the-job training (OJT)
open-admissions policy
Pell Grant
Perkins Loan
postsecondary
preprofessional programs
proprietary school
student-faculty ratio
technical school
university

Vocabulary

You can use the "Developing Your Vocabulary" worksheet in Chapter 6 of the *Preparing for Career Success Instructor's CD-ROM, Third Edition* as a pretest or as a reteaching worksheet.

Vocabulary Builder

Explain the meaning of lifelong education (seminars, workshops, in-service training, reading about recent technology or methods).

Discussion Starter

Ask your students: Increasing numbers of high-paying jobs require postsecondary education and training. Is this additional education necessary for hard-working, ambitious employees?

As you begin to narrow your career choices to a few specific occupations, you should make plans to obtain the specific education and training you'll need to enter those occupations. Throughout your working years, education and training will play a key role in your career success. Each career move will involve specific education and training requirements.

Several employment trends have emerged in recent years that will be important to you in planning your career:

1. The highest-paying jobs with the best chance for career growth will go to the workers who have the most education and training.
2. Job opportunities for highly trained and educated workers are increasing, and job opportunities for the unskilled are decreasing.

TAKE NOTE

The failure to develop basic skills in reading, writing, mathematics, science, and social studies will limit your career choices and your future earnings. An increasing number of employers are testing job applicants to determine their proficiency in basic high school skills.

Most job classifications will require you to have some form of postsecondary education and training. Are you taking the courses you will need to enter the occupation of your choice?

© JIST Works

3. More workers than in the past are obtaining education and training after high school graduation.
4. Although fewer low-skilled workers are needed in the U.S. workforce than in the past, the number of middle- and upper-level workers needed to develop and sell new products will continue to increase as the economy grows.
5. Workers will require lifelong education and training if they are to **adapt** (fit into) to the changing world of work.
6. Some form of **postsecondary** (after high school) education or training will be required for approximately 75 percent of all job classifications.

Nearly two thirds of today's high school graduates enter some form of educational program after high school. What will you do?

Career Fact

Research shows that roughly half of the differences in earnings among American workers can be attributed to education and training in school and on the job.

Comprehension Check

Explain that all of the occupations listed in Figure 6.1 require some postsecondary education. Ask the students to look at the first two occupations listed. Explain that the number of workers employed as medical assistants is expected to increase 52 percent between 2006 and 2016. The number of network systems and data communications analysts will increase by 53 percent.

Video Tour on DVD

Show students the Chapter 6 segment to introduce them to the content.

Section 1: The Importance of Education and Training

Global competition for worldwide markets, new technologies, and political forces have influenced the **employment structure** (types of jobs available). Jobs are now more likely than ever to require postsecondary education and training (see Figure 6.1).

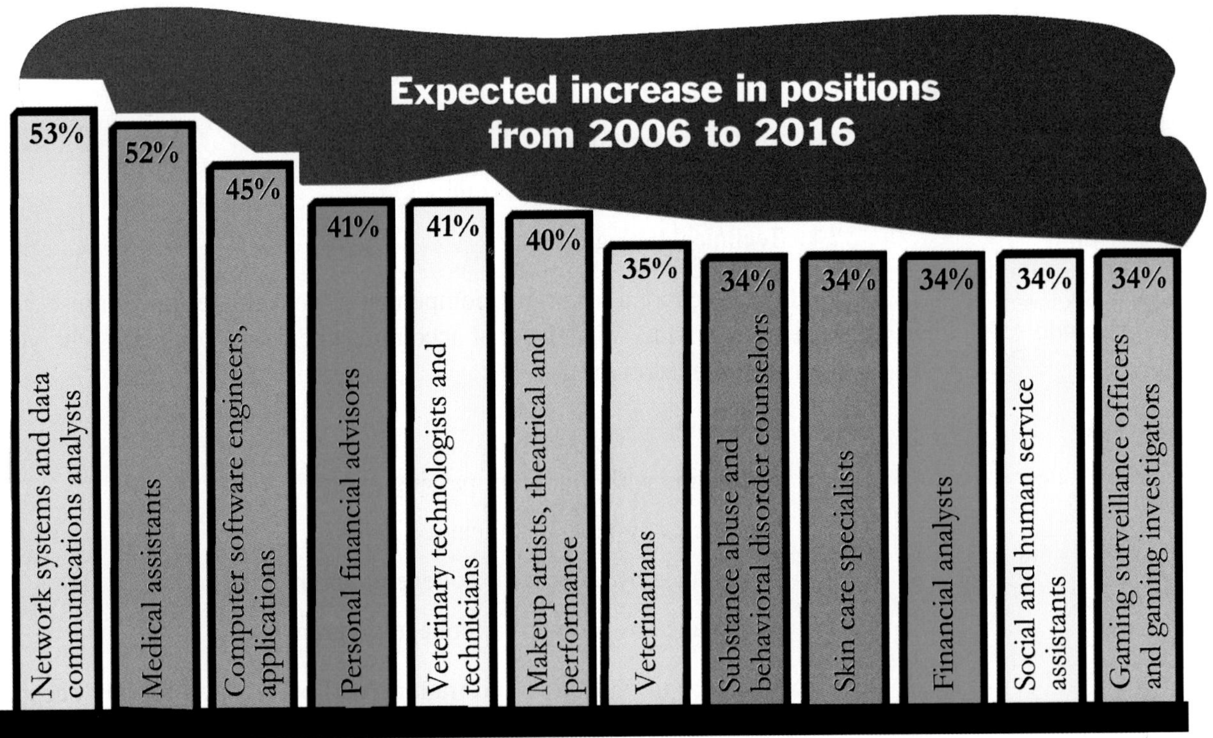

Figure 6.1 Fastest-growing occupations requiring postsecondary education or training.

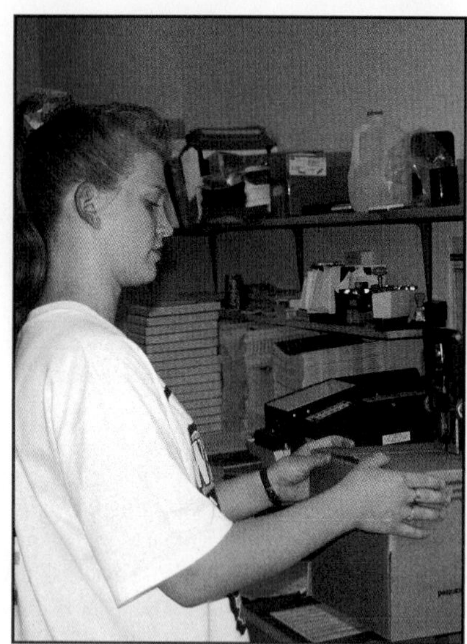
More than 385,000 packaging and filling machine operators and tenders work in the U.S. labor force. This low-skilled occupation is growing faster than the average and usually requires short-term on-the-job training.

Graduating from high school without specific job preparation (career and technical education) and/or preparation for further education (college preparatory education) increases your likelihood of being unemployed. Employers offering jobs beyond the minimum-wage level have little interest in the high school graduate who lacks specific job skills.

Dropping out of high school reduces employment opportunities even more. High school dropouts are more likely to obtain jobs that are low paying, offer little chance for advancement, and are projected to be declining or growing very slowly. The risk of unemployment is also higher for high school dropouts (see Figure 6.2). When an economic recession takes place, high school dropouts are usually the first workers to be laid off.

It is important that you begin now to identify and develop education and training skills that are marketable in the world of work. You can acquire employment skills through formal and informal instruction in programs as short as a few months or as long as several years. The type and length of education or training you select will determine the range of your occupational qualifications. Here is a list of the alternatives you have for education and training:

1. Community college
2. On-the-job training
3. Military training
4. Vocational education
5. Four-year college
6. Professional college
7. Apprenticeship
8. Graduate college
9. Tech-prep program
10. Vocational training opportunities
11. Technical college

Education and Training

Ask students to think of an occupation they are considering for their future. Ask individual students: Which of the 11 education and training alternatives presented will prepare you for that occupation?

Cooperative Learning

Have students complete the "Exploring Choices" worksheet in Chapter 6 of the *Preparing for Career Success Instructor's CD-ROM, Third Edition.*

Is high school a rewarding component of your life, or do you just want to get it over with? What level of accomplishment will you reach with your high school education?

- Dropout?
- A diploma with minimum passing grades?
- Specific entry-level technical job skills?
- Acceptance by a two-year college program?
- Acceptance by a four-year college program?

Some type of education and training will be required for any occupation you select. Will your present thoughts and attitudes about education and training affect your future career success in a positive or negative way?

© JIST Works

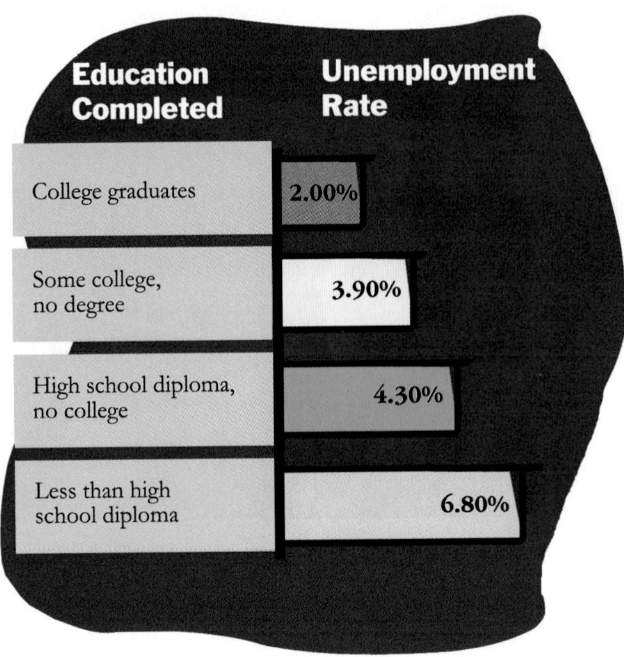

Figure 6.2 Schooling versus the rate of unemployment (U.S. Census Bureau, 2006).

Enrichment

Have students complete the "What Must the Worker Know?" worksheet in Chapter 6 of the *Preparing for Career Success Student Activity Book, Third Edition.*

School to Work: A Dead End on the "Easy Road"

Bennie Lee liked high school most of the time, but he didn't like to study. Bennie took the "easy road" when it came to mathematics, science, and English courses, but he always passed with a grade of C or D. Bennie felt that young people should enjoy life and that there would be plenty of time to be serious and work hard when he was older.

Bennie's counselor encouraged him to enter the career and technical education program in the 11th grade. Bennie looked at several technical programs but decided he would rather stay in the general course of study. He had a good part-time job and could see no problem in obtaining a better job after he received his high school diploma.

As a senior, Bennie discovered he was eligible to obtain financial assistance for college. However, the schools he applied to would not accept him because of his low grades, his lack of college preparatory courses, and his low score on the ACT test.

After Bennie graduated, he bought a four-year-old car. The payments took most of his paycheck, and he continued living at his parents' home. He checked out a private career school but found that even with financial aid he wouldn't be able to make the payments on his car, pay off the other debts he had acquired, and have enough left to live on—even if he stayed at home.

Bennie lost his job last month. Now he is out of money, the finance company *repossessed* (took back) his car, and he is waiting for his first unemployment check.

TECHNOLOGY

Some students have difficulty participating in a traditional internship because of the cost involved (if, for example, the student has to travel to and live in another city) or the required time commitment (many internships are full-time). If you want to gain some experience in your chosen career or have to fulfill an internship requirement for school, another option is the virtual internship. In a virtual internship, you use your own computer to complete projects for an employer during a certain period of time. The major advantage of virtual internships is that they're flexible. For the most part, you can work when and where you want. The major disadvantage is that you miss out on learning about the corporate culture and interacting with other employees in person.

© JIST Works

CAREER FACT

According to the U.S. Census Bureau, a high school graduate will earn 20 percent more money during his or her lifetime than a high school dropout. Today, that number amounts to more than $200,000. The U.S. Bureau of Labor Statistics adds this fact: Within months of their graduation, students who finish high school are about twice as likely to be working or enrolled in postsecondary education as those who drop out.

Critical Thinking

Why is Bennie having so many problems while many of his friends are experiencing career success?

What advice would you give Bennie? What future do you see for him?

Section 1: Get Involved

Answer the following on a separate sheet of paper, and be prepared to discuss your responses in class.

1. Name two occupations that you are presently considering. What education and training skills will you need for each occupation? What high school subjects will be important in preparing for each occupation?
2. Make a list of all of the education and training choices available in your high school. For what further education and training will your high school education prepare you?
3. Many American companies insist that they can't fill job openings because they can't find qualified, skilled, motivated workers. What does this statement mean to you?
4. Study Figure 6.1. Which one occupation would you select if these were your only career choices? What satisfaction would you receive from this occupation? What wouldn't you like about this occupation? How would this choice fit your personal orientation? What education or training would you need to enter this occupation?

Enrichment

Have students complete the "The Best Time to Learn Is Now!" worksheet in Chapter 6 of the *Preparing for Career Success Student Activity Book, Third Edition.*

Section 2: High School Preparation

Taking advantage of your high school education and training opportunities will help you learn important employment skills and will increase your employment options.

If you strive for high achievement in high school, the likelihood of connecting your education and training to employment opportunities will increase. Today's employers place a premium on skills in reading, math, communication, and problem solving. Employers understand that success in school is a strong indicator of success on the job. Students who have

© JIST Works

acquired a good understanding of basic high school subjects almost always are easier to train than those who have done poorly.

Courses

Why did you choose the course of study you are now pursuing in high school? Which courses are preparing you for postsecondary education and training? Which provide you with specific vocational skills? Which prepare you for your intended career? What is the connection between your values and interests, the occupations you are considering, and the subjects you are studying? If you are not satisfied with your answers to these questions, you should discuss possible changes with your parents, teachers, and high school counselor.

Many students are enrolled in occupational training programs called *tech-prep*. High schools and community colleges work together to develop the course of study for tech-prep programs. Courses are offered in engineering technology, applied science, mechanical arts and trades, agriculture, health, business, marketing, and many other technical career areas.

During the last two years of high school, tech-prep programs effectively blend academic and vocational education. Course sequences include mathematics, science, communications, and a "priority occupation" specialty. Education and training for these programs begins in high school and ends with an apprenticeship certificate or graduation from a community college program.

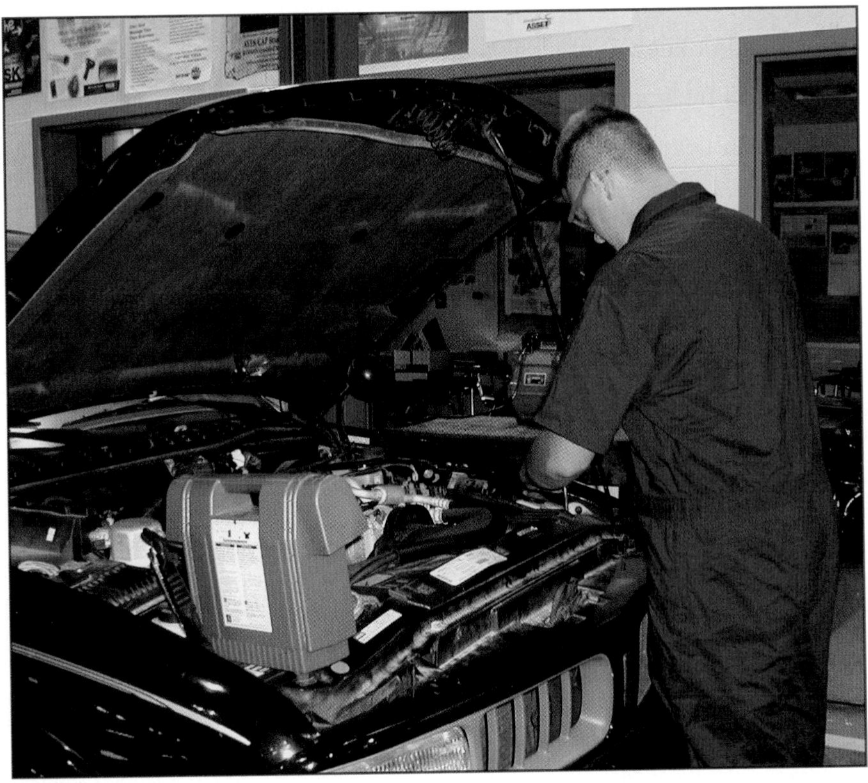

Tech-prep programs help students turn vocational interests into occupational skills. Does your school offer tech-prep courses of study?

Comprehension Check

Ask a volunteer to go to the chalkboard to list occupations. Ask the class to provide the occupations of workers they have interacted with at a shopping mall or any place of business during the past month. Next, ask a few to provide the name of a parent's occupation. Ask the students: How would a (choose an occupation from the list) job performance be affected by a deficiency in math skills? Reading skills? Ability to solve problems? Communication skills? Use as many examples as you feel are productive.

Community Resources

Have the class elect a committee of students to contact the personnel department of a local business, industry, or agency. Ask the committee to arrange for a speaker to demonstrate and discuss basic skill tests used by employers and education and training requirements for certain occupations.

Case Study

Have students read the case study, "New Information—New Goal," in Chapter 6 of the *Preparing for Career Success Instructor's CD-ROM, Third Edition* and discuss the "Critical Thinking" questions.

Career Fact

Studies by the U.S. Department of Education concluded that of students who acquire a GED credential between 50 to 65 percent go on to acquire some form of postsecondary education or training. In postsecondary schools, they earn grades similar to those of high school graduates, but are less likely than high school graduates to complete a program of study. They earn wages that are 5 to 11 percent higher than those of high school dropouts but lower than those of high school graduates.

© JIST Works

Cooperative Learning

Divide your class into small groups. Assign a school subject from Table 6.1 to each group. Instruct them to relate each of the occupations related to their assigned subject to one of the occupational clusters in the appendix. Have them report the reasons for their decisions to the class.

School-to-Work Transition

Explain to the class that students who rely on excuses at school become workers who use the same excuses on the job. Ask for volunteers to role-play the first three excuses on the job. Ask one student to role-play the worker and one to role-play the boss. Have each presentation begin with the worker saying the respective statement to the boss: 1. My supervisor is boring; 2. I can't concentrate on my job; 3. I don't understand the work order I'm reading.

Cooperative Learning

Divide the class into groups of three or four. Assign a specific excuse to each group. Specify a number of minutes to identify a situation when a member of the group used this excuse and to write several possible responses to this excuse. Allow time for each group to make a brief report to the class. Note: You may not feel comfortable assigning #12. Be certain to involve additional professional help if you discover a student with a serious depression.

Education—Who's Using It?

Table 6.1 demonstrates the strong relationship between high school subjects and certain occupations. Keep in mind that mathematics, English usage, and reading comprehension are needed at some level in all occupations. Which of the subjects listed interest you the most? Which of the occupations interest you the most? Which subjects are needed for the occupations you are considering?

Effective Learning Skills

One major key to career success is knowing how to learn. Equipped with this skill, you can achieve competency in school subjects and workplace skills. Successful students think, act, and study positively. Unsuccessful students have a million reasons why they can't learn. Twelve of the most common excuses for poor performance are listed here. Have you used any of these excuses?

1. "My teachers are boring."
2. "I can't concentrate."
3. "I don't understand what I'm reading."
4. "I'm too busy to study."
5. "I'll never use this stuff anyway."
6. "I can't study without a friend."
7. "I didn't know it was due today."
8. "Tests freak me out."
9. "I don't even know where to begin to study."

Employers evaluate performance. Do you give 100 percent of your effort to your studies? Do you stick with your schoolwork until you succeed? Would an employer consider you a good worker?

© JIST Works

10. "My memory is terrible."

11. "I don't need to study because I learn it all in class."

12. "Sometimes I'm so depressed about school that I feel badly about everything else in my life, too."

Table 6.1 Related High School Subjects and Occupations

Foreign Language	Biology	Physics	Chemistry
Customs inspector	Dental Assistant	Electrician	Pharmacist
Missionary	Landscape worker	Civil engineer	Ceramic engineer
Salesperson	Veterinarian	Astronomer	Assayer
Flight attendant	Rancher	Architect	Chemical salesperson
Travel agent	Game warden	Meteorologist	Laboratory technician
Social worker	Park ranger	Physical chemist	Food scientist
Immigration agent	Nursery worker	Electrical engineer	Metallurgist
Foreign correspondent	Dietitian	Electronics technician	Chemical engineer
Teacher	Biologist	Physicist	Oceanographer

Physical Education	Business Education	Health Education	English
Lifeguard	Accounting clerk	Chiropractor	Librarian
Dancer	Buyer	Dental assistant	Lawyer
Umpire	Stenographer	Practical nurse	Author
Coach	Legal assistant	Dentist	Proofreader
Professional athlete	Word-processing operator	Surgical technician	Stenographer
Recreation worker	File clerk	EKG technician	Administrative assistant
Swimming instructor	Office manager	Registered nurse	Advertising manager
Firefighter	Data entry keyer	Respiratory therapist	Reporter
Sports trainer	Administrative assistant	Physician	Editor

Social Studies	Mathematics	Art	Industrial Arts
Urban planner	Machinist	Fashion designer	Electrician
Psychologist	Actuary	Architect	Locksmith
Social worker	Bank cashier	Cartographer	Plumber
Political scientist	Accounting clerk	Graphic artist	Sheet-metal worker
Court clerk	Engineer	Photographer	Drafter
Counselor	Scientist	Industrial designer	Automotive technician
Politician	Electrician	Fine artist	Bricklayer
Lawyer	Carpenter	Landscape architect	Carpenter
Fire inspector	Electronic technician	Engineer	Machinist

Education and Training

Ask several students to go to the chalkboard. Using the information in Table 6.1, ask them to write their favorite and least favorite subjects. Next, ask them to write their favorite and least favorite occupations. Select one of the class members at the chalkboard, and ask the seated members of the class to point out any relationships they observe concerning his or her favorite and least favorite selections. Ask seated class members to provide career advice.

© JIST Works

Section 2: Get Involved

Answer the following on a separate sheet of paper, and be prepared to discuss your responses in class.

1. Keep a daily log describing your study skills and habits over the course of two weeks. Include a description of your learning strengths, weaknesses, fears, and goals. Describe where, how, and when (the actual hours) you study. Describe the learning strategies that work best for you, and evaluate your learning progress for the two-week period.
2. Make a list of reasons why schools should or should not have minimum proficiency tests in basic skill subjects such as English, mathematics, science, and social studies. Be prepared to defend your reasons in class.
3. If you were an employer, what opinion would you form about yourself after reviewing your high school transcript? Can you improve an employer's opinion of you? If so, how?

Student Evaluation

To evaluate student mastery of concepts, you might want to use the Section 1-2 quiz found in the Chapter 6 file in the *Preparing for Career Success Instructor's CD-ROM, Third Edition.*

School-to-Work Transition

Ask the students to raise their hand if they plan to continue their education and training after graduation. Record the number of raised hands on the chalkboard. Ask the students to calculate the percentage of their class planning on postsecondary education. How does this compare to the national average of approximately 66 percent?

Enrichment

Have students complete the "Where to from Here" worksheet in Chapter 6 of the *Preparing for Career Success Instructor's CD-ROM, Third Edition.*

Enrichment

Have students complete the "Education and Training After High School" worksheet in Chapter 6 of the *Preparing for Career Success Student Activity Book, Third Edition.*

Section 3: Postsecondary Education

All education and training that occurs after high school is referred to as *postsecondary education.* Almost two of every three students graduating from high school will enter some form of postsecondary education in the fall. Some will enter vocational or technical schools. Others will enter two- or four-year college degree programs.

Deciding whether to continue your education and training beyond high school will be one of the most important career decisions you make in your life. Acquiring postsecondary education and training will provide you with increased earnings and a more desirable lifestyle during the approximately 45 years you will work.

Are you planning to enroll in a postsecondary school? If so, the information in this section will help you select a program of study and an appropriate school. It will also explain the necessary steps between high school and higher education.

Almost one third of high school graduates choose to bypass postsecondary education and go directly to work. Within a few months or even years later, many of them will seek some form of postsecondary education and training. Will you be in this group? If so, learning as much as you can about postsecondary education now will benefit you later in your career.

Choosing a College Major or Vocational Program

Before you choose a program of education and training, you need to choose an occupation or occupational area that you want to enter. After you establish an occupational goal, you should determine the specific *program of study* (type and level of education and training) that your occupational goal requires. This is your *educational goal.* Selecting a particular occupation or a broad cluster of related occupations will narrow your choices of

© JIST Works

college majors (special areas of study) and/or technical career programs to a manageable number.

A good place to discover what education and training are required for the specific occupation you are considering is the *Occupational Outlook Handbook (OOH)*. Occupational descriptions and their page locations are listed alphabetically in the index. Each description includes a section titled "Training, Other Qualifications, and Advancement." The level of education required for each occupation is described. For example, here is an excerpt from the description for a registered nurse:

"There are three major educational paths to registered nursing: a bachelor's of science degree in nursing (BSN), an associate degree in nursing (ADN), and a diploma. BSN programs, offered by colleges and universities, take about 4 years to complete."

The next step is to identify schools that offer that program of study.

TAKE NOTE

To make international study more affordable, the Institute of International Education provides students with financial assistance through the many scholarship programs they administer, such as the National Security Education Program (NSEP) David L. Boren Undergraduate Scholarship, a need-based scholarship that provides experience studying in countries that are crucial to our national security. You can learn more about this and other scholarship programs by visiting the Institute's Web site at www.iie.org.

Picking a Level of Postsecondary Education and Training

The level of education and training required for all occupations is increasing at a rapid rate. At this point in your educational planning, you may wish to consider the following options:

- **Certificate, Diploma, and Apprenticeship programs** are offered in technical schools and community colleges. They lead directly into a specific occupation. The length of study ranges from a few months to about two years.
- **Associate Degree programs** normally require two years of study. They are usually offered at community or junior colleges or two-year programs within a university.
- **College Degree programs** require at least four years of study. Many professional programs require five or six years.

Hundreds of college majors and technical programs are offered by several thousand schools. Which one fits your plan? Review the college majors and programs listed in Table 6.2. Imagine that these are your only possible choices. On a separate sheet of paper, select the four that interest you most and the four that interest you least.

Using the four selections that interested you most, observe the related levels of education required, and answer the following questions:

1. Which educational level appears most often? You are expressing a preference for this level of education and training.
2. Which educational level appears least often? You are expressing less interest in this level of education and training.

Discussion Starter

Ask your students: Which of the high school courses that you have completed satisfy technical school or college requirements? Which additional courses should you complete?

School-to-Work Transition

Ask your students: How does your postsecondary education plan relate to your career goal? What level of postsecondary education satisfies your career goal: one-year technical school, two-year college, or four-year college?

3. As you consider your educational goals at the high school level and the career information you have studied, which postsecondary educational level are you considering? What are your reasons?

4. Which of the high school courses you have completed or are presently taking satisfy the entrance requirements for a two-year or four-year college program?

Table 6.2 Choosing a Postsecondary Education or Training Program

College Major or Program Title	Personal Orientation	Education Level		
Wildlife Management	Environmental			C
Parks and Recreation	Environmental	A	B	C
Agricultural Production	Environmental		B	C
Forestry and Related Sciences	Environmental		B	C
Aircraft Mechanics, Power Plant	Mechanical			C
Electrical/Electronics Equipment Repair	Mechanical		B	C
Plumbing, Pipe Fitting, Steam Fitting	Mechanical	A		
Robotics Technology	Mechanical		B	C
Appliance Repair	Investigative	A		
Chemical Technology	Investigative		B	C
Engineering Technology	Investigative		B	C
International Relations	Investigative			C
Commercial Art	Creative	A	B	C
Advertising	Creative		B	C
Fashion Design	Creative	A	B	C
Music Performance	Creative	A	B	C
Physical Therapy Aide	Sociable	A		
Teacher Assisting	Sociable	A	B	
Family and Community Services	Sociable		B	C
Psychology	Sociable			C
Greenhouse Operation and Management	Persuasive	A		
Insurance/Real Estate Marketing	Persuasive	A	B	
Business and Management	Persuasive		B	C
Institutional Management	Persuasive			C
Accounting, Bookkeeping	Structured		B	C
Administrative Support, Business	Structured	A	B	C
Library Assisting Technology	Structured		B	C
Business Data Processing	Structured		B	C

Education Level: A = Certificate, diploma, and/or apprenticeship; B = Associate degree; C = College degree

Reteaching

Ask your students these questions regarding Table 6.2: Which personal orientation appears most often in the four selections that interested you most? Which appears least often? Using the four selections that interested you least, which personal orientation appears most often? Least often? Based on your answers, which orientation seems to be most like you, and which seems least like you? Have students review descriptions of the personal orientations described in Chapter 4.

© JIST Works

Deciding Which School to Attend

After you determine your educational goal, you can begin to identify and evaluate schools that offer the program of study that fits your goal. Matching your educational needs and special interests to the offerings and facilities of specific schools will require accurate information about you and the schools you are considering.

It is prudent to use a **methodical** (systematic, orderly) approach that includes your occupational and educational goals; financial situation; and personal needs, interests, and values. Taking the time to locate resources and information relative to your choice of school will help you evaluate the individual schools you are considering and compare them to one another. Thoroughness in your evaluation of school choices will make it easier for you to select the best school for you. You may find your high school guidance counselor to be a valuable source of help in this process. Consider the following suggestions:

- Spend time researching school catalogs, guides, and directories for lists of colleges and other postsecondary schools according to major areas of study or training. Postsecondary school catalogs and brochures are usually located in the high school guidance office or library. Write to the schools you are considering to request additional information.
- If a catalog from the school of your interest isn't available, locate the school's address in a directory or on the Internet, and request a catalog from the school's admission office.
- Use a computerized career information system. Most systems contain information files describing apprenticeship programs, vocational and technical schools, and two- or four-year colleges.
- Listen to and question admissions counselors when they visit your school. Attend college fairs. Ask your guidance counselor for a schedule of visiting schools' representatives.
- Keep a file folder for each school you are considering.

Enrichment

Ask students to visit the high school library or guidance office and locate catalogs for three postsecondary schools they would like to attend. Instruct them to compare the list of courses they have completed and grades they have received with the requirements of each school. On the basis of their course work and grades, which schools would they expect to accept them? Why? Which schools would they expect to reject them? Why?

FIND OUT MORE

To acquire additional information about college programs and school accreditation, contact the U.S. Department of Education's College Opportunities On-Line system at www.nces.ed.gov/ipeds/cool. At the Web site, type in the name of a school to receive information about that school, including the organizations that accredit it. Additional information is available online. Type **Office of Postsecondary Education** in your search engine.

Considering All the Factors

When evaluating your choice of a postsecondary school, you need to consider many factors.You can start the process by finding out the answers to the following questions:

- What are the entrance requirements? The admissions office of a college or postsecondary school is responsible for admitting and recruiting students and working closely with the financial aid department.
- What is the size of the college or school? Sizes vary from fewer than 100 students to urban universities with enrollments as high as 80,000.

- Is the school public or private? Public schools are tax-supported. Private schools may be church-supported or independent of both church and the government.
- Where is the school located? School location determines the possibility of living at home while attending school—a very important financial consideration for many students.
- What is the ratio of women to men in the student body? This ratio is an important social consideration for many students.
- What are the tuition and fees? State-supported schools charge less for residents of that state and more for out-of-state students. Be sure to include expenses such as housing, meals, books and supplies, clothing, laundry, entertainment, medical insurance, and transportation in your student budget.
- What is the **student-faculty ratio** (the number of professional staff members compared to the number of students)? This information provides you with an indication of how much individual attention you can expect.
- What are the quality and credentials of the faculty? The qualifications and credentials of the faculty are more important than the number of faculty.
- What is the cost of housing if you live away from home? Housing costs on or off the campus are an important financial consideration.
- What student activities are available? Schools vary in the extent to which they promote or encourage student activities and social life.
- What is the quantity and quality of campus facilities? The quality of education the school is able to provide is directly related to the campus facilities. Unless the needed tools, equipment, building space, laboratories, and learning resources are available, the quality of the education program will be weakened.
- Is the school **accredited** (refers to a school's meeting minimum standards for its program of study, staff, and facilities)? The accreditation of the school where you receive your education and training will be important to future employers as they consider your credentials.

Cluster Link

Have you considered the amount of postsecondary education or training you will need to begin your adult career? Whether you plan to enter the workforce from high school or with a college degree, reviewing the level of education and training required for various occupations is important. Because there are many levels of responsibility (and paychecks) within occupations, you can enter several occupations with different levels of education and training. The occupation listings in the appendix show this fact.

Thoroughness in your evaluation of school factors will help you to select the best school for you.

Paying for Postsecondary Education

Finding a way to pay for additional education and training after high school is essential to your future career success. It is important for you to investigate the sources of these financial aid dollars. **Financial aid** is the

© JIST Works

combination of financial resources you can add to the money that you and your family can pay to meet the cost of your postsecondary education. Financial aid can generally be applied toward education leading to almost any degree or career training program.

A financial aid package can be a combination of merit scholarship, state and federal grants, employment, and loans. Not all students are eligible to receive all types of financial aid. Within the limits of available funds and the applicant's eligibility, the financial aid office of the postsecondary school will attempt to balance *gift aid* (grants and scholarships) with *self-help* (employment and loans). Students who apply before the priority date are likely to receive more attractive packages than those who apply later.

You will have to apply for financial aid during each year of your postsecondary schooling. Be aware that you are not guaranteed the same amount each year because your family's financial circumstances may change or the school you are attending may run short of funds.

Scholarships are awarded on the basis of merit or financial need plus merit. Scholarships are generally awarded for a combination of the following: academic standing, artistic talent, state of residence, leadership potential, athletic ability, organization membership, or religion.

Grants are awards based on financial need and do not require repayment. Grants are available from the federal government, state agencies, and educational institutions. The federal government is the major supplier of grants, awarding several billion dollars each year. Most of this money is awarded through the **Pell Grant**.

Loans are borrowed money that must be repaid with interest. Loans may be obtained from colleges, banks, loan companies, nonprofit agencies, and companies that are specifically in the business of making educational loans. The federal government funds the **Perkins Loan** at a low rate of interest. Repayment and interest begin nine months after you graduate, leave school, or drop below half-time enrollment.

College work study (CWS) programs are part-time campus jobs awarded to students by the financial aid office.

Cooperative education plans place students on supervised jobs in the field of work for which they are preparing. They are part of the educational process. Co-op plans usually add one year to the student's total college time.

After you are admitted, the college or school will notify you of the financial aid you are eligible to receive. Although costs vary from school to school, your total family contribution remains the same. Because of this, attending the college of your choice may not cost you more than attending one that is less expensive. Most financial aid is currently awarded on the basis of need, as determined by a financial analysis statement, which shows the amount you and your family can reasonably afford to pay.

As with most situations, you will get as much out of your postsecondary education as you put into it. The demands are great, but so are the rewards.

Enrichment

Instruct your students to write a letter to the Director of Student Financial Aid at a postsecondary school they are considering and to inquire about: A. What financial assistance is available? B. How does the school select financial aid recipients? C. What is the procedure and deadline for submitting an application for each available financial aid program? Ask them to request information on all federal, state, local, private, and institutional financial aid programs.

KEY TO SUCCESS

Don't delay sending applications to postsecondary schools. Financial aid will not be awarded until you have been accepted for admission.

FIND OUT MORE

If you need help filing your financial aid application, correcting a student aid report (SAR), or determining your eligibility for financial aid, or if you wish to receive free publications about financial aid, phone the Federal Student Aid Information center. The toll-free number is 1-800-4 FED AID. You also can find the application available online at www.fafsa.ed.gov.

© JIST Works

Section 3: Get Involved

Interview a student who is presently attending a postsecondary school you are considering, and find out the answers to the following questions. Write down the answers on a separate sheet of paper, and be prepared to discuss your responses in class.

1. How much time does the student spend in the library?
2. How much time does he or she spend on daily studies?
3. What type of homework is assigned?
4. Where does the student usually study or complete writing assignments?
5. What is the most difficult adjustment the student found going from high school to a postsecondary school?
6. What special advice does he or she have for you?

Comprehension Check

What advantages would an apprentice have over a young worker taking an entry-level job in the same industry?

Community Resources

Assign a committee of volunteer students to contact local craft unions and construction contractors. Also, have them locate a professional who works with apprenticeship programs. Provide the committee with a list of possible dates and times, and ask them to schedule their contacts to speak to your class about apprenticeship programs.

Section 4: Apprenticeship Programs

Benjamin Franklin was an apprentice printer under his older brother. From this beginning, he became the wealthiest man in the New World. Apprenticeship is a relationship between an employer and an employee during which the beginning worker, or apprentice, learns a trade. Apprentices train for occupations that require a wide range of skills and knowledge as well as maturity and independent judgment. Apprenticeship programs combine daily, supervised, on-the-job work experience with technical classroom instruction.

Apprenticeship is a centuries-old method of on-the-job training under the watchful eye of a master craftsman. The twelfth-century **guilds** (unions of craftsmen) of England were widespread in the skilled trades. Today's apprenticeship programs usually require about four years of training but range from one to six years. The apprentice receives wages during this learning period. A beginning apprentice earns about half the pay of a skilled craftsperson, with periodic raises throughout the apprenticeship.

In addition to on-the-job work experience, an apprentice receives classroom instruction from skilled craftspeople and specialists in related occupations. Trade manuals and other educational materials are required reading. Classes cover techniques of the trade, theory, and safety precautions.

An experienced worker who is known as a journey worker supervises the apprentice on the job. The **journey worker** is a certified, experienced, skilled craftsperson who has successfully completed an apprenticeship. Under the journey worker's guidance, the apprentice gradually learns the skills of the trade and performs the work under less and less supervision.

Apprenticeship programs are sponsored and operated by employers or employer associations or by management and labor on a voluntary basis. The sponsors plan, administer, and pay for the program. The government's role is to provide support services to these program sponsors.

© JIST Works

Apprenticeships are available for occupations from child care to construction. An apprentice is paid to learn a trade while under the watchful eye of a journey worker. Do you have the academic skills necessary to enter an apprenticeship program?

Find Out More

The Employment and Training Administration of the U.S. Department of Labor offers a CD-ROM and several brochures describing apprenticeship. For a copy of these materials, call 1-866-487-2365, or for more detailed information, go online at www.doleta.gov/atels_bat/. Additionally, America's Workforce Network toll-free help line is 1-877-872-5672. Operators can provide information about career counselors and apprenticeship programs in a caller's ZIP code.

Most programs require applicants to have a high school diploma or its equivalent. In some cases, college graduates are sought. All apprentices must be proficient in reading, writing, and mathematics. Courses in shop, math, algebra, geometry, drafting, physics, and other subjects related to the technical and mechanical trades are also highly recommended.

After the application is approved, the Joint Apprenticeship Committee or another administrative body representing the sponsor will interview each applicant. Once accepted, the applicant must wait for a place in the program. The length of the wait depends on the number of qualified applicants and the number of apprenticeship openings.

When an apprentice is accepted into a program, he or she and the sponsor sign an apprenticeship agreement. The apprentice agrees to perform the work faithfully and to complete the related course of study. The sponsor agrees to make every effort to keep the apprentice employed and to comply with the standards established for the program.

Upon successful completion of a registered program, the apprentice receives a certificate of completion from the U.S. Department of Labor or from a federally approved state apprenticeship agency. What similarities do you see between the twelfth-century guilds and today's apprenticeship programs?

More than 850 occupations may be entered through apprenticeship programs (see Table 6.3). However, apprenticeships related to construction and manufacturing are most common. Possibilities range from telecommunications, environmental protection, and pastry making to health care, child

The earning potential and skills required in apprenticeship programs are the same for men and women.

Education and Training

Ask the students to turn their attention to Table 6.3. Select a specific occupation, and ask the following questions: Which job tasks performed by a worker in this occupation would use skills learned in a high school mathematics class? How? English class? How? Art class? How? and so on.

care, and the arts. For all its advantages, apprenticeship takes time and effort. So before deciding whether apprenticeship is right for you, learn more about what apprenticeship is and how to find, choose, and qualify for a program.

One of the fastest growing preapprenticeship initiatives is the school-to-work apprenticeship program. School-to-work apprenticeship allows high school students to begin their apprenticeships as juniors and seniors. These students take occupational classes in addition to their regular high school curriculum. They concentrate on math and science or other classes important to the occupation they are considering. After graduation, they become full-time apprentices, with the advantage of having already completed many of the requirements.

Table 6.3 Apprenticed Occupations with the Most Job Openings*

Occupation	Average Annual Job Openings
Cooks, restaurant and cafeteria	238,542
Carpenters	223,225
Maintenance and repair workers, general	165,502
Automotive service technicians and mechanics	97,350
Electricians	79,083
Hairdressers, hairstylists, and cosmetologists	73,030
Licensed practical and licensed vocational nurses	70,610
Plumbers, pipefitters, and steamfitters	68,643
Welders, cutters, solderers, and brazers	61,125
Correctional officers and jailers	56,579
Machinists	39,505
Roofers	38,398
Police and sheriff's patrol officers	37,842
Automotive body and related repairers	37,469
Cement masons and concrete finishers	34,625
Heating, air-conditioning, and refrigeration mechanics and installers	29,719
Bus and truck mechanics and diesel engine specialists	25,428
Emergency medical technicians and paramedics	19,513
Firefighters	18,887

**Commonly apprenticed occupations expected to have the most job openings between 2006 and 2016 (U.S. Department of Labor).*

Section 4: Get Involved

Using a separate sheet of paper, do the following activities:

1. Select an occupation listed in Table 6.3 that you would consider for a career.
2. Contact the nearest Job Services office in your area, and ask about the age, education, aptitude, and physical condition qualification standards for the occupation you selected. Report your findings to the class.

© JIST Works

Section 5: Vocational Training Opportunities

Many high school graduates enter postsecondary vocational training offered by proprietary and technical schools. A **proprietary school** is privately owned and is operated for profit. A **technical school** focuses on training students in fields related to engineering and the physical sciences.

Several thousand proprietary and technical vocational schools operate in the United States. These small, single-purpose schools may be independent institutions or may operate as part of traditional high schools or colleges. Their major purpose is to send graduates into the job market with skills.

Tuition for proprietary and technical vocational schools ranges from a few hundred to several thousand dollars. Individual schools will provide information concerning financial aid upon request. Courses are usually offered five days a week (evenings may be an option), and programs are usually completed in less than two years. Courses of study seldom include traditional academic subjects, and course credit cannot be transferred to most colleges. Most schools emphasize small classes and offer job-placement assistance after graduation. A high school diploma or **GED** (general equivalency diploma) is usually required for admission.

Discussion Starter

Explain that proprietary and technical vocational schools prepare students for hundreds of highly skilled occupations. Two examples are aircraft mechanics and jet engine specialists. Ask your students: Should high school students who obtain high grades in difficult subjects consider attending a proprietary or technical school instead of a four-year college? Why or why not?

Find Out More

My Future is a Web site that strives to help you prepare for life after high school. It has information on getting a job and managing your money as well as information on different postsecondary options such as military opportunities, apprenticeships, and technical and vocational schools. Visit the site at www.myfuture.com.

Guidelines for Selecting a Proprietary or Technical Vocational School

Being selective in choosing a proprietary or technical vocational school is important because of the wide range of quality and high tuition cost. Use the following guidelines to help make a satisfactory choice:

1. Write or visit several schools offering training in your chosen occupation, and ask for their catalog. Compare each school's course offerings, hours of instruction, costs, and job-placement assistance.
2. Carefully read all of the terms of your enrollment application or contract before you sign it. Don't be pressured into signing an application or contract that you don't understand.

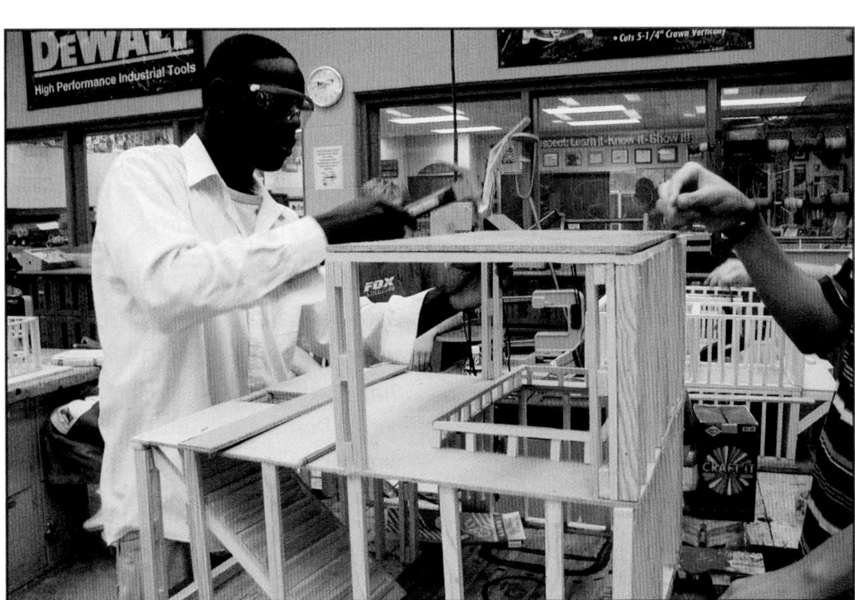

Have you considered enrolling in a vocational or technical school program?

© JIST Works

3. Phone your local Consumer Protection Office or Better Business Bureau before you enroll. Check to see whether local employers or government agencies offer similar training at no cost. For example, most airlines conduct their own training programs for flight attendants.
4. Check with employers and workers employed in the occupation to be certain that skills being taught by the school are currently being used in the workplace.
5. If using tools, machines, or instruments is part of the training, find out whether the school has enough equipment to enable every student to practice using it. Is the equipment up-to-date? Is there an extra charge for using the equipment? Will you be required to purchase tools?
6. How many recent students graduated? How many graduates found jobs in their field? Did the school help them find jobs, and how long did it take? If possible, discuss the school's program with current and past students.
7. Will the program improve your math, reading, and thinking skills? Will it teach you how to continue learning after graduation?
8. Does the program include on-the-job training? Do teachers work with business and industry on a regular basis to update their skills and information?
9. Will you have to take out a loan to pay for the program? Who will pay back the loan if the school doesn't deliver on its promises?
10. Find out whether the school is licensed by your state's postsecondary school licensing bureau.
11. Check on whether the school is accredited by an accrediting agency recognized by the U.S. Department of Education. (You can visit its Web site at www.ed.gov/admis/finaid/accred/ to find out which agencies are recognized.) A nonaccredited school may be as reputable as an accredited one. Applying for accreditation is voluntary, and the school must be in operation for five years before it can apply.

FIND OUT MORE

For more information on private vocational schools, visit the Web site of the Accrediting Commission of Career Schools and Colleges of Technology (ACCSCT) at www.accsct.org. This site's Resources section provides a School Directory that you can use to search for accredited schools for the programs you are interested in.

School to Work: Success Increases Confidence

Laura Warder graduated from Eisenhower High School last June. Laura's parents didn't think they would ever see her walk across the stage—and neither did Laura. She experienced several personal problems during 10th grade. She even ran away from home for two months.

When Laura returned to school, she was placed in an occupational work-experience program. Her teacher, Mr. Gary, helped her find a job and made regular visits to her employer to be certain that everything was OK.

© JIST Works

Her subjects included mathematics, English, geography, and a special work-experience class during the morning. She had an early release from school so that she could go to her job during the afternoon.

Obtaining job-seeking and job-holding skills, learning how to get along with others, and developing confidence in herself were all part of Laura's educational program. In addition to teaching Laura's English and work-adjustment classes, Mr. Gary was always there for her as a counselor and friend. Being in the work-experience program gave Laura a chance to redirect her life, save some money, and make plans for her future.

Laura returned to the regular school program during her senior year and maintained a B average. Although she missed her chance to take a vocational program in high school, Laura decided to continue her education in a postsecondary vocational program and to train for a career in cosmetology. Even though she is no longer in his class, Mr. Gary arranged for Laura to visit the Touch of Beauty Vocational School. Laura is excited about her plans to attend school in the fall. It's hard for her to imagine that she will begin her career in another year. Laura told Mr. Gary that she wants him to be her first customer and that he will get a great hairstyle at no cost.

TAKE NOTE

The Peace Corps and the American Association of Community Colleges have joined forces to attract qualified community college graduates whose skills are requested by developing countries. Volunteers must be at least 18 years old and be U.S. citizens. Sought-after skills are applied in Peace Corps assignments such as demonstrating sustainable agriculture and helping to set up clean-water systems. About 8,000 volunteers are presently serving in 74 countries. The Peace Corps service commitment is two years plus a few months of training. Completion of service provides educational, financial, personal, and professional benefits—including preparation for some of the fastest-growing occupations in the United States. For additional information, go online and type **Peace Corps** in your search engine.

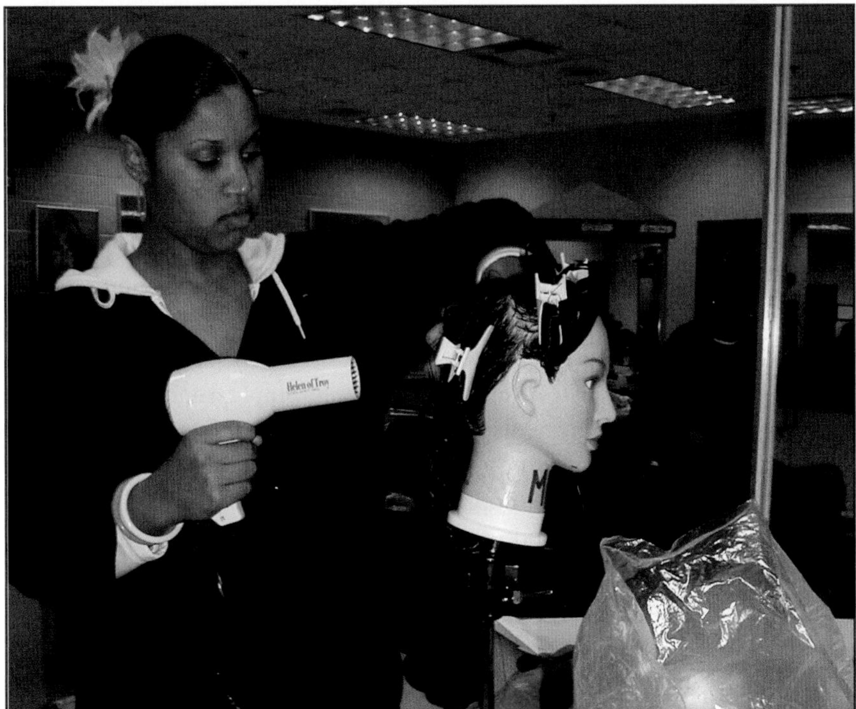

Critical Thinking

Did Laura have a high level of self-confidence during the 10th grade? What evidence can you show to support your opinion? How did this affect her attitude toward school and work?

How would you account for Laura's high level of self-confidence during her senior year? How did this affect her attitude toward school and work? What evidence can you show to support your opinion?

Find Out More

To check to see whether a certain correspondence school you are interested in is accredited, a good place to start is the Web site for the Distance Education and Training Council at www.detc.org/.

Cooperative Learning

Form a committee to gather more information about correspondence schools, home study courses, and school credibility. Have committee members report their findings to the class.

Correspondence Schools

Correspondence courses (home study) offer an opportunity to those who are unable to attend regular classes at a vocational school or college. Home study makes it possible for students to study at their own pace and on their own schedule, avoiding conflicts with existing job or family responsibilities. Students take the courses through the mail or by means of specially designed computer software that links students to instructors. Using a computer and an Internet connection, students "attend" lectures, take tests, and submit homework. Some correspondence courses may be offered in combination with television classes on educational channels.

The correspondence school provides materials for study. Instructors correct, grade, and comment on the examination material, which the students mail or e-mail back to the school as they complete the lessons. Corrected assignments are returned, and this written exchange establishes a personalized student-teacher relationship.

The most popular correspondence courses are business, high school equivalency, electronics, midlevel engineering technician training, other technical and trade courses, and art. These courses generally require one year to complete.

Key To Success

Use the same criteria for selecting a correspondence school as you would for selecting a proprietary or technical vocational school.

Government Job-Training Programs

Qualified young people may participate in a variety of government-provided training programs while they are in or out of school. These programs are usually limited to applicants from low-income families. Some are residence programs, in which classes are held at public training centers. Other programs provide funds and counseling services to participants and arrange for them to enroll in schools or to work in firms.

The **Job Corps** is a federally administered employment and training program that serves severely disadvantaged young people aged 16 through 24. It helps them to get a better job, make more money, and take control of their lives. Enrollees receive food, housing, education, vocational training, medical care, counseling, and other support. The program prepares these young people for stable employment and entrance into vocational or technical schools, junior colleges, or other education and training programs.

Enrollees in Job Corps Centers receive a living allowance, part of which is paid when the program is satisfactorily completed. Enrollees may stay in the Job Corps for up to two years, although the average length of stay is about eight months.

Find Out More

If you're interested in joining the Job Corps program or finding out more about it, call 1-800-733-JOBS. Alternatively, you can go online at jobcorps.doleta.gov/about.cfm.

Job Corps training is provided in occupations such as auto repair, carpentry, painting, masonry, nursing and other health-care occupations, word processing, business and clerical skills, welding, and heavy equipment operation.

© JIST Works

Section 5: Get Involved

Do the following activity, and be prepared to discuss your findings in class.

1. Contact the admissions office of a proprietary or technical school in your community. Acquire as much information as you can about the school using the guidelines presented earlier in this section.

Section 6: On-the-Job Training, Civilian and Military

On-the-job training (OJT) refers to a wide range of education and training provided by employers for their employees. It ranges from brief periods of job instruction for low-skilled jobs to extensive classroom instruction resulting in advanced certificates or licenses. Almost all employers provide new workers with some kind of training.

Education and Training

Ask whether any students have had on-the-job training. If so, ask those students to describe their OJT experience.

Civilian On-the-Job Training

Civilian OJT is provided through the following:

- Seminars and institutes conducted at the worksite
- Separate education and training facilities that are operated by the organization (McDonald's Hamburger University for merchandising and retail sales training and the Xerox Learning Center are examples)
- Accredited corporate-owned colleges that grant degrees, such as the General Motors Institute
- Satellite universities that beam course work by satellite to corporate classrooms around the country
- Numerous cooperative learning programs sponsored by employers and presented at local universities or community colleges

Although OJT programs may involve some classroom instruction, most on-the-job learning involves supervised work experience. OJT usually prepares younger workers to perform job tasks that can be learned in a brief demonstration period and that require minimal general education. After the tasks are learned, the workers are assigned to the jobs for which they were hired.

Advances in the technical requirements for entry-level jobs and the increasing lack of academic proficiency among high school graduates have caused employers to dramatically increase OJT for younger workers. Employers are finding it increasingly necessary to bridge the widening gap between knowledge learned in high school and knowledge needed on the job.

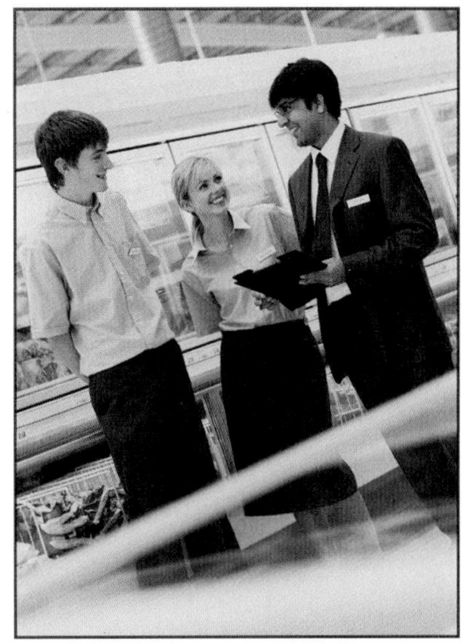

After tasks are learned through on-the-job training, workers are assigned jobs. Do you know anyone who has had OJT?

© JIST Works

New employees frequently learn to perform complex work tasks by observing and assisting skilled workers. In some cases, employers rotate new employees through a series of job experiences so they will know the overall operations of the organization. This experience generally helps new employees perform more effectively when assigned to a specific job.

Education and Training

Form a committee to contact two or more military recruiters. Have the committee arrange a combined presentation to the class describing education and training opportunities offered by the military services.

Military On-the-Job Training

The first responsibility of military personnel is to defend the United States. However, because the defense of our nation is so encompassing, numerous jobs are available. Each branch of the armed services provides training through on-the-job assignment, specialized schools, or a combination of both. Upon completion of basic training, an enlisted person may be given a duty assignment or sent to a school for specialized training.

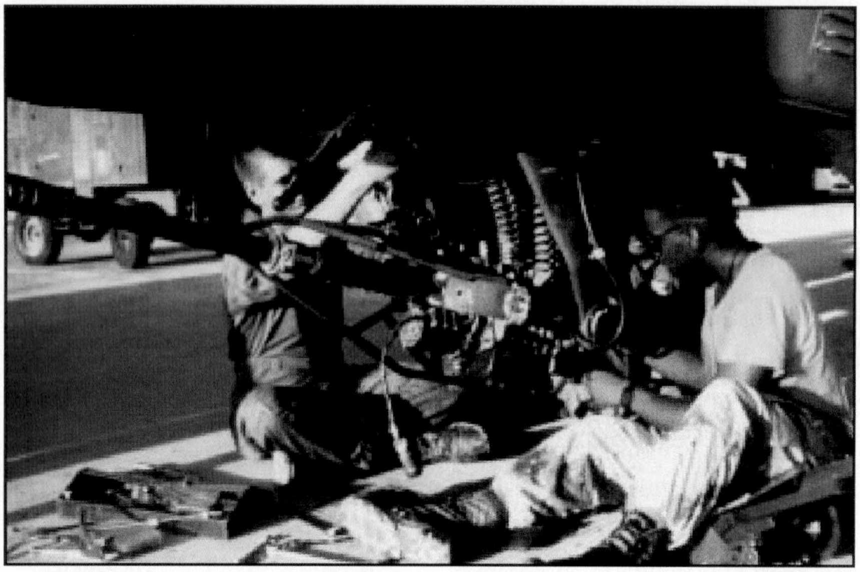

What advantages would military training offer? What disadvantages?

The education and training taught in the special technical schools provide the military services with a skilled workforce. The quality of training available in military schools usually equals or exceeds the training that can be acquired in similar civilian schools.

Many military occupations have some relationship to civilian occupations. However, the degree to which training can be transferred from military to civilian work will vary. Table 6.4 lists several occupations that can be entered with military education and training. Numerous job skills learned for these particular military occupations can be transferred to civilian occupations.

Military personnel are encouraged to study voluntarily while off duty. Each military service contracts with colleges and universities to operate correspondence schools. In addition, the United States Armed Forces Institute provides correspondence courses to enlistees in all branches of the armed forces.

Most military installations have tuition-assistance programs for military personnel who wish to take courses during off-duty hours. They may be correspondence courses or degree programs offered by local colleges or universities.

Each branch of the armed forces provides opportunities for full-time study to a limited number of exceptional applicants. Military personnel accepted into these highly competitive programs receive full pay, tuition, and related allowances. In return, applicants must agree to serve an additional amount of time in the service.

© JIST Works

Table 6.4 Civilian Occupations with Military Training Available

Mechanical and Craft	Electronics and Electrical	Business and Clerical	Health, Social, and Technology
Bulldozer operator	Electronic/electrical equipment repairer	Human resource specialist	Environmental health specialist
Crane operator	Aircraft electrician	Personnel specialist	Media specialist
Plumber	Flight engineer	Vehicle driver	Firefighter
Pipefitter	Powerhouse mechanic	Accounting specialist	Laboratory technician
Electrician		Payroll specialist	X-ray/ultrasound technician
Machine operator: engines, turbines, nuclear reactors, water pumps		Shipping/receiving specialist	Physician
Heating and cooling mechanic			Nurse
Welder			Physical therapist
Marine engine mechanic			Health-care personnel
Aircraft pilot			Dental technician
			Optical technician
			Dentist
			Air traffic controller

Section 6: Get Involved

Answer the following on a separate sheet of paper, and be prepared to discuss your responses in class.

1. Contact the human resources department of a large employer in your community. Find out what positions can be learned with OJT. Report your findings to the class.
2. Imagine that you are an employment counselor hired to help discharged military personnel find employment in the civilian sector. What businesses or industries would you contact to find employment for the following discharged veterans?

Name	Military Experience
Janet T. Brown	Sergeant, Marine Corps, 6 years experience, 4 years as a missile maintenance technician, 3 years overseas in a combat theatre of operations. Recipient: Bronze star/Purple heart.
Ronald J. Adams	Corporal, Army, 4 years experience, 3 years as heating and cooling mechanic serving in the United States.
John R. Cork	Petty Officer 3rd Class, Navy, 6 years experience, 4 years as a firefighter, 3 years sea duty on an aircraft carrier in a combat theatre of operations. Recipient: Silver Star.

Section 7: Community Colleges, Colleges, and Universities

Do you plan to enroll in a college after you graduate from high school? If so, which type of college program will prepare you for the career path you have selected?

© JIST Works

Reteaching

Have students complete the "Is School in Your Future?" worksheet in Chapter 6 of the *Preparing for Career Success Instructor's CD-ROM, Third Edition.*

Discussion Starter

Ask individual students the following question: What is an open-admissions policy? After they clearly understand this term, ask your students: Is it fair to allow students who didn't take high school seriously or even dropped out of high school to be accepted by tax-supported one- and two-year colleges? Why or why not?

FIND OUT MORE

For college information ranging from campus visits to online applications and financial aid, contact the College Board's Web site at www.collegeboard.com.

One- and Two-Year Community Colleges

The need for people holding two-year degrees or certificates continues to grow. Two-year and community colleges are becoming the hubs of "skilling and reskilling." Continuous lifelong learning will be necessary to keep you competitive in a global marketplace. With only two years of post-secondary education, you can train for some of the fastest-growing jobs in the economy, increase your earnings, and pave the way for further education.

A major share of all postsecondary education is provided by public and private colleges that award associate degrees after two years of full-time study. Many of these colleges also offer shorter-term certificate and diploma programs in specific career areas. Accreditation of these schools rests primarily with state or regional agencies.

Training is available for those with nearly any interest, from technical fields, such as electronics and health care, to liberal arts areas, such as design and social work. Community colleges offer specialized programs of education and training to fill the needs of businesses and industries, health organizations, and public service groups. They teach up-to-date employment **competencies** (qualifications) to students preparing to enter the workforce, workers who have been laid off, and employed workers who want to upgrade their job skills.

Most public two-year colleges have an **open-admissions policy**, meaning that they grant admission to all applicants without regard to grade point average, test scores, or class rank. However, they do require students to take

One- and two-year community colleges offer a wide variety of programs for many students who want to further their education after high school. Have you explored the offerings at one of these colleges?

© JIST Works

diagnostic placement tests after admission. Approximately half of all two-year college students enter directly from high school. Others become employed after high school and later enroll as part- or full-time students. These programs are well suited for students who want to further their education after high school but do not want to pursue a four-year degree. Various schedule options are offered, and more than half of the students are enrolled on a part-time basis.

Community colleges generally provide a four-part program that includes the following:

- A two-year university program for students who plan to transfer to a four-year college or university to complete a specific four-year program
- A technical program to prepare students to enter employment upon completion of the two-year curriculum
- A variety of short courses to retrain local workers or upgrade their job skills
- Adult education programs, consisting of formal or informal courses

FIND OUT MORE

At your school or public library, request the most recent publication of any of the following:

- *Peterson's Four-Year Colleges,* published by Peterson's Guides
- *Peterson's Competitive Colleges,* published by Peterson's Guides
- *College Handbook,* published by College Board Publications
- *Barron's Profiles of American Colleges,* published by Barron's Educational Series

Four-Year Colleges and Universities

The more than 3,300 accredited colleges, community colleges, and universities in the United States together enroll more than 12 million students at both the undergraduate and graduate levels. More than 2,000 of these schools offer four years of full-time study leading to the **baccalaureate degree**. This degree, sometimes called a *bachelor's degree* or an *undergraduate degree*, is a four-year degree in a specific subject. Many colleges offer two-year programs from which a student can transfer into a baccalaureate degree program. Four-year colleges and universities vary considerably in their policies on enrollment and attendance, curriculum offerings, and graduation requirements.

A **university** is the largest type of institution of higher learning. It is composed of several undergraduate colleges and graduate schools for advanced study. Universities usually include a liberal arts college and several other specialized colleges. Each college has its own specific admissions requirements, which must be met by every student seeking to earn a degree in that college. In addition, the university establishes certain requirements that every undergraduate student must meet.

State universities are supported by public funding and are usually less expensive than private universities. In addition, state universities may charge increased tuition fees and have higher entrance requirements for out-of-state students.

Liberal arts colleges offer Bachelor of Arts degree programs that combine a broad four-year education in the arts, humanities, social sciences, and sciences with a major in a subject or area such as government

Enrichment

Have students complete the "Using a College Directory" worksheet in Chapter 6 of the *Preparing for Career Success Student Activity Book, Third Edition.*

Education and Training

Ask the school guidance counselor or librarian to show your class how to locate and use the available college guides and references to other education and training programs.

School-to-Work Transition

Send several students to the chalkboard. Ask each of them to make headings for specific colleges at a university. Ask seated students to name occupations related to specific colleges. Have the students at the chalkboard write down the occupations that the other students name.

Education and Training

Explain to the students that all universities employ recruiters. Form a committee to arrange a class presentation by a college recruiter. Ask them to contact the nearest university's admissions office. Addresses and phone numbers are listed in most college guides. Ask the remaining class members for questions concerning this section of the text. Ask the committee to list the questions and forward them to the recruiter prior to his or her visit to the class.

Curriculum offerings and admissions requirements vary widely at the college and university level. Will you be one of the more than 12 million students who enroll in college?

and political science, mathematics, or biology. Many liberal arts colleges are small, private colleges with fewer than 5,000 students.

Specialized colleges and schools that offer Bachelor of Science degree programs focus more on preparation for a specific career and less on a broad liberal arts education. Examples of these programs are engineering, education, business, agriculture, and home economics.

Graduate Schools

A student may be eligible for graduate studies after completion of a four-year baccalaureate degree. Graduate studies usually lead to a master's degree, which requires one or two years of advanced study in a specific subject, or a doctoral degree, which requires three or four years of advanced study in a specific subject. To obtain a graduate degree, a student must meet the requirements established by the college or school awarding the degree.

Many occupations require a graduate degree. Here are some examples: economist, education administrator, historian, librarian, political scientist, psychologist, school counselor, sociologist, and urban planner.

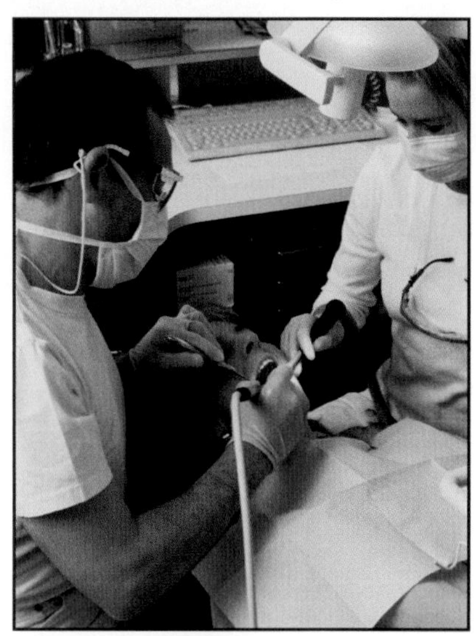

Dental hygienists must be licensed by the state in which they practice. They must graduate from an accredited dental hygiene school and pass both a written and a clinical examination.

Professional Schools

Professional schools prepare students for specific professions, such as lawyer, dentist, veterinarian, and physician. To obtain a professional degree, a student must meet the minimum requirements established by the college or professional school offering the degree.

Many colleges or universities offer courses of study that satisfy the admissions requirements for a specific professional school as part of the baccalaureate degree. These programs are known as **preprofessional programs**.

© JIST Works

Specialized Colleges and Schools

Specialized colleges and schools prepare students for specific occupations, such as minister, dental hygienist, artist, nurse, optometrist, and chiropractor. These colleges and schools are similar to professional schools in that they often provide training in only one field. However, they seldom require a baccalaureate degree as a condition of enrollment. Training usually takes three to five years.

Student Evaluation

To evaluate student mastery of concepts, use the Section 7 quiz in the Chapter 6 file of the *Preparing for Career Success Instructor's CD-ROM, Third Edition.* You can also find a chapter test in the Chapter 6 file.

Section 7: Get Involved

Ask your school librarian for one of the college guides listed in the "Find Out More" box in this section and use it to answer the following questions. Be prepared to discuss your responses in class.

1. Locate a two-year or four-year college in your state and one other state that interests you. Select one program of study that you would consider pursuing. What is the college tuition for this program in the college located in your state? At the college in the other state?
2. What is the cost of living on campus at the college in your state? At the college in the other state?
3. What are the entrance requirements for each school you chose?
4. What career opportunities would be available to you after you completed the program you chose?
5. What are the requirements for entering the professions of law and medicine at the largest university in your state? What is the tuition for a law or medical student for one year?
6. What professional programs are offered at the largest university in your state?
7. What specialized colleges in your state prepare students for the occupations of minister, nurse, and chiropractor?

Chapter 6 Review

Reteaching

Have students complete the "Finding the Right Words" and "Checking Your Location" worksheets in Chapter 6 of the *Preparing for Career Success Student Activity Book, Third Edition.*

Enrich Your Vocabulary

On a separate sheet of paper, number from 1 to 26, and write the term from the "Enrich Your Vocabulary" list at the beginning of the chapter next to the number of the phrase it matches.

1. General equivalency diploma
2. After high school
3. Fit into
4. Unions of craftsmen
5. Qualifications
6. A certified, experienced, skilled craftsperson who has successfully completed an apprenticeship
7. Types of jobs available
8. Relationship between an employer and an employee during which the worker learns a trade

Enrich Your Vocabulary Answers

1. GED
2. postsecondary
3. adapt
4. guilds
5. competencies
6. journey worker
7. employment structure
8. apprenticeship

(continued)

Enrich Your Vocabulary Answers *(continued)*

9. proprietary school
10. correspondence courses
11. accredited
12. Job Corps
13. technical school
14. on-the-job training (OJT)
15. university
16. baccalaureate degree
17. preprofessional programs
18. open-admissions policy
19. college majors
20. methodical
21. student-faculty ratio
22. financial aid
23. Pell Grant
24. Perkins Loan
25. College work-study programs (CWS)
26. cooperative education

Enrichment

Have students complete the Chapter 6 section of the *Preparing for Career Success Student Portfolio, Third Edition.*

9. A school privately owned and operated for profit
10. Home study
11. Has met certain minimum standards for its program of study, staff, and facilities
12. A federally administered employment and training program that serves severely disadvantaged young people
13. Intended to train students in fields related to engineering and the physical sciences
14. A wide range of education and training provided by employers for their employees
15. The largest type of institution of higher learning, composed of several undergraduate colleges and graduate schools for advanced study
16. A four-year degree that is sometimes called a bachelor's degree or undergraduate degree
17. A course of study that satisfies the admissions requirements for a specific professional school as part of the baccalaureate degree
18. A policy of granting admission to all applicants without regard to grade point average, test scores, or class rank
19. Special areas of study
20. Systematic, orderly
21. The number of professional staff members compared to the number of students
22. The combination of financial resources you can add to the money that you and your family can pay to meet the cost of your postsecondary education
23. A grant funded by the federal government for students based on the student's financial needs
24. A student loan funded by the federal government at a low rate of interest
25. Part-time campus jobs awarded to students by the financial aid office
26. Place students on supervised jobs in the field of work for which they are preparing

© JIST Works

Check Your Knowledge

On a separate sheet of paper, answer the following questions. (Do not write in your textbook.)

1. Occupations that require more education and training have been growing faster than those that require less education and training. What is the underlying message in this statement?
2. What is the unemployment rate shown in Figure 6.2 for students with less than 12 years of schooling?
3. All high school subjects provide specific training for certain occupations. List three high school courses. For each course, name an occupation that is closely related to each course and name a specific skill learned in each course that is used in the related occupation.
4. Why do employers use grades as a basis for evaluating a job applicant?
5. What are three different ways students can identify schools that offer them the types of programs they want to study?
6. Approximately how many occupations can be entered through apprenticeship programs?
7. Why is it that those with a high school diploma are not likely to receive on-the-job training beyond basic job requirements? As a worker's general level of education increases, why does the opportunity for more advanced levels of OJT also increase?
8. What needs have community, junior, and technical colleges filled in training and retraining workers?
9. What are five factors students should consider in narrowing their choices of a postsecondary school?
10. Why is going to an accredited school an important factor to consider?

Develop SCANS Competencies

Government experts say that successful workers can productively use resources, interpersonal skills, information, systems, and technology. This activity will give you practice in developing information skills.

Develop a chart that compares information from a variety of postsecondary schools. Contact any universities, colleges, community colleges, technical institutes, and apprenticeship programs in your area. Find the following information for each facility: courses of study offered; end result, whether it is a degree, certificate, and so on; time investment required; financial investment required.

Check Your Knowledge Answers

1. Answers will vary. Prospects for good jobs throughout a person's life will depend on continual education and training to maintain and improve job skills.
2. 10 percent.
3. Table 6.1 lists several possibilities.
4. Employers know that a good understanding of basic high school subjects is usually shown by a student's grades, and higher grades usually mean that the person will be easier to train than someone with low grades. Grades are also an important predictor of future success.
5. Research school catalogs, guides, and directories; use a computerized career information system; talk to college admissions counselors who visit your school; attend college fairs; search the Internet.
6. Approximately 850.
7. OJT prepares them to perform job tasks that can be learned in a brief demonstration period. Once the tasks are learned, the workers are assigned the lower-level jobs for which they were hired.
8. They provide education and training that keeps up with the fast-paced changes in technology in semiprofessional, technical, and highly skilled professions.
9. Answers will vary. Factors listed in this chapter are school size, whether the school is public or private, location, ratio of women to men, tuition and fees, student-faculty ratio, faculty credentials, cost of housing, student activities, facilities, accreditation.
10. Answers will vary. Not being accredited could indicate a substandard school. In such a case, future employers or educational institutions may reject your education and training or consider it as a substandard credential.

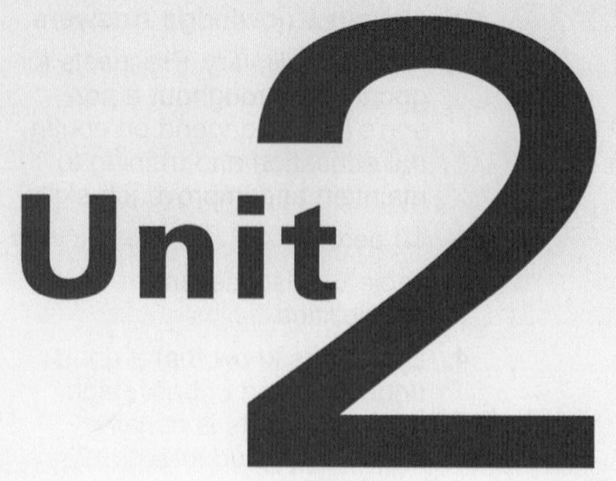

Unit 2 Finding a Job and Achieving Success

Chapter 7: Expressing Yourself: Effective Communication

Chapter 8: Conducting the Job Search

Chapter 9: Applying and Interviewing for a Job

Chapter 10: Taking Responsibility for Your Job Success

Chapter 11: Making Progress on the Job

Chapter 7 Resources

Lesson Plans and Preparation

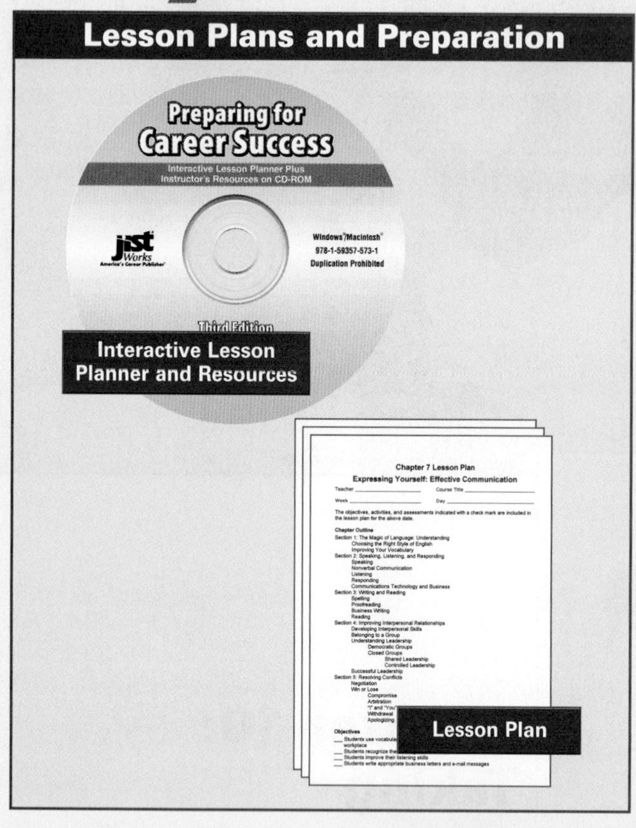

Multimedia

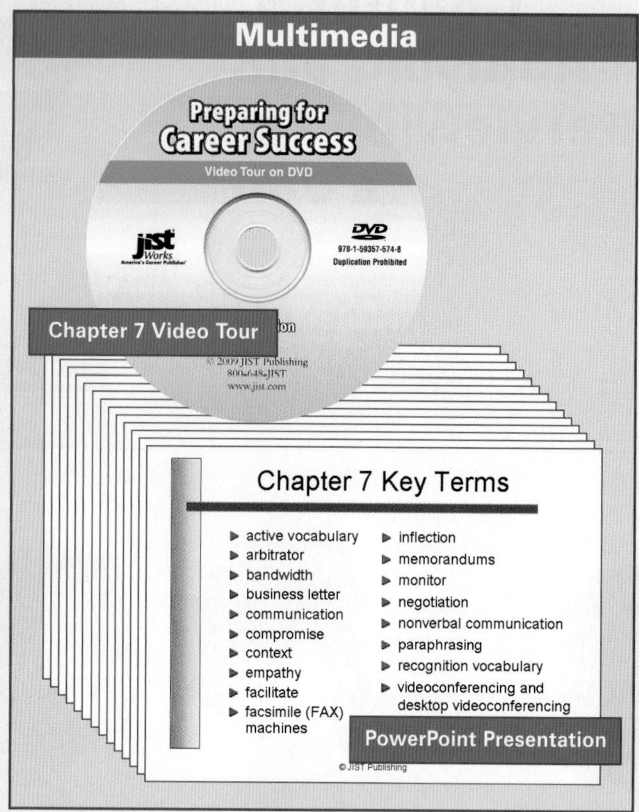

Preparing for Career Success
Video Tour on DVD
978-1-59357-574-8
Duplication Prohibited
Chapter 7 Video Tour
© 2009 JIST Publishing
800-648-JIST
www.jist.com
Chapter 7 Key Terms
active vocabulary
arbitrator
bandwidth
business letter
communication
compromise
context
empathy
facilitate
facsimile (FAX) machines
inflection
memorandums
monitor
negotiation
nonverbal communication
paraphrasing
recognition vocabulary
videoconferencing and desktop videoconferencing
PowerPoint Presentation
© JIST Publishing

Activities

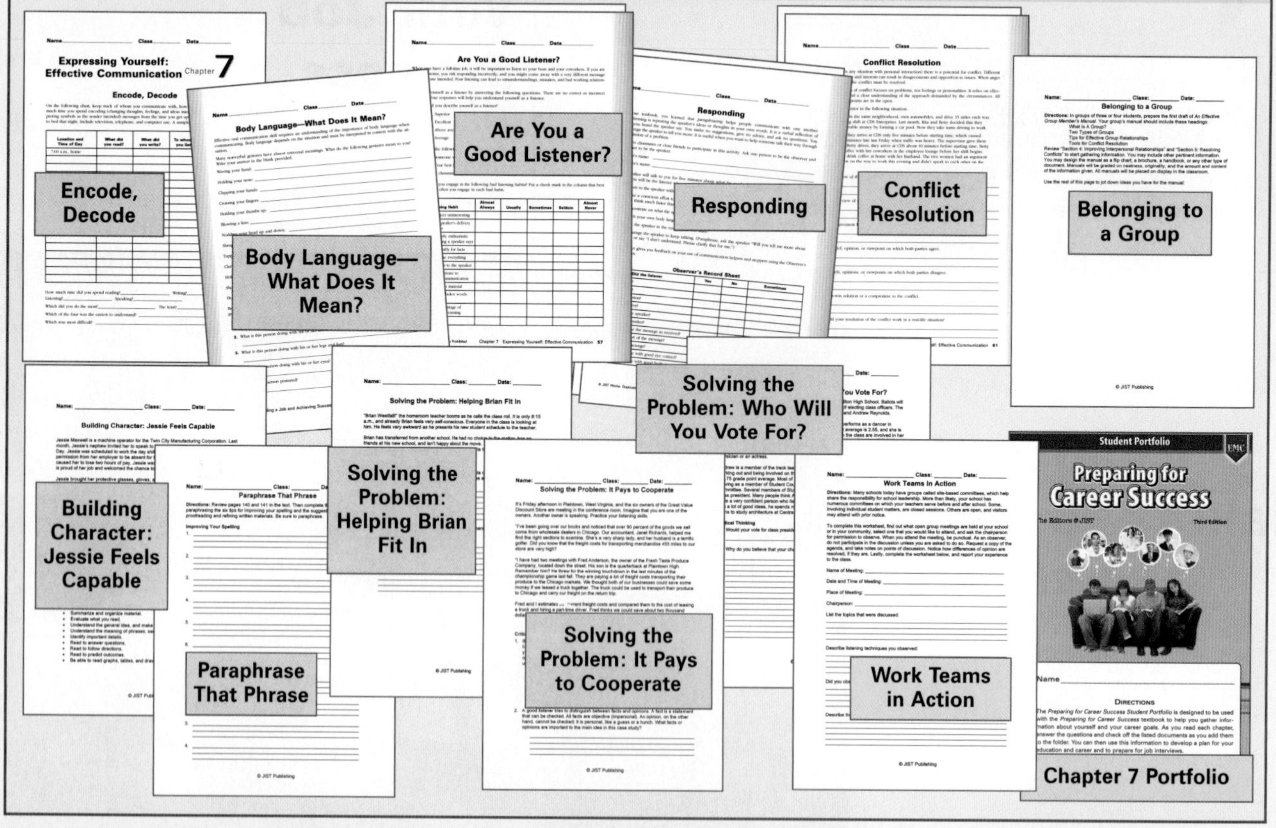

- Encode, Decode
- Body Language—What Does It Mean?
- Are You a Good Listener?
- Responding
- Conflict Resolution
- Belonging to a Group
- Solving the Problem: Who Will You Vote For?
- Building Character: Jessie Feels Capable
- Solving the Problem: Helping Brian Fit In
- Paraphrase That Phrase
- Solving the Problem: It Pays to Cooperate
- Work Teams in Action
- Chapter 7 Portfolio

© JIST Works

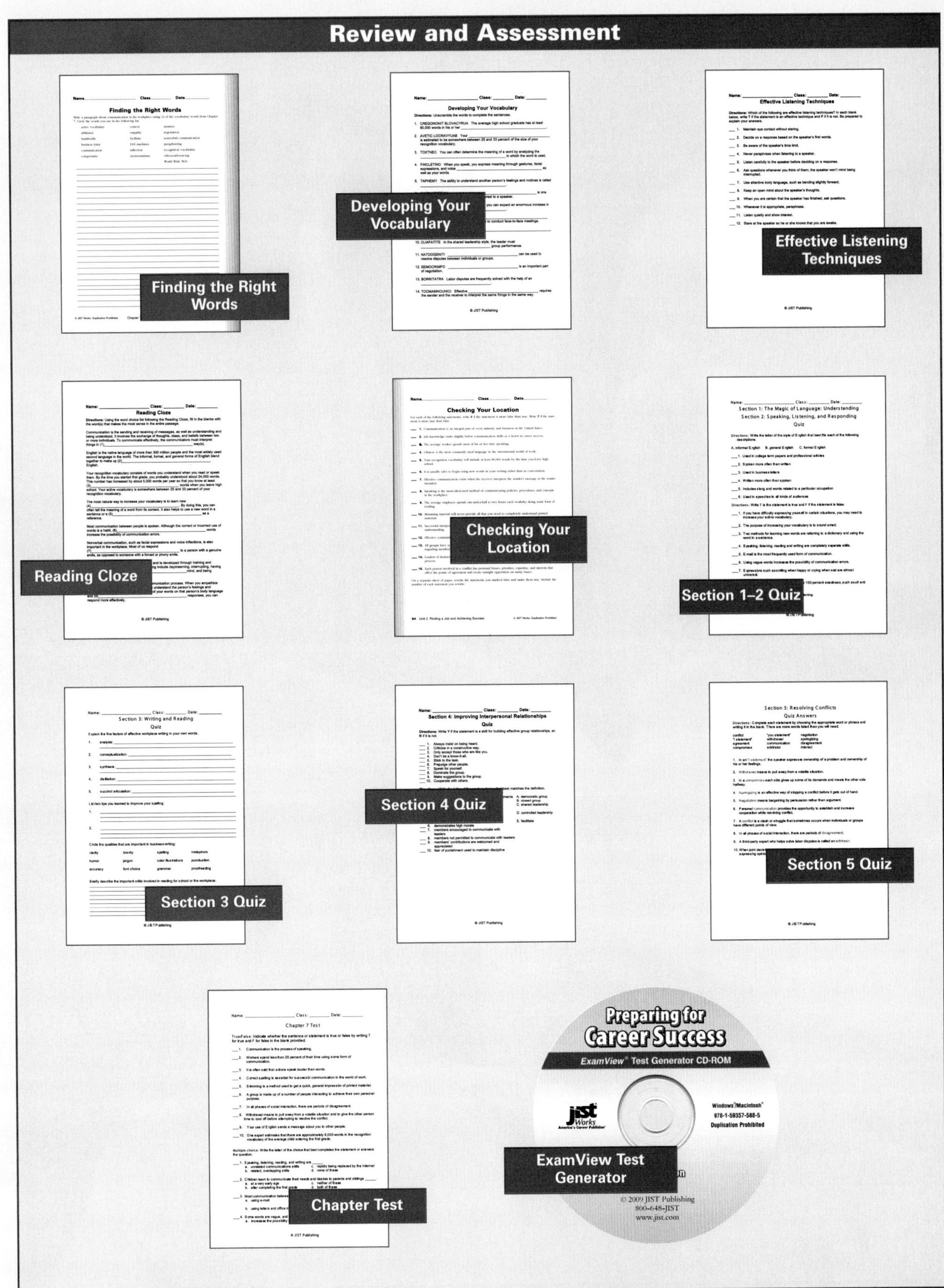
Review and Assessment
Finding the Right Words
Developing Your Vocabulary
Effective Listening Techniques
Reading Cloze
Checking Your Location
Section 1–2 Quiz
Section 3 Quiz
Section 4 Quiz
Section 5 Quiz
Chapter Test
Preparing for Career Success
ExamView® Test Generator CD-ROM
ExamView Test Generator
© 2009 JIST Publishing
800-648-JIST
www.jist.com

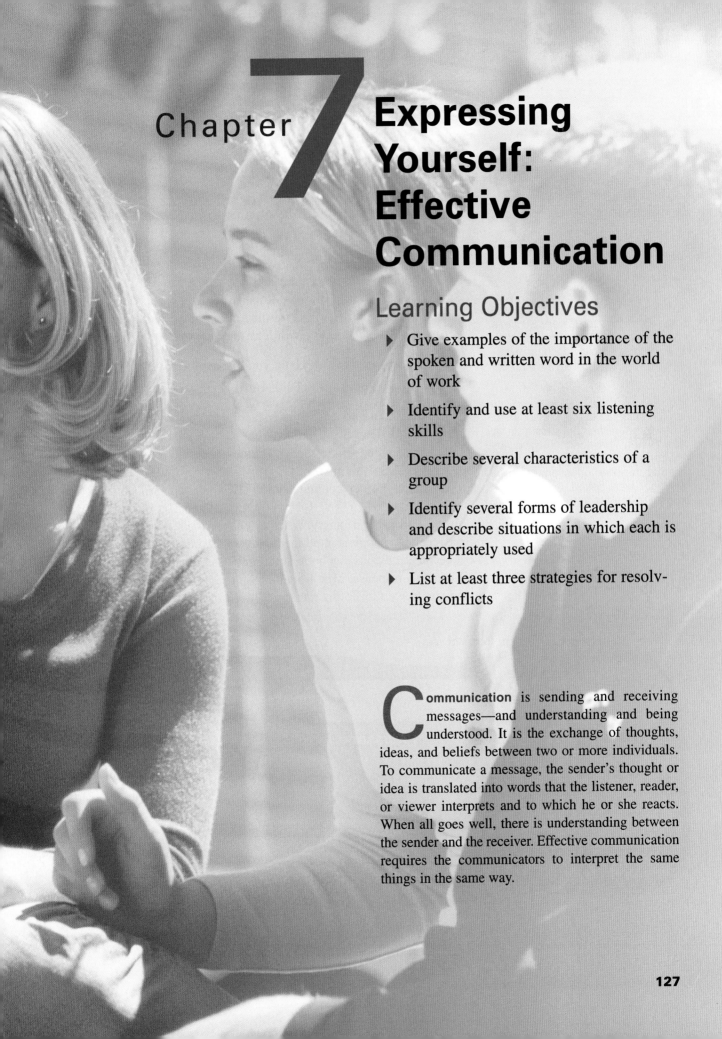

Chapter 7 Expressing Yourself: Effective Communication

Learning Objectives

- Give examples of the importance of the spoken and written word in the world of work
- Identify and use at least six listening skills
- Describe several characteristics of a group
- Identify several forms of leadership and describe situations in which each is appropriately used
- List at least three strategies for resolving conflicts

Communication is sending and receiving messages—and understanding and being understood. It is the exchange of thoughts, ideas, and beliefs between two or more individuals. To communicate a message, the sender's thought or idea is translated into words that the listener, reader, or viewer interprets and to which he or she reacts. When all goes well, there is understanding between the sender and the receiver. Effective communication requires the communicators to interpret the same things in the same way.

Enrich Your Vocabulary

In reading this chapter and doing the exercises, you will learn the following important terms:

active vocabulary
arbitrator
bandwidth
business letter
communication
compromise
context
empathy
facilitate
facsimile (FAX) machines
inflection
memorandums
monitor
negotiation
nonverbal communication
paraphrasing
recognition vocabulary
videoconferencing and desktop videoconferencing
World Wide Web

Vocabulary

You can use the "Developing Your Vocabulary" worksheet in Chapter 7 of the *Preparing for Career Success Instructor's CD-ROM, Third Edition* as a pretest or a reteaching worksheet.

Discussion Starter

Ask the students to raise their hands if they can remember being in a class when the teacher gave an assignment, asked the students whether they had questions, and no questions were asked. Ask your students: Did the teacher and all of the students in the class have an effective communication? Why or why not?

Consider a communication taking place at the Thrifty Buy Discount Store. The store manager, Mrs. Roberts, realizes that she will need someone on the day shift to work overtime during the evening rush. She directs her message to a clerk, Kenneth Johnson.

Mrs. Roberts: How would you like to work over?

Kenneth Johnson: I could probably use the extra cash.

Figure 7.1 describes the understanding of the sender, Mrs. Roberts, and the receiver, Kenneth, regarding Mrs. Roberts' question. It also describes the understanding of the sender, Kenneth, and the receiver, Mrs. Roberts, regarding Kenneth's answer.

Without further communication, Kenneth will probably go home at quitting time. When Mrs. Roberts discovers that he hasn't worked overtime, she will probably be angry. Whether you are the sender of a message or on the receiving end, it is important that you continue the communication until it becomes obvious that both parties have an accurate understanding. Given Kenneth's response, Mrs. Roberts might say, "Does that mean I can count on you to work over this evening?"

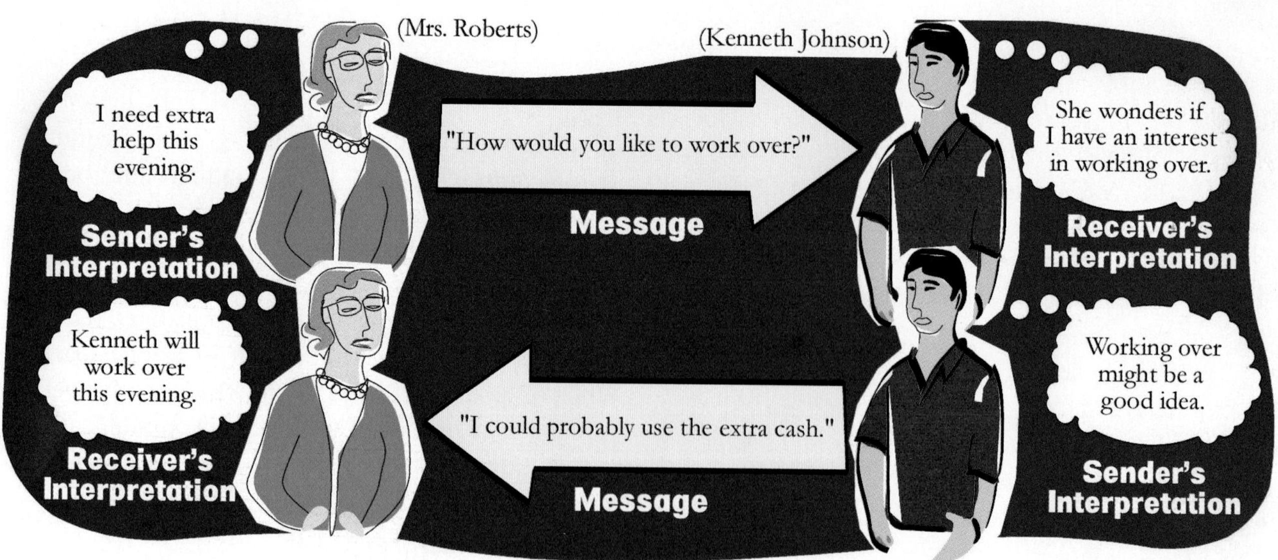

Figure 7.1 The understanding of both the sender and receiver in a communication.

© JIST Works

As individuals, we are unique, and this uniqueness can affect what we say, how we say it, and how others receive it. In the communication between Mrs. Roberts and Kenneth, the message sent and the message received are vastly different and could cause serious problems between the communicators unless they communicate further.

Communication involves knowledge of words, beliefs, attitudes, and values. You can increase understanding and reduce misunderstanding considerably by using common terms of reference, recognizing that unique qualities exist, and being as specific as possible.

As a high school student, you have studied grammar, spelling, vocabulary, composition, speech, and reading. These tools are all critical for effective communication. Without these tools, communicating in the world of work would be impossible. If you learn effective communication skills in high school, you will avoid embarrassment and job limitations after you are employed.

Workers spend most of their job time using some form of communication. They communicate with customers and with one another about procedures and problems. Communication is an integral part of every industry and business in the United States. It is central to the smooth operation of an organization. Vocational research indicates that only job knowledge ranks above communication skills as a factor in career success. Sometime in your career you will be expected to write, listen, and interact with coworkers and management. You may be asked to speak in front of a group. Will you be prepared?

Enrichment

Assign the roles of manager, clerk, and baker to three students. Have the clerk and baker leave the room. Ask the manager to read this order: "Mr. Green ordered a large, white tray cake. He wants 'Happy 10th Birthday, Paul' written on it with blue icing." Next, ask the clerk to reenter the room. Have the manager give the order from memory. Then call in the baker and have the clerk give the order to the baker from memory. How has the order changed? Stress the importance of accurate communications on the job.

Video Tour on DVD

Show students the Chapter 7 segment to introduce them to the content.

Section 1: The Magic of Language: Understanding

Your skill at expressing your thoughts and understanding the expressed thoughts of others is directly related to your knowledge of words, their meaning, and their usage. The relationship between a word and what it refers to is a mental one. A word has no real meaning of its own apart from the uses people give it.

The effective use of the English language in written and oral communication is very important for success in the workplace. On every continent and in nearly every time zone, English is the most commonly used language in the international world of work. It is the native language of more than 500 million people and is the most widely used second language in the world. Standard Chinese is spoken by more people (1,075,000,000), but no language on the globe can match English for the diversity of places where it can be understood.

TAKE NOTE

The combination of a rapidly growing global economy and increasing worldwide Internet usage is creating a small explosion in the employment market for language translators and interpreters. Successful translators and interpreters are proficient in their native language, a foreign language, and have a thorough understanding of the foreign culture. If you have a strong interest in a language career, be aware that the 10 most widely spoken languages in the world are Mandarin Chinese (more than a billion speakers), English (514 million speakers), Hindustani (496 million speakers), Spanish (425 million speakers), Russian (275 million speakers), Arabic (256 million speakers), Bengali (215 million speakers), Portuguese (194 million speakers), Malay-Indonesian (176 million speakers), and French (129 million speakers).

Choosing the Right Style of English

Using modern English to communicate effectively in the workplace requires knowledge of the different varieties of usage and traditions of

Different situations require the use of different styles of English.

Cooperative Learning

Divide the class into small groups. Assign one of the photos on this page to each group. Ask each group to write a conversation that would be appropriate for the people in the photo. Next, have each group read or role-play their conversations to the class. Ask the class whether the English style is correct and appropriate.

Enrichment

Explain to your students that *buzzwords* are particular words or phrases used by every business or industry and that they have little or imprecise meaning to outsiders. Ask your students to list a group they belong to and any special buzzwords they use to communicate within the group. Conclude the activity by explaining the importance of avoiding a miscommunication by not using buzzwords outside the group.

style, especially the informal, general, and formal styles. Informal, general, and formal English blend together to make up what is known as standard English. Informal English is spoken more often than written and includes words related to a particular occupation, slang, and other everyday words. General English is both written and spoken and is used in talks to general audiences, conversations, and most business letters. Formal English is more often written than spoken and is used to write formal essays, literature, scientific or professional articles, and college term papers.

Your use of English sends a message about you to other people. Your language skills and the style of English you use are a large part of the message you send. It is your responsibility to be perceived in a positive way. Which form of the English language do you use most frequently? What percentage of your verbal communication time is spent using each style of English? What percentage of your written communication time is spent using each?

Improving Your Vocabulary

Your **recognition vocabulary** contains the words you understand when you read them or hear them spoken. One expert estimates that there are 24,000 words in the recognition vocabulary of the average child entering the first grade. This number is thought to increase by 5,000 words per year. If you are average, your recognition vocabulary will include at least 80,000 words by the time you leave high school.

© JIST Works

Your **active vocabulary** contains the words you use in your speech or writing. It is estimated to be somewhere between 25 and 33 percent of the size of your recognition vocabulary. This means that you probably use somewhere between 20,000 and 30,000 words in your active vocabulary. Does this number seem high or low to you?

Having an adequate vocabulary is an important part of career success, but how do you determine what an adequate vocabulary is? One way is to consider any difficulty you have expressing yourself to others in school, at work, or in social situations. Have you ever been in a situation in which you said, "I know what I mean, but I can't put it into words"? If so, you probably need to increase your vocabulary in that area of your life. The most natural way to do this is to learn new information.

Learning new information is often a part of everyday life. Think about the time that you learned to ride a bike or drive a car. You probably learned the meaning of several new terms during this experience, such as *right of way* and *transmission.* New vocabulary words come from every life experience, including jobs, sports, books, school subjects, and conversations with other people. Consider how many words you might add to your vocabulary by pursuing a new interest in computers, sailing, cooking, skiing, chemistry, or history.

If your choice of words is limited, your communication skills will also be limited. Increasing your understanding of words will improve your communication effectiveness. Methods frequently used for learning and recognizing the meanings of new words include using the word in a sentence and using the dictionary as a reference.

You can usually determine the meaning of a word by analyzing the whole statement in which the word is used. Consider the following examples:

- The pilot took a vacation during the fall.
- The pilot frantically pulled back on the controls during the fall.

The statement or situation in which the word *fall* is used is known as its **context.**

Beginning to use new words in your writing is usually safer than using them in conversation because you can more easily check and revise your written words. As you work to improve your vocabulary, choose new words for their usefulness, not their impressiveness. After all, the goal of increasing your vocabulary is to improve your communication skills.

Vocabulary Builder

Clip a controversial statement from an article concerning work or workers from your daily newspaper, and write it on the chalkboard before class begins. Explain to your class that the context of a statement or word quoted is explained by the information stated immediately before or after it. Distribute copies of the article you used, and ask volunteers to quote individual words or statements from the article in a way that changes the intended meaning of the speaker.

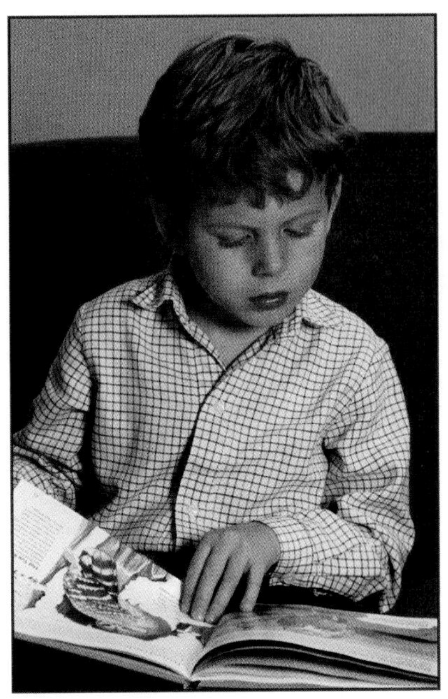

The average child entering first grade can recognize approximately 24,000 words. Are you satisfied with the number of words in your active vocabulary?

Section 1: Get Involved

Answer the following on a separate sheet of paper, and be prepared to discuss your responses in class.

1. Among the many languages that Americans use in their daily lives are Spanish, 47 million; Chinese, 2 million; French, 1.6 million; German, 1.4 million; Tagalog (Philippines), 1.3 million; and Russian, more than 700,000. However, the predominant language is English. Should all U.S. students be required to study more than one language, as students are required to do in Canada? Why or why not?
2. Use a standard unabridged dictionary to look up the word career. What part of speech is it? What is its derivation? Identify its meanings, synonyms, and antonyms.

© JIST Works

I know you believe you understand what you think I said, but I am sure you realize that what you heard is not what I meant.

—Anonymous

Section 2: Speaking, Listening, and Responding

Speaking, listening, reading, and writing are related, overlapping skills. The failure to master any one skill is likely to affect the others. How would an employer rate your speaking, listening, and responding skills?

Speaking

Discussion Starter

Ask your students: If you were physically unable to speak, what positive or negative effect might it have on your ability to

- Learn reading and writing skills?
- Listen and respond if you were a rescue worker?
- Read instructions if you were a machinist?
- Write if you were a reporter in a noisy office?

Most communication between people is accomplished the same way today as it was 2,000 years ago: It is spoken. Speaking skills are important for expressing your opinions, asserting yourself, and defending your rights in your personal life as well as in the world of work. Through conversation, discussion, debate, and lecturing, the spoken word continues to be used more often than any other form of communication.

Correct or incorrect usage of language is a habit. Frequently, we know better when we use incorrect language, but we don't always pay attention to the correctness of what we are saying. As an example, listen to Betty Brunson's job interview at the W.J. Hardware Store:

> **Owner:** What would you say to a customer who asks for a brand of paint we don't stock?
>
> **Betty:** Well, I think you oughta show 'em what we got and tell 'em how good it works. Ours is prob'ly better anyhow.

Stop the interview right here! If you were the owner of the store, would you have a problem with Betty's communication? If so, why? Would you correct Betty or simply ignore her incorrect speech and not hire her? Why?

Vocabulary Builder

Send a volunteer writer to the chalkboard. Ask the writer to make a heading titled "Vague words." Ask the class to provide the writer with vague words that are commonly used by young adults. Next, ask individual students to use a word from the list in a sentence that should be clearly understood by young coworkers. Ask another student to use the same word in a sentence that could easily be misunderstood by older coworkers.

Some words are vague, and their usage increases the possibility of communication errors. Vague words are open to personal interpretation and miscommunication. Consider the following conversation between two 11th grade students attending Amity High School:

> **Margo:** My parents are cool with me having the car on Friday night. Do you want to check out the game with me?
>
> **Zoe:** Yeah, that'd be okay. Maybe we'll see Jerome there. He's so hot.

The words *cool, check out, okay,* and *hot* are very general and fail to convey an exact meaning. Vague words of this type are more likely to be used in conversation than in writing. Using vague words to provide important job instructions could have disastrous results.

© JIST Works

Workers have different styles of *verbal communication* (speaking) and **nonverbal communication** (facial expressions and body posturing). In the workplace, effective oral communication skill requires an understanding of the meaning of voice **inflection** (a change in tone or pitch) and *body language* (thoughts or feelings communicated by posturing of the body).

Employees who lack proficiency in oral communication and listening skills cost employers millions of dollars each year in lost productivity and errors. Contributing to meetings, resolving conflicts, and providing meaningful *feedback* (a reaction or response to what is said) all require effective oral communication and listening skills.

People fail to get along because they fear each other. They fear each other because they don't know each other. They don't know each other because they have not properly communicated with each other.

—Martin Luther King, Jr.

Solving the Problem: It Pays to Listen

Angela Dawson is a very competent worker on an automobile assembly line. She normally speaks with a soft voice and pleasant tone. Last week, she began noticing occasional minor defects in the auto body parts passing her workstation.

Brent Johnson is Angela's supervisor. Brent normally speaks with a firm, authoritarian voice. He is conducting a meeting with the 14 workers who report to him. Let's listen to part of the meeting:

> **Brent:** I have a letter from the plant manager praising the quality of the body parts being assembled on our line. Let me read it to you.

Angela places her hand over her eyes and shakes her head back and forth while Brent reads the letter. Brent is busy reading to the workers and doesn't notice their nonverbal reactions.

> **Brent** (looking around the group): What are your feelings about the quality level of our products?
>
> **Angela** (quietly): I've been noticing lately that…
>
> **Betty** (loudly): I think we're doing a great job. The company should share more of the profit with us.

When other workers begin supporting Betty's point of view, Angela shakes her head back and forth and sits quietly. Brent changes the subject to the financial difficulty the company has faced due to competition from foreign automobile makers.

A year later, several thousand new autos, with body parts assembled by Brent's team, develop rust marks on the defective area that Angela noticed. Angela's inability to communicate her message to the rest of her team and the team's inability to recognize her attempt to communicate were costly mistakes for all concerned.

Key to Success

Say "Good morning" or another appropriate greeting to a coworker you don't know very well. Shaking hands and introducing yourself are good ways to learn another person's name. The next time you meet, make a point of greeting your coworker by name.

CAREER FACT

Good reading, writing, and verbal communication skills and the ability to work effectively with people are important in all occupations.

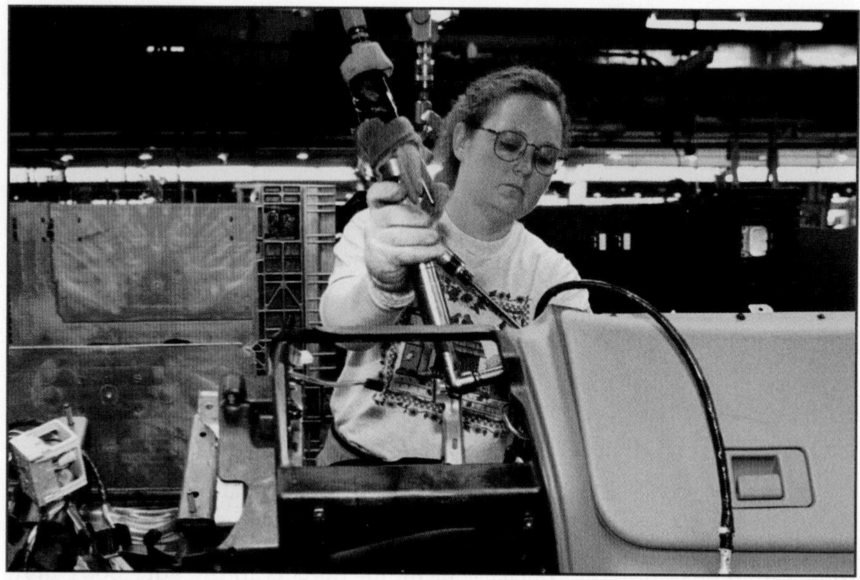

Critical Thinking

Could Brent have prevented this situation? If so, how?
What could Angela have done to communicate her views?
What value did Angela's team place on her ideas?
What would you have done in Angela's place?

School-to-Work Transition

Explain to the students that using positive body language is an important skill for both seeking and holding a job. Stress the importance of eye contact, body posture, and facial expressions. Place a chair in the front of the room and ask for volunteers to use nonverbal behaviors to communicate the following feelings: enthusiasm, boredom, high interest, agreement, disagreement, confusion, and understanding.

Enrichment

Have students complete the "Body Language—What Does It Mean?" worksheet in Chapter 7 of the *Preparing for Career Success Student Activity Book, Third Edition.*

Nonverbal Communication

You've likely heard the expression that actions speak louder than words. When you speak to someone and when someone speaks to you, you send and receive both verbal and nonverbal messages. Sometimes, you convey your meaning without using words at all. You express your meaning by gestures, facial expressions, and voice inflections. The reactions of others to your trustworthiness, expertise, or character rely not only on what is said, but also on how it is said.

The message you send with your voice may depend on your voice inflection. How would the following speakers use different inflections?

Situation: A football game.
Message: "He's running for a touchdown."

Speaker 1: An excited student from the runner's school.
Speaker 2: A discouraged player on the other team.
Speaker 3: A student who can't believe the runner could make the team, much less run for a touchdown.

Expressions such as smiling when happy and crying or looking dejected when sad are almost universal. Most people respond favorably to a person with an attractive and spontaneous smile, and they respond

© JIST Works

unfavorably to someone whose smile seems forced or phony.

Body language must be interpreted as it relates to different situations. To become more aware of body language, observe those around you. Try to analyze the nonverbal behaviors you observe. Do you interpret a person standing with his arms crossed as cold and unreceptive? How about someone with clenched hands and crossed legs? Are these gestures of suspicion? Do hands on hips indicate readiness? Does it seem as though a person is really interested in what you are saying when she leans forward and looks in your eyes when talking with you? What about when someone leans back and ignores your eyes? Most people use these and many more nonverbal signs to reinforce the meaning of the spoken word.

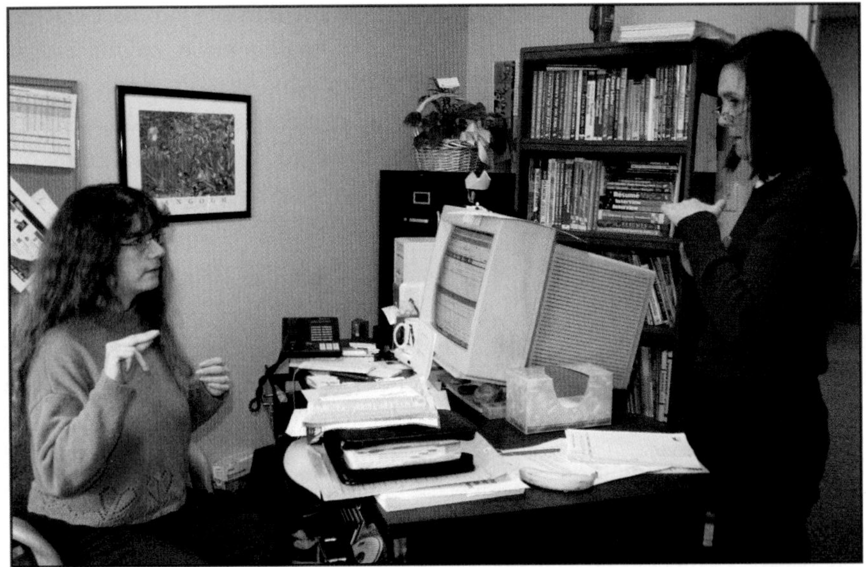

Using facial expressions, employing hand movements, and maintaining eye contact help Anna to express the meaning of her thoughts through sign language.

Listening

Don't assume that everything you say or everything you hear is clearly understood. In the role of listener, you are continually exposed to various kinds of listening, all requiring your attention. In the workplace, it is important to listen for content, long-term meaning, and emotional meaning and to follow directions.

When you are listening to a speaker, always pay particular attention to words such as *never*, *always*, *all*, *none*, *everyone*, and *no one*. These words assume 100 percent exactness. Listen with doubt to a speaker who forgets that information can be incorrect and subject to revision. Listen with distrust to someone who states opinions as though they were facts.

When the eyes say one thing and the tongue another, a practiced man relies on the language of the first.

—Ralph Waldo Emerson

Good listening demands alert and active participation and is developed through training and practice. You receive messages based on your personal expectations and feelings. Therefore, you must be careful not to read unintended ideas into the message you hear. Your interpretation of a verbal message depends on your interpretation of the words spoken, on the speaker's body language, and sometimes on your previous relationship with the speaker.

Effective communication exists when the receiver interprets the sender's message in the same way as the sender intended it. Miscommunication occurs when the message sent does not accurately describe the speaker's intention. Continuous checking is required to ensure accurate understanding. One technique for checking the speaker's meaning is to rephrase the speaker's statement in your own words and then ask, "Is that what you meant?"

Enrichment

Have students complete the "Are You a Good Listener?" worksheet in Chapter 7 of the *Preparing for Career Success Student Activity Book, Third Edition.*

© JIST Works

Reteaching

Have students complete the "Effective Listening Techniques" worksheet in Chapter 7 of the *Preparing for Career Success Instructor's CD-ROM, Third Edition.*

Case Study

Have students read the case study "It Pays to Cooperate" in Chapter 7 of the *Preparing for Career Success Instructor's CD-ROM, Third Edition* and discuss the "Critical Thinking" questions.

School-to-Work Transition

Ask your students: What occupations would require excellent listening skills? For each occupation a student identifies, ask how listening skills would be used by a worker with this occupation.

CAREER FACT

Unpleasant relationships in the workplace are frequently caused by poor communication.

Reteaching

Have students complete the "Paraphrase That Phrase" worksheet in Chapter 7 of the *Preparing for Career Success Instructor's CD-ROM, Third Edition.*

Many barriers can block effective listening. They include interrupting, not paying attention, having a closed mind, daydreaming, reacting emotionally to what is said, putting down the speaker, and being argumentative. Annoyances can also block effective listening. They include the ring of a cell phone, conversations going on around you, the way you feel, and being seated where it is difficult to hear the speaker.

Responding

Have you ever been told, "I might as well be talking to a brick wall!" If so, you were probably not responding in a way that showed that you understood what was being said. A person who is speaking expects feedback from the listener to show that what he or she is saying is understood. Learning to respond effectively is an important part of the communication process.

Most listening and speaking occur in social conversation, which can be both the easiest and yet the most difficult way to communicate with others. In social conversation, we switch from the role of listener to that of speaker over and over. Active participation from both the speaker and the listener is required at all times. Observe how Janet and Fred continually reverse roles in Figure 7.2.

Have you ever been in a conversation in which both participants took the role of speaker or listener at the same time? What effect did this have on the communication?

In one-to-one verbal communication, you can follow the effects that your words have on the other person by carefully observing his or her body language and verbal responses. The ability to understand another person's feelings and motives is called **empathy**.

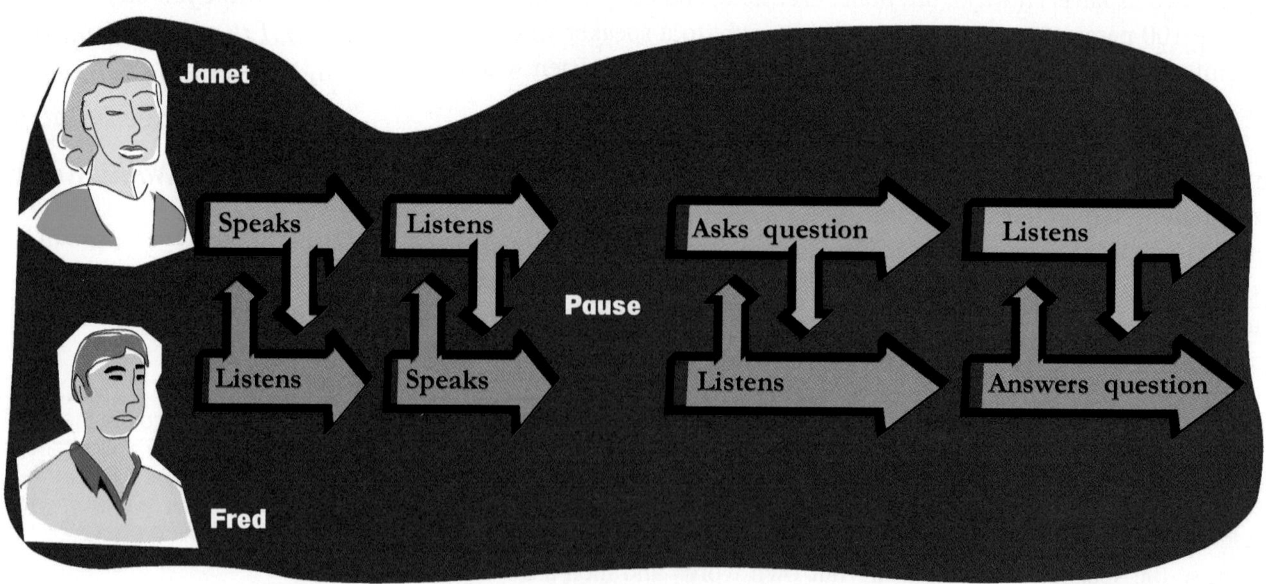

Figure 7.2 Roles for effective conversation.

© JIST Works

Paraphrasing is one technique used by a listener to convey interest to the speaker. It requires repeating the speaker's ideas or thoughts in your own words. Figure 7.3 shows an example of this technique.

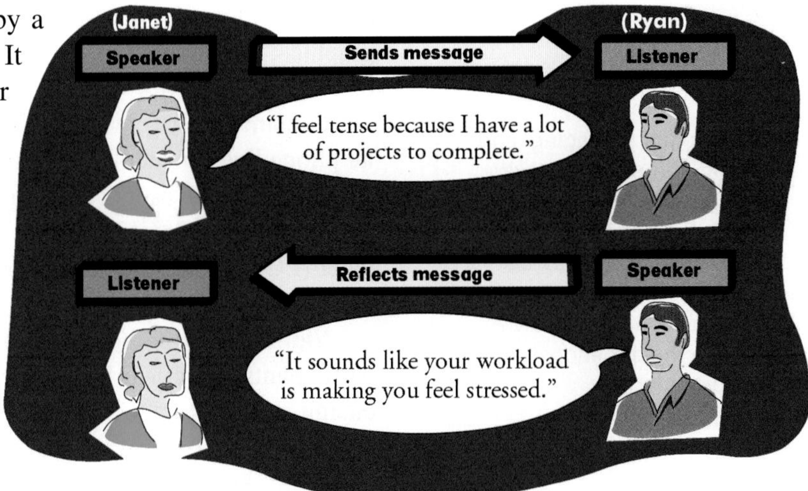

Figure 7.3 Paraphrasing.

In summary, effective listeners try to use these techniques:

1. Keep an open mind about the speaker's thoughts.
2. Listen quietly and show interest.
3. Maintain eye contact without staring.
4. Use attentive body language (usually by bending slightly forward).

5. Paraphrase when it is appropriate.
6. Listen carefully to the speaker before deciding on a response.
7. Ask questions only when certain that the speaker has finished.

Communications Technology and Business

Communications technology has made it practical for a provider of goods or services in "Small-town, U.S.A." to conduct business efficiently with a customer in "Big-town, Asia" and vice versa. It is the grease that makes the wheels of the international economy operate smoothly. Time and distance have become communication highways rather than roadblocks.

It is probable that new technology will continue to flood the market during your career, and you can expect an enormous increase in the **bandwidth** (the amount of information that can be transmitted each second over a communication channel), such as a telephone cable. Every day, spoken words, data, photographs, and graphics are exchanged using a range of carriers from ordinary copper wire to fiber-optic cables, satellites, and microwave radio signals. The demand for workers to have user skills with telecommunication equipment has skyrocketed for both small and large businesses. Which of the following business communication systems will you use in your career?

The Internet is a global network of computers linked by high-speed data lines and wireless systems. Established in 1969 as a method for military communications, it now allows individuals to connect a computer modem to vast online sources of information, from bulletin boards and discussion groups to e-mail (electronic mail) and up-to-the-minute information.

The **World Wide Web** is a *multimedia* (audio, video, graphics, and text) information storage system linking resources around the world. Browsers

Community Resources

Arrange a demonstration of communications media for your class. Your school office, library, business-office education program, or a local business would be possible resources for the demonstration.

Key to Success

The importance of understandable written and verbal communication will increase as the world continues to get smaller through advances in telecommunications technology.

Cluster Link

Are you interested in designing, developing, managing, and supporting computer hardware and software systems? Would you like to work with multimedia programs? If so, you may discover your future career in the Information Technology career cluster. See the appendix for more information.

allow highlighted words or icons, called *hyperlinks*, to display text, video, graphics, and sound on a local computer screen, no matter where the resource is located.

Facsimile (FAX) machines are used to transmit and receive, over regular phone lines, virtually any image that is on paper. FAX machines are easy to use and enable users to transmit words and images anywhere in the world within seconds. A FAX card used in an expansion slot of a personal computer (PC) enables the computer to function as a sending or receiving FAX terminal.

Videoconferencing and desktop videoconferencing enable distant participants and coworkers to conduct face-to-face meetings. Videoconferencing products let workers throughout the nation and around the world "meet" with clients and coworkers without leaving their offices. This technology saves thousands of travel miles and adds a personal dimension to phone conversations. It is especially useful for those whose jobs require regular client meetings and for managers who supervise workers in branch offices.

Community Resources

Form a committee of students to contact the local telephone company, and arrange for a speaker. Give the committee a list of convenient dates and times. Tell the students that the public relations department is a good place to begin. Students should describe the communications unit they are studying and request a speaker who is qualified to discuss telephone communication skills in the business world.

Digital media are rapidly replacing many printed and graphic information sources and increasing the capacity for storage. Compact discs (CDs) are less costly to produce and easy to customize for a user's equipment.

Voice mail, another communications technology, provides a barrier between a telephone caller and the person receiving a call. Whether you are job hunting or asking a friend to go to a Friday evening football game, the only choice you have is to leave a message on the machine and hope it is worth a return call. When you leave a phone message, always include your phone number, the day of the week, and the time. Make it easy for the person to return your call.

Like voice mail, Voice over Internet Protocol (VoIP) is simply a verbal e-mail. Using this technology, voice calls are carried over computer networks. VoIP costs less than traditional phone service because it rides on data networks and doesn't require the costly switches and other equipment necessary for a circuit-based network. Internet telephony also is free of the numerous regulations, fees, and charges applied to regular phone calls.

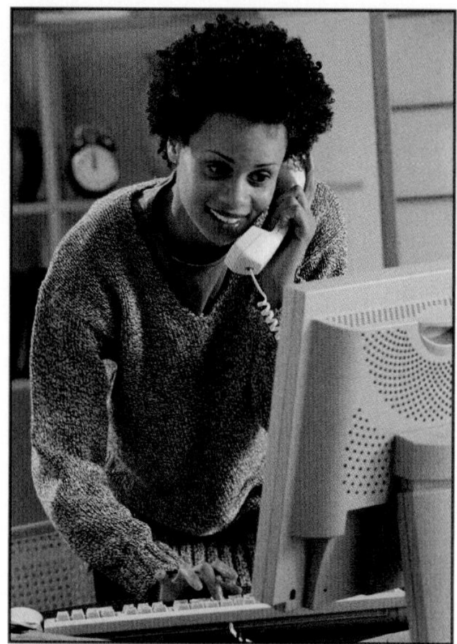

Using good telephone manners projects a positive image of your organization to the listener.

Even the telephone, more than a century old, has adapted and become a survivor of the high-tech revolution. Whether it is a cellular phone tucked into your purse or pocket, a portable phone carried around the office or home, or a phone simply fastened to your desk or computer with a wire, it's still the workhorse of the business world. The telephone is used to communicate or exchange information with customers and prospects, suppliers, colleagues, branch offices, and sales staff. In fact, just about everywhere in the world, the telephone supports business growth. By providing a regular communication alternative, it multiplies the effectiveness of face-to-face contact.

Every employee in a company who has contact with customers or potential customers is in a position to contribute to the company's sales effort. On the other hand, employees are also in a position to hurt sales and damage the company's image. Employers provide communications training for employees to achieve the following goals.

© JIST Works

Good Telephone Manners

Most employers are well aware that dollars of profit can be lost through their phone lines because of an employee who lacks communication skills. Inadequate interpersonal relationships and telephone manners lose more sales than inferior products or services. When used correctly, the telephone provides an effective means to speak, listen, and respond. Use the following guidelines:

- When making telephone calls, always identify yourself and the company you represent. With a business associate you call frequently, drop the name of your company, but still identify yourself by name, no matter how many times a day you speak to one another.
- Be certain you know the name and title of the person you are calling. Most people like to be addressed by their name and title.
- When you answer the telephone, identify yourself by name, organization, and department.
- Speak into the phone with a clear, normal voice. A loud telephone voice may disturb others in your office as well as the listener.
- Be courteous and alert, and respond in a positive manner, even when the circumstances are trying.
- Don't talk too long. In the business world, time is money, so don't waste it.
- Make notes before and during an important call.
- Remember that umm, uh-huh, and ah are not Standard English words.

- Get the maximum sales potential from each customer contact.
- Assess the satisfaction level of existing customers.
- Handle angry customers and resolve customer conflicts.
- Improve the company's image and make good impressions.
- Manage contact time effectively.

Whatever the communication equipment, keep in mind that every time you communicate with a customer, your communication can make or break a sale and affect the public image of your company. It can also cause a task to be completed efficiently or can disrupt progress within the organization. Skills that enable you to communicate effectively, solve problems quickly, and reflect a positive image will make you a successful employee in a successful organization (see the Retail/Wholesale Sales and Service career cluster in the appendix).

Discussion Starter

Ask your students: Who can describe a time when they were pleased or annoyed by an unsolicited telephone salesperson? After a few examples, ask the following question: The federal government and some states place restrictions on telemarketers. Should salespeople be permitted to make unsolicited telephone sales calls to a private residence? Why or why not?

Student Evaluation

To evaluate student mastery of concepts, you might want to use the Section 1-2 quiz in the Chapter 7 file of the *Preparing for Career Success Instructor's CD-ROM, Third Edition.*

Section 2: Get Involved

Answer the following on a separate sheet of paper, and be prepared to discuss your responses in class.

1. Observe the body language of close friends as they talk to one another. What are they doing with their arms, legs, hands, and feet as they talk? What do their nonverbal behaviors seem to mean?
2. What types of communications technologies have you used? What was the situation? What form of communications technology would be valuable in your future career? Why?
3. Imagine that you suddenly become deaf. How would you learn? Would you be able to follow through with your present career plans? Would being deaf change your personality? If yes, how? If no, why not? How would you communicate with your friends, family, and coworkers?
4. How do you rate as a listener? Ask two friends and two family members how they would rate you as an effective listener on a scale of 1 to 10, with 10 being outstanding and 1 being very poor. What can they suggest to improve your communication with them?

© JIST Works

Career Fact

According to the Business Roundtable, a national association of CEOs that surveyed 120 companies with 8 million employees, two-thirds of American employees have some writing responsibility. In addition, 80 percent of large companies take writing skills into account when hiring, and 50 percent consider writing skills when making promotions.

Section 3: Writing and Reading

Writing is a very important job skill. It is still the most often used method of communicating policies, procedures, and concepts. Effective workplace writing relies on these five factors:

- Carefully sorting out the facts (*analysis*)
- Figuring out the general idea (*conceptualization*)
- Combining all of the parts to develop written material (*synthesis*)
- Eliminating unnecessary words and ideas (*distillation*)
- Making your point in a short, clear statement (*succinct articulation*)

Words should be picked carefully in written communication. Remember, there is no voice or body language to convey your meaning. Consequently, it is a good idea to test whether your written words are understood by reading what you have written as a stranger might. If the meaning is so clear that your words can be understood without hearing them said, you have done a good job.

Spelling

Writing is a valuable job skill. Do you enjoy writing letters to family or friends?

Correct spelling is essential for successful communication in the world of work. However, most workers do make occasional spelling mistakes. The English alphabet of 26 letters can produce more than 40 sounds. This makes the spelling of some words very difficult. Three of the letters, *c*, *q*, and *x*, duplicate the work of other letters. Therefore, the other 23 letters alone or in combinations must represent all of the sounds. Examples include *sh, ea,* and *th.*

The vowels *(a, e, i, o, u)* create the most spelling problems. Consider the different vowel sounds created by the letter *a* in the words *lap, far, fare, was, lay,* and *many.*

Study the following tips to improve your spelling:

1. Pronounce words accurately. *Surprise*, not *suprise*.
2. Visualize the word before you spell it.
3. Use difficult words in a sentence. This technique will help you remember them.
4. Learn to spell words correctly as soon as you hear or read them.
5. Practice spelling words that are hard to keep separate, such as *there* and *their* or *peace* and *piece*.

© JIST Works

6. Keep a dictionary or pocket-size spell-checker handy. Use it when you have doubts about the spelling of a word.

CAREER FACT

A survey by the College Board's National Commission on Writing reports that a majority of U.S. employers say about one third of workers do not meet the writing requirements of their positions. Businesses are crying out; they need to have people who write better.

Proofreading

The average worker could greatly improve in the use of correct grammar, sentence and paragraph construction, and punctuation. Such improvement requires simply a commitment to proofreading and correcting.

Use the following techniques for proofreading and refining written materials:

1. Read the final copy for logic, meaning, clarity, and interest.
2. Read it again for good sentence structure and punctuation.
3. Check for typographical errors, misspellings, precise word choice, agreement of subjects and verbs, correct tense of verbs, and agreement of pronouns and their antecedents.
4. Compare the final copy to the final draft. Have someone read aloud the final draft as you check the final copy, or lay the two copies side by side and follow both copies with your index fingers as you compare them word by word.

School-to-Work Transition

Send a volunteer to the chalkboard and have him or her number from 1 to 10. Ask students to name 10 occupational titles for the writer to list. When the list is completed, ask the students: How would each worker on the list use writing and spelling skills? Which occupation would require the highest level of writing and spelling skill? Why? Which occupation would require the lowest level? Why?

Business Writing

The writing of business letters, memorandums, and reports is not confined to the workplace. You have had to write reports using proper English since elementary school, and practically everyone must occasionally write a business letter or e-mail.

Two thirds of American employees have some writing responsibility. With keyboards replacing face-to-face communication, people are writing more than ever. Employers need workers who write well, and this requires proficiency in using the English language.

E-mail has become an essential means of business and personal communications. Almost 3 billion e-mails are transmitted worldwide every day. Most offices use e-mail for interoffice communications although some still rely on written notes called **memorandums** (memos). See the sample memo in Figure 7.4.

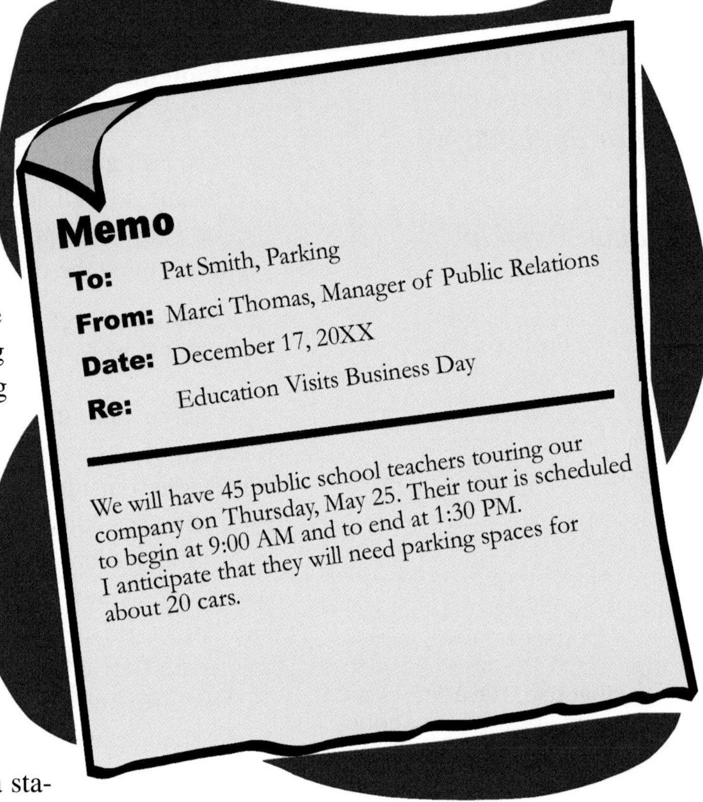
Memo
To: Pat Smith, Parking
From: Marci Thomas, Manager of Public Relations
Date: December 17, 20XX
Re: Education Visits Business Day

We will have 45 public school teachers touring our company on Thursday, May 25. Their tour is scheduled to begin at 9:00 AM and to end at 1:30 PM. I anticipate that they will need parking spaces for about 20 cars.

Figure 7.4 Many employers use the memo format for interoffice e-mail communications.

Not long ago, having an e-mail address was a status symbol, a sign that you were on the cutting edge of advancing technology. Now, you're considered to be out of the loop if you

KEY TO SUCCESS

E-mail can help you be efficient at work; it can also get you fired if you use it inappropriately. Many employers monitor their employees' e-mail to check whether it is being misused. Find out what your employer's policies on e-mail use are, and make sure that your messages are always professional.

Comprehension Check

Ask the students to turn their attention to the sample memo in Figure 7.4. Ask your students: How is the memo similar to a letter? How is the memo different from a letter?

If you would not be forgotten as soon as you are dead, either write things worth reading or do things worth writing.

—Benjamin Franklin

Enrichment

Invite the school principal or another school administrator to speak to your class about the importance and everyday use of the written word in school administration. Ask the speaker to bring copies of e-mails or memos he or she has written in the past. Ask the speaker to conclude by providing information for an e-mail he or she would like your class to write for actual use. Have the class use the seven skills on this page to write the e-mail.

don't have an e-mail address. Having access to e-mail and learning how to use it effectively are two different things, however.

The speed and informality of e-mail may encourage you to dash off haphazard notes. This method may be acceptable with friends and family, but it conveys the wrong image when used to communicate with colleagues, superiors, clients, and suppliers. In a fast-paced workplace, it is important to think before you write. Following are the most sought-after skills for e-mail, reports, and presentations:

- **Accuracy:** Be specific. Don't use vague terms such as "See you next Wednesday." A better choice would be to write "Meet you at 4 p.m. on Wednesday April 2 at the Pizza Parlor Restaurant on Main Street."
- **Clarity:** Use familiar, everyday words to ensure that your message is easily understood. E-mail places a mask over the other person's facial expressions, hand gestures, and verbal inflections that could otherwise communicate meaning in spoken conversations.
- **Brevity:** Use as few words as possible without losing the objective(s) of your communication. Keep e-mail messages to a single topic. Put the key point of the message in the first sentence, and put the action you're planning or requesting in the second sentence. If the value of the message isn't obvious, don't send it.
- **Spelling:** Correct spelling is essential for workplace communications.
- **Punctuation:** Use standardized punctuation marks to separate sentences or sentence sections or to make the meaning clearer.
- **Correct grammar:** Follow the accepted standards for writing. Use a business English book and dictionary, or use the grammar checker on your word-processing program. Don't allow brevity and clarity to undermine the correctness of your communications.
- **Proofreading:** Always proofread your e-mail before clicking the Send button.

A large and important part of business is transacted through the exchange of business letters. A **business letter** is a written document sent to someone outside an organization. It is usually formal in appearance, style, and tone. Some of the most common types of business letters are application, order, inquiry, reply, recommendation, introduction, claim, adjustment, acknowledgment, appreciation, collection, congratulation, and sales letters. Business letters may communicate good news or bad news to the reader. They are not written for reasons of friendship.

The form and appearance of business letters are very important. Most businesspeople use the following guidelines when preparing business letters:

1. Center the letter on the page, and frame it with adequate margins.

© JIST Works

2. Separate the various parts of the letter from one another with extra spacing: two lines between the return address and the inside address, between the inside address and the salutation, between the salutation and the body, and between the body and the complimentary close.
3. Take care when writing the opening sentence. It sets the tone for the entire message.
4. Type the letter on the company or organization's stationery.

Figure 7.5 shows the 10 main parts of a business letter.

Key to Success

Take pride in everything you write. Train yourself to proofread your work, and correct mistakes to meet the expectations of the most discriminating employers.

Reading

The average employee spends one and a half to two hours per workday reading forms, charts, graphs, manuals, computer terminals, e-mails, memos, letters, reports, signs, and bulletin boards. These reading tasks require the successful worker to

- **Monitor** (check for accuracy) his or her understanding of the reading task.
- *Summarize* information (identify the main parts of the topic).
- Be *analytical* (examine the separate parts of the topic).

How would you rate your ability to read? Excellent? Average? Below average? Reading is a complex process requiring many skills in order to understand and interpret ideas symbolized in writing. Reading the sports page of the daily newspaper for pleasure and reading the operator's manual for a complex machine do not require the same level of reading skill or concentration.

Skimming is a method used to get a quick, general impression of printed material. Although this method provides only a shallow understanding of written information, it can help you use your reading time efficiently. Take time now to evaluate your skimming and reading comprehension skills.

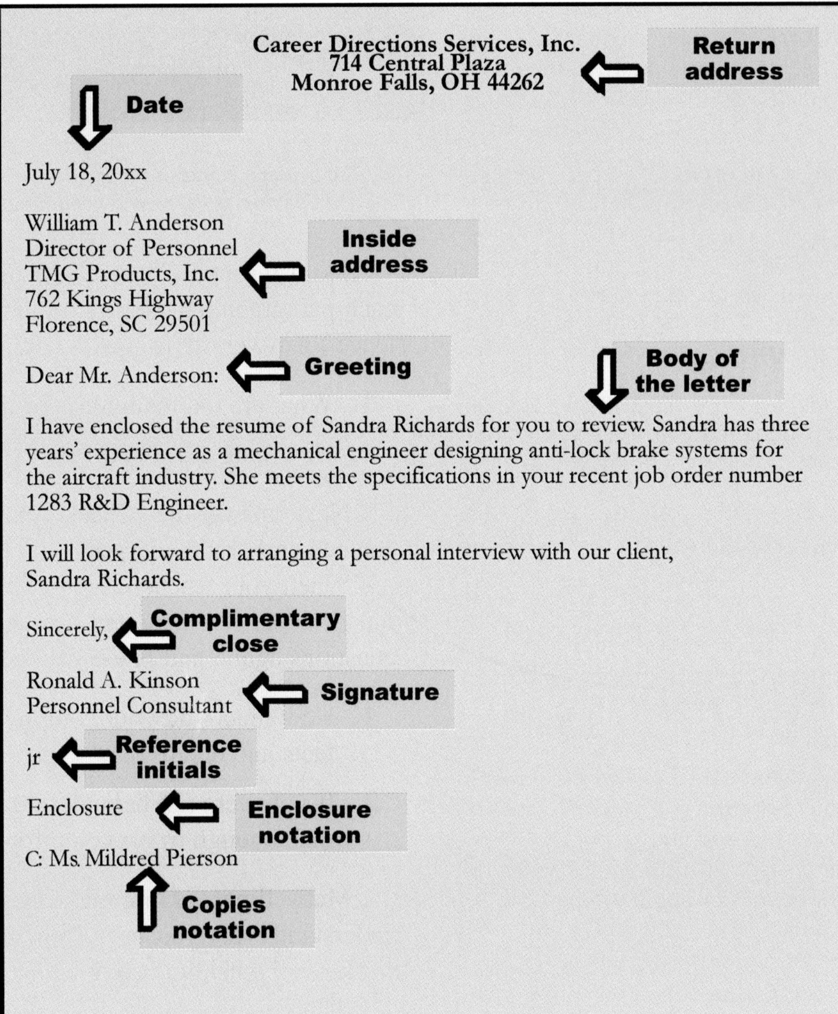
Career Directions Services, Inc.
714 Central Plaza
Monroe Falls, OH 44262

July 18, 20xx

William T. Anderson
Director of Personnel
TMG Products, Inc.
762 Kings Highway
Florence, SC 29501

Dear Mr. Anderson:

I have enclosed the resume of Sandra Richards for you to review. Sandra has three years' experience as a mechanical engineer designing anti-lock brake systems for the aircraft industry. She meets the specifications in your recent job order number 1283 R&D Engineer.

I will look forward to arranging a personal interview with our client, Sandra Richards.

Sincerely,

Ronald A. Kinson
Personnel Consultant

jr

Enclosure

C: Ms. Mildred Pierson

Figure 7.5 Sample business letter.

The man who doesn't read good books has no advantage over the man who can't read them.
—Mark Twain

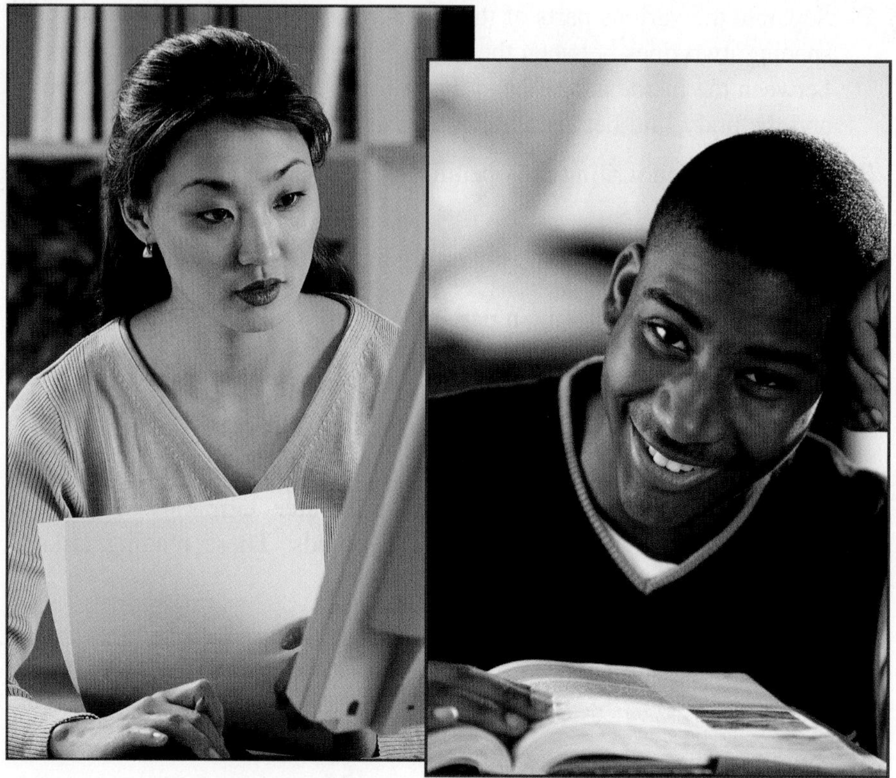

The average worker spends one and a half to two hours per workday using his or her reading skills. How much time do you spend each day using your reading skills?

Self-Understanding

Ask your students: How many situations can you think of in your everyday life when you use your ability to read? After the class develops a list of reading situations, assign the following project: During the next two days, maintain a log of the time you spend reading. Make a brief note describing each reading situation and the actual time spent reading. Explain that making frequent entries will increase the log's accuracy.

Self-Understanding

Ask your school guidance counselor, English teacher, or reading specialist to provide you with resources for remedial reading assistance. Explain to your students that having poor reading skills places a limit on the career advancement of numerous adult workers. Most of the workers with poor reading skills are embarrassed to let others know they have difficulty reading. Offer to arrange confidential reading assistance. Ask interested students to see you before or after school.

Skim through Chapter 8 of this book by reading the first sentence in each paragraph. (If the first sentence doesn't make sense, try the last sentence.) Answer the following after you have completed the chapter:

1. What are the main ideas of the chapter?
2. How long did it take you to skim the chapter?

Next, answer the "Check Your Knowledge" questions at the end of the chapter, and grade yourself.

When your teacher assigns Chapter 8 for reading, read the same material in depth for facts and details. Answer the "Check Your Knowledge" questions again, and grade yourself. Then answer these questions:

1. How much did your comprehension improve when you read for facts and details?
2. If you were not being tested, would skimming have provided you with enough information for a general understanding of the chapter?

Many times, skimming will provide all that is necessary for you to understand what you need from printed material. For example, skimming works well when you are reading newspapers and magazines.

KEY TO SUCCESS

If you are lacking in the reading skills you will need for career success, and you want to improve, talk with your teacher or counselor about ways to get extra help.

© JIST Works

Section 3: Get Involved

Complete the following activities on a separate sheet of paper. Be prepared to discuss your work in class.

1. Using the format shown in Figure 7.5, write a business letter to the public relations department of an organization you think you would like to work for in the future. Ask for information about the company's products or services. If you do not know the address of the company, ask your school or public librarian for help in locating the correct address.
2. Pair up with another student, and practice using e-mail to write business letters and memorandums. Take turns being the boss in a company, a customer, and so on. Correct each other's e-mail, and send it back. If home computers are not available, check out your school or public library.

Section 4: Improving Interpersonal Relationships

Successful interpersonal relationships are built on mutual trust, acceptance, empathy, and understanding. These four building blocks are necessary when two or more people seek common values, attitudes, and interests through personal communication.

Each of us needs to have a close relationship with someone in order to feel secure and comfortable. We need to trust and be trusted, accept and be accepted, empathize and be empathized with, and understand and be understood in that relationship. Think of a close relationship you have with someone. In what ways have you and that person expressed or demonstrated these qualities to each other? Did the importance you place on this relationship occur quickly, or did the relationship take a long time to become special? Why?

The ability to relate well with others is a characteristic of successful people in all walks of life. It is a part of the "fitting in" process at work, school, home, or play. Relating well with others doesn't require having a close personal relationship with everyone. However, it does require communicating effectively with other group members and earning their respect and acceptance.

Acceptance into a group makes people feel worthy. When you were growing up, you probably belonged to a school club, a youth organization such as Scouts, or an informal group of friends in your neighborhood. You probably didn't think about the building blocks of relationships at the time, but they were a part of being a group member. Can you remember a situation in which you wanted to fit in, but didn't—in which you wanted to be accepted, but weren't? Did it make you wonder if you would ever be accepted? Did you have doubts about your self-worth?

Case Study

Have students read the case study "Helping Brian Fit In" located in the Chapter 7 file of the *Preparing for Career Success Instructor's CD-ROM, Third Edition* and discuss the "Critical Thinking" questions.

Vocabulary Builder

Ask your students for personal examples of *mutual trust, acceptance, empathy,* and *understanding.* Next, ask the students to use each of the four terms in a sentence.

Developing Interpersonal Skills

Have you ever been in a situation in which you were able to get along well with everyone in a group except one person? As you have already learned in this chapter, effective communication is important in all

© JIST Works

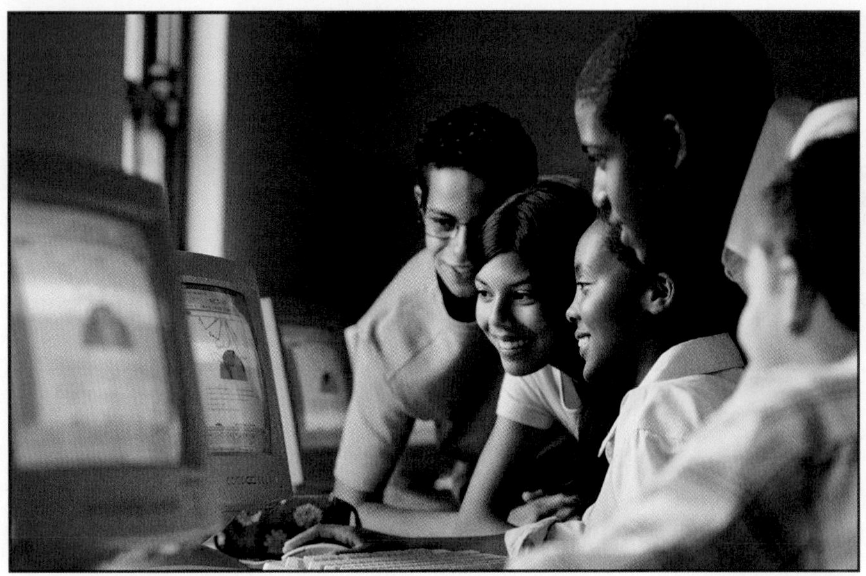

Developing your interpersonal skills and learning to work in groups are valuable in preparing for your future career.

interpersonal aspects of life. Unpleasant relationships are frequently caused by poor communication.

Interpersonal relationships are built on the understanding that grows between two or more people. Each of us tends to like people whose behavior satisfies or rewards us in someway, someone with whom we have similarities. It is easy for us to dislike people who are very different from us.

Mutual trust occurs when two people become convinced that the other person is reliable and honest. It takes several experiences with the other person over a period of time to develop trust. Think about a person that you trust, perhaps a friend, relative, or teacher. What experiences convinced you that this person is trustworthy? How much time did this take?

Self-Understanding

Instruct your students to write the name of a close friend on the top of a sheet of paper. They should then list the similarities and differences they have with their friend. Ask your students: What similarities pull you and your friend together? What differences push you apart?

Cooperative Learning

Have students complete the "Belonging to a Group" worksheet in Chapter 7 of the *Preparing for Career Success Instructor's CD-ROM, Third Edition.*

KEY TO SUCCESS

Recognizing your personal style of communication and understanding the style of other workers is important.

Belonging to a Group

Whether it is a family, clique, school class, social club, athletic team, church, musical group, employee union, political party, work team, or professional association, you will be a member of various groups throughout your life.

A group is made up of a number of people interacting with a common purpose in mind. Some groups have many rules and are highly organized; others are informal and have very few rules and little organization. However, all groups have some form of organization, rules for establishing leadership, and expectations regarding member behavior.

Effective groups have an atmosphere of equality among members. Each member has a sense of belonging, importance, and purpose. Members usually know one another on a first-name basis. Depending on the situation, leadership is frequently shared by different members of the group. Every member is a leader, and every member is a follower. Members are sensitive to the roles that other members perform and how they relate to their own particular role in the group.

Group meetings are related to the needs of members. Problems are expressed, alternatives are discussed, and solutions are arrived at through joint effort. Groups are more effective when tasks are divided among the members. Members are more likely to follow the established rules of the group and to identify with the group's goal when they are personally involved in the process of group communication and problem solving.

© JIST Works

Tips for Effective Group Relationships

Which four of the following tips do you practice most often? Which four tips do you practice the least?

1. Treat others with respect.
2. Be willing to listen attentively.
3. Stick to the task.
4. Don't dominate the group.
5. Think before you speak.
6. Don't be afraid to speak up.
7. Avoid making cynical remarks.
8. Apologize if you offend someone.
9. Recognize and correct your mistakes.
10. Take the initiative to participate.
11. Provide feedback to other speakers.
12. Don't prejudge other people.
13. Keep an open mind.
14. Don't be a know-it-all.
15. Cooperate with others.
16. Be open to suggestions.
17. Make suggestions to the group.
18. Evaluate all suggestions sincerely.
19. Criticize in a constructive way.
20. Tolerate differences in others.
21. Speak for yourself (say "I believe...").
22. Allow speakers time to pause and think.

Changes in the behavior of an individual frequently reflect membership in a particular group. Groups can exert considerable pressure on individual members to conform. Can you think of a group you belong to that expects you to behave in a certain way? Do you ever behave in a certain manner to please the group when you personally disapprove of the behavior?

As you will learn in Chapter 11, workers are often organized into teams so that appropriate talents and skills can be directed through group effort to accomplish important tasks and achieve goals. When the group achieves its goals, the members are more cohesive, feel more secure about their jobs, communicate more openly, and work more cooperatively.

School-to-Work Transition

Explain that learning to get along with others in group situations is important preparation for career success. Ask individual students to respond to the following questions: What's the name of a group in which you are a member? What attitudes and behaviors have you learned that cause other members of the group to accept and respect you? Will these same attitudes and behaviors influence your career success? If so, how? If not, why?

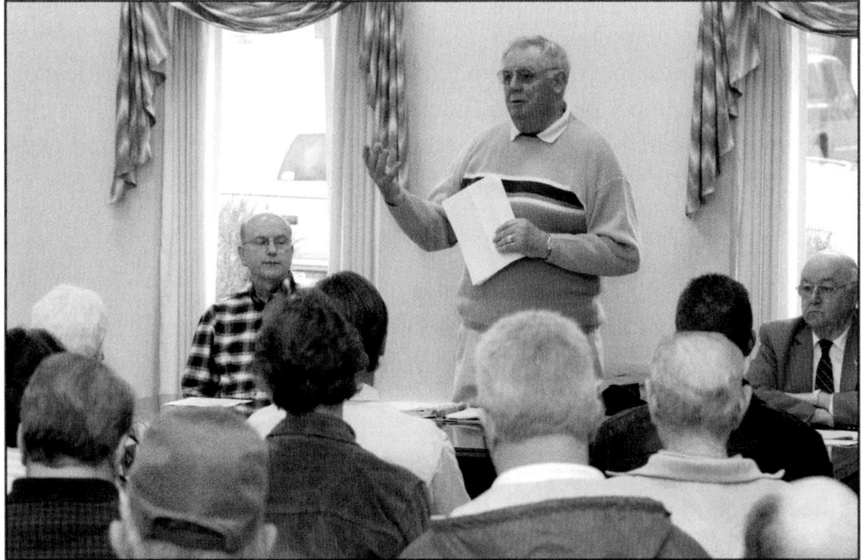

What makes a group successful?

TECHNOLOGY

Businesses use instant messaging software to help employees in different locations share information easily. Keep in mind that sending instant messages to coworkers is different than sending instant messages to friends. To be professional, you should avoid using abbreviations such as LOL or smileys such as :-).

© JIST Works

Discussion Starter

Ask your students to think about their future careers and the organizations where they will be employed. Ask them: What characteristics would you like the leader to have? Why? What characteristics would you not want the leader to have? Why?

Successful team members are aware of the skills that fellow members have, and they understand how those skills can be applied to resolve problems and make improvements. Each member of a successful work team must be able to use interpersonal and negotiation skills. Verbal feedback must be provided and received. Each individual must be able to recognize and cope with the unique personalities of other team members. Differences between team members are recognized as strengths to be added to group knowledge and skill rather than taking away from group harmony.

Understanding Leadership

"How did she ever get elected to Congress?" "He should be in jail instead of being the mayor!" "Why does a big corporation pay an idiot like him three million bucks a year to lose their money and our jobs?" If phrases like these sound familiar, that's because you have probably been listening to them and reading them all of your life. Such remarks are sometimes justified. Most of the time, however, they are based on a lack of accurate information.

The way group members speak and write, their life experiences, and the overall purposes of the group determine the way group members relate to each other and the type of leader they will accept. A feeling of mutual dependence emerges between members of the group and the leader. The relationship between those who lead and those who follow can range from very rigid control to anything goes. Each group has its own style.

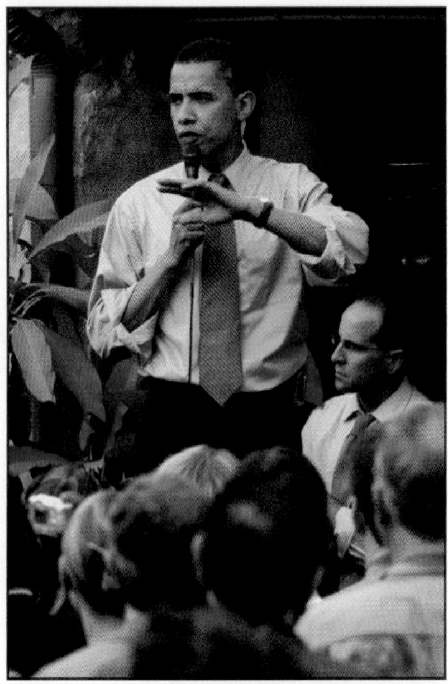

The leader of a democratic group encourages active communication among the other members. Who encourages you to communicate with others?

Democratic Groups

In a democratic group, leadership relies on the active participation of members in the decision-making process. Group members are encouraged to have active communication with their leaders. The United States Congress is an example of a group that uses the democratic style of leadership. Would a democratic group function better if the rank-and-file members were unskilled and poorly educated or highly skilled and well educated? Why?

Closed Groups

In a group with a closed system of leadership, group members are not permitted (or are at least discouraged from) active communication with the leaders. Street gangs and military governments are examples of groups with closed leadership. Would a closed system of leadership function better if the rank-and-file members were unskilled and poorly educated or highly skilled and well educated? Why?

Case Study

Have students read the case study "Who Will You Vote For?" in Chapter 7 of the *Preparing for Career Success Instructor's CD-ROM, Third Edition* and discuss the "Critical Thinking" questions.

Leaders of both democratic and closed groups are seen as having more influence than other members of the group. Successful leaders have the ability to persuade group members to accept their ideas, opinions, and orders. In addition, they have the power to delegate authority, motivate, and

© JIST Works

control their followers. The success or failure of group tasks and goals measures their credibility.

In a favorable situation, the leader enjoys good relations with other group members, the task on which the group works is successful, and the leader's power in the group is strengthened. In an unfavorable situation, the leader's relationship with other group members is poor, the task on which the group works is unsuccessful, and the leader's power in the group is weakened.

A group member may be a leader in one situation and not in another. All groups are not alike. The size of the group and its purpose are important determinants of the type and style of leadership needed. As an example, the larger the group, the more leadership it requires. Most often, leadership in an organization falls into one of two types: shared leadership or controlled leadership.

Who is the leader in this office scene? What is the reason for your conclusion?

Comprehension Check

Explain to your students that the work situation sometimes determines the type of leadership that is most effective. For example, a group of rescue workers entering a badly damaged building would probably use controlled leadership. Ask your students: What work situations can you think of in which you would prefer having shared leadership? Why? In what work situations would you prefer controlled leadership? Why?

Shared Leadership

In the shared leadership style, the leader's activities and those of the group members provide mutual satisfaction. The leader stops being a leader the moment the followers stop following. Shared leadership requires a greater ability to persuade and a greater knowledge of the job than do other leadership approaches. Group participation is encouraged. Discussion and informal planning by the whole group usually precede any important group action. Being a stakeholder in the project motivates members to make their best contribution. The leader works as a member of the group with special responsibilities for keeping the group on the right track. Individuals are encouraged to use their *ingenuity* (skill to think out new ideas), and they quickly discover that their contributions are welcomed and appreciated.

A group using shared leadership is usually cooperative and demonstrates high morale. Although the leader must **facilitate** (encourage) group performance, influential and involved members feel confident, secure, and useful.

Take Note

Throughout history, many important military battles were lost due to the death of a leader. The high degree of training and leadership ability among lower-ranking officers and noncommissioned officers is one reason for the success enjoyed by today's American military forces. When a leader is killed or wounded, another trained person quickly steps into the leadership role.

Controlled Leadership

In the controlled, or forced, leadership style, the leader uses means under his or her control to satisfy the needs of the group. The leader maintains a separate status, initiating and directing activities of the group rather than participating in them. The alternative to following this type of leader is to be punished.

Leadership is not rank, privilege, titles, or money. It's responsibility.
—Colin Powell

Military organizations and some privately owned businesses rely on forced leadership. Fear of punishment is used to maintain discipline and obedience. The leader directs with a firm hand, and the group carries out the orders (policies) but has no voice in formulating or changing them.

Those who work under a controlled type of leadership frequently develop hostile feelings toward the organization. They have no voice in running the organization, and they tend to feel a lack of responsibility for the quality of the product or service being manufactured or provided. The work will probably proceed smoothly as long as the leader is able to exert firm control. When a leader is removed from power, the group usually develops a sense of powerlessness and fails unless a new, powerful leader emerges quickly.

Paternalism (managing like a father) is a form of controlled leadership in which the leader hopes to gain the gratitude and loyalty of the group. Although many group needs are met, control and power remain with the leader.

Successful Leadership

Interpersonal relationships develop between leaders and group members in all styles of leadership. All leaders must assign tasks, come up with new ideas, seek information, give information, clarify situations, and make certain that tasks are carried out. All successful leaders

1. Influence other people. When they speak, others listen.
2. Enlist the support and cooperation of other people.
3. Communicate in a way that is clearly understood.
4. Seem fair, accessible, and honest.
5. Listen to other points of view without making judgments.
6. Accept future uncertainty without panic or unnecessary stress.
7. Interact with others to share responsibilities.
8. Set an example that inspires confidence in others.
9. Behave in a manner appropriate to the situation.
10. Accept criticism as constructive information.

Section 4: Get Involved

Answer the following on a separate sheet of paper, and be prepared to discuss your responses in class.

1. When your class has a discussion, who usually gives an opinion? Who usually asks others what they think? Who usually takes over or performs on their own?
2. If you were a leader, which leadership style would you prefer to use? Why?
3. Reread the "Tips for Effective Group Relationships." Then spend 20 minutes observing the actions of a family member or a classmate in a group situation with four or more participants. On a separate sheet of paper, record the tips you observe this person using and the number of times he or she uses each of the tips. Which tips did your subject practice the most? The least?

© JIST Works

Section 5: Resolving Conflicts

A conflict is a clash or struggle that sometimes occurs when individuals or groups have different points of view. These collisions can be at the spiritual (religious), intellectual, emotional, or physical level. Some conflicts are organized; others are not. Some are short-term (lasting a few days); others last for years. A failure to resolve the conflict by communication may lead to physical violence and long-term unresolved feelings of anger.

In all phases of social interaction, there are periods of disagreement. How often have you said, "Every time I try to talk with him, we get into an argument?" Whether it is between parents and children, siblings, friends, or coworkers, unkind words are said, feelings are hurt, and disagreements arise. Responding to these situations by expressing anger or showing irritation creates the possibility of conflict. Either of these emotions can prevent you from saying what you really feel.

Each person involved in a conflict has personal biases, priorities, expertise, and interests. They affect the points of agreement and create outright opposition on many issues. What do you do when a difference of opinion or an open conflict occurs among your family or friends? How do you feel?

Workers depend on one another to get their jobs done. When joint decisions are made, workers are expected to interact by offering ideas to the group and expressing opinions. However, new ideas, insights, and differing opinions sometimes cause friction instead of cooperation. When friction develops into conflict, strategic plans may be interrupted, and productivity lowered. Effective communication must be used to resolve the conflict.

Good friends have occasional disagreements. How do you solve personal conflicts?

Student Evaluation

To evaluate student mastery of concepts, you might want to use the Section 4 quiz in the Chapter 7 file of the *Preparing for Career Success Instructor's CD-ROM, Third Edition.*

Enrichment

Assign your students to clip newspaper or magazine articles about conflict and bring them to tomorrow's class. Next day, begin by assigning a writer to the chalkboard. Ask the writer to make four headings: Religious, Intellectual, Emotional, and Physical. Select students to read their conflict articles. Ask the class to determine which of the four categories is most related to the conflict. Ask the writer to mark the appropriate category for each conflict discussed.

Negotiation

Negotiation (bargaining by persuasion rather than argument) is one method frequently used to resolve conflicts. Negotiation can be used to resolve disputes between two or more individuals or groups.

When nations, labor unions, or individuals negotiate, they engage in a mutual trading of offers and concessions in an attempt to reach a formal agreement concerning issues of common concern. The sides have conflicting interests but share a desire for a reasonable settlement of their

Key to Success

Have you ever been involved in a lengthy discussion that turned into an argument and heard someone say, "What are we arguing about anyway? We're all saying the same things in different ways. We're arguing over nothing." Try using negotiation techniques to resolve your day-to-day personal conflicts. It is easiest to solve a minor disagreement before it grows into a major conflict.

differences. Negotiation is not successful until a solution is acceptable to both sides.

Successful negotiators begin by focusing on points of agreement to build a sense of togetherness. After points of agreement are established, major differences are identified. Unlike arguers, negotiators don't expect to win all of their points (see Table 7.1).

Whether personal or work related, most disagreements focus on the facts of a situation and do not revolve around personality conflicts. Personal communication provides the opportunity to establish and increase cooperation while resolving a conflict. However, the effect of communication depends on the nature of the conflict and the issue being communicated. Different opinions must be identified and completely disclosed; negative as well as positive feelings must be accepted. After this is done, the conflict can be examined, discussed, and studied, and a compromise can be reached.

Participants in a negotiation need to be confident, open, and honest. Sometimes, people agree in a negotiation because they are intimidated (feel threatened) by others, because they don't want to hurt another person's feelings, or simply because they want a quick end to a bad situation. Have you ever felt like this? Did you act with confidence, openness, and honesty? Did you live up to the agreement after you realized it was not consistent with your real beliefs?

Table 7.1 Negotiation Versus Argument

Negotiation	Argument
Focuses on the issues. Personal feelings and personalities are left out.	Personal feelings and emotions are frequently included.
Focuses on important interests.	Focuses on fixed positions.
Strives to propose options for mutual gain.	Strives to win a point of view.
Insists on objective information.	Presents information supporting one side of the dispute.
Relies on each participant having good interpersonal skills.	Relies on verbal domination without considering the other viewpoint.
Depends on each side openly expressing all their beliefs.	Expects the other side to accept a new set of beliefs.
Focuses on points of agreement.	Focuses on points of difference.

Community Resources

Form a committee of students to contact a labor union's negotiator. Tell the students to look under "Labor Organizations" in the telephone book. Give the committee a list of convenient dates and times for a speaker presentation. Have the committee explain the communications unit they are studying and ask for information concerning any aspect of business communication and especially negotiation versus argument.

Win or Lose

During a conflict, each side has choices. The following are types of choices you will face as you try to manage conflicts:

You can't lose.	Either choice is to your advantage. However, one choice may be more of an advantage than the other.
You can't win.	Either choice is to your disadvantage. However, one choice may be less of a disadvantage than the other.

© JIST Works

You could win or lose.	One choice is clearly to your advantage, and the other is clearly to your disadvantage.

Think of a time when you were faced with one of these three situations. If you had to make the decision over again, would you make the same choice?

A strategy is a skillful plan used to manage a situation. Professional athletes, for example, use several strategies. They practice for years to develop the skills they need to make their strategies work during a game. Studying and practicing the following strategies will help you develop the necessary skills for resolving conflicts.

Enrichment

Have students complete the "Work Teams in Action" worksheet in Chapter 7 of the *Preparing for Career Success Instructor's CD-ROM, Third Edition.*

Cooperative Learning

Divide the class into small groups. Ask each group to write a paragraph about a conflict that is real or could be real. Then have them write a role-playing skit about people trying to resolve the conflict. They may use negotiation, argument, compromise, or arbitration. Have each group read their conflict and role-play their solution for the class.

Compromise

In a **compromise**, each side gives up some of its demands and meets the other side halfway. Compromise is an important part of negotiation. It can be as simple as two children deciding to take turns or as complex as two nations deciding where to place their border.

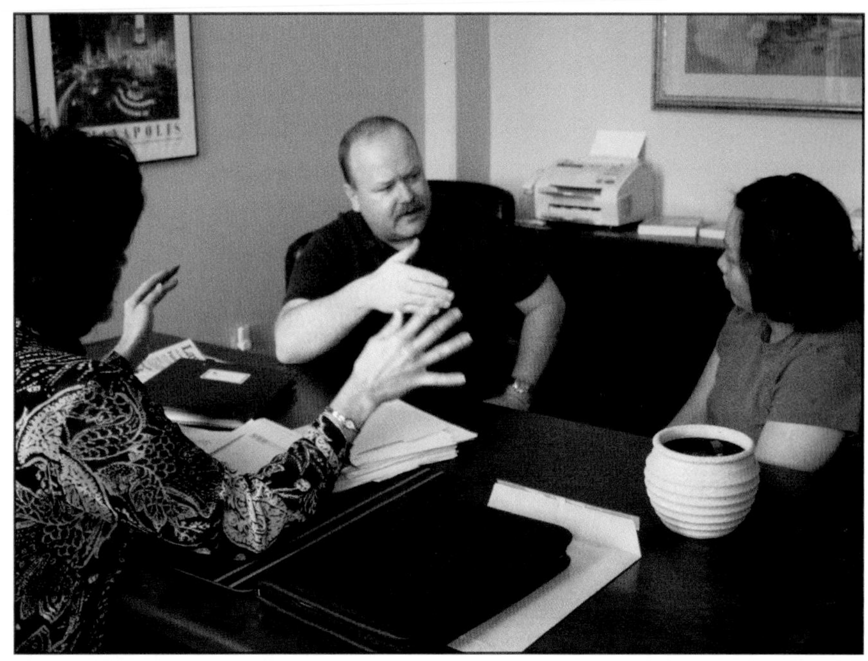

An arbitrator can help opposing groups work out a compromise.

Arbitration

In other types of conflict resolution, a third person, respected by both sides, is asked to join the discussion and give an opinion. For example, students frequently ask a teacher to enter a dispute and give an opinion. Likewise, business owners and employee groups frequently solve labor disputes by using a third-party expert called an **arbitrator**.

"I" and "You" Statements

The words *I* and *you* can mean the difference between resolving a problem and making it worse. Imagine that Mike is waiting at a red light, and Carl drives into the back of his car. Neither Mike nor Carl is hurt, but both cars have a lot of damage. The two men get out of their cars and walk toward each other. Here is The "I statement" approach:

> **Mike:** I was scared to death when I saw you in my rearview mirror. I'm glad to get out of this alive. I just bought this car last month.

Key to Success

Persuasion is not accomplished by arguing, making insulting remarks, or making the other person look foolish. If you are seeking a friendly agreement, be pleasant, respectful, and tolerant of differences.

Student Evaluation

To evaluate student mastery of concepts, you might want to use the Section 5 quiz in the Chapter 7 file of the *Preparing for Career Success Instructor's CD-ROM, Third Edition.* You can find a chapter test in the Chapter 7 file as well.

How do you think Carl will respond to these "I" statements? Note the difference in the "you statement" approach:

> **Mike:** You drove right into my new car. You could have killed us both!

How do you think Carl will respond to these "you" statements?

When an "I" statement is made, the person making the statement expresses ownership of a problem and ownership of his or her feelings. When a "you" statement is made, the person making the statement blames the other person. The speaker takes no responsibility for the problem or for his or her feelings.

Enrichment

Have students complete the "Conflict Resolution" worksheet in Chapter 7 of the *Preparing for Career Success Student Activity Book, Third Edition.*

Withdrawal

Another strategy for conflict resolution is withdrawal. It means to pull away from a volatile situation and to give the other person time to cool off before attempting to resolve the conflict. This strategy is not a cop-out. It should not be confused with surrendering and letting others take advantage of you.

Have you ever experienced a conflict in which good friends or family members were so angry that they lost their temper? An "I" statement followed by withdrawal would be an appropriate response to this situation. Try using the following example: "I would like some time to think through this situation. I feel it would be best if we discussed this later. I hope you feel the same."

Apologizing

Apologizing, another strategy, isn't necessarily a way of saying, "You're right, and I'm wrong." It may mean, "I know your feelings are hurt and you're angry, and I'm sorry about that." This approach can be a very effective way to stop a conflict before it gets out of hand. When you're in this type of situation, you might try saying

- "I feel bad about this situation."
- "I'm sorry. I really didn't want this to happen."
- "I regret this, and I hope we can put it behind us."

 © JIST Works

Section 5: Get Involved

Answer the following on a separate sheet of paper, and be prepared to discuss your responses in class.

1. Do you always have to win in a conflict? Give an example of a conflict you were involved in that supports your answer.
2. Imagine that none of your family or friends could disagree with you, and you couldn't disagree with them. How would this improve your life? How would this cause a problem for you?
3. We usually behave toward others in a manner that is similar to their past treatment of us. Can you think of a situation in which this was true for you and you behaved in a positive way? In a negative way?
4. What effect do emotions have on quarrels between friends? On disputes between parents and children? On disputes between labor and management?

Chapter 7 Review

Reteaching

Have students complete the "Checking Your Location" worksheet in Chapter 7 of the *Preparing for Career Success Student Activity Book, Third Edition.*

Enrich Your Vocabulary

On a separate sheet of paper, number from 1 to 19, and write down the most appropriate term from the "Enrich Your Vocabulary" list at the beginning of the chapter that matches each of the following phrases.

1. Understanding another person's feelings and motives
2. Third party to solve disputes
3. Informal written communication
4. The statement or situation in which a word is used
5. To encourage group performance
6. An agreement in which each side gives up some of its demands
7. Bargaining by persuasion rather than argument
8. A written document sent outside an organization
9. Meaning expressed by facial expressions and body posturing
10. Words you understand when you read them
11. A change in tone or pitch
12. Words you use in your speech
13. Repeating the speaker's ideas or thoughts in your own words
14. Sending and receiving messages and understanding and being understood
15. Check for accuracy
16. The amount of information transmitted each second over a channel or cable
17. A multimedia information system linking resources around the world

Enrich Your Vocabulary Answers

1. empathy
2. arbitrator
3. memorandums
4. context
5. facilitate
6. compromise
7. negotiation
8. business letter
9. nonverbal communication
10. recognition vocabulary
11. inflection
12. active vocabulary
13. paraphrasing
14. communication
15. monitor
16. bandwidth
17. World Wide Web

(continued)

© JIST Works

Enrich Your Vocabulary Answers *(continued)*

18. Facsimile (FAX) machines
19. Videoconferencing and desktop videoconferencing

Check Your Knowledge Answers

1. Informal English is spoken. It includes slang and words specific to certain jobs and is used in casual conversation. General English is spoken and written and is used in public speaking and business letters. Formal English is written and is mainly used in term papers and formal essays.
2. Understanding the meaning behind voice (inflection) and recognizing the meaning of body language.
3. Barriers include interrupting, not paying attention, having a closed mind, daydreaming, reacting emotionally to what is said, putting down the speaker, and being argumentative. Annoyances include the ringing of a telephone, conversations going on around you, the way you feel, and being unable to hear the speaker.
4. (1) Monitor your understanding of the reading task. (2) Summarize information. (3) Be analytical.
5. (1) To express problems. (2) To discuss alternatives. (3) To arrive at solutions through joint efforts.
6. A leader influences other people; enlists the support and cooperation of other people; communicates in a way that is clearly understood; seems fair, accessible, and honest; listens to other points of view; accepts future uncertainty; interacts with others to share responsibilities; inspires confidence in others; and behaves appropriately.
7. See Table 7.1.

18. Machines that transmit and receive virtually any image over regular phone lines

19. Enables distant participants to conduct face-to-face meetings without travel

Check Your Knowledge

On a separate sheet of paper, complete the following activities. (Do not write in your textbook.)

1. Effective communication in the workplace requires knowing the three styles of English. List these three styles and describe how each of the three is typically used.
2. When we communicate with other people, we send and receive both verbal and nonverbal messages. Describe the two skills that are essential for effective oral communication in the workplace.
3. Good listening demands alert and active participation and is developed through training and practice. List some of the barriers and annoyances that can block effective listening.
4. The average employee spends one and a half to two hours per workday reading. Describe three skills needed to be a successful reader in the workplace.
5. Group meetings are related to the needs of the members. Name three major reasons why groups meet in the workplace.
6. List four of the characteristics of a leader.
7. Negotiation is one method frequently used to resolve conflicts in the world of work. List the seven major differences between negotiation and argument.

© JIST Works

Develop SCANS Competencies

Government experts say that successful workers can productively use resources, interpersonal skills, information, systems, and technology. This activity will give you practice in developing system skills.

Study the following diagram. Use this format to diagram three conversations you were involved in today. Be sure to identify the sender and the receiver. Briefly explain the message and the feedback.

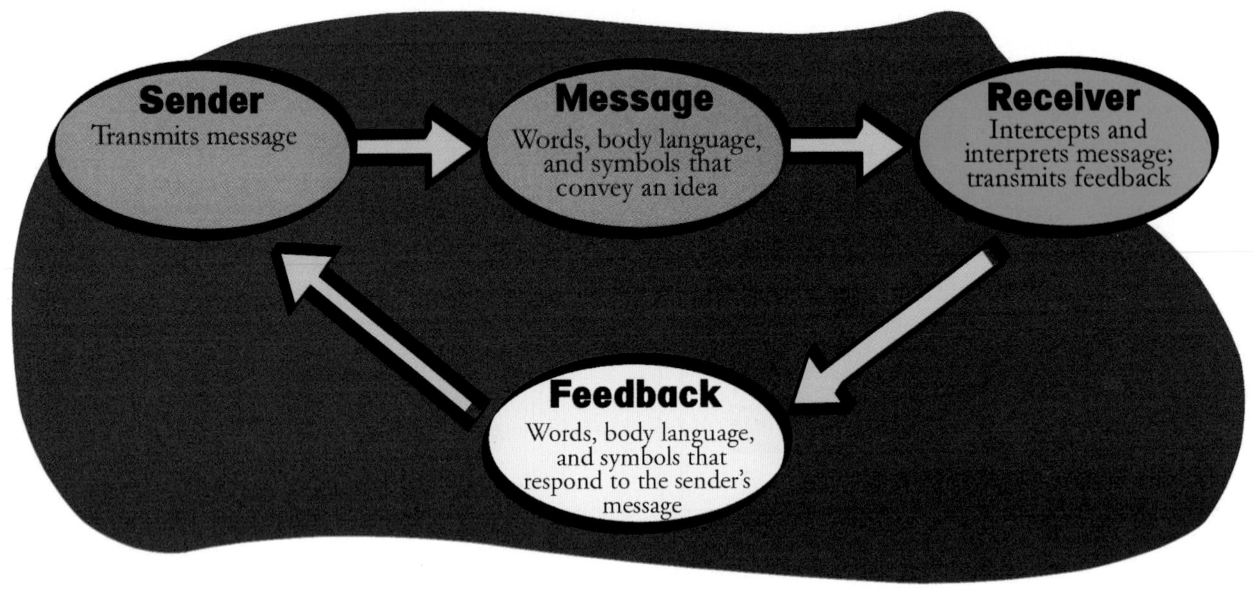

Enrichment

Have students complete the Chapter 7 section of the *Preparing for Career Success Student Portfolio, Third Edition.*

Chapter 8 Resources

Lesson Plans and Preparation

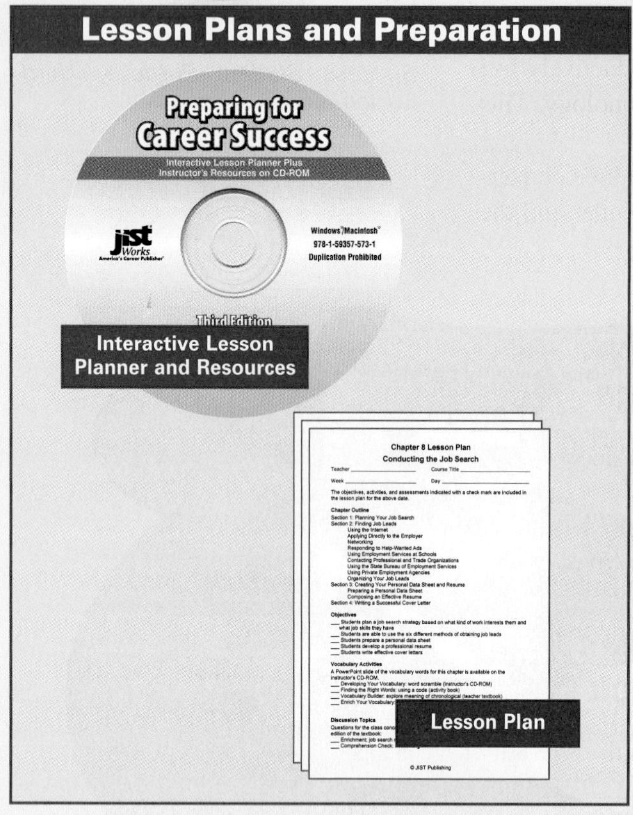

Preparing for Career Success
Interactive Lesson Planner Plus Instructor's Resources on CD-ROM
Windows/Macintosh
978-1-59357-573-1
Duplication Prohibited
Interactive Lesson Planner and Resources
Chapter 8 Lesson Plan
Conducting the Job Search
Lesson Plan
© JIST Publishing

Multimedia

Preparing for Career Success
Video Tour on DVD
978-1-59357-574-8
Duplication Prohibited
Chapter 8 Video Tour
© 2009 JIST Publishing
800-648-JIST
www.jist.com
Chapter 8 Key Terms
blind ads
chronological resume
cover letter
digital resume
employment service
functional resume
identified ads
job applicant
job banks
job fairs
job lead
job market
job search
networking
personal data sheet
references
resume
resume bank
screening interview
PowerPoint Presentation

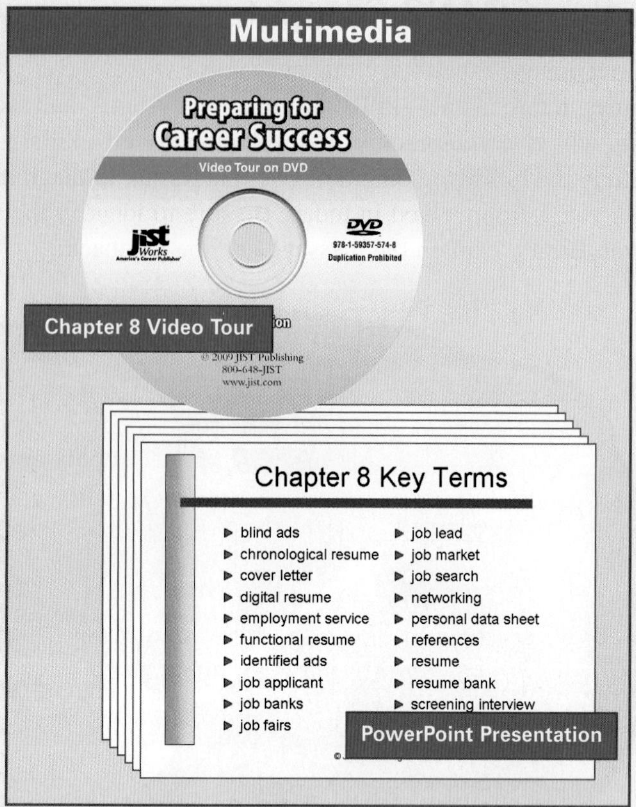

Activities

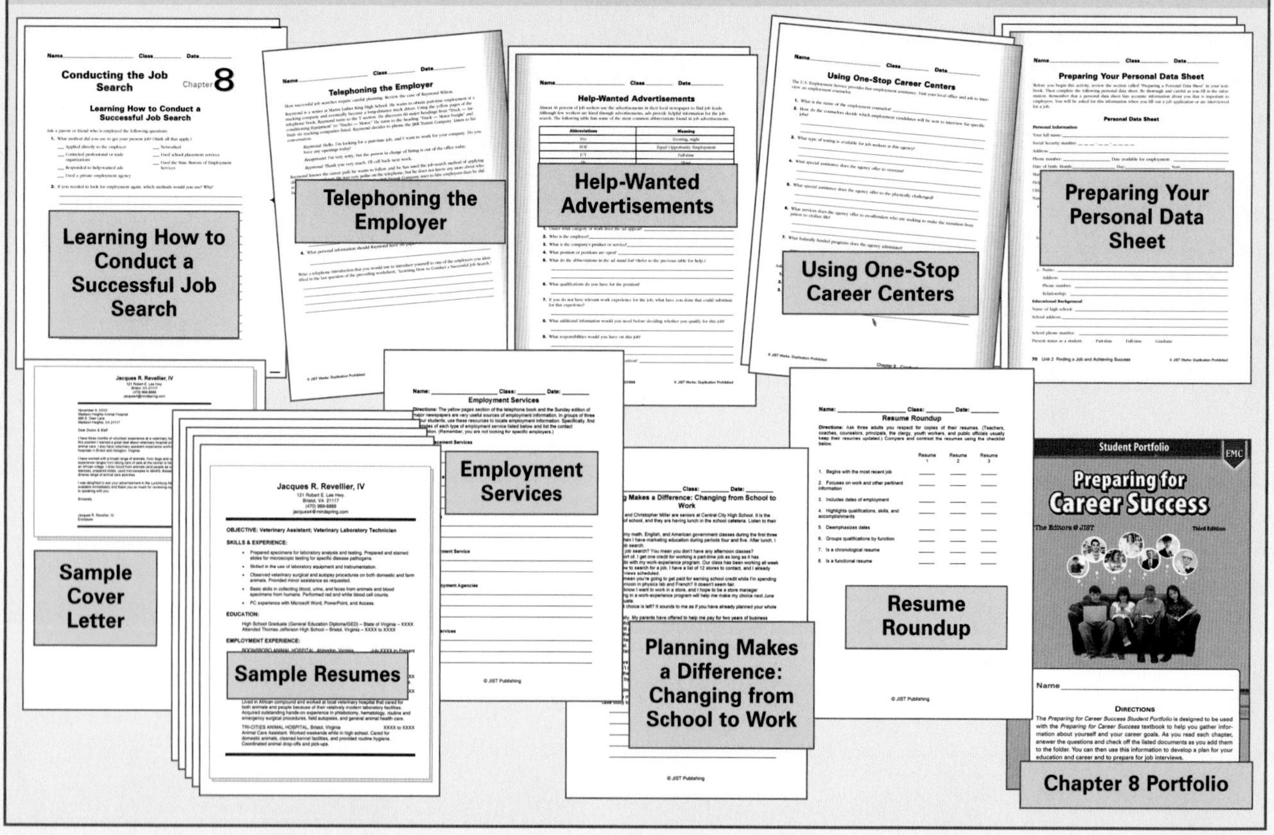

Learning How to Conduct a Successful Job Search
Telephoning the Employer
Help-Wanted Advertisements
Using One-Stop Career Centers
Preparing Your Personal Data Sheet
Sample Cover Letter
Sample Resumes
Employment Services
Planning Makes a Difference: Changing from School to Work
Resume Roundup
Student Portfolio
Preparing for Career Success
Chapter 8 Portfolio

© JIST Works

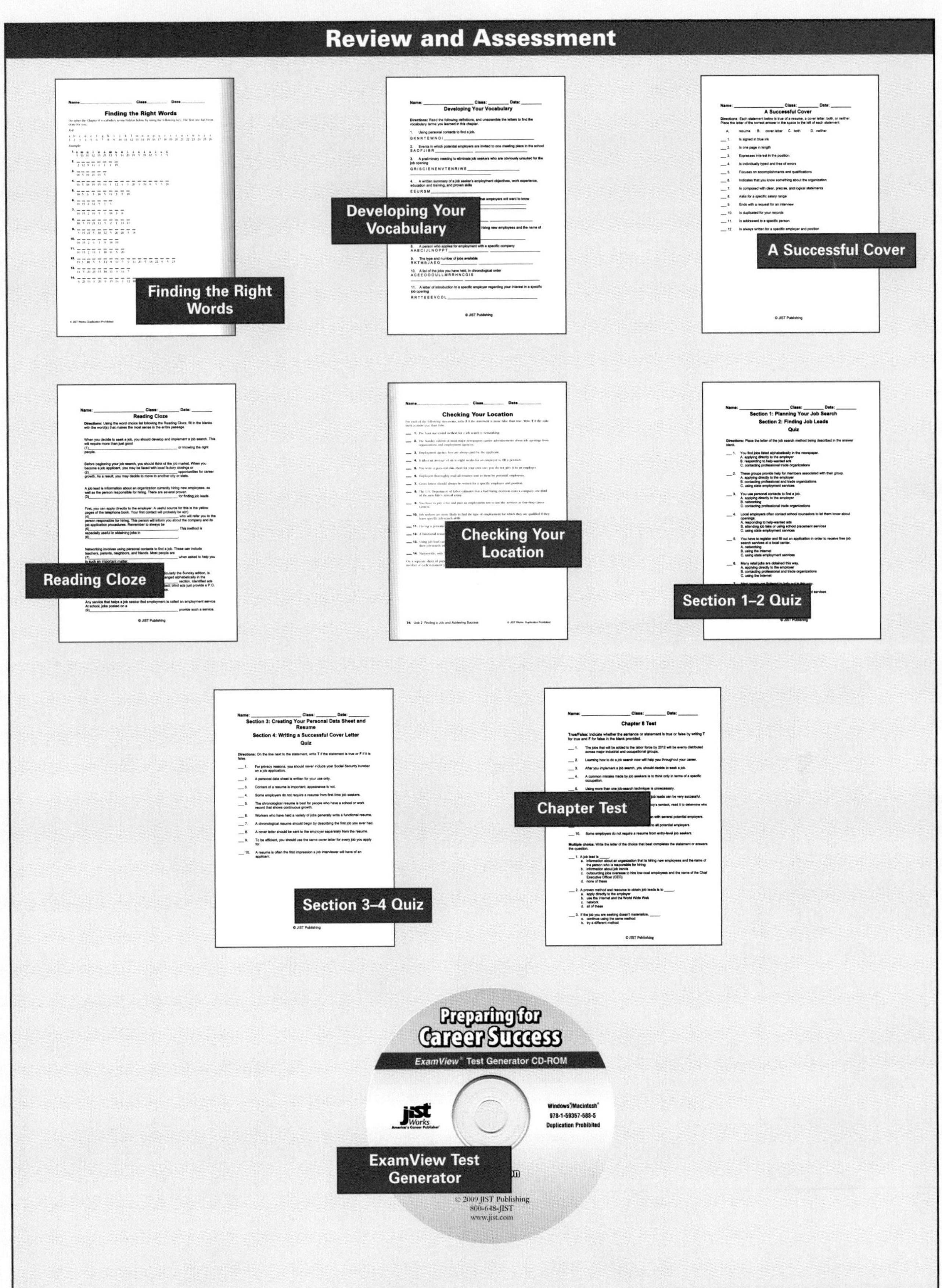

Review and Assessment
Finding the Right Words
Developing Your Vocabulary
A Successful Cover
Reading Cloze
Checking Your Location
Section 1–2 Quiz
Section 3–4 Quiz
Chapter Test
Preparing for Career Success
ExamView Test Generator CD-ROM
ExamView Test Generator

Chapter 8 Conducting the Job Search

Learning Objectives

- Plan a successful job search
- Use six different methods to obtain job leads
- Keep track and follow up on job leads
- Prepare a personal data sheet and resume
- Write a successful cover letter

The jobs that will be added to the labor force by 2016 will not be evenly distributed across major industrial and occupational groups. Changes in consumer demand, new technology, and many other factors will contribute to the continually changing employment structure in the U.S. economy. At some point, you will be a worker seeking one of those jobs.

Learning how to do a job search now will help you throughout your career. After you learn the process, you can repeat it over and over whether you are seeking a promotion, have been fired, have been laid off, or just want to relocate. Current research shows that your generation will average 8 to 10 or more job changes during your working years. Chances are good that you will put job search skills to good use over and over again.

Enrich Your Vocabulary

In reading this chapter and doing the exercises, you will learn the following important terms:

blind ads	job applicant	networking
chronological resume	job banks	personal data sheet
cover letter	job fairs	references
digital resume	job lead	resume
employment service	job market	resume bank
functional resume	job search	screening interview
identified ads		

Vocabulary

You can use the "Developing Your Vocabulary" worksheet found in the Chapter 8 file of the *Preparing for Career Success Instructor's CD-ROM, Third Edition* as a pretest for chapter concepts or as a reteaching worksheet.

When you decide to seek a job, you will need to develop and implement a **job search** (the process of seeking employment). More than "good luck" or knowing the "right people" will be necessary. Planning and persistence are almost always required in a successful job search.

As you begin organizing your job search, treat it as you would an important paying job. Commit your time and energy to being successful. After you plan your job search, you can begin making the plan work.

CAREER FACT

Some employers keep a file of potential job candidates so that as openings occur, they can fill a job vacancy without paying for advertising or using an employment agency.

Section 1: Planning Your Job Search

Before you begin your job search, take time to think about yourself. Make certain that you can answer the following questions:

1. What type of work interests me?
2. What skills can I offer an employer?
3. What rewards do I expect from the job?
4. Who can help me make contacts with possible employers?
5. How can I convince an employer that hiring me would benefit the organization?

Video Tour on DVD

Show students the Chapter 8 segment to introduce them to the content.

Case Study

Have students read the case study "Changing from School to Work" located in Chapter 8 of the *Preparing for Career Success Instructor's CD-ROM, Third Edition* and discuss the "Critical Thinking" questions.

Cross Reference

You may wish to review "Section 3: Interests" in Chapter 2.

When you think of the word *market,* you probably have thoughts about stores, the places where they are located, the process of buying and selling goods, and prices. You can think of the job market in the same way. The term **job market** refers to the type and number of jobs available. Ask yourself the following questions as you prepare for your job search:

1. What businesses, industries, or agencies are hiring (buying) new workers with my job skills?
2. Where are these potential employers located?

© JIST Works

3. What wages and benefits (prices) will they offer for my skills?
4. How can I become a **job applicant** (a person who applies for employment with a specific company) with the employers I choose? How will I sell my skills to these employers?

Job seekers often make the mistake of thinking only in terms of a specific occupation. For example, someone who has a college degree in chemistry and wants to be a chemist should identify and contact all industries that employ chemists. Most manufacturing industries and numerous nonmanufacturing industries employ chemists. The health-care industry is one example. Looking at industries rather than occupations expands your search to a greater number of potential employers.

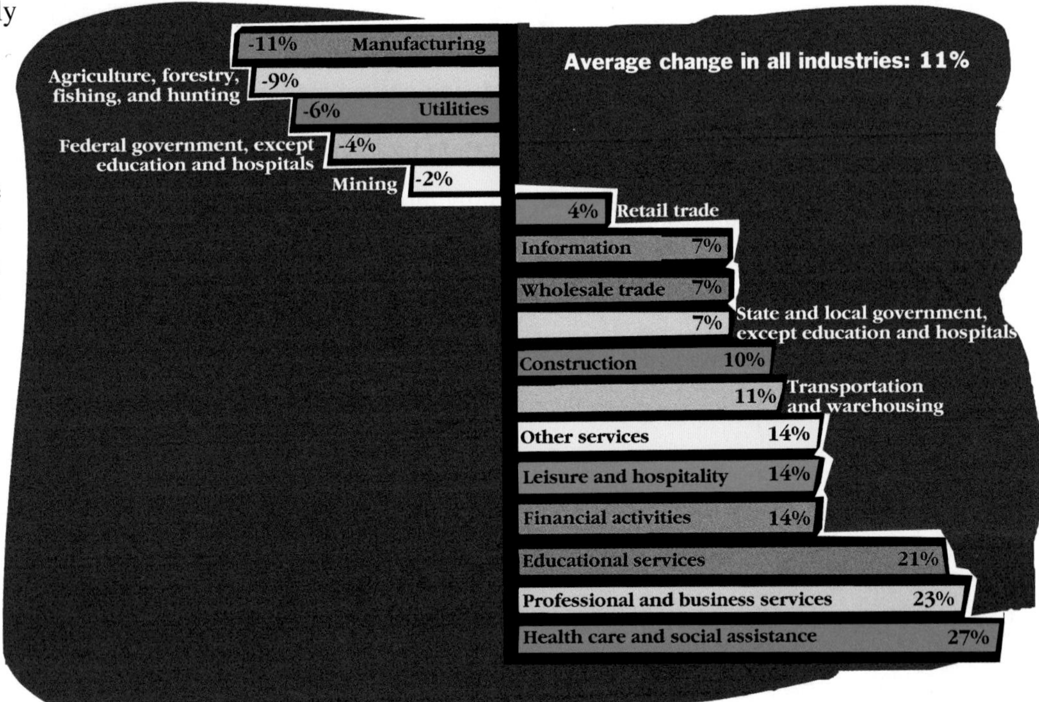

Figure 8.1 Percent change in wage and salary employment organized by industry sector and projected for 2006–2016. (Source: U.S. Department of Labor, Bureau of Labor Statistics)

Workers frequently move to other cities or states when faced with local factory closings or limited opportunities for career growth. Such moves require knowledge of local and national job markets. As you read the information in Figure 8.1, imagine that you are conducting a nationwide job search for yourself. Each industry listed is composed of several thousand corporations, *subsidiaries* (companies in which more than half the stock is owned or controlled by another company), and other businesses employing millions of workers.

Section 1: Get Involved

Analyze the information presented in Figure 8.1. Answer the following on a separate sheet of paper, and be prepared to discuss your responses in class.

1. What recent technology has influenced your life? How? What job opportunities will be created because of this technology?
2. What do you think has brought about the continued growth in services? If this trend continues, would a young worker be wise to pursue any occupations in manufacturing? If so, what? If not, why not?
3. In terms of employment growth, what are the three leading service industries? What are the three leading nonservice industries?

© JIST Works

Section 2: Finding Job Leads

Wanting a job isn't enough. You must find employers and convince them to hire you. At this point, job leads become important. A **job lead** is information about an organization that is hiring new employees and the name of the person who is responsible for hiring. Use the following proven methods and resources to obtain job leads:

Enrichment

Send a volunteer to the chalkboard. Ask the writer to print a heading for each of the seven most successful job-hunting methods. Ask your students: By show of hands, who has tried to find a job by applying directly to the employer? Ask the writer to record the number of students using this method under the heading. Repeat this process for each of the remaining six methods. Then ask which system is used most by the class and which system is used least. Reinforce the importance of learning to use several job-hunting methods.

1. Use the Internet and the World Wide Web.
2. Apply directly to the employer.
3. Network.
4. Respond to classified ads.
5. Use placement services at schools and job fairs.
6. Contact professional and trade organizations.
7. Use public and private employment services.

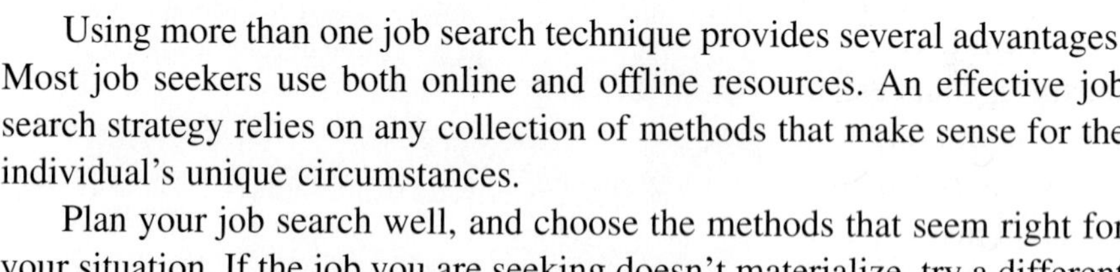

Using more than one job search technique provides several advantages. Most job seekers use both online and offline resources. An effective job search strategy relies on any collection of methods that make sense for the individual's unique circumstances.

Plan your job search well, and choose the methods that seem right for your situation. If the job you are seeking doesn't materialize, try a different method. The sooner you become skilled at using several proven methods, the sooner you will find the type of employment you are seeking.

Help-wanted ads are a good source of information about local and regional employment.

Using the Internet

The Internet can aid a job search or prolong joblessness, depending on how it is used. Today's savvy job seekers add online methods to the traditional job search process.

The World Wide Web offers an overwhelming number of resources for job seekers. As a result, some job seekers get lost. They click from one interesting site to the next and allow whatever pops up to determine the course of their job search. The hours they spend in front of a computer monitor produce few job leads and no interviews. It is important to use offline resources at least as much as online ones. Create a plan for your job search, and allow your plan to determine which resources to use when and for what purpose.

Begin your search using keywords you have discovered in this chapter. When you feel comfortable with the process, investigate the following resources. Using your search engine, key in the terms that appear in bold italic type, and click the Search button.

© JIST Works

America's Talent Bank (***ATB***) holds electronic resumes posted at local employment services offices and on the Internet. Employers search online to find candidates with the skills needed to fill available jobs.

Job banks hold listings of available jobs. In addition to private sector job banks, every state has its own Internet-accessible ***job bank***. Job seekers can find all of these thousands of job openings listed in job banks by going online to www.jobbankinfo.org. This site also includes links to related Web sites.

Monster.com posts as many as 400,000 jobs at any given time.

Additional keywords to search include ***Careerbuilder***, ***Job Hunter's Bible***, ***flipdog.com***, ***career journal***, and ***career path***.

Now that you are excited about the Internet's job search magic, it's time to get started. A good place to begin is your school's library or computer center. Librarians can help you locate Internet directory indexes for specific topics and show you how to put a search engine into gear.

Applying Directly to the Employer

The yellow pages section of the telephone book provides a very useful source of employers to contact for your job search. It does not tell you who is presently hiring, but it is a source of *who* hires. Organization names, addresses, and telephone numbers are listed under the services they offer or the products they produce.

Take time to prepare yourself before using the telephone to make your initial contact with an employer. Consider the type of job you are seeking, and then select appropriate organizations to call. Record the names of these organizations on a sheet of paper, and include the phone numbers and names of the persons (if known) to call. As you make the calls, write down the following information:

- Any openings for the type of job you are seeking
- When or if you are to call back
- When or if an interview is set up

"A fair day's wages for a fair day's work": it is as just a demand as governed men ever made of governing. It is the everlasting right of man.

—Thomas Carlyle

Keep the information on a sheet of paper, or make job lead cards for each organization. (Look ahead to Figure 8.3 for a sample job lead card.) Have your personal data sheet handy in case you have the opportunity to discuss your qualifications over the telephone. (Personal data sheets are discussed later in this chapter.)

Enrichment

Have students complete the "Telephoning the Employer" worksheet in Chapter 8 of the *Preparing for Career Success Student Activity Book, Third Edition.*

Your first contact will probably be with a receptionist. Introduce yourself, and request the name and title of the person who is responsible for hiring new employees. Make certain that you have the correct pronunciation of that person's name. Ask to speak with him or her. If the person responsible for hiring is unavailable, ask for an appropriate time to call back.

After you make contact with the person responsible for hiring, again introduce yourself and explain why you are calling. Inquire about the procedures for obtaining a job with the organization. In some organizations, you

When men are employed, they are best contented, but on our idle days, they were mutinous and quarrelsome.

—Benjamin Franklin

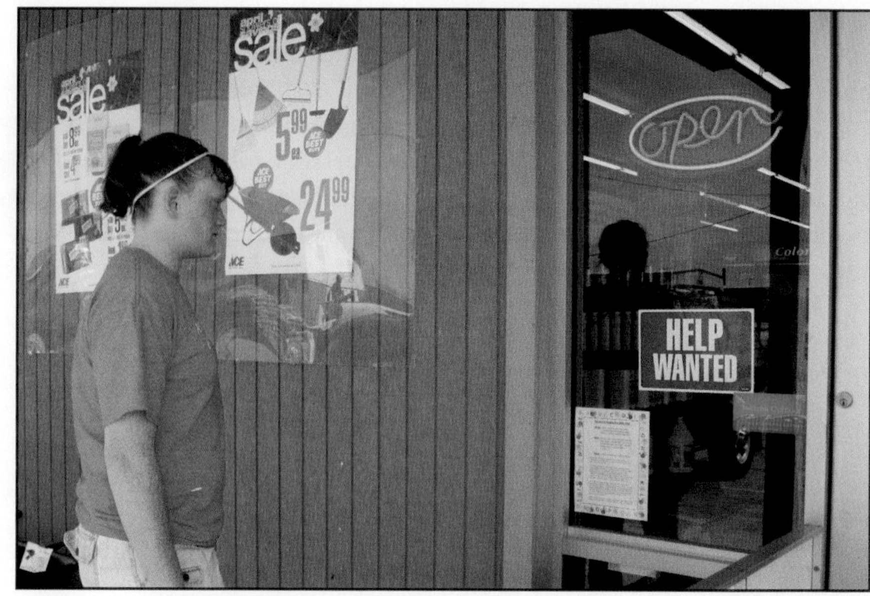

Local customers frequently become the best employees of retail merchants. Should this girl apply for the job now?

Cooperative Learning

Divide the class into groups of three. Ask each group to role-play a phone conversation between a job seeker, receptionist, and hiring manager. Each group should decide who will play each role, write a list of personal information and questions for the job seeker, and create a name and purpose for the employer's business. Using the procedures described in "Applying Directly to the Employer," have the groups perform their role play for the class. Ask the class to critique each group's role play.

may be able to schedule an appointment for an interview over the telephone. If you cannot schedule an interview, ask that an employment application be mailed to you, and ask permission to submit a resume to the organization. Whatever the outcome of the conversation, always be courteous.

Many job openings in retail trade are obtained by direct contact. The owner or manager of the retail business is usually responsible for hiring new employees. Retail merchants know that local customers frequently become their best employees. If you are seeking a job in one of the retail trades, walk into the business appropriately dressed and with your personal data sheet or resume in hand. Ask to speak with the manager or owner. If the manager has a secretary, introduce yourself and ask to speak with the manager, or schedule an appointment for an interview. You may be asked to fill out a job application before being granted an interview.

Networking

Comprehension Check

Tell the students to close their books. Ask them: When you are networking to find a job, what three types of information can personal contacts frequently offer? (Suggestions, direct leads, or referrals to other people.)

Networking involves using personal contacts to find a job. When you begin a job search, make a contact list of the names and phone numbers of all the people you know. Teachers, parents, friends, neighbors, local merchants, and members of the organizations you belong to are examples of personal contacts you have right now. As you gain work experience, you will develop other valuable contacts.

Networking people you know to obtain job leads can be very successful. In fact, personal contacts help millions of individuals get jobs each year. In many cases, your contacts can offer you suggestions, direct leads, or referrals to other people. Clearly, this is a good approach for making your skills and availability for work known to as many people as possible.

 © JIST Works

The thought of asking personal contacts for help in seeking employment is embarrassing to some people. In fact, most people are flattered when asked for help in such an important matter.

Planning Makes a Difference: Networking Pays Off

Samantha Wilson is a good example of a successful networker. She recently graduated from Middletown High School, where she had taken a general education program. During her senior year, she had a part-time job at a local grocery store.

Samantha didn't want to continue bagging groceries and stocking shelves for the rest of her life. She sat down in her favorite chair one evening and took a personal inventory of her employment skills and her career interests. She really enjoyed driving and frequently drove her dad's pickup truck. She had an excellent safety record and wondered whether a company might hire her to drive a small truck or van for its business.

Samantha made a list of acquaintances who might know of a possible job opening. In the next three days, she called 17 people to tell them of her interest and to enlist their help in looking for a driving job. She also checked the help-wanted ads every day.

Three weeks passed, and during that time, Samantha visited 24 different businesses to seek a driving job. Then her big break came. The manager of the store where Samantha worked part-time mentioned Samantha to her brother, who operated an auto parts store. Mrs. Greene told her brother that Samantha had an excellent attendance record and was one of the best workers in her store.

Networking paid off, and Samantha is now a successful driver for South Shore Auto Parts, Inc.

CAREER FACT

Two types of job openings are advertised and unadvertised. The majority of job openings are unadvertised. You will miss more than half of all job opportunities if you search only for advertised jobs.

CLUSTER LINK

Whether you are interested in driving a delivery truck, an ocean-going oil tanker, or a jet airplane, you could find an interesting career in the Transportation, Distribution, and Logistics career cluster. All of the occupations involved with planning, managing, and moving people, materials, and goods by road, pipeline, air, rail, and water are in this career cluster. See the appendix for more information.

Critical Thinking

If Samantha asked 17 friends and relatives to help with her job search, and each of them told 5 people about Samantha, and each of them told 2 people, how many people would be networking to help Samantha?

What specific job search techniques did Samantha use?

Responding to Help-Wanted Ads

CAREER FACT

You can find most newspaper job advertisements on the newspaper's Web site.

Enrichment

Have students complete the "Help-Wanted Advertisements" worksheet in Chapter 8 of the *Preparing for Career Success Student Activity Book, Third Edition.*

The Sunday editions of most major newspapers print advertisements about job openings from organizations and employment agencies (see Figure 8.2). The job descriptions are generally broad and request that interested candidates respond by calling or sending a resume to the listed address.

Newspapers usually arrange job openings alphabetically by job title and category in the classified section. Job advertisements placed by employers normally include the following:

- Job title
- A brief description of the job
- Required qualifications
- A short statement about the organization
- The name and address of the organization
- How and with whom to make contact in the organization

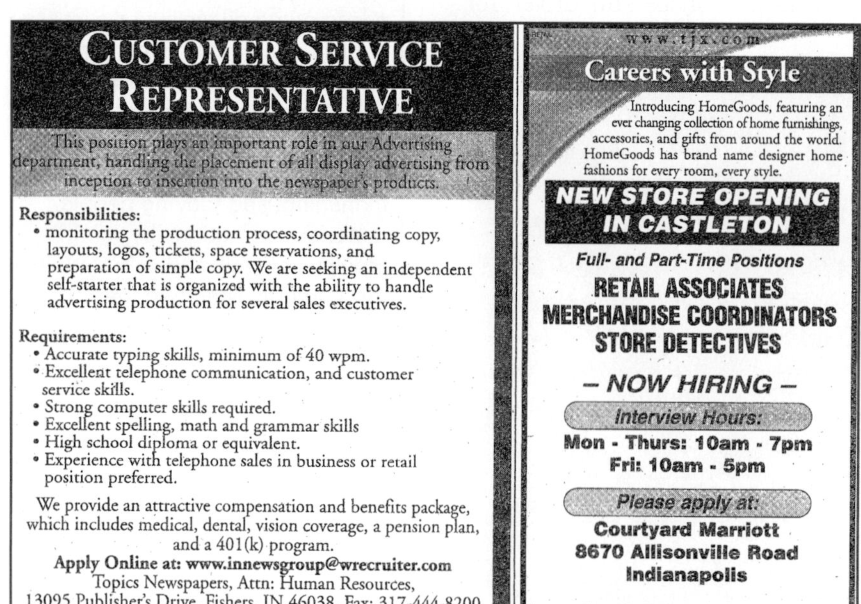

Figure 8.2 Sample job advertisements.

Identified ads and blind ads are two types of ads specifically used to attract entry-level and middle-level employees. **Identified ads** provide the name of the employer or the employment agency and a person or department to contact. Because most professional employment agencies have hundreds of job openings to fill at any given time, they often place several general ads in the newspaper covering a wide range of specific skills.

Blind ads provide only a post office box or e-mail address for sending a response; they do not include employer information. Unemployed or entry-level professionals can safely respond to blind ads. Employed workers, however, should not

© JIST Works

respond to blind ads. They could be sending their resumes to their present employers.

Employers may receive anywhere from 10 to 1,000 resumes or letters of response for each classified ad they place. This high number of responses for each job results in keen competition among job seekers. The most efficient procedure for responding to help-wanted ads is to create and save a letter of response on a word-processing program and use it for a template. Then you can customize your letter for each response you send.

Cooperative Learning

Divide the class into groups of four. Assign each group to write an employment ad for an entry-level worker(s). Have each group read an ad to the class. Ask class members why they would or would not respond to the ad.

Using Employment Services at Schools

An **employment service** is any assistance that helps a job seeker find a job. Assistance with your job search may be as close as your high school. Some schools post jobs with area employers on a bulletin board. Frequently, these listings are for part-time, summer, and temporary jobs. Local employers sometimes contact school counselors and technical teachers to tell them about job openings. Work study teachers are also in contact with employers and are a good source of jobs related to their particular area of career training. Ask your counselor to help you locate these resources in your school.

High schools, technical schools, and colleges occasionally arrange **job fairs**. Several potential employers are invited to meet at one location in the school. Tables are set up where each employer can distribute information describing the organization and briefly discuss career opportunities with interested job seekers. If your school has a job fair, the principal or counselor will announce the dates and times that you can attend.

Job fairs are a good way to learn about several places of employment at one time. They provide an opportunity to meet employers and to obtain job application forms. Interviews at job fairs are usually not lengthy and rarely lead to on-the-spot job offers.

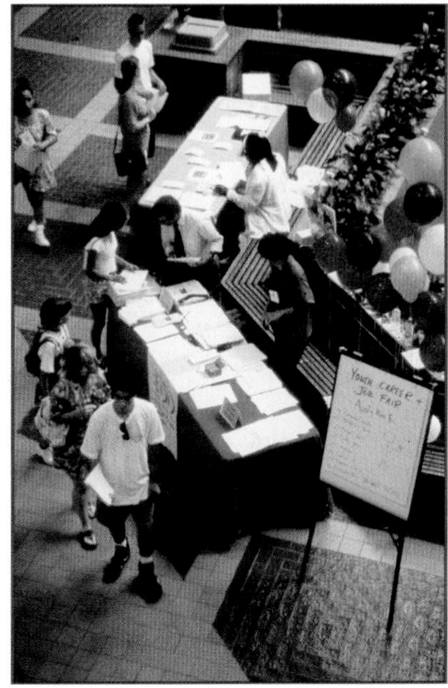

Job fairs are a good way to learn about several job openings at one time and place.

Contacting Professional and Trade Organizations

Labor unions, professional and trade organizations, and groups for the physically challenged often receive and post job openings. These groups provide employment assistance to individuals who are associated with their organization. Many publish trade journals or magazines that include listings of job openings and other career information. The *Occupational Outlook Handbook (OOH)* lists the mailing and Internet address for many of these organizations.

Professional and trade organizations also conduct local meetings and sponsor state or national conventions for their members. Job fairs are frequently included on the agenda of large meetings and conventions. Local speakers are frequently available to speak about their career to students. If you are interested, ask your counselor or career teacher to help you make the appropriate contact.

Cooperative Learning

Have students complete the "Employment Services" worksheet in Chapter 8 of the *Preparing for Career Success Instructor's CD-ROM, Third Edition.*

Enrichment

Assign a group of students to decorate a section of your class bulletin board with background paper, trim, and lettering related to the theme of "Employment Information." Instruct them to leave enough space for class members to post related information.

Enrichment

Allow extra credit for students who volunteer to use the library and report to the class about a trade or professional journal. Have the students post the information they obtain on the "Employment Information" bulletin board.

Trade and professional journals also provide considerable information about current happenings and job openings in their career area. Your school or public librarian can help you select a trade or professional journal in an area of your interest. Examples include *The Journal of the American Chemical Society* and *The Tappi Journal* of the pulp and paper industry. Many of these journals also provide online information. Key in the name of the organization in your Internet search engine and click the Search button. Additionally, look in your phone book for local branches of the organizations that interest you.

Using the State Bureau of Employment Services

Community Resources

Form a committee of students to contact the local State Bureau of Employment Services (titled Job Services in many states). Provide the committee with a list of convenient dates and times for a speaker presentation. Have the committee arrange for a speaker to describe the agency's employment services and summer youth employment programs. The committee should also request printed materials for the "Employment Information" bulletin board.

The U.S. Employment Service (USES) operates more than 2,000 local offices in partnership with state employment services to provide free testing, counseling, and job placement. These state-operated employment services, frequently called One-Stop Career Centers in most states, form a national network of public employment offices that follow federal guidelines.

The Job Service also channels applicants into various training programs. Summer youth programs provide summer jobs in city, county, and state government agencies for low-income youth. Students, school dropouts, or graduates entering the labor market who are between 16 and 21 years of age are eligible.

One-Stop Career Centers (employment services) are listed in the telephone directory under "State Government." They receive job listings from employers and match registered job seekers to these openings. Many of these state agencies have employment counselors who specifically assist young people in entering the job market.

CAREER FACT

In the past 50 years, the U.S. Employment Service and local state employment services have combined to counsel more than 33 million people in job-seeking skills needed to fill more than 126 million jobs.

One-Stop Career Centers provide employment services and resources to help you in your job search.

© JIST Works

To register for employment services, fill out an application at your local One-Stop office. You will be asked to list your skills, training, and work history and to identify one or two specific types of jobs for which you would qualify. All applications are filed in the system by occupation, so you need to be specific when identifying the types of jobs you are seeking. The application form you complete will be kept and sent to employers seeking someone with your credentials. When there is an interest from an employer, you will be contacted, and an interview will be arranged.

After you are registered, you will have free use of computers equipped with word-processing software and career information delivery systems. You can explore potential careers, research sources of training and education, write resumes and cover letters, and implement a job search. Active job seekers have free use of telephones, fax machines, photocopiers, and the Internet. In addition, some centers have videoconferencing facilities, allowing for long-distance job interviews.

Notify your local One-Stop staff if you change your address or phone number, and keep in touch. Your application will remain in the "actively seeking work" files for 60 days from the last date on which you contacted the bureau. Be aware that unanticipated openings may occur at any time.

What skills, training, and work experience would you list on a Bureau of Employment Job Services application? What specific types of jobs are you qualified to do?

FIND OUT MORE

To identify the nearest provider of public employment services, call toll-free 1-877-USA-JOBS, or look up America's Service Locator online at www.servicelocator.org.

Using Private Employment Agencies

There are several thousand privately owned employment services in the United States. Although these agencies are in business to make money, they can also be very helpful to established professionals. They operate on a commission basis, and the fee depends on a successful match. Always find out the exact cost and who is responsible for paying the fee before using the service. The employer, the applicant, or both may pay fees.

You may wish to contact a private employment agency after your career is established. If so, you will probably have an initial **screening interview**. The purpose of this interview is to eliminate job seekers who are unsuited for the job opening. If your qualifications match an opening, the agency will arrange an interview with the employer. The agency files your information if no match is found.

Temporary services are another type of private employment agency. These services have grown rapidly in recent years. Temporary employment services "rent" employees for a short or limited amount of time, thus the term *temporary.* The temporary service acts as the employer and hires the temporary worker. The organization where the temporary worker is assigned pays the temporary service, which in turn pays the temporary worker.

Temporary agencies usually check an applicant's references, evaluate his or her skills and personality traits, and conduct a placement interview. The level of screening required and the training and benefits offered depend on the applicant's expertise and the employer's demand for those skills.

Comprehension Check

Have your students close their books and then ask them: If a private employment agency places a client on a job, who pays the fee? (The employer, applicant, or both may be responsible for paying the fee.) Explain to your students that it is more cost effective for many small businesses to contract with private employment services than it would be to operate their own personnel department.

TAKE NOTE

Before you sign a private employment agency's contract, read it to determine who is responsible for the fee.

Nine out of ten companies use temporary help. What temporary employment services are available in your community?

Career Fact

Twenty-first century employers are very cost-conscious as they face competitive global challenges. Almost 90 percent are using some temporary workers to increase efficiency and lower labor costs. Don't overlook temporary employment agencies as part of your job search.

Discussion Starter

Explain that temporary workers (temps) are employees of a temporary employment agency. Temps frequently perform the same work as the employer's full-time workers. However, temps are usually paid lower wage rates with fewer benefits. Ask your students: Should temps and full-time workers be treated equally? If no, why not? If yes, who should pay the additional cost? The employer, the temporary agency, or both?

Temporary employment has advantages for both workers and employers. Temporary assignments allow entry-level workers to work in a variety of settings, choose projects that provide the work experiences they need, live where they want, and earn wages. Gaining experience and acquiring new skills on temporary assignments and maximizing your networking opportunities can be a stepping-stone to your career. Many permanent employees start out as temporary workers (often called temps).

Organizing Your Job Leads

A job search usually requires communication with several potential employers. Some experts have estimated that 25 job leads may be needed to generate one interview, and five interviews to get one job offer. These numbers make it difficult but important to remember all of the people and organizations you have contacted. Consider the following high-tech and low-tech methods for organizing job lead information:

- The low-tech approach is to purchase a small notebook and some three-by-five-inch cards to organize your job leads. Arranging a card file in alphabetical order makes it easy to retrieve job lead information (see the sample job lead card in Figure 8.3). If you choose to use a notebook, arrange job leads sequentially by date of initial contact. In either case, record the same information.
- The high-tech approach is to use your computer. Set up files similar to the job lead card in Figure 8.3, and record the same data as the low-tech method. You will still need to gather your initial information using a small notebook and then key it into your computer files.

© JIST Works

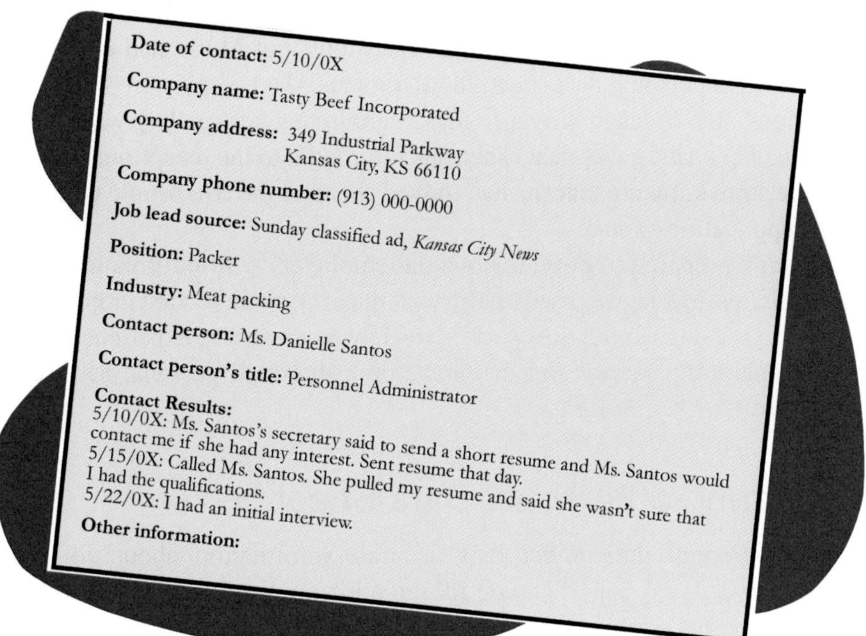
Date of contact: 5/10/0X

Company name: Tasty Beef Incorporated

Company address: 349 Industrial Parkway
Kansas City, KS 66110

Company phone number: (913) 000-0000

Job lead source: Sunday classified ad, *Kansas City News*

Position: Packer

Industry: Meat packing

Contact person: Ms. Danielle Santos

Contact person's title: Personnel Administrator

Contact Results:
5/10/0X: Ms. Santos's secretary said to send a short resume and Ms. Santos would contact me if she had any interest. Sent resume that day.
5/15/0X: Called Ms. Santos. She pulled my resume and said she wasn't sure that I had the qualifications.
5/22/0X: I had an initial interview.

Other information:

Figure 8.3 Sample job lead card.

Section 2: Get Involved

Do the following activities, and be prepared to discuss what you discovered with your class.

1. Using the yellow pages of your telephone book, select and develop a list of appropriate employers for whom you would be qualified to work following high school graduation. List four questions you would ask the receptionist if you called, and then consider what personal information the employer will ask about you.
2. Learn to network by thinking of a job you are qualified to perform. Ask two relatives, two friends, and a teacher for suggestions on finding an employer who might hire you. Then ask these people whether they have friends or relatives who work for these employers. Make a list of friends and relatives they mention.
3. Read the help-wanted ads in the Sunday edition of your local or regional newspaper. (They are probably available on the Internet as well.) Using the newspaper or your printout, clip out four employment opportunities you would be interested in pursuing. Bring them to class for discussion.

Section 3: Creating Your Personal Data Sheet and Resume

Maria waited patiently for her turn to speak with the receptionist. The Great Value Discount Store had advertised for two part-time stock clerks in the morning paper. The working hours would be perfect for her senior year at Edison High School. Maria hoped that the three men and two women ahead of her would not be hired before she had a chance.

Finally, it was Maria's turn. She introduced herself and explained why she was seeking the part-time stock clerk position. She could tell that the receptionist liked her attitude because she gave her a job application form and asked her to bring it back as soon as possible.

School-to-Work Transition

Ask your students: Which members of the class have completed job application forms to acquire part-time employment? Then ask: Were you able to complete the form immediately, or did you need to take it home to obtain all of the necessary information? Stress the importance of having personal employment information on hand when applying for a job.

The application asked numerous questions, but Maria had come prepared with a personal data sheet. In 20 minutes, she had answered all of the questions. She checked it over to make certain that her spelling was correct and that her writing was neat. Then she returned it to the receptionist. Maria left the store knowing that she had moved ahead of the five people who took their applications home.

Being prepared to provide potential employers with information about yourself, as Maria was, will help you make a positive first impression. Before you begin your job search, review your skills, experiences, and employment objectives, and then develop a thorough personal data sheet and a well-written resume.

Accurate, concise information in your personal data sheet will help you complete job applications and write an effective resume. Have you organized the information you will need to write an effective resume?

Preparing a Personal Data Sheet

A **personal data sheet** lists accurate information about you that employers will ask for when you fill out a job application or when you are interviewed for a job.

The data sheet contains a wide range of information, including your Social Security number, the addresses and phone numbers of friends or past employers who will give you a recommendation, and the number of days you were absent from school last year. The personal data sheet is written for your use only. You will *not* give it to an employer. It will help as you fill out job applications and prepare for job interviews. Just as identifying and keeping track of job leads will help you find possible jobs, your personal data sheet and resume will help you get the job you want after you find it. Study the personal data sheet outline in Figure 8.4.

Comprehension Check

Ask your students to turn their attention to Figure 8.4. Explain that part-time work experience could include babysitting, mowing grass, and performing similar types of neighborhood work. Ask your students: What additional skills have you developed that you could use on a job? What type of worker would use this skill?

Composing an Effective Resume

A **resume** is a written summary of a job seeker's employment objectives, work experience, education and training, proven skills, and certain personal information. Your resume is a written picture of you. The content and appearance are very important because your resume may create the first impression an employer has of you.

Employers typically request a resume from job seekers. Competition among companies, the cost of hiring unqualified employees, laws that protect employees from unfair labor practices, and lengthy lawsuits have made it necessary for employers to screen and thoroughly investigate potential employees before putting them on the payroll.

Discussion Starter

Ask your students to imagine they are in charge of hiring new employees for a business. Is it fair not to interview a job applicant because he or she submitted a messy resume or a job application with a few spelling mistakes? Why or why not?

Some employers do not require a resume from entry-level job seekers, although many do. If you need to submit a resume, the employer will probably ask for it before scheduling you for an interview. This procedure enables the employer to read several resumes and narrow down the number of job candidates to interview. It is worth your time and effort to prepare an interesting, well-written resume because the quality of your resume could determine whether you are interviewed. Employers will read only as far as their first yawn!

© JIST Works

Your full name: ________________
Social Security number: ________________
Address (number and street): ________________ City: ________ State: ____ Zip: ____
Phone number: ________________
Date available for employment: ________________
Date of birth: ________ Marital status: ________
Citizenship status: ________________

Emergency Contact Information
Name: ________________
Address: ________________

Educational Background
Name of high school: ________________
School address: ________________ City: ________ State: ____ Zip: ____
School phone: ________________
Present status of student: ______ Part-time ______ Full-time ______ Graduated
Grade point average: ________
Dates of attendance: From (month and year) ________ To ________
Course of study: ______ General ______ Vocational ______ College Preparatory
Extracurricular activities (clubs, sports): ________________
Awards or honors: ________________
Favorite subjects: ________________

Part-Time or Full-Time Work Experience
Name of company: ________________
Position: ________________ Dates employed: ________________
Responsibilities: ________________
Wages or salary: Start: ________ Last: ________
Reason for leaving: ________________
Name of company: ________________
Position: ________________ Dates employed: ________________
Responsibilities: ________________
Wages or salary: Start: ________ Last: ________
Reason for leaving: ________________

Volunteer Work
Name of organization: ________________
Reason for volunteering: ________________
Your responsibilities: ________________
Your future educational goals: ________________
Your present job goals: ________________

References
Name: ________________ Job Title: ________________
Address: ________________ Phone Number ________________
Relationship: ________________
Major qualifications you have for a position (skills you have such as typing or operating equipment):
____
Leisure time activities and hobbies:
____

Figure 8.4 Sample personal data sheet.

Take time to prepare your resume before you begin your job search so that you will be ready when an employer asks for a copy. Most of the information you need to write your resume is on your Personal Data Sheet.

Employers will not expect you to have strong work experience for an entry-level position. However, they will expect you to have a good attitude, school courses that relate to the job responsibilities, and some part-time and/or volunteer work experiences.

The two most accepted resume styles are chronological and functional. Each style organizes your experience differently. You will need to choose which style projects the best impression of your education and work experience. Whichever style you select, review it carefully and limit it to one page.

Vocabulary Builder

Write the word *chronological* on the chalkboard, and explain that it means to arrange events in order of time. Ask individual students for examples of three events they have experienced today, arranged in chronological order. Next, ask for three events they have experienced in their lives, arranged in chronological order.

FIND OUT MORE

Many Internet sites provide guidance on the format and content of different types of resumes and cover letters. Some provide instructive samples. For one example, type **America's Career InfoNet** on your search engine, and click the Search button. For another, Microsoft Word offers the Resume Wizard to help you to write four styles of resumes: entry-level, chronological, functional, and professional.

KEY TO SUCCESS

Career portfolio documents such as school records, training certificates, and letters of recommendation can be a great help when you are writing a resume. These documents can help you focus on your skills and experience and highlight your accomplishments.

The **chronological resume** is a history of your career. It lists the jobs you have held in chronological order. It begins with your most recent experience and works backward. The focus is on work history and other relevant information, such as education or training. The chronological resume is best for people who have a school or work record that shows steady growth. It is the easiest style to write, and many hiring managers prefer it.

The chronological resume follows this basic outline:

Name: Include your first, middle, and last names.

Address: Give the address at which you can most readily be contacted by mail and your e-mail address.

Phone number: Give the number for a phone or answering machine that will always be answered during normal business hours.

Career objective: Write a brief statement that describes the type of work you want to do. This should be a realistic objective based on your career goals and employment skills.

Education: Give the name and location of your high school and the date when you graduated or expect to graduate. Include your class rank, grade point average, and any awards or honors you earned.

Activities and work experience: Stress your skills and accomplishments. Account for important school, volunteer, and work activities. Begin with your most recent experience, and work backward. Include dates, job titles if employed, the name of your employer's business, and a full description of all jobs held. Always write in the first person.

Personal information: Include hobbies, social skills, extracurricular activities, and date of birth.

Date available for employment: State the earliest date you will be available. If you are a student seeking part-time employment, specify the hours and days of the week that you are available.

References: References are people who have agreed to provide an employer with a written or verbal statement about your character or ability. Identify at least three references. Ask teachers, counselors, principals, previous part-time or full-time employers, or professional people who know you personally or have met you through school activities. Request their permission before citing them as references. Make certain that you have their names spelled correctly, and include their job titles, mailing addresses, and phone numbers. The names and contact information of references need not be included on your resume. A statement such as "References are available on request" will do. You don't want your references contacted unless the employer is sincerely interested in hiring you.

© JIST Works

Next, review the chronological resume written by Ronald Grant in Figure 8.5. Notice that Ronald's resume

- Is one neatly typed page in length
- Focuses on accomplishments and qualifications
- Is composed with clear, precise, and logical statements
- Is well organized and free of errors

The **functional resume** highlights qualifications, skills, and accomplishments rather than dates and previous jobs. People with lengthy work experiences, those who may be short on experience, and others who have held a variety of jobs generally write this style of resume. The functional resume groups qualifications by functions, such as repairing, organizing, managing, and selling. Dates are usually not given. This format allows job seekers to leave out experiences that do not relate to the kind of work they prefer.

Resume
of
Ronald T. Grant

40 North High Street
Mount Vernon, Ohio 43050

(614) 000-0000
rtgcompute@xxxxx.net

Career Objective
Employment using my word-processing skills. Opportunity for long-term career growth and advancement.

Education
High school diploma. Majored in Cooperative Office Education. GPA 3.14 Knox County Joint Vocational School, Mount Vernon, Ohio. June 7, 2005

- Treasurer of senior class.
- Third place 2004 Ohio State competition in word processing.

Activities and Work Experience
September 14, 2004 - Present
Anderson Printing, Inc., Mount Vernon, Ohio.
Employed as a part-time word processor during my senior year of high school and presently working 20 hours per week. Using Dell computers with Microsoft Word, Excel, and Graph software.

September 2003 - Present
First Baptist Church, Mount Vernon, Ohio.
Work as a volunteer to type the weekly church bulletin.

May 2002 - June 2003
Knox County Joint Vocational School, Mount Vernon, Ohio.
Student helper for the school newspaper. Word processing final copy using Apple II computer with PFS Write software.

Personal Information
Date of birth: August 7, 1987
Health: Excellent
Marital status: Single
Hobbies: Hiking, singing in church choir, collecting old coins
willing to relocate for good employment opportunity.

Data Available for Employment
Available for immediate employment. Present employer can replace me with a COE student from Knox County JVS on short notice.

References
Excellent references available on request

Figure 8.5 Sample chronological resume.

TECHNOLOGY

Career Web sites such as Vault and CareerBuilder.com have recently added features to let jobseekers post video resumes in addition to traditional ones. A video resume is a one- or two-minute video in which jobseekers introduce themselves, describe their qualifications, and explain why they would be good employees. Some video resumes include music or special titles, but most of them are a simple shot of a person from the waist up in one location.

If you decide to create a video resume, follow these guidelines to make the best impression:

- Practice being in front a camera so that you will be more comfortable and confident.
- Dress professionally.
- Minimize distractions by clearing away any clutter that will appear on screen and controlling background noise.
- Speak clearly and slowly and look straight into the camera.
- Be enthusiastic and show your personality, but stay focused on presenting your job skills.

Enrichment

Have students complete the "Resume Roundup" worksheet in Chapter 8 of the *Preparing for Career Success Instructor's CD-ROM, Third Edition.*

You may decide to write a **digital resume** (sometimes called *virtual* or *electronic*) using a chronological, functional, or combination style. You can easily store it on a database and e-mail or fax it to potential employers. This style should convey the same information as a traditional resume.

A **resume bank** (job board) is a database that job seekers can use to post their digital resume. In turn, employers can search the resume bank when they have vacancies to fill. Writing a digital resume allows you to respond to job boards and other employer Web sites immediately.

There are a few important differences between digital and traditional printed resumes. A digital resume must be prepared in a way that will allow it to be posted on the Internet, scanned, stored in a database, and e-mailed or faxed to potential employers. Traditional resumes have eye appeal because the various styles of type and rows of bulleted information accent your strongest qualifications and most relevant experiences. However, these same eye-pleasing resume styles are frequently obliterated when cast into cyberspace.

Whether you choose to use the U.S. mail or the Internet to send your resume, in many cases an electronic scanner will perform the initial read of your resume. Using the following suggestions can increase the probability that a scanner will read your resume accurately:

- Use nontextured white or off-white paper and black printing (no color).
- Use a common type font, such as Times Roman, Helvetica, or Arial.
- Use an appropriate font size. A font size of 12 points is ideal, but 10- or 14-point type is acceptable. Use all capital letters to make headings.
- Do not underline or italicize text, and do not use asterisks or bold type.
- Do not use boxes, graphics, or more than one column of type.
- Allow separate lines for your name, address, phone number, and e-mail address at the top of the page.
- Align all copy flush left on the page.
- Never mail a resume that is folded, stapled, or has damaged edges.

A potential employer will have certain questions and concerns whether you send your resume by e-mail, fax, the U.S. mail, or you simply hand deliver it. For each resume you submit, imagine that you are the employer, and then evaluate the resume in terms of whether it satisfies these three objectives:

1. Can you perform the duties and responsibilities as specified in the job description?
2. Do you have previous experience related to the position?
3. Can you solve the everyday problems that you will encounter in the job?

Technology

Keep these guidelines in mind when you post your resume to a job site or e-mail it to an employer:

- Save your resume as text only or plain text so that it can be read in any type of program.
- Don't send your resume as an attachment to an e-mail unless the employer requests that you do so. Because of the threat of computer viruses, attachments are often never opened. Instead, put it in the body of the e-mail after your cover letter.
- Keep in mind that lines in e-mail messages are short. Adjust your resume so that each line is 65 characters long or less before including it in an e-mail. You may want to send it to yourself before sending it to an employer to make sure that it looks acceptable.
- Include important keywords so that employers will find your resume when they do online searches. For example, make sure you list the names of all the software you know how to use. Use terms that are common in the work you are seeking.

© JIST Works

Section 3: Get Involved

Answer the following on a separate sheet of paper, and be prepared to discuss your responses in class.

1. Use the outline in Figure 8.4 to develop your own personal data sheet.
2. If an employer could read your personal data sheet, what do you think he or she might expect from you on the job? Explain the reasons for your answer.
3. In the sample chronological resume in Figure 8.5, what words are used to describe Ronald's career objective? What skills can Ronald offer an employer? What are Ronald's positive personal characteristics? What three questions would you ask Ronald if you were an employer?
4. Use your personal data sheet and the resume outline presented in this section to write your chronological resume.

Section 4: Writing a Successful Cover Letter

The purpose of a **cover letter** is to introduce yourself to a specific employer regarding your interest in a specific job opening. Include a cover letter with each resume you send. Sending a resume without a cover letter is like starting an interview without shaking hands.

When you write a cover letter in response to an advertisement, always relate the requirements stated in the ad to your career skills and goals.

Begin your letter with a brief statement telling the prospective employer why you are writing and why he or she should read your resume. Use your words to display your attitude, energy, interest, and enthusiasm. These positive qualities often overcome the negative factors of being an entry-level worker with little job experience. If your letter is successful, it will create enough interest in your resume to produce an interview.

As you begin to write, keep the following 15 suggestions in mind. A cover letter should

1. Be one page long, written in a business format and free of errors.
2. Always be written for a specific employer and position.
3. Be individually typed and error free—ideally using word-processing software with a basic font.
4. Have single-spaced paragraphs with double spacing between paragraphs.
5. Be addressed to a specific person.
6. Acknowledge any previous contact with the recipient or state the name and title of a referral.
7. Explain the way you learned of the employer and your particular interest in the organization.
8. Express interest in the position (paragraph 1).
9. Include a list or statement of your qualifications that relate to the job (paragraph 2).

Cooperative Learning

Divide the class into learning pairs. Assign one or more of the 15 suggestions for writing a cover letter to each learning pair. Ask the learning pairs to write an important reason for each of their assigned rules.

Reteaching

Have students complete the "A Successful Cover" worksheet in Chapter 7 of the *Preparing for Career Success Instructor's CD-ROM, Third Edition.*

Each resume you send to an employer should include a cover letter that expresses your interest in a specific job opening. What is the most difficult task in writing a cover letter?

© JIST Works

10. Include only statements that you can support in an interview.

11. End with a request for an interview and a statement about your desire to work for the organization (paragraph 3).

12. Include your name and the address, phone number, and e-mail where you can be contacted.

13. Include the original ad or a copy if you are responding to an advertised job.

14. Be duplicated for your records (keep a file of the organizations and people you respond to).

15. Be signed in ink (if not being sent via e-mail), preferably blue, so it won't appear to be a copy.

KEY TO SUCCESS

Do not waste valuable space in the cover letter claiming sincerity, dedication, and 100 percent honesty unless you can prove your statement. If you want employers to take you seriously, make serious statements.

Ronald Grant used the cover letter shown in Figure 8.6 for his response to an ad he read in the *Columbus Dispatch*. He attached a copy of the ad and his resume before he mailed the letter.

Write a new cover letter or revise your last cover letter for each resume you send to an employer. Be sure to have someone proofread the cover letter and resume before you mail them. Remember, this may be the only chance you have to make a good impression.

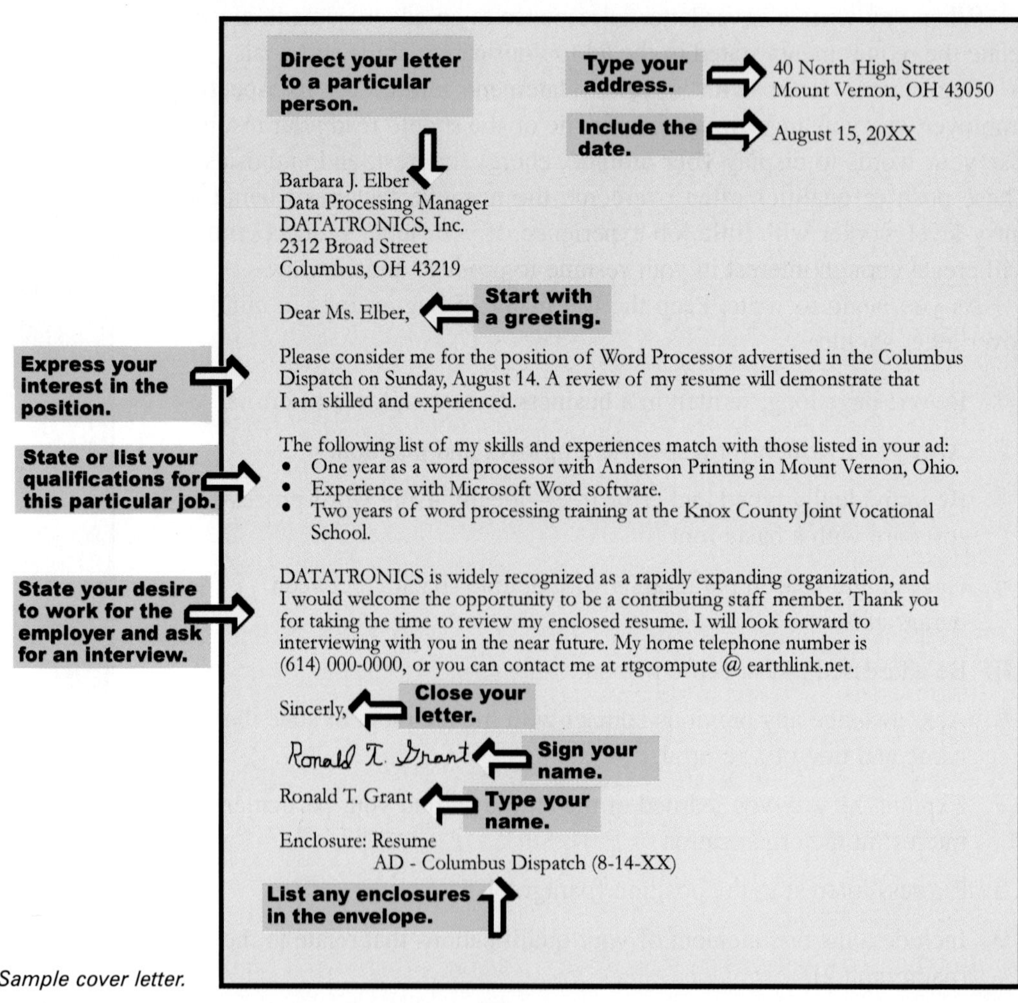
40 North High Street
Mount Vernon, OH 43050

August 15, 20XX

Barbara J. Elber
Data Processing Manager
DATATRONICS, Inc.
2312 Broad Street
Columbus, OH 43219

Dear Ms. Elber,

Please consider me for the position of Word Processor advertised in the Columbus Dispatch on Sunday, August 14. A review of my resume will demonstrate that I am skilled and experienced.

The following list of my skills and experiences match with those listed in your ad:

- One year as a word processor with Anderson Printing in Mount Vernon, Ohio.
- Experience with Microsoft Word software.
- Two years of word processing training at the Knox County Joint Vocational School.

DATATRONICS is widely recognized as a rapidly expanding organization, and I would welcome the opportunity to be a contributing staff member. Thank you for taking the time to review my enclosed resume. I will look forward to interviewing with you in the near future. My home telephone number is (614) 000-0000, or you can contact me at rtgcompute @ earthlink.net.

Sincerly,

Ronald T. Grant

Ronald T. Grant

Enclosure: Resume
AD - Columbus Dispatch (8-14-XX)

Figure 8.6 Sample cover letter.

© JIST Works

Section 4: Get Involved

Select an ad that interests you from your local or regional newspaper. Write a cover letter responding to it. Have a friend or teacher check your cover letter for content, appearance, grammar, and format.

Chapter 8 Review

Reteaching

Have students complete the "Finding the Right Words" and "Checking Your Location" worksheets in Chapter 8 of the *Preparing for Career Success Student Activity Book, Third Edition.*

Enrich Your Vocabulary

On a separate sheet of paper, number from 1 to 19, and complete the following activity. (Do not write in your textbook.) Match each statement with the most appropriate term from the "Enrich Your Vocabulary" list at the beginning of the chapter by writing that term next to the number of the correct statement.

1. A summary of a job seeker's work experience, education and training, and proven skills
2. Information about an organization that is hiring
3. People who recommend you to an employer
4. The process of seeking employment
5. A person applying for employment with a specific company
6. Using personal contacts to find a job
7. The type and number of jobs available
8. A preliminary meeting to eliminate unqualified candidates
9. A good way to meet several potential employers at one time
10. Any assistance that helps a job seeker find a job
11. Lists accurate information about you that is important to employers
12. Lists jobs you have held in the order you held them, beginning with the most recent
13. Groups qualifications by functions
14. A letter of introduction to a specific employer regarding your interest in a specific job opening
15. Job listings that provide the name of the employer or employment agency and a person or department to contact
16. A collection of listings of available jobs
17. Sometimes called a virtual or electronic resume
18. Job listings that provide only a post office box or e-mail address for sending a response
19. A database where job seekers can post their digital resume

Enrich Your Vocabulary Answers

1. resume
2. job lead
3. references
4. job search
5. job applicant
6. networking
7. job market
8. screening interview
9. job fairs
10. employment service
11. personal data sheet
12. chronological resume
13. functional resume
14. cover letter
15. identified ads
16. job banks
17. digital resume
18. blind ads
19. resume bank

© JIST Works

Check Your Knowledge Answers

1. Transportation and construction are growing; agriculture, forestry, fishing, hunting, utilities, and mining are declining. The rationale for answers will vary.
2. Answers will vary. Private employment agencies and the World Wide Web would be least helpful.
3. The local state employment service and on the Internet.
4. See "Responding to Help-Wanted Ads." (1) Job title. (2) A brief job description. (3) Required qualifications. (4) A short statement about the organization. (5) The name and address of the organization. (6) How and with whom to make contact in the organization.
5. Testing, counseling, and job placement.
6. In many cases, an optical scanner will perform the initial read of your resume.

Enrichment

Have students complete the Chapter 8 section of the *Preparing for Career Success Student Portfolio, Third Edition.*

Check Your Knowledge

On a separate sheet of paper, answer the following questions. (Do not write in your textbook.)

1. Review Figure 8.1. If you were a person who enjoyed working outdoors, which industry or sector would you select? Why? Which would you reject? Why?
2. Section 2 describes seven methods and resources to obtain job leads. Which two methods would you consider most helpful to a high school student? Why? Which two methods would you consider least useful to a high school student? Why?
3. Where should a job seeker look to find job openings posted on America's Job Bank?
4. What six pieces of information would you expect to find in an identified employment ad?
5. List three free services that are available from the State Bureau of Employment Services.
6. Why should a job seeker send a digital resume using the U.S. postal service?

Develop SCANS Competencies

Government experts say that successful workers productively use resources, interpersonal skills, information, systems, and technology. This activity will give you practice in developing information and systems skills.

You need to be systematic and organized when searching for a job. Being organized not only helps you, but it also impresses prospective employers and could be the difference between your getting or not getting a job.

A number of hints listed in this chapter will help you stay organized during your job search. You may want to review these hints. Then compare the flow charts in Figures 8.7 and 8.8 for finding a job. Use the best aspects of both charts to develop your own flow chart. Make your flow chart as specific as possible. Then write a paragraph explaining how your flow chart improves upon the two examples.

© JIST Works

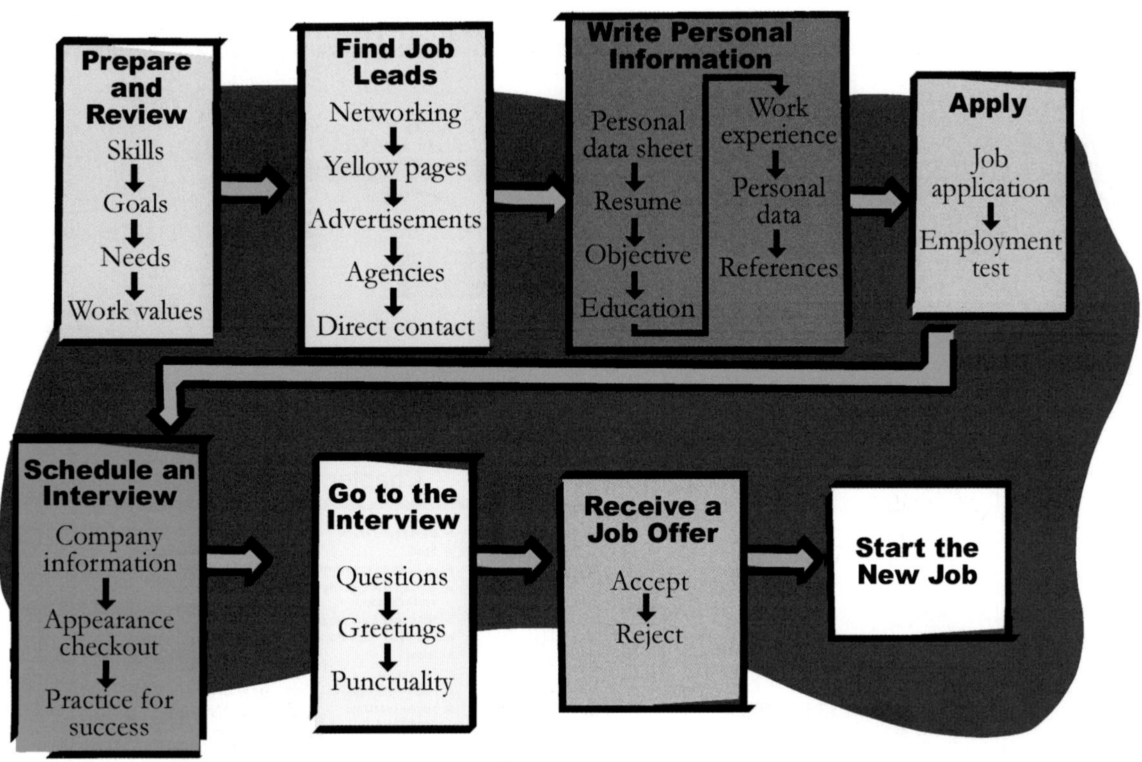

Figure 8.7 This job hunt trail shows the steps on the path to employment.

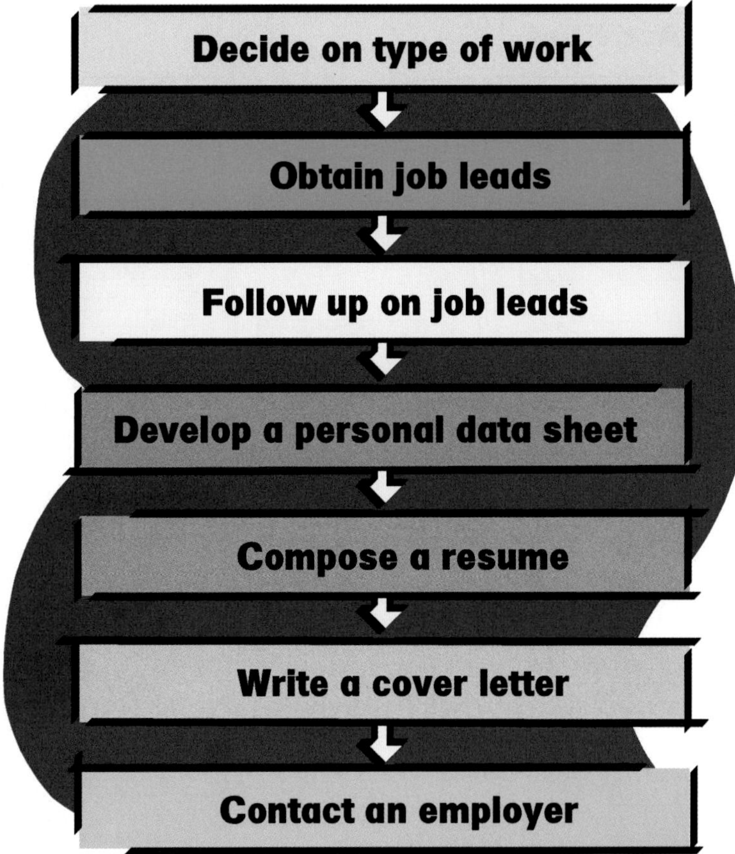

Figure 8.8 These are the steps in finding a job.

Chapter 9 Resources

Lesson Plans and Preparation

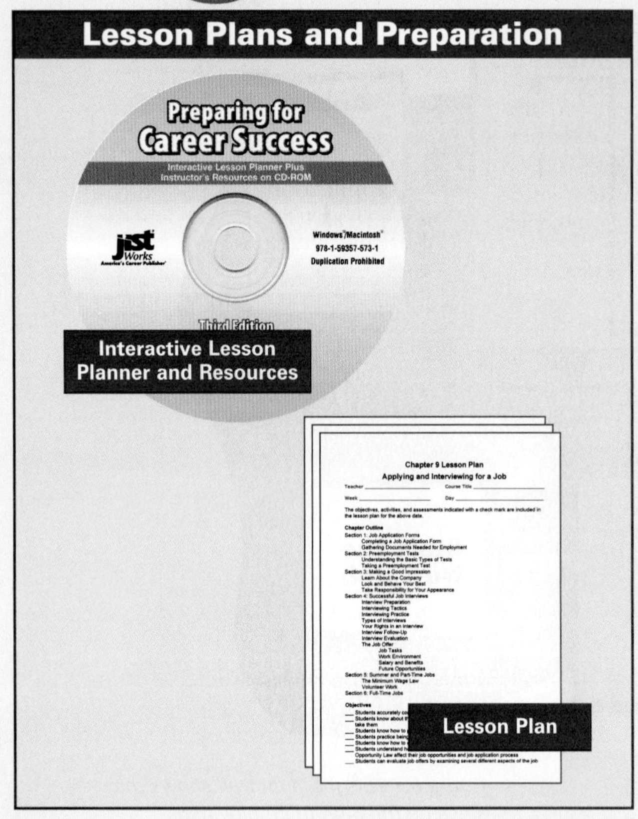

Preparing for Career Success
Interactive Lesson Planner Plus Instructor's Resources on CD-ROM
Third Edition
Interactive Lesson Planner and Resources
Chapter 9 Lesson Plan
Applying and Interviewing for a Job
Lesson Plan

Multimedia

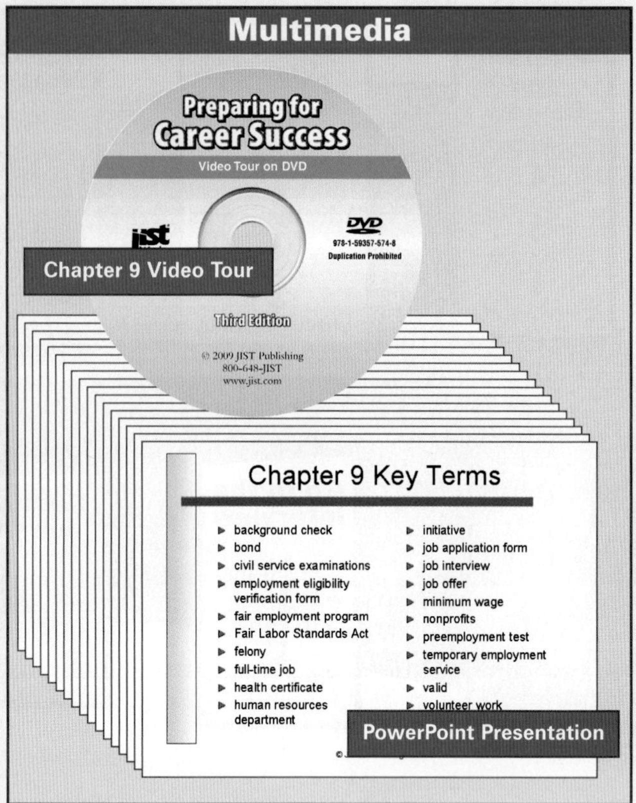

Preparing for Career Success
Video Tour on DVD
Chapter 9 Video Tour
Third Edition
© 2009 JIST Publishing
800-648-JIST
www.jist.com
Chapter 9 Key Terms
background check
bond
civil service examinations
employment eligibility verification form
fair employment program
Fair Labor Standards Act
felony
full-time job
health certificate
human resources department
initiative
job application form
job interview
job offer
minimum wage
nonprofits
preemployment test
temporary employment service
valid
volunteer work
PowerPoint Presentation

Activities

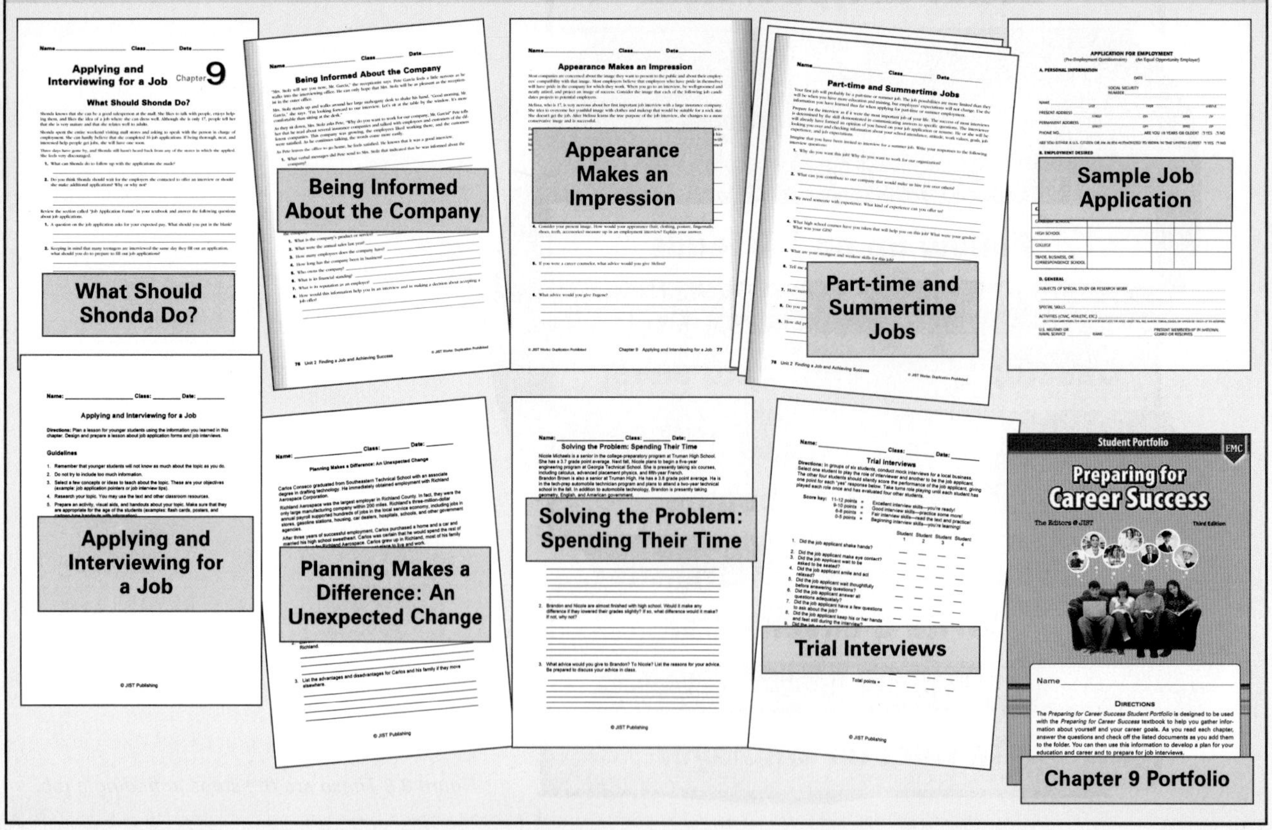

- What Should Shonda Do?
- Being Informed About the Company
- Appearance Makes an Impression
- Part-time and Summertime Jobs
- Sample Job Application
- Applying and Interviewing for a Job
- Planning Makes a Difference: An Unexpected Change
- Solving the Problem: Spending Their Time
- Trial Interviews
- Chapter 9 Portfolio

© JIST Works

Review and Assessment

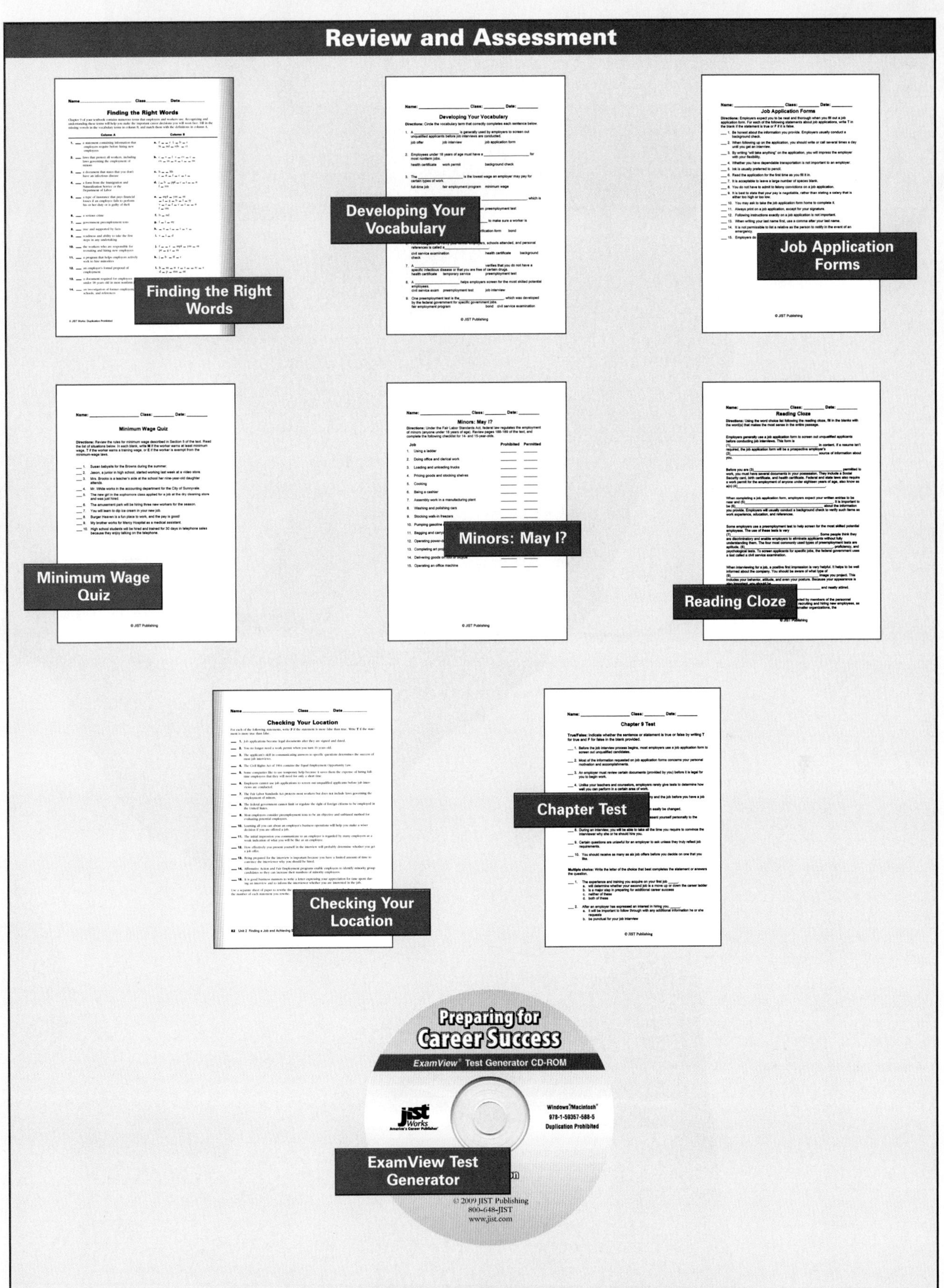

Finding the Right Words
Developing Your Vocabulary
Job Application Forms
Minimum Wage Quiz
Minors: May I?
Reading Cloze
Checking Your Location
Chapter Test
Preparing for Career Success
ExamView® Test Generator CD-ROM
Windows®/Macintosh®
978-1-59357-588-5
Duplication Prohibited
© 2009 JIST Publishing
800-648-JIST
www.jist.com
ExamView Test Generator

Chapter 9

Applying and Interviewing for a Job

Learning Objectives

- Complete an acceptable job application form
- Describe preemployment tests and explain why employers use them
- Locate several sources of information about companies and other organizations
- Present yourself well in a job interview, follow up with the interviewer, and evaluate your performance
- List the advantages and disadvantages of volunteer, part-time, and full-time work

Finding your first job, whether it is full-time or part-time, is a major step in preparing for career success. The experience and training you acquire will determine whether your second job is a move up or down the career ladder.

Enrich Your Vocabulary

In reading this chapter and doing the exercises, you will learn the following important terms:

background check	full-time job	minimum wage
bond	health certificate	nonprofits
civil service examinations	human resources department	preemployment test
employment eligibility verification form	initiative	temporary employment service
fair employment program	job application form	valid
Fair Labor Standards Act	job interview	volunteer work
felony	job offer	work permit

Vocabulary

You can use the "Developing Your Vocabulary" worksheet in Chapter 9 of the *Preparing for Career Success Instructor's CD-ROM, Third Edition* as a pretest for chapter concepts or as a reteaching worksheet.

Before you begin searching for your first or next job, you should be able to answer the following questions:

1. What personal documents will employers require?
2. What preemployment tests am I likely to encounter?
3. How can I obtain information about major employers?
4. How can I improve my job interviewing skills?
5. What are my legal rights as a job seeker?

Key to Success

When you apply for a job, be sure to have your personal data sheet with you (see Chapter 8). It contains the information that most job application forms request.

In Chapter 8, you learned how to plan your job search, develop a personal data sheet, and write a resume. The next step is to pursue job leads and prepare for interviews with potential employers. After an employer has expressed an interest in hiring you, you will need to follow through with any additional information he or she requests and be punctual for your job interview. Finally, you will need to be mentally prepared for job offers and rejections. The information in this chapter will help you prepare for each of these events.

Video Tour on DVD

Show students the Chapter 9 segment to introduce them to the content.

Section 1: Job Application Forms

School-to-Work Transition

Ask your students: What forms have you completed at school during the past two years? Explain to the students that learning to complete forms properly at school is good preparation for handling the many forms they will be required to complete in the world of work.

Before the job interview process begins, most employers use a **job application form** to screen out unqualified applicants. Your job application form creates an impression of you with the person who selects interview candidates. In most hiring situations, several qualified applicants apply for the same job. A neat, accurate application will help you join the group being interviewed.

Employers usually request certain basic information on a job application form. First, you will need to fill out the following personal information:

- Name
- Home address
- Home phone number (cell phone only if it is left on or has voice mail)

© JIST Works

- E-mail address
- Social Security number
- Date of birth (if under 18)

You will also need to provide information about your education and training. Some employers will request a copy of your high school transcript.

In the references section of the application, list individuals who will say positive things about you. Include the name, address, and phone number of each reference.

Most job applications have a space for you to fill in the job you are applying for and the hours you are available to work. State the specific job for which you are applying. Also, be specific about schedule conflicts such as your school schedule or transportation problems.

In the current and past employment section, list all full-time, part-time, and volunteer work experience. Include the name, address, and phone number of each former employer.

Sometimes applications have space for you to fill in information about your hobbies and personal interests. This information provides an employer some insight into your personality.

Employers may request other information on an application as well. Some employers will ask whether you have ever been convicted of a crime other than a minor traffic violation. In addition, the employer may ask you to authorize a consumer-reporting agency to perform a credit check.

Most of the information requested on job application forms is factual. Your personal motivation or accomplishments receive very little space. Instead, a restricted amount of space is provided for your personal information, job skills, and work experience. If a resume is not required, your job application form will be the potential employer's major source of information about you.

If you are hired, your employer will keep your job application form on file for the duration of your employment. After you sign and date it, the job application form becomes a legal document. Be certain that all of your responses are honest. If you misrepresent yourself in any statement and later this information comes to your employer's attention, it is a breach of trust and grounds for dismissal.

TECHNOLOGY

Instead of paper job applications, most major retail stores now have online applications that job applicants complete on the store's Web site or at an in-store kiosk. Following these tips will help you advance beyond this computerized screening-out process:

- **Do your research.** Review the entire application so that you can take time to think about how best to answer the questions. Find a description of the job you are applying for so that you know what keywords to use.
- **Keep your resume and personal data sheet handy.** At a kiosk, you will need to type this information into the computer. From a Web site, you may be able to copy and paste information from your electronic resume file into the job application.
- **Be prepared to take some tests.** Online applications often include skill and psychological tests in addition to standard job application questions.
- **Follow up in person.** This action will show that you are serious about the job and will make you stand out in the manager's mind when he or she reviews the applications.

Completing a Job Application Form

Employers expect you to be neat and thorough when you fill out a job application form. Follow these guidelines:

1. Read the entire application before you begin, and follow the instructions. Employers know that an applicant who does not follow directions on the job application form is not likely to follow directions on the job.

Read job application forms carefully before filling out all the questions.

2. Write something in every blank space. If a question doesn't apply to you, write "N/A" (not applicable), or draw a line through the blank. Completing all of the blanks will demonstrate your thoroughness.
3. Print is easier to read than longhand, and ink is usually preferred to pencil. However, if you use ink and make a mistake, you likely will not be able to correct it without ruining the neat appearance of the application form.
4. If possible, find out in advance what jobs are available. Emphasize your qualifications for one specific job. Some employers take a dim view of applicants who apply for "just any job" or who write "will take anything."
5. Some employers may schedule an interview with you before they ask you to complete a job application form. In this case, ask for a copy of the form before the interview. This way, you will have enough time to consider your answers and to type in the requested information.
6. If you are not satisfied with the first application you complete, request another from the office worker who is helping you. Keep in mind, though, that some employers frown on applicants who make mistakes and require additional forms.
7. The application form may ask for "your expected pay." If so, it is best to state that you will accept the standard rate for the position or that your pay is negotiable. A salary or hourly rate may be fixed, but pay is usually open for discussion. If possible, wait until you are offered a job before discussing pay. Asking for too much money could eliminate you from consideration. On the other hand, willingness to accept a noncompetitive, low wage will not gain an employer's respect or advance your career.

Reteaching

Have students complete the "Job Application Forms" worksheet in Chapter 9 of the *Preparing for Career Success Instructor's CD-ROM, Third Edition.*

KEY TO SUCCESS

Respectfully request two copies of the job application form. Use one copy as a rough draft and the other as the final product.

Case Study

Have students complete the "What Should Shonda Do?" worksheet in Chapter 9 of the *Preparing for Career Success Student Activity Book, Third Edition.*

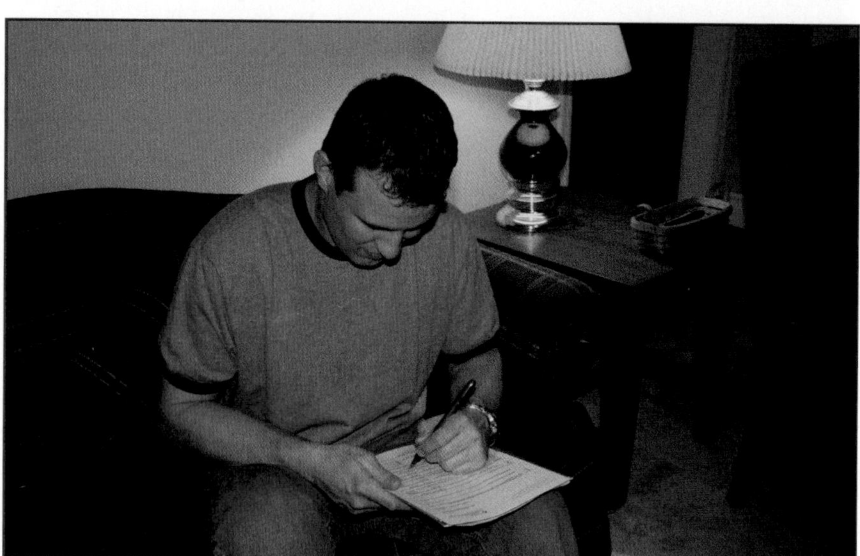

Carl asked the secretary for permission to take the job application form home so that he could write a few paragraphs about his qualifications for the job opening.

© JIST Works

8. If the application form asks for the name of a person to notify in case of emergency, list the name of your closest relative or a best friend living in the area. Include that person's home and work telephone numbers.
9. Be honest about the information you provide. Employers usually conduct a **background check** (an investigation to verify your former employers, schools attended, and personal references).
10. Some job application forms request a list of your memberships in social or civic clubs and organizations. Some employers consider your involvement as an indication of how well you get along with other people.
11. Employers prefer applicants who have reliable transportation. If you own or have access to a reliable car or public transportation, emphasize that fact.
12. Most job application forms ask if you ever have been convicted of law violations. In addition, many employers initiate a routine police investigation before hiring a new employee. This is very important if you must be bonded. A **bond** is a type of insurance that pays financial losses if an employee fails to perform his or her duty or is guilty of theft. The law requires you to admit to felony convictions. A **felony** is a criminal offense and requires a penalty of one year or more in prison. However, you are not required to acknowledge violations for which you were arrested but not convicted. Traffic violations other than felonies do not require disclosure.
13. Job application forms usually ask whether you are willing to undergo a physical examination. Tests for chemical dependency are frequently included in the physical. Lost production, poor job performance, and safety violations caused by workers' substance abuse are very costly to employers.
14. Some employers want to know how many days of school or work you missed during the past 12 months. Missing 7 or more days usually indicates an unreliable worker.
15. When you submit your job application to the employer, ask about the procedure for finding out the status of your job application. Persistence indicates your interest in the job and may result in a job offer. Don't be a nuisance, but do follow up on your application.

As a teenager seeking part-time or entry-level employment, you may become the exception to the normal job seeker's rule. Be prepared for an interview when you pick up a job application form. An employer might have immediate needs and take time to talk with you. Be informed about the employer's business, be appropriately dressed, and learn some interviewing techniques before you start the process of picking up job applications.

School-to-Work Transition

Ask your students if any of them have ever had an illness at school and the school office was unable to contact a parent or responsible adult because of incomplete or outdated information on their emergency card. Explain that the employer's emergency information serves the same purpose as their school emergency card. It protects them in case of a serious accident.

Career Fact

Job applicants frequently think they can hide past problems from potential employers, particularly if they've moved since the problems occurred. Yet most employers perform some type of background check. Many dig into applicants' personal history with preemployment checks. Concerns about everything from workplace violence to embezzlement prompt the checks. These employers hire background-checking firms to comb records for arrests for stealing, using drugs, harassing coworkers, and the like.

School-to-Work Transition

Explain that when an employee does not show up for work, coworkers must work harder or the employer must pay another employee a premium wage to work overtime. Make this statement: Raise your hand if you missed seven or more days of school last year. Write that number of students on the chalkboard. Ask the students in this group if they missed several days in a row with an illness or missed a day or two at a time. Explain that employers consider students with numerous short absences to be unreliable.

Gathering Documents Needed for Employment

After you are hired and before you start work, employment laws require that you provide certain documents to your employer to verify that you are eligible to work in the United States and to establish your identity. An employer must review these documents and complete an **employment eligibility verification form** (Form I-9) for you. You will also have to sign this form during your first day of work.

When you begin a job search, make sure you have the following documents in your possession:

FIND OUT MORE

If you do not have a Social Security number, phone your local Social Security Office and ask for an SS-5 Form to apply for one. You can also go online, enter **Social Security Form** on your search engine, and then print the form.

- **Social Security card:** The number on your Social Security card is used to identify your tax and retirement records and provides a way for numerous agencies and organizations to identify you.
- **Birth certificate:** Your birth certificate is proof of your age and place of birth (and citizenship). To obtain a copy of your birth certificate, contact the Department of Health, Division of Vital Statistics, in the county where you were born.
- **Driver's license or other photographic identification:** Other acceptable forms of identification include a U.S. passport, student identification card, voter registration card, or state identification card. If you are under 18, you may be able to use a school report card or medical record as identification.
- **Health certificate:** Certain jobs require a **health certificate**. This document may certify that you do not have a specific infectious disease or that you are free of certain drugs. Your employer will know whether you need this kind of documentation. If you do, your family doctor or the local health department can help you obtain the proper health certificate.
- **Work permit:** Employees under 18 years of age must have a **work permit** for most nonfarm jobs. Your school counselor or principal can help you get the application. You will not be able to obtain the work permit until you are hired. The employer must complete some information on the application.

Laws concerning work permits are part of the **Fair Labor Standards Act** (FLSA). This important federal legislation protects all workers. It includes laws concerning work permits that regulate the employment of *minors* (anyone under 18 years of age). In addition, state laws also regulate the employment of minors.

Federal law states it is illegal to employ 14- and 15-year-old minors

- During school hours, except for students enrolled in work-experience and career-exploration programs
- Before 7 a.m. or after 7 p.m., except from June 1 through Labor Day (minors may work until 9 p.m.)

© JIST Works

- More than 3 hours per day on school days
- More than 18 hours per week when school is in session
- More than 8 hours per day on nonschool days
- More than 40 hours per week when school is not in session

Federal law states that (among others), it is legal to employ 14- and 15-year-old minors to

- Perform office and clerical work (including the operation of office machines)
- Work at cashiering, sales, art work, window trimming, price marking, packing, and stocking shelves
- Work bagging and carrying out customer orders and perform delivery work by foot, bicycle, or public transportation
- Dispense gasoline and oil and wash and polish cars (may not use pits, racks, or lifting devices or inflate tires with removable retaining rings)

Among the occupations legally prohibited to 14- and 15-year old minors are those involving

- Any manufacturing, mining, or processing occupations
- Work operating or tending hoisting apparatuses or power-driven machinery
- Work requiring the use of ladders or scaffolds
- Work involving cooking, operating food slicing or grinding equipment, and being in food coolers or freezers
- Work loading goods to and from trucks, railroad cars, or conveyers

The Fair Labor Standards Act requires a minimum age of 18 for any nonagricultural occupations declared particularly hazardous for 16- and 17-year-olds or detrimental to their health and well-being.

Work Permit and Age Certificate

CA-7 for 16 and 17 years of age

Regular/Temporary

Directions: Please print using an ink pen, or type.
See back of this form for details.

Permit Number for school use (optional)

Section I: To be completed by the Employer

Name of Business | Address | City | Zip

Applicant's Job Title | Will minor be working under an existing Michigan Department of Consumer and Industry Services-granted hour deviation? [ ] No [ ] Yes (copy attached) If Yes, hours listed require the hour deviation and parent/guardian consent.

Hourly Wage | Hours of Employment: (total per week)

Job Duties/Tasks to be performed by minor: | Earliest Starting Time a.m./p.m. | Latest Ending Time a.m./p.m.

Employer Signature (x)

Title | Date

Telephone ( )

Employer Information:
- The employer must have a completed work permit form before a minor begins work.
- The employer must provide competent adult supervision at all times.
- The employer of the minor must comply with federal, state, and local laws and regulations, including nondiscrimination against any applicant or employee because of race, color, sex, age, religion, marital status, national origin, ancestry, or disability.

Section II: To be completed by Applicant

Name of Minor | Address | City | Zip

Name of School* | Address | City | Zip

Age | Date of Birth (Month, Day, Year) | School Status (check one) [ ] in school [ ] left school | Last Grade Completed

Signature of Minor (x) | Name(s) of Parent(s)/Guardian(s)

*present or last attended

Section III: To be completed by School's Issuing Officer

This is to certify that:
(1) the minor personally appeared before me,
(2) this form was properly completed,
(3) listed job duties are in compliance with state and federal laws and regulations,
(4) listed hours are in compliance with state and federal laws and regulations,
(5) this form was signed by student and employer, and I authorize the issuance of this work permit.

Signature of Issuing Officer
(x)
Issue Date:

Evidence of Age confirmed by: (issuing officer checks one)
[ ] Birth Certificate [ ] Certificate of Arrival in the U.S.
[ ] Driver's License
[ ] School Record [ ] Other
[ ] Baptismal Certificate
[ ] Hospital Record of Birth

Number of Hours in School (per week)

School
Address
City, State, Zip
Telephone ( )

Form CA-7 (revised September 1998) Combined Offer of Employment & Work Permit and Age Certificate Print on Canary Bond

The Fair Labor Standards Act requires employees under 18 years of age to obtain a work permit.

Reteaching

Have students complete the "Minors: May I?" worksheet in Chapter 9 of the *Preparing for Career Success Instructor's CD-ROM, Third Edition.*

Discussion Starter

Ask your students: Does the Fair Labor Standards Act protect or interfere with the employment rights of minor workers? What are the reasons for your answer?

© JIST Works

Building Character: Small Lies—Big Problems

When Russell Wakefield answered the following question on his job application form, he didn't tell the truth: "Are you now dependent on or a user of any addictive or hallucinogenic drug other than for medical treatment under the supervision of a doctor?" That was 14 months ago.

A cough broke the silence in the back of the courtroom as the judge looked down from his bench and pronounced Russell's sentence. "Russell Wakefield, you are sentenced to spend the next six months in the county jail and to pay your former employer, Tri-City Delivery, $12,200 for damage to the truck you were driving. In addition, you will pay the United Utility Company $3,800 for damage to their utility pole and electrical wires. Because you were driving under the influence of alcohol, you will lose your chauffeur's license in this state for a period of one year." Russell did not know how he would pay the damages. Tri-City Delivery had fired him, and it seemed doubtful that another company would hire him. The $1,700 Russell had saved after high school graduation was a source of personal pride to him. Now it was gone. Russell felt angry, foolish, and humiliated. How would he ever face his parents or friends?

Again, the gray eyes of the judge looked down from the bench as he announced to everyone in the courtroom, "Because this is your first such offense, the court suspends the six months in jail. However, the court places you on probation for a period of one year. During your probation, you must attend weekly counseling sessions sponsored by this court."

Find Out More

The U.S. Department of Labor has established a Web site titled "Youth Rules!" to describe the regulations governing teen work. You can find this site, in both English and Spanish, at www.youthrules.dol.gov.

Cluster Link

Have you ever thought about becoming a firefighter, lawyer, police officer, or judge? If so, take time to read the information about the Law and Public Safety career cluster in the appendix.

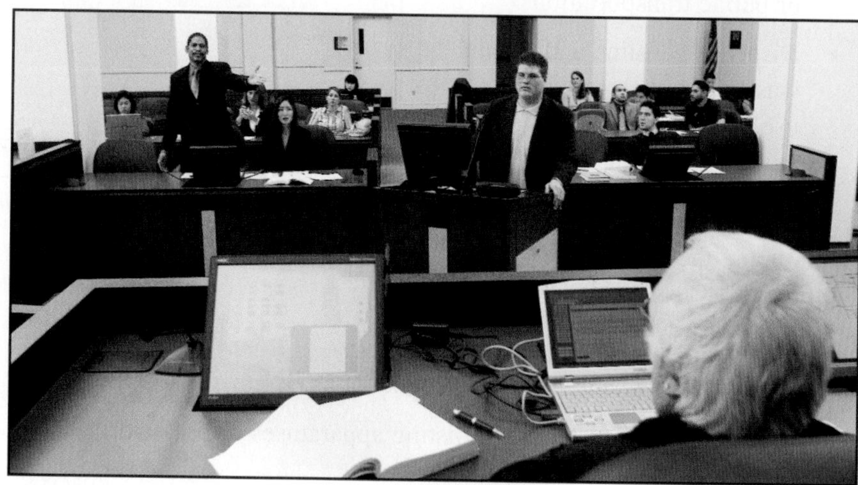

Critical Thinking

Before a new employer hires Russell, he will probably be asked on the job application form or during the job interview about his use of drugs or alcohol. Years later, the employer could fire Russell if he elects to cover up his past and the employer discovers the truth.

If you were Russell, how would you handle this situation? How might your solution help Russell to strengthen his character? To improve his career? How might your solution weaken his character? Damage his career?

© JIST Works

Section 1: Get Involved

Practice filling out job application forms before you begin a job search. Your school librarian, counselor, or the owner of a local business may be able to provide you with a blank form. Fill out the application with the same care and thoroughness you would use if you were submitting it to an employer.

When you finish filling out the job application form, use the following criteria to evaluate your work:

1. Is my typing or printing neat and easy to read?
2. Are all of the words spelled correctly?
3. Is all of the information accurate?
4. Does the finished application make me look like a good job candidate?

Section 2: Preemployment Tests

Discussion Starter

Ask your students: Are preemployment tests valid or do they discriminate against certain job candidates? What facts can you offer to support your position? Do you think job candidates should be required to take preemployment tests? Why or why not?

Just as your counselors and teachers have given you tests to determine how well you can perform in a particular school subject, employers may test you to determine how well you can perform in a specific area of work. Some employers use a **preemployment test** to help them screen for the most skilled potential employees. The use of preemployment tests is growing rapidly. Why do you suppose this is?

Many employers consider testing to be the most objective and unbiased method for screening potential workers. Personal feelings do not influence the selection of employees when this approach is used. For most employers, preemployment testing is only one of the methods used to select new employees. Most employers know that attitude, experience, education, training, and appearance are all important to job success.

The use of preemployment tests is very controversial. Some people argue that tests are the only **valid** (true and supported by facts) method an employer can use to determine the skill level, honesty, personality, attitude, and communication ability of job applicants. Others argue that preemployment tests are discriminatory and eliminate job applicants without totally understanding them.

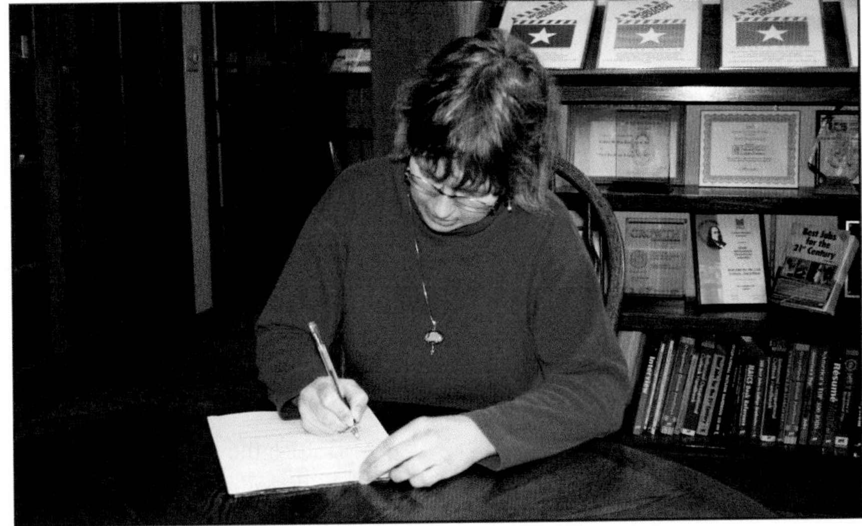

Some people argue that preemployment tests are the only fair way to determine a job applicant's qualifications, and others consider them to be discriminatory. What is your opinion?

Understanding the Basic Types of Tests

An employer may give you a preemployment test before or during a job interview. The test may require you to answer questions, solve problems,

© JIST Works

> **CAREER FACT**
>
> Many employers rely on written examinations to weed out unskilled applicants. Thirty-five percent of large and midsize companies test applicants' math skills, and 31 percent test literacy, according to a survey by the American Management Association. The survey also reports that more than one third of applicants fail these exams because they lack the reading, writing, or math skills needed to do the job. Although some companies will hire and train applicants who fail, more than 85 percent will not.

perform certain tasks, or perform a combination of all three. Some tests limit your time, whereas others allow as much time as you need. Employers commonly use four types of preemployment tests:

1. Aptitude tests predict success in some occupation or course of training. For example, there are tests of musical aptitude, math aptitude, and engineering aptitude.
2. Intelligence tests measure the intellectual abilities used for all types of thinking. Examples include memory and communication skills.
3. Proficiency tests measure a person's ability to perform some particular task. Some examples are troubleshooting engine problems, operating a word processor, reading, and playing a musical instrument.
4. Psychological tests measure your interests, attitudes, honesty, and personality traits. Employers are particularly concerned about hiring honest employees when job responsibilities include handling cash or merchandise.
5. Personality inventories measure such characteristics as emotional stability, responsibility, creativity, and openness to new situations.
6. **Civil service examinations** are preemployment tests developed by the federal government for specific government jobs. The Civil Service Commission administers civil service tests and announces job openings. Then it posts the announcements in government office buildings, Civil Service Career Information and Testing Centers, and local offices of the Bureau of Employment Services. Each civil service examination is specifically designed for a particular job classification. Most government workers qualified for their jobs by achieving a certain score on a civil service examination.

Taking a Preemployment Test

The following tips will help you achieve your best possible score on a preemployment test:

1. Make certain that you are well rested and relaxed on the day of the test. Arrive at the test site a few minutes early.
2. Before the test, ask the test administrator what is expected. Some tests do not allow the examiner to answer questions after testing has begun.
3. Find out if there is a penalty for giving a wrong answer. If so, skip questions that you are not sure you can answer correctly.
4. If the test has a time limit, skip difficult questions that might slow you down. If time allows, go back to the difficult questions after you finish the easier ones.
5. When the test is over, ask the test administrator when he or she will notify you of the results. You will probably be interviewed if you score well on the preemployment test.

© JIST Works

Solving the Problem: Selecting the Best Approach

The timer sounded, and Mrs. Greene told Helen to stop. Helen Clark was the sixth employment candidate to complete the word-processing skill test that day.

Helen asked Mrs. Greene if she would be permitted to repeat the test if her score was not satisfactory. Mrs. Greene explained that company policy would not permit job applicants to repeat the test.

Helen was certain that she had not performed at her best. She explained to Mrs. Greene the difficulty she experienced with timed tests. Despite Helen's anxiety with timed tests, her community college instructor recommended her as a highly skilled, very thorough word-processing operator. As Helen left the office, she thanked Mrs. Greene for giving her the test and considering her for a word-processing job.

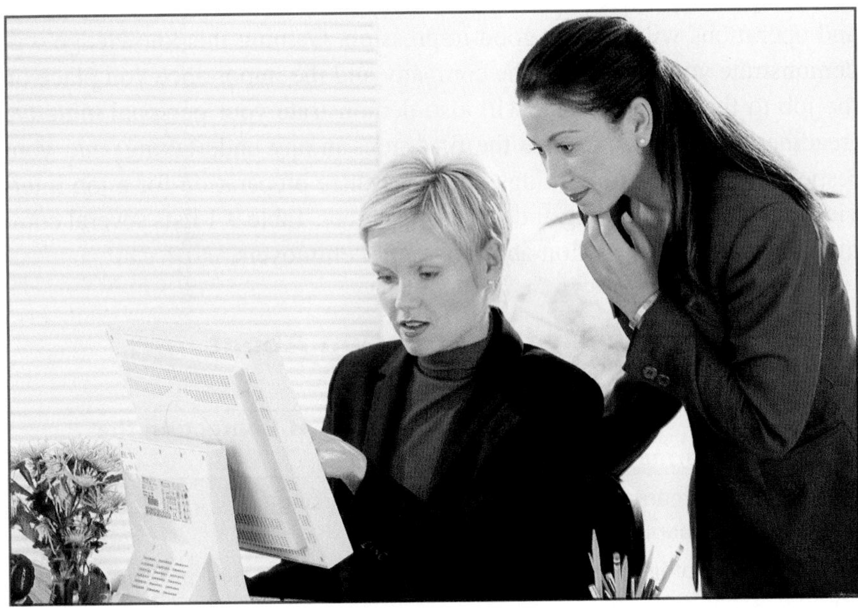

Critical Thinking

Helen's test results were average. Two other applicants scored higher. However, Mrs. Greene felt that Helen would be a pleasant, sincere, and thorough worker. If you were Mrs. Greene, would you schedule Helen for an interview with the manager? Explain your reasons.

How might Mrs. Greene's decision affect her own future career?

> **KEY TO SUCCESS**
>
> Remember the old saying "Don't count your chickens until they hatch"? Keep your job search active until you accept a job offer and you are actually hired.

Section 2: Get Involved

Answer the following on a separate sheet of paper, and be prepared to discuss your responses in class.

1. Should employers permit job applicants to retake employment tests? Explain your answer.
2. Which type of employment test is most important for job success? Explain your answer.

© JIST Works

Section 3: Making a Good Impression

At your job interview, you need to be well informed about the company and the job. The more you know, the better. Your overall appearance and your verbal and nonverbal behaviors send a message of the importance you place on getting the job. In the interview, be sure to put your best foot forward. Let the employer know that you value this opportunity. A positive first impression influences the rest of the interview. Your first impression may determine whether you are hired.

Key to Success

Do not be a "No-show." If unexpected circumstances require you to cancel a scheduled interview, phone the interviewer at least 24 hours in advance, and apologize for the inconvenience. No-shows are irresponsible and unprofessional.

Learn About the Company

Before you attend a job interview, learn all you can about the organization's day-to-day operations. Your understanding of the employer's purpose and operations will make a good impression. Gaining this knowledge will demonstrate your interest in the company and the importance you place on the job to the interviewer. It will also demonstrate your personal **initiative** (readiness and ability to take the first steps in any undertaking) and your responsibility for getting things done. Advance preparation for a job interview could result in a long and satisfying career. Table 9.1 lists several common sources of information about potential employers.

There is no substitute for hard work.

—Thomas Alva Edison

Table 9.1 Sources of Information About Organizations

Source of Information	Means of Contacting the Source
Employees who currently work for the organization	Networking
Annual reports of finances, products, and services	Public library, stockbrokers, Internet
Brochures published by the organization	The organization's public relations office
Advertisements for the organization's products or services	Newspapers, magazines, and Web sites
The Better Business Bureau	Telephone directory and the Internet
Friends or relatives	Networking
The organization itself	Your contact at the organization The organization's Web site
Business periodicals and directories	Public library
The local chamber of commerce	Telephone directory and the Internet

Enrichment

Have students complete the "Being Informed About the Company" worksheet in Chapter 9 of the *Preparing for Career Success Student Activity Book, Third Edition.*

Cross-Reference

You may wish to have students review "Networking," in Section 2 of Chapter 8.

If information about a specific employer is not easily available, investigate the operations of similar organizations or the industry as a whole. For example, you may not be able to find out how a particular insurance agency

© JIST Works

operates, but information on the types of insurance and services that insurance companies provide is readily available in your public library or on the Internet.

Your employer will have a direct influence on your lifestyle (review "Lifestyle" in Section 4 of Chapter 3) and future career alternatives. Consider each potential employer's geographic location, size, products and services, reputation, financial outlook, and other factors that have specific importance to you.

The impression you have of the organization is as important as the impression its management team has of you. Your relationship with an employer should meet the needs and expectations of both the employer and you. Your first day on the job is not the time to learn that your new job is not what you thought it would be. Becoming informed about the organization and the job you will be doing is your responsibility.

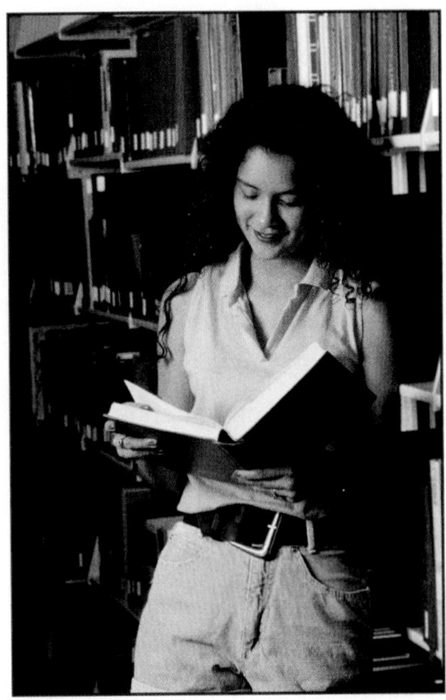

Julie has a job interview at Crest Manufacturing Company tomorrow morning. She wants to be well informed and make a good impression, so she is reading about Crest's business operations and the occupation of assembler.

Look and Behave Your Best

Many factors contribute to your overall image, and you have control over most of them. When you enter an office to apply for a job or for an interview, do you project an image of

- Self-confidence or insecurity?
- Concern or indifference?
- Cooperation or arrogance?

First impressions are not easily changed. Office workers and the interviewer will begin to form opinions about you based on your appearance and actions.

For example, good posture indicates self-confidence. Walking with a springy step indicates an upbeat and energetic person. On the other hand, slumping when you walk, letting your head hang down, and crossing your hands send a message of low self-esteem and insecurity. A tightly closed mouth and stiff jaw indicate anger or frustration, but having a twinkle in your eye and a smile on your face indicate a pleasant, cooperative nature. Your walking and standing posture will change as situations change. At different times, you have probably projected all of these messages.

Employers want to hire interested, enthusiastic workers. They are also concerned about the image their employees present to customers, clients, and the public. During your job interview, the employer will try to determine how well you match the organization's image. For example, if you are hired, will you fit in and be accepted by your coworkers? Will your appearance help or harm the organization?

Cooperative Learning/ Self-Understanding

Ask students to read "Look and Behave Your Best." Next, divide the class into groups of three. Have each group use the information in the first paragraph to discuss six ways people can project their personal image. Ask each group member to share his or her perception of the type of self-image he or she projects. The other two members of the group should provide feedback about the speaker's self-assessment. When you feel the students are done, ask volunteers to share what they have learned.

Take Responsibility for Your Appearance

T-shirts, sweats, jeans, and running shoes may be appropriate dress for school, but not for a job interview. If you do not have appropriate clothes for an interview, consider buying an outfit with money you earned from a part-time job or gift money you receive for graduation. In addition, your peers might admire the rings and jewelry embedded in your ears, nose, and lips, but the interviewer may not consider them appropriate.

Your personal appearance is your responsibility. The following guidelines are especially important for a job interview, but you should also follow them after you are hired:

1. Be freshly showered or bathed, and use a modest amount of deodorant.
2. Have clean teeth, and use a modest amount of mouthwash.
3. Make sure your fingernails are clean and neatly trimmed. "Fashion nails" could indicate that you do not intend to work with your hands.
4. Your hair should be clean, neat, and trimmed.
5. Your clothes should be clean and ironed and should fit well.
6. Your shoes should be cleaned and polished.

Tips for females: Hemlines just below the knee and conservative or tailored blouses are appropriate. Save your short skirts and shorts for other events. Hosiery that is neutral in color is always correct, as are medium-heel, closed-toe shoes. Select simple jewelry, and use a modest amount of cosmetics and cologne. Use conservative nail polish and eye shadow.

Enrichment

Send four volunteer writers to the chalkboard. Assign one of the following headings to each writer: "Fast-food worker," "Clothing store clerk," "Service station attendant," and "General office clerk." Ask seated class members for personal appearance suggestions that would be appropriate for an interview for one of these four jobs. (Limit class members to one suggestion until you have involved all of the class members.) Have each writer list the suggestions under the heading for his or her assigned job.

Discussion Starter

Should employers care about the way you dress as long as you are able to do the job? Why or why not?

Compare the appearance of these job applicants to the interviewing guidelines and tips described in this section. Which examples of appearance are appropriate? Which examples are inappropriate?

© JIST Works

Tips for males: If you wear a suit or sport jacket, select one that is conservative in style and color. Make certain that your slacks are long enough to cover the top of well-polished, dark-colored shoes. Under no circumstances should you wear jewelry, including distracting neck chains.

When you attend a job interview, you should be well groomed and neatly attired and project an image of success. Trying to make a good impression on the interviewer may seem phony to you, but to the interviewer, the appearance you project in the job interview is the same appearance you will project to coworkers, customers, clients, and the public. When you display a satisfactory personal appearance, many employers will regard it as a sign of your having a positive attitude and a willingness to follow rules. If you do not know what is appropriate, dress conservatively but a little better than you will be expected to dress for the job. Avoid wearing trendy fashions.

Enrichment

Have students complete the "Appearance Makes an Impression" worksheet in Chapter 9 of the *Preparing for Career Success Student Activity Book, Third Edition.*

Section 3: Get Involved

Answer the following on a separate sheet of paper, and be prepared to discuss your responses in class.

1. Select a major employer. Use the information sources listed in Table 9.1 to learn as much as possible about the organization's product or service, annual sales, and number of employees. Report the information to your class.
2. Interview a white-collar worker and a blue-collar worker. Ask each to list the necessary clothing and to describe the personal appearance expected for a person with his or her job. How do the clothing requirements and personal appearance expectations relate to the employee's job tasks? Be specific.

Section 4: Successful Job Interviews

The **job interview** is an opportunity for you to present yourself personally to the employer. Not everyone (fewer than 25 percent) who applies for a job is interviewed. All of the work you put into your job search is in preparation for this important meeting. How effectively you present yourself will probably determine whether you receive a job offer.

In large organizations, well-trained interviewers work in the **human resources department**. This department is usually responsible for recruiting and hiring new employees, for administering employee benefit programs, and for employee relations. Human resources assistants (see the appendix) or human resources administrators conduct most initial interviews. Department managers usually conduct additional interviews. In smaller organizations, the owner or manager usually conducts the interviews.

Whether you are interviewing for a job with a neighborhood pizza parlor or a worldwide corporation, the interviewer will evaluate your suitability for the job opening by considering

- Your job skills and whether you take pride in your work
- Your willingness to follow company rules

TECHNOLOGY

Because many employers run an Internet search on the people they plan to interview, you need to consider the impression you give online as well as in person. Having a well-designed personal Web site or a thoughtful blog can make an employer think more highly of you. On the other hand, an embarrassing YouTube video can create a negative impression about you and can prevent you from getting the job you want. Do an Internet search on yourself and try to remove (or request that others remove) anything that employers might consider objectionable before you apply for a job.

© JIST Works

KEY TO SUCCESS

You never get a second chance to make a good first impression.

- Your ability and willingness to work with others
- Your sincerity, honesty, and attitude
- How well you "fit in" with the organization and other staff members
- How you compare to other job candidates

When you arrive for your job interview, be businesslike and friendly with everyone you meet. After you leave, the interviewer will probably ask the receptionist or secretary for his or her impression of you. Introduce yourself in a friendly, relaxed manner, and offer a firm handshake. Remember that your nonverbal actions, such as posture and facial expressions, send messages to the interviewer about your attitude and self-confidence. Use your body language to make a good impression.

Cross-Reference

Have students review "Nonverbal Communication" in Section 2 of Chapter 7. Next, send two writers to the chalkboard, and assign one of these headings to each: "Positive Nonverbal Behaviors" or "Negative Nonverbal Behaviors." Ask individual students for an example of one positive or negative behavior that a job seeker might display in an interview. Explain to your class that job applicants should also watch the nonverbal behaviors of the person conducting the interview. They are a good indicator of the interviewer's feelings.

Allow the interviewer to guide the conversation after the introductions. He or she will explain the responsibilities of the job, company benefits, and vacation policies. Later, if a job is offered, the interviewer will negotiate an acceptable wage or salary with you. The interviewer is also the person who will notify you when a hiring decision has been made, will answer your questions about the job or benefits, and will address any other concerns you have regarding the opening.

You can expect the interviewer to be knowledgeable about the job opening and about the characteristics that the employer is seeking in a job applicant. Most interviewers will try to put you at ease and will treat you in a very professional and friendly manner.

During the interview, you will be asked several questions about your background and your interest in the job. While the interviewer is talking with you, he or she will be making judgments about your character, personality, and skills. The entire conversation will probably last between 30 minutes and 1 hour. This is not a long time to communicate your interests and abilities.

The interviewer will signal the end of the interview by standing up, shaking hands, and making a concluding statement. Thank the interviewer for his or her time and consideration in meeting with you. Before you leave, restate your interest in the job, and ask when you can expect someone to contact you.

Lisa is calm because she arrived a few minutes early for her interview.

Interview Preparation

Gather all of the information and papers you will need for your interview, and place them in a folder or briefcase. Keeping them contained will prevent you from dropping or losing them. Include your resume, personal data sheet, recommendations from teachers and previous employers, school grades, Social Security number, birth certificate, and a work permit application. Having all this information available will demonstrate to the interviewer that you are organized and prepared. Both of these qualities are important on the job. If you complete a job application before the interview, make certain that it is neat and accurate before turning it over to the interviewer.

© JIST Works

The day before the interview, phone the interviewer's secretary to confirm the appointment. Do not trust your memory. Make a note of the date, time, address, name of the interviewer, and directions. Be sure to carry this information with you on the day of the interview as well.

Interviewing Tactics

Read the following interviewing tactics carefully. They will increase your chances for a successful job interview.

1. Arrive on time—preferably a little early. If you are not familiar with the organization's location, make a trial run a few days before the interview.
2. Know what skills are required to do the job. Know how your school, work, and other activities can relate to the job you are seeking.
3. Go to the interview alone. This demonstrates your independence and maturity.
4. Listen to each question carefully. If you do not understand a question, ask for clarification before you answer.
5. Take time to think about each question before responding.
6. When you answer questions, make positive, brief, but complete statements. Be prepared to expand on your answers when asked.
7. Show an enthusiastic interest in the job and a sincere desire to learn.
8. Relax. You do not have to be perfect. Being nervous is normal.
9. Keep your personal problems out of the conversation.
10. Be sincere, and give honest answers. Never argue with the interviewer.
11. Use proper English and avoid slang. Speak clearly.
12. Don't interrupt! If you want to ask a question or make a statement, wait for an appropriate opening in the conversation.
13. Look directly at the interviewer's eyes, and listen carefully.
14. Always thank the interviewer for his or her time, and ask for a business card. Thank the secretary and the receptionist if you get a chance. Their opinions may count.

Building Character: Confidence Wins

Mr. Waters called his secretary on the intercom and told him to send Roberta Castile in for the interview. Mr. Waters had more than 20 years of experience as a human resources administrator for the International News Publishing Company. He wondered how many job applicants he had interviewed over the years.

Cross-Reference

Suggest to your students that they review "Knowing Yourself and Career Decisions," in Section 2 of Chapter 4. Explain that reviewing their strong personal characteristics will help them to answer many of the interviewer's questions.

Stephen feels tense because he was almost late for his interview.

Cooperative Learning

Divide the class into learning pairs. Assign one of the 14 interviewing tactics to each pair. Allow a specific amount of time for each learning pair to write as many reasons as they can for using their assigned interviewing tactic. Have each learning pair report their reasons to the class.

Community Resources

Ask a committee of students to contact a local chapter of The American Society for Personnel Administration (ASPA), a local employer's human resources department, or the manager of an employment agency. Ask the committee to schedule an interviewer to visit your class and conduct mock interviews, obtain information on the specific job students will be interviewed for, and ask three student volunteers to dress appropriately and make preparations for the mock interviews. You may wish to videotape the mock interviews for a critique.

KEY TO SUCCESS

A portfolio is a great tool to have when you go to a job interview. Before the interview, identify items in your portfolio that relate to the interview. Think about how you can describe each of those items to an interviewer. Your descriptions should include the problems you faced, the actions you took, and the results you attained. During the interview, point out examples in the portfolio that demonstrate your experience, accomplishments, and training. Employers want to know that you can apply your skills and achievements to their organization's problems and needs. Use your portfolio examples to reinforce your descriptions of your achievements. You gain credibility with the employer when you are able to both describe and show examples of what you have done and what you can do.

Roberta was applying for a position as a copy editor. A brief review of Roberta's resume told Mr. Waters that she had a college education, three years' work experience as a high school English teacher, and two years' summer experience editing articles for a small newspaper.

Roberta walked into the room with a confident stride and a pleasant smile. After a firm handshake and a personal introduction, Mr. Waters asked Roberta why she wanted to work for his company. It was easy for Roberta to explain what she liked about the publishing business and to describe the skills she could bring to the job. Roberta had given a great deal of thought to this career change, and she was confident that it was the right thing to do.

Roberta told Mr. Waters how she enjoyed working with people on writing projects. She especially liked to organize and coordinate materials, make them more understandable, and work with people in the art department to develop interesting graphs and pictures.

When Mr. Waters concluded the interview by standing up and extending his hand, Roberta responded with a firm handshake and thanked him for the interview.

Critical Thinking

On a separate sheet of paper, list the reasons you would or would not hire Roberta for the job of copy editor.

Roberta displayed a high level of self-esteem during the interview. List the behaviors that demonstrated her confidence to the interviewer. Next, place a check mark beside each behavior on your list that you would display in an interview as well as Roberta did. Circle each behavior that you would not display as well as Roberta and that you would like to improve.

Interviewing Practice

During an interview, you have a limited amount of time to convince the interviewer why he or she should hire you. How you communicate your answers to specific questions will determine the success or failure of most

© JIST Works

interviews. The interview is the time for you to elaborate on the information in your resume or job application form.

Do not memorize your part for an interview, but do anticipate certain questions and be prepared. Practicing with your family or friends will help you build self-confidence and will reduce your level of anxiety. Being well prepared for an interview is very similar to being well prepared for a test at school. When you understand the material, you do well.

In particular, practice answering these frequently asked interview questions:

Why did you apply for this job? Briefly, describe the method you used to research information about the organization, and provide some positive specifics such as a good financial report and high-quality products or services. Then point out how your career goals fit with this type of organization.

Tell me about yourself. Do not turn your response into a mini-series. Briefly, describe where you were born, your nuclear family, school years, hobbies and interests, and career aspirations. Practice answering this question in no more than two minutes.

Why should I hire you for this job? Point out your qualifications for the job and how they fit with the job requirements. Focus on how hiring you will be beneficial to the organization.

You seem to be the perfect employee. Have you ever made any serious mistakes? Take time to think through your answer, and give an honest and sincere response to an error you made at school or on the job. Stress what you learned from the mistake and how it made you a better worker and a better candidate for the job at hand.

What job do you expect to have 10 years from now? Think about your long-term career goals, and answer the question in terms of where you hope to be in this particular organization. Never say, "I want a business of my own."

In this position, you will be working closely with several coworkers. How do you feel about that? Very few organizations are looking for a "loner." Regardless of whether you hate working with others, point out a group project you worked on at school or on a job and how the skills of the group were more effective than any individual within the group. The world of work is team-oriented.

If you think the answer to a question could be damaging, keep your answer brief and positive. For example, "Why have you had so many jobs in the past year?" A good response might be something like, "Although I performed the duties of each of those jobs well, they were not a good fit for me. The position you're offering is a good match for my skills, and I know I can contribute to the company's success for a long time."

Answer potentially beneficial questions fully. For example: "Can you operate a computer using Microsoft Word software?" "Yes, one of my main tasks in my current part-time job is creating form letters using the mail merge feature in Microsoft Word. I also know how to use the other programs in Microsoft Office, including Excel and PowerPoint." Always relate

Being well prepared for the job interview helped Ethan relax and convey his feeling of confidence to the interviewer. When you are well prepared for a school assignment, are you more relaxed and confident?

The "W" Questions

During a job interview always listen for the "W" questions. Interviewers commonly ask them. How would you answer the following examples?

- Who influenced you to look for this type of work?
- What were the highlights of your high school years?
- When will you expect a promotion?
- Where did you learn the skills that are required to do this job?
- Why are you interested in working for us?

your answers to the job at hand. The more the interviewer pictures you in the job, the better.

Types of Interviews

Employers use several types of job interviews. As your career progresses, you will probably experience many of these types. Practicing mock interviews will help you to prepare for all of the types.

Cooperative Learning

Assign a specific type of job interview to each group. Instruct each group to conduct a *mock interview* for the class using their assigned type.

Cooperative Learning

Have students complete the "Trial Interviews" worksheet in Chapter 9 of the *Preparing for Career Success Instructor's CD-ROM, Third Edition.*

Discussion Starter/ Self-Understanding

If you were an interviewer, what characteristics would you look for in a potential employee? Why do you consider these characteristics important? Do you demonstrate these characteristics in your daily life? If so, how? If not, why not?

- **Behavioral:** Verbal questions are used to probe for specifics about your past work or school behaviors. This questioning is based on the premise that your future behavior can be determined by your past behavior.
- **Screening:** In this first interview (telephone, job fair, campus visit), a representative of the organization determines whether you have the qualifications to warrant an in-depth interview.
- **Stress:** The interviewer intentionally attempts to upset you to see how you react under pressure. The interviewer may bark out questions and interrupt your attempts to answer.
- **Situational:** The interviewer presents common situations that you may encounter on the job. Then your interviewer measures your responses against predetermined standards.
- **Peer:** Two or more of the employer's representatives may be present during the interview of a single job candidate.
- **Group:** The organization forms a group of prospective employees to test their networking and social skills.
- **Online:** Because of your job application form, you receive an online questionnaire about your skills and experience that you submit by e-mail. Employers use these questionnaires as a screening interview.
- **Psychological:** Verbal and/or written questions are used by the employer to determine your personality type and whether you will fit the organization and job.
- **Video:** The organization uses professional media services or in-house resources to conduct preliminary interviews with job candidates. The employer is able to see and hear many job candidates before inviting a few to the home office for costly and time-consuming selection interviews.

Your Rights in an Interview

Employers have traditionally used application forms and preemployment interviews to eliminate unsuitable or unqualified job applicants from consideration at an early stage of the hiring process. Unfortunately, some employers have also used them to deny or restrict employment opportunities for women and minorities.

© JIST Works

The purpose of the Equal Employment Opportunity Law, a part of the Civil Rights Act of 1964, is to remedy this problem. The law prevents employers from asking questions and considering factors that would disproportionately screen out members of minority groups or members of one sex. Questions and factors that are not valid predictors of successful job performance or that cannot be justified by "business necessity" are forbidden.

In other words, certain questions are unlawful for an employer to ask unless they truly reflect job requirements. If these unlawful questions are asked, the interviewer is in violation of your equal employment opportunity (EEO) rights. You may choose to answer the question or to tell the interviewer that you see no relationship between the question and the job requirements. As an example, should an employer be able to ask the question, "Do you plan to get married soon?"

Questions that are not needed to judge an applicant's competence or qualification for the job are a violation of the EEO laws. In general, these laws make it illegal to discriminate against job applicants because of their race, religion, sex, national origin, disability, age, or ancestry. However, an employer may be required or permitted to request such information because of involvement in a legitimate affirmative action program or because the company is under order from a state, federal, or local fair employment practices agency.

Involvement in an affirmative action program or a **fair employment program** may require employers to hire minorities, women, or the physically challenged. In such cases, the employer has the right to request information to help identify employment candidates from the desired group.

Review the interview questions in the "Interviewing Practice" section. Can you think of additional interview questions the interviewer might ask because of your gender, ethnic background, physical appearance, or race? Are these questions legal? How would you respond? What effect might your response have on the interview?

Discussion Starter

Make this statement: Although it is unlawful for employers to ask certain questions during a job interview, would it be to your advantage as a job seeker to make an issue of the unlawful question or to simply answer it? When the discussion slows, ask your students to state one unlawful question they would answer and one they would refuse to answer.

Enrichment

Have students complete the "Applying and Interviewing for a Job" worksheet in Chapter 9 of the *Preparing for Career Success Instructor's CD-ROM, Third Edition.*

Interview Follow-Up

After the interview, write the interviewer a brief letter or an e-mail expressing your appreciation. Use the format illustrated in Figure 9.1. If you are still interested in the job, emphasize your interest, and restate your background qualifications that match the job requirements. In closing, let the interviewer know that you look forward to hearing the decision soon.

If you have not been contacted within two weeks, phone the interviewer, and politely inquire as to when the company plans to notify you about its hiring decision. This is also a good time to restate your qualifications and interest in the job.

If you are not interested in the job, it is still good business manners to write a letter expressing your appreciation for time spent and to inform the interviewer that you no longer wish to be a candidate. In addition, you may wish to express your interest in other positions more related to your background and career interests.

© JIST Works

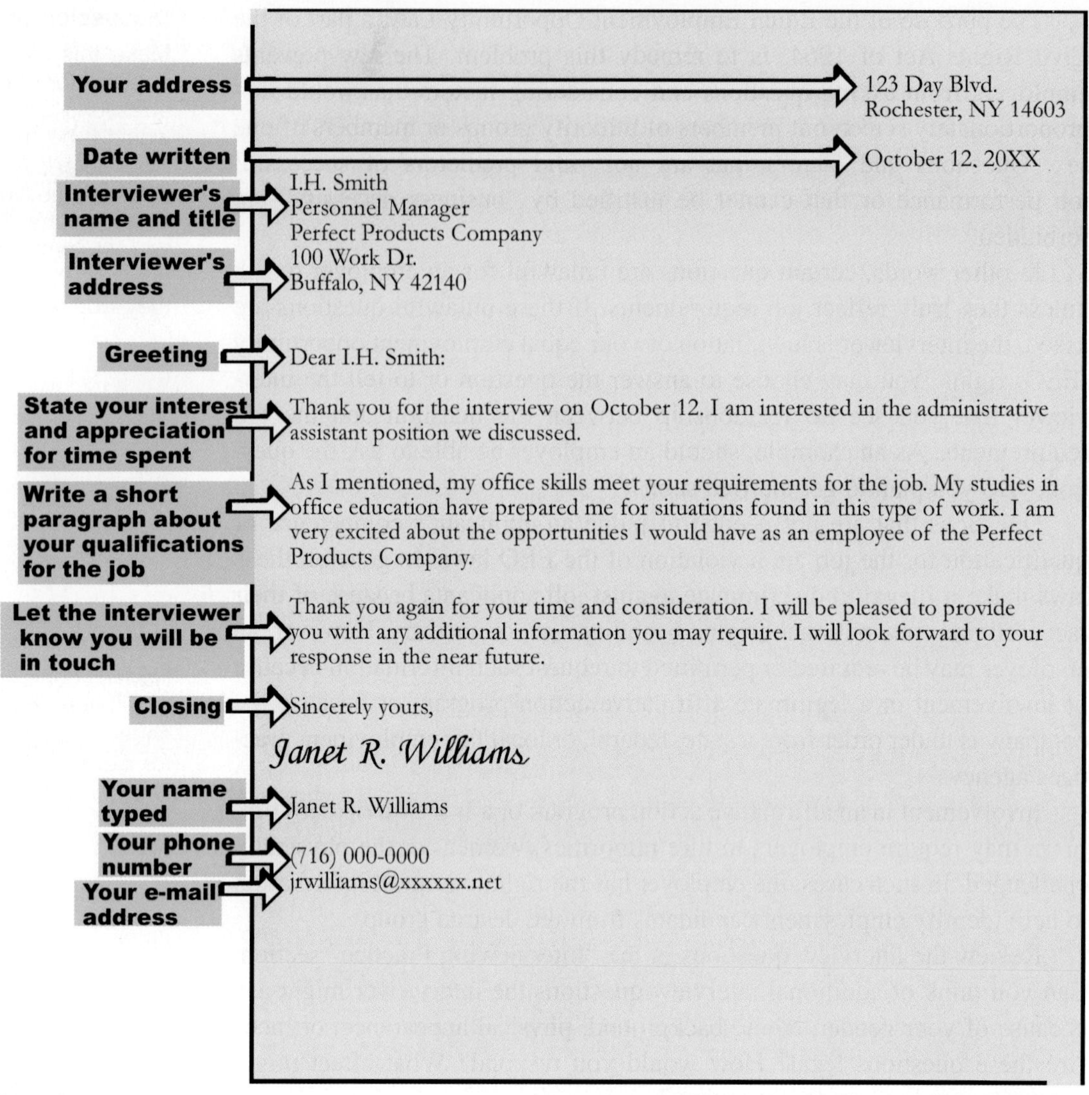

Your address
123 Day Blvd.
Rochester, NY 14603
Date written
October 12, 20XX
Interviewer's name and title
I.H. Smith
Personnel Manager
Perfect Products Company
Interviewer's address
100 Work Dr.
Buffalo, NY 42140
Greeting
Dear I.H. Smith:
State your interest and appreciation for time spent
Thank you for the interview on October 12. I am interested in the administrative assistant position we discussed.
Write a short paragraph about your qualifications for the job
As I mentioned, my office skills meet your requirements for the job. My studies in office education have prepared me for situations found in this type of work. I am very excited about the opportunities I would have as an employee of the Perfect Products Company.
Let the interviewer know you will be in touch
Thank you again for your time and consideration. I will be pleased to provide you with any additional information you may require. I will look forward to your response in the near future.
Closing
Sincerely yours,
Janet R. Williams
Your name typed
Janet R. Williams
Your phone number
(716) 000-0000
Your e-mail address
jrwilliams@xxxxxx.net

Figure 9.1 Thank-you letter for an interview.

KEY TO SUCCESS

Never take a job rejection personally. Always evaluate your performance during your last interview, and identify areas you can improve.

Comprehension Check

Ask your class to read the thank-you letter in Figure 9.1. Next, ask them to imagine that they are I. H. Smith, Human Resources Manager. Ask individual students: What is one specific statement in Janet Williams's letter that would impress you and increase her chances of being hired? Why did this statement impress you?

Interview Evaluation

Be sure to keep a written record or electronic file of all of your job interviews. Include the date, time, place, interviewer's name, and a copy of your thank-you letter. Learn as much as possible from each job interview. You can begin by

- Evaluating the interviewer's reaction to what you said
- Considering any additional information you might have stated
- Reviewing any statements you wish you had not made

Also, consider these points:

- What did you emphasize that seemed to interest the interviewer?
- How well did you present your qualifications?

© JIST Works

- Did you talk too much or too little?
- Did you learn everything about the job that you wanted to know?
- Did you project a positive attitude?
- Was your appearance appropriate for the position?
- What improvement can you make for the next interview?

After reviewing your interview, what grade will you give yourself? Excellent, good, or needs improvement? What grade will you give the person who interviewed you?

Kyle keeps a record of each job interview on his computer. What method could you use to record information about job interviews?

The Job Offer

You will probably have several job interviews before you are hired. You may receive up to 16 rejections before your first suitable job offer. Learning to accept rejection is one of the important lessons you can learn from the job-seeking process.

After each job interview, be optimistic and plan to receive a **job offer** (a specific offer of employment). Most job offers are made within two weeks after the interview. The person who interviewed you usually extends the job offer over the telephone. If you accept the offer, a congratulatory letter, welcoming you to the organization, will usually follow. This letter should include details of the salary or wage agreement, job benefits, and a request for any information the employer will need before you can begin the job.

A job is occasionally offered during the interview, requiring the applicant to make an immediate decision. It is a good idea to plan for this possibility. If you are certain that you want the job, you should be prepared to accept the offer. However, you will probably want time to think about information you have learned during the interview.

If you do not wish to make an immediate decision, ask the interviewer if you might think about the offer overnight and phone the next day with your decision. If the interviewer still insists on an immediate decision, take a few minutes to determine your answers to the following questions about four major areas of the job being considered:

Key to Success

Never accept a job thinking that it will be suitable until you find a better job. Workers with this mindset frequently spend their career "waiting for their ship to come in," not realizing that "the boat has already sailed."

Job Tasks

1. Are you prepared to handle the responsibilities of the job?
2. Will the employer provide training to help you learn the specific job?
3. Are the employer's work rules too strict or too lax?

Work Environment

1. Did you have a chance to tour the company to observe and meet other workers? If not, could the interviewer or another person take you on a tour before you make your decision?

After being turned down on nine previous job interviews, Zoe finally receives a job offer. How would you feel if you had been turned down for nine jobs in one month?

Cooperative Learning

Divide your class into 11 groups. Assign one of the 11 questions listed under the four major areas of consideration to each group. Ask each group to write a brief statement about the importance of considering their assigned question before accepting a job. Have each group report their conclusions to the class.

Self-Understanding

Which area of a job offer would be most important to you: the job tasks, work environment, salary and benefits, or future opportunities? Why? Which area of a job offer would be least important to you: the job tasks, work environment, salary and benefits, or future opportunities? Why?

2. Do the people who will be your coworkers seem to get along with one another? Do you think you will fit in with them? How do the managers seem to get along with the workers?
3. Will you have any transportation problems getting to this job? Does the work setting seem safe to you?

Salary and Benefits

1. Did the interviewer specify the wage or salary range of the job? If so, is it similar to the pay range you observed in newspaper ads for similar jobs? What future pay increases can you expect? Because you are a beginner, salary is not as negotiable as it will be later in life.
2. What employee benefits are included with this job? Are the costs of employee benefits paid by the employer or shared with the employee? If shared, what is your cost?

Future Opportunities

1. How will this position fit in with your plans or enhance your career growth?
2. How will the offered job provide an opportunity for you to learn valuable job skills?
3. What opportunities will you have within this organization?

Long-range factors may determine whether your first position will be a springboard or a hurdle. On your first job, it is important to have the opportunity to grow and continue your education. Take the job with the most promise for the career track you have chosen, not necessarily the job that pays the most money.

Think carefully about the advantages and disadvantages of working for a certain employer before you accept or reject a job offer. Decide whether you will earn enough to maintain your present lifestyle and whether your pay will increase as you increase your job skills. Whatever your criteria for accepting or rejecting a job offer, be realistic about your ability to perform the job and your worth to the employer.

Section 4: Get Involved

Answer the following on a separate sheet of paper, and be prepared to discuss your responses in class:

1. Select three interview questions from the list in "Interviewing Practice," and write them on a sheet of paper. For each question you select, write the answer you would give in an actual interview and the reason you believe an interviewer would ask the question.
2. Imagine that you have interviewed with I. H. Smith of the Perfect Company, for a specific job. Use a job title you are considering for your future career. Using the format shown in Figure 9.1, write a thank-you letter to I. H. Smith.
3. Review the types of interviews highlighted under the heading "Types of Interviews." Which type of interview would you prefer most? Why? Which type of interview would you prefer least? Why?

© JIST Works

Section 5: Summer and Part-Time Jobs

Recent studies state that more than half of all employed teens work in service and retail occupations. Their main source of employment is jobs such as clerks, cashiers, and servers in food-service establishments. Table 9.2 lists the major types of work that are available for teenagers wanting to work part-time or during the summer.

Table 9.2 Where the Part-Time Jobs Are

The Employers	The Jobs
Local government agencies	Summer youth employment
New stores or businesses	Clerking, cleaning, stocking
Temporary-help firms	Clerical work
Restaurants	Waiter, busser, kitchen work
Fast-food restaurants	Counter and kitchen work
Day-care centers	Teacher's helper
Summer camps and resorts	Kitchen work, lifeguard, counselor
Food stores	Stock clerk, cashier, bagger
Automobile service station, car wash	Attendant, cashier
Movie theaters	Cashier, usher, concession clerk
Retail stores	Sales or stock clerk, janitor
Farms	Fruit or vegetable picker
Construction companies	Helper, cleanup person
Manufacturing companies	Helper, cleanup person
Amusement parks, tourist sites	Cashier, guide, performer, helper

Many teens attend school and work during the summer. These teens may be able to

- Increase their academic opportunities
- Earn additional money
- Learn valuable time-management skills
- Learn new work skills
- Develop positive work habits

Some skills learned on entry-level jobs can be transferred to jobs that are more complex. For example, when the interviewer for a retail management position asks about your summer job delivering packages, emphasize the customer service and punctuality the job required, not the heavy lifting and clean driving record.

Your first part-time, temporary, or summer job will provide you with an opportunity to learn about the challenges and rewards of work and to explore possible careers. You may be required to work a few hours each

Career Fact

Every year, thousands of high school seniors work away from home at a variety of camps and major tourist attractions. What is the point of a summer away from friends and family? Here are some of the benefits:

- Getting valuable job experience
- Enjoying a unique atmosphere
- Making new friends from a variety of backgrounds
- Saving money for future education or training
- Learning how to be independent

Enrichment

Have students complete the "Part-Time and Summertime Jobs" worksheet in Chapter 9 of the *Preparing for Career Success Student Activity Book, Third Edition.*

Case Study

Have students read the case study "Spending Their Time" in Chapter 9 of the *Preparing for Career Success Instructor's CD-ROM, Third Edition.*

Community Resources/Cooperative Learning

Divide your class into small groups. Assign specific types of employers (The Employers column in Table 9.2) to each group. Using telephone books, have each group develop a list of local employers for their category. Lists should include telephone numbers and addresses. Post the lists on your bulletin board.

© JIST Works

Laurie works as a swimming instructor during her summer break. Can you think of other seasonal jobs for students?

TAKE NOTE

If you accept a part-time or temporary job while you are still in school, you will need to reorganize your time to meet the demands of school and the job. Will working a part-time job lower your grades or prevent you from graduating?

day, several days each week, or an occasional full shift. In any case, working will provide you with money for clothing, graduation expenses, or savings toward your education and training after high school.

Employers usually hire part-time and temporary workers during vacation periods, when someone is sick, or when they need additional help. Many organizations hire part-time workers through a **temporary employment service** (an agency that "rents" employees to employers). Review "Using Private Employment Agencies," Section 2, Chapter 8.

Kenneth is working for a national chain of pizza parlors. His employer is required to pay him no less than the minimum wage. Labor shortages force many employers to pay more than minimum wage.

Reteaching

Have students complete the "Minimum Wage Quiz" worksheet in Chapter 9 of the *Preparing for Career Success Instructor's CD-ROM, Third Edition.*

The Minimum Wage Law

Do all jobs for teenagers pay minimum wage? No, some pay less. A youth minimum wage, authorized by 1996 amendments to the Fair Labor Standards Act of 1938 (FLSA), allows employers to pay workers who are under age 20 a lower wage for 90 calendar days. Basic wage standards are set by the federal government's FLSA. The **minimum wage** (the lowest wage an employer may pay for certain types of work) has increased from 40 cents per hour in 1938 to $6.55 per hour on July 24, 2008. On July 24, 2009, an increase to $7.25 per hour is scheduled. Some states require employers to pay a higher minimum wage, but none may pay less than the federal rate.

Not all employment of youth workers is covered under the FLSA. Certain full-time students, apprentices, and workers with disabilities may be paid less than the minimum wage under special certificates issued by the Department of Labor. Employers of certain amusement and recreational places of business, certain retail or service businesses, and babysitters are also exempt from minimum wage laws. In addition, jobs held by youths—such as delivering newspapers and performing in motion picture, theatrical, radio, and television productions—are specifically exempted from child labor laws.

© JIST Works

Volunteer Work

Not all work is paid work. Many young people are concerned about what is going on in their neighborhoods and communities and get involved. They want to make a difference and feel good about themselves. You can learn a lot about the responsibilities and rewards of paid work by volunteering in an organization.

Volunteer work (a contribution of free labor, usually to a nonprofit organization) gives you a chance to observe various workers and to learn new skills. Volunteering demonstrates commitment to a cause. It can also help you clarify your career interests and build your self-confidence. Volunteer work can be included in a resume and treated as work experience on a job application form. Occasionally, it even leads to paid employment.

Before you commit to volunteer work, study the requirements of the volunteer job. How do they match the personal characteristics you identified in Chapters 2 and 3? Volunteer for a job you will enjoy and where you can develop your talents and skills. Before you make a commitment, interview with several organizations that depend on volunteers.

Where are the volunteer jobs in your area? Use the following list of organizations as a starting point to begin your own volunteering adventure:

- Hospitals
- Museums
- YMCA or YWCA
- Regional food banks
- Amateur theater groups
- Government housing authorities
- Special Olympics
- Libraries
- United Way
- Urban League
- School
- State or national parks
- Habitat for Humanity
- Symphony orchestra groups
- Zoos
- American Cancer Society
- Churches
- American Red Cross
- Nursing homes
- Local parks
- Salvation Army
- Animal shelters
- Women's networks
- Mobile meals programs
- Student-watch programs

List the local agencies that use volunteer help. Ask your school counselor whether your community has a volunteer center.

Nonprofits provide unique employment experiences, sometimes in occupations not usually found in other sectors. **Nonprofits** (organizations not intending to earn a profit for their members or owners) are neither businesses nor part of government. Charities, foundations, private schools, churches, professional and trade associations, many scientific institutions, and more than half of the nation's hospitals belong to the nonprofit sector. If hands-on service appeals to you, you will find many employment opportunities in the nonprofit world. Some of the most well-known occupations in the nonprofit sector provide the following opportunities.

FIND OUT MORE

The Foundation Center and Association for Volunteer Administration provide career or educational information about nonprofits. To contact the Foundation Center, phone 1-800-424-9836, or go online at fdncenter.org. Also, to contact the Association for Volunteer Administration, go online at www.avaintl.org.

Discussion Starter

Explain to your class that some politicians, economists, and employers argue that the minimum wage law prevents employers from hiring thousands of additional workers. Ask your students: Should the minimum wage law be abolished, expanded to cover all workers, or left in its present form? Why?

Volunteerism and community service have been a strong and important tradition in America since its founding.

—George W. Bush

Community Resources

Invite a community agency leader or volunteer to speak to the class about the importance of volunteering and ways to become involved in volunteering.

Comprehension Check

Have your students close their books, and ask the following questions: What are the similarities between paid work and volunteer (unpaid) work? What are the differences?

Discussion Starter

Ask the students if they think that volunteer work is something they would want to do, now or in the future? Why or why not? Ask students to study this list for skills they could learn by volunteering.

- People-to-people services in counseling, health, and educational services
- Meal preparation and serving
- Trade and transportation work using skill with tools and equipment
- *Advocacy* (gathering support) for a cause and helping nonprofits grow

Section 5: Get Involved

Each year, thousands of students and adults accept part-time employment. On a separate piece of paper, describe the advantages and disadvantages of part-time employment for each of the following people:

1. A woman who is a homemaker and has a husband who works full-time and a son who will be in college next year
2. A high school senior who plans to join the armed forces after graduation
3. The owner of a restaurant where most of the business occurs during a two-hour lunch period and a four-hour dinner period

Be prepared to discuss your responses in class.

Section 6: Full-Time Jobs

Imagine being hired for your first **full-time job**. This will probably be your first opportunity to assume the responsibilities of an independent adult. Perhaps you will rent an apartment or buy a car. On the other hand, you may decide to stay at home and help with family finances. Whatever the situation, a full-time job requires a major commitment of your time and labor.

When you begin a new job, you will know the amount of your wages and fringe benefits and what the job site is like. You will probably know less about advancement opportunities, the personality of your supervisor and coworkers, and the satisfaction you will receive from performing the job.

Enrichment

Send two writers to the chalkboard. Assign one of these headings to each writer: "Reasons Workers Accept Full-Time Jobs They Dislike" and "Reasons Workers Are Able to Find Jobs They Enjoy." Ask individual class members to provide reasons for each writer. After you are satisfied with the lists, ask your students: Which reasons on your lists could be controlled by the worker? How? Which reasons are beyond the control of the worker? Why?

Some workers accept a job they dislike because they do not have the education or training for a job they would like. Others need to earn a living and cannot wait for the ideal job to come along. If you are fortunate enough to receive more than one job offer, the likelihood of meeting your interests, using your skills, and obtaining your career goals will be increased.

Some experts believe that most people of your generation will make six or more major job changes during their working lives. If this is true, success or failure on your first job could determine your future jobs, including

- Your career progress
- What work tasks you will be performing
- The skill level of your coworkers
- The type of employer you will have
- How much will you earn

© JIST Works

Your decision to stay with one employer will be determined by the opportunities you create. What you presently consider job satisfaction and success will change as you increase your job skills. At some point, you may decide to acquire additional education or training to enter a higher level of your present occupation or to help you enter a different occupation. As you have been learning, today's economy and technology are changing rapidly. As changes in your skills, technology, and the economy occur, you will need to re-examine your job skills in terms of the current job market.

New hire Reva plans to be the office supervisor within two years. Do you have a plan?

Few of today's workers will remain on one job, working for the same employer, for most of their careers. In fact, most first-time job seekers change jobs within two years. Reasons for changing jobs include: more money available elsewhere, an unfair boss, an unsatisfying job, a transfer to another city or state, and the elimination of a position or closing of the operation.

Technology has changed the jobs of many workers, resulting in the growth of service occupations and a rapid decline in the number of manufacturing jobs. Many jobs have completely disappeared. Throughout your working years, improved technology and the efficiency it brings will continually change the job market.

Key to Success

After you accept your first full-time job, work at it as though it were your lifetime career choice.

Section 6: Get Involved

Answer the following on a separate sheet of paper, and be prepared to discuss your responses in class.

1. Divide a sheet of paper into three columns titled "Entry-Level Job," "Higher-Paying Job," and "Education or Training." Write the following jobs in the "Entry-Level Job" column: fast-food counter attendant, word processor, retail salesperson, and nursing aide. For each of these jobs, list a higher-paying job in the appropriate column that could be obtained as a result of more experience and a good work record. Next, use the last column to list the education and training that would be required to acquire the higher-paying job. (This information is in the *Occupational Outlook Handbook* in your school library.) For example, a lubrication worker could move up to a higher-paying job such as automotive mechanic after attending a technical school.
2. Review "Section 2: Goals" in Chapter 3. Then list the goals that were most important to you. Which of these goals do you expect to satisfy on your first full-time job? What career steps will you take to reach your highest goals?

Case Study

Have students read the case study "An Unexpected Change" in Chapter 9 of the *Preparing for Career Success Instructor's CD-ROM, Third Edition* and discuss the "Critical Thinking" questions.

Reteaching

Have students complete the "Finding the Right Words" and "Checking Your Location" worksheets in Chapter 9 of the *Preparing for Career Success Student Activity Book, Third Edition.*

Enrich Your Vocabulary Answers

1. job application form
2. Fair Labor Standards Act
3. health certificate
4. employment eligibility verification form
5. bond
6. felony
7. civil service examinations
8. valid
9. initiative
10. human resources department
11. fair employment program
12. job offer
13. full-time job
14. volunteer work
15. temporary employment service
16. work permit
17. background check
18. preemployment test
19. job interview
20. minimum wage
21. nonprofits

Chapter 9 Review

Enrich Your Vocabulary

On a separate sheet of paper, number from 1 to 21. (Do not write in your textbook.) Match each of the following statements with the most appropriate term from the "Enrich Your Vocabulary" list at the beginning of the chapter by writing that term next to the number of the correct statement.

1. A document containing information that employers require before hiring new employees
2. A law that protects all workers, including minors
3. A document stating that you don't have an infectious disease or that you're free of certain drugs
4. A document stating that a person is eligible to work in the United States
5. Insurance that pays financial losses if an employee fails to perform his or her duty or is guilty of theft
6. A serious crime
7. Preemployment tests for government jobs
8. True and supported by facts
9. Readiness and ability to take the first steps in any undertaking
10. The people responsible for recruiting and hiring new employees
11. A program in which employers actively seek to hire minorities
12. An employer's formal proposal of employment
13. A job that provides you with an opportunity to assume adult responsibilities
14. A contribution of free labor
15. An agency that "rents" employees to employers
16. A document that is necessary for employees under 18 in most non-farm jobs
17. An investigation of a job applicant's former employers, schools, and references
18. A test to determine how well an applicant is likely to perform in a certain area of work
19. An opportunity to personally present yourself to an employer
20. The lowest amount an employer may pay for certain types of work
21. Organizations not intending or intended to earn a profit

© JIST Works

Check Your Knowledge

On a separate sheet of paper, complete the following activities. (Do not write in your textbook.)

1. List four kinds of information requested on most job applications.
2. When do job applications become legal documents?
3. How can you prove your date of birth to an employer?
4. At what age do you no longer need a work permit?
5. List five occupations permitted for 14- and 15-year-olds.
6. List three types of preemployment tests.
7. Name five resources that you can use to find information about a company or an organization.
8. How much time does a job interview usually take?
9. What determines the success of most job interviews?
10. What act of Congress contains the Equal Employment Opportunity Law?
11. Why do some companies like to use temporary help?
12. Approximately how many job changes will most of your generation make during their career?
13. What sector of the job market has had the greatest decline as a result of automation?

Develop SCANS Competencies

This activity will give you practice in developing the technology competencies needed to be a successful worker.

Choose four to five careers in which you have an interest. They could be part-time jobs you will look for in the near future, or they could be jobs that will require more education on your part.

Make a list of the technology you will need to be familiar with to be successful in each of these jobs. The technology might include different types of equipment, such as cash registers or computers. List technology with which you are already familiar. How can this knowledge help in your search for a job?

Check Your Knowledge Answers

1. Personal, education, references, employment desired, previous employment, hobbies and interests, and job skills.
2. When they are signed and dated.
3. By presenting your birth certificate.
4. 18.
5. Office and clerical work; cashiering; sales; art work; window trimming; price marking; packing and stocking shelves; bagging and carrying out customer orders; delivery work by foot, bicycle, or public transportation; and dispensing gasoline and oil and washing and polishing cars.
6. Aptitude, intelligence, proficiency, and psychological tests.
7. Employees who currently work for the company, the Internet, annual reports, brochures, advertisements, the Better Business Bureau, friends or relatives, the company itself, business periodicals and reference books, the local chamber of commerce, and the operation of similar companies.
8. 30 minutes to 1 hour.
9. The applicant's skill in communicating answers to specific questions.
10. The Civil Rights Act of 1964.
11. It saves them the expense of hiring full-time employees that they will need for only a short amount of time.
12. Six or more.
13. The manufacturing sector.

Enrichment

Have students complete the Chapter 9 section of the *Preparing for Career Success Student Portfolio, Third Edition.*

© JIST Works

Chapter 10 Resources

Lesson Plans and Preparation

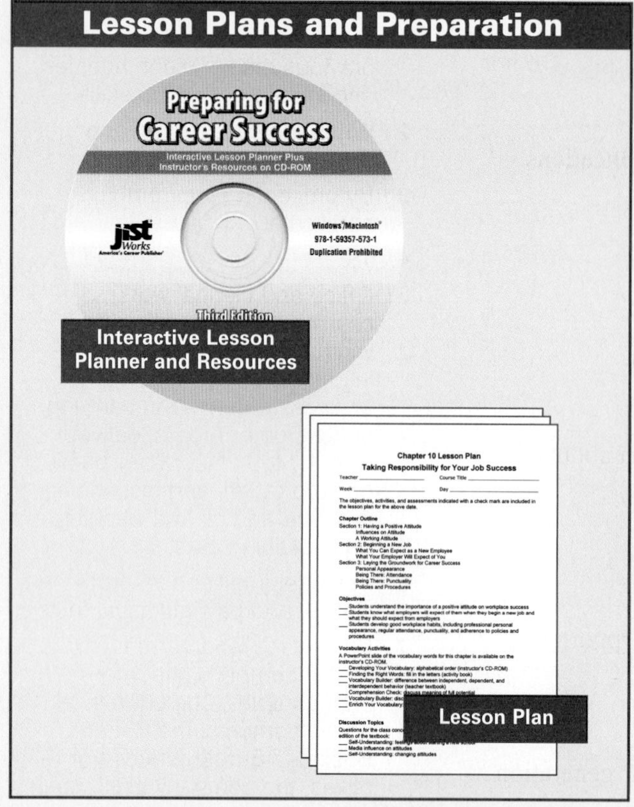

Preparing for Career Success
Interactive Lesson Planner Plus Instructor's Resources on CD-ROM
JIST Works America's Career Publisher
Windows/Macintosh
978-1-59357-573-1
Duplication Prohibited
Third Edition
Interactive Lesson Planner and Resources
Chapter 10 Lesson Plan
Taking Responsibility for Your Job Success
Lesson Plan

Multimedia

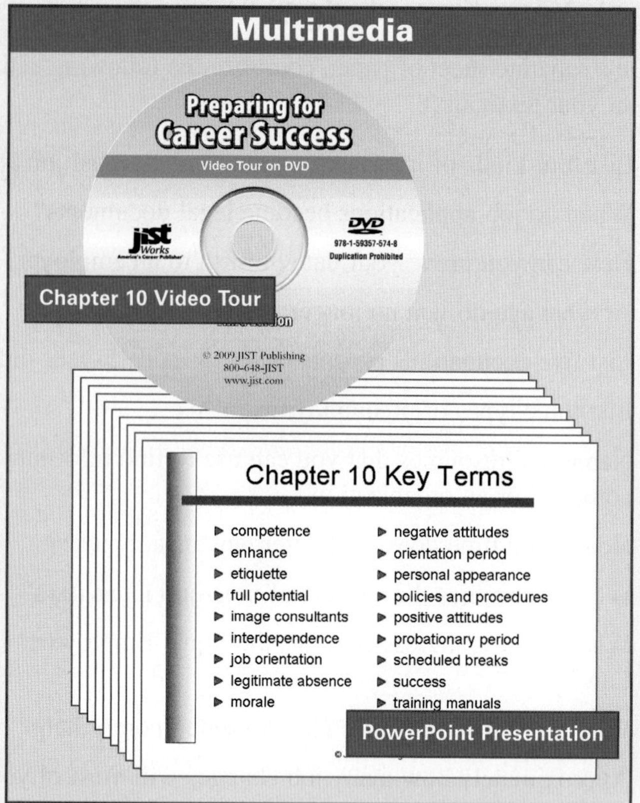

Preparing for Career Success
Video Tour on DVD
JIST Works America's Career Publisher
DVD
978-1-59357-574-8
Duplication Prohibited
Chapter 10 Video Tour
© 2009 JIST Publishing
800-648-JIST
www.jist.com
Chapter 10 Key Terms
competence
enhance
etiquette
full potential
image consultants
interdependence
job orientation
legitimate absence
morale
negative attitudes
orientation period
personal appearance
policies and procedures
positive attitudes
probationary period
scheduled breaks
success
training manuals
PowerPoint Presentation

Activities

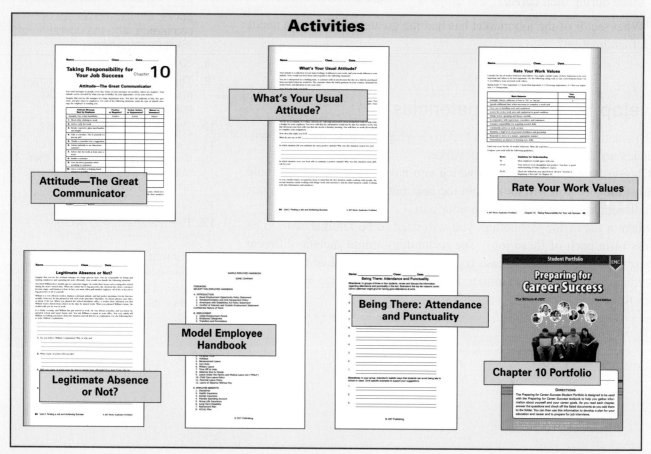

Taking Responsibility for Your Job Success Chapter 10 — Attitude—The Great Communicator

Attitude—The Great Communicator

What's Your Usual Attitude?

Rate Your Work Values

Legitimate Absence or Not?

Model Employee Handbook

Being There: Attendance and Punctuality

Chapter 10 Portfolio — Student Portfolio, Preparing for Career Success, Third Edition

© JIST Works

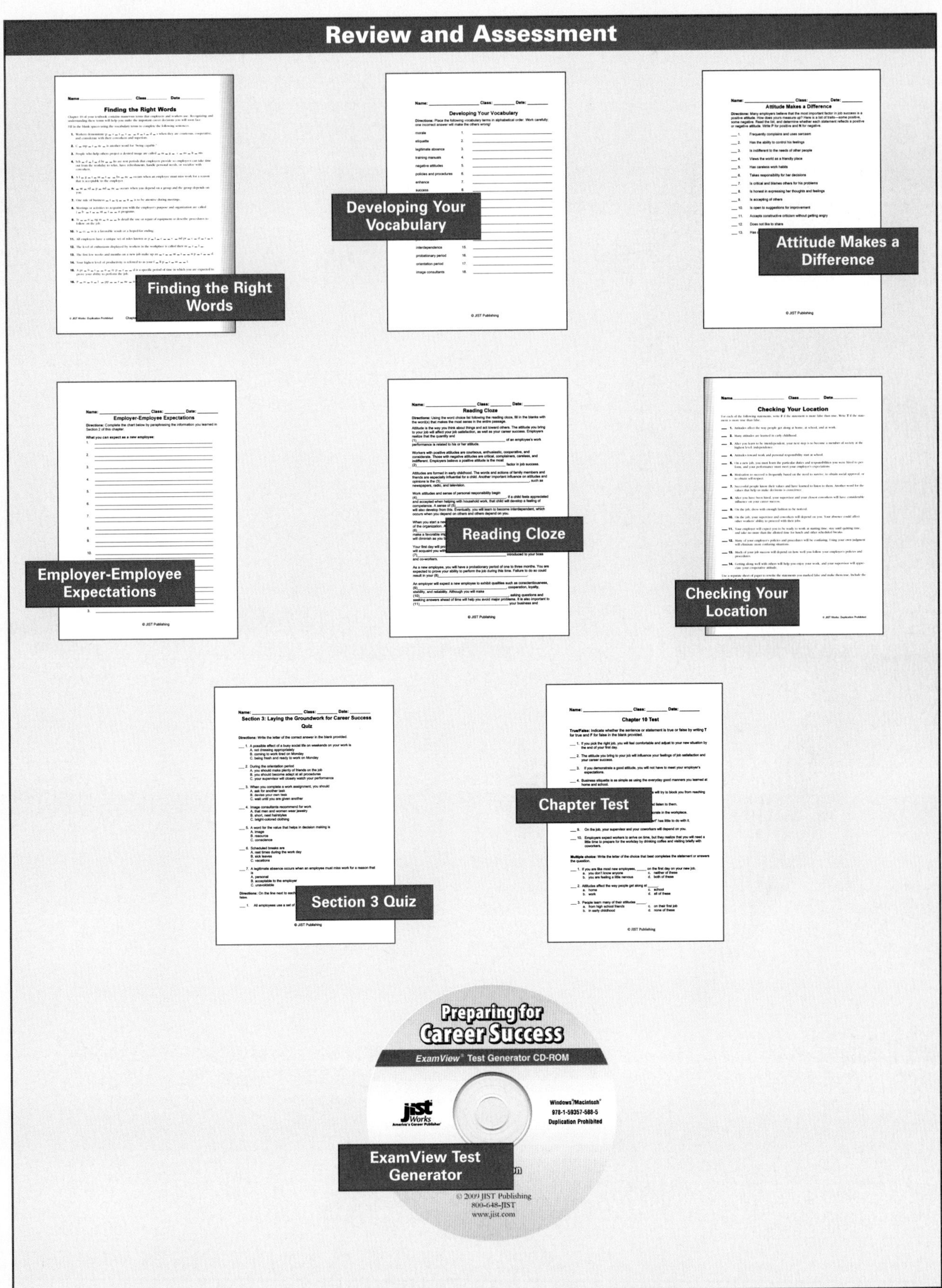
Review and Assessment
Finding the Right Words
Developing Your Vocabulary
Attitude Makes a Difference
Employer-Employee Expectations
Reading Cloze
Checking Your Location
Section 3 Quiz
Chapter Test
Preparing for Career Success
ExamView® Test Generator CD-ROM
Windows®/Macintosh®
978-1-59357-588-5
Duplication Prohibited
ExamView Test Generator
© 2009 JIST Publishing
800-648-JIST
www.jist.com

Chapter 10 Taking Responsibility for Your Job Success

Learning Objectives

- Explain the relationship between your attitude, future job satisfaction, and career success
- Describe the procedures for beginning a new job and list several of the employer's expectations
- Describe a suitable appearance for a job and explain the importance of being present and punctual
- Explain the purpose of a company's policies and procedures

Congratulations, you are hired! From a list of several applicants, the employer has selected you for the job. This selection demonstrates your ability to be successful. Your new job will provide you with opportunities for continuing success.

If you are like most new employees, you do not know anyone at your new job, and you are feeling a little bit nervous about starting. Perhaps you are concerned about having the necessary skills. Maybe you have doubts about your ability to fulfill your supervisor's assignments. You might wish you did not have to begin at all. If any of these statements are true, do not panic. Your feelings are normal.

Enrich Your Vocabulary

In reading this chapter and doing the exercises, you will learn the following important terms:

competence	job orientation	policies and procedures
enhance	legitimate absence	positive attitudes
etiquette	morale	probationary period
full potential	negative attitudes	scheduled breaks
image consultants	orientation period	success
interdependence	personal appearance	training manuals

Self-Understanding

Ask your students: Who can remember entering a new school? Next, ask individual students: What feelings did you have during the first few days? Did attending the new school affect your attitude toward other family members, your schoolwork, or leisure-time activities? If no, why not? If yes, how? Were you able to make personal adjustments and accept the new situation? If yes, how long did it take? If no, why not?

Did you ever enroll in a new school? Think back to your first few days at the new school or even the first few days of this school year. In many ways, the first few days of a new job are very similar. When you began school, you had a general idea of what it was going to be like. However, the students, teachers, school rules, and procedures were not familiar. You were probably excited, yet uneasy, about the new experience. After a few weeks, you probably adjusted to your new situation and felt comfortable. As you did with school, you will need some time to become adjusted and comfortable with a new job.

Section 1: Having a Positive Attitude

It is not your aptitude, but it is your attitude that will ultimately determine your altitude.

—Zig Zigler

Attitudes affect the way people get along at home, school, and work. The attitude you bring to your job will influence your feelings of job satisfaction and your career success. Attitude is the way you think about things and act toward others. The effort you make to do a good job will be no better than your attitude allows.

Video Tour on DVD

Show students the Chapter 10 segment to introduce them to the content.

Enrichment

Have students complete the worksheets "Attitude–the Great Communicator" and "What's Your Usual Attitude?" in Chapter 10 of the *Preparing for Success Student Activity Book, Third Edition.*

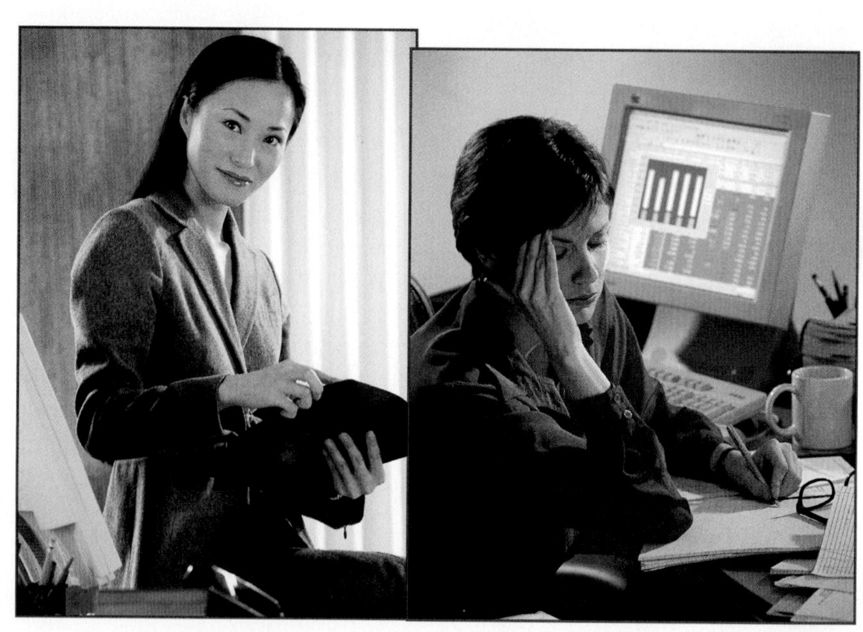

Maria views her job as an opportunity. She is interested and enthusiastic about her work. Elena views her job as a responsibility. She frequently complains, is critical, and has careless work habits. Are your attitudes toward schoolwork, home responsibilities, and paid employment more like Maria's or Elena's?

© JIST Works

Comparing High School and Work	
High School	**Work**
You are required to attend school.	You may enter or leave a job by choice.
Public schools must accept all students.	Employers select workers they want.
Teachers must retain students with poor attendance.	Poor attendance is cause for dismissal.
Teachers evaluate the quality of your work.	Employers evaluate the quality of your work.
Teachers continue to help students who perform poorly.	Poor performance is cause for dismissal.
The rewards are knowledge, skills, and satisfaction.	The rewards are paychecks, promotions, and satisfaction.
Education is most successful when students and teachers respect and trust each other.	Employment is most successful when workers and employers respect and trust each other.
Students receive a summer, winter, and spring vacation, plus several holidays.	Workers receive a week or two of vacation after a year of service, plus fewer holidays.
School problems are resolved by the student and the teacher. A counselor, principal, or parent may help.	Job problems are resolved by the worker and the supervisor. A union representative may help.

Influences on Attitude

You learned many of your attitudes in early childhood. People who are important to a child, such as parents, siblings, relatives, and friends, teach attitudes by what they say and do. The child accepts the feelings, values, and preferences of these important people as the correct and proper way to think and behave. Mass media, such as newspapers, radio, the Internet, and television, also influence attitudes and opinions.

Attitudes toward work and personal responsibility start at home. Suppose that a teenager is expected to help with household work, such as washing dishes, taking out the trash, mowing the yard, or cleaning the basement. The teen is learning to be a responsible member of the family. She will notice an increased acceptance and appreciation from other family members. Being appreciated and accepted causes the teen to value productive work. A feeling of **competence** (being capable) grows within her. In later years, she will use the work values learned as a teen to acquire acceptance and appreciation from employers and coworkers as well as from family and friends.

Suppose that another teenager lives in a home where he is discouraged from taking responsibility as a member of the family. He might be told to stay out of the way when household work is being done. This teen learns to depend on others instead of being independent, grows into an adult who lacks self-confidence in his ability to work, and places little value on being a productive worker.

When you learn to be independent, the next step is interdependence. **Interdependence** occurs when you depend on a group, and the group depends on you. It is the highest level of human relations at the personal level or in the world of work.

Discussion Starter

Ask your students: During the past month, have any television or radio programs, newspapers, or magazines tried to influence your attitudes or opinions? Next, ask individual students: What specific program or article tried to influence you? What attitude or opinion did the program or article want you to accept? Did you accept the attitude or opinion presented? Why or why not?

Take Note

People tend to use media sources and listen to speeches or conversations that agree with their own attitudes and opinions. They usually avoid exposing themselves to information and opinions that disagree with their own point of view. When exposed to information and opinions that disagree with their own, they prefer to talk about the matter with others who agree with them. If you were expressing your attitude and opinion toward an issue, would you talk it over with a friend who agrees with your view or with a friend who disagrees and offers opposing information?

© JIST Works

KEY TO SUCCESS

Busy professionals often conduct business during a breakfast, lunch, or dinner meeting. Do not ruin your opportunity to make a favorable impression by displaying bad manners such as talking with a full mouth, making loud eating noises, being argumentative, eating food off your knife, licking your fingers, eating before others are seated, serving yourself without offering food to others, or not engaging in the conversation.

Learning to appreciate work begins at home. Are you a responsible member of your family?

Interdependent people are not so independent as to do everything "their way." They are also not dependent in the sense of being helpless. Instead, they are contributing members of a family of relatives and friends at the personal level and are part of a team of workers in the world of work and in society. Think of situations in which you acted in a dependent way, an independent way, and an interdependent way. How did your attitudes influence your feelings, judgments, and behaviors in these situations?

Vocabulary Builder/ Self-Understanding

Ask your students: Who can give an example of a situation when your behavior was independent? Dependent? Interdependent?

A Working Attitude

Many employers believe that the most important factor in job success is a positive attitude. They relate the quality and quantity of an employee's work performance to his or her attitude. They also link the organization's profits to employee attitudes. Companies with a dedicated workforce enjoy better business performance. In these companies, there is a good feeling among employees.

The effort you make to do a good job will be no better than your attitude allows. Table 10.1 lists several differences between workers who display **positive attitudes** and **negative attitudes**. Which of the positive or negative attitudes will you demonstrate on a job? How will this influence your career success?

The way you look and think about situations will largely determine their outcomes. If you are gloomy and irritable, you cannot expect coworkers to be enthusiastic and friendly. Projecting a positive attitude will help you to develop better relationships with friends, family, coworkers, and employers. Demonstrating a positive attitude at school and work will **enhance** (strengthen or make better) your image with others.

TAKE NOTE

The principle of feng shui (pronounced fung shway) is finding acceptance in the modern workplace. Feng shui is the Chinese art of placement, or arranging your surroundings to enhance your life. Proper feng shui is supposed to improve the flow of energy, making the occupants of the space more comfortable, creative, successful, and happy. If your workplace is a space-restricting cubicle, simple changes such as positioning a desk correctly, getting rid of unnecessary objects, and organizing the essentials can make a big difference in your health, productivity, and well-being.

© JIST Works

Table 10.1 Positive and Negative Worker Attitudes

People with a Positive Attitude	People with a Negative Attitude
View a new job as an opportunity	View work as drudgery or a requirement
Enjoy learning new information	Are skeptical about new information
Are courteous, cooperative, and considerate	Are less courteous, uncooperative, and indifferent
Enjoy developing new skills	Dislike situations requiring new skills
View the world as a friendly place	View the world as an unfriendly place
Are accepting of coworkers and leaders	Are less accepting of coworkers and leaders
Take responsibility for all of their decisions	Place the responsibility for their failure on others
Are open to suggestions for improvement	Consider suggestions as unwarranted criticism
Accept constructive criticism without being angry	Make angry reactions to constructive criticism
Perform above and beyond their responsibility	Perform below their ability and responsibility
Are honest in expressing their thoughts and feelings	Withhold their thoughts and feelings
Have the maturity to control their emotions	Lack the maturity to control their emotions

Section 1: Get Involved

Answer the following on a separate sheet of paper, and be prepared to discuss your responses in class.

1. Name three family members or close friends that you feel express a positive attitude toward work or school.
2. Select one word from the following list that best describes each of the three people you selected. Tell how each person expresses this positive characteristic in his or her attitude toward school or work.

   Acceptance of others
   Cheerfulness
   Confidence
   Courtesy
   Flexibility
   Helpfulness
   Open-mindedness
   Patience
   Responsibility

3. Briefly, describe a situation in which you displayed one or more of the positive attitudes listed in Table 10.1. How might this attitude have a positive effect on the quality of your work in your first job and your schoolwork? Be specific.
4. Briefly, describe a situation in which you displayed one or more of the negative attitudes listed in Table 10.1. How might this attitude have a negative effect on the quality of your work in your first job and your schoolwork? Be specific.

Section 2: Beginning a New Job

On a new job, you must learn the particular duties and responsibilities you were hired to perform, and your performance must meet your employer's expectations. You must also learn the protocol of the organization. *Protocol* is another word for the rules of diplomatic **etiquette** (manners). You have already learned how to be diplomatic at school; now you must learn the protocol of the working world.

Self-Understanding

What causes an "I don't care" attitude? How can you change an attitude? Should employers have the right to discipline a worker with a bad attitude? How? Why is it important for an employee to have a positive attitude?

School-to-Work Transition

Send two writers to the chalkboard. Ask one writer to write the word "School" as a heading and the other writer to write "Workplace." Ask seated class members to describe a situation involving protocol at school for the first writer's list. Next, ask for a related situation and protocol in the workplace for the second writer's list. Some examples: attendance, punctuality, accepted dress, type of language used, and safety procedures.

FIND OUT MORE

Ask employers about the importance they place on positive attitudes and communication skills. Use your phone book to contact and schedule an interview with a recruiter at an employment agency, a job consultant at the state employment service, or the owner of a small business.

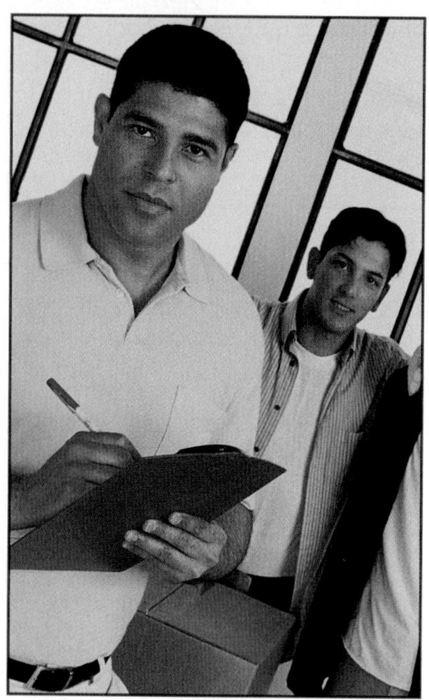

Calvin will begin his new job tomorrow. Do you think he will get along with Mr. Garcia? Why?

In the world of business, etiquette involves using the everyday good manners you learned at home and school. Good manners put people at ease and send a positive message of your consideration. Here are a few easy-to-remember rules of business etiquette:

- Never use first names unless permission is granted.
- Always say "please" when asking and "thank you" when being appreciative.
- Pick up after yourself.
- Start the day by saying "good morning."
- Make proper table manners a requirement when dining with coworkers or management.
- Compliment others when they have done a good job or something special.
- Be attentive during meetings.

As a new employee, you can expect to learn a lot during your first days and weeks on the job. Your new job will probably place unusual demands on your emotions. Some of this emotional pressure might be self-imposed, but a certain amount is unavoidable.

Building new relationships, adjusting to the unexpected, and making an extra effort to create a favorable impression can certainly contribute to emotional stress. As you learn new information, new procedures, and the names of your coworkers, the stress will diminish. Remember, your coworkers and boss do not expect a new employee to know everything.

You will probably report to the personnel office on your first day. This could be a large department in a big corporation or simply the boss's desk in a small business. A personnel worker or the boss will help you complete the necessary paperwork, including payroll and hospitalization forms. Bring your personal data sheet (see Chapter 8) with you, and the task of filling in personal information will be easier.

After you complete the necessary paperwork, you will probably spend the remainder of your first day on job orientation. **Job orientation** programs are meetings and activities to acquaint you with the employer's purpose and organization. Depending on the organization's size, your job orientation may take an hour or several days. During this time, you will learn about the management structure, the services provided or products manufactured, and the rules and regulations.

You can expect to be formally introduced to your boss and coworkers. One of these people will probably work closely with you until you can perform your assigned tasks on your own.

If you apply extra concentration on your work performance during the first few days and weeks of a new job, you will win the respect of your supervisor. Using this time to build good relationships with coworkers is

© JIST Works

also very important. Getting along well with others will help you enjoy your work, and your supervisor will appreciate your cooperative attitude.

What You Can Expect as a New Employee

Most employers realize that helping a new employee make full use of his or her skills improves the productivity and quality of the entire organization. For this reason alone, most employers want you to reach your **full potential** (highest level of productivity).

As a new employee, you can expect

- To be paid for your time. When you accepted the job, you and your employer agreed to the hours you would work and the wages or salary.
- To have a safe work environment. The law requires employers to maintain certain safety standards established by the government.
- To be provided equipment and supplies to perform your job. Certain mechanics and other skilled workers may be required to provide the tools designated in their employment agreement.
- To have a probationary period of one to three months. A **probationary period** is a specific period of time in which you prove your ability to perform the job. During this time, you will probably receive training and assistance from supervisors and coworkers. Failure to perform the job to the employer's satisfaction will be cause for terminating your employment at the end of the probationary period.
- To receive job training, on-the-job coaching, or other help that the employer normally provides for that specific job. This help may include special courses away from the actual worksite, special orientation meetings, self-study, correspondence school courses, college credit courses, and programs to earn special certificates or licenses. **Training manuals** are normally provided during training sessions. These handbooks detail the use or repair of equipment or describe procedures to follow on the job. The employer may place you in a training program that moves you from one job to another until your final job assignment.
- To make mistakes. Should you damage equipment or offend a customer, report the mistake to your supervisor. Covering up mistakes can result in serious consequences. Asking questions ahead of time will help you avoid making mistakes or violating job rules. If possible, look for the answer you are seeking in your manuals or brochures. After you ask for help, listen carefully.

CAREER FACT

Employers view irregular attendance, habitual lateness, and frequent abuse of policies regarding lunch periods and scheduled breaks as reasons for dismissal. The reason is that this behavior causes work slowdowns, which cost the employer money.

Comprehension Check

Have your students close their books and ask them these questions: In your own words, what is the meaning of the term *full potential*? Allow a few students to respond. Next, ask several students to use the term *full potential* in a sentence.

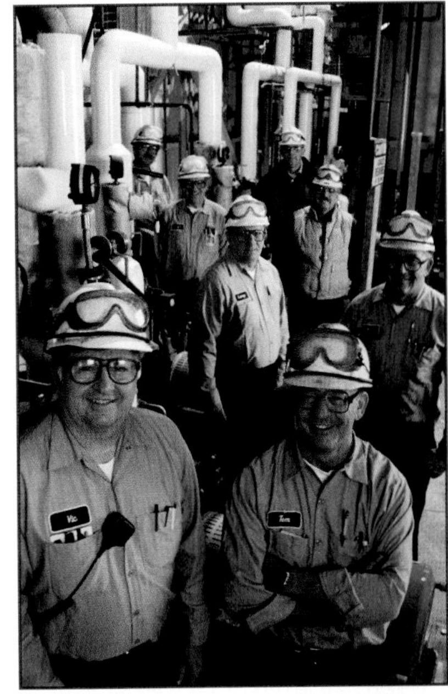

Does this employer provide a safe work environment?

School-to-Work Transition

Explain to your class that at one time or another, most students do not ask questions about an assignment they do not understand. Then ask your students: Who can think of a time when they remained silent instead of asking a question about an assignment they did not understand? Why did you choose not to ask a question? Explain to your class that just as most teachers appreciate honest questions, so do most supervisors and coworkers. In the world of work, ignorance can be dangerous and expensive.

Cooperative Learning/ Education and Training

Divide your class into groups of four or five. Assign each group to review the expectations you should have as a new employee. Ask each group to write a list of those expectations that are influenced by the amount and type of a worker's education and training. In each case students identify, have them write how the expectation is influenced. Allow time for each group to share their conclusions with the class.

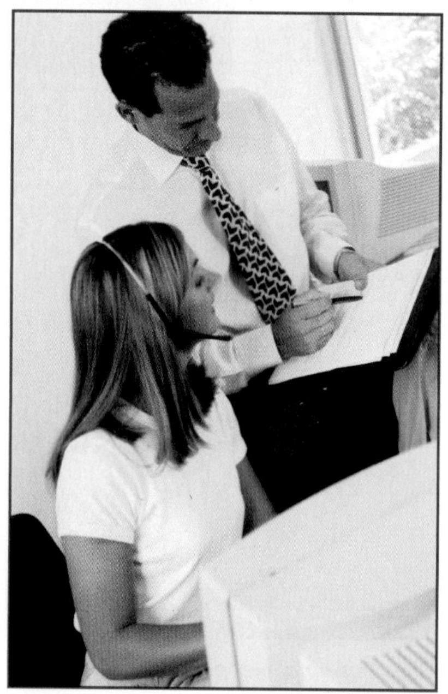

As a new employee, Terry expects to dislike some of her assignments, but she realizes that it's all part of the job. Terry's supervisor is demanding, but fair.

- To be evaluated. Although formal evaluations seldom occur during the early weeks of a new job, your immediate supervisor makes informal evaluations.
- Discipline methods to vary. Some companies maintain high levels of discipline that may be unfamiliar to new employees. For example, manufacturing firms, where safety is a key concern, maintain discipline standards that are more restrictive than standards of service firms, such as retail stores.
- To dislike some of your assignments. Be flexible, and take the bad with the good. It is all part of the job. You are not being realistic if you think you will enjoy all of your work assignments.
- To have assigned responsibilities. A specific job description, detailing the duties, purpose, equipment, and demands of your job, should be explained to you. Knowledge of the various tasks, the workload, and the pace of your work will give you a chance to prove your potential and to demonstrate your willingness to do a good job.
- To be supervised. Your immediate supervisor may be lenient or demanding. In either case, try to build a good working relationship with him or her. Resist the temptation to challenge your supervisor.

Being Responsible: All Work Is Important

At 2:45 in the afternoon, John Strand entered the door of the Golden Candle. Hired as a dining room attendant only three months ago, John already had a dream of owning his own restaurant. He did not begin work until 3:00, but he liked to arrive early and have some time to get ready for his shift.

Considered by some to be at the lowest level, John quickly learned that his job is very important. As soon as customers finished dining, John quickly and thoroughly cleaned and reset the table. During busy dinner hours, waiting to clean unused tables translates into lost dollars for the business. On the other hand, seating customers at poorly cleaned tables can anger them and cause lost business.

Mrs. Crimaldi, the owner and manager, asked John to step into her office before his shift started. She told him that she was very pleased with his attendance, the efficiency with which he handled his work tasks, and the attitude he displayed toward customers and other employees. She needed a person to train under the head chef and offered John the job. The new job would pay more, and it would provide him with an opportunity to learn the various operations of a restaurant kitchen.

John was very happy when he went home that evening. He knew that he was one step closer to his dream of owning his own restaurant.

© JIST Works

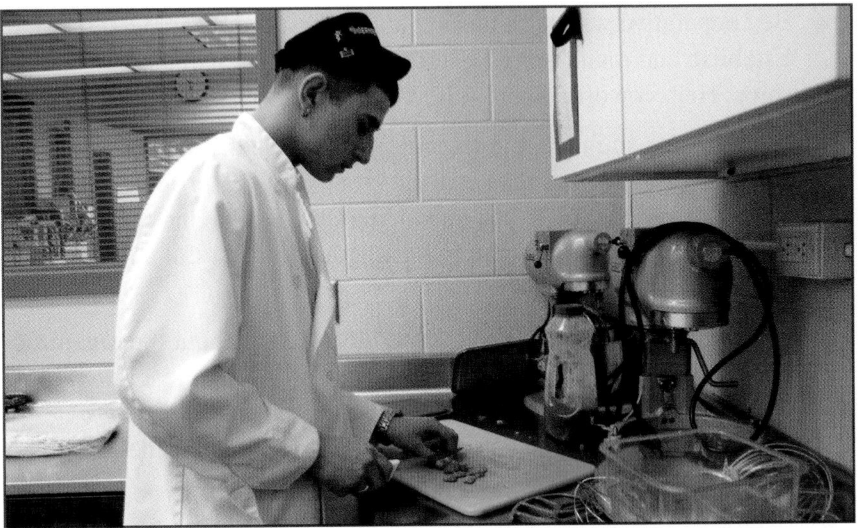

Critical Thinking

Would John be better off if he found a higher-paying job, saved his money, and then opened his own restaurant? List the reasons supporting your opinion.

Key To Success

Expect several introductions during the first few days of a new job. Learn the names of your supervisors and coworkers and to pronounce them correctly.

Reteaching

Have students complete the "Employer-Employee Expectations" worksheet found in Chapter 10 of the *Preparing for Career Success Instructor's CD-ROM, Third Edition.*

What Your Employer Will Expect of You

Employers know that doing the job is not enough to build a successful organization. During your time on the job, your employer will expect you to

- Be conscientious and self-disciplined in meeting performance expectations. Spend additional time, when necessary, to accomplish assigned work tasks at a high standard.
- Use effective written and oral communications. Think before you speak. Then speak clearly, and listen carefully.
- Be enthusiastic and express a positive attitude toward your work.
- Be emotionally stable and respond to stress in an appropriate manner.
- Be pleasant in appearance and personal hygiene. For career success, you must comply with the dress code and maintain acceptable levels of personal cleanliness and grooming.
- Arrive prepared to work and use the job as a learning opportunity.
- Be responsible and use care in handling tools and equipment. If equipment breaks while you are using it, report the damage. When you complete a task, leave your work area and equipment in good condition.

Take Note

Training a new employee costs money and productivity, so the length of time a new worker will stay is an important concern to the employer.

Enrichment

Have students complete the "Rate Your Work Values" worksheet in Chapter 10 of the *Preparing for Career Success Student Activity Book, Third Edition.*

School-to-Work Transition

Ask students to reread the factors employers expect of their employees. Discuss which factors relate most to job-specific skills. Which factors relate most to personality characteristics? Why do so many factors relate to personal characteristics?

- Be cooperative with supervisors, coworkers, and customers. Establish and maintain respectful and honest interpersonal relationships. Help coworkers, but follow the supervisor's instructions.
- Demonstrate an interest in learning. Determine the skills required for your new job, and then evaluate your skills in terms of the company's requirements. If you lack certain skills, take the responsibility for acquiring them. Observe the methods of successful coworkers, and copy them.
- Be loyal. When asked, keep certain information about the organization confidential. Follow company rules and procedures. If you violate a standard procedure, apologize to those whom you have offended. Learn all you can about your employer's business, and speak well of it.
- Perform a full day's work. If you must leave your workstation for something other than a regular break or lunch, let others know where you are.
- Be reliable by consistently arriving at work on time and attending all expected functions. By being punctual and involved and having good attendance, you let management know that you are conscientious and dependable.
- Separate your business and personal life. Your lifestyle outside the company is your business, but when you bring personal concerns to work, they become your employer's business. Reserve personal telephone calls for emergencies. Keep them to a minimum.

These expectations may be difficult to become accustomed to at first. As you read each one, which do you expect to have the most difficulty in meeting? Which will be easiest?

Key To Success

Don't let personal responsibilities and interests interfere with your job performance. Your employer will notice if you do.

Career Fact

Employee theft of property and secrets costs employers millions of dollars each year.

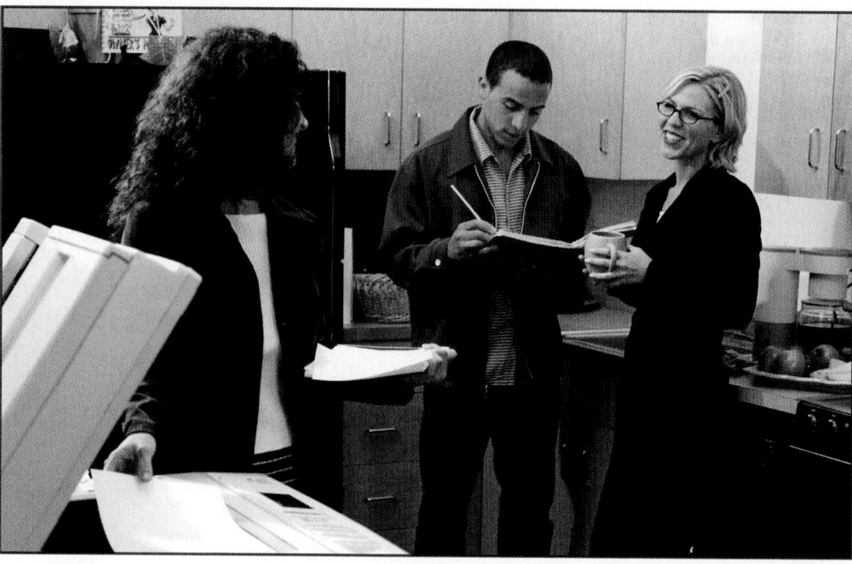

Do not abuse the time allotted for scheduled breaks. Successful workers give a full day's work for a full day's pay.

© JIST Works

Section 2: Get Involved

Compare being a student to being an employee. For example, an employee is rewarded for time and effort spent at work with wages or salary. A student is rewarded for time and effort spent in school with grades. Answer the following questions about this comparison on a separate sheet of paper, and be prepared to discuss your responses in class.

1. What is done by the school to provide a student with a safe work environment?
2. What equipment and supplies does a school provide students?
3. When may a student be given a probationary period?
4. What methods of discipline do schools use with students?
5. Who supervises students?
6. Are the expectations of employers different from those of your teachers? Explain your answer.

Section 3: Laying the Groundwork for Career Success

Success can mean different things to different people, but all of them could agree that **success** is a favorable result or a hoped-for ending. Success results when someone fulfills a wish, a need, or a desire. Your needs to survive, gain social approval, or obtain self-respect are all motivators for career success. Several motives usually operate at once.

Personal values are major motivators. Successful people understand their values and listen to them. They depend on their values when they make career decisions. Another word for values that help you make decisions is *conscience.* Review the work values described in Chapter 3. Which four work values are major motivators for you?

Your definition of career success may involve several factors:

- Promotion to a position with greater responsibility
- An increase in pay
- Job security
- Recognition of your accomplishments
- Knowing you are competent

For some, success means fame and fortune. For others, it is making the world a better place. You will need to determine what success means to you before you can strive to achieve it.

Successful workers balance their personal activities with their work. How you choose to live your life outside your employer's organization is your decision. However, personal lifestyle activities sometimes intrude on job responsibilities and hamper career success. How might you solve the possible career problems in each of the following situations?

Key To Success

When you begin a new job, use formal names in addressing others until granted permission to use first names. Even then, be slow in using first names, and revert to formal names when you are involved in important or formal business situations.

Vocabulary Builder

Ask several students this question before you assign Section 3: When you consider your personal and career goals, what does the word *success* mean to you?

Self-Understanding

Ask your students: What does school success mean to you? Ask for examples of experiences that have been a success for them.

Key To Success

Personality conflicts can harm morale, reduce production, and lower quality. Make the effort to get along with all of your coworkers.

© JIST Works

Discussion Starter

Ask students how their present lifestyle activities affect their school performance. Ask which lifestyle activities have negative effects on their schoolwork? Which ones have positive effects?

Lifestyle Activity	Possible Effect on Job
A busy social life on the weekend	You arrive tired on Monday morning.
A very emotional love relationship	You concentrate on personal concerns.
Alcohol or drug abuse	Your job performance is impaired.
Personal business appointments	You leave work early or take time off.
Cell phone communications	An activated cell phone could interfere with your work tasks.

The first few weeks and months on a new job make up an **orientation period**. This is a time to learn what is expected, establish your credibility, and begin building your performance record. During the orientation period, you will become more aware of your strengths and weaknesses. It is a good time to learn new skills. You will probably encounter certain job tasks that you perform well and others that cause you difficulty. During that time, your supervisor will closely observe your job performance.

Key To Success

Attitudes are transferable. Make sure yours is worth transferring.

Employers strive to maintain high **morale** (level of enthusiasm) in the workplace. To maintain that level of morale, carry out your duties and responsibilities with sincerity and enthusiasm. When you complete a work assignment, ask your supervisor for another task. Taking on new tasks will help you learn more about the job. It will also demonstrate to your supervisor that your morale is good and that you want a more important role in the organization. Like a successful student, a successful worker is not satisfied with completing the minimum requirements.

After you are hired, your supervisor and closest coworkers will have considerable influence on your career success. The supervisor will explain the overall job objectives and your specific role. If you do not have a clear understanding of what is expected, ask questions. Show courtesy and respect for the expertise of your supervisor and your coworkers. Doing so will help you build good working relationships.

Take Note

Your appearance should be in keeping with your job, the public image of the organization, good taste, and any dress codes your employer has. Personal appearance expectations differ from one employer to another and for various jobs within each organization. What would be suitable clothing the following jobs?

- Male or female administrative assistant in a large office
- Female or male sales clerk in a large discount store
- Male or female machine operator in a factory
- Female or male home appliance repairperson

Personal Appearance

Many studies have identified why some people have more career success than others. One study included more than 660 managers of Fortune 500 firms. The basis for their rankings was their personal background, experience, and knowledge. Here's the order of importance they placed on 11 personal qualities or conditions that influence career success:

1. Performance record
2. Personality
3. Communication skills
4. Technical skills and ability to stay up-to-date with skills

© JIST Works

5. Human relations skills
6. Significant work experience and assignments
7. Ability to stay cool under pressure
8. Personal appearance
9. Ability to make tough business decisions
10. Health and energy level
11. Ability to judge people

Observe that **personal appearance** ranks 8 out of the 11 success factors. This means that promotion and acceptance in an organization tend to increase when workers have an acceptable appearance.

Image consultants (people who help others project a desired image) generally recommend the following as acceptable grooming standards:

- Conservative style and color for clothing
- Short, neat hairstyle
- A minimum amount of conservative jewelry
- Pressed clothes, polished shoes, and clean nails

Before you start a new job, take an inventory of your wardrobe. Begin by placing all of your appropriate work clothes in one area of the closet. Mix and match items that may be suitable for your new job. Make a list of any additional clothing you will need. Decide how much you can afford to budget for new clothes, and make a tentative list of what you will buy with that amount.

School-to-Work Transition

Ask your students: Is it more important to be accepted by your employer as "who you are" or to conform to the expected personal appearance and dress code?

Discussion Starter

Ask your students: Should employers establish dress codes for their employees? Why or why not?

Self-Understanding

Ask your students: What message does your "usual" appearance send to people in authority? Is this the message you wish to send during a job interview or to an employer? What is the explanation for your answers?

Key To Success

As you begin a new job, picture yourself as others will see you. Maintain a good sitting and standing posture, and develop a businesslike image. Your appearance is a form of nonverbal communication. It reveals your personal pride and self-confidence.

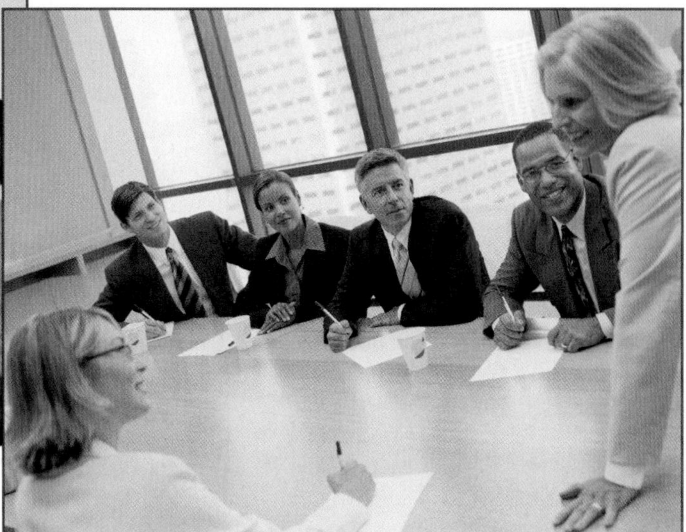

Which group of workers is writing a million dollar advertising campaign for a large corporation? Why do you think so? Which group of workers is responsible for increasing sales at an insurance company? Why do you think so?

Cooperative Learning/ Discussion Starter

Present a variety of endings to the "Critical Thinking" role-play for "Where Does Tiffany Belong?" Facilitate a brief discussion for each ending.

Cluster Link

Are you considering a career working in an office environment? Whether you plan to enter from high school in an administrative support role or from college on the professional track, you should investigate careers in the Business and Administration career cluster. See the appendix for more information.

Solving the Problem: Where Does Tiffany Belong?

Tiffany Fenton carefully moved through the lunchroom, balancing her tray, avoiding other workers and looking for Jeff Lange. Lunch was the one part of her new job at CompuData where she felt comfortable. Jeff had graduated from Wilson High last year, and he knew his way around the company. Tiffany wanted all the advice she could get to help her be successful on the new job. It seemed strange that last week she was an important senior at Wilson, and now she was *nobody* at CompuData.

"Over here, Tiff!" Jeff called to her. "How's everything in the accounting department today?"

"Not very good, Jeff," she replied. "Reynolds has been picking on me all morning. Sometimes I feel like running his tie through the shredder. He started out the morning being upset about my new outfit and ended it being angry because I broke a nail. In the first place, these are not shorts. That shows you how little Reynolds knows about fashion! In the second place, I am the one who cannot use the word processor with a sore finger, not him. What can I do to please the man?"

"For openers, he's not down on you, Tiff," Jeff said. "He told me that you have become more accurate on the spreadsheet program in one week than some of the accounting clerks have in one year. Reynolds is OK. He has been here a long time, and he is playing the corporate game. If his manager should walk in and see you dressed in your new outfit and not keying in data because of your fashionable nails, he would come down on Reynolds like a ton of bricks."

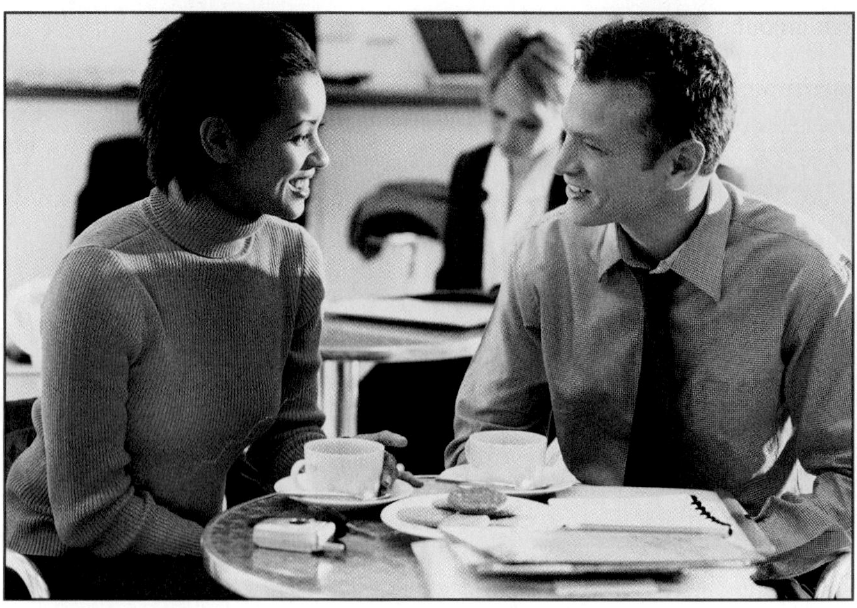

© JIST Works

"We're all people, Tiffany," Jeff continued, "and we all want to belong someplace. A year ago, I decided to belong at CompuData. Maybe that isn't what you want. If it is, then you have to get in the mainstream. Watch Jan Morris and other successful workers in your department. Look at the clothes they wear and how they behave on the job. If you want that identity, go for it. If not, don't blame Reynolds. He knows what he wants."

The next day, Mr. Reynolds called Tiffany into his office. He started the discussion by telling Tiffany that her job was very important to the success of his department and that he was very pleased with the level of her computer skills. Then he asked Tiffany if she really wanted to work at CompuData, and if so, how could he help her fit in?

Critical Thinking

Work with another class member to role-play the end of the conversation between Mr. Reynolds and Tiffany. Present your interpretation to the class.

Being There: Attendance

Is your presence at work so important you cannot afford to miss a day? When is a family crisis more important than a job? Do you deserve a day off if you are a conscientious worker and you have not been absent for months? What are legitimate reasons for being absent from work?

Since the first grade, you have probably been told about the importance of your being present and on time for school. Have you ever received a certificate for perfect attendance or for never being tardy? Were there times when you missed school because of sickness or family situations? If so, you probably had to make up the schoolwork you missed. Did you depend on others to help you catch up? The lessons you have already learned about the importance of attendance and punctuality are a big part of preparing for career success.

On the job, your supervisor and coworkers will depend on you. Your absence could affect other workers' ability to proceed with their jobs. If you are absent, other workers may be required to perform your assigned task in addition to their share of the work. If you work as part of a team, work may slow down or stop during your absence.

A **legitimate absence** occurs when an employee must miss work for a reason that is acceptable to the employer. In cases of legitimate absence, employers have procedures for employees to follow. In most organizations, you notify your supervisor or coworkers as soon as possible. If instructed, telephone the workplace before starting time on a day when you will be absent to explain your situation. If you know in advance that you must miss work on a particular day, it is a good practice to let your supervisor know as far ahead of time as possible. If you become ill late in your shift, notify your supervisor that you are ill and might be absent the next day.

Read the following list of common reasons workers offer for being absent. Which of the reasons would most likely apply to you? Why?

Key To Success

Sometimes you need to take time off for a doctor's appointment or for necessary personal business. Always try to make these appointments outside your scheduled working hours. If making such arrangements is impossible, notify your employer in advance, and obtain permission to be away from work.

Comprehension Check

Have your students close their books. Ask individual students to name one reason for being absent from work that would be acceptable to most employers. Ask whether anyone disagrees. Have students who disagree state their reasons. Then ask individual students to name one reason for being absent from work that would not be acceptable to most employers. Discuss.

Case Study

Have students read the case study "Legitimate Absence or Not?" in Chapter 10 of the *Preparing for Career Success Student Activity Book, Third Edition* and answer the questions.

Accident on the job
Accident off the job
Transportation problem
Leave of absence
Discipline
Excused absence
Family illness
Personal illness
Jury duty
Birthday
Unexcused absence
Military obligation
Medical appointment
Personal problem
Leaving work early
Honor being bestowed
Temporary suspension
Death in the family
Weather
Vacation
Layoff

Being There: Punctuality

Employers insist on punctuality for many of the same reasons that they expect regular attendance. Employers with specific business hours need to have workers at those times to answer the telephones, help customers, and carry out the work of the organization. Your employer will expect you to be ready to work at starting time, stay until quitting time, and take no more than the allotted time for lunch and other scheduled breaks.

Cooperative Learning

Have students complete the "Being There: Attendance and Punctuality" worksheet found in Chapter 10 of the *Preparing for Career Success Instructor's CD-ROM, Third Edition.*

Scheduled breaks are rest periods that employers provide so employees can take time out from the workday to relax, have refreshments, handle personal needs, or socialize with coworkers. These breaks usually last 10 or 15 minutes. In some work operations, another employee will perform your job during your scheduled breaks.

Most employers expect workers to arrive on the job promptly and be ready to work as scheduled. If getting started in the morning is not easy for you, prepare for your job the night before. Practice the following suggestions, and make a commitment to be on time:

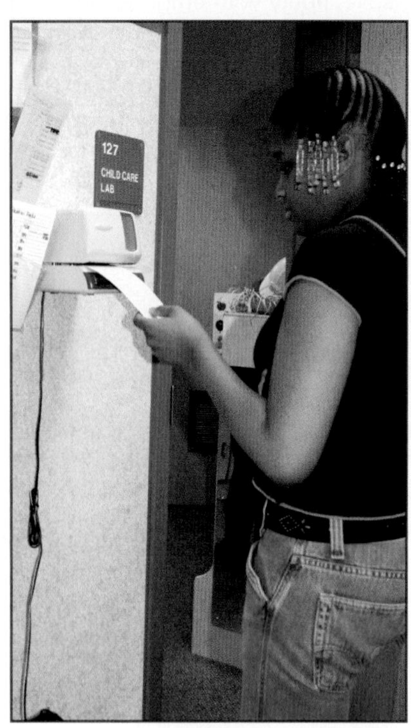

Employers expect workers to be on time and have good attendance.

1. Get enough sleep. Plan your activities so you are home in time for a full eight hours of sleep—no late TV or parties on work nights.
2. Buy a clock radio that has an alarm or an alarm clock that has a light plus an alarm. Place your alarm where you must walk across the room to turn it off.
3. Before you go to bed, decide what you will wear to work the next day. Lay out your clothing, clean, pressed, and ready to wear. Place shoes and accessories, such as jewelry, next to your outfit.
4. If you drive to work, leave your car keys on the nightstand along with your wallet or purse. If you use public transportation, have the correct change laid out so it is ready to go in the morning.
5. Set all but the refrigerated parts of your breakfast on the table the night before. If you want coffee in the morning, prepare the pot and have it ready to turn on.
6. Skip the newspaper until evening, read it at lunch, or read it on your way to work if you use public transportation.
7. Time yourself. For several days, write down the amount of time you take to complete each of the tasks listed.

© JIST Works

Policies and Procedures

All employers have a *unique* (one-of-a-kind) set of rules known as **policies and procedures.** They serve the organization's unique needs, purpose, and management system. Employers spend a considerable amount of time developing and testing different procedures. If you expect to receive the rewards of working for an employer, you should also expect to follow the organization's policies and procedures.

As you become familiar with the day-to-day operations of your employer, the organization's policies and procedures can provide a sense of order and eliminate many confusing situations. In addition, they can provide employee protection. For example, a company that manufactures hazardous chemicals would expect employees to follow a long list of safety policies and procedures. A different company, such as the owner of a chain of retail stores, would be more concerned with policies and procedures that focus on customer relations.

Much of your job success will depend on how well you follow the policies and procedures of your employer. Learning and adjusting to your employer's methods are an important part of establishing yourself as a member of the organization. It is best to follow policies and procedures even when you do not understand why. The failure to follow established rules could result in the termination of your employment.

Many employers give their employees policies and procedures manuals (also known as employee handbooks) when they begin working. If you did not receive one, your supervisor or a coworker may be able to inform you about the organization's policies and procedures. Manuals concerning absence, punctuality, evaluation, grievances, use of equipment and tools, safety, rest periods, and theft are usually available.

TECHNOLOGY

Most companies have established policies concerning the use of technology in order to control company information, increase employee productivity, and protect themselves from lawsuits. These policies involve activities such as visiting Web sites, sending e-mails and instant messages, blogging, and using cell phones and MP3 players. Make sure you know your employer's policies concerning these activities.

School-to-Work Transition

Send two writers to the chalkboard. Ask one writer to write "School policies and procedures" as a heading and the other writer to write "Employer policies and procedures." Begin by asking the class to name school policies and procedures for the first writer's list. Next, ask the students which school policies and procedures also fit the second writer's list. Then ask for employer's policies and procedures that would not be appropriate for a school.

Section 3: Get Involved

Answer the following on a separate sheet of paper, and be prepared to discuss your responses in class.

1. Five of the 11 career success determinants in the list in the "Personal Appearance" section are personal qualities and are not related to job skills or education and training levels. Evaluate yourself in terms of items 2, 5, 7, 8, and 10. What personal improvements could you make in these areas?
2. Numerous studies indicate the relationship between school attendance and attendance on the job. How much emphasis should employers put on school attendance and tardy records when making hiring decisions? Why?
3. Some reasons people offer for being late to their jobs are anxiety about work, conflicts with coworkers, job boredom, dislike of getting up early, conflicts with the boss, and transportation problems. Which of these reasons would be most likely to result in your being late for work? Explain your answer.
4. Other than family emergencies, what are two legitimate reasons for being late to work? Explain your answer.
5. Ask a family member or an employed friend about his or her employer's policies and procedures regarding absence, punctuality, evaluation, grievances, use of equipment and tools, and safety. Report your findings to the class.

Chapter 10 Review

Enrichment

Have students complete the Chapter 10 section of the *Preparing for Career Success Student Portfolio, Third Edition.*

Enrich Your Vocabulary

On a separate sheet of paper, number from 1 to 18, and then match each of the following statements with the most appropriate term from the "Enrich Your Vocabulary" list at the beginning of the chapter by writing that term next to the number of the correct statement.

1. Relying on one another
2. Manners
3. A favorable result or a hoped-for ending
4. People who help others to project a desired image
5. Handbooks
6. Getting acquainted with a new job and the employer's organization
7. Expressing interest and enthusiasm
8. Complaining and using sarcasm
9. A period of time in which you are expected to learn the job
10. Highest level of productivity
11. The first few weeks and months on a new job
12. The way you look to others
13. Missing work for an acceptable reason
14. Rest periods that employers provide
15. Rules and regulations
16. Being capable
17. Level of enthusiasm
18. Strengthen or make better

Enrich Your Vocabulary Answers

1. interdependence
2. etiquette
3. success
4. image consultants
5. training manuals
6. job orientation
7. positive attitude
8. negative attitude
9. probationary period
10. full potential
11. orientation period
12. personal appearance
13. legitimate absence
14. scheduled breaks
15. policies and procedures
16. competence
17. morale
18. enhance

Check Your Knowledge

On a separate sheet of paper, answer the following questions. (Do not write in your textbook.)

1. What do many employers believe is the most important factor in job success?
2. How do people demonstrate a positive attitude? List three ways.
3. How do people demonstrate a negative attitude? List three ways.

Check Your Knowledge Answers

1. A positive attitude.
2. By viewing a new job as an opportunity; acting interested and enthusiastic; being courteous, cooperative, considerate; viewing the world as a friendly place; being accepting of others; taking responsibility for their decisions; being honest in expressing their thoughts and feelings; believing that they have the ability to control their feelings; and being open to suggestions.
3. By seeing a job as drudgery; frequently complaining and using sarcasm; being critical and blaming others; having careless work habits; being indifferent to the needs of others.

(continued)

© JIST Works

4. Why do employers want employees to be successful?
5. What can employees expect from their employers? List five things.
6. What do employers expect from their employees? List five things.
7. What is the first-ranked determinant of career success in the list in the "Personal Appearance" section?
8. Which determinant of career success is earned only through education?
9. Why are attendance and punctuality very important on the job? Give one reason.

Develop SCANS Competencies

Government experts say that successful workers can productively use resources, interpersonal skills, information, systems, and technology. This activity will give you practice in developing information skills.

Employers often use forms with items similar to the following to appraise their employees' performance. Rate your school performance on the items listed and analyze the information to determine where you might need to improve your performance.

Quality of Work

- ☐ Very high
- ☐ Sometimes superior—usually accurate
- ☐ Careful worker—seldom needs redone
- ☐ Frequently unacceptable
- ☐ Very low

Cooperation

- ☐ Very cooperative
- ☐ Usually cooperative
- ☐ Cooperates when asked
- ☐ Frequently uncooperative
- ☐ Very uncooperative

Attendance and Punctuality

- ☐ Excellent
- ☐ Above average
- ☐ Average
- ☐ Below average
- ☐ Unreliable

Check Your Knowledge Answers *(continued)*

4. Because an employee's success enhances the productivity and quality of the entire organization.
5. To be paid for their time; a safe work environment; equipment and supplies; a probationary period; some job training; to make mistakes; to be evaluated; discipline; to dislike some assignments; to have assigned responsibilities; and supervision.
6. Conscientiousness in meeting performance expectations; responsibility and care in handling tools and equipment; effective written and oral communication; positive attitude; cooperation with supervisors, coworkers, and customers; an interest in learning; loyalty; a full day's work; emotional stability; reliability; pleasant appearance and hygiene; and separation of business and personal life.
7. An excellent performance record.
8. An advanced college degree.
9. Your supervisor and coworkers depend on you. Your absence could affect other workers' ability to proceed with their jobs. In your absence, other workers may be required to perform more than their share of the work. Work may slow down or stop if a team member is absent.

Reteaching

Have students complete the "Finding the Right Words" and the "Checking Your Location" activities for Chapter 10 in the *Preparing for Career Success Student Activity Book, Third Edition.*

© JIST Works

Chapter 11 Resources

Lesson Plans and Preparation

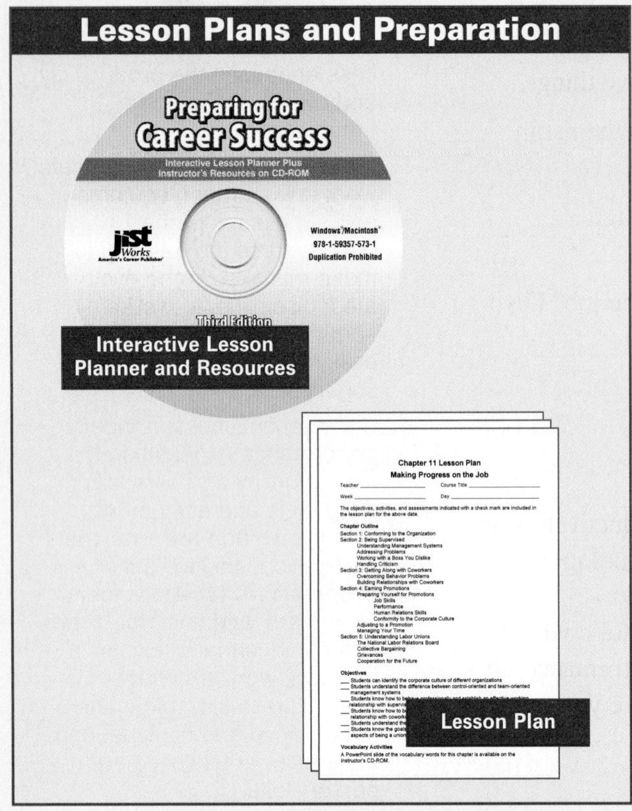

Preparing for Career Success
Interactive Lesson Planner Plus
Instructor's Resources on CD-ROM
Third Edition
Interactive Lesson Planner and Resources
Chapter 11 Lesson Plan
Making Progress on the Job
Lesson Plan

Multimedia

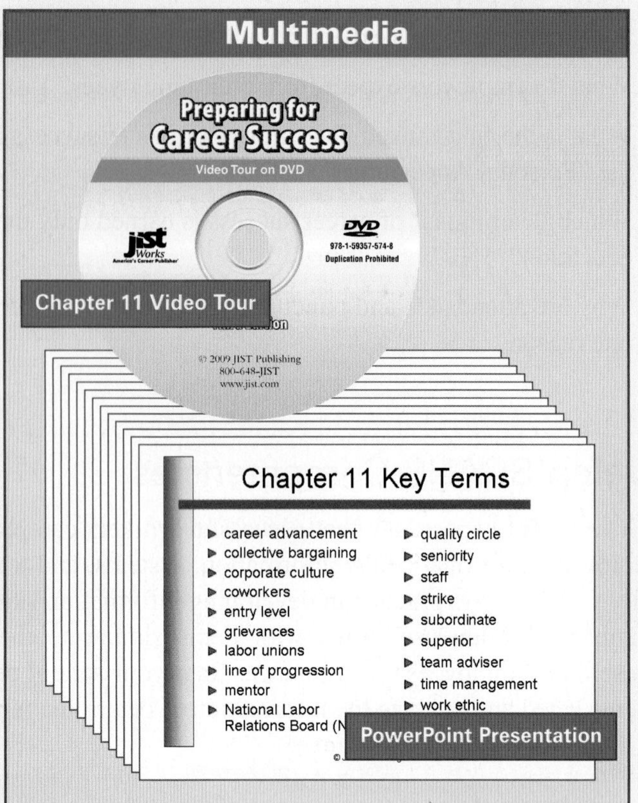

Preparing for Career Success
Video Tour on DVD
Chapter 11 Video Tour
© 2009 JIST Publishing
800-648-JIST
www.jist.com
Chapter 11 Key Terms
career advancement
collective bargaining
corporate culture
coworkers
entry level
grievances
labor unions
line of progression
mentor
National Labor Relations Board
quality circle
seniority
staff
strike
subordinate
superior
team adviser
time management
work ethic
PowerPoint Presentation

Activities

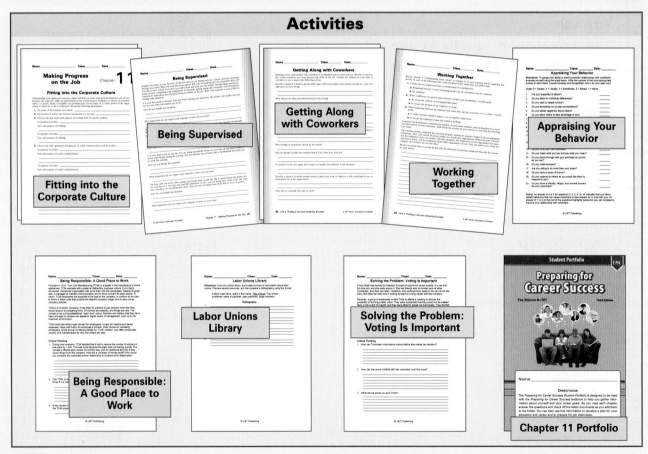

Fitting into the Corporate Culture

Being Supervised

Getting Along with Coworkers

Working Together

Appraising Your Behavior

Being Responsible: A Good Place to Work

Labor Unions Library

Solving the Problem: Voting Is Important

Chapter 11 Portfolio

© JIST Works

Review and Assessment

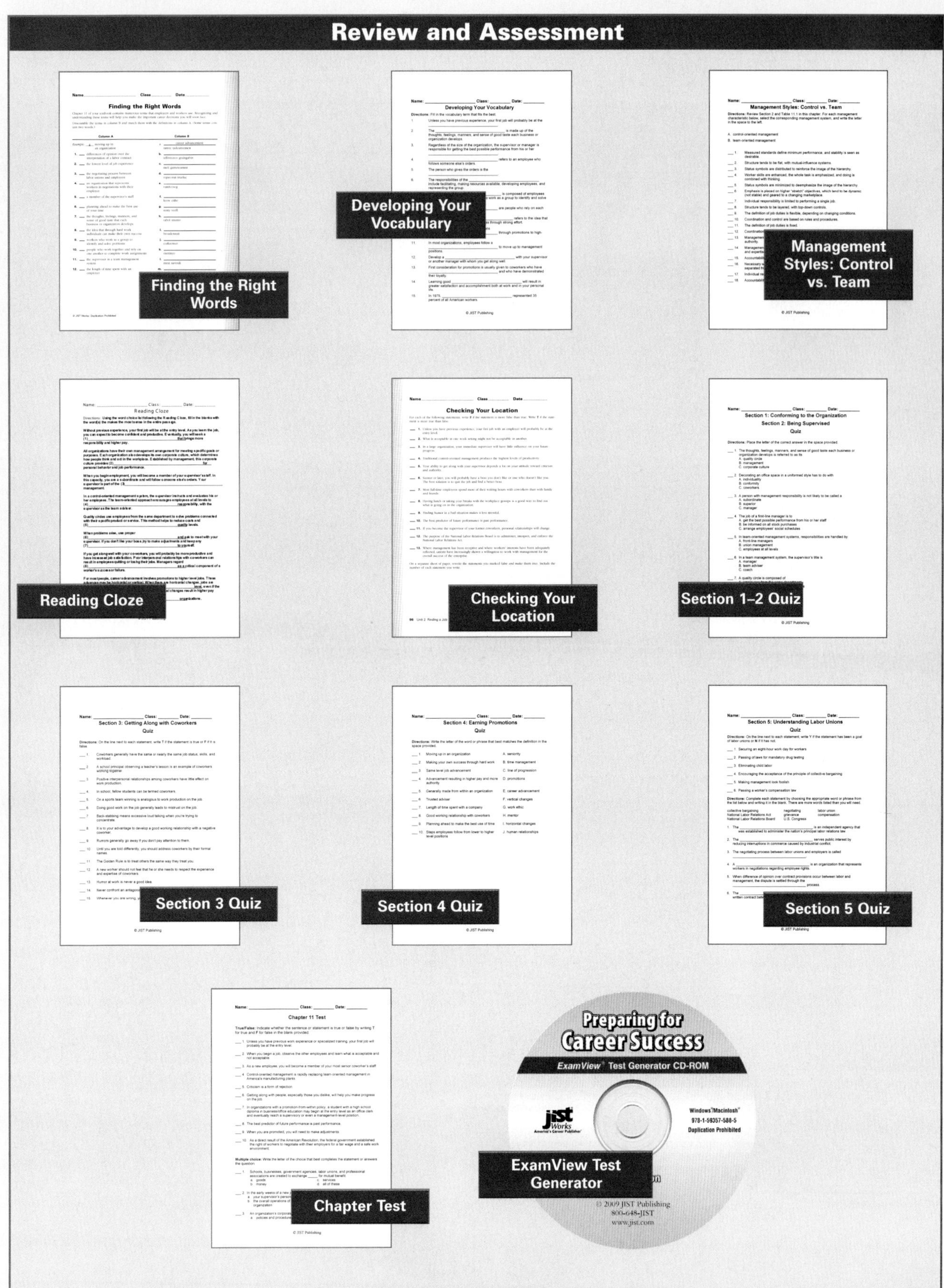

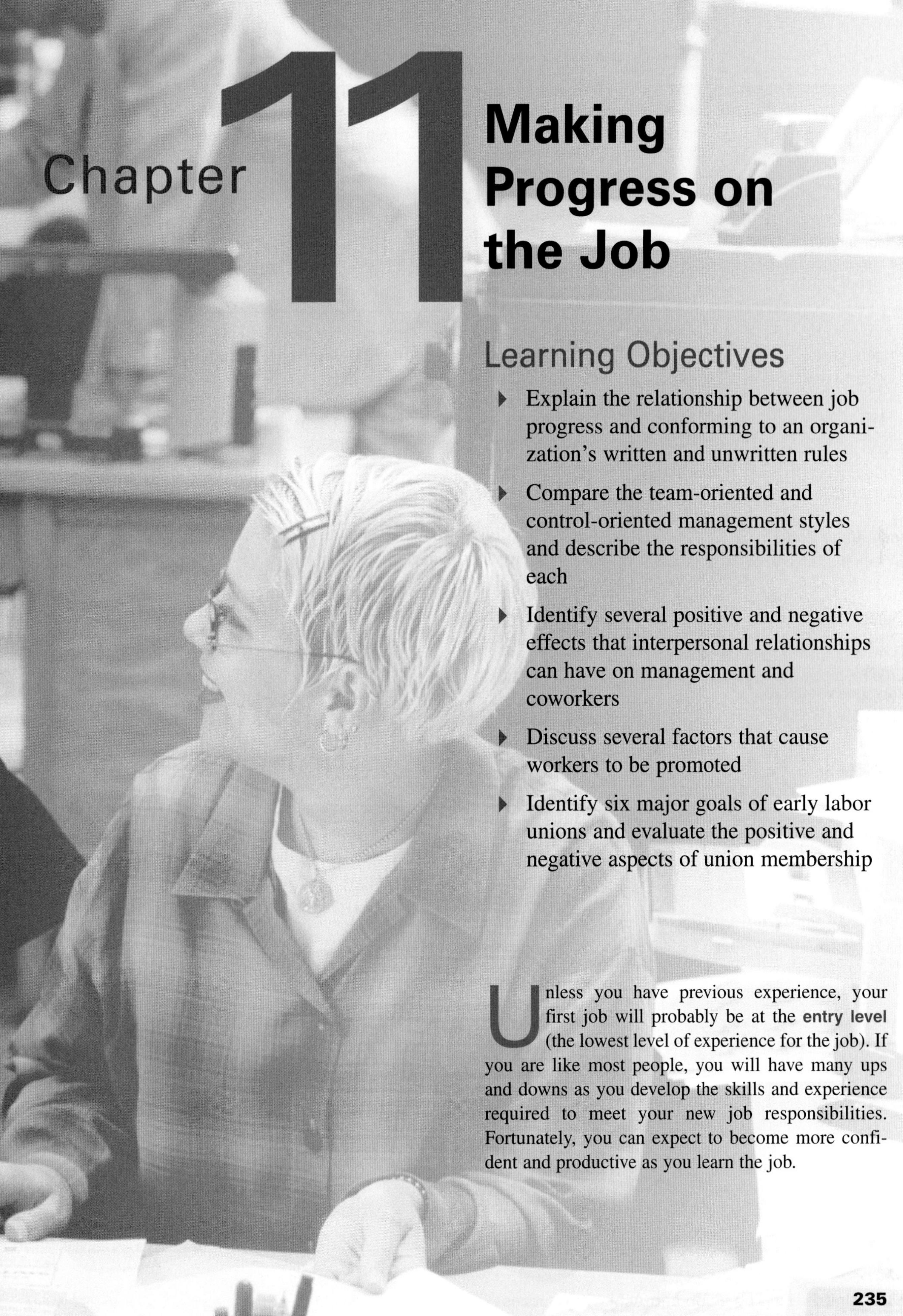

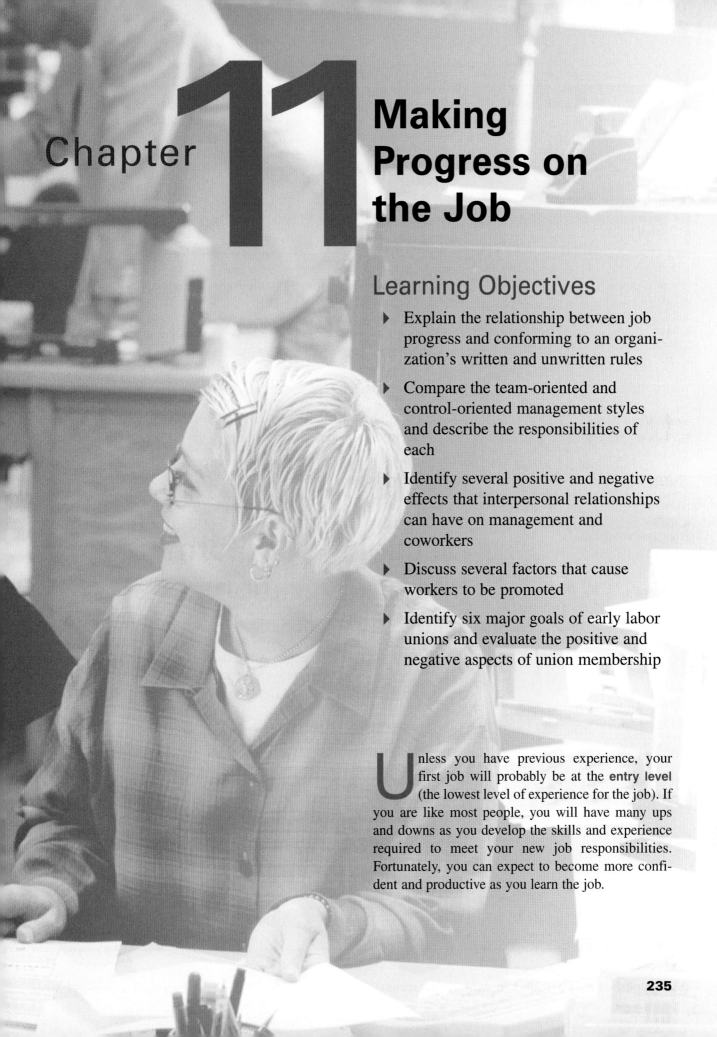

Chapter 11 Making Progress on the Job

Learning Objectives

- Explain the relationship between job progress and conforming to an organization's written and unwritten rules
- Compare the team-oriented and control-oriented management styles and describe the responsibilities of each
- Identify several positive and negative effects that interpersonal relationships can have on management and coworkers
- Discuss several factors that cause workers to be promoted
- Identify six major goals of early labor unions and evaluate the positive and negative aspects of union membership

Unless you have previous experience, your first job will probably be at the **entry level** (the lowest level of experience for the job). If you are like most people, you will have many ups and downs as you develop the skills and experience required to meet your new job responsibilities. Fortunately, you can expect to become more confident and productive as you learn the job.

Enrich Your Vocabulary

In reading this chapter and doing the exercises, you will learn the following important terms:

career advancement	line of progression	strike
collective bargaining	mentor	subordinate
corporate culture	National Labor Relations Board (NLRB)	superior
coworkers	quality circle	team adviser
entry level	seniority	time management
grievances	staff	work ethic
labor unions		

Vocabulary

You can use the "Developing Your Vocabulary" worksheet found in the Chapter 11 file of the *Preparing for Career Success Instructor's CD-ROM, Third Edition* as a pretest for chapter concepts or as a reteaching worksheet.

Vocabulary Builder

Explain that all career clusters have *entry-level* jobs. For example, entry-level attorneys usually act as research assistants to experienced lawyers or judges. Ask individual students to name an entry-level job for a recent high school graduate and a high school dropout.

Enrichment

Have students complete the "Fitting into the Corporate Culture" activity in Chapter 11 of the *Preparing for Career Success Student Activity Book, Third Edition.*

Video Tour on DVD

Show students the Chapter 11 segment to introduce them to the content.

When you seek a promotion with more responsibility and higher pay, keep the following criteria in mind:

1. You will need to demonstrate to your employer that you have mastered your present assignment.
2. You will need to demonstrate your ability to get along with managers and coworkers.
3. You will need to understand and conform to the organization's philosophy and management structure.
4. You will need to understand the requirements of the next highest job level in the organization.

Section 1: Conforming to the Organization

Schools, businesses, government agencies, labor unions, and professional associations are created to exchange goods, services, or money for mutual benefit. All of them have a *management arrangement* (system of organization) within which they operate to meet specific goals or purposes (see Figure 11.1).

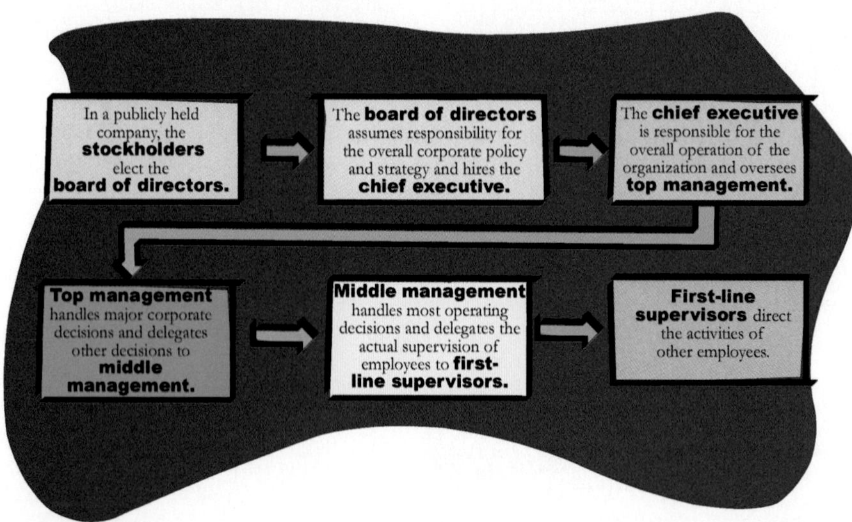

Figure 11.1 Business organization.

© JIST Works

Since elementary school, you have been conforming to the management organization of a school system. The school system you currently attend has an organizational structure similar to that of a private business. It is structured to meet the educational goals of the community or group it serves.

In the early weeks of a new job, you should learn all you can about the overall operations of the organization. Learn how it is *structured* (organized) and who reports to whom in the system of management. To help you learn, keep a notepad and write down the names of people you meet, along with their positions, titles, and functions. Then use this notepad as a reference when you want to clarify something you were told, obtain additional information, or remember a specific person's name. Understanding the structure of the organization will help you understand your position within it.

Every worker in an occupational group has certain characteristics that make him or her different from other workers in the same occupation. Similarly, every organization has certain *characteristics* (policies and procedures) that make it different from other organizations with similar *missions* (purposes, goals). This personality is the organization's **corporate culture**. The culture is made up of the thoughts, feelings, manners, and sense of good taste each business or organization develops. The stated mission of Microsoft Corporation, for example, is "to enable people and businesses throughout the world to realize their full potential."

Reteaching

Invite the school principal to your class to explain how your school system is organized.

Enrichment

Have students develop a mission and vision statement for your school.

Cross-Reference

Explain that people frequently have prejudiced attitudes and stereotypes concerning organizations just as they do about certain groups of people. See "Section 3: Attitudes" in Chapter 3.

School-to-Work Transition

Ask your students: What concerns do you have about conforming in a new job?

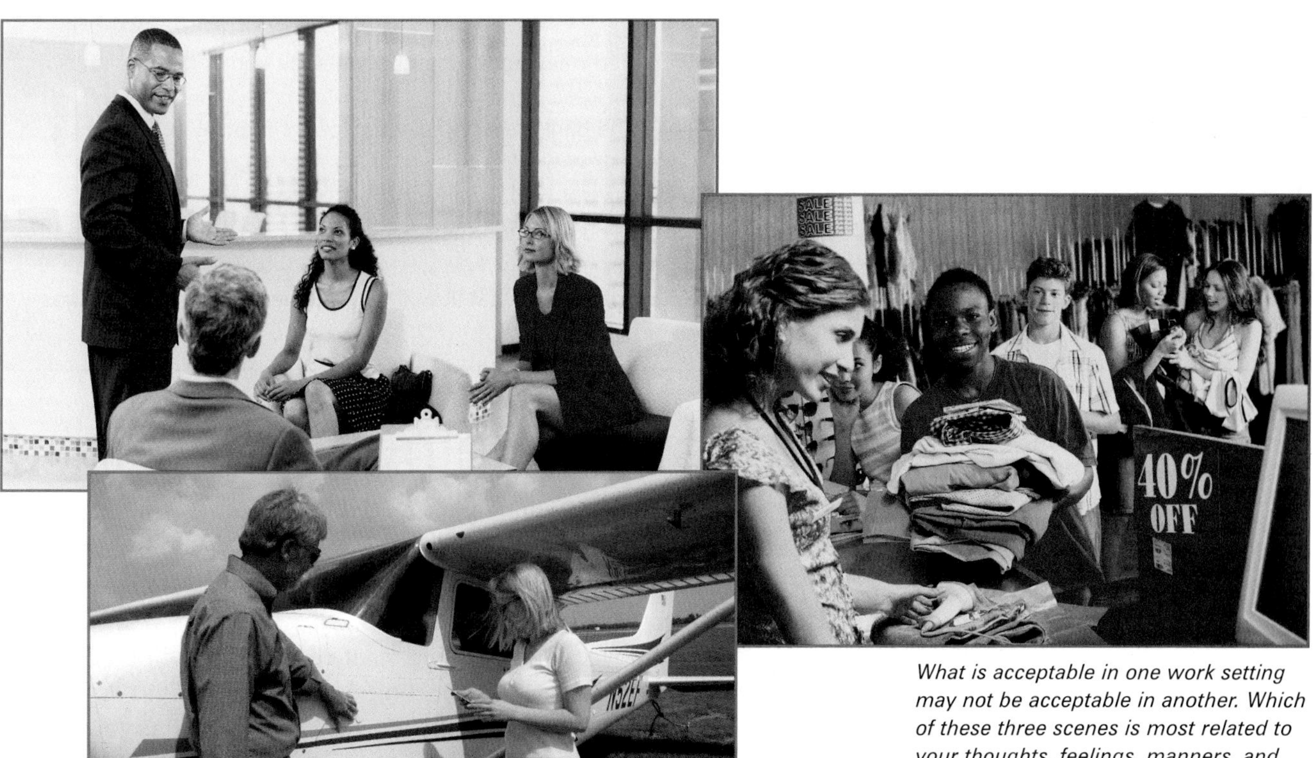

What is acceptable in one work setting may not be acceptable in another. Which of these three scenes is most related to your thoughts, feelings, manners, and sense of good taste?

Community Resources

Assign a student to use the local telephone book to locate a local corporate office. Invite an employee to speak with your class about the corporation's (mission, vision) culture.

Case Study

Have students read the case study "A Good Place to Work" found in Chapter 11 of the *Preparing for Career Success Instructor's CD-ROM, Third Edition.* Discuss the "Critical Thinking" questions.

As the twenty-first century began, many employers added a *vision statement* to their *mission statement*. The vision statement is about the organization's future. For example, the vision statement of Airborne Express is "Airborne Express is its people"; for Mylan Laboratories, a pharmaceutical product corporation, it is "Expanding our horizons."

The corporate culture, which the management establishes, becomes the guideline for personal behavior and job performance for the entire organization. Your job progress will depend in large part on your ability to understand and fit into your employer's corporate culture.

When you begin a job, observe other employees, and learn what is acceptable and not acceptable. For example, one employer may encourage you to decorate your work area with pictures, posters, or other items that show you have a personal space in the organization. Another employer may have a strict policy regarding decorating your work area, and individuality may be discouraged. How is student individuality encouraged in your school?

Section 1: Get Involved

Public expectations influence certain stereotypes of conformity. Answer the following on a separate sheet of paper, and be prepared to discuss your responses in class.

1. Describe your image of working in a large bank.
2. In what ways does the bank appear to be uncluttered, well organized, and managed by people who dress conservatively?
3. Do the bank employees seem to conform to clearly defined rules about their appearance and conduct with customers?
4. Think about the function of a bank. Does your image of the bank give you a sense of confidence in the bank's ability to handle your money safely and accurately? Why or why not?
5. Would you want to deposit your money in a bank that was not well organized?
6. If bank employees dressed as casual as students, would you question their commitment to being precise and accurate with your money? Why or why not?
7. What are some rules you follow (conform to) to avoid problems? What are some advantages or disadvantages you have experienced when you conform to rules?

Vocabulary Builder

Write these terms on the chalkboard: *entry level, corporate culture, staff, subordinate,* and *superior.* Divide the class into learning pairs. Allow 10 minutes for each pair to write as few correct sentences as possible using these terms. (Terms cannot be used more than once.) Scoring: 1 point for each correct sentence; 1 point for each word or term used in a grammatically incorrect sentence; 1 point for each unused word. The pair with the lowest score wins.

Section 2: Being Supervised

The person who will direct your work has a position of management responsibility in the organization. Whether this person is a manager, supervisor, or foreman, he or she will be important to your success, satisfaction, and progress on the job.

Assigning employees and deciding what each person will do in a specific position is a management function known as *staffing*. As a new employee, you will become a member of your supervisor's **staff** (a group of employees who work for and with someone in charge). As a staff member, you will also be a **subordinate**. This term refers to an employee who follows someone else's orders. The person who gives the orders is the subordinate's **superior**.

© JIST Works

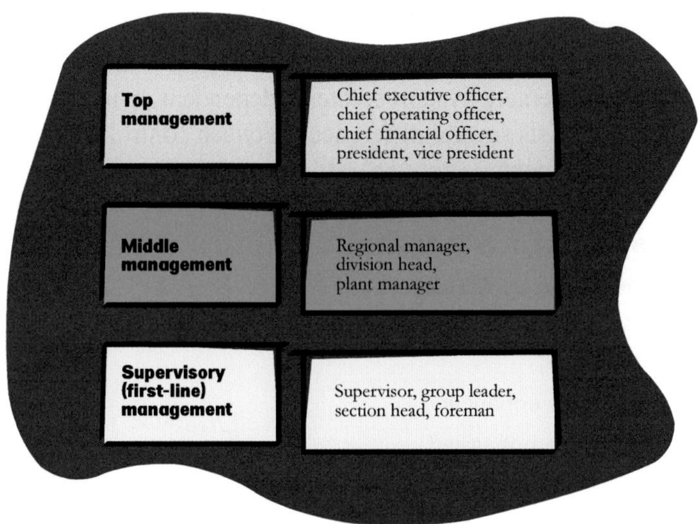

Top management
Chief executive officer, chief operating officer, chief financial officer, president, vice president
Middle management
Regional manager, division head, plant manager
Supervisory (first-line) management
Supervisor, group leader, section head, foreman

Figure 11.2 The three layers of management.

Find Out More

For additional information concerning management and supervision, enter **American Management Association** in your Internet search engine, visit www.amanet.org, or write to the following address to request information:

American Management Association
1601 Broadway, 6th Floor
New York, NY 10019

Regardless of the size of the organization, the supervisor or manager is responsible for getting the best possible performance from his or her staff. As both a member of a staff and a subordinate, you will be assigned specific job duties and responsibilities by your supervisor. After the supervisor makes assignments, he or she will provide any special directions that you need. Your supervisor is a part of the first-line management (see Figure 11.2).

Discussion Starter

Explain that worker communication begins and ends with the *supervisory, first-line manager* (see Figure 11.2) in an organization using a control-oriented management system. Ask your students: What advantages or disadvantages would you have if you were a worker in an organization using control-oriented management?

Understanding Management Systems

Control-oriented management was widely used in the early part of the twentieth century. One person controlled the entire organization, which was composed of several layers of management from the top to the bottom. Each layer had specific responsibilities, and they reported to the layer above them. The lowest layers of management were the *supervisors* in charge of the *workers.*

Some businesses still use a form of the control-oriented management system. Most of them also include modern management styles in their system.

Most American employers have moved away from the traditional control-oriented management system to a more *team-oriented* management approach. Management studies link this approach to higher productivity, improved product quality, and increased worker satisfaction. In the

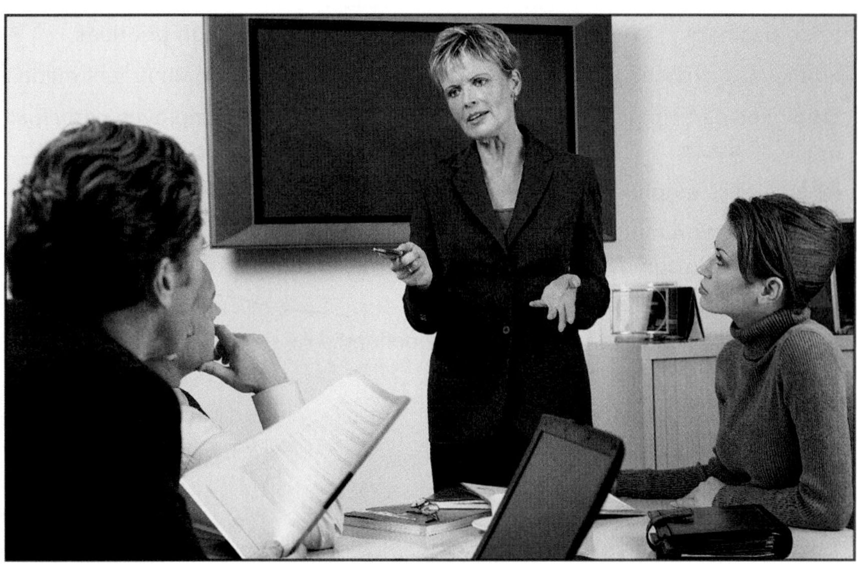

In a control-oriented corporate culture, your supervisor will determine your work schedule and inform you about work procedures (including the quality of the product or service provided).

Reteaching

Have students complete the "Management Styles: Control vs. Team" worksheet in Chapter 11 of the *Preparing for Career Success Instructor's CD-ROM, Third Edition.*

team-oriented management system, employees at all levels share responsibilities. This sharing encourages interdependence in workers. In contrast, the control-oriented management system creates a dependent or independent workforce. Table 11.1 lists several differences between control-oriented and team-oriented management.

Table 11.1 Differences in Workforce Management Systems

Control-Oriented Management	Team-Oriented Management
Individual responsibility limited to performing a single job	Individual responsibility extended to upgrading group performance
Necessary worker skills diluted	Worker skills enhanced
Work tasks fragmented	Whole task emphasized
Doing separated from thinking	Doing combined with thinking
Accountability focused on individual	Accountability focused on team
Job duties with fixed definitions	Flexible job duties that depend on changing conditions
Measured standards defining minimum performance, and stability seen as desirable	Emphasis placed on higher "stretch" objectives, which tend to be dynamic and geared to changing marketplace
Layered structure with top-down controls	Flat structure with mutual influence systems
Coordination and control based on rules and procedures	Coordination and control based on shared goals, values, and traditions
Management decisions based on individual privilege and positional authority	Management decisions based on problem solving, current information, and expertise
Status symbols distributed to reinforce the image of the hierarchy	Status symbols minimized to de-emphasize the image of the hierarchy
Individual pay linked to job evaluation	Individual pay linked to mastery of skill
Variable-pay systems providing individual incentive and achievement	Variable-pay systems creating equity and reinforce group achievement
Employees regarded as variable costs necessary to do business	Training and keeping the existing workforce as high priorities
Employees expecting occasional layoffs	Commitment made to avoid layoffs or assist in re-employment
Employee participation allowed on narrow range of issues	Employee participation encouraged on wide range of issues
Related risks emphasized	Related benefits emphasized
Communication methods that include open-door policy, attitude surveys, grievance procedures, and collective bargaining	Communication methods that include new group concepts of corporate governance
Business information shared on strictly defined "need-to-know" basis	Business information shared widely
Adversarial labor relations	Mutuality in labor relations
Emphasis on interest conflict	Emphasis on joint planning and problem solving
Communication on narrow agenda	Communication on broad agenda
Unions, management, and workers maintaining clearly defined roles	Unions, management, and workers redefining their respective roles

© JIST Works

In the team management system, the supervisor's title is **team adviser** or team consultant. The team adviser's responsibilities include many of those previously listed for supervisors, but focus on the following tasks:

- *Facilitating* (motivating and encouraging) workers rather than directing them
- Ensuring that resources are available so the team can produce quality work on time
- Developing the employees into a team and providing leadership in problem solving
- Representing the team in the organization

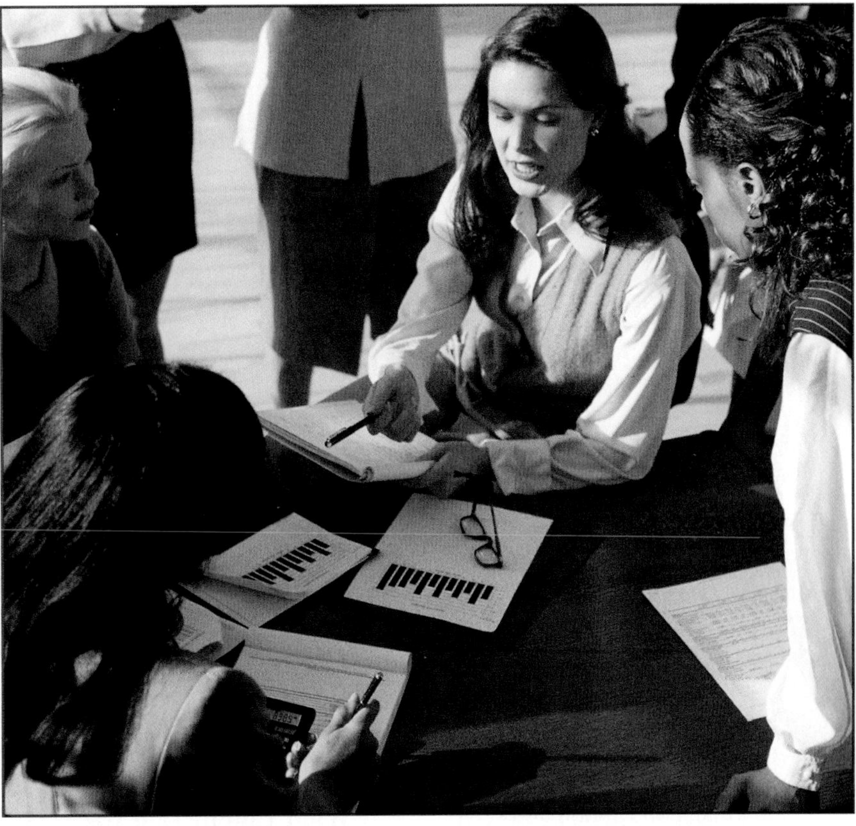

In a team-oriented corporate culture, workers from the same department work together to identify and solve quality problems with the product they manufacture or the service they provide.

A quality circle is one team-oriented management style used in the United States. A **quality circle** is composed of employees from the same department who work as a group to identify and solve quality problems with the product they manufacture or the service they provide. The rank-and-file workforce is often the group most qualified to solve work-related problems involving quality.

Solving the Problem: Being Pleasant Is Important

Connie Lee is very pleased with her new job as an office clerk in the training department. After three days on the job, Connie believes her supervisor, Mr. Darrow, approves of her skills. Now he has another assignment for her. "Connie," he says, "type this material for me exactly as it is. Do not change a thing. I'll need it early this afternoon." He drops the handwritten pages in her in-box and returns to his office.

As Connie reviews the material, she notices that it has several spelling errors and some very poor grammar. Typing the material takes her about an hour longer than she had expected because of the corrections that are necessary. However, she completes the job on time and has it ready for Mr. Darrow when he returns. He takes a few minutes to read it before saying, "Good job, Connie! I really appreciate the way you handle things."

"Thanks!" Connie replies. "I would have finished much sooner, but half the words were spelled wrong. I haven't seen such poor grammar since the eighth grade." Mr. Darrow immediately turns around and walks rapidly back to his office.

Comprehension Check

Have your students close their books. Then ask your students: Which job responsibilities of a first-line manager in a control-oriented management system and a team advisor in a team-oriented management system are similar? Which job responsibilities are different?

Community Resources

Form a volunteer committee to contact the American Management Association (allow extra credit). Assign the committee to write a letter describing the management unit they are studying and request related information. Allow time for them to report their findings to the class.

© JIST Works

It's easier to do a job right than to explain why you didn't.

—Martin Van Buren

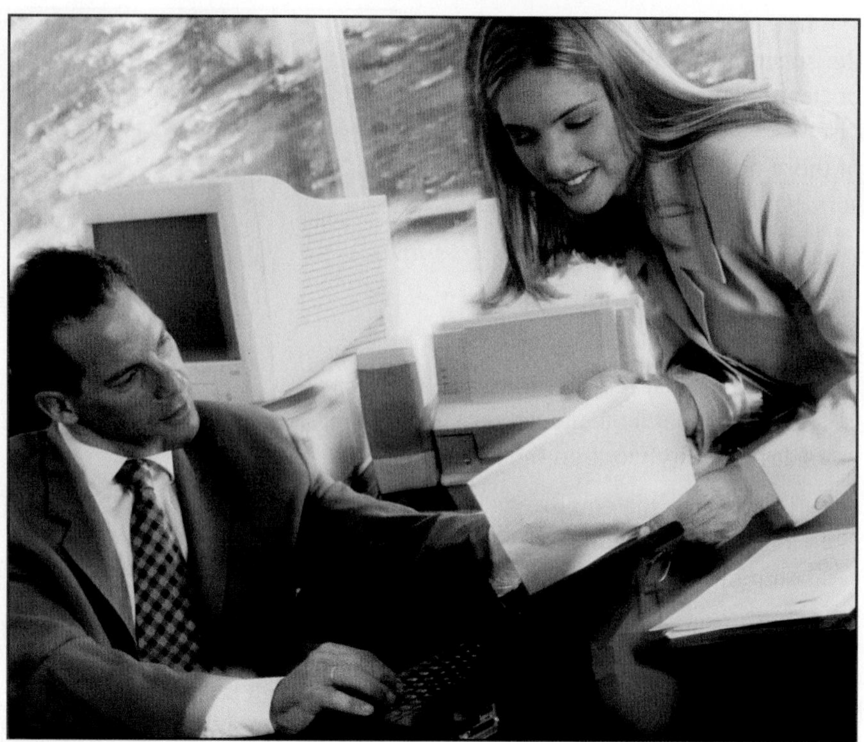

Critical Thinking

What Connie said was true, but was it wise?

Should Connie have made the corrections without first discussing the problem with Mr. Darrow? Why do you feel this way?

What impression did Connie give Mr. Darrow when she criticized the spelling and grammar in the original material?

If you were Connie, how would you have handled this situation?

TAKE NOTE

Traditional, control-oriented American business leaders rejected the American idea of building quality circles. Following World War II, Japanese business leaders were quick to embrace this American idea. They used it as a philosophy to rebuild their industries. When the high quality of Japanese products began to cause a loss of sales for American business and a loss of American jobs, many American business leaders took a second look at quality circles and the team-oriented style of management. American companies such as Ford, Honeywell, Corning Glass, Chrysler, Northrop, and Lockheed discovered that their use of quality circles increased production, raised quality levels, reduced costs, and increased worker satisfaction.

Addressing Problems

If you do not fully understand what your supervisor expects of you, or if you have a problem you want to discuss, be sure to use proper business etiquette and request a meeting with your supervisor. Follow these guidelines:

1. Do not request a meeting when you are angry. Wait until you have calmed down, even if it takes a day or two.
2. Ask your supervisor or the administrative assistant when a meeting would be convenient.
3. Handle the problem in private, and do not discuss your meeting with your coworkers.
4. Arrive on time for your scheduled appointment. When you enter the supervisor's office, remain standing until offered a seat.

© JIST Works

5. Be prepared to state the problem as you see it. Maintain a positive attitude in your presentation and during the entire meeting. Your cool head will attract respect from your superiors in the organization.
6. Respect the chain of command by accepting the outcome of the meeting. Do not go over your supervisor's head unless you are prepared to live with the possible consequences. End the meeting with a handshake and a positive comment.

KEY TO SUCCESS

Getting along with people, especially those you dislike, will help you to make progress on the job.

Working with a Boss You Dislike

Have you ever had a teacher you did not get along with, someone you could never please? Who was at fault: the teacher, you, or both of you? Did you attempt to solve the problem?

In some situations, a boss may make unreasonable demands and may put pressure on a subordinate to do more work than he or she can handle. Perhaps upper-level management is pressuring the boss, or perhaps he or she expected a promotion or pay raise and did not get it. A boss with a short temper may yell whenever something goes wrong. This behavior will cause feelings of anger, fear, and inferiority among the workers. A workaholic boss may expect subordinates to work extra hours without pay for the pure pleasure of being at work. Sometimes, though, a boss may just not understand the value of complimenting a worker for a job well done.

Every relationship has glitches, and eventually, you will probably encounter a boss you do not like or one who does not like you. In such cases, you will have to fight off feelings of despair, anger, and frustration. Quitting the job will not solve this type of problem; it will only help you take the problem somewhere else. Perhaps you will not have this problem on your first full-time job. If you do, though, turn it into an opportunity by learning how to develop relationships with difficult people. Going the extra mile is in your own best interest. These guidelines will help:

1. Accept the fact that you and the boss have personal differences.
2. Become tolerant of your differences, and make adjustments.
3. Keep any resentment to yourself.

As an employee facing these situations, you can either speak up in your defense or change your behavior. Before you do either, it is best to take a close look at yourself. Could you be the one at fault? Could you be overreacting to the situation? Be objective. If you were the boss in the same situation, how would you have handled it? Criticizing your superior to coworkers will not solve the problem, and if you decide to quit, you will need the boss for a reference.

School-to-Work Transition

Explain to your class that student-teacher relationships in the classroom are very similar to worker-supervisor relationships in the world of work. Teachers have unique personalities and classroom management styles, just as supervisors have unique personalities and management styles. Learning how to make personal adjustments and succeed in a variety of classrooms is realistic preparation for success in a variety of work situations.

Discussion Starter

Ask students to think of the three most important characteristics they would like in a boss. Discuss their responses in terms of what they can really expect from a boss.

Self-Understanding

Ask students to give examples of how they respond to authority figures.

© JIST Works

Key To Success

Before you react to criticism, take a deep breath and put the situation in perspective. Then accept or disagree with the criticism.

Self-Understanding

Discuss the questions in paragraph 2 of "Handling Criticism." Next, ask students to express what they can learn about their feelings and emotions from their reaction to these questions.

Enrichment

Have your students complete the "Being Supervised" worksheet in Chapter 11 of the *Preparing for Career Success Student Activity Book, Third Edition.*

Handling Criticism

Did you ever thank someone for criticizing you? Most people would answer no. Criticism makes people feel angry, embarrassed, anxious, and guilty. All of these feelings deflate the ego and lower self-esteem. Criticism is a form of rejection. It makes adults feel like unloved children caught with their hands in the cookie jar. Criticism from a supervisor for unsatisfactory work performance does not make your relationship with that person any easier, but it is a part of learning and making progress on a job.

How do you react to criticism? Did an adult ever scold you for crossing the street without looking both ways or for quarreling with a brother, sister, or playmate? Did you ever miss recess because your schoolwork was unsatisfactory? How did you feel in these situations? Were you angry? How did you react? Did you retaliate with similar criticism, or did you become silent and withdrawn? Did you take out your frustrations on someone else, such as a younger brother or sister? Did you say something nasty? Did you want to get even?

You have responded to criticism from people in authority since you were a child. Perhaps you have always disliked having other people tell you what to do, or perhaps you believe that everything a person in authority tells you must be right. You probably have the same attitude toward authority today as you did when you were a child.

Keep in mind that criticism can be good for you. In sports, coaches criticize. Their feedback improves the players' game and helps them develop new performance skills. Being criticized by a supervisor is somewhat like being coached. It can help you become a better employee. What if your supervisor did not tell you what you do well and what areas you need to improve? How would you know whether you were meeting your employer's standards or progressing?

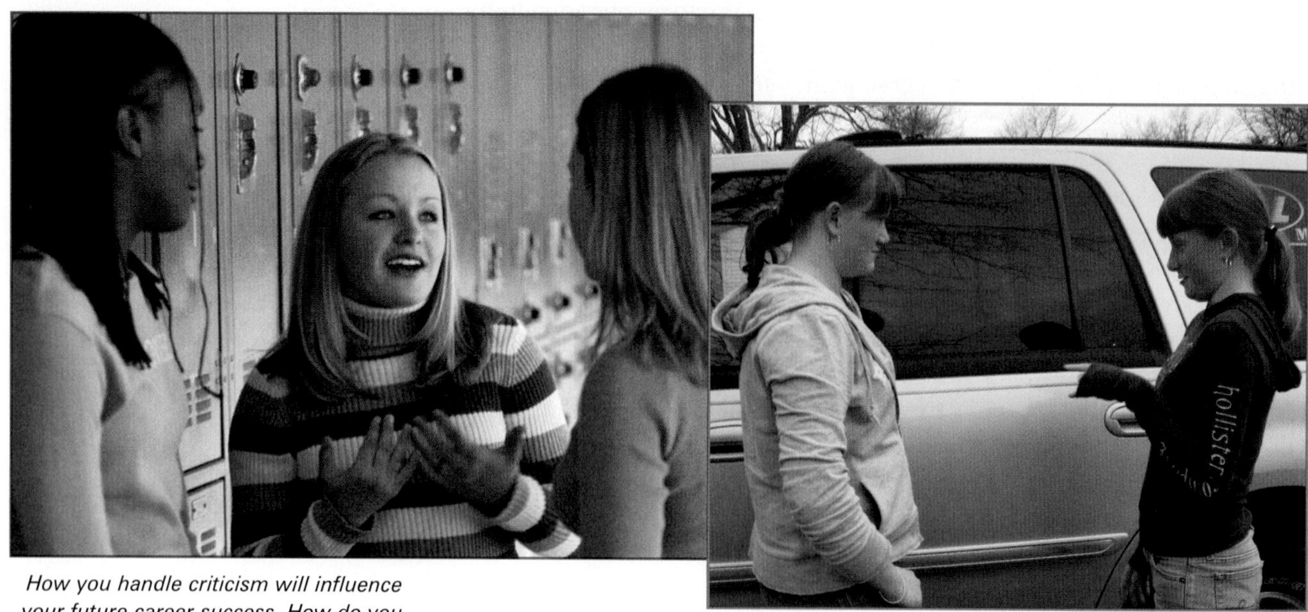

How you handle criticism will influence your future career success. How do you handle criticism from your parent(s) or guardian? Your teachers? Your friends?

© JIST Works

When you deal with criticism, examining your thoughts and feelings is important because they influence your attitude and, in turn, your behavior. When you are taking criticism, focus on the criticism itself, rather than on feelings of anxiety or hostility. When you understand your thoughts and feelings, you can learn to manage your behavior. Learn to separate "what you do" from "who you are."

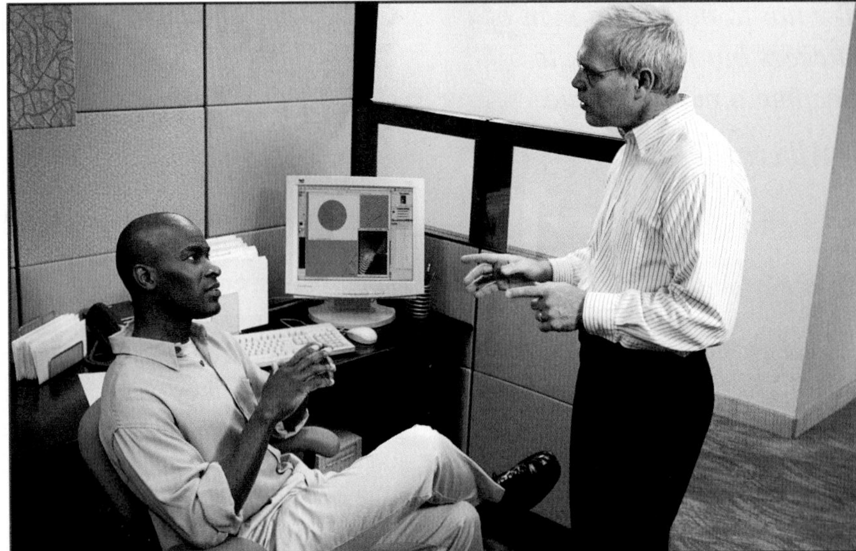

Successful workers view a supervisor's constructive criticism, offered in private, as a helpful learning experience.

Your ability to get along with your supervisor depends a lot on your attitude toward criticism and authority. Your supervisor has the right and the obligation to offer constructive criticism when your work needs improvement. As a new employee, you can expect some criticism. Learning to handle criticism will influence your working relationships and future positions within the organization. View criticism as a potential source of valuable information. Supervisors are not enemies, but individuals with their own pressures and "bosses."

A considerate supervisor offers constructive criticism in private. This approach prevents unnecessary embarrassment and negative feelings on your part. The supervisor will clarify the work being criticized and will offer solutions. You will be given time to respond. After you receive the criticism, take action to improve your performance. You can expect your supervisor to monitor your performance to be certain that you are following the suggestions offered.

Cooperative Learning

Divide your class into small groups. Ask each group to write a paragraph about a work situation involving a supervisor who must criticize a worker's performance. Have each group role-play the same situation two different ways. In one role play, the supervisor uses negative criticism, and the employee is embarrassed and angry. In the other role play, the supervisor uses constructive criticism, and the employee feels more confident about his or her work task and gains respect for the supervisor.

Section 2: Get Involved

Interview a parent, relative, or friend who has at least five years of full-time work experience. Record his or her answers to the following questions on a separate sheet of paper:

1. What are three ways you must conform to the rules of your employer?
2. What are three characteristics you like in a supervisor?
3. What are three characteristics you dislike in a supervisor?
4. Describe a time when you were glad someone in authority was supervising a situation at work.

Now imagine that you are a supervisor who has criticized an employee's performance. The employee is taking the criticism personally and acts dejected and uninterested in doing a good job. What can you do to get this worker back on the right track? Write your answer on a separate piece of paper and be prepared to discuss your answers in class.

© JIST Works

Try not to become a man of success but rather try to become a man of value.

—Albert Einstein

Cross-Reference

Point out the importance of effective communication as a job-keeping skill. Have students review Chapter 7 by reading the introduction and "Section 2: Speaking, Listening, and Responding."

Cooperative Learning/ Self-Understanding

Divide your class into small groups. Assign the following group discussion topics: 1. A person that I trust; 2. How I developed a feeling of trust with this person; 3. How I could use what I learned in this relationship to build trust with coworkers. (Write the three discussion topics on the chalkboard.) Conclude by having each group select and give a short report on one response to the third topic.

Section 3: Getting Along with Coworkers

Coworkers are people who work together and rely on each other to complete work assignments. They generally have the same or nearly the same job status, skills, and work load. Most full-time employees spend more of their waking hours with coworkers than with family and friends.

You have seen teachers cooperate with one another to fulfill a job obligation. Perhaps they were conducting a school assembly, supervising a student dance, or monitoring a large-group testing program. Would things have worked as well if these teachers had not had positive interpersonal relationships?

Positive interpersonal relationships with coworkers increase personal job satisfaction, affect the manner in which workers cooperate on assignments, and lead to increased production and sales. Poor interpersonal relationships and failure to communicate effectively cause more employees to quit or lose their jobs than any other factor. Managers regard skills related to job performance and human relations as the two most critical components of a subordinate's success or failure. On any job, it will be important for you to build positive interpersonal relationships with coworkers as well as managers.

How do you get along with teachers (management) and fellow students (coworkers)? Today's employers are looking for skilled employees who are capable of fitting into highly skilled work teams. They consider interpersonal skills as important as job skills. Cooperative work teams benefit the team and the organization. However, if one team member fails to carry out his or her designated responsibilities or contribute to team meetings, job satisfaction and team production are lowered.

Whether you are a white collar, blue collar, or no collar worker, lunchtime is a good time to build friendly relationships with coworkers.

Your employer expects you to work well in a team and to cooperate with your coworkers. To meet these expectations, build positive coworker relationships, and learn how to deal with coworkers you dislike or with whom you disagree.

Friendly relationships with coworkers will take time. When you are a new employee, most coworkers will be polite. Some may be critical, though, or may simply ignore you. They expect you to conform to their expectations. As members of your work team see you doing competent work and being reliable, they will begin to trust you as a worker. As you continue to be a trustworthy member of the team, personal acceptance will grow.

© JIST Works

Overcoming Behavior Problems

You may not like all of your coworkers' personal habits. Some annoying behaviors are

- Excessive and loud talking and laughing when you are trying to concentrate
- Constant throat clearing
- Constant humming, whistling, and singing
- Smoking in a nonsmoking area
- *Back-stabbing* (being nice to your face and criticizing you behind your back)
- Nervous picking at nose, ears, or skin irritations
- Unpleasant body or clothing odors

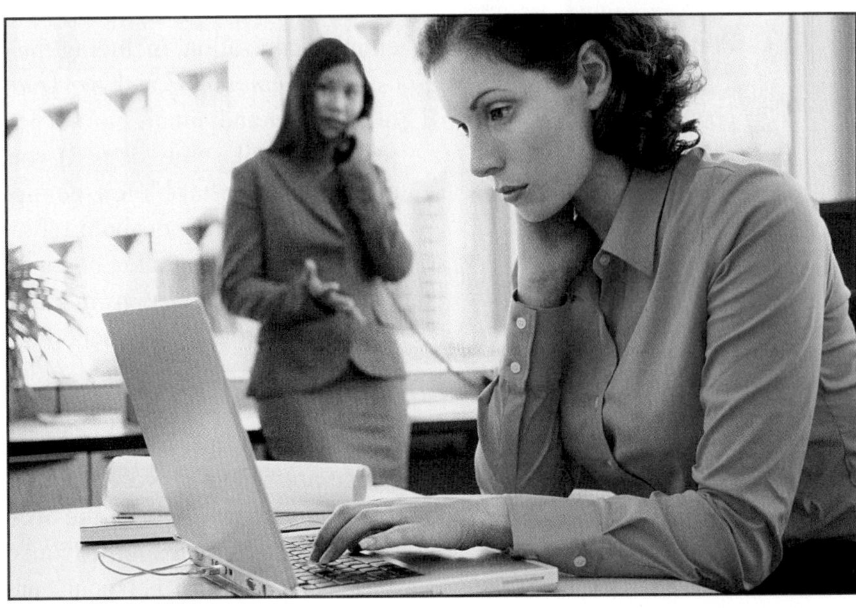

Loud talking and laughing are not appropriate when other workers are trying to concentrate. Save this behavior for scheduled breaks and lunchtime.

Remember that every coin has two sides. Coworkers will be equally offended or irritated if you demonstrate these types of behaviors. Can you think of additional behaviors that "turn you off?"

Vindictive behavior toward you or the organization is unacceptable. A typical comment from a vindictive person may express surprise that you joined such a "cheapskate" organization. Perhaps this person wanted your job or had recommended a friend. This person's open rejection lets you know that he or she does not want a relationship with you. However, time and experience may change his or her negative attitude. If not, management will eventually become involved, and this vindictive behavior will result in this person losing his or her job.

In the meantime, do not overreact. Perform your job, and be prepared to communicate whenever the other person is ready. Refuse to be intimidated. It is in your favor to build a good (not close) working relationship with this type of person. He or she will probably be more receptive to your good manners later. Have you ever had a relationship start off poorly but eventually work out? If so, what happened to turn the relationship around?

Prejudicial behavior concerning your gender, race, religion, or *ethnic* (cultural) background might arise. If the offending person (coworker or supervisor) stays within the legal boundaries of behavior and words, do not overreact. A coworker might direct a prejudicial statement outside your team, but it is still offensive and wrong. Using sexist or racist comments or behaviors can result in losing your job and/or being sued. Laws governing workplace behavior have no tolerance for low tolerance.

Jealous behavior from your coworkers may have its roots in your success. Achieving success early in your career can cause resentment among

Key To Success

Develop leadership and human relationship skills by doing volunteer work. Join a group whose cause you believe in and where you can become active in ways that require managing and motivating others.

Enrichment

Have your students complete the "Getting Along with Coworkers" worksheet in Chapter 11 of the *Preparing for Career Success Student Activity Book, Third Edition.*

Apologizing for an honest mistake demonstrates your maturity and self-confidence.

School-to-Work Transition

Ask your students: How do you deal with annoying behaviors of friends, family, and others? Then ask students: How will you deal with the annoying behaviors of coworkers on a job? Next, discuss acceptable methods for dealing with annoying behaviors.

Self-Understanding

Make this statement to your class: Think of a time when you had a misunderstanding with another person, handled your anger in a positive way, and solved the problem. Allow a minute or two of silence; then ask your students: Who would be willing to tell us about their situation and how they handled their anger?

Self-Understanding

Ask your students: Who is a member of a group in which you feel a strong sense of belonging and acceptance? Allow several students to respond to this question before the class reads and discusses "Building Relationships with Coworkers."

your former coworkers and your new peers. This is not a time to put salt on their wounds. Making progress on the job requires rebuilding and maintaining good relations with your former coworkers, new level of coworkers, and the next level of management.

You do not need to apologize for well-deserved promotions you receive because of your hard-earned accomplishments. Your success benefits the entire organization, including the occasional jealous faultfinder.

The *rumor mill* and *workplace politics* are common to all organizations, large and small. Do not let them disrupt you. *Rumors* (unapproved reports) are like stray dogs. If you do not feed them, they will probably go away. You may have a few gossips in your school. They thrive on creating and spreading rumors about fellow students and the school. Worrying over rumors and gossip that is beyond your control or might never happen anyway takes energy away from important tasks. Can you think of a rumor that circulated through your school, had students upset, and turned out to be false?

On the job, try to avoid eating lunch or having coffee breaks with the workplace gossips. Be courteous and objective in conversations with them, but do not become involved in their gossip.

Personal conflicts in the workplace are frequently caused by breakdowns in communications. If misunderstandings are not resolved quickly, they can grow into personal conflicts. Becoming angry and confronting your antagonist will not resolve the conflict. When you feel the anger building, follow these tips:

- Take a deep breath and, if possible, leave the immediate area to regain your composure.
- Try to imagine the other person's point of view.
- Consider whether your expectations are realistic.
- Be certain you understand the entire situation.

At such times, remember that no one is perfect. If you conclude that you are wrong, admit your mistake. Apologize, shake hands, and forget it. When the other person is wrong, be tolerant. Behaving with good manners and dignity is the mark of a mature person.

Building Relationships with Coworkers

Being liked by others and belonging to groups that have a common purpose (school, church, club, or profession) are basic social needs of people. You will begin to meet these needs on the job as you learn the names of your coworkers and enter into daily conversations with them.

In some instances, you may build personal relationships based on common interests outside the job as well as your experiences working together. You may share an interest in music, fishing, church, volunteer work, golf, or any of a number of leisure activities. With other coworkers, you may find that simple courtesies, such as talking about the weather or something to do

© JIST Works

with the job, will be the highest level of interpersonal relationship you can expect. Just as your relationships with family and friends are special, so, too, are your relationships with coworkers. They are in a position to provide you with encouragement, empathy, and companionship on the job.

In Chapter 10, you learned to follow accepted *protocol* (business etiquette) to earn the respect of your supervisor. You can use the same rules of etiquette to gain acceptance from coworkers. Some organizations expect a new employee to address coworkers by their formal names. In other organizations, first names are preferred. If you are not sure which is most acceptable, use formal names until asked to use first names. Showing respect for the wisdom and skill of senior coworkers will usually cause them to accept you personally and share their knowledge with you.

In your new position, you can learn to use effective interpersonal skills. Regular practice and experience using these skills will enhance your interpersonal relationships with family and friends as well as coworkers.

Remember the Golden Rule: "Do unto others as you would have others do unto you." How many words or phrases can you substitute for the word *do* to turn this principle into a golden rule for building positive interpersonal relationships? An example would be "Provide assistance to others as you would have others provide assistance to you."

To find out how effective you are at getting along with others, ask yourself the following questions:

1. Are you usually respectful of others?
2. Do you allow for individual differences?
3. Do you avoid starting or repeating rumors?
4. Do you refuse to allow others to take advantage of you?
5. Do you give credit where credit is due?
6. Do you apologize when you are wrong?
7. Are you sensitive to the problems of others?
8. Do you withhold your comments until the other person has finished speaking?
9. Can you quietly resolve personal conflicts between yourself and others?
10. Do you mind your own business?
11. Do you mean what you say and say what you mean?
12. Do you avoid making excuses?
13. Are you willing to do more than your share?
14. Do you have a sense of humor?
15. Do you respond to others as you would like them to respond to you?
16. Do you make an effort not to complain?
17. Do you refrain from judging others on looks alone?

Discussion Starter/ Self-Understanding

Ask your students: What were your responses to the questions about getting along effectively with others? The mature response to all of the questions is yes. Here are some additional points you can make about each question:

1. Respect the experience and expertise of coworkers.
2. Everyone is unique.
3. Don't eavesdrop on private conversations or talk negatively about others. Be sure of your facts before you speak.
4. Be assertive but not aggressive.
5. When coworkers praise your work, acknowledge their work and praise them in return. We all like to be recognized and appreciated.
6. Coworkers will respect you more if you apologize when you're wrong.
7. Be a good listener.
8. Listen to all of the information before responding.
9. Learn to accept other points of view and compromise.
10. Avoid asking questions involving matters not related to your assignment.
11. Follow through with your promises as quickly as you can.
12. Learn to establish priorities and make time lines.
13. All players on a winning team do more than their share.
14. Finding humor in a bad situation makes it less stressful. Coworkers always prefer laughter to complaints.
15. Show a friendly, helpful, and sincere concern for your coworkers.
16. If you have a complaint, have proof of what you are complaining about, and complain to the person who can do something about it.
17. Judge people by their contributions rather than by their looks.

© JIST Works

Comprehension Check

Ask individual students to describe an argument or discussion they were having with another person when they (or the other person) improved the situation by using one of the 17 human relations skills described in this section.

Reteaching

Have students complete the "Appraising Your Behavior" worksheet in Chapter 11 of the *Preparing for Career Success Instructor's CD-ROM, Third Edition.*

Cross-reference

See "Submissive, Aggressive, or Assertive?" in Section 1 of Chapter 1.

Being involved in leisure-time activities with coworkers will help you build personal relationships. Which of your leisure interests would you enjoy pursuing in an employee group?

You will learn numerous behaviors from your closest associates. Select them with care. In turn, you will be evaluated by your coworkers and managers in part by how they view your closest associates.

Section 3: Get Involved

Interview a relative or friend who has at least five years of full-time work experience. Write this person's responses to the following interview questions on a separate sheet of paper, and be prepared to discuss them in class.

1. Did you ever lose your temper with a coworker and later regret it? Please explain.
2. Have you become friends with any of your coworkers? If so, what caused this friendship to grow? If not, why not?
3. What advice can you give to young people to help them get along with their coworkers?
4. How would you handle a situation in which a coworker made a costly mistake and blamed you?

Section 4: Earning Promotions

Key To Success

Business protocol dictates that you contribute to customary coffee funds, gifts for coworkers, and flower funds. Your contribution shows others that you are part of the team and helps build positive relationships.

Most Americans believe in the **work ethic**. This is the idea that America is the land of opportunity and that through hard work individuals can make their own success. For most people, this success means **career advancement** (moving up in an organization) through promotions to higher-level jobs. The increased income and prestige connected with career advancement can provide a great deal of personal satisfaction.

© JIST Works

Career advances may be horizontal or vertical. In most organizations, career advancement is a **line of progression** (steps that employees follow from lower- to higher-level positions). Horizontal changes may offer a pay increase or more personal challenge, but these jobs are on the same level.

Vertical changes result in higher pay and more authority. These promotions are to a higher level. In terms of a management track, this is the chain of command. For example, if you are hired as a grocery bagger in a supermarket, you might gain experience through a series of horizontal changes. They might include stock clerk, meat counter clerk, and cashier. After gaining a broad range of experience in the business, obtaining additional education and training, and demonstrating your ability and dependability, you might receive a vertical promotion to manager trainee.

As you become familiar with a particular job and master the required skills, you can begin to look at ways to grow and achieve your next-highest career goal. Opportunities for promotion occur when

- A vacant position exists due to a promotion.
- Someone leaves the organization.
- The employer creates a new position.

Some organizations use a bulletin board to post job openings, whereas others invite potential candidates to apply. Supervisor recommendations are the basis for some promotions. By staying alert and networking with other employees, you frequently can discover promotional opportunities.

In general, promotions occur within an organization. This encourages employees to strive for high levels of performance and commitment to the job. Whether organizations promote from within or outside, they usually review all qualified candidates, not just those who are next in line for the position.

In organizations with a promotion-from-within policy, a student with a high school diploma in business/office education may begin at the entry level as an office clerk and eventually reach a supervisory or even management-level position. This person could improve his or her knowledge and skills by taking evening courses at a technical school or college, participating in relevant company-sponsored training programs, and perhaps by obtaining a two-year associate degree or even a four-year college degree. Most promotions require a combination of continuing education and training, outstanding performance appraisals, and personal motivation.

Preparing Yourself for Promotions

The best predictor of future performance is past performance. Suppose that your employer considers you for a promotion or more challenging career opportunity. The quality of work and attitude that you have displayed at your present job will be the main factors used to evaluate you for the new position.

Education and Training

Send a writer to the chalkboard, and instruct him or her to write these headings side by side: "Job Title" and "Education and Training." Ask your class to begin making a line of progression by naming an entry-level job title for a high school graduate. Ask the writer to record each job title and the required education and training. Continue asking the class for the next level of career advancement and the required education and training. You may wish to make more than one career line of progression.

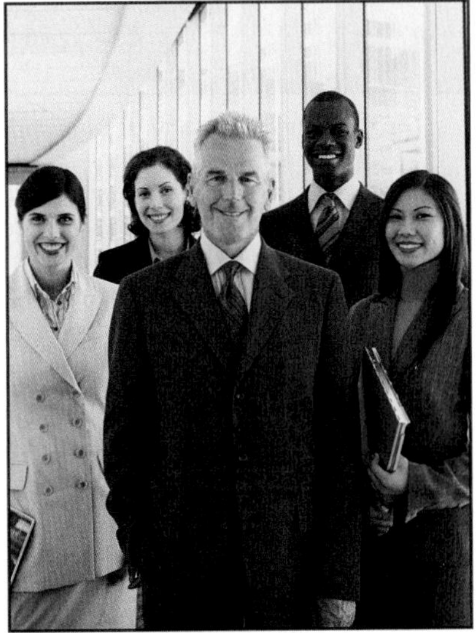

Examine the photo. Where do you think the line of progression begins? Ends?

Cooperative Learning/ Education and Training

Have your students answer the following on a separate sheet of paper:

1. Write the title of a job you expect to have eight years from now.
2. Describe the education and training you will need to qualify for this job.
3. Write the job title of your first major promotion.
4. Describe the additional education and training you will need to qualify for this promotion.

Next, divide the class into learning pairs. Have each learning pair exchange their responses to the four statements.

© JIST Works

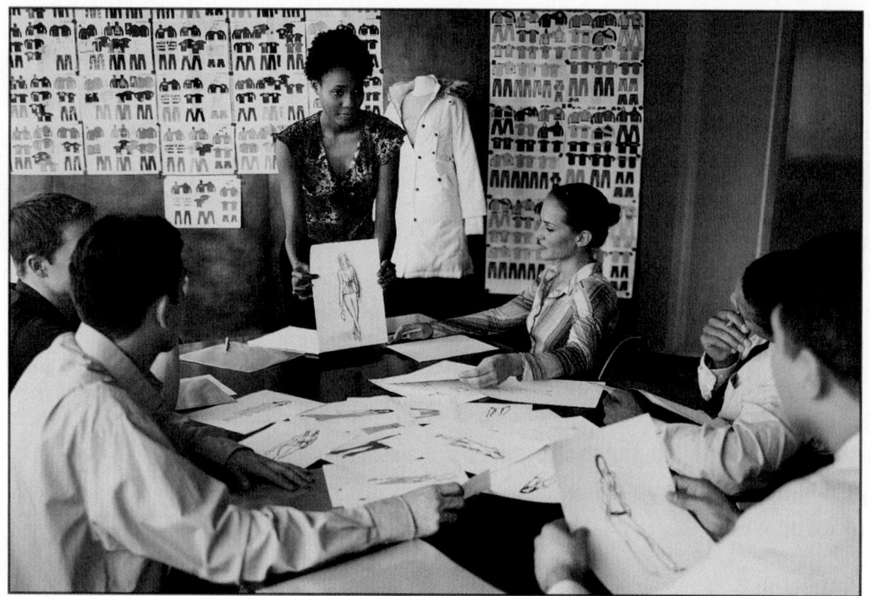

The quantity and quality of Saleema's work and her working relations with coworkers and management are excellent. She is attending night school to qualify for a promotion.

In determining your readiness to compete for promotions, consider the values that large corporations frequently express. The following list of corporate values appears in order, with 1 being most important:

1. Ability to take the initiative
2. Pride in performance
3. Self-confidence
4. Open-mindedness
5. Flexibility
6. Satisfaction in creating something new
7. Cooperation
8. Honesty
9. Coolness under stress
10. Pleasure in learning something new
11. Sense of humor
12. Loyalty to others
13. Openness and spontaneity
14. Independence
15. Friendliness
16. Attitude toward authority
17. Compassion
18. Generosity
19. Idealism

School-to-Work Transition

Ask your students: Who can share a personal experience when you were evaluated in some type of school competition? Allow several students to share their experience. Ask each student how he or she felt about winning or losing. Next, explain to your students that getting career promotions is a similar form of competition. They will compete with coworkers and be evaluated, accepted, or rejected, and personal feelings will be involved.

Which of these values are most like you? Which are least like you? Can you identify a time when you expressed these values?

A **mentor** (a trusted adviser) can help you prepare for promotions and move up the chain of command. Develop a mentor relationship with your superior or another manager with whom you get along well. A mentor is like a special teacher because he or she functions as a role model. The mentor relationship is usually personal enough so that you can request feedback, ask questions, air misgivings, and get honest advice about how best to use your employment situation for personal career advancement.

Career Fact

No one will ever care or be more responsible for your career than you.

When the opportunity for a promotion occurs, you can expect competition. First consideration is usually given to coworkers who have **seniority** (length of time spent with a company) and who have demonstrated their loyalty. However, these qualities alone do not merit promotions. Competition will also include the evaluation of job skills, education and

© JIST Works

training, quality of work produced, personal initiative, interpersonal skills, positive attitude, proven reliability, and leadership potential.

If you apply, you will be evaluated in each of these areas in relation to the position requirements and the level of your competition. You will have to decide whether you have the expertise to compete with more-experienced employees. You will also have to decide whether you are ready for more responsibility and different duties. Consider each of the following areas if you want to apply for a promotion.

CAREER FACT

Total Quality Management is a highly adaptive management tool that has shaped the way many organizations operate today. It is a support structure for continuous improvement and renewal. Governments, health-care organizations, and educational institutions have adopted the fundamentals of quality management. Making significant contributions to the quality of your employer's products or services will help you to make progress on your job.

Job Skills

Be prepared with the necessary education and training. Attend company-sponsored seminars; participate in on-the-job training programs; or take classes at a community college, a vocational school, or a four-year college or university. Decide which job skills you need to improve, and work on improving them. Join a professional or trade association.

Performance

Prepare for the job of your immediate boss. Observe your boss's leadership qualities and the methods he or she uses to inspire confidence, obtain cooperation, and make effective decisions.

The quantity and quality of your work performance are important considerations. High-quality work is critical, but completing the work on time is also important, especially on an assembly line or a construction site. Frequently review your job performance. Compare the quality of your work to that of your coworkers. Is it better, worse, or about the same?

Be visible to people in management positions. Make sure that they know your name, are aware of your interest in career advancement, and hear about your successes on the job. They will decide who is promoted.

In some jobs, levels of productivity are not easily measured. What could you do that would be considered exceptional as an office clerk or as an automotive technician?

Human Relations Skills

Build good working relationships with your coworkers and management. Reread the section in this chapter titled "Getting Along with Coworkers."

KEY TO SUCCESS

Knowing how to handle criticism in a positive manner will help you grow in your career and in your personal life.

Conformity to the Corporate Culture

Make fitting in with the organization and all levels of employees a top personal priority. Learn all there is to know about the organization. Make a pact with yourself to be committed to doing your very best for the company. Then carry out orders cheerfully, be honest and loyal, and put the needs of the organization ahead of personal plans. Also, demonstrate initiative by volunteering for new responsibilities and doing more than is expected.

© JIST Works

Cluster Link

Planning, managing, and performing the processing of materials into products is at the heart of the Manufacturing career cluster. If you are interested in operating a machine, managing the plant, or performing the necessary engineering services, you could find a career in this cluster. See the appendix for more information.

Career Fact

Drug-free workplaces have become a major concern to both labor and management in the collective bargaining relationship. Many contracts spell out a joint responsibility of union and management in assuring a drug-free work environment. The following are some examples of clauses asserting cooperation in agreements involving a drug-free workplace. Labor and management

- Recognize alcohol and drug abuse as a sickness and a treatable condition
- Commit to a joint policy to discourage the abuse of drugs and alcohol and to provide a treatment program (normally an employee assistance program)
- Agree to a drug-testing program where appropriate
- Commit to provide a safe workplace and promote employee health and well-being

Building Character: A Feeling of Pride

"Paul, you have earned this promotion to supervisor," Mrs. Watson said. "Mr. Clark recommended you highly, and I have been very pleased with the progress you've made during your four years at MCS Manufacturing Systems." Mrs. Watson was the vice president of manufacturing. Paul felt 10 feet tall when she walked him to the door of her office and shook his hand again.

Paul Fermin was filled with excitement as he approached the door of the department manager, Donald Clark. He was eager to tell Don about his promotion to supervisor and to thank him for being such a great boss. Four years ago, when Paul started work as a machine operator, Mr. Clark was production supervisor. Now that was Paul's job.

Mr. Clark's promotion to department manager created the supervisor vacancy. Several employees were well qualified for the job, but only Paul had Mr. Clark's recommendation. That tipped the scales in his favor.

Although Mr. Clark was only six years older than Paul, he seemed like a combination of father and big brother on the job. Mr. Clark was one of the people who interviewed Paul for his first job with MCS. From the very beginning, Paul asked him for advice on shop problems and on what he could do to get ahead in his career. Paul always followed through on Mr. Clark's advice, and taking these steps helped him develop the skills he needed to become a senior machine operator. Paul and his wife had invited Mr. and Mrs. Clark to their house for dinner a few times, and Mr. Clark had invited them to his home. Paul and Mr. Clark went fishing together a couple of times every summer. In the privacy of Mr. Clark's office, they called each other "Don" and "Paul." In front of the other employees, though, it was always "Mr. Clark" and "Paul."

Paul planned to continue his career advancement. He knew that Mr. Clark would continue to be his mentor and friend. He also knew that if he received good performance evaluations as a supervisor and continued to learn from Mr. Clark, someday Mr. Paul Fermin would be the department manager.

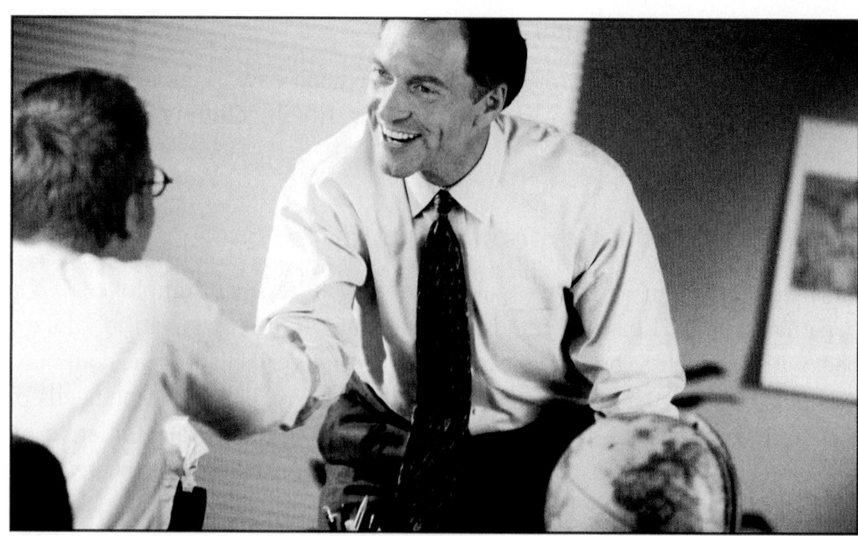

© JIST Works

Critical Thinking

To get a job promotion, what do you think is more important: what you know, who you know, or a combination of both? Explain your answer.

Why do you think Mr. Clark became a mentor to Paul rather than to some other employee?

Would Mr. Clark have been promoted if he had failed to train Paul for the position of supervisor? Explain your answer.

Adjusting to a Promotion

When you are promoted, you will need to make adjustments. If you become the team leader or supervisor of your former coworkers, personal relationships will change. Before the promotion, you could overlook a coworker who takes extra long breaks. In the role of supervisor or team leader, however, you must deal with this problem as a violation of company rules. If you are a *junior* (less-experienced) employee, senior employees may resent you.

To complete certain jobs effectively in your new position, you might need to spend time beyond your required working hours. You will be evaluated and criticized by the employees who work for you, by those who are at your level, and by your boss. Will you be ready to accept these disadvantages?

Laura was promoted to team leader six months ago. She works about an hour beyond quitting time each evening. Her working over usually eliminates the need to take work home.

Discussion Starter

Ask your students: When is it fair for employers to expect employees to place the organization's business needs ahead of personal plans? When is it not fair?

Managing Your Time

Time is irreversible. You can use time wisely, but you cannot save it. Have you ever heard the expression "just killing time"? For a business, killing time can mean the difference between profit and loss, growth and layoffs. In today's high-tech world, the job of managing e-mail is one big task confronting workers trying to organize their time.

Time management is planning to make the best use of your time. Achieving this goal requires knowing what needs done, setting priorities, planning the work, and completing projects in the time allotted. Your employer expects you to use your time wisely.

Observe how coworkers and supervisors manage their time, schedule priorities, and handle interruptions. Use what you learn to identify how your time is wasted and how it could be managed. Learning good time management will result in greater satisfaction and accomplishment both at work and in your personal life.

KEY TO SUCCESS

Your objective should not be merely to move faster. You must also move smarter.

© JIST Works

Section 4: Get Involved

Managing time is important in both your personal life and your work life. Start now to manage time to your best advantage:

1. Analyze your use of time over a one-day period by listing your activities in 15-minute intervals from the time you get up in the morning until you go to bed at night. (Do not include your sleeping time.)
2. Review your log after a period of one day. Cross out the activities that you now consider unnecessary.
3. Rank the 10 most important activities you did during the day, with 1 being most important. Which activities would you like to spend more time doing? Which activities could take the place of those you crossed out as unnecessary?
4. List the specific ways you could use time better in your daily schedule.
5. Plan your schedule for tomorrow. Be sure that your plan includes priorities and allows for schedule changes. Commit yourself to your new priorities. Then check your new plan again at the end of the day. How did you do?

Section 5: Understanding Labor Unions

At the close of the Civil War in 1865, factories were producing products that had been handmade by skilled craftsmen for hundreds of years. The craftsmen were unable to compete with the factories and forced to seek employment as factory workers. Children worked full-time jobs for very low wages. A working day of 10 hours or more and weekly wages of 10 dollars or less were common. Working conditions in factories, sweat shops, and mines were frequently unhealthy and dangerous. American workers struggled against these conditions.

During these years of struggle, numerous **labor unions** (organizations that represent workers in negotiations regarding employee rights) formed to represent various segments of the American labor force. Among the goals of these unions were

- Elimination of child labor
- Elimination of laws used to break up unions
- Acceptance of the principle of collective bargaining
- Establishment of state and federal bureaus of labor
- Passing of workman's compensation laws
- An eight-hour workday

American workers achieved a national unity during the early decades of the twentieth century when a flood of legislation from the federal government established the right of workers to negotiate with their employers for a fair wage and a safe work environment. America's labor relations and collective bargaining practices matured during labor's struggle for recognition in the Great Depression of the 1930s. They flourished in the heyday of high productivity and market supremacy that characterized the nation's dominant position in the world's economy after World War II.

Enrichment

Have students complete the "Labor Unions Library" worksheet in Chapter 11 of the *Preparing for Career Success Instructor's CD-ROM, Third Edition.*

Find Out More

For additional information concerning the legal rights of workers, key in **National Labor Relations Board** on your Internet search engine.

Career Fact

The mission of most unions is to improve the standard of living of workers, to represent their members' varied work interests in dealings with employers, and to promote equity and social justice for all workers in society.

© JIST Works

Membership in labor unions peaked in 1975. In that year, labor unions represented 35 percent of all American workers. By 2007, the situation had changed, and only 12.1 percent of wage and salary workers belonged to labor unions.

Figure 11.3 depicts union members as a percentage of all employed wage and salary workers in various groups. Why do you think such a small percentage of agricultural workers belong to unions? Why are such large numbers of teachers, police officers, and firefighters union members?

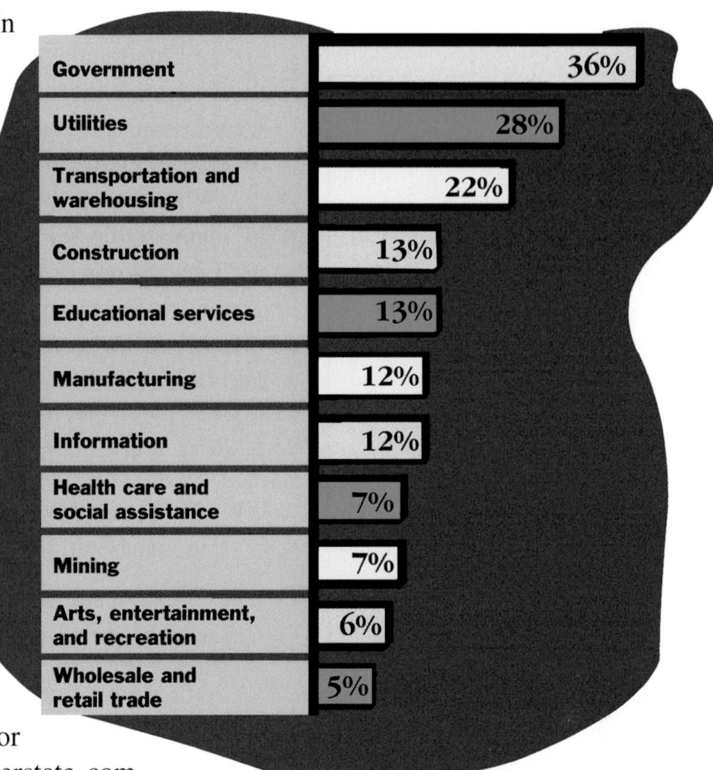

Figure 11.3 Percentage of union members in various types of employment, 2007.

The National Labor Relations Board

The **National Labor Relations Board (NLRB)** is an independent federal agency established in 1935 to administer the National Labor Relations Act (NLRA), the nation's principal labor relations law. This act generally applies to all interstate commerce except railroads and airlines. The Railway Labor Act covers these two industries.

The purpose of the NLRA is to serve the public interest by reducing interruptions in commerce caused by industrial conflict. It does this by providing orderly processes for protecting and implementing the rights of employees, employers, and unions in their relations with one another. The purpose of the National Labor Relations Board is to administer, interpret, and enforce this act.

Each year the U.S. courts of appeals make decisions related to the enforcement and/or review of NLRB orders in unfair labor practice proceedings. Most favor the NLRB in whole or in part.

Collective Bargaining

With the exception of minimum legal standards, employers in nonunion organizations set the level of wages and the hours of labor and establish production quotas for workers. When promotions or pay raises are involved, employers can reward favorites and ignore qualified workers with longer service. If work is slow, employers in nonunion organizations can lay off whomever they choose.

Collective bargaining is the negotiating process used between labor unions and employers. This negotiating process generally results in a written contract between the employer and the labor union. Collective bargaining was developed to introduce the ways of democracy into employer-employee relations.

Community Resources

Form a volunteer committee to contact the National Labor Relations Board (allow extra credit). Assign the committee to research information related to the "Understanding Labor Unions" section they are studying, including the legal rights of workers. Allow time for them to report their findings to the class.

Case Study

Have students read the case study "Voting Is Important" in Chapter 11 of the *Preparing for Career Success Instructor's CD-ROM, Third Edition.* Discuss the "Critical Thinking" questions.

Discussion Starter

Ask your students: If you were a rank-and-file worker, would you prefer working for an organization that allows collective bargaining? Why or why not? How would you feel about this issue if you were the owner of a large business?

Career Fact

Following are the matters over which employees file the most contract grievances:

- Denied sick benefits
- Discipline
- Discrimination
- Evaluation
- Excused and compensatory time
- Grievance process
- Pay
- Performance
- Safety
- Scheduling
- Suspension
- Termination
- Training
- Transfer
- Union representation
- Vacation
- Work out of classification

Which grievance categories do you consider most important? Which categories do you consider least important? Why?

Community Resources

Form a volunteer committee to contact the American Arbitration Association (allow extra credit). Assign the committee to acquire information concerning the arbitration process and the education and training necessary to become an arbitrator.

Find Out More

For information about arbitration and mediation, visit the Web site of the American Arbitration Association at www.adr.org or call toll-free at 800-778-7879.

In an organization that allows collective bargaining, individual workers are no longer subject to arbitrary decisions. They share with the employer the responsibility for establishing orderly procedures for determining wages, hours of work, rates of production, promotion and layoff policies, and fair penalties for the violation of necessary work rules.

When collective bargaining fails, the union may call for a vote, asking its membership for authority to strike. A **strike** is a temporary stoppage of work by a group of workers (not necessarily members of a union) to express a grievance or enforce a demand. A union-authorized strike occurs when all members stop working and leave their jobs. This causes a loss in production or a curtailment of services to the employer. You may have seen striking workers carrying picket signs that say the union is on strike. The two kinds of labor-management disputes are

- Those resulting from differences of opinion over how contract provisions should be interpreted
- Those resulting from differences over what provisions should be included in a new contract agreement

When the labor union and the employer reach an agreement, both the employer and labor union representatives sign a labor contract. These contracts usually last for one to three years.

Grievances

When **grievances** (differences of opinion over how contract provisions should be interpreted) occur, the grievance process is used to settle the labor-management dispute. Grievance procedures vary, but they always involve a method by which the individual workers can process a complaint through the union. The final appeal, in most contracts, consists of the company and the union submitting the issue to an impartial *arbitrator* (person chosen to settle a dispute). After hearing the evidence from both sides, the arbitrator issues a decision that is binding and legally enforceable for both sides.

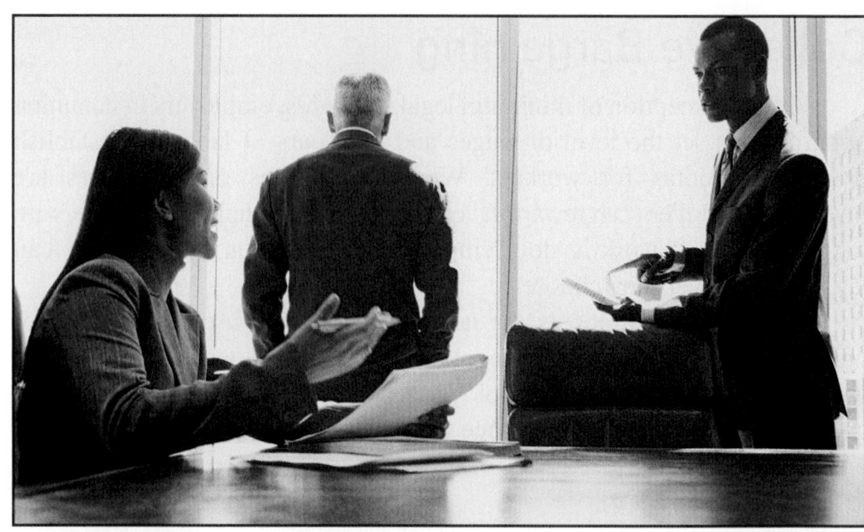

Sometimes a dispute between two parties must be settled by an independent arbitrator.

© JIST Works

Cooperation for the Future

Since the early 1970s, the country's industrial base, its workforce, and the strength of foreign competition have changed dramatically. The rapid advance of technology has changed many of our traditional manufacturing processes. International competition has challenged U.S. supremacy in world markets, and a better-educated, demographically changing workforce has compelled employers and unions to improve the quality of life both at work and at home.

To meet these social and economic challenges, workers and their unions, management, and government have begun to forge more cooperative and productive relationships through numerous organizations. Unions are working with management to improve the economic performance of American enterprises and to help firms adapt to changes in technology, market conditions, and worker values and expectations. Where management has been receptive and where workers' interests are reflected, unions have increasingly shown a willingness to work with management for the overall success of the enterprise.

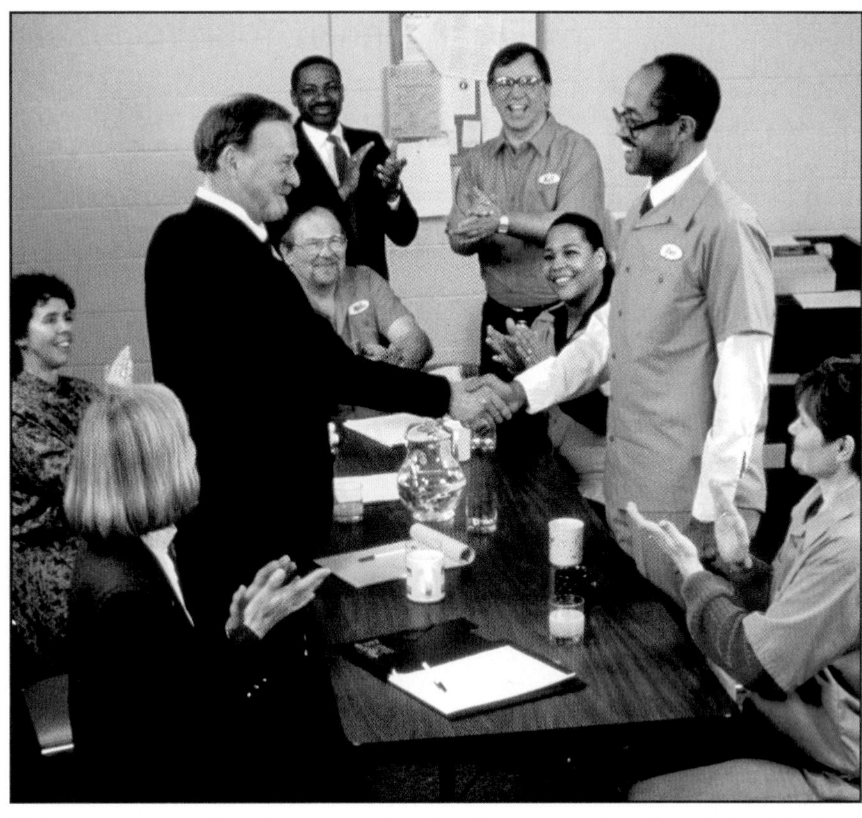

Unions, management, and government are forming more cooperative relationships to meet the challenges presented by foreign competition for products, services, and jobs.

Section 5: Get Involved

Answer the following on a separate sheet of paper, and be prepared to discuss your responses in class.

1. Check the yellow pages of your telephone book under the heading "Labor Organizations." How many unions are listed? Which are craft unions? Industrial unions? Service unions? Contact one of these unions, and invite a union representative to speak to your class. Find out why some industries are heavily unionized and others are not. Find out why membership in some unions has declined, whereas in others it has risen.
2. Discuss union membership with a friend or relative who has been working full-time for at least three years. List the ways this person feels unions help workers, and list the reasons he or she dislikes unions.
3. Expect to pay an initiation fee when you join a union. You will also have to pay regular dues as a condition of membership. What are the initiation fee and monthly dues for membership in the unions in your area?

Case Study

Have your students read the case study "Working Together" in Chapter 11 of the *Preparing for Career Success Student Activity Book, Third Edition* and answer the questions.

© JIST Works

Chapter 11 Review

Enrich Your Vocabulary

Enrich Your Vocabulary Answers

1. entry level
2. corporate culture
3. work ethic
4. subordinate
5. line of progression
6. team adviser
7. quality circle
8. coworkers
9. collective bargaining
10. superior
11. National Labor Relations Board (NLRB)
12. grievances
13. seniority
14. career advancement
15. time management
16. strike
17. labor unions
18. staff
19. mentor

On a separate sheet of paper, number from 1 to 19, and complete the following activity. (Do not write in your textbook.) Write the term from the "Enrich Your Vocabulary" list at the beginning of the chapter next to the number of the statement you think best matches it.

1. The lowest amount of experience for the job
2. The guidelines that an organization's management establishes for behavior and job performance
3. Belief that through hard work individuals make their own success
4. An employee who follows someone else's orders
5. Steps that employees follow from lower to higher positions
6. A supervisor in a team-oriented management system
7. A group of workers who identify and solve quality problems
8. People who work together as equals
9. The negotiating process between labor unions and employers
10. A person in an organization who gives orders to others
11. An independent federal agency that administers labor relations law
12. Differences of opinion over how contract provisions should be interpreted
13. Length of time spent with an organization
14. Moving up in an organization
15. Planning ahead to make the best use of the hours you have
16. A temporary stoppage of work by a group of workers (not necessarily members of a union) to express a grievance or enforce a demand
17. Organizations that represent workers in negotiations
18. A group of employees
19. A trusted adviser

© JIST Works

Check Your Knowledge

On a separate sheet of paper, complete the following activities. (Do not write in your textbook.)

1. Why are businesses or organizations created?
2. In a corporation, who directs the activities of other employees?
3. What are the three management levels most often found in organizations?
4. Which management system most encourages worker interdependence and group problem solving?
5. What is the purpose of constructive criticism?
6. What is the most frequent reason people quit or lose their jobs?
7. What do managers consider to be the two most critical components of a subordinate's success?
8. Would a job change from cashier to supervisor be a vertical or horizontal change?
9. If you expect to be promoted to a more important and better-paying job, what must you demonstrate to your employer?
10. What are the three most important characteristics that corporations consider when they promote employees?
11. Why were labor unions created?

Develop SCANS Competencies

Government experts say that successful workers can productively use resources, interpersonal skills, information, systems, and technology. This activity will give you practice in developing information and systems skills.

Talk with a friend or family member about the organizational structure of his or her place of employment. Using the information this person gives you, develop an organizational chart of that business. As an alternative, develop an organizational chart of your school.

Check Your Knowledge Answers

1. To exchange goods, services, or money for mutual benefit
2. A supervisor or team leader
3. Top management, middle management, and supervisory or first-line management
4. Team-oriented management
5. Improvement
6. Poor interpersonal skills
7. Skills related to job performance and human relations
8. Vertical
9. That you have mastered your present assignment and that you fit into the organization
10. Initiative, performance, and self-confidence
11. To represent employees with regard to employee grievances, wages, hours, and conditions of work

Reteaching

Use the "Finding the Right Words" and the "Checking Your Location" worksheets in Chapter 11 of the *Preparing for Career Success Student Activity Book, Third Edition* to help students review the content of this chapter.

Enrichment

Have students complete the Chapter 11 section of the *Preparing for Career Success Student Portfolio, Third Edition.*

© JIST Works

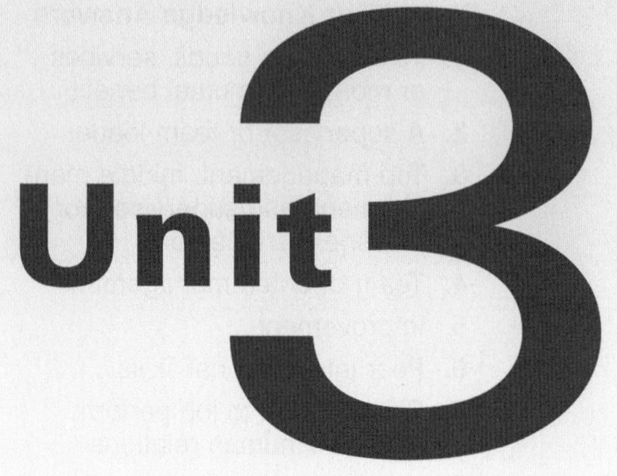

Understanding the World of Work

Chapter 12: Defining Roles, Rights, and Responsibilities

Chapter 13: Managing Career Change and Growth

Chapter 14: Adapting to a Changing Workplace

Chapter 15: Connecting Economics and Work

Chapter 16: Starting a Business

Chapter 12 Resources

Lesson Plans and Preparation

Multimedia

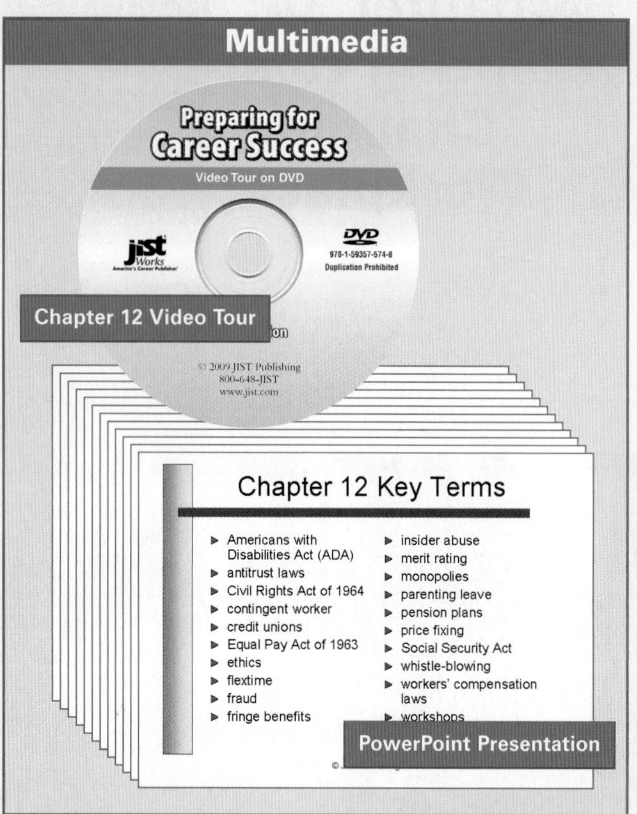

Activities

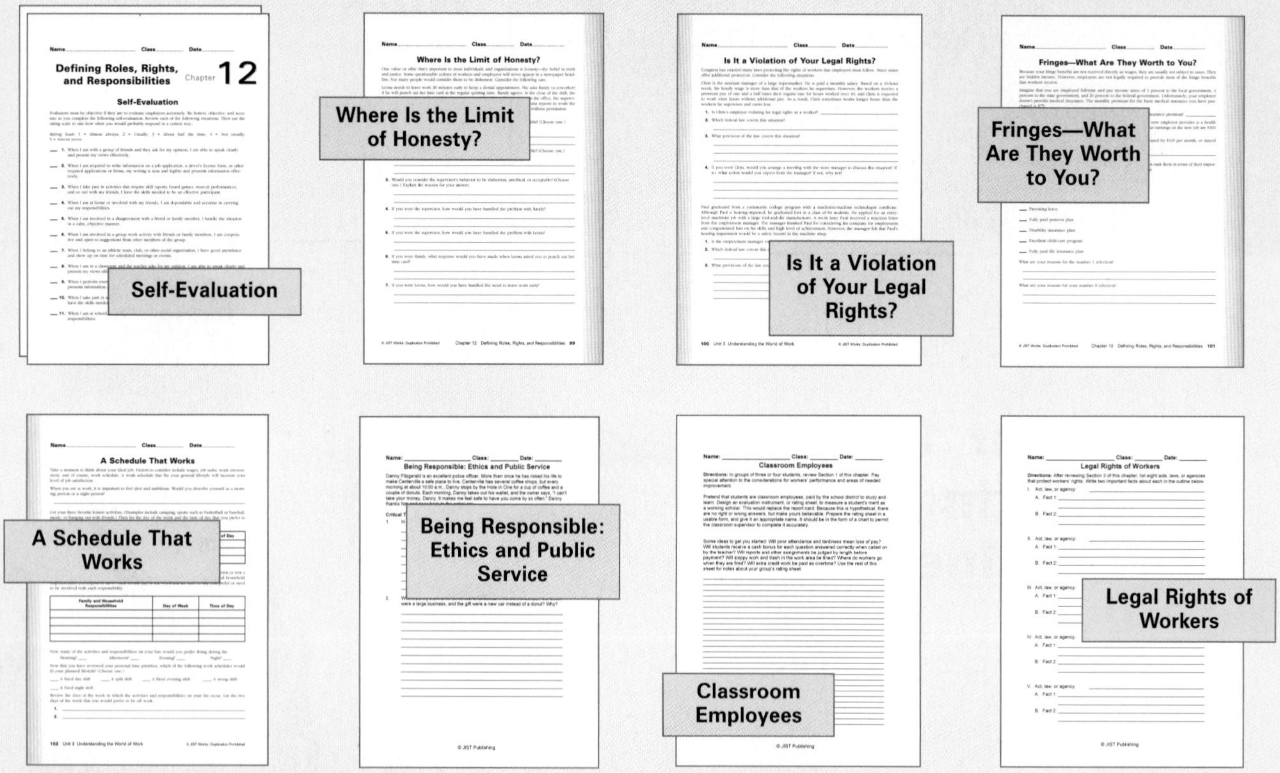

Self-Evaluation

Where Is the Limit of Honesty?

Is It a Violation of Your Legal Rights?

Fringes—What Are They Worth to You?

A Schedule That Works

Being Responsible: Ethics and Public Service

Classroom Employees

Legal Rights of Workers

© JIST Works

Review and Assessment

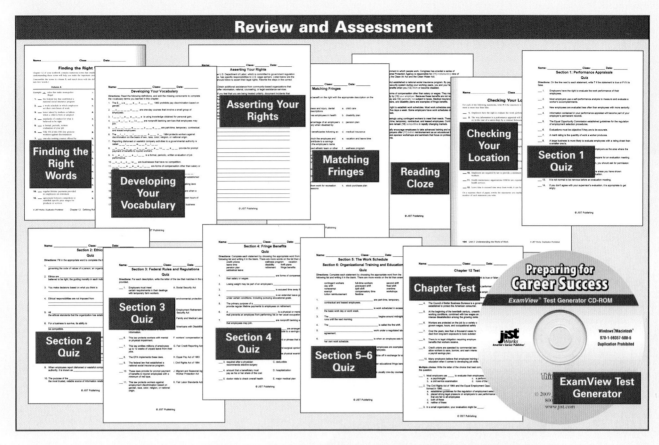

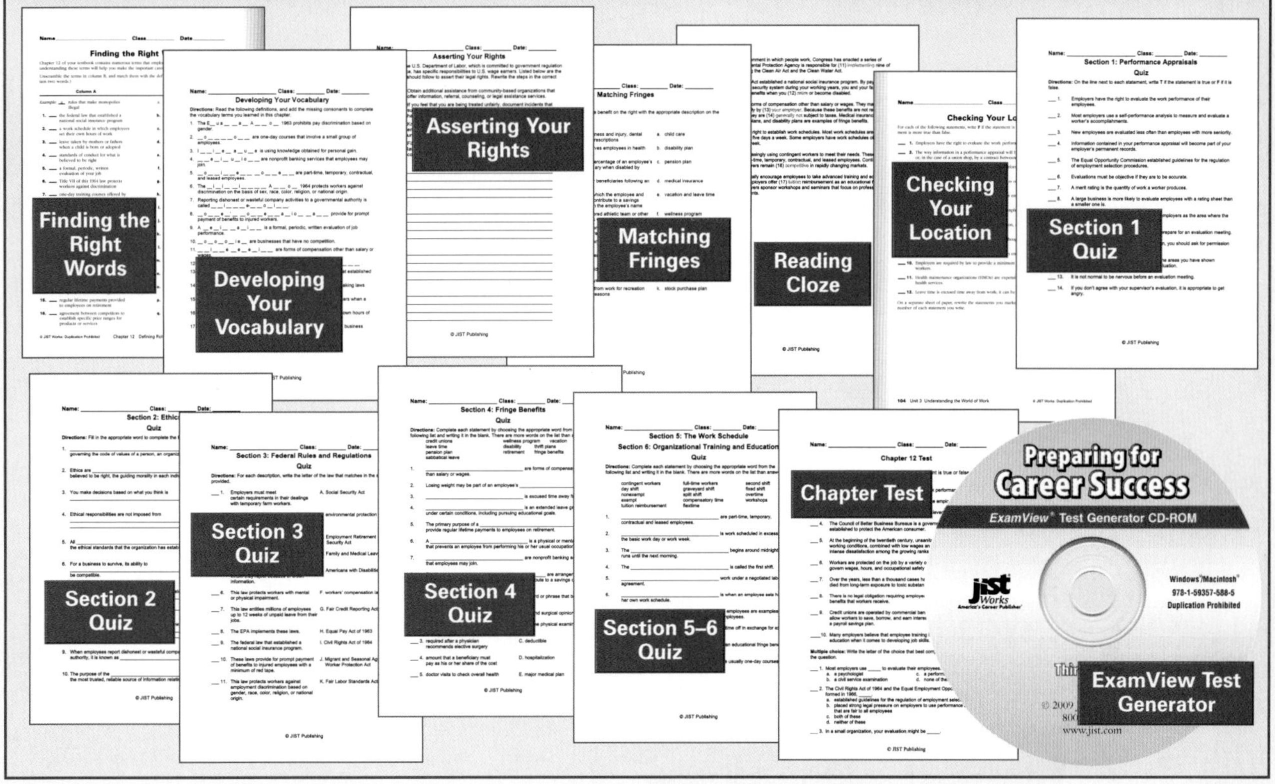

Finding the Right Words

Developing Your Vocabulary

Asserting Your Rights

Matching Fringes

Reading Cloze

Checking Your Location

Section 1 Quiz

Section 2 Quiz

Section 3 Quiz

Section 4 Quiz

Section 5–6 Quiz

Chapter Test

ExamView Test Generator

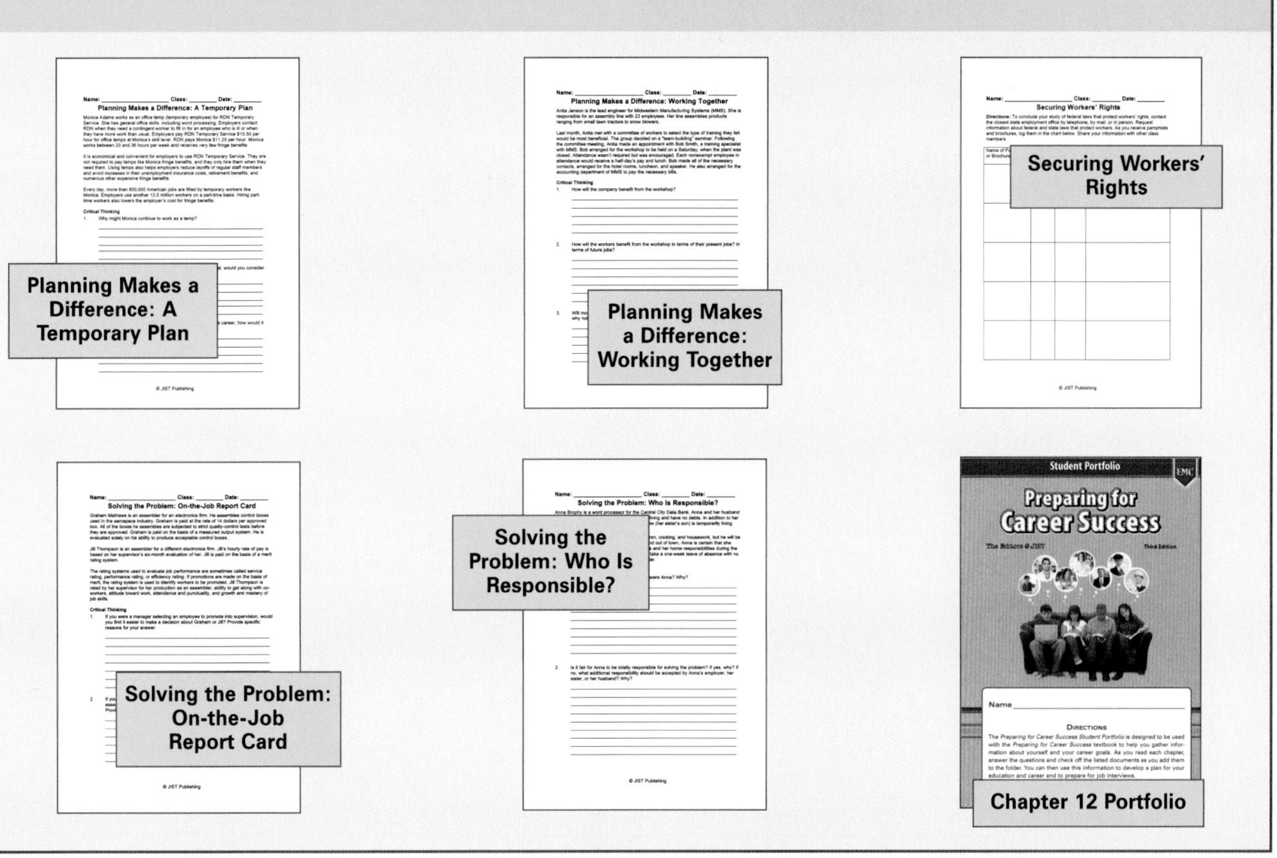

Planning Makes a Difference: A Temporary Plan

Planning Makes a Difference: Working Together

Securing Workers' Rights

Solving the Problem: On-the-Job Report Card

Solving the Problem: Who Is Responsible?

Chapter 12 Portfolio

Chapter 12 Defining Roles, Rights, and Responsibilities

Learning Objectives

- Explain the purpose and process of job performance appraisals
- List examples to demonstrate the financial, legal, and moral importance of business ethics
- Discuss your legal employment rights and the federal rules and regulations that protect them
- Understand common fringe benefits offered by employers
- Describe various work schedule options and explain the reasons for having them

What role will you play in the world of work? Who will evaluate your performance? Will you make fair and honest decisions during your career? Will others treat you with honesty and fairness?

Unfortunately, the major interest of some people is to acquire personal gain at the expense of their fellow workers and society. Their idea of the Golden Rule is "The person with the most gold rules." This unfortunate fact of human nature has caused state and federal governments to *legislate* (make laws) to protect your rights as a worker. State and federal laws set standards for such issues as fringe benefits, *compensation* (payment for loss or injury), and work schedules.

Enrich Your Vocabulary

In reading this chapter and doing the exercises, you will learn the following important terms:

Americans with Disabilities Act (ADA)
antitrust laws
Civil Rights Act of 1964
contingent worker
credit unions
Equal Pay Act of 1963
ethics
flextime
fraud
fringe benefits
insider abuse
merit rating
monopolies
parenting leave
pension plans
price fixing
Social Security Act
whistle-blowing
workers' compensation laws
workshops

Vocabulary

You can use the "Developing Your Vocabulary" worksheet in Chapter 12 of the *Preparing for Career Success Instructor's CD-ROM, Third Edition* as a pretest for chapter concepts or as a reteaching worksheet.

Do you plan to be a leader in the world of work? What philosophy will you use to make important management decisions? How will you manage a large organization? Would society be better off to stop relying on politicians and return to the management methods used by employers in "the good old days"?

You have probably listened to adults discussing these issues at home. Perhaps you have raised them yourself. As you read and discuss the information in this chapter, consider all of the different points of view.

School-to-Work Transition

Explain the relationship between school evaluations and employer evaluations (Teacher = Supervisor; School = Employer; Report Card = Performance Appraisal; Employer's Production Goals = Teacher's Learning Goals; School's Permanent Record = Employer's Permanent Record).

Section 1: Performance Appraisals

Employers have the right to evaluate the work performance of their employees. Most employers use performance appraisals to measure and evaluate a worker's accomplishments over a specific time. The appraisal is based on the job description and the employer's goals. During your career, you can expect your immediate supervisor to conduct an annual performance appraisal. As a new employee, you can expect the supervisor to evaluate you more often. Information contained in your performance appraisal will become part of your employer's permanent records.

We judge ourselves by what we feel capable of doing, while others judge us by what we have already done.

—Henry Wadsworth Longfellow

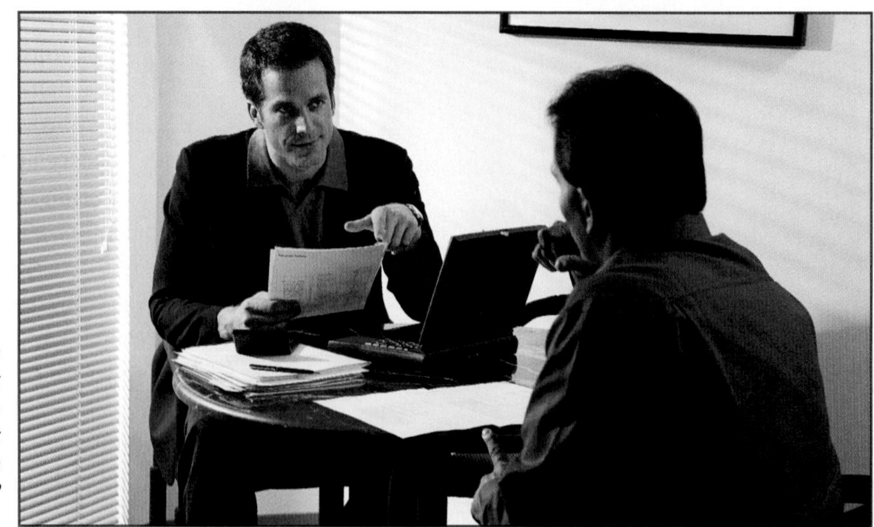

Measurement and evaluation of performance are a part of an employee's permanent record just as evaluation of academic performance is part of a student's permanent record. How high would an employer rate your student performance?

© JIST Works

Performance appraisals are not new. As far back as the third century A.D., Chinese emperors employed an "imperial rater" to evaluate the performance of official family members. In the early 1800s, Robert Wen, owner of cotton mills in Scotland, established the first performance appraisals in industry by hanging a cube of colored wood over each employee's workstation. The color of the wood represented each worker's performance level. In the United States, General Lewis Cass of the U.S. Army used performance appraisals as early as 1813. He submitted to the War Department an evaluation of each man under his command. General Cass described his men in such colorful terms as "a good-natured man" or "a knave despised by all."

The Civil Rights Act of 1964 and the Equal Employment Opportunity Commission (EEOC), formed in 1966, established guidelines for the regulation of employment selection procedures. The act and the EEOC placed strong legal pressure on employers to use performance appraisal systems that are fair to all employees.

KEY TO SUCCESS

Good job performance appraisals are important. If you leave your current job for any reason, potential employers will usually check with your past employers to find out about the quality of your work.

Video Tour on DVD

Show students the Chapter 12 segment to introduce them to the content.

Enrichment

Have students fill out the "Self-Evaluation" worksheet in Chapter 12 of the *Preparing for Career Success Student Activity Book, Third Edition.*

Purpose of Evaluation

Using one method or another, your employer will measure the degree of your career success. In a large organization, your supervisor might use a standard evaluation form and established procedures to evaluate your work performance. In a small organization, your evaluation might be your manager's personal observations and informal discussions with you. In both cases, evaluation judgments will influence decisions regarding your

- Promotion to a better job
- Salary increase
- Possible *discharge* (firing)
- Transfer to a different job or department
- Admission into a training program

The amount of your annual pay usually depends on your measured *output* (the quantity of work you produce) or on your **merit rating** (a formal, periodic written evaluation of your job performance). How the employer uses the information in your performance appraisal will be determined by the employer or, in the case of a union shop, by a contract between workers and the employer.

Evaluators must be *objective* (not allow personal feelings to interfere) if they are to evaluate employees accurately. If you are rated against others, as in the case of measured output, your rating must be in numerical terms.

Graham Matthews's employer is very concerned that assemblers put together high-quality control boxes. The sale of defective products could result in the loss of important contracts with the aerospace industry or could be the cause of a major accident. Graham's employer uses the rating sheet shown in Figure 12.1 to determine each assembler's accuracy. The rating is based on the amount of work that passes inspection the first time and does not require rebuilding.

TAKE NOTE

The Electronic Communications Privacy Act of 1986 permits an employer to listen to business-related phone calls, but the employer is to hang up the instant the conversation turns personal. By the time the employer realizes the conversation is personal, however, you may have said things you would have preferred to keep private.

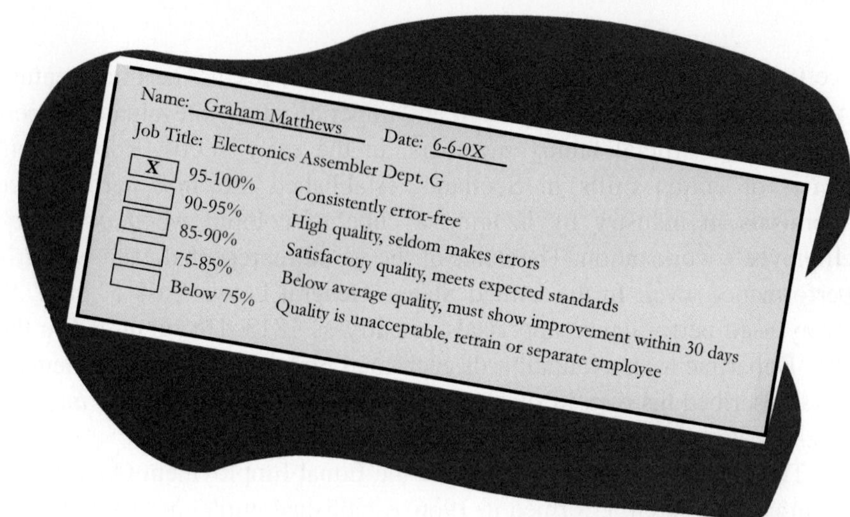
Name: Graham Matthews Date: 6-6-0X
Job Title: Electronics Assembler Dept. G

X	95-100%	Consistently error-free
	90-95%	High quality, seldom makes errors
	85-90%	Satisfactory quality, meets expected standards
	75-85%	Below average quality, must show improvement within 30 days
	Below 75%	Quality is unacceptable, retrain or separate employee

Figure 12.1 A sample ratings sheet.

Enrichment

Explain to your students that defective products can create consumer problems and accidents, which in turn can cause lawsuits resulting in enormous financial losses to the employer. Assign your students to search recent magazines and newspapers for information about lawsuits involving defective products.

Case Study

Have students read the "On-the-Job Report Card" case study in Chapter 12 of the *Preparing for Career Success Instructor's CD-ROM, Third Edition* and discuss the "Critical Thinking" questions.

Career Fact

According to the American Management Association, more than half of U.S. companies engage in some form of e-mail monitoring of employees and enforce e-mail policies with discipline or other methods. Although 75 percent have written policies concerning e-mail, less than half train their employees on them. More than 20 percent have terminated an employee for e-mail infractions.

Rating sheets are not appropriate for all employers, however. For example, the owner-operator of a small business would not necessarily need a rating sheet to evaluate an employee's performance. In this case, it would probably be more efficient for the employer to use personal, daily contact to evaluate such factors as the worker's attendance and punctuality, attitude, and productivity.

One survey asked employers about needed improvements in a variety of areas that prepare people for entry into full-time work. Employers based their responses on entry-level jobs for which workers acquire their education and training in a high school or labor program. Much of what employers said applies to any entry-level job. Employers selected the following improvement areas in order of importance, with 1 needing the most improvement:

1. Concern for productivity
2. Pride of artisanship and quality work
3. Responsibility and ability to follow through on assigned tasks
4. Dependability
5. Work habits
6. Attitude toward the employer
7. Ability to write and speak effectively
8. Ability to follow instructions
9. Ability to read and apply printed information to the job
10. Ambition, motivation, and desire to get ahead

Cooperative Learning

Have students complete the "Classroom Employees" worksheet in Chapter 12 of the *Preparing for Career Success Instructor's CD-ROM, Third Edition.*

The Evaluation Meeting

After you complete the first few months of a new job or at the completion of your probation period, your supervisor will probably schedule a meeting to discuss your work record to date. Advance scheduling will allow

© JIST Works

you time to prepare. The purpose of the meeting will be to discuss your strengths and weaknesses.

Every job has certain critical performance areas. For example, an office clerk should expect his filing and word-processing skills to be evaluated. An auto-body mechanic should expect the quality of her sanding skills and finish work to be evaluated. Ask your supervisor what aspects of your job performance he or she will appraise and how he or she will collect and use the information. Make a list of what you want to learn from the evaluation meeting that will benefit you on the job. For example, you may wish to know specific ways to improve your performance.

You may be nervous about the evaluation meeting. This feeling is normal and to be expected. At the beginning of the meeting, your supervisor will probably explain the appraisal process. This information will prevent future misunderstandings. Then your supervisor will fill out a written form that lists the job criteria. Next, the two of you will discuss your evaluation. The supervisor will probably ask you to rate your own performance. Be prepared to emphasize your successes, personal strengths, and skills. (Review the sample performance appraisal form in Figure 12.2.)

Listen carefully to suggestions your supervisor makes about ways you can improve your performance. Be frank and open in this discussion. If your supervisor recommends that you improve your work, do not let hurt feelings cause you to display resentment. Becoming angry or arguing with your supervisor about the conclusion he or she has reached about your performance is definitely not appropriate. If your appraisal contains factual errors such as stating that you have been absent from work seven days, and you are certain it has been less, make the correction tactfully.

Remember that your supervisor's role is to evaluate your performance. You are responsible for performing at minimum standards or above.

If your supervisor focuses on your weaknesses, try to profit from the criticism and become a better worker by improving in those areas

Cooperative Learning

Divide your class into small groups. Ask each group to write a performance appraisal on a separate sheet of paper, using Figure 12.2 as an example. Assign half of the groups to write a very positive appraisal and the other half to write a very critical appraisal. Have each group use their performance appraisal to role-play an evaluation meeting between the supervisor and the worker.

RMJ

RMJ Industrial Products Inc.
Employee Evaluation

Employee's name: Margaret Reynolds Position held: Machine Operator
Years under my supervision: 2 Total years of RMJ service: 2

The evaluator uses Column 1. The employee uses Column 2 for self-appraisal, using this key: O = outstanding, VG = very good, S = satisfactory, N = needs improvement, U = unsatisfactory

		1	2
1. Work performance	Demonstrates work skills needed for present assignments	O	VG
2. Communication	Communicates clearly with others using effective oral and written skills	VG	VG
3. Initiative	Sees what needs to be done and is judicious in doing it with or without direction	O	VG
4. Employee relations	Has a cooperative and open-minded attitude in working with others	O	S
5. Reliability	Is consistent, dependable, and accurate in carrying responsibilities to a successful conclusion	O	VG
6. Personality	Has a pleasant, cheerful disposition, shows enthusiam, and has an appealing manner with coworkers	VG	S
7. Personal appearance	Grooming is neat and dress is appropriate	VG	VG
8. Stamina	Posture and bearing show evidence of energy and vitality in carrying out daily responsibilities	O	VG
9. Stability	Handles situations in a calm, objective manner	VG	S
10. Career growth	Seeks higher level skills through additional education and training	O	VG
11. Attendance pattern and punctuality	Has a good attendance record and meets responsibilities promptly	VG	S

Comments and recommendations by evaluator:
Margaret Reynolds started her employment with RMJ Industrial Products upon her graduation from high school. She has attended Tri-State Community College as a part-time student and has completed two years of study in accounting. She would like a permanent position in the Accounting Department. I would recommend her highly for the first available position.

Comments by employee:
I am presently attending school two evenings per week. It will take me two more years to complete my associates degree in accounting. My present assignment has enabled me to pay for my education.

I am aware of this evaluation.

Employee Signature: Margaret Reynolds Evaluator Signature: Joseph Michaels

Date: June 6, 20XX Evaluator's title: Production Supervisor

Figure 12.2 Sample performance appraisal form.

mentioned. If your supervisor points out your weaknesses but does not make any recommendations to help you improve, ask for suggestions.

If you disagree with your evaluation, ask your supervisor for permission to respond to the points of disagreement. Be prepared to back up your position with supportive information. Be calm, open, and prepared to resolve differences in a mature way.

Regardless of whether you feel the supervisor has evaluated you fairly, close the meeting on a positive note. When the boss indicates that the meeting is finished, stand up, extend your hand, offer a firm handshake, and express your appreciation for offering suggestions to improve and taking this time to collaborate on establishing new goals.

Self-Understanding

Ask your students: Who can remember a time when you were called to a teacher's desk for an evaluation and the teacher recommended ways to improve your work? Who felt the teacher's criticism was unfair? Next, ask individual students: Did you become resentful or angry? How did your reaction influence your relationship with the teacher? The quality of your schoolwork? Your enjoyment of the class?

Your supervisor may schedule a follow-up meeting to discuss how you are improving your weak points. Be prepared to show specific examples that demonstrate your improvement. For example, suppose a trainee in restaurant management receives a U (unsatisfactory) for her communication skills. Under Comments on the appraisal form, the supervisor suggests that she should avoid using slang when speaking with customers. In the follow-up meeting, the supervisor will want to discuss her improvement or lack of improvement communicating with customers.

Plan immediately to improve the areas in which you have shown weakness. Make it your business to show improvement before the next evaluation meeting. By taking this step, you will demonstrate your commitment and responsibility to doing a good job.

Section 1: Get Involved

Answer the following on a separate sheet of paper, and be prepared to discuss your responses in class.

1. Review the list of 10 areas in which entry-level workers could improve. List the 4 areas that you consider most closely related to the employee's attitude. Next, list 4 areas that you consider most closely related to the employee's self-esteem. Did you list any areas of concern twice? Explain the reason for your selections.
2. Review the annual evaluation of Margaret Reynolds in Figure 12.2. If you were the director of personnel, would you transfer Margaret to the accounting department, or would the company be better off keeping her in her present job? What evidence in the evaluation supports your conclusion?

Section 2: Ethics

Do unto others as you would have them do unto you.

—The Golden Rule

A ship loaded with grain entered the harbor of a Middle Eastern nation that was suffering from a depressed economy. The grain harvest in this nation had been poor, the people needed food, and merchants were willing to pay far more than the grain was normally worth. The businessman who owned the ship was aware that other ships would soon bring additional grain to the suffering city. Their arrival would cause the value of his grain to return to normal. Should the businessman tell the local merchants that additional grain would be available soon, or should he act quickly and sell his grain to the highest bidder? Why?

This event happened more than a thousand years ago when a Greek trading ship entered the port of Rhodes. The philosopher Cicero presented

© JIST Works

the question you have answered to businessmen of ancient Rome. Cicero's answer—that the duty of any businessman is to make an honest and full disclosure—set ethical standards for business that are as appropriate for entrepreneurs today as they were for the Roman businessmen of Cicero's day.

The word **ethics** refers to the unwritten rules governing the code of values of a person, an organization, or a society. Ethics are the standards of conduct for what is believed to be right, the guiding *morality* (good) in each individual, organization, and society. Each day, you make decisions based on what you believe to be right. Your decisions are ethical or unethical, moral or immoral. Organizations do the same.

What are the responsibilities of the company importing these goods to the community? How might unethical behavior affect homeland security?

Understanding Business Ethics

Organizations establish ethical codes, or standards of conduct, that reflect the interests of the group they represent. For example, the ethical code of a police department might be the protection of the people it serves. The ethical code of a major discount store might be customer satisfaction, whereas the ethical code of an automobile manufacturer might be public safety.

Unlike legal responsibilities, ethical responsibilities are not imposed from outside the organization, but from within. All employees are to practice the ethical standards the organization has established.

Discussion Starter

Ask your students: Should you conduct business in an ethical manner at all times? If so, why? If not, why not?

Ethical dilemmas are not always choices between right and wrong. Sometimes they are choices between right and right. In some situations, both alternatives seem to be the best solution—for different reasons. Still, one must be selected and one rejected.

For example, automobile manufacturers have sometimes been accused of concealing safety hazards. They have been required to recall millions of vehicles at great expense. Ethically, automobile manufacturers believe and state that safety is their first priority. However, safety costs increase manufacturing costs. If one manufacturer offers new safety features, and a major competitor offers the same features for a lower price, the first manufacturer must reduce prices to stay competitive. This could result in the use of less-expensive materials and manufacturing processes at the risk of reduced safety and quality.

Unethical business practices put billions of dollars at risk. Yet for a business to survive, its ability to earn a profit and its code of ethics must be compatible.

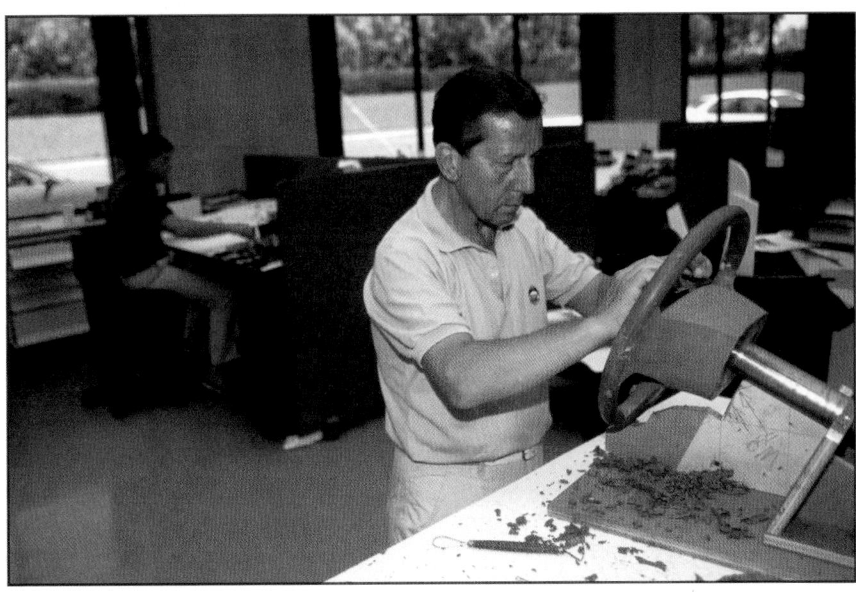

What ethical considerations should designers use when creating new products?

Comprehension Check

Send two writers to the chalkboard. Ask one writer to make a heading titled "Unethical" and the other writer to make a heading titled "Illegal." Ask the class to provide the writers with examples of unethical and illegal practices for a business. Next, ask the class to provide the writers with examples of unethical and illegal customer practices.

Discussion Starter

Explain that *reverse engineering* or *benchmarking* is the widespread process of studying the products of other manufacturers and copying the best features into your products. In many cases, large companies are able to use this method to legally improve their products. Ask your students: Is this process stealing or a legitimate way to improve products? Is it ethical?

Case Study

Have students read the case study "Ethics and Public Service" in Chapter 12 of the *Preparing for Career Success Instructor's CD-ROM, Third Edition* and discuss the "Critical Thinking" questions.

Discussion Starter

Read the following situation to your students: Imagine that you are responsible for buying new carpeting for your employer's office building. The carpeting is expected to cost about $15,000. Your manager has told you to contact three carpet firms, review the quality and price for similar carpets, and use your best judgment in the purchasing decision. You receive a phone call from the salesperson of the second company you contact. He invites you and your spouse to have dinner and go to an event with very expensive tickets on Saturday evening. He explains that he realizes you are a very busy person, and this event would provide a good opportunity to discuss the carpet deal. What is your reply? Explain the reason for your reply.

Unethical Business Practices

To help you understand what unethical business behavior is, the following sections describe two unethical business practices.

Trade Secret Theft

Information is one of an organization's most valuable resources. As we entered the twenty-first century, electronic terrorists, cyberspace spies, and computer hackers were costing American businesses an estimated $10 billion a year. That dollar amount continues to rise. Sophisticated hackers enter an organization's data system and with a few clicks of their mouse obtain valuable trade secrets.

Sometimes online thieves are employees of the organization. They have access to the organization's internal computer network. These thieves could be angry about their career progress, treatment from a supervisor or coworkers, or they could be unethical *profiteers* (pirates) who set out to commit a crime.

Trade secrets include any information or invention that gives a business a competitive advantage—from a list of customers to a formula or manufacturing process. Employers have legal rights to protect this type of information and prosecute people who steal it. Under the Economic Espionage Act of 1996, trade secret theft is a federal crime and punishable by a $500,000 fine and a jail term of up to 15 years.

Kickbacks

Cash fees, percentage commissions, gifts, and services are forms of kickbacks when the giver expects the receiver's company representative will buy from the giver. In this case, the company's representative accepts the gift first, knowing that he or she will buy from the salesperson later. Examples of kickbacks are tickets to the Super Bowl, a weekend of golf at a resort, or dinner and a theater production.

In another example, a construction firm's employee could overlook the use of less expensive materials or substandard work from a subcontractor, even though the practice violates safety standards. In return, the subcontractor would pay a significant kickback.

Consumer Protection

Unethical business practices can lead to unsafe products, high prices, and job loss. What protection do consumers have against this behavior? The three main defenses are employees, watchdog organizations, and the government.

Whistle-blowers

When employees report dishonest or wasteful company activities to a governmental authority, this behavior is known as **whistle-blowing**. This is

© JIST Works

one way to handle unethical business practices. Many states have whistle-blower laws that provide job protection for employees who report work-place hazards or wrongdoing. In 1989, President George Bush signed the Whistleblower Protection Act, which grants additional job protection to federal employees who report their superiors' wrongdoings. In 2002, the public learned of the financial deception of utility company Enron and telecommunications company WorldCom in large part through the action of a woman in each organization who did the right thing by going over her boss's head. At WorldCom, the bookkeeping entries constituted what appears to be the largest accounting **fraud** (something said or done to deceive; trickery; cheating) and **insider abuse** (using knowledge obtained as a result of your position for personal gain) in U.S. history. The company's bookkeeping was concealing a $3.9 billion problem.

Considering all employees in an organization to be unethical because of the unethical behaviors of a few would be unfair. Most employees consider themselves ethical and conduct themselves accordingly.

Career Fact

Many organizations are making a commitment to a set of core values and are holding their employees accountable to them. A 2002 survey of the American Management Association's member corporations revealed that 76 percent identified ethics and integrity as their primary corporate values and 50 percent posted their corporate values on their Web sites.

Community Resources

Form a committee of students to obtain additional information about ethical business practices from the Better Business Bureau (BBB). Designate a time for the committee members to report their findings to the class. If the local telephone book does not list a BBB, have the students use the Internet.

Better Business Bureau (BBB)

Can you imagine a world that permitted business owners to deceive you, cheat you out of money, and sell you faulty merchandise with no fear of a penalty? As far back as the early 1900s, American businesses began policing themselves by forming watchdog groups. In 1906, Samuel Dobbs, a sales manager and later the president of Coca-Cola Company, made the public aware of dishonest practices and called for truth in advertising. His efforts resulted in the formation of vigilance committees throughout the United States. In 1916, these committees were renamed Better Business Bureaus.

Today, the Council of Better Business Bureaus is a private, nonprofit, self-regulatory organization dedicated to promoting fairness and honesty in the marketplace. The purpose of the BBBs is to be the most trusted, reliable source of information relating to ethical business and advertising practices and to be a major provider of services to resolve marketplace disputes. The BBB protects consumers through voluntary self-regulation and monitoring of business activities. The BBB is supported by its membership of private businesses and individual member bureaus. It is not a government agency supported by tax dollars. If you need help with a consumer question or complaint, phone your local Better Business Bureau.

Should using steroids to develop strength be considered illegal, unethical, or acceptable? Why do you think so?

Building Character: Unethical, Criminal, or Acceptable?

Alvin Gates attends evening classes at Tri-State Community College and works full-time in the accounting department of RMJ Industrial Products. Alvin frequently takes home about 25 sheets of paper or a couple of ballpoint pens. He uses his employer's paper and pens to do his school-work. Alvin believes that RMJ underpays him. He also considers his job performance to be better than most of the other workers.

TAKE NOTE

Whistle-blowing takes courage; whistle-blowers often face negative consequences as a result of their actions. C. Fred Alford, author of *Whistleblowers: Broken Lives and Organizational Power,* notes "Half of all whistle-blowers get fired. Half of those fired will lose their homes, and most of those will lose their families, too." "The forms of organizational harassment are limited only by the imagination," says Tom Devine, head of the Government Accountability Project, a whistle-blower advocacy group (*Fortune Magazine*).

Critical Thinking

In your opinion, is Alvin's behavior unethical, criminal, or acceptable? Explain the logic for your answer.

Imagine that you are a department manager. Consider the following list of behaviors:

- **Using the company phone to make long-distance calls**
- **Leaving work two hours early without permission**
- **Making lengthy personal phone calls during working hours**
- **Taking a laptop computer home without permission**

How would you handle each of these situations if you discovered that a worker in your department was involved? Would you discharge the employee? Would you punish him or her? If so, how?

Case Study

Have students read the "Where Is the Limit of Honesty?" case study in Chapter 12 of the *Preparing for Career Success Student Activity Book, Third Edition* and answer the questions.

Government Regulation

Two ethical qualities our society demands from employers are honesty and *equality* (fair treatment). When organizations fail to define and practice ethics, the result may be regulation through laws.

During the late nineteenth century and early years of the twentieth century, many businesses were **monopolies** (businesses with no competition). This practice is opposed to the democratic principle of free enterprise. When a business eliminates its competitors, buyers are left without choices.

Imagine having to pay $5.00 for a gallon of gasoline because one company owns the entire gasoline-refining industry and controls the price. As a consumer, you would have two choices: pay the price or do not drive. Would you pay the price? To prevent businesses from establishing monopolies, Congress passed the Sherman Act in 1890 and the Clayton Act in 1914. Today, if a company attempts to monopolize a particular market, it is breaking these **antitrust laws**.

© JIST Works

Another illegal business practice is **price fixing** (agreements between competitors to establish specific price ranges for their products or services). If the three largest manufacturers of gasoline in your area agreed to fix the price for a gallon of gasoline between $4.90 and $5.10, the choice for a consumer would be almost the same as a monopoly charging $5.00 per gallon.

President George W. Bush signed the Sarbanes-Oxley Act into law on July 30, 2002. Its objective is to make financial information released by public companies as accurate as possible by making small adjustments to the checks and balances already in place. Chief executive and chief financial officers must certify financial statements, and the act holds them criminally liable for inaccuracies. Violators receive penalties of up to 20 years in prison for altering, destroying, or inaccurately stating records.

In 1991, Congress increased the severity of penalties for white-collar crimes and assured that the penalties would be applied with consistency. As a result of government pressure and individual and class-action lawsuits

- Individual corporate decision makers face harsh financial penalties and possible criminal charges for white-collar crime.
- Large corporations face severe penalties in terms of losing defense contracts or paying large government fines for certain unethical practices.
- Large corporations face legal settlements that can amount to millions and in some cases billions of dollars.

Keep in mind that only a few leaders in the world of work are guilty of the white-collar crimes that have prompted government regulation. Personal characteristics that help to elevate the majority of executives to the highest positions in their organization include a strong personal code of ethics, integrity, and honesty. In your career, take care of your personal and professional reputation; they are as valuable as your education, skills, and work record.

Vocabulary Builder/Comprehension Check

Send a writer to the chalkboard, and ask your students to close their books. Ask individual students to use one of the following vocabulary terms in a sentence: *monopolies, antitrust laws,* and *price fixing.* Ask the writer to write each sentence on the chalkboard. Have the entire class correct the usage of the term and any grammatical errors. Have the writer make corrections at the board. Develop at least one correct sentence for each of the three terms.

What would happen to the price of soda if one company owned the entire soft-drink industry?

Building Character by Making Ethical Decisions

Did you ever stretch the truth a little bit or perform less than your share of the work on a project? One ethic that most workers and employees agree with is honesty—the belief in truth and justice. At one time or another, you have probably heard someone say, "Do an honest day's work for an honest day's pay," or "You have my word on it." These expressions mean different things to different people. What do they mean to you?

Career success requires education, training, and job skills, but alone they cannot guarantee job satisfaction or happiness in your personal life. Achieving these goals requires that you develop a positive character.

You will encounter ethical decisions of varying importance during your career and in your everyday life. The best way to prepare for crucial ethical decisions is to practice the small ones each day. This practice will help you

Career Fact

Most employers conduct background checks before hiring new workers. Ethics, honesty, and integrity are requirements for positions of trust.

Self-Understanding

Present the following situation to your students: In line at the clothing store, the cashier gives you a $20 bill in your change when the correct change is $10. How would you handle the situation if you noticed the error immediately? What if you noticed the error after you arrived home?

Cross-Reference

You may wish to have your students review "Section 1: Values," in Chapter 3.

Career Fact

As reported in *USA Weekend*, the top three forms of wrongdoing among regular folks are as follows:

1. **Workplace theft**: Financial scams are a $600 billion problem, according to the Association of Certified Fraud Examiners.
2. **Tax evasion**: Internal Revenue Service (IRS) estimates that this is a $200 billion problem.
3. **Academic dishonesty**: 75 percent of high school students admitted cheating in 2007.

to draw the line between right and wrong. Practicing the following six guidelines will help you make honorable choices:

1. Have a thorough understanding of the situation. Does your decision make sense? Is it legal? Could the result of your decision jeopardize your job? Is the outcome worth the risk?
2. List all of the events that created the situation.
3. Ask yourself whether you would openly accept the result of your decision and disclose your course of action to your best friends, family members, and business colleagues. If your answer is yes, your decision is likely to be an ethical one.
4. Discuss your decision with trusted colleagues, and ask for their opinions about the ethics involved and whether your decision will bring about a successful outcome. Do they openly support your decision and consider it ethical? Are the responses of your colleagues divided?
5. Whether or not you decide to implement the plan, ask yourself if your final decision reflects your best character and makes you feel proud. If not, does your decision have the potential for inflicting self-doubt and shame?
6. Determine how you will benefit from your decision. Whom will your decision benefit or harm? Are your motives based on truth, respect for others, and integrity?

Use the small, everyday events in your life to build your character. Later, you will have no difficulty making major ethical decisions. Most of the ethical problems you will encounter on your job will focus on small dilemmas. When you face difficult circumstances that require you to do the right thing, your true character will be revealed. Will you be ready?

Section 2: Get Involved

Answer the following on a separate sheet of paper, and be prepared to discuss your responses in class.

1. If you see a coworker stealing something, should you confront him or her directly, ignore it, or report the situation to management? Explain your answer.
2. Is a whistle-blower disloyal to the employer? What is the reason for your answer?
3. Give an example of an ethical and unethical business or professional practice for each of the following:
   a. Appliance repairperson
   b. College coach
   c. Dentist
   d. Gas station attendant
   e. Journalist
   f. Politician

© JIST Works

Section 3: Federal Rules and Regulations

At the beginning of the twentieth century, the rapid spread of the factory system in the United States created a labor class that lived in cities and towns and depended on wages for its livelihood. Unsanitary, dangerous, and uncomfortable working conditions, combined with low wages and long working hours, caused intense dissatisfaction among the growing ranks of factory workers. The workers prompted change by forming labor unions and electing politicians who were committed to government regulation of the workplace.

In 1913, Congress created a separate executive department, the Department of Labor, to deal with the problems of workers. The Department of Labor has specific responsibilities regarding U.S. wage earners. They include

- Fostering, promoting, and developing their welfare
- Improving their working conditions
- Advancing their opportunities for profitable employment

Since the Labor Department's creation, Congress has enacted many laws that employers must follow. These federal laws protect the rights of all men and women when they are seeking a job, while they are on the job, and when they retire. Many states offer similar, and sometimes broader, protection than the federal laws. State laws have exclusive rights to govern several areas of employment.

Career Fact

It is unlawful for an employer to discharge or otherwise discriminate against an employee for filing a complaint or participating in a proceeding under the FLSA.

Enrichment

After students read this section, have them complete the "Is It a Violation of Your Legal Rights?" worksheet in Chapter 12 of the *Preparing for Career Success Student Activity Book, Third Edition.*

Understanding the Legal Rights of Employees

Workers are protected on the job by a variety of laws that prohibit discrimination and govern wages, hours, occupational safety and health, and other employment-related issues.

Minimum Wages and Overtime Pay

In Chapter 9, you learned about some of the protection provided by the Fair Labor Standards Act (FLSA). This law establishes and regulates the minimum wage, overtime pay, record-keeping procedures, and child labor standards. The FLSA covers most full-time and part-time workers in the private sector and in federal, state, and local governments. Workers not covered include casual babysitters; companions for the aged and infirm; executive, administrative, and professional employees; employees of certain small, retail, or service establishments; outside salespeople; and some agricultural workers.

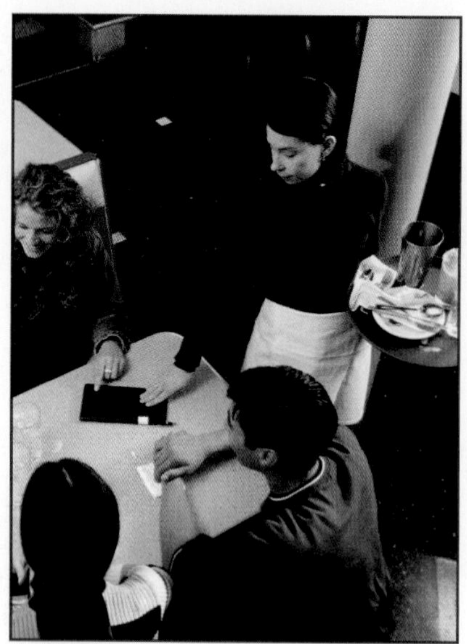

Unless restaurant employees are participating in a valid tip pool, the employer pays at least 50 percent of the minimum wage to servers regardless of the amount of tips.

Discussion Starter

Many of your students probably have been casual babysitters. Ask your students: The minimum wage provision of the Fair Labor Standards Act does not cover casual babysitters. Day-care workers are covered, however. Casual babysitters and day-care workers have very similar job tasks and responsibilities. Should the minimum wage law cover casual babysitters? Why or why not?

The FLSA does not limit the hours or work for employees who are 16 years old or older. Most covered workers are entitled to one and a half times their regular rate of pay for each hour they work in excess of 40 hours per week. If your employer is not paying you the minimum wage rate or the required overtime pay, you may file a complaint with the Wage and Hour Division of the Department of Labor. It is listed under the heading "U.S. Government" in the government pages of most telephone directories. The Internet home page for the Wage and Hour Division is www.dol.gov/dol/esa/public/shd-rog.htm.

Agricultural Workers

The Migrant and Seasonal Agricultural Worker Protection Act (MSPA) safeguards most migrant and seasonal agricultural workers in their interaction with farm labor contractors, agricultural employers, agricultural associations, and providers of migrant housing. Employers must meet certain minimum requirements in their dealing with migrant and seasonal agricultural workers. Employees have the right to receive written notice of the terms and conditions of their employment and the right to file a complaint with the Wage and Hour Division of the Department of Labor.

Equal Pay

On April 9, 1866, Congress passed the nation's first civil rights act. The act declared that "all persons born in the United States are citizens of the United States and citizens of every race, creed and color shall have the same right in every State and Territory in the United States." Among the rights guaranteed were "full and equal benefits of all laws and proceedings for the security of person and property." The Fourteenth Amendment to the U.S. Constitution (1868) included most of the act's provisions. The Civil Rights Acts of 1870, 1871, and 1875 followed this legislation. Definitions of discrimination were expanded to include employment discrimination. Congress ignored civil rights legislation for the next 90 years.

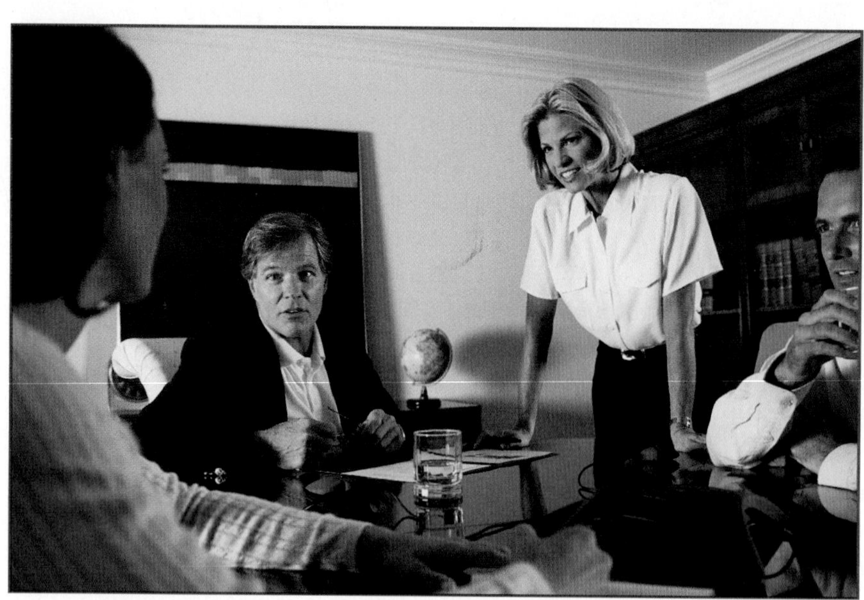

The Equal Pay Act prohibits pay discrimination because of gender. Why is this law especially important to women?

Title VII of the **Civil Rights Act of 1964** protects workers against discrimination based on sex, race, color, religion, or national origin. Specific areas of employment protection include hiring, discharge, compensation, and conditions or privileges of employment. Subsequent laws and *executive* (presidential) orders continue to close loopholes concerning discriminatory employment practices. Almost every aspect of the workplace is subject to civil rights

© JIST Works

requirements. They include employment testing, transfers, compensation, physical facilities, hiring, grooming, fringe benefits, layoffs, promotions, maternity leave, scheduling of work, and sexual harassment.

The Equal Employment Opportunity Commission (EEOC) has primary responsibility for enforcing Title VII. If you have received unfair treatment on the job based on your gender, race, color, religion, national origin, disability, or age, contact the EEOC for information about protection provided and the enforcement process.

The **Equal Pay Act of 1963** amended the FLSA to prohibit pay discrimination because of gender. Employers are required to pay equal wages to men and women doing equal work on jobs requiring equal skill, effort, and responsibility that are performed under similar working conditions. Pay differences based on seniority, merit, or a system that measures earnings by quantity or quality of production are permitted. If you believe that you are not receiving equal pay for equal work, you may file a complaint with the EEOC (the agency responsible for enforcement).

Credit Reporting

The Fair Credit Reporting Act (FCRA) of 1971 requires employers to tell rejected job applicants if they were denied a job based on credit information. Despite the FCRA, employers are increasing their use of credit reports to screen potential employees. Employers must also provide rejected applicants with the name and address of the credit bureau that supplied the report so the applicant can request a free copy of the report and check it for inaccuracies.

Compensation for Injuries

Workers' compensation laws cover workers who are injured or who contract an occupational-related disease on the job. These laws provide for prompt payment of benefits to injured workers with a minimum of red tape and no need to fix the blame for the injury.

Because each state has its own law and operates its own system, the employees covered, the amount of compensation, the duration of the benefits, and the procedures for making and settling claims vary. Benefits usually include medical payments for the period of disability or for permanent disability, occupational rehabilitation, specified services and death benefits for a worker's family, and burial expenses.

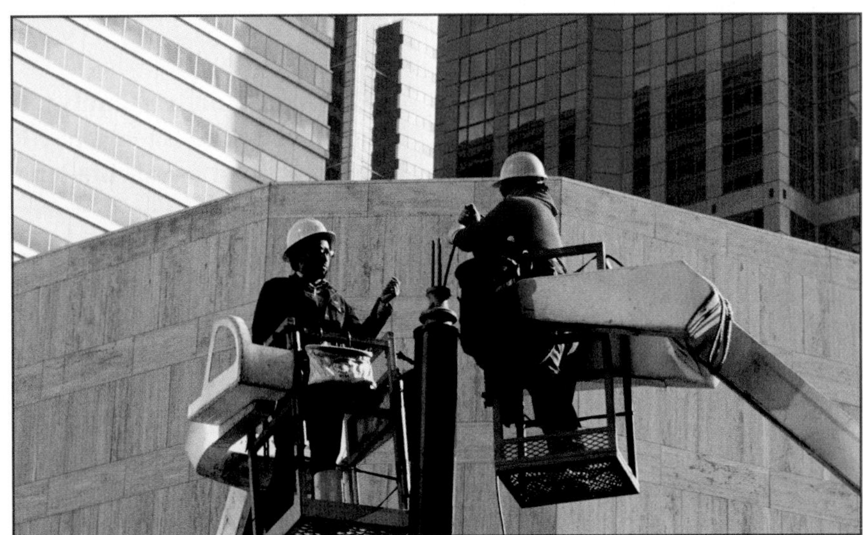

Employers are required to pay workers' compensation so employees will be compensated for being injured on the job.

Reteaching

Have students complete the "Legal Rights of Workers" worksheet found in the Chapter 12 file of the *Preparing for Career Success Instructor's CD-ROM, Third Edition.*

Comprehension Check

Read the case of *Shults vs. Wheaton Glass Co.* to your students: A glass manufacturing company paid male selector-packers 21 cents per hour more than female selector-packers. The company justified the difference on the basis that men performed additional duties, such as lifting and stacking cartons and using hand trucks. The Court of Appeals ruled that under the Equal Pay Act, *equal* does not mean *identical* but rather "substantially equal" and that minor differences in duties do not justify pay differences. Next, write the title of an occupation on the chalkboard. Ask your students to describe (1) a job task that a worker in this occupation would perform, (2) a job task that would be different but substantially equal, (3) a job task that would be different and justify a different pay rate.

Discussion Starter

Ask students the following questions: What information might appear on a job applicant's credit report that might cause a potential employer to reject him or her? What is the reason for your answer?

Community Resources

Form a committee of students to acquire additional information about workers' compensation.

Most states require employers to cover their employees with workers' compensation protection and assess heavy penalties for failure to comply with the law.

CAREER FACT

In some states, a person can receive workers' compensation for disability caused by work-related stress, including stress related to sexual discrimination.

Solving the Problem: Who Pays the Bills?

Randy Browne was a telephone equipment installer for a private company. He supported a wife and a three-month-old daughter. One day, Randy's supervisor instructed him to install lines through the ceiling of a new office building. The ladder provided by the employer did not have safety feet. Randy was busy installing the lines when the ladder slipped, causing him to plunge 12 feet to the floor below. He spent six months in the hospital before the doctor told him that he would never be able to use his legs to do physical work again. He will be able to walk, but only with a severe limp.

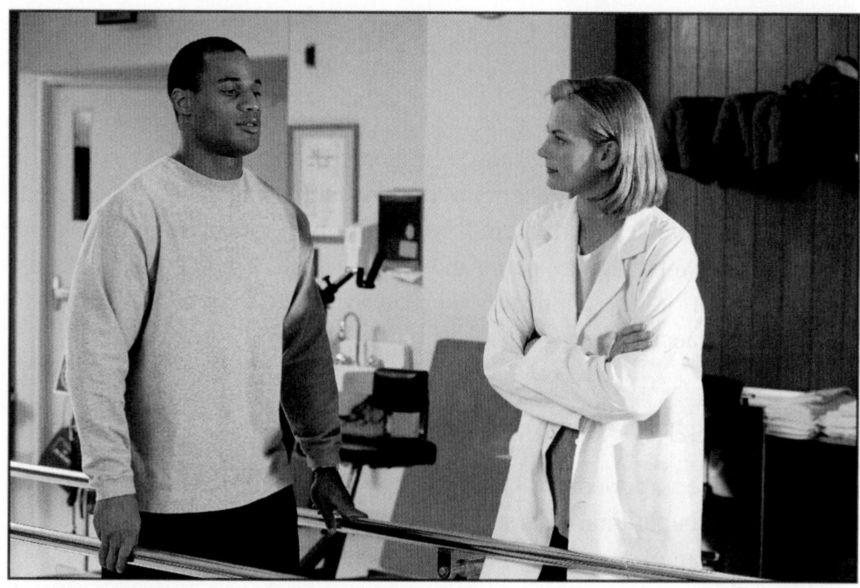

Critical Thinking

How will Randy's family pay their bills while he is unable to work? Who do you think should pay Randy's medical expenses? Will Randy be compensated for his life-long injury? If so, how? If not, why not?

TAKE NOTE

According to the United States Department of Labor, Bureau of Labor Statistics, employer costs for employee compensation averaged $28.03 per hour worked in September 2007. Wages and salaries, which averaged $19.56, accounted for 69.8 percent of these costs, while fringe benefits, which averaged $8.47, accounted for the remaining 30.2 percent. Costs for legally required benefits, including Social Security, Medicare, unemployment insurance, and workers compensation, averaged $2.22 per hour (7.9 percent of total compensation), representing the largest nonwage employer cost. Employer costs for life, health, and disability insurance benefits averaged $2.35 (8.4 percent); paid leave benefits (vacations, holidays, sick leave, and other leave) averaged $1.95 (7.0 percent); and retirement and savings benefits averaged $1.22 (4.4 percent) per hour worked.

Protection for the Disabled

Hailed as a landmark victory for people with disabilities, the **Americans with Disabilities Act (ADA)** went into effect in 1990. This law protects qualified individuals with a disability from employment discrimination, unless hiring the individual would impose an undue hardship on the employer.

Additionally, the ADA protects workers with physical or mental impairment. The covered conditions, diseases, and infections include

© JIST Works

orthopedic problems, cerebral palsy, multiple sclerosis, HIV infection, visual impairment, epilepsy, alcoholism, cancer, diabetes, drug addiction, emotional illness, speech or hearing impairment, muscular dystrophy, mental retardation, heart disease, and specific learning disabilities.

Discussion Starter

Explain that most workers and employers are pleased with the Americans with Disabilities Act of 1990. Many workers with physical or mental impairment are more punctual, have better attendance, and are more productive than many of their physically or mentally unimpaired coworkers. Ask your students: Should employers be required to hire workers who are suffering from alcoholism or drug addiction on an equal basis with other job applicants? Why or why not?

Family Leave

The Family and Medical Leave Act (FMLA) of 1993 provides a means for employees to balance their work and family responsibilities by taking unpaid leave for certain reasons. The act promotes the stability and economic security of families as well as the nation's interest in preserving the integrity of families. The FMLA entitles millions of employees up to 12 weeks of unpaid leave from their jobs to deal with a birth, adoption, or medical emergency in the family.

Employers with 50 or more workers within a 75-mile radius must provide unpaid time off for the birth or adoption of a child; the care of a seriously ill child, spouse, or parent; or an employee's own illness. Employers must continue to offer group health benefits during the leave.

Discussion Starter

Explain that although environmental protection laws have brought about significant environmental improvements, many challenging problems remain. Ask students to think of situations in which the laws still do not protect the environment. Ask for specific examples, and discuss ideas for solving the problem.

Environmental Protection

Human activities have threatened the working environment for many decades. Thousands of workers have died from illnesses caused by long-term exposure to toxic substances and breathing polluted air. Many times, people have acted without regard for the effect on the life-sustaining, economic, and recreational value of the air, land, and water. To protect and restore the quality of these essential and irreplaceable resources, Congress enacted a series of laws.

The U.S. Environmental Protection Agency (EPA) is responsible for implementing the federal laws designed to protect our working world. The agency now administers nine environmental protection laws including the Clean Air Act, Clean Water Act, Safe Drinking Water Act, Toxic Substances Control Act, and the Uranium Mill Tailings Radiation Control Act.

The Clean Air Act was passed to restore the quality of the air we breathe. Can workers who drive to work daily help curb air pollution? What are the long-term effects of breathing polluted air?

Guaranteed Pensions

The Employee Retirement Income Security Act (ERISA) of 1974 protects interests of participants and their beneficiaries who depend on benefits from private employee benefit plans. ERISA sets standards for

KEY TO SUCCESS

When you have a financial emergency, you will appreciate having money saved, especially if your employer contributed some of it.

administering these plans, including a requirement that financial and other information be disclosed to participants and beneficiaries. Some employee benefit plans are not covered by the act. Two examples are church and government plans. As a new employee, you should know your plan, what it requires of you, how to become eligible for benefits, and what steps you can take to assure that you will receive your earned benefits.

Social Security (FICA)

TAKE NOTE

Social Security is not intended to provide adequate retirement income. Many workers include employer pensions and personal savings in their retirement plan.

The basic idea behind Social Security is simple: You pay taxes into the system during your working years, and you and members of your family receive monthly benefits when you are retired or disabled. Your dependent survivors collect benefits when you die. The **Social Security Act** is the federal law that established this national social insurance program. To receive full compensation benefits, you must pay the FICA tax for a stipulated length of time (10 years or 40 quarters for most people).

Social Security provides benefits for about 9 out of 10 workers, including household and self-employed workers. Employers and employees each pay a share of the FICA tax. FICA places taxes in trust funds to pay benefits to eligible people. FICA tax contributions are not refundable.

You have most likely had a Social Security number since you were born. Every worker needs a Social Security card and number if FICA covers his or her job or if certain taxable income is received. Your bank accounts, insurance policies, and credit cards will use your Social Security number for identification.

Asserting Your Rights

Comprehension Check

Ask several students: Who can describe an employment practice that you consider unfair but legal? Who can describe an employment practice you consider unfair and illegal?

Reteaching

Have students complete the "Asserting Your Rights" worksheet found in the Chapter 12 file of the *Preparing for Career Success Instructor's CD-ROM, Third Edition.*

The first step in asserting your legal rights is to know the difference between *prohibited* (illegal) employment practices and those that might seem unjust but are not. An employer has the right to take action against an employee for good cause. For example, laws that protect you against job discrimination do not prevent your employer from discharging you for not doing your job, nor do they require the employer to hire you if you are not qualified.

The second step is to know the procedures you need to follow to assert your legal rights. Most agencies with enforcement or administrative responsibilities for federal laws print free information pamphlets for consumers. If you are unsure about how the law might apply to a specific situation, phone the agency that handles those complaints, and ask to speak with a compliance officer. Table 12.1 lists the agency to contact if you believe an employer is in violation of your rights. Agencies can also be located by using the Internet.

© JIST Works

Table 12.1 Agencies That Enforce the Legal Rights of Employees

Law Violated	Agency to Contact
Equal Pay Act	The Equal Employment Opportunity Commission (EEOC)
Civil Rights Act	The Equal Employment Opportunity Commission (EEOC)
Workers' compensation laws	Your state's Department of Labor or Industrial Commission
Family and Medical Leave Act	U.S. Department of Labor, Employment Standards Administration, Wage and Hour Division
Environmental protection laws	U.S. Environmental Protection Agency (EPA)
Migrant and Seasonal Agricultural Worker Protection Act	U.S. Department of Labor

You might obtain additional assistance and information from community-based organizations that have information and referral, counseling, or legal assistance services. Your local bar association might provide information about resources in your area as well.

If you believe that you are the victim of discrimination, you are entitled to file a complaint with the agency that has responsibility for enforcing the relevant law. Procedures for making complaints vary. If you feel that you are not receiving fair treatment, document incidents that support your complaint. Written notes on what happened, when it happened, and who was there are very useful in refreshing your memory and showing a pattern of unfair treatment. There are time limits on filing complaints, so it is important to act promptly.

Enrichment

Have students complete the "Securing Workers' Rights" worksheet found in the Chapter 12 file of the *Preparing for Career Success Instructor's CD-ROM, Third Edition.*

Solving the Problem: Fair Choices or Discrimination?

Tanya Robinson arrived early for her job interview at the Casablanca. The restaurant had an opening for the position of assistant manager. With more than 100 employees working at the Casablanca, Tanya knew that she would have opportunities for promotion.

While waiting in the manager's outer office, Tanya noticed the three other applicants being interviewed were white. She assumed that she was the only African American applying for the job. When the interview was over, Tanya was certain she would be selected.

Three days later, Tanya received a letter from the manager telling her that another person was hired for the job. The manager would keep Tanya's application on file in case of another opening. Not getting the job seemed unfair to Tanya.

© JIST Works

Critical Thinking

Tanya thinks that the Casablanca's manager is guilty of discrimination. She plans to contact her state's Department of Labor and file a complaint. If you were Tanya, what course of action would you follow? Why?

Section 3: Get Involved

Answer the following on a separate sheet of paper, and be prepared to discuss your responses in class.

1. How could a worker's credit rating affect his or her job performance or honesty? Is using credit reports a fair way to screen job applicants? Why or why not?
2. Should manufacturers be required to remove pollutants that are proven health hazards from the air and water if the cost of cleaning the air or water would drive the company out of business? What if the company were the largest employer in the area?

Reteaching

Have students complete the "Matching Fringes" worksheet in Chapter 12 of the *Preparing for Career Success Instructor's CD-ROM, Third Edition.*

Enrichment

After your students read this section, have them complete the "Fringes—What Are They Worth to You?" worksheet in Chapter 12 of the *Preparing for Career Success Student Activity Book, Third Edition.*

Section 4: Fringe Benefits

Can you remember a time when you went on a vacation or celebrated a holiday with your family? Were you ever a patient in a hospital? If you answered yes to either of these questions, you probably used a family member's fringe benefits.

Fringe benefits are forms of compensation other than salary or wages. There is no legal obligation requiring employers to provide most of the fringe benefits that workers receive. Your employer may pay them partially or totally, and because fringe benefits are not considered wages, they are usually not taxed. As a new employee, you should learn as much as possible about the fringe benefits your employer offers.

Medical Insurance

If the employer offers medical insurance, it is available to employees and their eligible dependents. Many organizations offer employees a choice

© JIST Works

of medical plans. The amount of an employee's contribution depends on the plan selected. In addition to hospital costs, many medical plans also provide dental care, surgical benefits, prescription drug plans, and much more.

Familiarize yourself with the terms in Table 12.2. They will help you make the *wellness* (good health) choices that are most beneficial to you.

Five types of medical insurance plans are

- A *health maintenance organization (HMO)* provides a full range of health coverage in exchange for a monthly fixed fee. In many organizations, an employee may elect to have his or her medical care provided by an HMO at little or no cost to the employee. Enrollees are limited to specific care providers, and most services are fully paid. HMOs are responsible for both delivering the care and bearing the associated financial risk.
- *Traditional fee-for-service (FFS)* plans allow participants to select any provider for care. These plans reimburse the patient, provider, or both.
- *Preferred provider organizations (PPOs)* are fee-for-service plans that provide coverage to participants through a network of selected hospitals, doctors, and diagnostic clinics. Enrollees may choose providers outside the network, but they must pay a greater percentage of the cost.
- *Managed care plans* are an alternative to or a replacement for traditional insurance plans, HMOs, and PPOs. These plans arrange with selected health-care providers to furnish a comprehensive set of services and implement cost-containment and quality measures.

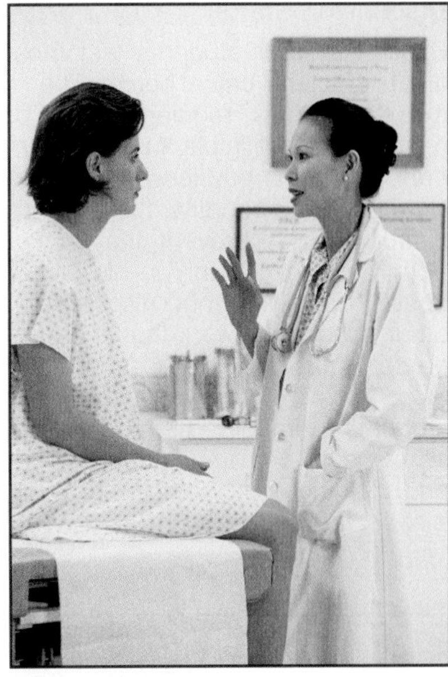

The worry about paying for the cost of medical care is relieved when the employer pays for your medical benefits. What fringe benefits are most important to you?

Community Resources

Form a committee to invite a speaker to your classroom to discuss medical insurance. Contact a large insurance carrier or the insurance benefits department of a local employer. Have the committee prepare a list of questions about medical insurance and send it to the speaker.

Table 12.2 Health Benefit Terms

Insurance Term	Definition
Hospitalization benefits	Payments that cover all or a portion of hospital room and board for a certain number of days and for specific services.
Major medical plans	Programs that cover costly services over and above what is normally covered by a hospitalization plan.
Second surgical opinion	Judgment of a different surgeon made after a physician who is qualified to perform surgery recommends elective (optional) surgery. This is a requirement of most health-care plans.
Deductibles	The amount of an expense that a beneficiary must first meet as his or her share of the cost.
Routine physical examinations	Physical checkups or other tests made in the absence of definite symptoms of disease or injury.
Outpatient care	Medical service performed in the emergency department of a hospital, an ambulatory care center, an emergency care center, or a physician's office. Patients return home following outpatient care.
Prescription coverage	Program that pays all or part of the cost for prescribed medication.
Coinsurance provisions	Requirements that the insured pay a portion of covered medical expenses, with the plan paying the remaining portion. For example, the employee may pay 20 percent, and the plan pays the remaining 80 percent.

© JIST Works

Discussion Starter

Explain to your students that most disability plans pay a percentage of the employee's regular wages or salary. To be eligible for long-term benefits, which pay less than short-term disability benefits, the worker's disability must prevent the worker from working not only in his or her usual occupation but also in any other substantial work that is appropriate for his or her education, training, and work experience. Ask students to imagine being disabled. Who would pay the housing, food, and clothing expenses? How would it affect family members?

- *Cafeteria plans*, also known as *flexible benefits*, let you put aside money, by way of a deduction, from each paycheck before taxes to cover various types of costs. These costs may be payment of health insurance premiums, life insurance premiums, vision care, dental care, or child or dependent care costs.

Additional Fringe Benefits

Fringe benefits are very costly for employers. Benefits paid to workers by private industry amount to about 30 percent of total employee wages. Receiving benefits from your employer is sometimes better than receiving cash. You must pay taxes on cash wages, but many benefits are tax-free.

Although medical insurance is likely to be the top benefit priority for most workers, you should know about the benefits described next because they will enhance the quality and security of your career.

Disability insurance, sometimes referred to as *income-protection insurance*, protects you from loss of income if you are sick or are injured. Disability insurance pays you an income until you are able to return to work or until the benefits run out. Most employers offer some form of short- or long-term disability benefits. Long-term disability programs do not pay benefits for a disability resulting from an act of war (declared or undeclared); criminal acts; or participation in an insurrection, rebellion, or riot.

Parenting leave allows new parents time to adjust to the demands of their child.

Wellness programs, also known as *employee-assistance programs (EAPs)*, involve employees in health activities. Many programs include confidential counseling to help employees resolve personal concerns that may affect job performance. Employers have discovered that encouraging employees to take increased responsibility for their good health results in less absenteeism and lower insurance costs.

Vacations provide workers with one or two weeks of annual vacation time after six months to one year of continuous service. Vacation time usually increases to four or more weeks after 15 or 20 years of service. Can you imagine arranging your first paid vacation with a travel agent?

Leave time is excused time away from work. It may be paid or unpaid. Common reasons for using leave time include personal illness, family care, death in the family, jury duty, pregnancy, and personal reasons.

Discussion Starter

Ask your students: Are wellness programs unfair to employees who already use good health practices? For example, is it fair to give one employee $500 to quit smoking and nothing to a nonsmoking employee?

- Employers grant **parenting leave** to mothers or fathers when a new child is born or adopted. Parenting leave time is usually subtracted from accumulated sick leave days for pay purposes. Should new parents have the right to spend time with their child? Why or why not?
- Federal laws govern *military leave* for members of the U.S. Armed Forces. National Guards and other state or federal peacetime military personnel who must participate in annual training periods are usually granted a leave of 15 workdays, with pay, per year. This pay, provided by the employer, is usually the difference between the

© JIST Works

employee's regular pay and his or her military pay during the duty time. Is military leave important? Why or why not?

- *Sabbatical leave* is an extended leave granted under certain conditions to employees who wish to acquire additional education and training or to travel extensively.

Pension plans provide regular lifetime payments to retired employees. Employers may pay the entire cost of a pension plan or require employee contributions.

A 401(k) plan allows a worker to put a certain percentage of *gross* (pretax income) into a trust fund or other qualified investment fund. Many employers match the contribution up to a certain percentage. When or if you change employers, you can take your 401(k) plan with you.

Accumulated pension benefits are *vested* (legally yours) when you have a nonforfeitable right to receive benefits at retirement, even if you leave your job before retirement age. Most pension plans require that you work five years, with a minimum of 1,000 hours of service each year, before you earn pension rights.

Another fringe benefit is *child care*, which is provided by some employers at an on-site day-care center. Employees drop off their preschool children only minutes away from the worksite. The parents may visit the center during the day to play, read, or have lunch with their children or just check up on them. Other employers provide information about locating child-care services and possible tax deductions.

Employers lose millions of dollars annually from work-family conflicts caused when a child is sick, day-care arrangements fall through, or on-the-job time is spent worrying about a child's well-being. Employer-sponsored child-care programs are not widespread, but many employers are involved in finding practical solutions to the problem.

Group life insurance provides financial support for *beneficiaries* (people who receive benefits from insurance policies) following an employee's death. The term *group* refers to the insured individuals who have a common employer.

The amount of basic life insurance provided by an employer-paid plan is usually equal to the employee's annual base pay. As annual wages increase, the amount of coverage is also increased.

The insured employee names a beneficiary for the policy. Soon after the employee's death, the beneficiary receives the total amount of the policy. Frequently, the spouse uses the money to pay current bills, funeral expenses, and a home mortgage and to produce income for the surviving family.

Savings/thrift plans are investment or savings plans for the employee. Both the employee and employer contribute. Employees authorize the employer to make payroll deductions for their contribution.

Credit unions are nonprofit banking services that employees may join. They permit members to save, borrow, and earn interest on contributions

The father of a preschool child enjoys the benefit of a child-care center at his worksite. Will this benefit be important to you some day?

Vocabulary Builder

Send a writer to the chalkboard, and ask your students to close their books. Ask individual students to use one of the following terms in a sentence: *parenting leave, military leave,* or *sabbatical leave.* Ask the writer to write each sentence on the chalkboard. Have the entire class correct the usage of the term and any grammatical errors. Develop at least one correct sentence for each term.

Discussion Starter

Explain to students that most people have dreams for their retirement years. Making your dreams come true requires financial security. Ask your students: Should a young worker think about retirement? Why or why not?

Cluster Link

Would you enjoy a career planning, managing, or providing services related to banking, financial planning, investments, or insurance? If so, you should explore opportunities in the Finance career cluster. See the appendix for more information.

Discussion Starter

Explain that child-care programs are costly for employers to operate. Ask your students: Who should pay the cost of child care for a single parent? For two working parents?

Case Study

Have students read the case study "Who Is Responsible?" in Chapter 12 of the *Preparing for Career Success Instructor's CD-ROM, Third Edition* and discuss the "Critical Thinking" questions.

Discussion Starter

Explain to students that many employers offer their employees the option of purchasing additional life insurance at attractive rates. Ask students: Should responsible people carry life insurance? Who should pay for a worker's life insurance? Why?

School-to-Work Transition

Explain that employers and schools agree that involvement in recreational activities increases the level of motivation and productivity of workers and students. Allow several students to answer this question: Describe a situation when you noticed a difference in your level of motivation, attitude toward school, or grades because of your involvement in an extracurricular activity.

Credit unions provide nonprofit banking services to members.

they make through payroll deductions. Credit unions accept savings from and make loans only to members. At the end of the year, a credit union often has a surplus of funds to distribute to its members.

Stock purchase plans enable employees to purchase *stocks* (shares of ownership) in the company, with or without employer contributions. The purchase terms are generally more favorable than those available in the open market. Stock option plans allow employees the privilege of purchasing company stock at a certain price and at a time of their own choosing.

Social and recreational programs are sponsored by some employers. These programs include athletic teams such as softball, basketball, golf, and bowling. Some employee groups with common interests may form clubs or meet informally. Likewise, groups of employees may operate similar activities in small organizations.

Company-paid education/training is yet another fringe benefit offered by employers. See Section 6, "Organizational Training and Education," later in this chapter for more details on these programs.

Section 4: Get Involved

Answer the following on a separate sheet of paper, and be prepared to discuss your responses in class.

1. Discuss pension plans with a retired person. Record his or her answers to the following questions: If you were a young worker again, would you handle your retirement savings plan in the same way? If so, how did you handle it? If not, what would you do differently?
2. If you were a working parent, which two fringe benefits would be most important to you? Why? Which two benefits would be least important. Why?

Student Evaluation

To evaluate student mastery of concepts, you might want to use the Section 4 quiz in the Chapter 12 file of the *Preparing for Career Success Instructor's CD-ROM, Third Edition.*

© JIST Works

Section 5: The Work Schedule

Some people work best in the early morning, some work best late at night, and for others, their work schedule varies. Given this information, why do you suppose most employers adopt an 8-hour day and a 5-day week of 40 hours? Is the restriction of a fixed work schedule or a time clock necessary?

Employers have the right to establish work schedules. In doing this, their first consideration is the purpose and needs of the organization. For most office or white-collar employees, 8:00 a.m. is the normal starting time. For blue-collar employees, it's usually 7:00 or 7:30 a.m. Service businesses schedule their hours of work according to the convenience of their customers. Although most work schedules are 8 hours per day, schedules of 7½ hours per day are not unusual. Some employers even use work schedules consisting of four 10-hour shifts per week.

To understand some of the reasoning for specific work schedules, review the following factors that the owner of an automobile repair shop considered when making a work schedule for employees. Keep in mind that each of these activities must take place when other businesses are open or when it is convenient for customers:

- Ordering and receiving parts and supplies
- Making money transactions
- Placing advertisements with radio, TV, and newspapers
- Conducting sales meetings with commercial customers
- Performing daily custodial tasks and maintenance of shop equipment
- Scheduling and providing automobile repair services

Customer demands, products, and services can change quickly. Today, the economic problems faced by employers generating goods and services and the needs of their employees are changing faster than at any time in the past. Worldwide competition demands that workers and employers work together developing alternatives to the traditional nine-to-five workday. These alternatives meet workers' changing goals and lifestyles, but not at the expense of employers' profits. The new ways of working include, but are not limited to, flexible work scheduling, telecommuting, job sharing, and compressed workweeks. The utilization of contingent employees, overtime pay, and compensatory time also is available when needed.

Contingent Employment

To remain efficient and competitive in rapidly changing markets, an increasing number of employers are building their work schedules around a ring-and-core base. Permanent, full-time employees make up the core,

Cooperative Learning

Divide your class into learning pairs. Designate a time period for each pair of students to write the title of two occupations they are considering for future careers. Write the probable shift(s) for a worker in each occupation and the reason for working that particular shift(s). Have each learning pair report to the class about one occupation.

Enrichment

Have students complete the "A Schedule That Works" worksheet in Chapter 12 of the *Preparing for Career Success Student Activity Book, Third Edition.*

TECHNOLOGY

People increasingly are relying on electronic devices and computer technology to help them manage information, complete work and personal tasks, and fulfill their multiple life roles as employees, friends, family members, and members of the community. Devices such as the iPhone or BlackBerry and social networking sites such as Facebook can be helpful and fun to use, but they also can become a distraction. Remember that such technology is a tool to help your reach your goals; it's not the end result.

Case Study

Have students read the case study "A Temporary Plan" in Chapter 12 of the *Preparing for Career Success Instructor's CD-ROM, Third Edition* and discuss the "Critical Thinking" questions.

A nursery schedules contingent workers during the peak season. What other seasonal jobs provide opportunities for students?

and workers whose time can adjust to short-term changes make up the ring. This type of scheduling has led to a substantial increase in the number of part-time, temporary, contractual, and leased employees. Any employee in this category is a **contingent worker**.

For years, retail stores and agricultural businesses have used contingent workers to meet changing seasonal as well as daily labor needs. However, the use of contingent workers across all industries is new to the American labor force. It is common for an employer to build a work schedule that includes part-time workers in the office to keep up with billings or to use contractual engineers and technicians to help full-time staff meet the demands of a specific contract.

Whatever the reason, contingent workers are available for part of a week, several weeks, or several months. Some workers prefer this type of work schedule. Others prefer the security that comes with being a permanent employee.

Comprehension Check

Ask your students to close their books. Have several students explain, in their own words, the legal meaning of overtime pay and when an employee is eligible to receive it.

Overtime

Work scheduled in excess of the basic workday or workweek, as defined by law, the collective bargaining agreement, or the company, is considered overtime. Hours of work considered to be overtime are those beyond 8 hours in one shift or 40 hours in one week. Overtime is determined by whether the employee is an exempt or nonexempt employee. Most *exempt employees* (those who are excused from the rule) fall into one of four classifications: executive employees, administrative employees, professional employees, and salespeople (outside, not retail).

© JIST Works

Nonexempt employees work under a negotiated labor agreement. Many employers schedule nonexempt employees at overtime rates for Saturday work, even when they are not unionized or working on a government contract. However, employers are not legally required to do so.

Compensatory Time

Employees scheduled for extra hours sometimes receive time off in exchange for the extra time worked. This time is called *compensatory time.* For example, if you worked 44 hours in one week instead of the normal 40 hours, you would not receive extra pay. Instead, you would take off 4 hours of excused time, with pay, at a future date.

Some workers are required to use a time card to certify the time they begin working and the time they end. In this case, the employee inserts his or her card into a machine that records the exact time. This machine enables the employer to keep an accurate record of each worker's schedule.

Find Out More

For career information on becoming an Employee Benefits or Compensation Analyst, key in **International Foundation of Employee Benefit Plans** on your search engine, or go online at www.ifebp.org.

Planning Makes a Difference: A Flexible Plan

Carlin Abbott is a single parent with skills that are in high demand in the field of engineering technology. She wants to be a good mother and a good employee. Carlin also wants to advance her career. Knowing that she must handle time conflicts between her work and family responsibilities, Carlin plans to interview with organizations that offer the option of a **flextime** work schedule. The total hours of work remain the same on a flextime schedule, but the employee sets his or her own hours of work.

On the job, Carlin uses a computer to make technical drawings. She requires little or no supervision after her work is assigned. However, she does need to work a few hours each day at a time when her supervisor is available to discuss her assignments. It makes little difference in the overall operation of the organization if Carlin comes in early and leaves early or comes in late and leaves late.

After Carlin completed several job interviews, a small engineering firm that uses flextime scheduling offered her a position. The personnel manager told her that the composition of the workforce—in particular the increase in the number of working mothers—has brought about a greater acceptance of flextime work schedules among many employers. Many single and older employees choose flextime schedules to adjust their work hours to their personal lifestyles. One survey showed that half of 521 large firms surveyed offered flextime scheduling. These companies believe that flextime scheduling has a positive effect on employee turnover, absenteeism, morale, and tardiness.

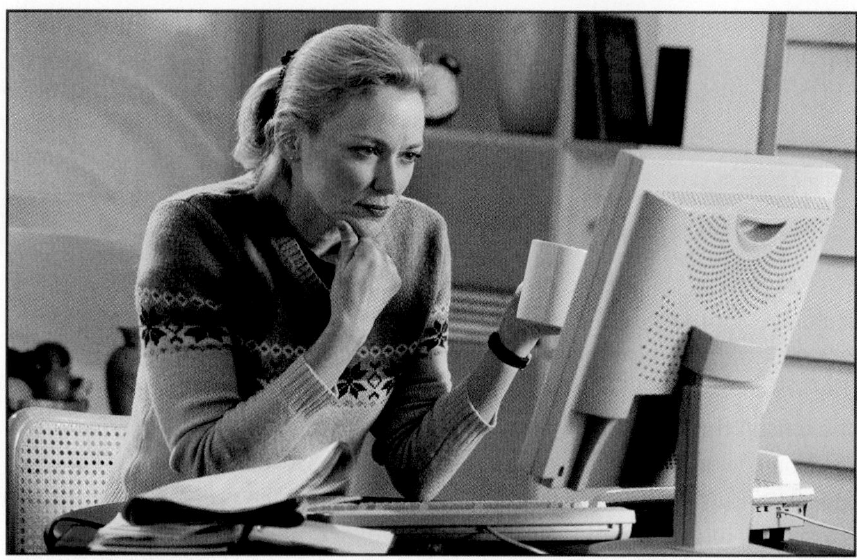

Critical Thinking

Carlin did not find her flextime job by accident. How will her plan help her meet her goals as a worker? As a mother?

If employees could make doctor appointments, dentist appointments, or take care of family emergencies and still work an eight-hour flextime shift, how would their scheduling benefit their employers?

Section 5: Get Involved

Answer the following on a separate sheet of paper, and be prepared to discuss your responses in class.

1. What hours would you schedule your employees if you were the owner of a small bakery? Would you schedule any particular workers at different times from others? If so, which workers, and why?
2. How would you establish a work schedule for nurses, police officers, and firefighters who must provide service 24 hours a day, 7 days a week?
3. Work shifts make up the daily schedule of a plant and its employees: The day shift (first shift) occurs during the morning and afternoon hours, the evening shift (second shift) extends from late afternoon until about midnight, and the third shift (night shift or graveyard shift) is from about midnight until the next morning. A swing or rotating shift changes (usually every week) on a regular schedule. Which of these four shifts would you prefer? Why? Which would you not prefer? Why?

Section 6: Organizational Training and Education

Very few new employees have the necessary skills, knowledge, and experience to immediately excel in their jobs. In fact, many employers believe that employee training is more important than formal education when it comes to developing job skills. In addition, the availability of useful training fosters positive employee attitudes toward the organization.

© JIST Works

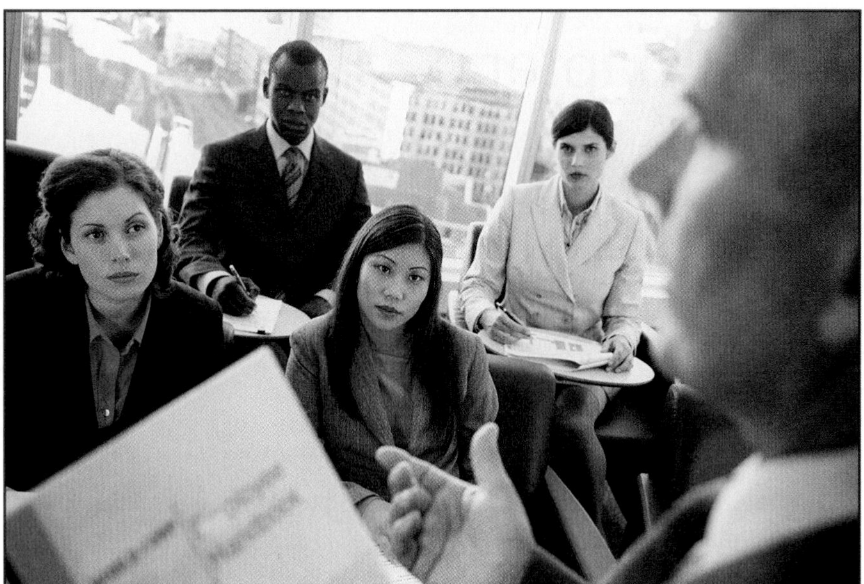

Workshops and seminars sponsored by employers usually focus on professional or personal development. Would you enjoy participating in this three-day seminar with your coworkers?

Organizations usually encourage employees to take advanced training and education programs. They are aware that developing each employee's talent serves the best interests of the employee and the organization.

Tuition reimbursement is an educational fringe benefit that some employers offer. They agree to pay part or all of the costs of the job-related training or college courses that their employees undertake. Most organizations restrict tuition reimbursement to training or education courses related to the employee's current job or another job within the organization for which the employee is preparing.

Chapter 6 described apprenticeship and on-the-job training programs within organizations as well as advanced training at colleges and universities. Unlike that type of education and training, most employee training does not require in-depth study. Instead, most employers sponsor practical training in the form of workshops or seminars.

Workshops are usually one-day courses that involve a small group of employees. They provide an excellent opportunity for interaction between the presenter and the participants. Seminars are similar to workshops but often last two to five days. Most workshops and seminars focus on professional or personal development. The presenters may be employees of the organization or hired consultants. Upon completion of these programs, participants usually receive certificates of attendance or participation.

Education and Training

Explain to your students that many large employers make tuition reimbursement programs available to all levels of employees from high school graduates to those with doctorate degrees.

Case Study

Have students read the case study "Working Together" in Chapter 12 of the *Preparing for Career Success Instructor's CD-ROM, Third Edition* and discuss the "Critical Thinking" questions.

Section 6: Get Involved

Write a response to the following activity and prepare to discuss it in class:

1. Interview an employed friend or relative who has been involved in some form of employer-sponsored education or training. Describe the training program he or she has completed. What career skills were learned or improved?

Chapter 12 Review

Enrich Your Vocabulary

On a separate sheet of paper, number from 1 to 20, and complete the following activity. (Do not write in your textbook.) Match each statement with the most appropriate term from the "Enrich Your Vocabulary" list at the beginning of the chapter by writing that term next to the number of the correct statement.

1. One-day, company-sponsored training sessions
2. The act that established a tax-sponsored pension and disability insurance plan
3. Using knowledge obtained as a result of your position for personal gain
4. The act that protects workers against several types of job discrimination
5. Forms of compensation other than salary or wages
6. Reporting wasteful or dishonest company activities to the government
7. Nonprofit banking services
8. A work schedule in which employees set their own hours of work
9. Agreement between competitors on the price range of products
10. Part-time, temporary, contractual, and leased employees
11. Businesses with no competition
12. The act that requires employers to pay equal wages for equal work
13. Time taken when a child is born or adopted
14. Code of values; standards for conduct
15. Formal, periodic, written evaluation of job performance
16. Laws that provide for payments to injured workers
17. Laws that make monopolies illegal
18. Something said or done to deceive; trickery; cheating
19. Protects any "qualified individual with a disability" from employment discrimination
20. Provide regular lifetime payments to employees on retirement

Enrich Your Vocabulary Answers

1. workshops
2. Social Security Act
3. insider abuse
4. Civil Rights Act of 1964
5. fringe benefits
6. whistle-blowing
7. credit union
8. flextime
9. price fixing
10. contingent workers
11. monopolies
12. Equal Pay Act of 1963
13. parenting leave
14. ethics
15. merit rating
16. worker's compensation laws
17. antitrust laws
18. fraud
19. Americans with Disabilities Act
20. pension plans

Reteaching

Have students complete the "Finding the Right Words" and "Checking Your Location" worksheets in Chapter 12 of the *Preparing for Career Success Student Activity Book, Third Edition.*

© JIST Works

Check Your Knowledge

On a separate sheet of paper, complete the following activities. (Do not write in your textbook.)

1. How should you prepare for an evaluation meeting?
2. What five major employer decisions are influenced by performance appraisals?
3. Who enforces a business organization's code of ethics?
4. Why did the American people begin to elect politicians who were committed to government regulation of the workplace?
5. What is the purpose of the Fair Labor Standards Act?
6. In addition to medical insurance, what fringe benefits do employers offer?
7. Which kind of employees are not eligible for overtime pay?
8. In the opinion of many employers, how do employees learn most of their job skills?

Develop SCANS Competencies

Government experts say that successful workers can productively use resources, interpersonal skills, information, systems, and technology. This activity will give you practice in developing information and interpersonal skills.

Working with classmates, develop a questionnaire to find out the environmental concerns of students in your school. Design a comprehensive questionnaire that can be given to 100 students in your school. You might ask questions about local companies' waste disposal routines, companies that cause air or water pollution, or companies that cause noise pollution.

As a class project, duplicate the questionnaire, administer it, tally the results, and report the findings. Based on the results, write to local businesses to inform them of the students' concerns and of their legal and ethical responsibility to the community in which they are located.

Check Your Knowledge Answers

1. Make a list of what you want to learn from the meeting; prepare to emphasize your accomplishments.
2. Promotion, salary increase, possible discharge, transfer to a different job or department, and admission into a training program.
3. Ethics are imposed and enforced from within an organization.
4. Low pay; long working hours; and unsanitary, dangerous, and uncomfortable working conditions.
5. The FLSA establishes a minimum wage, overtime pay, record-keeping requirements, and child labor standards for workers.
6. Disability insurance, wellness programs, paid vacations, leave time, pension plans, child care, group life insurance, savings plans, credit unions, stock purchase plans, recreational programs, paid training.
7. Exempt employees, including executives, administrative employees, professionals, and outside salespeople.
8. Through employer-sponsored training programs.

Enrichment

Have students complete the Chapter 12 section of the *Preparing for Career Success Student Portfolio, Third Edition.*

Chapter 13 Resources

Lesson Plans and Preparation

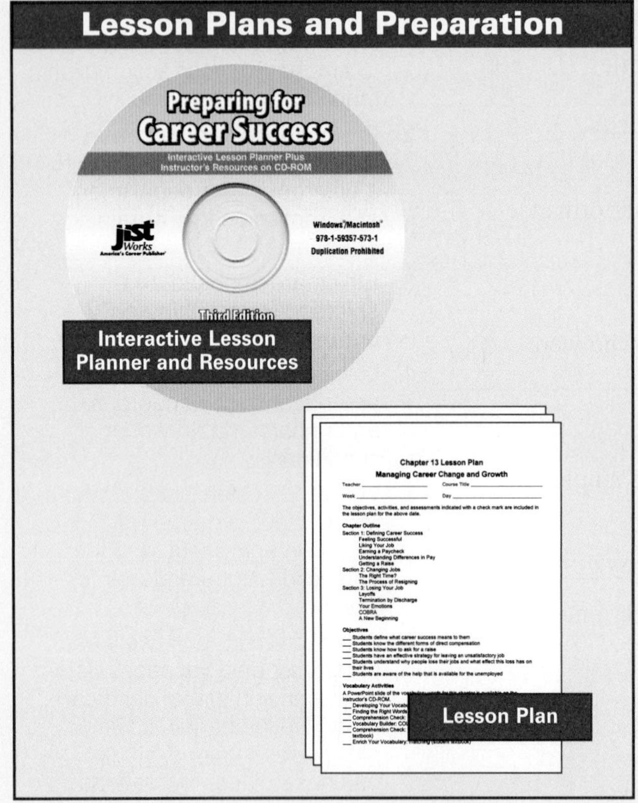

Multimedia

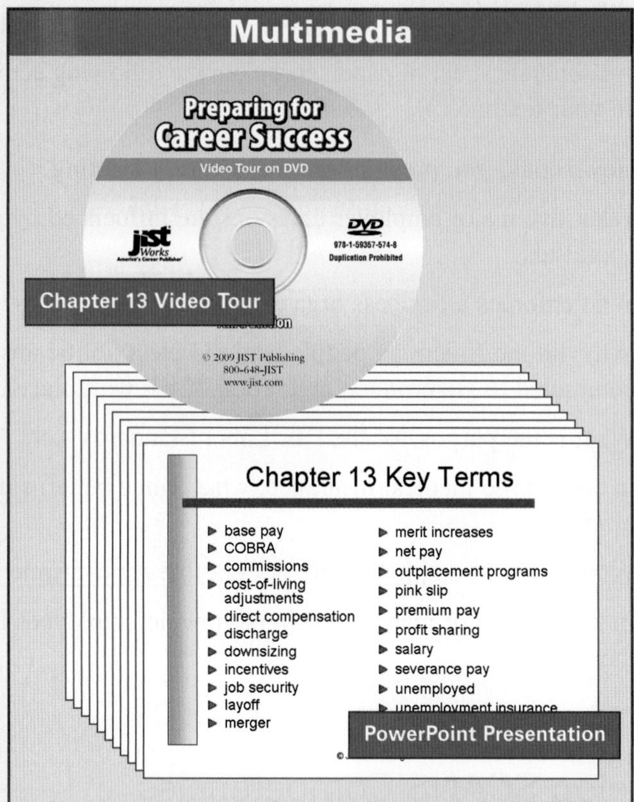

Activities

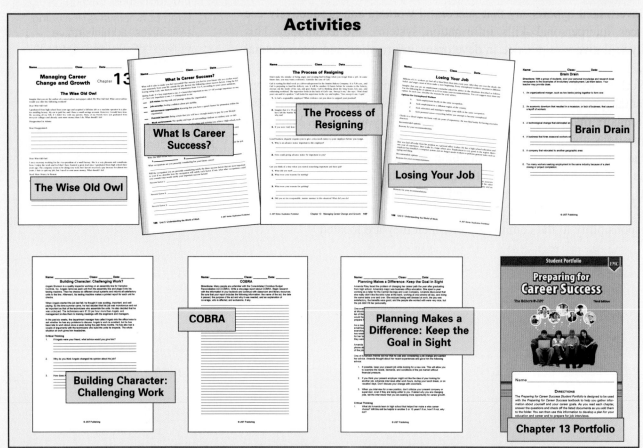

- The Wise Old Owl
- What Is Career Success?
- The Process of Resigning
- Losing Your Job
- Brain Drain
- Building Character: Challenging Work
- COBRA
- Planning Makes a Difference: Keep the Goal in Sight
- Chapter 13 Portfolio

© JIST Works

Review and Assessment

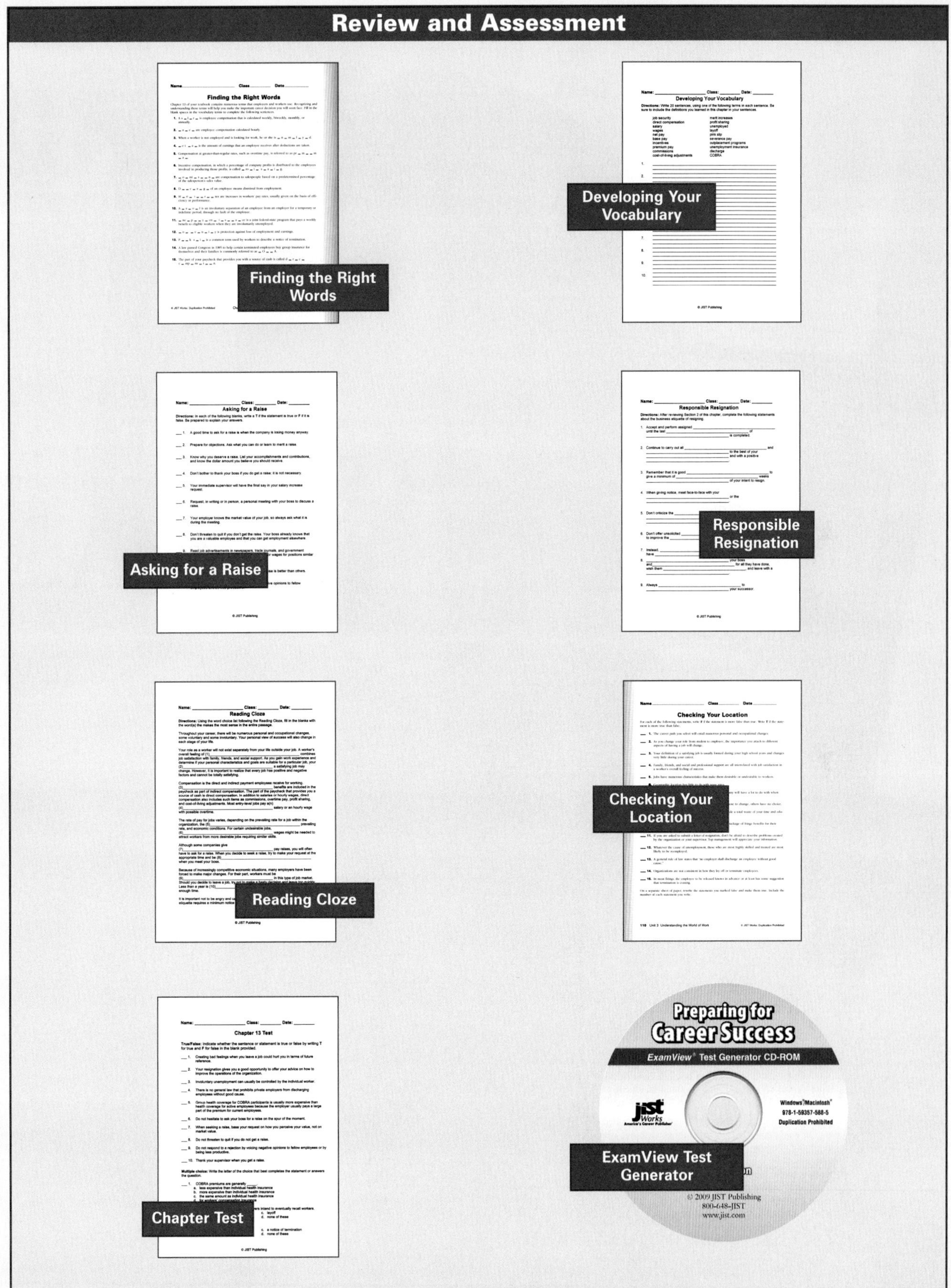

Chapter 13

Managing Career Change and Growth

Learning Objectives

- Explain the relationship between work, family, and friends in a successful career
- List several forms of direct compensation
- Make a systematic, positive job change
- List the benefits and job-placement assistance that are available to displaced workers

Your career path will entail numerous personal and occupational changes. Some changes are *voluntary* (planned); others are *involuntary* (unplanned). Those who study the future world of work estimate that workers in your generation will change jobs up to 10 times or more before they reach retirement. This number is even greater if you count career moves in large organizations that have promotion-from-within policies. You may have 10 or more different positions within one company if you start at the entry level and move up the job ladder.

Enrich Your Vocabulary

In reading this chapter and doing the exercises, you will learn the following important terms:

base pay	job security	premium pay
COBRA	layoff	profit sharing
commissions	merger	salary
cost-of-living adjustments	merit increases	severance pay
direct compensation	net pay	unemployed
discharge	outplacement programs	unemployment insurance
downsizing	pink slip	wages
incentives		

Vocabulary

You can use the "Developing Your Vocabulary" worksheet found in the Chapter 13 file of the *Preparing for Career Success Instructor's CD-ROM, Third Edition* as a pretest for chapter concepts or as a reteaching worksheet.

People, jobs, and life situations change continually, making career and life planning a lifelong process. Just as you cannot completely separate school from other parts of your life, neither can you isolate your career. Through periodic review and self-assessment, you exercise control over the direction of your life instead of allowing the forces of life to direct you.

Section 1: Defining Career Success

Success is full of promise till men get it: and then it is last year's nest, from which the bird has flown.

—Henry Ward Beecher

What will make you feel successful? Accumulating great wealth? Creating something beautiful? Establishing meaningful relationships with family and friends? Being in a position of power and prestige? Finding the meaning of success and desiring success are individual pursuits. Your answers today probably differ from what you would have said five years ago and what you will say five years from now. Each life stage has an impact on your personal view of success.

Cross-Reference

See "Interests," Section 3 of Chapter 2. Also, see "Goals," Section 2 of Chapter 3.

Video Tour on DVD

Show students the Chapter 13 segment to introduce them to the content.

In general, success in work

- Brings about a feeling of satisfaction with life
- Provides a satisfactory lifestyle
- Makes you feel as though you're a valuable part of society
- Assures a means of paying essential bills and providing the necessities of life
- Can be gauged by how well it supports leisure activities

Key to Success

You may need to leave a job where you enjoy the work, your coworkers, and the boss if your employer cannot provide your next upward career step.

Feeling Successful

Family, friends, and social and professional support are all interrelated with job satisfaction in a worker's overall feeling of success. The success you feel in your future role as a worker will not exist separately from your

© JIST Works

life outside the job. Success will, in part, be determined by how well you plan a lifestyle that balances your time, energies, capabilities, and needs with the demands and rewards of your job.

Liking Your Job

Do you believe that interesting and fulfilling work, job security, or considerate management can be more important than the amount of a paycheck? Your definition of a satisfying job may change as you gain work experience and learn how your personal characteristics and goals fit or do not fit a particular job. You may find that progress is more important than you had believed or that coworkers and managers make a bigger difference in job satisfaction than you had imagined. You also may find that you are uncertain about your career choice. Keep in mind that every job has negative and positive factors. Expecting a job to be totally satisfying and free of frustrations is unrealistic.

Every job provides you with an opportunity to learn more about your personal likes and dislikes and to improve your skill in getting along with others. After a few months, you will be able to evaluate all aspects of having a job. You will realize that any job is the sum of all its parts and that the paycheck is just one of those parts.

Earning a Paycheck

Without adequate pay, the importance of the work tasks, **job security** (protection against loss of employment and earnings), and good management greatly diminishes. Compensation is the direct and indirect payment that employees receive for a job performed. In Chapter 12, you learned how fringe benefits become part of your paycheck in the form of indirect compensation. The part of the paycheck that provides you with a source of cash is **direct compensation**. The following terms are associated with direct compensation.

Signs of Job Dissatisfaction

Employees who are experiencing job dissatisfaction display the following symptoms. Watch for these symptoms in yourself as you participate in the world of work. If you are experiencing these symptoms on a regular basis, you may want to consider changing jobs or even careers:

- Increase in absenteeism or tardiness
- Inability to finish tasks in a timely manner
- Sick leave without medical causes
- Interpersonal conflicts and strained work relationships
- Low morale and productivity
- Physical complaints, such as headaches, back pain, and indigestion
- Alcohol or drug dependence

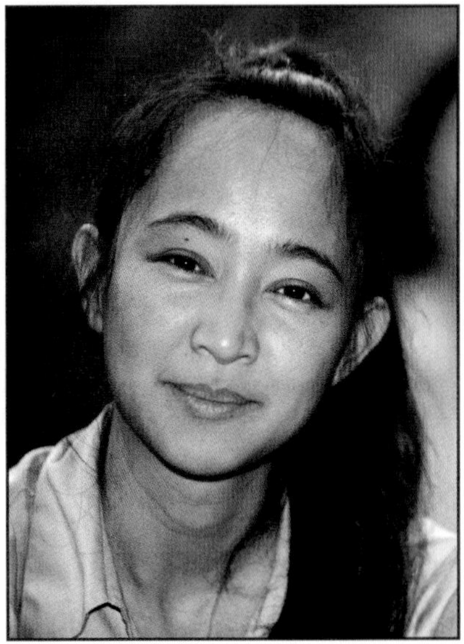

What will it take to make you feel successful?

Self-Understanding

Ask students to define success, as they perceive it. Then discuss how their personal expectations, attitudes, goals, family expectations, and accomplishments define personal success.

Discussion Starter

Ask your students: Is having interesting and fulfilling work, job security, considerate management, and pleasant coworkers more important than the amount of the paycheck? What are the reasons for your answer?

Community Resource

Ask a parent, relative, or adult friend about job rewards other than a paycheck. Report your findings to the class.

Key to Success

Building on past successes and failures helps you meet greater life challenges.

© JIST Works

Laura considers her job as a data control team leader to be interesting and fulfilling work. What job would you consider to be interesting and fulfilling?

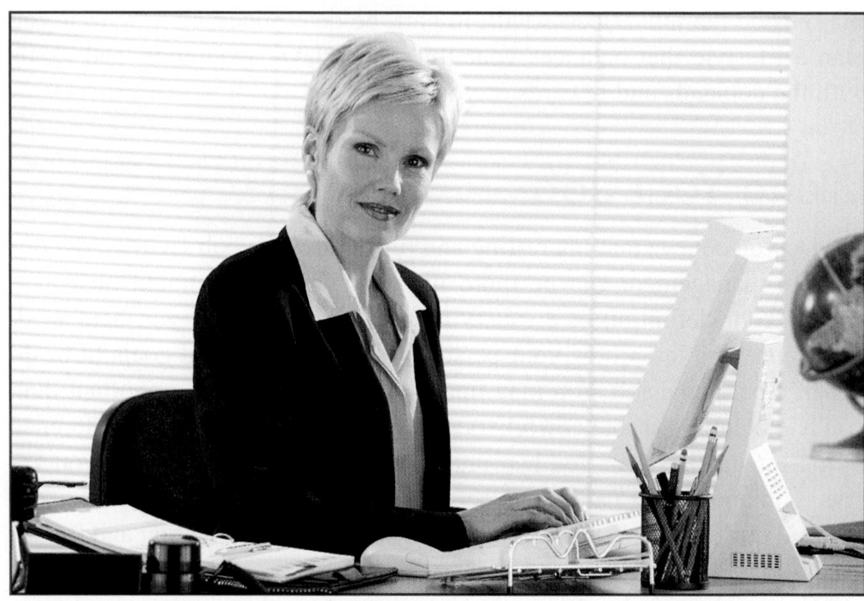

- **Salary:** Pay received by clerical, technical, professional, managerial, and other employees. Salary is usually calculated weekly or monthly.
- **Wages:** Employee compensation calculated hourly. Piecework wages are a set amount of money for each piece of work completed.
- **Net pay:** The amount an employee receives after deductions.
- **Base pay:** The regular salary or wage, excluding bonuses, fringe benefits, overtime pay, and all other extra compensation.
- **Incentives:** Extra financial payments for production above a predetermined standard. They depend on output rather than number of hours worked.
- **Premium pay:** Compensation at greater than regular rates. Examples are time and one-half when overtime is paid or an increased hourly rate for working certain shifts.
- **Commissions:** Percentage of sales paid to a salesperson. They are additions to a guaranteed salary rate or the total pay.
- **Cost-of-living adjustments** (COLAs): Pay increases based on an increase in the cost of living according to the U.S. Department of Labor's consumer price index studies.
- **Merit increases:** Increases in a worker's pay rate based on management's performance appraisal.
- **Profit sharing:** A bonus based on a percentage of the organization's profits.

Most entry-level jobs pay a straight salary or a specific hourly wage with overtime for hours worked beyond the regular schedule. However, many of today's organizations link the paycheck to achieving the employer's strategy. The role of pay is shifting from a way to compensate employees to a way to motivate them to achieve specific goals.

Comprehension Check

Ask your students to close their books. Ask several students to define *base pay* and *premium pay* in their own words.

Vocabulary Builder

Write the following terms on the chalkboard: *salary*, *commissions*, *wages*, *base pay*, *premium pay*, and *incentives*. Divide the class into learning pairs. Allow them 10 minutes to write as few correct sentences as possible using the six terms. (Terms are not to be used more than once.) Score: 1 point for each correct sentence; 1 point for each word used in a grammatically incorrect sentence; 1 point for each unused word. The pair with the lowest score wins.

Vocabulary Builder

Write the following terms on the chalkboard: *cost-of-living adjustments (COLAs), merit increase,* and *profit sharing.* Ask several students to make a statement of no more than four sentences using one of the terms on the chalkboard.

© JIST Works

Understanding Differences in Pay

Employers know that good pay attracts many people, which allows them to pick the most highly qualified applicants. When pay packages that include salary and wage scales are set, they are determined by the prevailing rates for a particular job in the organization, the competition's prevailing rate, and economic conditions.

Jobs have several characteristics that make them desirable or undesirable. Undesirable jobs involve monotony, danger, hard physical labor, irregular employment, low social prestige, or other features. For such work, a higher wage may be necessary to attract workers away from more desirable jobs that require similar skills. What jobs can you think of that fit this description?

Not all workers have identical talents, skills, and effectiveness. Thus, the supply of labor to various occupations is not the same. High wages tend to go to those who possess rare talents and skills that are in demand. For example, during the 1960s through the 1980s, the demand for computer-related positions was very great because few candidates were qualified for the numerous positions that needed filled. Then schools began turning out skilled programmers, operators, and analysts, and the demand eventually lessened. This area of employment is still growing rapidly, but organizations can now be more selective in hiring new employees.

Geographic location also affects wage rates. In most cases, higher wages in an area of the country are linked to a higher cost of living (food, housing, taxes). When you are considering a position, determine the amount of earnings that would be enough to cause you to relocate. Some people are reluctant to leave their homes and seek employment elsewhere because they would have to leave family and friends. Does this description apply to you?

TAKE NOTE

Retail workers shop for new jobs during the Christmas holiday season. Twenty-one percent of retail workers say they plan to change jobs between November and January, while 34 percent hope to find a new employer within six months. This is a good time to switch employers, considering 49 percent of retail hiring managers say they will continue adding new workers through the end of the year. According to CareerBuilder.com's recent survey, most employees leave retail companies because they desire a bigger paycheck, a job outside retail, and more options for growth in their careers.

Enrichment

Have students complete "The Wise Old Owl" activity in Chapter 13 of the *Preparing for Career Success Student Activity Book, Third Edition.*

Getting a Raise

You may hope that your boss recognizes what an outstanding contributor you are. However, waiting for a greater financial reward without asking for it may take a long time.

When you decide to seek a pay raise, improve your chance of success by following these guidelines:

1. **Know the organization's policy.** The type of job you have and the policy of your company will have a lot to do with when you will receive a raise in pay. If you do not know your company's policy on pay increases, the human resources department is a reliable source of information. Ask about your employer's compensation policies regarding cost-of-living increases, merit raises, hourly increases, and salary levels.

CAREER FACT

Are you looking for a job? In a tough economy, networking is the key. A study of 22 large companies by recruiter Wetfeet found that employee referrals were the single largest source of jobs. Thirty to forty percent of new hires' job leads come from "a friend who had a friend who had an uncle," according to *Fortune* magazine.

© JIST Works

Reteaching

Have students complete the "Asking for a Raise" worksheet found in the Chapter 13 file of the *Preparing for Career Success Instructor's CD-ROM, Third Edition.*

Enrichment

Assign a group of students to decorate a section of the bulletin board titled "Your Job's Market Value." Ask them to make subheadings of a few jobs commonly found in the help-wanted section of a newspaper. Assign the class to search for ads providing salary information, and post them under the appropriate job subheading on the bulletin board.

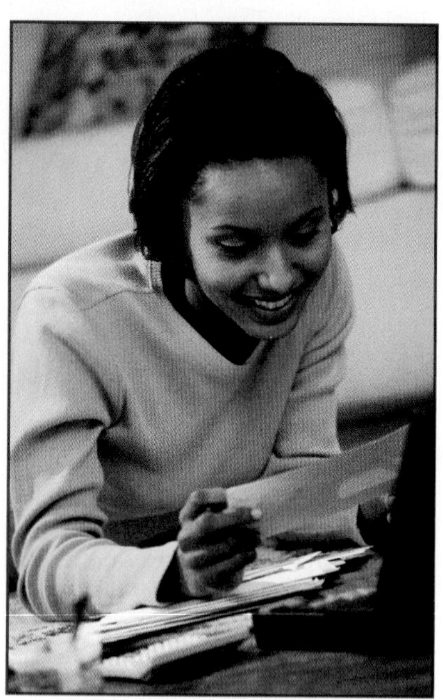

Rachel is glad that she followed the guidelines for getting a pay raise. Being a well-qualified worker and knowing how to acquire a pay raise are important success factors.

2. **Request a meeting with your supervisor.** Give your supervisor advance notice by writing a note requesting a personal meeting and stating your intent. Formally requesting a meeting is good business etiquette and gives your supervisor time to analyze the budget and consider your pay-raise request before meeting with you.
3. **Prepare for the meeting.** Know why you deserve a raise. Make a list of your accomplishments and contributions to the organization from the time you were hired or your last raise. Know the dollar amount you believe you should receive.
4. **Know your market value.** Learn what your skills are worth and how much replacing you would cost by asking workers in similar jobs and reading government compensation reports and job advertisements in newspapers and trade journals to find out the typical salaries or wages for positions similar to yours.
5. **Time your request well.** Because most raises are based on merit, a good time to ask for one is during the performance appraisal meeting or when the supervisor offers you a promotion or asks you to take on extra responsibilities. Avoid asking for raises when you know that the organization has budget problems. Try to ask when the organization is doing well.
6. **Avoid confrontation.** Never threaten to quit if you do not get a raise. Your supervisor knows whether you are a valuable employee and whether you can sell your expertise elsewhere. Your boss may not have the authority to give you a raise and will need to convince superiors about your worth.
7. **Anticipate objections.** Your supervisor may present several different arguments for refusing to grant your request for a raise. If the supervisor tells you that the company cannot afford your salary increase, ask for a date to renegotiate. Repeat that you like your job but feel that you are worth more. If the supervisor tells you that you are not ready for a raise, ask what you can do or learn to merit a raise.
8. **Stay positive.** Do not respond to a rejection by voicing negative opinions to fellow employees or by being less productive. This type of behavior can only hurt you if you stay with the employer, and it will influence your boss's recommendation if you leave for another job. The reason for the rejection could be valid.
9. **Be gracious.** Thank your supervisor when you do get a raise. Being gracious is good business etiquette.

A growing number of employers are using new procedures for pay raises that link the employee's paycheck to the employer's goals. See Table 13.1 to compare the traditional methods of qualifying for a pay raise with a sample of new methods.

© JIST Works

Table 13.1 Pay Raises in the Modern Workplace

Traditional Methods	New Methods
Years of service with the organization	Gain sharing (you and your boss share profits)
Cost-of-living adjustments (COLAs)	Team-based pay (your group's production)
Job title	Lump-sum merit pay
Job responsibilities	Competency-based pay (your skills)
Annual performance evaluation	Employer's quarterly profits

Section 1: Get Involved

The following questions evaluate your feelings about work. If you are not employed, substitute the word schoolwork for work. After answering these questions, ask an adult worker to answer them, and then compare your answers:

Family Satisfaction

1. Is it easy for you to talk with family members about your work (schoolwork)?
2. Do family members seem interested in your work (schoolwork)?
3. Would you discuss a new job opportunity (or a new course at school) with family members before making a change?

Friendship Satisfaction

4. Do you consider any of your coworkers (fellow students) to be close friends?
5. If you had a problem, would you ask one of these friends for help?

Work Satisfaction

6. Are you generally satisfied with your job (school)?
7. Do you like your job (school) environment (surroundings)?
8. Considering your present age, are you satisfied with your success as a worker (student)?

If you answered yes to all eight statements, you have exceptional career or school satisfaction. If you answered no to more than one statement in each category, you should consider ways to improve your satisfaction in that area.

Section 2: Changing Jobs

Millions of Americans choose to change jobs each year. Additional millions have no choice in the matter. Increasingly competitive economic situations cause employers to reorganize, close, and make major technological changes. In turn, workers must become flexible in a competitive job market. Increasing numbers of American workers are acquiring more education and training after high school to prepare for jobs with higher skill requirements.

If you are like most workers, you will leave your first job after high school within two years. Whether you are considering a move to another department, moving to a different employer, or retraining for a different profession, changing jobs is a large part of career success.

Self-Understanding

Ask your students: Have any students in the class moved to this area because of a family member's job? Ask those students: What feelings did you have when you moved? Have your feelings changed or remained the same? If you were an adult worker, would you be willing to relocate for a better job? Why or why not?

© JIST Works

KEY TO SUCCESS

Whenever you are considering a career change, reevaluate your interests, goals, and skills before making a final decision.

Case Study

Have your students read the case study "Keep the Goal in Sight" found in the Chapter 13 file of the *Preparing for Career Success Instructor's CD-ROM, Third Edition* and discuss the "Critical Thinking" questions.

Comprehension Check

After your students finish reading "The Right Time?" ask them to close their books. Ask several students: In your own words, what do *worth* and *experience* mean and what improvements should you make before you change jobs?

CAREER FACT

In most occupations, replacement needs provide more job openings than growth. Replacement openings occur as people leave jobs. Some individuals transfer to other occupations as a step up the career ladder or to change careers; some stop working temporarily, perhaps to return to school or care for a family; other workers—retirees, for example—leave the labor force permanently.

Reteaching

Have students complete the "Responsible Resignation" worksheet found in the Chapter 13 file of the *Preparing for Career Success Instructor's CD-ROM, Third Edition.*

The Right Time?

When you begin thinking about making a job change, one of your first considerations should be whether you are genuinely dissatisfied with your career path or just unhappy with your present job. After you answer this question, you should determine the reasons behind your feelings. Otherwise, you could end up in a different job with the same problems.

After several months or a year in a job, you may discover that what you thought you wanted in a job is not what you want at all. If that's the case, it may be a good time to reconsider your career path.

However, do not make a hasty career decision and quit a job too quickly. People who quit their jobs appear to be just that—quitters. Always make certain that there is a significant, clearly defined benefit to making a job change. If you are seeking a pay increase or promotion, keep in mind that you need enough time on the job to gain experience. Less than a year is rarely enough.

Even if you are dissatisfied with your current job, you can still use it to learn more about yourself and gain valuable work experience, such as improved human relations skills and more training. When you search for a new job, you need to be able to document your experience and worth as an employee.

If you decide to separate from your current employer, proceed with caution. Develop a strategy to ensure that your next job is a significant improvement. You are better off quietly beginning the job search while enjoying the pay and benefits of your existing job. If you look for a new job while you are still working, you will have the additional advantage of continuing income and not losing accumulated benefits such as vacation time, retirement, and insurance.

The Process of Resigning

You race past the receptionist and throw open the great oak door that separates your boss from the rest of the workers. "I quit," you scream as you slam your letter of resignation down on the enormous desk. That scenario may work in your dreams, but in the real world of work, resigning from a job should be a mature, well-planned decision.

Never permit your anger to determine your career path. Bad feelings between you and your coworkers and/or management have the potential for harming your future career choices. Your complaints, negative comments, and ill will have a way of coming back to haunt you. You might need to ask your present boss for a reference. Or you may want to return to your employer later in your career. The new employee that you treated well could be the president of the company 10 years from now. If you resign, leave a trail of goodwill, friendly faces, and professional respect behind.

Self-Understanding

Ask students to look again at the section on work values in Chapter 3. Then ask your students: Which of your work-related values would be most likely to cause you to resign from a job? Why?

© JIST Works

A responsible employee still accepts and performs assigned work tasks until the last day of employment is completed. Carrying out all duties and responsibilities to the best of your ability with a positive attitude will continue your record of accomplishment, even though you are seeking a change or even working out a *notice* (the period when you are still employed but have established a date for terminating your employment).

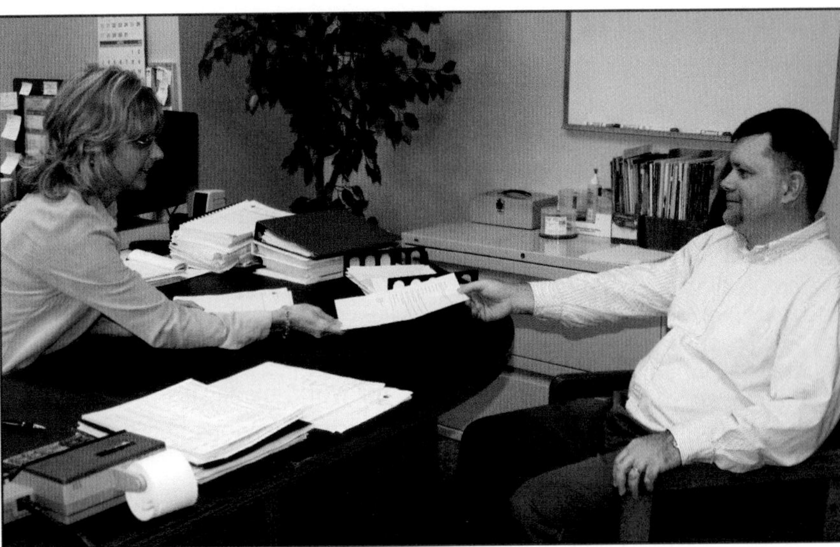

Daniel Ward is submitting his letter of resignation to accept a higher-level position with another employer. He is proud of his work and appreciates his boss and coworkers.

Giving a minimum of two weeks' advance notice of your intent to resign is good business etiquette. Do this face-to-face with your supervisor or the personnel administrator. In your meeting, do not criticize the organization, your coworkers, or the management. Likewise, do not offer unsolicited advice on how to improve the organization. Instead, mention the good things that have happened, thank your boss for the positive things he or she has done, wish him or her good luck, and leave with a handshake. Always volunteer to train your successor and complete any unfinished work. No one will blame you for seeking a better job.

If your employer requests a letter of resignation, keep it very positive. Simply write out the statements you plan to make when you resign. The managers in an organization will change over a period of years, and so will the workers. Having a good record on file may help you at some future date.

When you leave a job, schedule an appointment with your employer's benefits coordinator. Make sure that you receive payment to which you may be entitled for any unused vacation and that you understand what you need to do to roll over any accumulated retirement funds to a new retirement account.

Key to Success

When you resign from a job, tell your supervisor you are leaving before you tell coworkers. You do not want management to find out your plans from office gossip.

Section 2: Get Involved

From the early 1900s until the 1970s, employees commonly stayed with one employer for 25 or even 40 years and retired with a lifetime pension. Ask your grandparents or someone who is now retired the following questions about those days. Record your answers on a separate sheet of paper, and be prepared to discuss your responses in class.

1. Do you feel that career opportunities were better in the past?
2. Did you have more job security than most workers do today?
3. Did you change employers after you were 30 years old?
4. What was the longest number of years you worked for one employer?
5. Did your employer honor you when you retired?

Section 3: Losing Your Job

Comprehension Check

Explain to your class that the term *unemployed* has a technical meaning for the Bureau of Labor Statistics. People without jobs who are not available for work and make no specific effort to obtain a job during the reporting period are not counted as "unemployed." Ask your students: Can you think of reasons why some people without jobs don't try to find a job?

Discussion Starter

Have your students review Figure 13.1. Call to their attention the importance of having a low unemployment rate. Ask your students: How many additional workers would be unemployed if the rate jumps from 5 percent to 7 percent (three million)? Also ask your students: How will this increased number of unemployed workers affect your daily life? How might it affect the daily lives of three million families?

Cooperative Learning

Have students complete the "Brain Drain" worksheet found in the Chapter 13 file of the *Preparing for Career Success Instructor's CD-ROM, Third Edition.*

During the first year of full-time employment, millions of workers in the American labor force will change jobs. Many of these workers will be victims of layoffs or firings. For many, being out of work will have negative, even devastating, effects on their standard of living and self-esteem. At some time during your career, you may temporarily join the ranks of the unemployed (see Figure 13.1).

The Bureau of Labor Statistics classifies people as **unemployed** if, while it was conducting its survey, they had no employment, were available for work, made specific efforts to find employment, had been laid off from their former jobs and were awaiting recall, or expected to report to a job within 30 days.

Unemployment can occur for reasons beyond the control of the individual worker. These reasons include the following:

- An organizational **merger** (the joining together of organizations), or *acquisitions* (purchase of one organization by another), such as two banks joining to form one or one bank buying the other.
- An economic downturn resulting in a nationwide recession.
- A technological change that eliminates a whole industry. The automobile industry replaced the carriage industry, for example, and computer technology lessened the need for numerous workers.
- Seasonal work, such as agriculture and construction, that can occur only during certain months.
- An organization or industry moving to another location.
- A labor market imbalance caused by closing a factory or completing a large construction project.

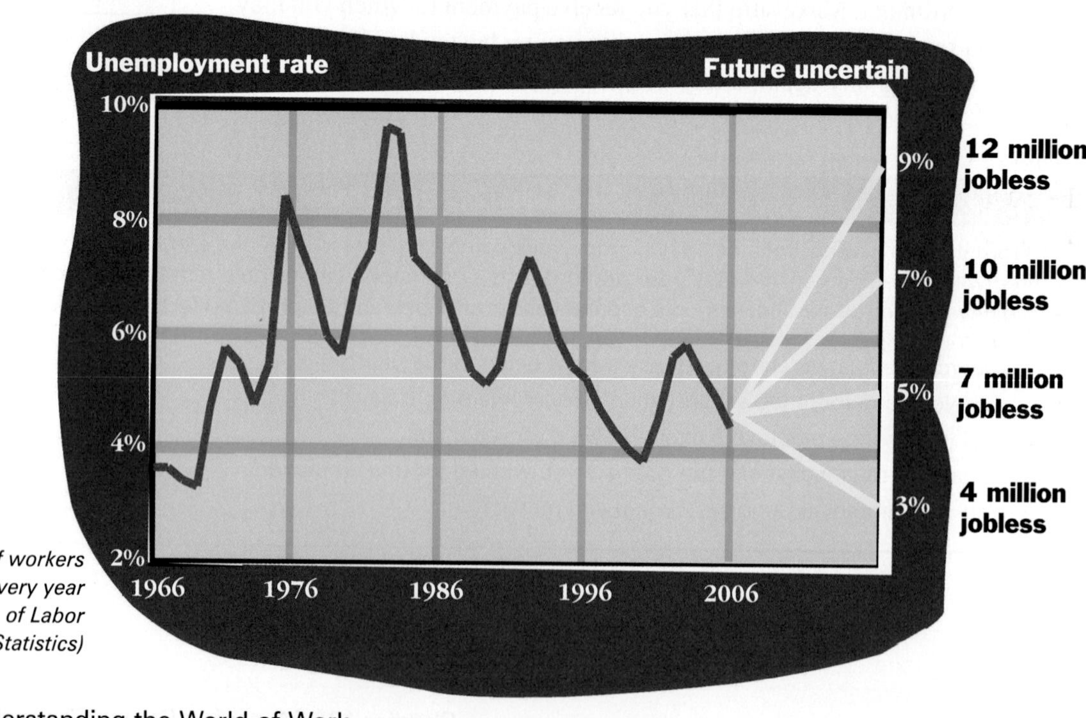

Figure 13.1 Millions of workers are unemployed every year (Source: U.S. Bureau of Labor Statistics)

© JIST Works

- **Downsizing**, or reducing an organization's size to increase efficiency. Job cuts are driven by a desire for increased operating efficiency and/or labor cost.

Whatever the cause of unemployment, those who are most highly skilled and trained have the most probability of being reemployed. Why do you think a worker's level of education has such a significant effect on his or her employment opportunities?

Enrichment

Have students complete the "Losing Your Job" worksheet in Chapter 13 of the *Preparing for Career Success Student Activity Book, Third Edition.*

Layoffs

A **layoff** is an involuntary separation of an employee from an employer for a temporary or indefinite period, through no fault of the employee. The term *layoff* suggests that employers intend to eventually recall workers. The term *reduction in force* usually signifies a permanent layoff. Employers often lay off employees during a time of economic *recession* (slowdown).

Organizations are not consistent in the policies they use to lay off or terminate employees. The methods used by some employers are almost horror stories. For example, when employees at one New England newspaper tried to log on to their desktop computers, they could not get into the system. Instead, the computer directed them to an editor's office, where they received an envelope containing either a new password for the computer, which meant that they still had a job, or a note to see a supervisor, which meant they would be receiving a **pink slip** (notice of termination).

Most organizations are not this insensitive. They try to ease the pain of reducing their workforce at considerable expense to the organization. They may offer employees voluntary buyouts or outplacement programs.

Voluntary buyouts include early-retirement programs and severance pay. Early-retirement programs add additional years to an older employee's length of service at the company to increase an eligible worker's pension benefit. **Severance pay** offers an eligible employee who retires or leaves the organization before retirement a certain number of weeks' pay for each year of service with the company. One large organization offered 30 months' pay to any employee who agreed to leave. In these programs, employees have a "window of time"—typically 60 to 90 days—in which to accept or reject the offer. The employer may also offer these employees an extension of health insurance and other benefits.

Outplacement programs provide assistance and training to released employees who are seeking new positions. These programs help terminated employees face the shock of being unemployed, deal with personal feelings, and put the termination into perspective. Counseling helps employees reassess their interests, values, and skills and set short- and long-term goals. Occupational and organizational information is made available, and assistance with resume writing, job searching, and interviewing techniques is provided.

Unemployment insurance is a joint federal-state program under which state-administered funds pay a weekly benefit for a limited time to eligible workers when they are involuntarily unemployed. The purpose of the payment is to assist unemployed workers until they find jobs for which they are

CAREER FACT

The Worker Adjustment and Retraining Notification Act (WARN) protects workers, their families, and communities by requiring employers to provide notification 60 calendar days in advance of plant closings and mass layoffs. WARN includes managers and supervisors as well as hourly and salaried workers.

TAKE NOTE

The earliest instance of U.S. Congressional action regulating trade in goods produced abroad under substandard labor conditions was the Tariff Act of 1890, which banned imports of goods manufactured by convict labor. This act protected U.S. workers from foreign competition that relied on low-cost convict labor.

reasonably suited in terms of training, past experience, and past wages. Cash benefits are paid. Federal law establishes certain minimum requirements, but each state determines who is eligible, how much money each person receives, and how long benefits are paid. To be eligible, a person must be unemployed, able to work, available for employment, and seeking work. All employers are required to pay premiums for this insurance.

Vocabulary Builder/ Cooperative Learning

Write the following terms on the chalkboard: *layoff*, *pink slip*, *severance pay*, and *outplacement program*. Divide the class into learning pairs. Pass a sheet of paper to each pair, and explain the following rules:

1. Each pair must write three grammatically correct sentences.
2. Each sentence must contain at least one of the four terms on the chalkboard.
3. Do not use a term more than once.

Explain that the first team to finish wins if all three sentences are correct. Then start the students as you would a race.

Comprehension Check

Instruct your students to close their books. Then ask them: In your own words, what is the purpose of giving unemployment insurance payments to unemployed workers? Do you think this is a good idea? Why or why not?

Career Fact

Trade Adjustment Assistance (TAA) is available to workers who lose their jobs or whose hours of work and wages are reduced by increased imports. Under the Trade Act of 1974, workers who lose their jobs or whose hours of work are reduced by increased imports may apply for TAA benefits and reemployment services. TAA provides job training, a job search allowance, a relocation allowance, and weekly trade adjustment allowances. For more information, use your search engine to contact the U.S. Department of Labor, Employment and Training Administration Program.

Building Character: Persistence Pays

As Ken Schaum cast his line into the still waters around the boat, he glanced at his grandfather. He hated to tell him that he was out of work and could not find a job. Grandpa had always had a good job, and Ken did not want to seem like a failure. Ken was thinking about how proud Grandpa had been two years ago when Ken started working at DRS Bearings, the same firm that Grandpa had retired from after 42 years of service. Now Ken had to tell him that DRS had laid him off.

Ken started talking, and the story poured out. DRS planned to close the plant. Ken's interviews with six other employers had all ended in rejection. He was so embarrassed that he almost hated to have another employer interview him for fear that the employer would reject him.

Grandpa listened quietly, and then he reminded Ken about the vegetable garden they had planted when Ken was in the fifth grade. They worked an entire day preparing the soil and planting the seeds. Ken checked the garden every day, but nothing seemed to be growing. He became discouraged. Then one morning, Ken and Grandpa went out to look at the garden and saw the first green sprouts coming through the ground.

They were both quiet for a while, and then Grandpa said, "I was proud of you then, and I'm proud of you now. You're not a quitter, Ken."

That evening at home, Ken thought a lot about being laid off, searching for a new job, and the garden he had helped to plant years ago. He sorted through several employment ads he had cut out of the newspaper but had not answered. He would send his resume to those employers in the morning, and this time he would be proud of himself.

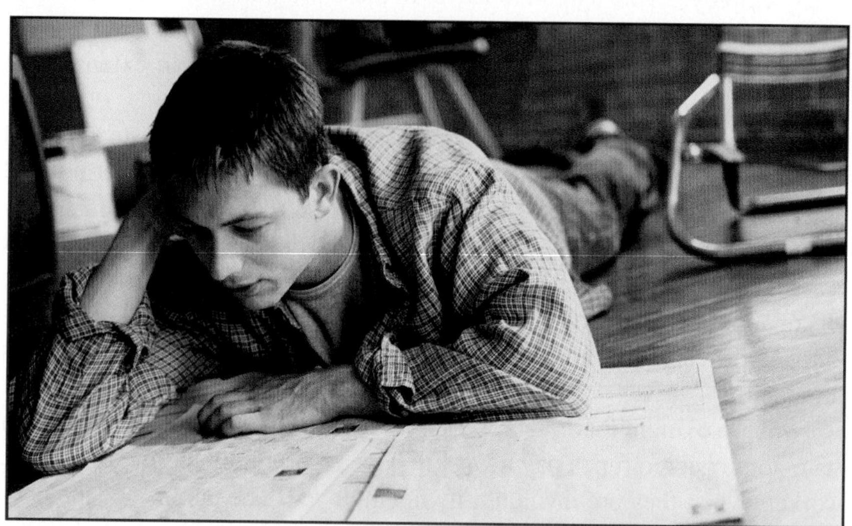

© JIST Works

Critical Thinking

On a separate sheet of paper, describe something you have accomplished that makes you feel proud. List any failures you experienced before you succeeded. How did you overcome your failures? What advice would you give to someone who wanted to accomplish what you have done?

Ken overcame his feeling of depression and increased his sense of personal confidence. Using events in the story, list as many reasons as you can for Ken's change of attitude. Can you use any of these reasons to increase your sense of confidence? If so, how? If not, why not?

Cluster Link

Although production occupations are experiencing job losses to foreign competition, they are projected to add 164,184 new jobs between 2006 and 2016.
If you are interested in the occupations of welder, machinist, or food processing worker, review the Manufacturing career cluster. See the appendix for more information.

Termination by Discharge

Discharge of an employee means dismissal from employment. The term implies discipline for unsatisfactory performance. Virtually all courts have supported the employer's right to discharge an employee who is demonstrably unacceptable, incompetent, lazy, uncooperative, or abusive to other employees.

There is no general law that prohibits private employers from discharging employees without good cause. Employers have historically had the right to fire employees at will unless a written contract protected against this type of dismissal. This broad right has been limited by federal laws that prohibit discrimination based on gender, race, color, religion, national origin, age, physical or mental disability, union activity, wage garnishment, and filing complaints or assisting in procedures related to enforcing these laws.

Cooperative Learning

Divide your class into small groups. Assign each group to write about a work situation in which one employee is obviously unacceptable, incompetent, lazy, uncooperative, or abusive to other employees. Allow time for each group to present their work to the class.

In addition to federal laws, some states and municipalities have passed laws prohibiting employers from discharging employees who serve on jury duty, file workers' compensation claims, or refuse lie detector tests or from discriminating against employees based on marital status or sexual orientation. Employee complaint procedures and collective bargaining agreements between employers and unions also place limitations on an employer's absolute right to fire workers.

Some employees who have challenged their discharges in court have succeeded in placing additional limitations on the employer's right to discharge. For example, an employer cannot discharge an employee

- For refusing to commit *perjury* (swearing that something is true when you know it is false)
- For refusing to approve market testing of a potentially harmful drug when it is not based on good faith and fair dealing
- For refusing to date a supervisor
- To save the employer from paying a large commission

Career Fact

In most firings, the released employee has an idea that termination is coming because he or she has received a bad performance rating or a warning from the supervisor. Alternatively, the boss may avoid talking to the employee, may give fewer assignments without any explanation, or may increase the number of reviews of the employee's work performance.

In some organizations, employers give a series of progressively more serious warnings to hourly employees before termination. The supervisor gives the employee formal notification of the need for improvement in

TECHNOLOGY

Many employers use different types of workplace surveillance technology to monitor their employees' activities. For example, businesses such as banks, casinos, and convenience stores use closed-circuit television, a system of video cameras connected to a set of monitors and video recorders. Call centers often record their employees' phone conversations with customers. Other types of businesses use computer monitoring programs to check employees' keystrokes, e-mail messages, or Internet use. Employees are often disciplined or even fired as a result of inappropriate actions that are recorded with surveillance technology.

specific areas of performance and provides an opportunity for the employee to improve. Discharge is a last resort. Some notified employees quit before the situation deteriorates into a discharge.

If your supervisor calls you into the office and discharges you because of a fault in your work performance, follow this advice:

1. Do not lose your temper. Accept the firing calmly, and maintain your dignity. The time to deal with your emotions is when you are away from the boss's office.
2. Ask your boss or the personnel staff for help in finding a new job. You may be eligible for severance pay, unemployment insurance, unused vacation time, and COBRA benefits.

Your Emotions

If your employer discharges you or lays you off, feeling angry, shocked, and betrayed is normal. Talking through your experience and feelings with someone you trust can be helpful at this time. Feelings of failure, fears for the future, concerns about financial problems, and self-pity are to be expected. Most people experience the following four stages of recovery from the loss of employment:

- **Shock:** If the layoff or firing was unexpected, you may be so shocked that you are not fully aware of what has happened.
- **Denial:** You may have difficulty believing what has happened. This stage can become an emotional burden that requires outside help. Time and help will bring relief. When you throw away the burden of denial, you can become excited about your career again.
- **Anger:** Anger is a healthy emotion if vented in channels that are nonharmful to you or others. It cleanses the mind of a lot of nonproductive, negative thoughts. For some, depression creeps in at this stage; if this happens to you, tell your physician.
- **Acceptance:** In the final stage, you come to terms with reality and generate the energy and desire to move beyond the loss of your job.

When you face difficult career choices, reappraise yourself and your career path by talking openly with a friend, relative, religious leader, or counselor you trust.

Without question, the stage of acceptance is the most desirable place for your emotions to be when you look for new employment. Unfortunately, responsibilities such as paying rent, making car payments,

© JIST Works

and putting food on the table prevent most people from dealing with their emotions in a timely and orderly manner.

Although you may feel down, continue to spend time with friends and family, pursue leisure activities, and, above all, maintain your sense of humor. When you reestablish your career and become a decision maker in an organization, do not forget what you have learned from this experience. Your past failures can become stepping stones to career success.

COBRA

In 1985, Congress passed the Consolidated Omnibus Budget Reconciliation Act (**COBRA**). This law enables certain terminated employees, or those who lose insurance coverage because of reduced work, to buy group insurance coverage for themselves and their families. When the former employee selects COBRA coverage, he or she must pay the insurance premiums. The former employer can charge up to 102 percent of the insurance premium cost.

Group health coverage for COBRA participants is usually more expensive than health coverage for active employees because the employer usually pays a large part of the premium for employees. However, it is ordinarily less expensive than individual health coverage. For example, if you are terminated but have participated in the group health plan maintained by your employer, you may choose to pay for a maximum of 18 months coverage at the company's group health rate plus 2 percent.

Career Fact

If your employer has fewer than 20 employees, you will not be entitled to COBRA coverage.

Enrichment

Have students complete the "COBRA" worksheet found in the Chapter 13 file of the *Preparing for Career Success Instructor's CD-ROM, Third Edition.*

A New Beginning

Reappraise yourself and your career path after you overcome your feelings of fear and doubt. Take inventory, and make sure you understand the reasons for the discharge. If the firing was your fault, take measures to correct your failings before starting a new job. To do that, consider these questions:

1. Were you qualified for the job? If not, what can you do to become qualified?
2. Did you have enough experience for the job level? If not, what job level would be appropriate for your experience?
3. Did you get along with management and coworkers?
4. Did you follow the organization's rules and carry out your job responsibilities?
5. Were you dependable?

If you allow it, a new career direction will emerge from your experience and change your life in positive ways. Take this opportunity to reevaluate your attitudes, values, and career goals. When you begin planning for the future and set out on a new job search, review and use the techniques

Key To Success

When you interview for your next position, do not make the mistake of attaching more importance to being laid off or fired than is necessary. The interviewer is more interested in your qualifications for the job opening than in your past. Do not volunteer information, but when the interviewer asks you about losing your job, make a brief, honest response while keeping the details and negative feelings to yourself.

© JIST Works

you learned in Chapters 8 and 9. Think of losing your job as presenting a new opportunity to advance professionally and move upward toward your long-term goal.

Section 3: Get Involved

Answer the following on a separate sheet of paper, and be prepared to discuss your responses in class.

1. What do you think could be done to help the unemployed find employment sooner?
2. If you exhausted your unemployment benefits, what changes in lifestyle would you have to make?
3. Employers gave the following reasons to the Department of Labor for laying off employees: automation, business ownership change, contract completion, import competition, material shortages, overseas relocation, seasonal work, vacation period, bankruptcy, contract cancellation, domestic relocation, dispute between labor and management, model changeover, plant or machine repairs, slack work, and weather-related curtailment. Which of these reasons would most likely result in a temporary layoff? Which would result in a permanent layoff? Explain your answers.

Reteaching

Have students complete the "Finding the Right Words" and "Checking Your Location" worksheets in Chapter 13 of the *Preparing for Career Success Student Activity Book, Third Edition.*

Enrich Your Vocabulary Answers

1. direct compensation
2. unemployment insurance
3. wages
4. incentives
5. commissions
6. premium pay
7. cost-of-living adjustments
8. profit sharing
9. net pay
10. base pay
11. salary
12. unemployed
13. job security
14. layoff

(continued)

Chapter 13 Review

Enrich Your Vocabulary

On a separate sheet of paper, number from 1 to 22, and write a term from the "Enrich Your Vocabulary" list at the beginning of the chapter next to the number of the statement it matches.

1. The part of your paycheck that provides you with cash
2. Provides a weekly benefit to qualified workers who don't have jobs
3. Employee compensation that is calculated hourly
4. Extra financial payments for production above a standard
5. Compensation to salespeople based on a percentage of sales
6. Compensation at greater than regular rates
7. Wage changes based on the consumer price index
8. Incentive compensation in which a company shares financial gains with employees
9. The amount an employee receives after deductions
10. The regular salary or wage, excluding all other compensation
11. Employee compensation that is calculated weekly, biweekly, monthly, or annually
12. Without a job and looking for work
13. Protection against loss of employment and earnings
14. An involuntary separation from a job for an indefinite time

© JIST Works

15. A lump-sum payment in exchange for quitting or retiring from a job
16. Assistance and training to help released employees find new jobs
17. Dismissal from a job for discipline or unsatisfactory performance
18. Consolidated Omnibus Budget Reconciliation Act of 1985
19. A written notice of discharge or layoff
20. A pay raise given for efficiency or performance
21. The joining together of organizations
22. Reducing an organization's size to increase efficiency

Enrich Your Vocabulary Answers *(continued)*

15. severance pay
16. outplacement programs
17. discharge
18. COBRA
19. pink slip
20. merit increase
21. merger
22. downsizing

Check Your Knowledge

On a separate sheet of paper, answer the following questions.

1. What are five indicators that suggest an employee is dissatisfied with the job?
2. What factors determine wage scales or salary for a particular job?
3. What would be a good time to ask for a pay raise?
4. What factors have increased the number of job changes that workers make?
5. What effect does a layoff or firing have on workers?
6. What has limited the employer's right to fire employees at will?
7. What are the normal feelings of a worker who is fired or laid off?

Answers to Check Your Knowledge

1. Increased absenteeism or tardiness, inability to finish tasks, sick leave without medical causes, interpersonal conflicts, low morale and productivity, physical complaints, and alcohol or drug dependence.
2. Prevailing rates for the job, the organization, competition, and economic conditions.
3. During a performance appraisal meeting, when you are given a promotion or asked to take on additional responsibilities, and during times of economic prosperity.
4. Tight and competitive economic situations have caused employers to reorganize, close, and make major technological changes. Workers are forced to be flexible in a competitive market.
5. It negatively affects their standard of living and their self-esteem.
6. A broad range of federal, state, and local laws that prohibit discrimination and limit reasons for discharge.
7. Anger at the boss, shame, feelings of failure, fears for the future, concern over financial problems, sadness, and self-pity.

Develop SCANS Competencies

This activity will give you practice in developing the information and interpersonal skills you need to be a successful worker. Conduct a telephone survey of businesses in your area to find what types of direct compensation are paid to employees. Choose a variety of businesses, such as those that hire unskilled labor, those that hire skilled labor, and those that hire professional help.

Ask each business you call what type of direct compensation employees receive. You might want to give respondents a choice of answers, such as hourly pay, salary, overtime pay, bonuses, and commissions. Be sure to write down the type of businesses you call (service, retail, manufacturing, and so on) and the answers you get from each business. After you have accumulated all of your data, analyze the results. Try to determine whether one type of business seems to offer a better pay package than other types of businesses.

Enrichment

Have students complete the Chapter 13 section of the *Preparing for Career Success Student Portfolio, Third Edition.*

Chapter 14 Resources

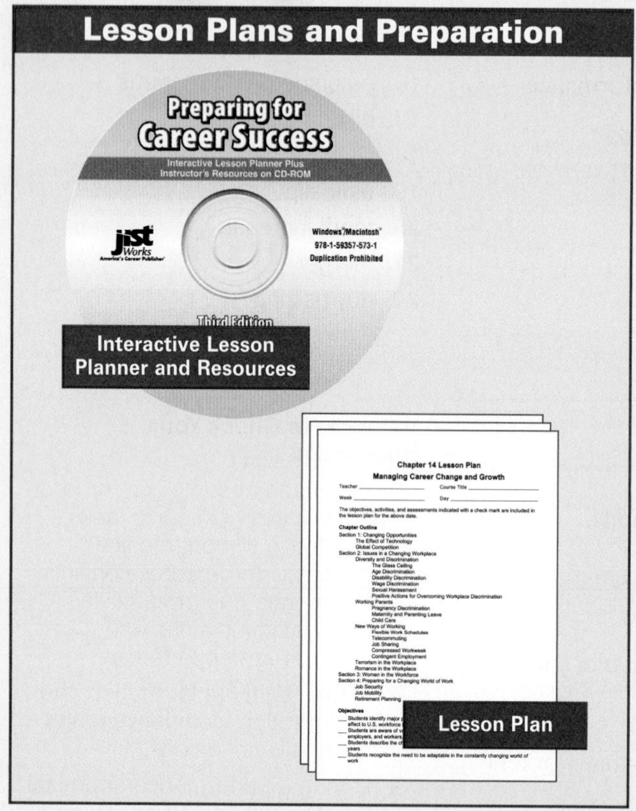

Lesson Plans and Preparation
Preparing for Career Success
Interactive Lesson Planner Plus Instructor's Resources on CD-ROM
Windows/Macintosh
978-1-59357-573-1
Duplication Prohibited
Third Edition
Interactive Lesson Planner and Resources
Chapter 14 Lesson Plan
Managing Career Change and Growth
Lesson Plan

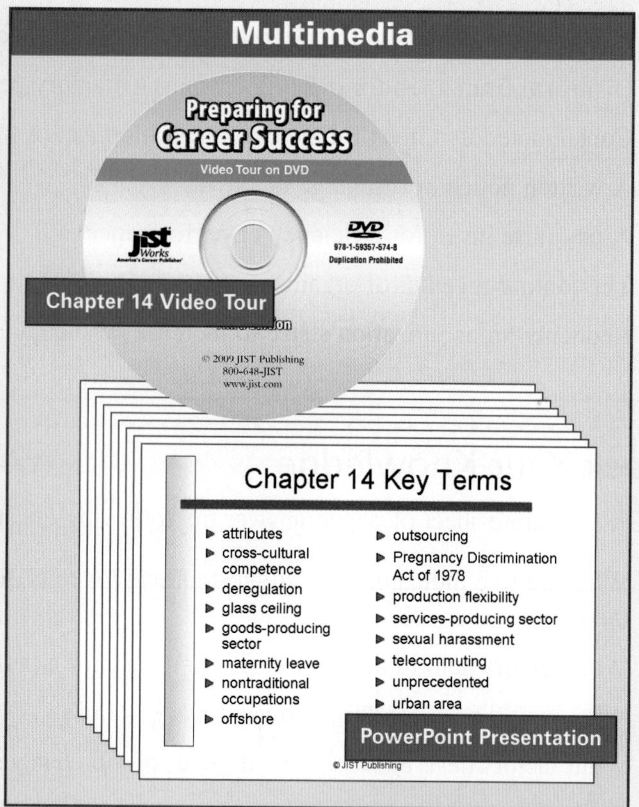

Multimedia
Preparing for Career Success
Video Tour on DVD
978-1-59357-574-8
Duplication Prohibited
Chapter 14 Video Tour
© 2009 JIST Publishing
800-648-JIST
www.jist.com
Chapter 14 Key Terms
attributes
cross-cultural competence
deregulation
glass ceiling
goods-producing sector
maternity leave
nontraditional occupations
offshore
outsourcing
Pregnancy Discrimination Act of 1978
production flexibility
services-producing sector
sexual harassment
telecommuting
unprecedented
urban area
PowerPoint Presentation
© JIST Publishing

Activities

- The Past—The Future
- Issues: Sexual Harassment, Pregnancy, and Contingent Employment
- Making the Labor Market Fair for All Workers
- Men's Roles—Women's Roles
- Job Mobility and Adapting to Change
- A Change of Pace
- Solving the Problem: Protecting Unborn Children
- Stopping Sexual Harassment
- Chapter 14 Portfolio

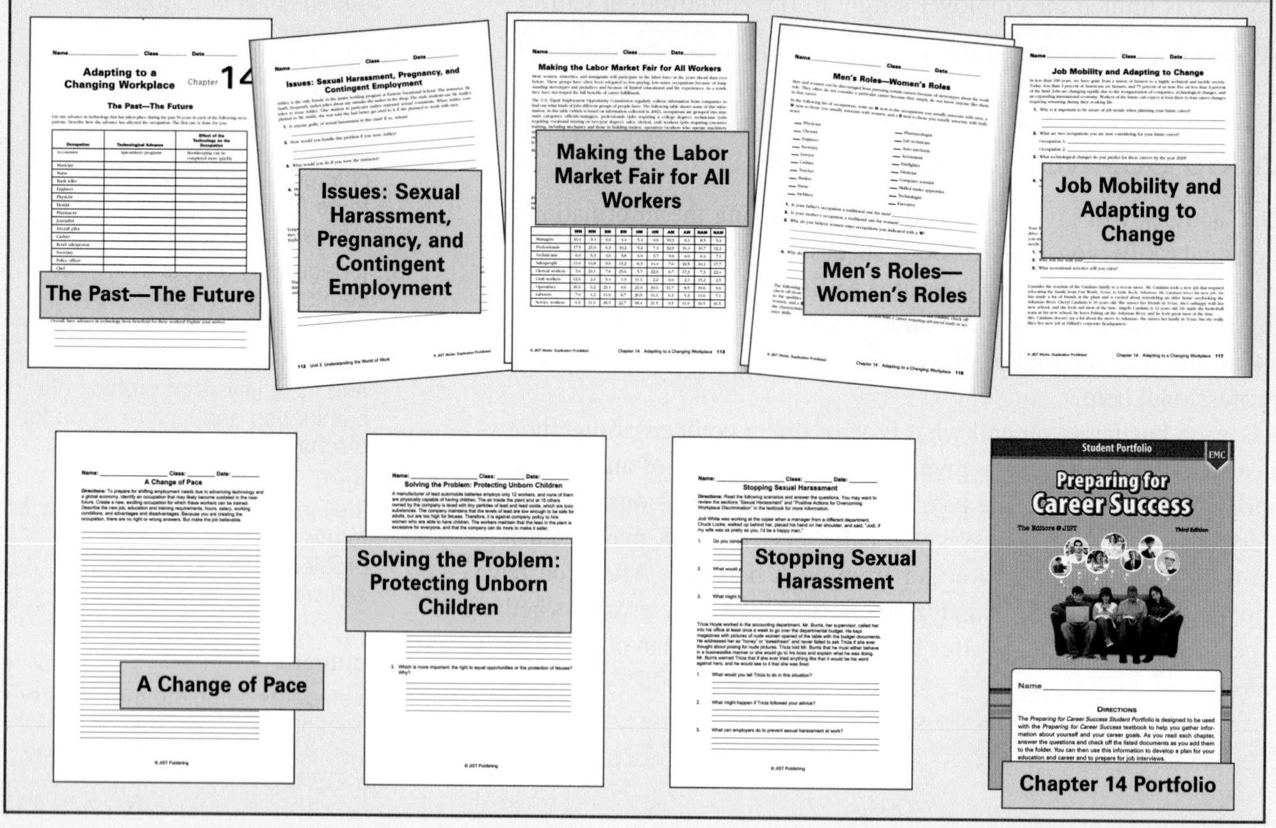

© JIST Works

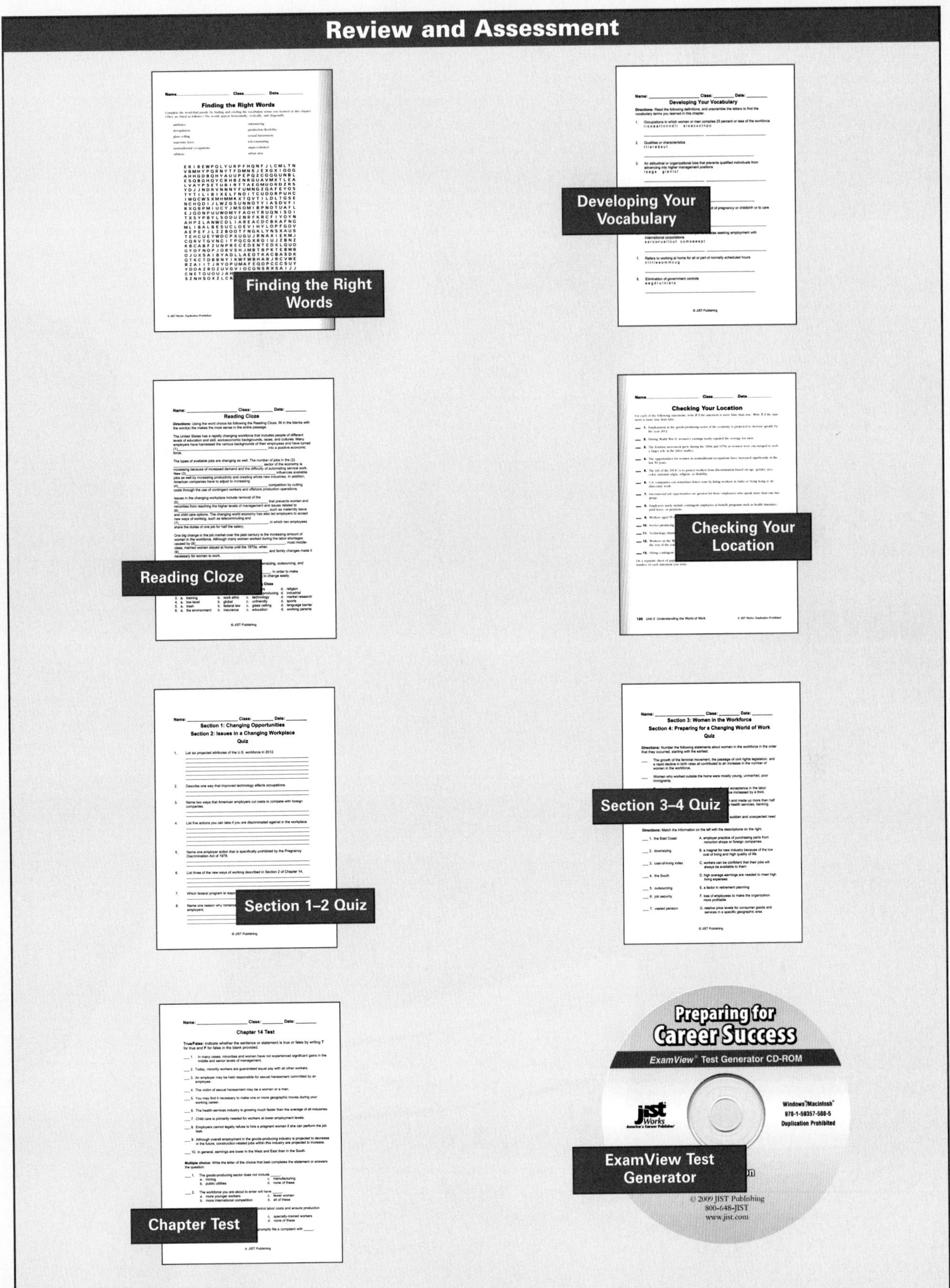
Review and Assessment
Finding the Right Words
Developing Your Vocabulary
Reading Cloze
Checking Your Location
Section 1–2 Quiz
Section 3–4 Quiz
Chapter Test
ExamView Test Generator
Preparing for Career Success
ExamView Test Generator CD-ROM
© 2009 JIST Publishing
800-648-JIST
www.jist.com

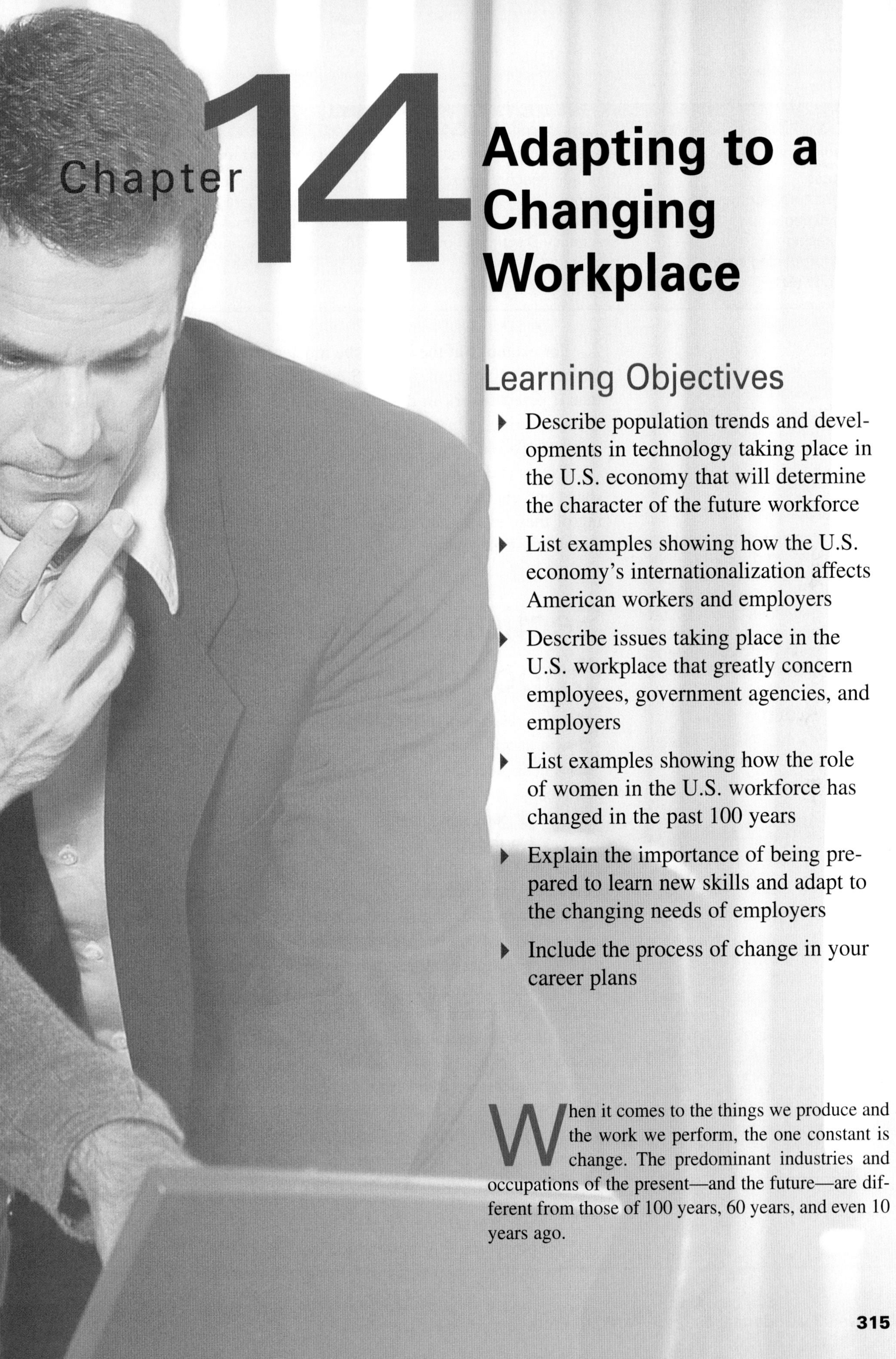

Chapter 14 Adapting to a Changing Workplace

Learning Objectives

- Describe population trends and developments in technology taking place in the U.S. economy that will determine the character of the future workforce
- List examples showing how the U.S. economy's internationalization affects American workers and employers
- Describe issues taking place in the U.S. workplace that greatly concern employees, government agencies, and employers
- List examples showing how the role of women in the U.S. workforce has changed in the past 100 years
- Explain the importance of being prepared to learn new skills and adapt to the changing needs of employers
- Include the process of change in your career plans

When it comes to the things we produce and the work we perform, the one constant is change. The predominant industries and occupations of the present—and the future—are different from those of 100 years, 60 years, and even 10 years ago.

Enrich Your Vocabulary

In reading this chapter and doing the exercises, you will learn the following important terms:

attributes
cross-cultural competence
deregulation
glass ceiling
goods-producing sector
maternity leave
nontraditional occupations
offshore
outsourcing
Pregnancy Discrimination Act of 1978
production flexibility
services-producing sector
sexual harassment
telecommuting
unprecedented
urban area

Vocabulary

You can use the "Developing Your Vocabulary" worksheet in Chapter 14 of the *Preparing for Career Success Instructor's CD-ROM, Third Edition* as a pretest for chapter concepts or as a reteaching worksheet.

Discussion Starter

Wars and calamities can affect business, industry, and employment. What industries and occupations are most affected by the war on terrorism? What industries and occupations are most affected by natural calamities such as earthquakes, hurricanes, and floods?

Video Tour on DVD

Show students the Chapter 14 segment to introduce them to the content.

School-to-Work Transition

Ask several students to describe a school situation in which they were involved that was created by a change in the school staff, a change in school policy, a change in technology used by the school, or a relocation from one school to another. After several students have responded, explain that changes in staff, policy, technology, and job location will also occur and influence them after they join the workforce.

For example, at the end of the nineteenth and beginning of the twentieth century, 40 percent of all U.S. workers were in agriculture. Today, fewer than 2 percent work in that industry. At their height during World War II, manufacturing industries employed nearly 4 of every 10 workers in this country. By 2002, that figure had fallen to 1 in every 10 workers.

Events and trends taking place in today's economy and population will shape and characterize the workforce of the future. Having an understanding of these events and trends will help you prepare for career success in the twenty-first century.

Section 1: Changing Opportunities

Several factors cause changes in an industry's demand for workers in a specific occupation. They include changes in the economy, business practices, technology, goods or services provided, and the competitiveness of U.S. products. For example, changing business practices will benefit paralegals as they take on more of the work presently done by lawyers. On the other hand, banks are increasing their numbers of branch offices, and the number of tellers is now increasing despite the use of automated banking machines.

Gardeners and groundskeepers also will benefit from shifts in the products and services that consumers demand. The reason is that growing numbers of two-career families have increased the demand for gardening and lawn services. In contrast, apparel workers are among the most rapidly declining occupational groups in the economy, and increasing imports, the use of offshore assembly, and automation will contribute to additional job losses.

Forecasters use trends in data to help predict what will happen in the future. Although projections cannot guarantee what will happen, they suggest what is likely to happen. Compared to the workforce of previous years, the workforce of 2016 will have the following **attributes** (qualities or characteristics). How might they affect your career?

- **Larger workforce:** The U.S. workforce will include 166 million people working or looking for work by the year 2016, an increase of 16 million, or 10 percent, from 2006 levels. The increased workforce

© JIST Works

will add about 15.6 million jobs. The percentage of workers who are aged 16 to 24 will decrease to 12.7 percent of the total labor force, due in part to older workers postponing retirement.

- **Older workforce:** As the baby-boom generation ages, the number of people in the labor force aged 55 or older is projected to leap from 16.8 percent to 22.7 percent.

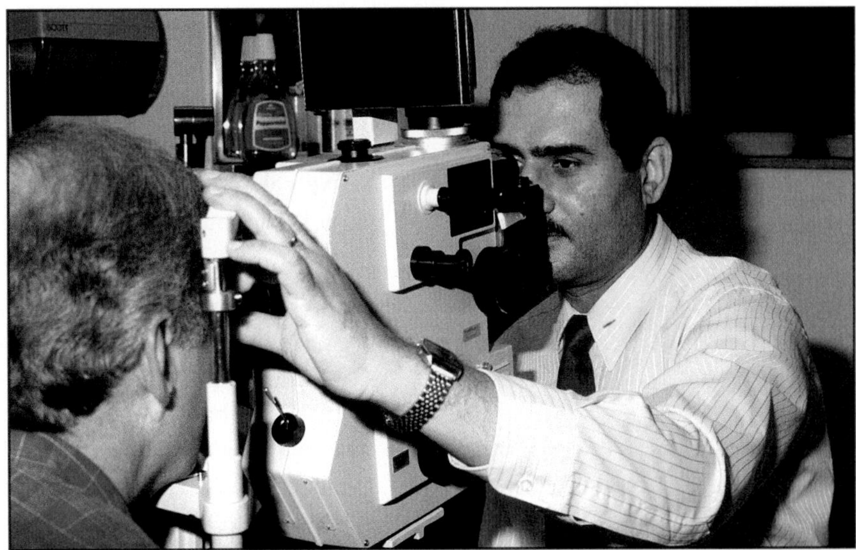

Ramon likes people and enjoys working in the services-producing sector. Working in a growing industry provides him with a sense of job security.

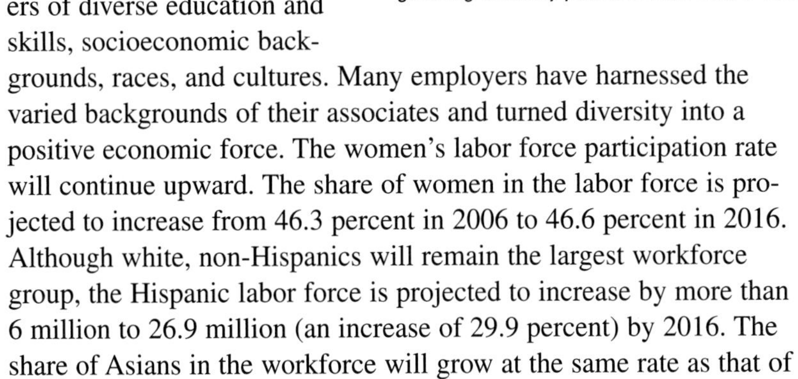

- **A more diverse workforce:** America has a rapidly changing workforce that includes workers of diverse education and skills, socioeconomic backgrounds, races, and cultures. Many employers have harnessed the varied backgrounds of their associates and turned diversity into a positive economic force. The women's labor force participation rate will continue upward. The share of women in the labor force is projected to increase from 46.3 percent in 2006 to 46.6 percent in 2016. Although white, non-Hispanics will remain the largest workforce group, the Hispanic labor force is projected to increase by more than 6 million to 26.9 million (an increase of 29.9 percent) by 2016. The share of Asians in the workforce will grow at the same rate as that of Hispanics.

- **Increase in service jobs:** The **services-producing sector** of the economy includes health services; transportation; public utilities; wholesale and retail trade; finance, insurance, and real estate; and government. Employment growth will be concentrated in the services-providing sector of the economy, generating almost 16 million new jobs by 2016. This growth is due, in part, to increased demand for services and the difficulty of automating service work.

- **Decline of goods-producing jobs:** The **goods-producing sector** of the economy includes mining, construction, manufacturing, agriculture, forestry, and fishing. Employment in goods-producing industries is projected to decrease from 16 to 14 percent of total employment by 2016. Construction is the only goods-producing sector in which employment is projected to grow.

- **Output by industry sector:** Manufacturing, financial activities, and professional and businesses services are projected to account for almost half of all output in 2016. Their high productivity enables them to reach this level of output with less than one-third of the employment across all industries.

Comprehension Check

Ask several students to name one occupation unique to mining, construction, and manufacturing. Next, ask several students to name one occupation unique to transportation and public utilities, wholesale and retail trade, finance, insurance, real estate, and government.

School-to-Work Transition

Identifying occupations that have a favorable growth rate and many job openings is important in career planning. Knowing which occupations are declining is also important. As an example, the health-services industry is growing much faster than the average. Therefore, health occupations are among those providing favorable job prospects at all levels of education. The manufacturing sector is declining. However, millions of jobs will be available due to the retirement and replacement of workers. Have your students explore the Health Science career cluster and the Manufacturing career cluster in the appendix of this book. Give them assignments relating high school courses to these clusters.

Cooperative Learning

Divide your class into groups. Assign one of the features of the future workforce to each group. Instruct each group to tell how their assigned feature will affect their future paychecks, education and training, family life, and overall lifestyle. Have them report their conclusions and the reasons for their conclusions to the class.

TAKE NOTE

Demand is rising for workers with skills related to the design, development, and maintenance of Web sites and the servers that house them. Occupations frequently specified include Webmaster, Web developer, network systems administrator, programmer, and customer service representative.

Enrichment

Have students complete "The Past—The Future" worksheet in Chapter 14 of the *Preparing for Career Success Student Activity Book, Third Edition.*

- **Consumer spending:** Of all goods components, consumer spending on computers and software is projected to have the largest and fastest growth at 8.2 percent or $469 billion. The overall annual growth rate for goods will be 0.4 percent.
- **New ways of working:** The line between work life and private life will continue to blend. Workers' job requirements will spill over into the rest of their lives.
- **Increasing levels of education and training:** Among the causes of gains in labor quality will be higher levels of educational attainment among workers, improving worker skills and productivity. An associate's or bachelor's degree is the most significant source of postsecondary education or training for 5 of the 10 fastest-growing occupations. Short-term on-the-job training is the most significant source of postsecondary education or training for 9 of the 10 occupations with the largest job growth.

Table 14.1 illustrates the projected increase in numbers of workers in various occupational groups. Can you think of an occupational group that will benefit or suffer because of a major event that took place in the past five years?

Table 14.1 Numeric Growth in Employment by Major Occupational Groups (2006–2016)

Occupational Group	Increased Number of Workers
Food preparation and serving	1,436,191
Healthcare practitioners, technologists, and technicians	1,422,626
Education, training, and library	1,264,510
Personal care and service	1,094,051
Business and financial operations	1,062,764
Healthcare support	997,094
Building and grounds cleaning and maintenance	850,134
Computer and mathematical science	821,809
Community and social services	541,221
Management	533,052

Source: U.S. Department of Labor

The Effect of Technology

Improved technology, new inventions, and discovery have a long-term influence on occupations. Entire industries come into existence, creating new occupations.

- **New technology changes the way people work.** It is a driving force in determining the job tasks and numbers of workers in a specific occupation. For example, business offices have increased their use of computers and other communications technologies at a rapid

© JIST Works

pace. Consequently, the growth of clerical and managerial jobs has declined, but the demand for workers with knowledge of computers, office technology (systems analysts), and office machine repair has increased.

- **Superior technology is an important source of competitive advantage.** It eliminates jobs that are no longer efficient and creates new jobs to replace them. One change that has had an impact on employment is the shift in importance from producing computer hardware to producing computer software and providing technical services. This shift has caused a decrease in computer manufacturing employment, whereas the number of jobs related to software production and technical services has continued to grow.
- **New technology creates business opportunities and jobs.** Emerging opportunities and occupations may be entirely new, created by changes in technology, society, markets, or government regulations. For example, Webmasters or coordinators write the computer code necessary to publish or update text and images on Internet Web sites. As more organizations establish a presence on the Internet, more Web-related businesses and occupations emerge.

Cooperative Learning

Divide your class into groups of three. Ask each group to write a brief paragraph detailing how technology has both increased and decreased their career opportunities. Allow time for each group to report to the class.

Enrichment

Have students complete the "A Change of Pace" worksheet found in Chapter 14 of the *Preparing for Career Success Instructor's CD-ROM, Third Edition.*

Many workers believe that they cannot keep up with these changes and that they are a very unimportant part of the economy. Nothing could be further from the truth, however. Labor is one of the most important factors of production. Therefore, a quality workforce is the foundation for our nation's economic strength and international competitiveness.

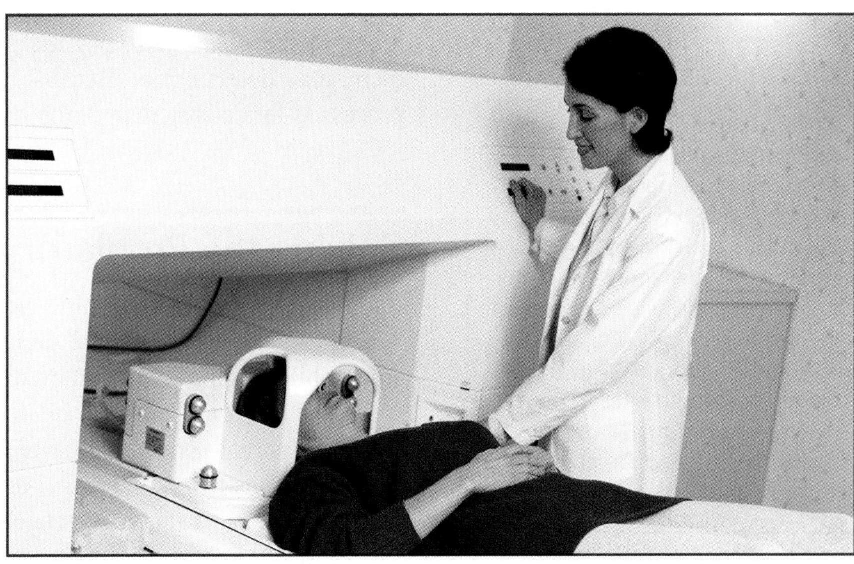

Learning to use new technology is an important factor in career success.

Management and labor are increasingly involved in teamwork decision making for matters related to product quality, operating procedures, and job responsibilities. In today's global market, competition requires continual improvement by U.S. companies. They must place the most up-to-date communication and production technology in the hands of their employees. In turn, employees must maintain and develop the skills necessary to use this technology to produce the maximum number of high-quality products or services.

Key To Success

When you consider an occupation, find out how many jobs exist in that occupation. Are the number of jobs growing or declining?

Global Competition

Competition in the global marketplace continually tests the quality and cost of U.S. products. Countries in Europe, Asia, and other parts of the world have emerged as strong challengers in international commerce. As a

© JIST Works

Discussion Starter

More than one million American workers in the garment industry have lost their jobs since 1993 because of foreign competition. Ask your students the following questions:

- What reaction would you expect from our world trading partners if the U.S. government placed a high *tariff* (a tax on imported products) on imported clothing to protect our garment industry?
- If our government took action to protect the workers in the garment industry, what effect might it have on workers in other occupational areas?
- When foreign competition causes U.S. workers to be displaced, what assistance, if any, should they receive? Who should pay for the assistance you are suggesting?

Cluster Link

If you have an interest in international business and working overseas, note that international and domestic businesses employ essentially the same categories of employees: management, professional, technical, sales, administrative support, service, and production workers. You will find the most opportunities in the Business and Administration career cluster. See the appendix for more information.

Community Resources

Form a committee of students to contact the local chamber of commerce. Instruct them to schedule a speaker on the subject of foreign-owned business and the way it affects the local job market, local services or products that are exported to foreign markets, and foreign services or products that are sold in the local market.

result, American businesspeople recognize that competition from abroad is exerting as much influence on the quantity and quality of jobs as competition from within the U.S. economy. To improve their global competitiveness, U.S. industries must continually adjust production and job requirements to reflect consumer demand.

American employers use several strategies to cut costs and maintain **production flexibility** (ability to respond quickly to production demands). For example, contingent workers can move on and off the payroll as needed. Hiring contingent workers is less expensive than maintaining permanent workers.

Employers also lower costs by moving production to **offshore** (not on the U.S. mainland) manufacturing and service operations. The U.S. employers that do the largest amount of offshore assembly are electrical machinery, transportation equipment, and metals companies. Their principal products include semiconductors, textiles, television sets and components, and motor vehicles.

Other examples of service operations that U.S. companies move offshore are computerized data- and text-entry work. These operations may be as far away as India or Hong Kong. There, wage rates are as little as one-tenth of U.S. rates. Workers in these offshore sites usually use American-made word processors or computer workstations. In some cases, two or more workers *key in* (type) the same information and, after comparing them, may detect errors. Because wage rates are so low at these sites, this process is less costly than doing the work in the United States.

Solving the Problem: Made in America?

Mike Parker worked nine years in the Great Lakes region for an American-owned automobile company. He and his coworkers assembled automobile engines. Mike started out working on the assembly line and spent his last six years as a quality-control technician. He ran tests on a variety of parts to ensure they were machined to specific *tolerances* (allowable deviations from a standard) before they were used in an engine. Many of the engine parts that Mike checked were manufactured offshore.

During a period of economic recession, the owners closed the plant where Mike worked and replaced it with an offshore engine-assembly plant. The savings from wages and taxes enabled the company to assemble engines at a healthy profit. The engines assembled offshore were then shipped to the United States to be part of "American-built" automobiles.

The American owner laid off Mike and 900 other workers. Workers with 10 years or more of service were able to retain their pension benefits. Mike received three months' pay but no benefits. However, he was allowed to keep his health and life insurance as long as he paid the premiums (see "COBRA," Chapter 13). Five months later, Mike was still out of work and out of money.

At this time, it seemed as though everyone in town wanted to sell their homes. Unfortunately, the price of houses fell until most people owed more

© JIST Works

on their homes than they could recover by selling them. Because the engine plant had been the largest taxpayer in the community, the loss of the plant's tax revenue forced the local government and the schools to reduce services and lay off employees.

After 10 months of job hunting, Mike was hired by a Japanese-owned automobile company in Tennessee. More than 95 percent of the workers in the Japanese-owned factory are American. It is a very modern factory, and Mike is very satisfied with his wages and benefits. Mike quickly noticed that many of the parts used in the Japanese car he helps assemble are made in the United States. Because the factory where Mike works is the largest taxpayer in the region, the taxes it pays help support a fine school system and pay for services in the town where Mike lives.

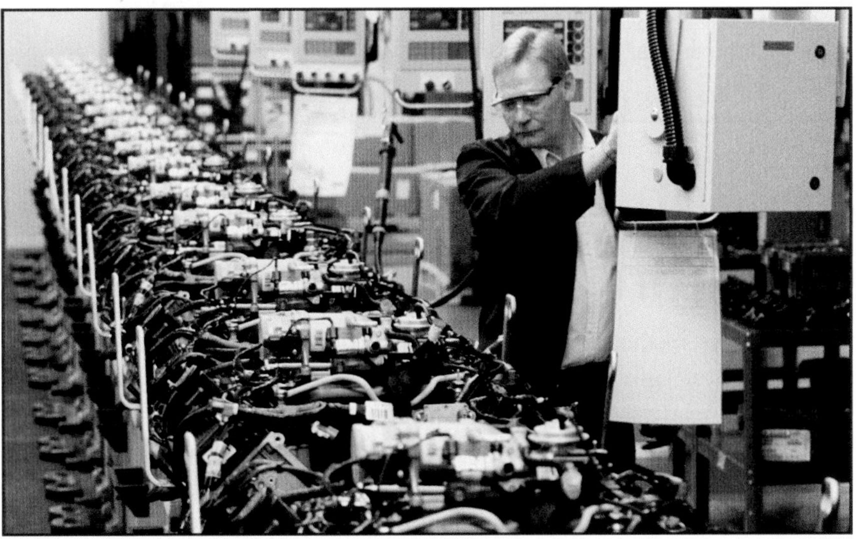

Critical Thinking

Slogans like "Buy American" are popular. Which one of Mike's employers builds an "American" car? Defend your answer.

Which of Mike's employers is the best citizen? Why do you think so? How do you think people in the Great Lakes region would answer this question? How about the people in Tennessee or in Japan?

If you are interested in pursuing international employment, now is a time of **unprecedented** (unheard of, novel) opportunity. It is probably best to begin your career working for an international corporation at home. Employers often take a long time to groom employees for international positions. Job opportunities are greatest for those employees who have prepared themselves by acquiring additional education and training (including reading, writing, and speaking more than one language) and multicultural experience (including personal travel).

You will need to be knowledgeable about the cultural, economic, legal, and political differences between nations. **Cross-cultural competence** is the new critical requirement for job candidates seeking employment with international corporations. It involves an understanding of the international

Key To Success

International organizations prefer well-educated people with previous international experience in fields such as economic and social development, international political affairs, and regional security.

Career Fact

The following occupations are expected to lose the largest numbers of workers by the year 2016. (Keep in mind that many of these losses will be absorbed by retiring workers and those making job changes.)

- Stock clerks and order fillers (130,722 jobs)
- Cashiers, except gaming (118,239 jobs)
- Packers and packagers, hand (103,632 jobs)
- File clerks (96,563 jobs)
- Farmers and ranchers (89,606 jobs)
- Order clerks (5,951 jobs)
- Sewing machine operators (3,284 jobs)

Source: U.S. Bureau of Labor Statistics

business environment, plus the skills and subject knowledge needed to be effective in new situations. In addition to the normal job skill requirements, international employees need to possess a multicultural awareness, sensitivity, and tolerance.

Section 1: Get Involved

Answer the following on a separate sheet of paper, and be prepared to discuss your responses in class.

1. The wage gap between jobs in the service sector and jobs in the manufacturing sector is wide. In some cases, service workers earn only 51 cents for every dollar that manufacturing workers earn. Should service-sector jobs pay as much as manufacturing jobs? Support your viewpoint.
2. Ask a parent, friend, or neighbor to help you locate a worker who lost his or her job in the past three years because of new technology or offshore production. How is this person presently earning a livelihood? How does his or her present job compare to the previous job?
3. Is it wise to use U.S. trade laws to promote international fair labor standards with our global trading partners? How could this help or hurt U.S. workers?

Section 2: Issues in a Changing Workplace

Changes in the labor force, the rapid development of new technologies, and global competition have caused dramatic changes in the American workplace. This evolution has given rise to many issues affecting both workers and employers that are yet to be resolved. An awareness of these issues and their possible effects is essential for all workers, government agencies, and private sector employers that are seeking to level the playing field for American participation in the global economy. These issues also may affect your lifestyle or the lifestyle of someone you know.

Diversity and Discrimination

Join the union, girls, and together say Equal Pay for Equal Work.

—Susan B. Anthony

A major strategy used by companies to be more competitive in the global economy is to develop a diverse workforce. They use this strategy to reduce barriers to promotion within the organization, take advantage of differing backgrounds and talents to solve problems and make decisions, and attract and retain top-quality employees. At issue is learning to take advantage of diversity to solve problems and make decisions. A major obstacle to achieving this goal is the discrimination that is still prevalent in the American workplace.

Discussion Starter

In the areas of employee-selection procedures, development programs, or work-family policies, what employer initiatives do you believe tend to increase organizational diversity? Why? What policies tend to stifle organizational diversity? Why?

The United States is recognized globally for political freedom and equality in the voting booth. However, equality in the workplace remains a distant goal for many workers. Although women and minority groups comprise growing segments of the labor force, unequal pay and limited advancement opportunities continue to be major issues for these workers. The government and business community are still learning how to satisfy labor needs while eliminating obstacles that hinder some workers from becoming part of the economic mainstream.

© JIST Works

The Glass Ceiling

In many cases, minorities and women have not experienced significant gains in the middle and senior levels of management even when they possess the required experience, credentials, and general qualifications. At issue is the removal of the **glass ceiling** that creates artificial barriers based on attitudinal or organizational bias that prevents qualified individuals from advancing into higher management positions.

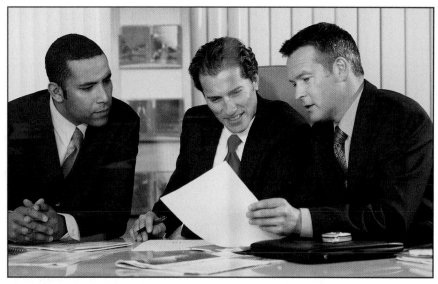

Less than 2 percent of all corporate board officers are women. If you were the owner of this company, would you hire a highly qualified female vice president or a less qualified male? Why or why not?

Age Discrimination

Some older workers lose their jobs only to have younger workers replace them. The Age Discrimination in Employment Act (ADEA) outlaws discrimination in recruitment, hiring, pay, benefits, training, promotion, job retention, and other employment practices.

Comprehension Check

After your students have finished reading "The Glass Ceiling," ask them to close their books. Ask several students: What is the glass ceiling? How do you suppose it got the name *glass ceiling?*

Disability Discrimination

Many persons with disabilities are fully qualified to perform a wide range of jobs. However, some employers believe that persons with a disability do not need or deserve equal employment opportunities. The Americans with Disabilities Act (ADA) protects any "qualified individual with a disability" from employment discrimination based on the disability, unless hiring the individual would impose an undue hardship on the employer.

Wage Discrimination

The earnings gap between genders, races, and ethnic groups remains a major issue in the U.S. workforce. Females and minorities earn less than 80 percent of a Caucasian male's wage. These numbers alone are not enough to determine the extent of wage discrimination between groups. For example, men and women as a group tend to make different career choices. Women tend to value caring for children and other family members higher than getting a toehold on the next higher rung of the career ladder. Consider this 2006 data about the median weekly earnings of female workers:

- Women who worked full-time jobs earned $600, or about 81 percent of the $743 earned by male workers.
- Women with less than a high school diploma earned $358 compared with $905 for those with a college degree.

Take Note

There is a growing wage gap between highly educated and poorly educated women. Less educated women, especially high school dropouts, have seen their wages fall and their level of participation in the labor market rise at a much slower pace than women with more education. Women who try to pull out of a cycle of welfare and low-wage jobs are finding what matters most is education.

- Married women earned more than unmarried women. Among unmarried workers, women without children earned 13 percent more than those with children.

Community Resources

Form a committee to send for additional information about procedures to follow if a person is sexually harassed. Have them report their information to the class.

Reteaching

Have students complete the "Stopping Sexual Harassment" worksheet in Chapter 14 of the *Preparing for Career Success Instructor's CD-ROM, Third Edition.*

Sexual Harassment

Sexual harassment is a kind of sex discrimination. Legally, **sexual harassment** is defined as unwanted sexual attention at work between members of the same or the opposite sex. In addition to asking for sex, this behavior includes touching, making sexual comments, or making advances toward a fellow worker. Any form of sexual harassment that you are required to accept in order to obtain or keep a job or to receive a raise or vacation or that influences other decisions about your job or makes it difficult for you to work should be stopped. To avoid legal responsibility for sexual harassment, employers must have a policy against harassment, have a proper complaint procedure, and communicate disapproval of harassment to their employees.

Positive Actions for Overcoming Workplace Discrimination

FIND OUT MORE

For information on procedures to follow if you are sexually harassed, key in the following on your search engine: **Equal Employment Opportunity Commission** or **Women's Bureau U.S. Department of Labor.**

The Equal Employment Opportunity Commission (EEOC) is the federal agency whose job it is to protect workers from discrimination based on age, sex, race, color, national origin, religion, or disability. Many states and cities have similar fair employment practices agencies. In some states, a state or local agency investigates discrimination cases and attempts to resolve them before referring them to the EEOC.

If you ever feel that you are a victim of discrimination in the workplace, it is important for you to take steps to correct the situation:

- Document the event in writing. Include date, time, place, what took place, what was said, and who was present.
- Seek support from family and friends if you are a victim of discrimination. This situation can be very emotional.
- Discuss the problem with your union representative if you are a union member.
- Follow the procedure for making a complaint if your employer has an employee handbook.
- Continue doing a good job, and keep a written record of your work. Keep copies of your job evaluations and any letters, memos, or e-mails that document your good work.
- File a complaint even if you no longer work for the employer. However, keep in mind that your right to file a legitimate complaint does have a time limit.

© JIST Works

- Contact the U.S. Department of Labor for additional information.
- Contact a free legal service or a lawyer who specializes in job rights if necessary. For information, contact your local or state bar association.

Working Parents

Economic survival above the poverty level dictates that many twenty-first century parents work outside the home, unlike parents of the nineteenth and most of the twentieth centuries. Most employers, workers, and politicians agree that the following issues are essential to the well-being of America's children. The focus of the public debate is on delivering and paying for the services.

CAREER FACT

According to the Bureau of Labor Statistics, 67 percent of women with children under the age of 18 are employed.

Pregnancy Discrimination

The **Pregnancy Discrimination Act of 1978** specifically prohibits companies with 15 or more employees from discrimination because of pregnancy. Employers cannot

- Refuse to employ a woman because of pregnancy
- Terminate her because of pregnancy
- Force her to go on leave at an arbitrary point during her pregnancy
- Penalize her because of pregnancy in reinstatement rights, including credit for previous service, accrued retirement benefits, and accumulated seniority

This law does not require an employer to provide a specific number of weeks for maternity leave or to treat pregnant employees in any manner different from other employees with respect to hiring or promotion. In addition, it does not establish new medical leave or other benefit programs where none currently exist. The phrases "different from other employees" and "where none currently exist" have led to interpretations of this law that resulted in the loss of many pregnant women's positions.

Discussion Starter

After your students finish reading about the Pregnancy Discrimination Act of 1978, make the following statement: Employers cannot refuse to hire a pregnant woman because of their prejudice against pregnant workers or the prejudice of coworkers, clients, or customers. Then ask your students: Is this law fair to employers? Why or why not? What effect would you expect the four features of this law to have on your income, job security, work load, and future career success if you owned a small business with 16 employees? If you were a pregnant, employed working mother? If you were a pregnant, unemployed job seeker? If you were the coworker of a pregnant employee?

Case Study

Have students read the case study "Protecting Unborn Children" found in Chapter 14 of the *Preparing for Career Success Instructor's on CD-ROM, Third Edition* and discuss the "Critical Thinking" questions.

Maternity and Parenting Leave

As more women enter the labor force, the need for maternity and parenting leave for the birth or adoption of a child is increasing.

- **Maternity leave** is a disability leave granted to women as a result of pregnancy and/or childbirth.
- *Parenting leave* is time given to mothers or fathers to care for a newborn or newly adopted child.

Cross-Reference

Chapter 21, "Balancing Your Career and Your Life," has more information on the personal aspects of being a working parent.

David's mother works for a large insurance company. This will be her first day on the job and David's first day to stay at the company's day-care center. What do you suppose David is thinking? What is David's mother thinking?

Child Care

The increase in the number of two-career families makes the availability and affordability of child care an important matter of national policy. Research shows that child-care needs are an issue at all income levels, even though the type of care selected varies according to family income. When employees face difficulty in arranging for child care, the frequent results are absenteeism, tardiness, low morale, and reduced productivity.

New Ways of Working

The economic problems faced by employers producing goods and services and the needs of their employees are changing faster than at any time throughout history. Worldwide competition demands that workers and employers abandon the adversarial relationships of past generations. In what ways do you see the following issues as part of the problem or as part of the solution?

Discussion Starter

Ask your students: Who should be responsible for solving issues such as unequal pay, limited advancement opportunities, and child care: workers, employers, or the government?

Flexible Work Schedules

Twenty-first century workers place a higher priority on time than past generations. They are redefining age-old questions such as "How do I want to live my life?" and "How do I allocate my time?" Faced with a shortage of skilled workers, many employers have offered some form of flexible scheduling. In general, an employee's total number of work hours is set, but the worker can choose from certain options when he or she will work those hours. Flexible scheduling allows workers to coordinate the demands of their paid employment with family responsibilities and recreational preferences.

Telecommuting

Telecommuting refers to working at home for all or part of normally scheduled hours. The employee is available by phone, computer, or FAX and stays in regular contact with the place of business. For employers, the location of their employees during the workday is far less important than what they accomplish. For employees, working at home allows them to schedule personal and family appointments at convenient times and to avoid an often time-consuming commute to the office.

 © JIST Works

Job Sharing

Successful job sharing starts with finding the right partner and requires a blending of work ethics, personality traits, and egos. Because companies are reluctant to promote this arrangement, it's up to the employees to determine how to split everything from job duties, vacation days, emergency situations, and business travel. Then they must convince management the idea will work. Overwhelmingly, more women than men choose to share positions. Job sharing provides the benefits of a part-time schedule without giving up high-profile, challenging work. Job sharers work for half the pay and benefits, but they say that having more time for family responsibilities or furthering an education is worth the trade-off.

TAKE NOTE

Many companies have a selected benefits approach to benefits, whereby employees can select from a number of benefit options based on a total monetary cost. In other words, the company will spend a certain amount of money on each employee for benefits, and the employees have some flexibility about the benefits options they select. For example, employees with young children may select child-care reimbursement; others may select educational assistance, longer vacations, or other options.

Compressed Workweek

A common form of the compressed workweek is working four 10-hour days and having three days off each week. Long days can be grueling, and arranging child care to cover extended hours can be difficult. In practice, hourly employees take advantage of the benefit, but executives rarely do.

Contingent Employment

As you learned in Chapter 12, contingent workers include part-time, temporary, contractual, and leased employees. Contingent employment has its benefits and pitfalls. Contingent work allows many employees to maintain dual roles, such as work and family or work and special interests. Flexible work schedules, supplemental income, and the opportunity to maintain skill levels when full-time work is neither needed nor desired are beneficial aspects of this type of employment. Contingent work also serves as a stopgap when full-time employment cannot be found. Frequently, it leads to offers of full-time employment.

On the downside, employers rarely include contingent employees in benefit programs, such as health insurance, paid leave, or pensions. The lack of benefits requires contingent employees to purchase benefits at much higher costs than group rates or to do without. The salaries and wages of contingent workers are also generally lower than those of full-time employees, except when a contract is negotiated for a specific amount. Finally, contingent workers do not acquire seniority in an organization. As the number of contingent employees in the U.S. workforce continues to increase, these issues will demand more public attention.

Comprehension Check

After your students have finished reading "Contingent Employment," instruct them to close their books. Ask several students to reply to these questions in their own words: What is one advantage of contingent employment for the employer? What is one advantage to the employee? What is one disadvantage of contingent employment for the employer? What is one disadvantage to the employee?

Terrorism in the Workplace

The focus on performing worthwhile work and valuing time spent with family and friends is greater since the terrorist attacks on the World Trade Center and Pentagon on September 11, 2001. Workers would like to feel that what happened then could never happen at their job site. They also realize that they are threatened by homegrown terrorists (such as those responsible for the Oklahoma City bombing) as well as terrorists from overseas.

Discussion Starter

As a worker, what can you do to make the worksite a safer place? Do you think that terrorism will change the relationship between employers and employees? If yes, how? If no, why not?

Enrichment

Have students complete the "Issues: Sexual Harassment, Pregnancy, and Contingent Employment" worksheet in Chapter 14 of the *Preparing for Career Success Student Activity Book, Third Edition.*

Much of the organization for antiterrorism is in the hands of the new federal program for Homeland Security. The hard work of making the American workplace safe has just begun. The role of each worker in establishing and maintaining a secure work site is not yet defined. It will be up to you and your coworkers to seek answers for this difficult problem.

Romance in the Workplace

Office romance is on the rise, with more than 30 percent of employees reporting they have been romantically involved with a coworker. Romances that concern management most are those that involve a supervisor and a subordinate. Such relationships call the supervisor's judgment into question and may expose the company to sexual harassment accusations. These relationships sometimes create morale problems among other staffers who believe that the boss is favoring his or her romantic partner or inappropriately sharing information. Most employers consider romantic relationships between employees with decision-making authority and company customers to be off-limits.

Section 2: Get Involved

Answer the following on a separate sheet of paper, and be prepared to discuss your responses in class.

1. Four major forms of workplace discrimination are described in this section. Which of these four types do you consider to be: Most serious? Why? Least serious? Why?
2. Which issue in this section concerns you most? Why?
3. Research the four highest-level jobs in a regional business or large institution. What is the number of women, minorities, and white men in these positions?

Section 3: Women in the Workforce

Key To Success

It is important for young women to prepare for job satisfaction and career success. They can expect to spend 30 or more years gainfully employed.

In the nineteenth century, economic equality between the sexes was a distant goal. Women who worked outside the home were generally young, unmarried, poor immigrants. Married middle-class women remained at home. Society considered that the role of women was to perform nonpaid work in the home. The role of men was to participate in the labor market to earn income to support their dependent spouse and families.

Social values regarding the roles of men and women slowly changed. A major reason for this change was the mobilization of men to fight in World War II. The war created severe labor shortages, and women found acceptance in the labor market. Between 1940 and 1944, the number of women in the labor force increased by more than a third. Even then, most employed women were in traditional occupations and usually in lower-paying industries. Their earnings, even for full-time, year-round jobs, were less than two-thirds the average for men.

© JIST Works

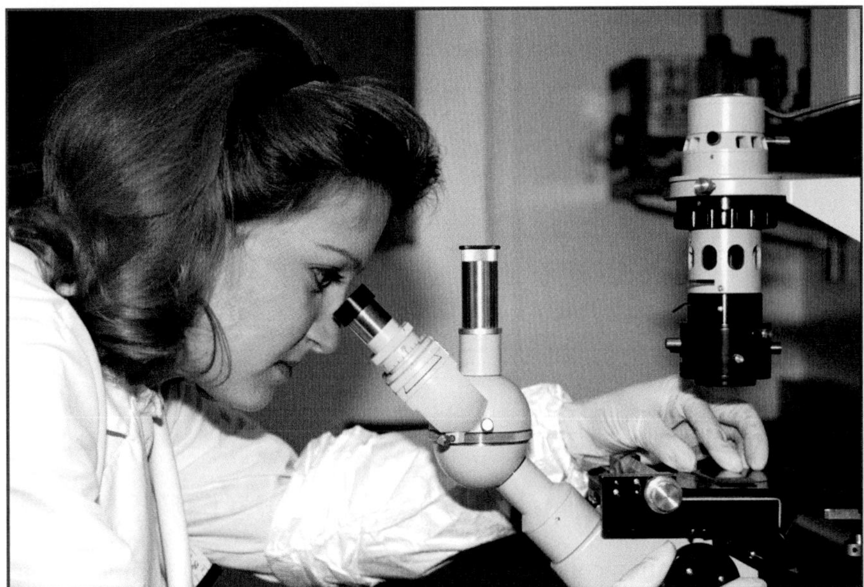

Once clustered in only a handful of traditional jobs (such as clerical work), women have branched out into such fields as accounting, law, medicine, and science.

Enrichment

Assign a group of students to decorate a section of the bulletin board titled "The Changing Role of Women." Assign the class to search for newspaper or magazine articles and pictures depicting the role of women in the workforce for the bulletin board.

CAREER FACT

In past decades, most women left the labor force during their childbearing years. Today, an increasing number of women in this group are working or looking for work.

During the mid-1960s, U.S. families continued a trend toward fewer children. The rapid decline in birth rates made it more acceptable for married women to work. Women were achieving higher levels of education, the overall economy was expanding, and jobs were available for those who sought them. During this period, the feminist movement grew, and women were encouraged to seek a larger role in the labor market. Civil rights legislation provided legal support for equal opportunities in the job market.

In 1970, less than 40 percent of wives living with their husbands and children worked outside the home, and the participation rate for those with preschool children was only 3 percent. The 1970s—a decade of inflation, an unpopular war, changing lifestyles, and family stress—changed these patterns. Divorce became more common; by the end of the 1970s, one out of every two marriages ended in divorce. Although many divorced women later remarried, they often found themselves faced with the sudden and unexpected need to earn money to maintain their families. In addition, a marked increase occurred in the number of never-married women with children. Single-parent families, most of them maintained by women, became an increasingly common family type.

U.S. women in the twenty-first century continue to make changes and overcome barriers as their numbers in the workforce approach those of men. An increasing number of women have completed higher levels of education and have sought opportunities for higher salaries and long-term career progress. They have also made it very clear that their income is important and in many cases vital to their survival.

Women make up more than half of the workforce of nearly a dozen industries, including such fast-growing industries as health services, banking, legal services, insurance, and retail. Yet opportunity or lack of opportunity for women in **nontraditional occupations** (those in which women or men comprise 25 percent or less of the workforce) has not changed significantly. Would you consider a nontraditional occupation? Why or why not?

Community Resources

Form a committee to acquire information about women's employment issues. Have them report their information to the class.

TAKE NOTE

Nontraditional occupations for women include chief executives (25 percent are women) and dentists (21 percent are women). Women are also underrepresented in the fields of computer science, engineering, law enforcement, transportation, manufacturing, and construction. Nontraditional occupations for men include clinical lab technologists (about 22 percent are men) and elementary school teachers (about 12 percent are men). Men are also underrepresented in nursing and administrative occupations.

© JIST Works

Section 3: Get Involved

Interview three women who are at least 15 years apart in age (ideally one who is in her 20s, one in her 40s, and one in her 60s). Ask them the following questions. (Be prepared to discuss your responses in class.)

1. What are your views on women in the workforce?
2. What jobs have you had outside the home (if any) since you were in high school?
3. What obstacles do you feel are most difficult for women to overcome in the workforce?
4. What have you enjoyed most and least about working outside the home?
5. What advice would you give to high school students to help them prepare for career success?

Enrichment

Have students complete the "Job Mobility and Adapting to Change" worksheet in Chapter 14 of the *Preparing for Career Success Student Activity Book, Third Edition.*

Section 4: Preparing for a Changing World of Work

Job skill requirements and responsibilities are changing rapidly due to corporate mergers and reorganizations and technological changes. Employment experts predict that during your career you can expect to have three or four employment changes that will require your retraining. Many workers will have second and even third careers, sometimes simultaneously. It will be common for workers of your generation to live to the age of 80 or 90 and spend 40 to 50 years in the workforce. Do you want to spend nearly half a century on the same job track?

Job advancement during your career will be more like climbing a large net than climbing a ladder. Making progress will not always mean going up. It may mean staying at the same level and shifting sideways or even moving into an entirely new area of job responsibility that relates to technology, products, or services that did not exist when you started your career.

CAREER FACT

During the early years of your career, the education requirements for most new jobs will continue to rise. Changing markets and new technologies will make lifelong education a requirement for many, if not most, occupations.

Job Security

Job security means that workers can be confident that their jobs will always be available to them. The following factors can pose a major threat to individual job security:

- **Downsizing:** Pressure on companies to be profitable and maintain managerial flexibility sometimes results in a reduction in the number of employees.
- **Global competition:** Pressure on companies to control costs and remain competitive may result in layoffs or plant closures.
- **Deregulation:** **Deregulation** (removing government controls) in industries such as the communications, financial, and transportation industries will continue to create new and unfamiliar business climates for employers and employees.

© JIST Works

- **Outsourcing: Outsourcing** is the employer practice of purchasing parts or finished goods from domestic nonunion shops or from foreign companies. Workers frequently lose their jobs or have hours or wages reduced when businesses move offshore or outsource domestically.

As a twenty-first century worker, you will be more responsible for your own career development and job security. Your job security will depend on your marketable skills.

Job Mobility

In 1900, job mobility meant moving from the farm to job opportunities in the city. Today, it means moving from one **urban area** (a community of 2,500 or more) to another. In fact, more than 50 million Americans change addresses every year. Due to changes in technology and global market demands, you may find it necessary to make one or more geographical moves during your career. Two factors to consider before you make a geographical move are the regional differences in average earnings and the cost of living. Table 14.2 presents the median annual pay for workers in selected states.

In today's world of work, finding a job or a promotion could require moving from one urban area to another. What factors will you consider before you move?

Differences in pay levels within individual geographic areas reflect a number of factors, such as the type of industry, extent of unionization, average size (number of employees) of employers, and length of service of

Vocabulary Builder

Ask several students to explain the term *job mobility* in their own words.

Table 14.2 Median Annual Family Income in Selected States for One Earner

State	Median Annual Income	State	Median Annual Income
Alabama	$35,190	Nebraska	$36,179
Alaska	$43,766	New York	$43,352
Arizona	$33,474	North Carolina	$35,267
California	$45,518	Ohio	$39,056
Colorado	$42,979	Oklahoma	$33,597
Florida	$38,927	Pennsylvania	$41,971
Indiana	$38,293	Texas	$35,820
Massachusetts	$51,176	Utah	$44,458
Michigan	$41,929	Virginia	$44,780
Minnesota	$43,965	Washington	$46,700

Source: U.S. Department of Commerce, Census Bureau, 2006

Comprehension Check

Ask your students: Who would have the most spending power, a worker earning $50,000 per year in Cincinnati, Ohio, or a worker earning $50,000 per year in New York, New York? What is the reason for your answer? Tell them that spending power is equal to earnings divided by the cost-of-living index. The Cincinnati worker has about $55,556 in spending power (50,000 divided by .90), and the New York worker has $23,256 of spending power (50,000 divided by 2.15). You may wish to use additional problems to demonstrate the importance of knowing the cost of living prior to making a job transfer. Tell your students that the raise they get could be a pay cut.

employees in their current jobs. Earnings have generally been highest on the West and East coasts. The South has attracted more new businesses than any other region in the United States because of immigration of industries from the North to the South, and workers following the jobs. The South has been a magnet for new industry because the cost of living is the lowest of any region in the nation, and the quality of life is high.

The cost-of-living index measures the relative price levels for consumer goods and services in a geographic area for a middle-management standard of living. The national average equals 100. Table 14.3 presents the cost-of-living index for several metropolitan areas. Each participant's index is read as a percentage of the national average.

Retirement Planning

Most workers from your generation will have several jobs and more than one employer during their working years. The result is that individual retirement planning becomes a complex career issue. Concerns expressed by workers include

- When I retire, will Social Security have the funds to pay my retirement check?
- Can I transfer my employee retirement benefits to another employer?
- How many years must I work to have a vested pension with my employer?
- Am I eligible to invest in tax-deferred pension benefits such as IRAs and 401(k) plans?

Even though you have many working years ahead of you before you retire, you need to understand the issues involved now in order to make the employment decisions that will help you reach your goals.

Table 14.3 Cost-of-Living Index for Selected Metropolitan Areas

Metropolitan Area	Cost-of-Living Index	Metropolitan Area	Cost-of-Living Index
Houston, TX	88%	Denver, CO	104%
Cincinnati, OH	90%	Chicago, IL	110%
Indianapolis, IN	94%	Miami, FL	116%
Dayton, OH	95%	Boston, MA	136%
Atlanta, GA	96%	Washington, DC	137%
Louisville, KY	99%	San Francisco, CA	169%
Pittsburgh, PA	99%	New York, NY	215%
Cleveland, OH	100%		

© JIST Works

Section 4: Get Involved

Answer the following on a separate sheet of paper, and be prepared to discuss your responses in class.

1. Interview a friend or relative who has worked for more than 15 years. Use the following questions:
   - How has your work changed because of advances in technology?
   - How has your work remained the same?
   - Have you found it necessary to learn new skills during your career? If so, what new skills have you learned? How did you learn them?
   - What effect has learning or not learning new skills had on your career?
2. Make a brief list of your most important personal and career interests. What areas of the country would be best suited to your personal interests? Why? What areas of the country would be best suited to your career interests? Why?
3. Which geographic area would provide you with the most desirable career future? Which would provide your family with the most desirable lifestyle? Give specific reasons for each answer.
4. How important are the issues of job security and retirement planning to you? How important do you think these issues will be to you when you are 35 years old? When you are 50?

Chapter 14 Review

Reteaching

Have students complete the "Finding the Right Words" and "Checking Your Location" worksheets in Chapter 14 of the *Preparing for Career Success Student Activity Book, Third Edition.*

Enrich Your Vocabulary

On a separate sheet of paper, number from 1 to 16, and match each of the following statements with the most appropriate term from the "Enrich Your Vocabulary" list at the beginning of the chapter by writing that term next to the correct number.

1. The part of the economy that includes transportation and public utilities
2. Not on the U.S. mainland
3. A community of 2,500 or more
4. Ability to respond quickly to production demands
5. Jobs in which women or men comprise 25 percent or less of the workforce
6. An artificial barrier to high-level promotions
7. A unlawful form of gender discrimination
8. Disability leave for pregnancy or childbirth
9. Elimination of government controls
10. The part of the economy that includes mining, construction, and manufacturing
11. Qualities or characteristics
12. Unheard of, novel

Enrich Your Vocabulary Answers

1. services-producing sector
2. offshore
3. urban area
4. production flexibility
5. nontraditional occupations
6. glass ceiling
7. sexual harassment
8. maternity leave
9. deregulation
10. goods-producing sector
11. attributes
12. unprecedented

(continued)

Enrich Your Vocabulary Answers *(continued)*

13. cross-cultural competence
14. telecommuting
15. outsourcing
16. Pregnancy Discrimination Act of 1978

13. Critical requirement for job candidates seeking international employment

14. Working at home for all or part of normally scheduled hours

15. Buying parts or finished goods from domestic nonunion shops or foreign companies

16. A law that prevents employers from discriminating against pregnant women

Check Your Knowledge Answers

1. World War II, a rapid decline in birth rates, and an increasing rate of divorce.
2. Attributes should include larger workforce, older workforce, a more diverse workforce, increase in services-producing sector and decrease in goods-producing sector, new ways of working, increasing levels of education and training.
3. See Table 14.1.
4. (1) New technology changes the way people work. (2) Superior technology is an important source of competitive advantage. (3) New technology creates business opportunities and jobs.
5. They use contingent workers and move certain operations offshore.
6. Employers reduce the cost of their products or services by paying low wages to offshore workers.
7. (1) To reduce barriers to promotion within the organization, (2) to take advantage of differing backgrounds and talents to solve problems and make decisions, (3) to attract and retain top-quality employees.
8. 15 or more.

Check Your Knowledge

On a separate sheet of paper, complete the following activities. (Do not write in your textbook.)

1. List three major factors that increased the number of American women in the workforce between 1940 and 1980.

2. List five attributes of the workforce of the year 2016.

3. List the six major occupational groups that are projected to increase the greatest numbers of workers between the years 2006 and 2016.

4. Describe three major benefits of improved technology, new inventions, and discovery for industries and occupations.

5. What two major strategies do U.S. firms use to cut costs and maintain production flexibility?

6. Why are some employers moving their production offshore?

7. List three reasons that U.S. corporations are encouraging diversity as a means to be more competitive in the global economy.

8. How many employees must a company have before it must comply with the Pregnancy Discrimination Act of 1978?

© JIST Works

Develop SCANS Competencies

This activity will give you practice in developing the resources, information, and interpersonal skills that successful workers use. Form cooperative learning groups to develop a time line of the changing workplace. Assign group members to research changes that have occurred in the workplace over the past 100 years. Changes can include such things as the number of women and minorities in the workforce and the change in the types of jobs available. Use the information from your text, and add information from your group's research.

After you have completed the historical aspect of changes in the workplace, find information that will allow you to continue your time line into the future. What types of jobs will be available in the year 2016? How will women and minorities be affected by these changes? Illustrate your time line by drawing pictures and diagrams or taking them from photos and magazines.

Enrichment

Have students complete the Chapter 14 section of the *Preparing for Career Success Student Portfolio, Third Edition.*

© JIST Works

Chapter 15 Resources

Lesson Plans and Preparation

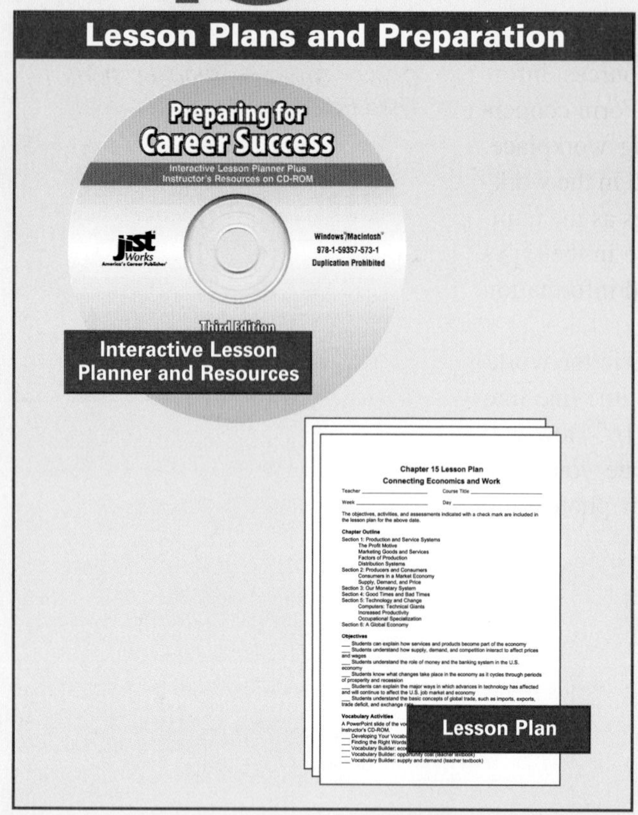

Preparing for Career Success
Interactive Lesson Planner Plus Instructor's Resources on CD-ROM
Third Edition
Interactive Lesson Planner and Resources
Chapter 15 Lesson Plan
Connecting Economics and Work
Lesson Plan

Multimedia

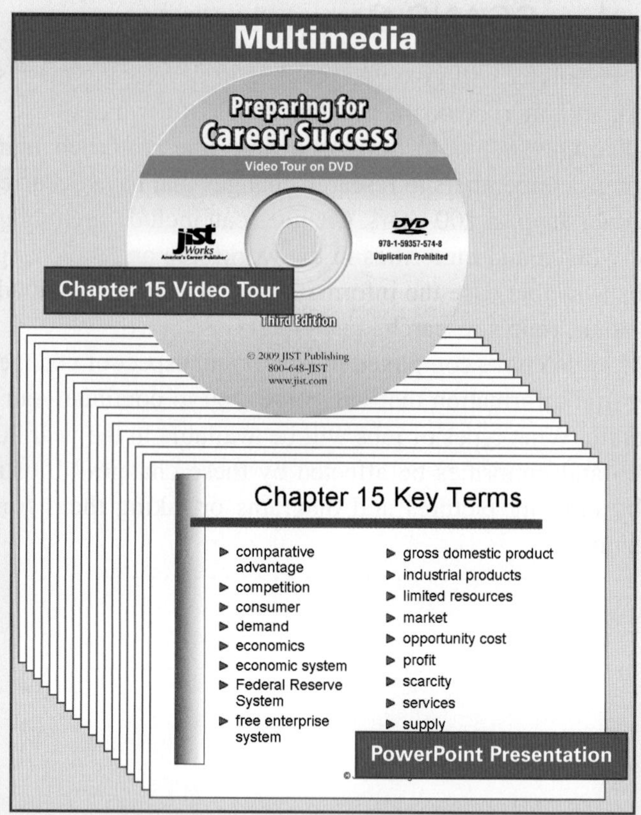

Preparing for Career Success
Video Tour on DVD
Third Edition
© 2009 JIST Publishing
800-648-JIST
www.jist.com
Chapter 15 Video Tour
Chapter 15 Key Terms
comparative advantage
competition
consumer
demand
economics
economic system
Federal Reserve System
free enterprise system
gross domestic product
industrial products
limited resources
market
opportunity cost
profit
scarcity
services
supply
PowerPoint Presentation

Activities

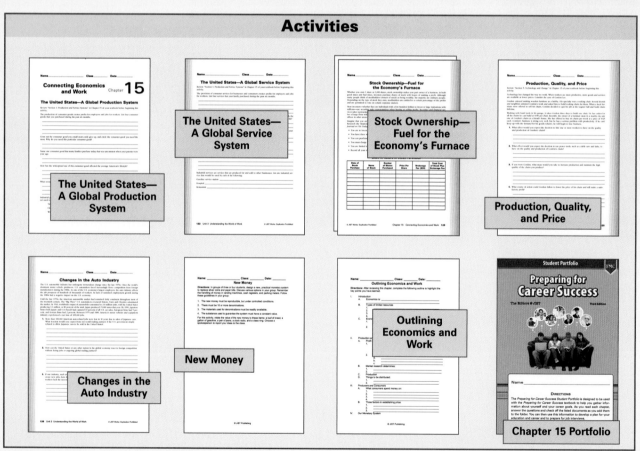

- The United States—A Global Production System
- The United States—A Global Service System
- Stock Ownership—Fuel for the Economy's Furnace
- Production, Quality, and Price
- Changes in the Auto Industry
- New Money
- Outlining Economics and Work
- Chapter 15 Portfolio

© JIST Works

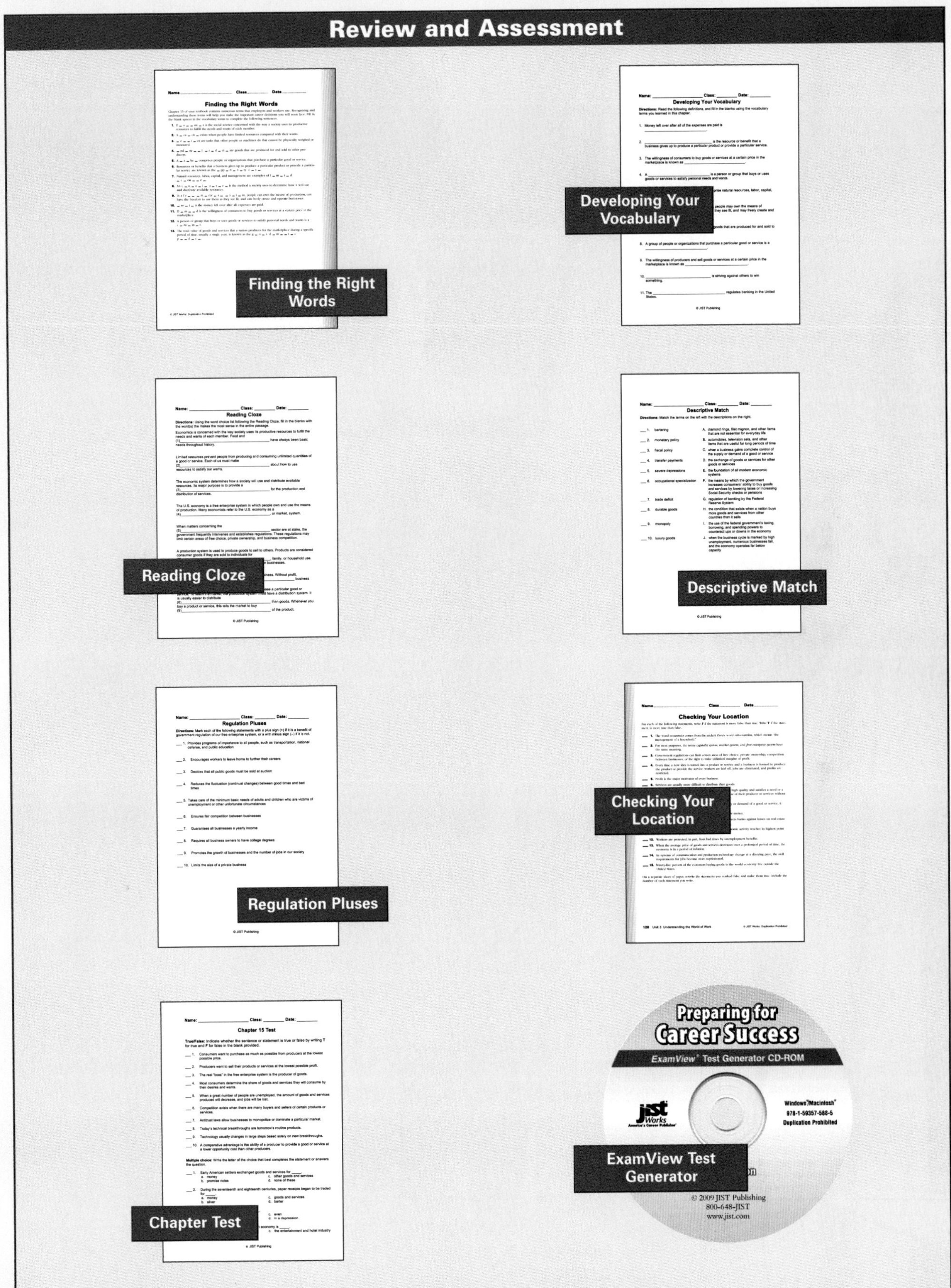

Review and Assessment
Finding the Right Words
Finding the Right Words
Developing Your Vocabulary
Developing Your Vocabulary
Reading Cloze
Reading Cloze
Descriptive Match
Descriptive Match
Regulation Pluses
Regulation Pluses
Checking Your Location
Checking Your Location
Chapter 15 Test
Chapter Test
Preparing for Career Success
ExamView® Test Generator CD-ROM
Windows®/Macintosh®
978-1-59357-588-5
Duplication Prohibited
© 2009 JIST Publishing
800-648-JIST
www.jist.com
ExamView Test Generator

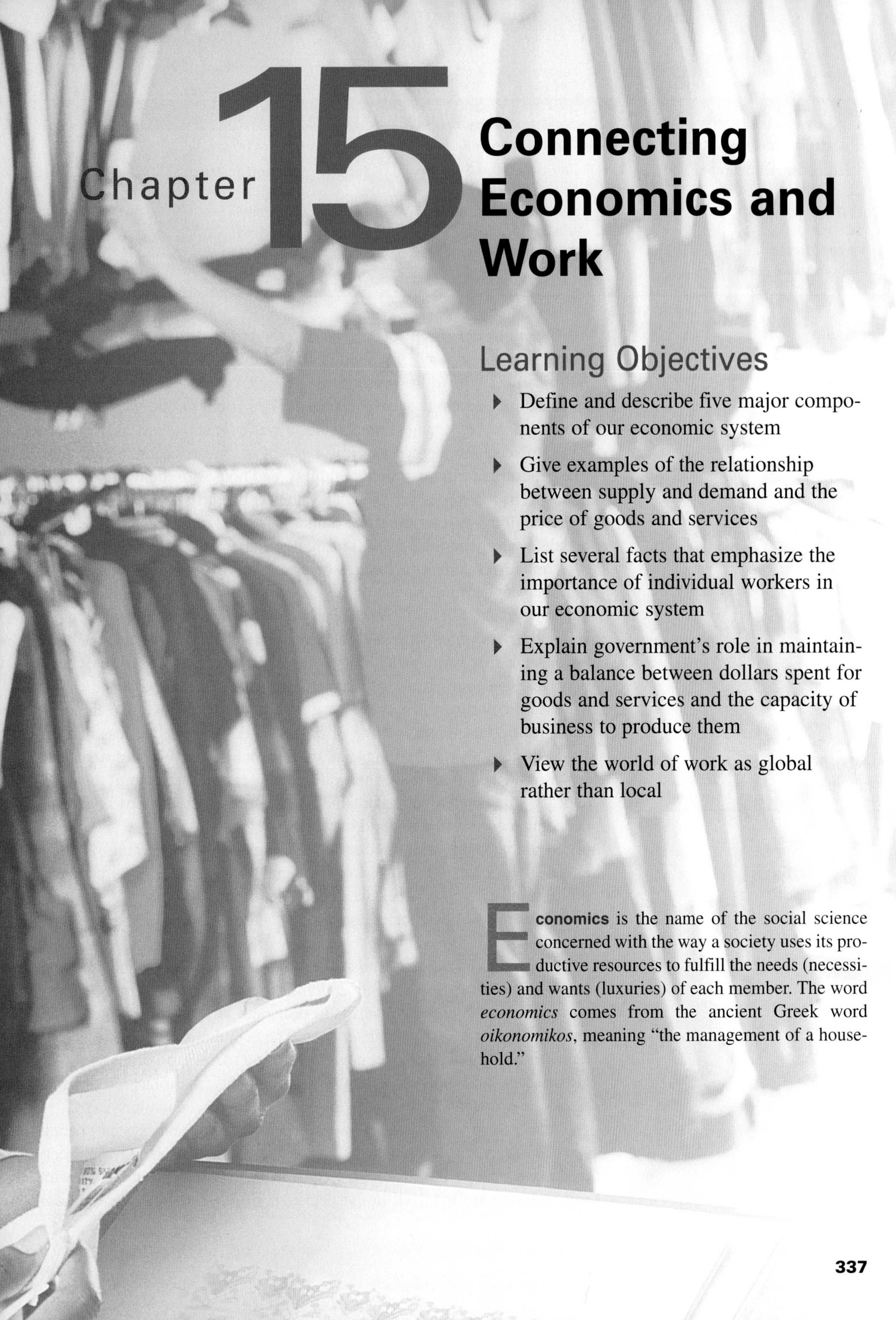

Chapter 15 Connecting Economics and Work

Learning Objectives

- Define and describe five major components of our economic system
- Give examples of the relationship between supply and demand and the price of goods and services
- List several facts that emphasize the importance of individual workers in our economic system
- Explain government's role in maintaining a balance between dollars spent for goods and services and the capacity of business to produce them
- View the world of work as global rather than local

Economics is the name of the social science concerned with the way a society uses its productive resources to fulfill the needs (necessities) and wants (luxuries) of each member. The word *economics* comes from the ancient Greek word *oikonomikos*, meaning "the management of a household."

Enrich Your Vocabulary

In reading this chapter and doing the exercises, you will learn the following important terms:

comparative advantage	Federal Reserve System	opportunity cost
competition	free enterprise system	profit
consumer	gross domestic product	scarcity
demand	industrial products	services
economics	limited resources	supply
economic system	market	technology

Vocabulary

You can use the "Developing Your Vocabulary" worksheet in the Chapter 15 file of the *Preparing for Career Success Instructor's CD-ROM, Third Edition* as a pretest or as a reteaching worksheet.

Cooperative Learning

Assign a group of students to decorate a bulletin board with the title "Economics and Work."

Key To Success

Understanding our economic system is an important part of understanding the world of work and planning for career success.

Video Tour on DVD

Show students the Chapter 15 segment to introduce them to the content.

Vocabulary Builder

After your students have completed the introduction, have them close their books. Ask several students to use their own words to describe the meaning of the term *economic system*.

From ancient times to the present, societies all over the world have shared the basic need for food and shelter. From the various Native American cultures to the present time, people on our continent have used an economic process to satisfy this need. The system for producing and distributing food has changed greatly, but it was as much a part of the Native American economic process as it is a part of our present economic process. The condominiums, apartment buildings, and houses of today are very different from the tepees, pueblos, and hogans of early societies, but all of these dwellings satisfy the same human need. All were made available to people by the economic process of their societies.

Limited resources (natural resources, labor, capital, and management) prevent people from producing and consuming unlimited quantities of a good or service. For example, the early colonists considered their source of wood to be unlimited. After all, the forests stretched for thousands of miles beyond the first settlements. Today, the shortage of timber in the United States presents our nation with difficult decisions. The unrestricted cutting of timber may result in the loss of a great natural resource. On the other hand, restrictions on the cutting of timber could result in the loss of thousands of jobs in the logging and milling industries. Finding a balance between the consumption, conservation, and recycling of natural resources and the jobs created and maintained by expanding businesses is a major economic concern in the world of work.

When people have limited resources compared to their wants, a condition of **scarcity** exists. All serious economic problems can be traced to a problem of scarcity. It affects us as individuals and as a society. As a result, each of us must make choices concerning the use of our resources to satisfy our wants.

The method a society uses to determine how it will use and distribute available resources (resource allocation) is its **economic system**. The major purpose of an economic system is to provide a process for the production and distribution of goods and services. The economic system of a society represents the input of private, government, and social institutions as well as laws, values, and individual priorities. Individually, these factors influence economic decisions; collectively, they determine the economic system.

The U.S. economy is a **free enterprise system**. In our system, people can own the means of production, use these means as they see fit, and freely create and operate businesses. All consumers, workers, producers, savers, and investors are involved in the decisions of our free enterprise system.

© JIST Works

Many economists refer to the U.S. economy as a capitalist, or market, system. For most purposes, the terms *capitalist system, market system,* and *free enterprise system* have the same meaning.

In our free enterprise system, large corporations sell shares of their stock to investors through a stock exchange. Nationwide, more than 300,000 securities and financial services sales representatives are employed. Would you enjoy working at this major stock exchange?

Freedom of choice is important in our free enterprise system. However, social and ethical pressure and laws limit the freedoms of consumers and producers. These regulators of free choice occur where the freedom of one individual or group ends and the freedom of another individual or group begins.

When matters concerning the public sector are at stake, government frequently intervenes and establishes protective regulations. These regulations may limit certain areas of free choice, private ownership, competition between businesses, or the right to make unlimited margins of profit. Numerous government agencies carry out the government's role in the economy. Government regulation of our free enterprise system

- Reduces the *fluctuations* (continual changes) between good times and bad times
- Promotes the growth of businesses and the number of jobs in our society
- Ensures fair competition between businesses
- Provides programs of importance to all people, such as transportation, national defense, and public education
- Takes care of the minimum basic needs of adults and children who are victims of unemployment or other unfortunate circumstances

Reteaching

Have students complete the "Regulation Pluses" worksheet in Chapter 15 of the *Preparing for Career Success Instructor's CD-ROM, Third Edition.*

The government usually places controls on a private business or industry that makes use of public resources or provides a service that is essential to the public good. More than ever before, the American public is concerned about economic questions such as

- What should be produced and who should produce it?
- How should it be produced and for whom should it be produced?
- What effect will production have on our environment?

TAKE NOTE

Wants rather than needs frequently determine how resources are used, yet natural resources are limited. If a business uses a natural resource to produce a product, that resource may not be available for another product. For these reasons, conservation and recycling of resources are important considerations for all businesses.

Developing a basic understanding of our economic system will help you achieve your career goals. It will also help you make wise decisions in your role as consumer and citizen. These decisions will benefit you individually and society as a whole.

Section 1: Production and Service Systems

Comprehension Check

Send two writers to the chalkboard. Instruct one writer to make a heading titled "Goods" and the other to make a heading titled "Services." Ask several students to name one consumer product or service for the writers to list. Next, ask your students: What is the difference between a consumer product and an industrial product? between a consumer service and an industrial service?

Satisfying the changing demand for goods and services is the goal of economic activity. Every time a new idea is turned into a product or a service and a business is formed to produce the product or provide the service, jobs are created for workers, and the opportunity to earn profits is created for employers.

The purpose of a production system is to produce *goods* (items that can be physically weighed or measured) to sell to others. **Industrial products** are goods that are produced for and sold to other producers. For example, a factory may produce only *synthetic fibers* (plastic threads such as nylon or polyester). These synthetic fibers are industrial products sold to companies that manufacture carpets, clothing, or tires. Products sold to consumers and used for personal, family, or household use are consumer goods. What consumer goods have you used this week? What industrial products were used to manufacture those consumer goods?

The purpose of a service system is to provide **services** (tasks that other people or machines perform that cannot be physically weighed or measured) to consumers or other businesses. Businesses use industrial services. Companies that sell these services include accounting firms, trucking companies, and architectural firms. Individuals use the services of a physician, beauty shop, or repair shop; these are consumer services. What services do both businesses and consumers use?

The sector of our free enterprise system that provides services is growing at a much faster rate than the sector that produces goods. In fact, the service sector will account for about four out of every five jobs by the year 2016 (see Figure 15.1).

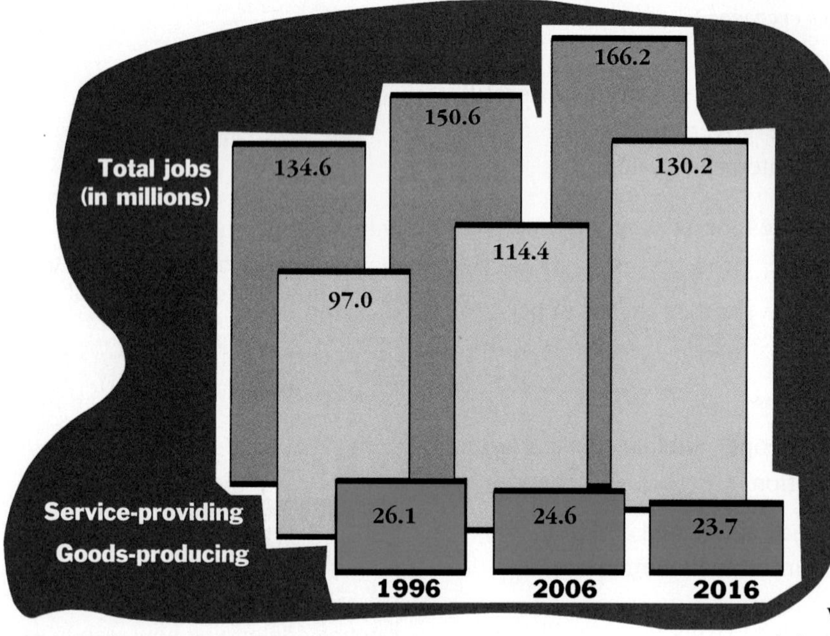

Figure 15.1 Projected growth of service-producing and goods-producing sectors.

The Profit Motive

Enrichment

Have students complete "The United States—A Global Production System" worksheet in Chapter 15 of the *Preparing for Career Success Student Activity Book, Third Edition.*

Profit is the major motivator of every business. Businesses of all types and sizes desire to make a **profit** (money that is left over after all of the expenses are paid). Profit is necessary for the creation of new jobs, the training of workers, and the cleanup of industrial pollution. Without profit, companies go out of business, jobs are lost, and office buildings and factories decay. Responsible, efficient, profitable companies are the foundation of a healthy free enterprise system.

© JIST Works

In both good times and bad times, investors purchase shares of stock in the hopes of making a profit. Depending on the type of stock, stockholders are entitled to certain shares of the profits and permitted to vote on certain corporate matters. Most people think of *stockholders* (owners of stock) as wealthy, yet most stockholders are ordinary people. In fact, more than 80 million individuals own *stocks* (ownership shares in a corporation). How would you like to own part of a business with the opportunity to make a profit?

Discussion Starter

Ask your students: Have you ever heard someone criticize a company for making a profit?

Marketing Goods and Services

Enrichment

Have students complete "The United States—A Global Service System" worksheet in Chapter 15 of the *Preparing for Career Success Student Activity Book, Third Edition.*

A **market** is a group of people or organizations that purchase a particular good or service. If you purchased a pair of shoes in the past year, you are part of the shoe market. The U.S. Army purchased several thousand pairs of shoes last year. It is probably the biggest organization in the shoe market. What other markets involve you?

Before new companies are formed, or established companies expand their production, they conduct *market research* (collecting and using information to link the marketer to the marketplace) and determine the *market demand* (what consumers want to buy).

Market research tells the organization which consumers are most likely to buy their product or service. These consumers make up the organization's target market. Examples of target markets are small children who watch cereal or toy commercials on TV and senior citizens who read ads for health products. What are some of the products or services that have targeted the teenage market?

Companies use information provided by market research analysts to make decisions about their products and services.

In our free enterprise system, numerous companies compete for business in their market. Each company strives for a certain *market share* (a percentage of sales in a market). Frequently, one company is the leader in its market. Who is the current leader in the shoe market, the cereal market, and the entertainment market? What might cause a leader's market share to rise or fall?

Enrichment

Assign your students to clip pictures from ads in newspapers and magazines that market specific goods or services. Include pictures of workers. Then have students post the ads on the "Economics and Work" bulletin board under a heading of "Goods" or "Services."

Solving the Problem: Investment Creates Jobs

Fran Gomez graduated from an 18-month technical school in 2001 with a major in drafting technology. She received similar job offers from the R. W. Anderson Corporation, a manufacturer of industrial machinery, and

Take Note

Inventions such as the transistor in 1947 and the microprocessor in 1971 led to the creation of the world's first personal computer (PC) in 1975 by Ed Roberts. Next, Apple and IBM introduced their first versions of the personal computer. From that time forward, computers have evolved rapidly, with new technologies reducing size and cost while increasing memory and processing power. Computers have had an enormous impact on society, providing tremendous technological possibilities and opportunities throughout the economy.

Take Note

The Technology Student Association is a nationwide organization that helps middle school and high school students explore careers in science, technology, and engineering. Through activities such as designing a house or developing a video game, students build their technical skills and gain experience in teamwork, communication, and leadership. Contact a local chapter or visit www.tsaweb.org on the Internet to find out more about this career and technical student organization.

SNC Plastic Products, a manufacturer of plastic kitchen products. Fran wanted to work for a stable, growing company that offered the opportunity for career growth. She looked forward to buying a home, having a family, and being a member of the community. Before accepting a job with either company, Fran checked the profits and growth of each company for the 10 previous years. At R. W. Anderson, the number of employees had grown very little, but the company had much higher profits than SNC Plastics. The Anderson family owned the R. W. Anderson Corporation, and they were a very wealthy family. SNC hired new employees each year, and it borrowed money from banks to expand its business.

Fran decided that R. W. Anderson would be her best choice. It was the town's largest employer, owned by local people, and had no outstanding debts.

Eight years later, in 2009, Fran's life dreams were coming true. Anderson had promoted Fran to senior design technician. She and her husband had purchased a small home and were expecting their first child in August. Six weeks before the baby was born, all of Fran's dreams exploded when R. W. Anderson announced that it was closing its factory in two weeks.

Fran learned an important economic lesson the hard way. Some companies make high profits year after year instead of investing money in new equipment and technology to keep factories and offices modernized or developing new products for growing markets. Eventually, the market for the products they have made year after year shrinks or disappears. The result is that they are unable to compete with modern factories, and they cannot afford the cost of modernization.

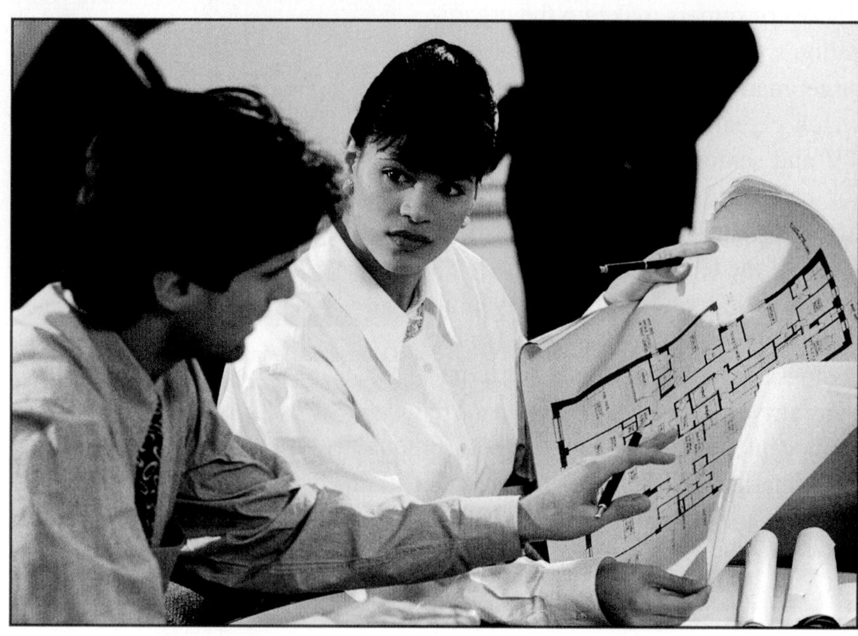

Critical Thinking

What should Fran have been looking for during her eight years of employment with R. W. Anderson to foresee the closing of the company?

© JIST Works

What criteria can employers use to figure out how much of their profits to invest each year in developing new products or services, expanding their markets, buying new equipment, updating their buildings, and training their employees?

In what way was R. W. Anderson an irresponsible business?

There is nothing permanent except change.

—Heracleitus

Factors of Production

As a business strives to make a profit, it must give up certain resources or benefits to produce a particular product or to provide a particular service. Resources or benefits given up by the business are **opportunity cost**. For example, an automobile company may have to choose between developing and producing a new sports car or a new van if it cannot afford to develop and produce both. The decision to produce a new van has the opportunity cost of not producing a new sports car. Suppose a small business must choose to either hire an additional salesperson or modernize its office equipment. If the business chooses to modernize its office equipment, what opportunity cost will it pay? Companies must continually decide what opportunity costs they should pay.

Comprehension Check/Vocabulary Builder

Instruct your students to close their books. Then ask several students: In your own words, explain the meaning of the term *opportunity cost.*

Distribution Systems

A production system cannot operate without a *distribution system* (steps involved in bringing products and services from their point of origin to the consumer). For example, every day you use toothpaste that may have been produced hundreds of miles from your home. Fortunately, drugstores are located throughout the nation to sell toothpaste. Without a transportation system, such as trucking or railroads, the toothpaste would not be available in your local drugstore. A labor force of engineers, machine operators, packaging experts, truck drivers, railroad workers, engine mechanics, construction workers, store managers, retail clerks, and hundreds of other workers are involved in making certain that you can purchase toothpaste at your local drugstore. To understand the distribution of goods, see Figure 15.2.

Enrichment

Explain to your students that distribution systems are paths that goods and services follow from the producer to the consumer. Ask several students: Name a familiar product or service used by your family, and describe the distribution system it follows.

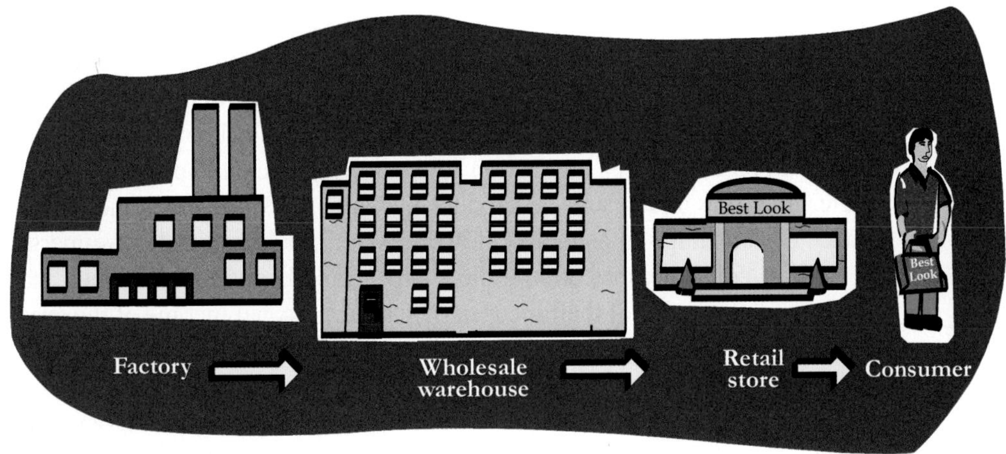

Figure 15.2 Distribution of goods.

Services are usually much easier to distribute than goods. For example, a dentist, beautician, or appliance repairperson may simply rent an office or shop and hire someone to schedule appointments. Likewise, large furniture, automobile, or appliance dealers may make repairs on their premises.

Section 1: Get Involved

One major corporation, Hyatt Hotels, developed a once-a-year training day called In-Touch Day. On this training day, corporate headquarters is closed, and everyone—from top executives to office secretaries—spends the day working at a rank-and-file job in one of the corporation's hotels. Answer the following questions related to this type of training, and be prepared to discuss your responses in class.

1. How would this type of work experience help executives and managers understand the total operation of their organizations?
2. How would this experience help managers understand their employees and customers and the problems that their organization needs to solve?
3. What message do machine operators in a factory receive when a vice president spends the day learning and doing job tasks with them?
4. What message does a vice president receive when he or she is unable to effectively perform the work tasks of a rank-and-file employee?
5. What would corporate workers and rank-and-file employees learn by talking and working together for one day as a team?
6. What effect would this experience have on making the organization cohesive and profitable?

Section 2: Producers and Consumers

Consumers and producers are interconnected in our market economy. Consumers want to purchase as much as possible from producers at the lowest possible price. In turn, producers want to sell their products or services and make as much profit as possible.

TAKE NOTE

As far back as 2000 B.C., people used gold as money. It was scarce, desirable, and perfectly acceptable for buying goods or services or for paying debts. During the seventeenth and eighteenth centuries A.D., wealthy people deposited their gold with local goldsmiths for safekeeping. The goldsmiths provided a paper receipt for the money deposited with them. Years later, the receipts began to be traded for goods or services because of the gold that they represented. This was the beginning of paper money.

Consumers in a Market Economy

The real "boss" in the free enterprise system is you—the **consumer** (a person or group that buys or uses goods or services to satisfy personal needs and wants). Every time you buy a product or service, you are telling the market to supply more of that product. When you and other consumers stop buying a product or service, the merchant must sell something else or go out of business. This interaction between consumers and producers helps determine how much will be produced. Figure 15.3 illustrates the importance of consumption as money flows between producers and consumers.

Most consumers determine the share of goods and services they will consume by the size of their income. When the personal income of the average consumer increases, his or her level of consumption also increases. When personal income decreases, the level of consumption decreases. When a great number of people are unemployed, the amount of goods and services produced will decrease, and jobs will be lost.

© JIST Works

Consumers spend their money on different types of goods:

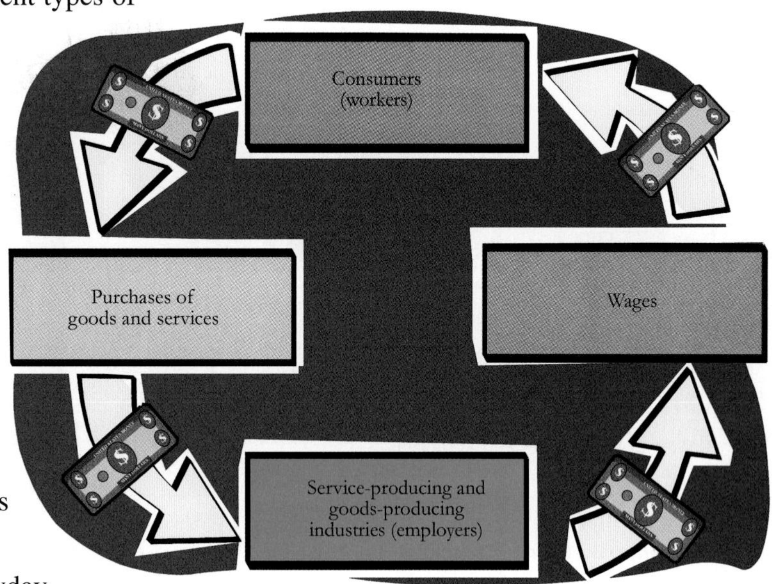

Figure 15.3 Money flowing between producers and consumers.

- Durable goods are useful for a very long time. Automobiles, television sets, clothing, and home appliances are examples of durable goods. When times are bad, consumers can postpone replacing these items. What durable goods do you own? Which ones would you like to replace?
- Nondurable goods require continual replacement. Toothpaste, gasoline, and food items are examples of nondurable goods. What nondurable goods have you used this week?
- Necessity goods are essential for everyday life. Food, clothing, shelter, and medical care are examples of necessity goods. What was the most expensive necessity good you used this week?
- Luxury goods are not essential for everyday life. Diamond rings, filet mignon, and compact discs are examples of luxury goods. What luxury goods would you like to have? In Chapter 18, you will learn methods to help you become a prudent consumer in our free enterprise system.

Supply, Demand, and Price

The willingness of consumers to buy goods or services at a certain price in the marketplace is a **demand. Supply** is the willingness of producers to produce and sell goods or services at a certain price in the marketplace. The *monetary value* (dollar amount) placed on goods or services in the marketplace is the *price.*

Changes in supply and demand influence prices in the marketplace. For example, wheat is the major raw material used to produce bread. Imagine that you are a Nebraska wheat farmer. Perfect weather conditions have resulted in a wheat crop that is twice your average annual yield. You are delighted because now you have twice the amount of wheat you normally sell (the supply). However, people do not plan to buy any more bread than usual (the demand). Other farmers also have had a bumper crop to sell. You suddenly have a great deal of competition for selling wheat in the marketplace (oversupply). With twice the normal amount of wheat available in the market and a demand for only half of it, what will happen to the price of your wheat? It will go down, of course. When the supply of a product or service is greater than the demand, the price goes down. What would have happened to the price of your wheat if the demand for it were greater than the quantity harvested?

Comprehensive Check/ Vocabulary Builder

After your students have finished reading "Supply, Demand, and Price," ask several students to respond to this statement: In your own words, describe the meaning of the economic terms *supply* and *demand.*

Career Fact

When producers and consumers are confident that their government has gold and silver to support the money, the value of the money is strengthened.

Competition for the consumer's business exists on every busy street in America.

Competition (striving against others to win something) plays a key role in establishing the prices of products and services. In our market economy, competition occurs when a business or service strives to win customers by offering lower prices or better quality than its competitors offer. Competition exists when there are many buyers and sellers of a certain product or service. McDonald's, Wendy's, and Burger King are big competitors in the fast-food industry. Can you remember a time when one of these fast-food restaurants offered lower prices or better quality to attract customers?

When a business obtains complete control of the supply or demand (most often the supply) of a good or service, it becomes a monopoly. The business price of the monopoly's goods or service increases to more than the real value. It represents the controlled conditions of supply and demand. Imagine a situation in which one company controls the production and supply of all the automobile tires in the United States. This single company can demand the highest possible price that consumers can afford for tires. There would be no competition to keep prices down. In this case, consumers would have two choices: buy the tires at the market price or do not operate their automobiles.

The government regulates fair competition between businesses through numerous antitrust laws. These laws prohibit attempts by businesses to monopolize or dominate a particular market. Antitrust laws are necessary to ensure the growth of businesses and the number of jobs in our society. They are especially important to small and new business owners because without the assurance of fair competition between businesses, they could not survive.

Community Resources

Form a committee to obtain additional information about monopolies from the Federal Trade Commission. Have the committee report the information to the class.

FIND OUT MORE

For more information about monopolies, key in **Federal Trade Commission** on your Internet search engine.

Section 2: Get Involved

Answer the following on a separate sheet of paper, and be prepared to discuss your responses in class.

1. Interview an automobile mechanic or car salesperson with 10 or more years of experience. Ask the following questions:
   What effect did the importing of automobiles from foreign countries have on competition in the United States?
   What effect did it have on the quality of U.S. cars?
   What about the effect on size, fuel efficiency, and price? Why?
2. A major purpose of advertising is to increase the demand for a product or service and to get consumers to buy it. Choose a product or service, and find at least four ads describing it. Are the ads truthful? Do they make you want to buy the product or service? What groups of people will be attracted by the advertising? Why?

© JIST Works

Section 3: Our Monetary System

Early settlers on the American frontier had little need for money. Instead, they exchanged goods or services for other goods or services. This system of exchange is called *bartering*. In the early 1900s, it was common for a rural physician to accept a supply of eggs, a couple of chickens, or even a pig in exchange for medical services.

Governments eventually began to print and issue paper money that was supported or could be exchanged for gold. In 1934, the U.S. government called in all gold coins and certificates and stopped redeeming paper money in gold. This enabled the government to vary the amount of money in circulation to meet both domestic and international needs.

Paper money, no longer redeemable in gold, continues to circulate as freely as ever. We have come to believe that our monetary authorities, even without the old-time discipline of gold at home, will not destroy the purchasing power of the dollar by printing and circulating too much money. Money itself has little value. The value of money exists only in the value of goods and services that it represents.

The federal government uses two methods to regulate and influence the economy to maintain a balance between the total dollar amount spent by individuals, households, businesses, and governments for goods and services and the growing capacity of business to produce goods and services.

Fiscal policy is the use of the federal government's taxing, borrowing, and spending powers to counteract *ups* (periods of inflation) or *downs* (periods of recession) in the economy. When the government acts to put more money in consumers' hands, the demand for goods and services increases, more jobs are created, and the economy moves toward an up cycle—a period of inflation. The federal government is the biggest consumer in our economy. Imagine the thousands of jobs created by the government when it buys a new fleet of airplanes, ships, or tanks; builds a new interstate highway; or gives money to state and local governments to build bridges or sewer and water systems.

The government can also increase consumers' ability to buy goods and services by reducing taxes. In addition, the government can increase the money it pays consumers in the form of Social Security checks or pensions. These are *transfer payments.* On the other hand, when the government reduces spending on goods or services, increases taxes, or reduces the money it spends on transfer payments, the economy moves toward a down cycle—a period of recession. Balancing the economy is a lot like flying an airplane. The pilot (the federal government) makes small adjustments to go up or down in response to changing pressures. Making large, sudden adjustments in either direction could result in a serious crash.

The second method the federal government uses to influence the economy is its monetary policy. The **Federal Reserve System**, a network of 12 regional banks, regulates banking in the United States. The Federal Reserve System increases or decreases the amount of money in our economy by

Comprehension Check

After your students have completed this section, ask them to close their books. Ask several students to answer the following question in their own words: What is the true value of money? (Answer: The value of the goods and services it represents.)

Cooperative Learning

Have students complete the "New Money" worksheet in Chapter 15 of the *Preparing for Career Success Instructor's CD-ROM, Third Edition.*

CAREER FACT

By law, the Federal Reserve cannot create paper money and bank reserves in excess of four times the value of gold held by the Treasury in Fort Knox and elsewhere. The reason for connecting the dollar to gold is to ensure that the buying power of the dollar, relative to that of other currencies, remains stable. Because all nations still desire and will accept gold, it is international money. Many countries, including the United States, pay their debts to one another by transferring gold.

Community Resources

Form a committee of students to contact a local bank or savings and loan. Ask them to invite a vice president or a loan officer to speak to your class about the Federal Reserve System.

printing more money or removing money from circulation. The Federal Reserve System not only regulates the amount of money flowing through the economy, but it also sets the interest rate it charges commercial banks. In turn, the commercial banks respond to the interest rates they must pay the Federal Reserve banks by lowering or raising interest rates to individual consumers or businesses. If you owned a business and wanted to buy new machinery or build a new building, would you be more likely to expand when interest rates were high or low? What effect does business expansion have on employment?

When individuals or businesses need to borrow money, they go to a *commercial* (privately owned) bank. When commercial banks need money, they go to a *Federal Reserve bank* (owned by the federal government).

Individuals or businesses make most purchases or payments with money or checks. Checks are not money, but they represent money and are widely accepted as a form of money. The banking system can increase the supply of money in the economy by making loans to individuals, businesses, or the government. In turn, making loans increases spending power and the demand for goods and services. What effect would this have on employment?

Are you interested in a banking career? The banking industry employs more than 546,000 tellers, 133,000 loan officers, and 73,000 financial managers.

When you deposit your money in most banks, it is insured by the Federal Deposit Insurance Corporation (FDIC). The FDIC is a government agency that protects small depositors against the failure of an insured bank or savings and loan institution. Before you open an account with a bank, be certain that you see the initials FDIC on its signs. The FDIC safeguards deposits up to $100,000 in each account.

Section 3: Get Involved

Answer the following on a separate sheet of paper, and be prepared to discuss your responses in class.

1. If our society operated without money, what could you or your family barter to obtain food, shelter, transportation, and clothing? Why did bartering work on the American frontier? What conditions have changed to make bartering almost impossible in our society?
2. How would an individual or a group of people start a business if there were no banks? What effect would this have on starting or expanding a business? What effect would this have on the number and variety of jobs available in our society?

© JIST Works

Section 4: Good Times and Bad Times

Like the pendulum on a clock, our economy swings between periods of "good times" and "bad times." These continual economic changes between prosperity and recession make up the business cycle.

During periods of good times and business peaks, economic activity reaches its highest point in the business cycle. Prosperity is evident as businesses produce goods and services at full capacity. At this point, new businesses are started, and the number of unemployed workers is low.

Bad times range from mild *recessions* (when the nation's output does not grow for at least six months) to severe *depressions* (when the business cycle is marked by high unemployment, numerous businesses fail, and the economy operates far below capacity), such as the Great Depression that lasted from 1929 to 1941. During bad times in the business cycle, declining industries lay off thousands of workers.

The business cycle affects and is affected by the production and distribution of goods and services; the earning and spending of wages by workers; the number of workers who are unemployed; the trading of goods and services with other nations; and the price of stocks, bonds, and commodities.

During the past 50 years, several safeguards built into our economy have helped protect business owners and workers alike from large swings in the business cycle:

- Workers receive some protection from bad times by unemployment insurance benefits.
- Investors receive some protection from sharp declines in business profits by corporate policies that attempt to keep dividend payments more stable than corporate profits.
- The federal government's fiscal and monetary policies regulate the rates of interest paid by businesses or individuals when borrowing money. These policies also determine the amount and types of taxes to be paid and the allowed tax exemptions. Lowering interest rates to encourage spending by individuals and businesses is an *easy-money policy.* During periods of easy money (low interest rates), businesses tend to invest in items such as new equipment and buildings. A major result of this investment is an increase in the number of jobs. On the other hand, the strategy of decreasing the amount of money in the economy and increasing the rate of interest for loans is called a *tight-money policy.* Tight money pushes the economy in the direction of less borrowing, less purchasing of goods and services, fewer jobs, and recession.

The **gross domestic product** (GDP) is the total value of goods and services that a nation produces for the marketplace during a specific period of time (usually a single year). Figure 15.4 illustrates this concept.

Cooperative Learning

Divide your class into learning pairs. Allow 10 minutes for each pair to write their answers to these questions: During good times, would you rather be a worker in a small business or the owner? Why? During bad times, would you rather be a worker in a small business or the owner? Why? Ask each pair to read their answers to the class.

Discussion Starter

Experiencing the Great Depression influenced the career choices and the buying and saving habits of the World War II generation. Ask your students how they have been influenced by good times or bad times.

Key To Success

Successful workers take advantage of every opportunity to learn about new technology in their selected occupations.

Comprehension Check

Instruct your students to close their books. Ask several students: In your own words, explain the economic terms *easy-money policy* and *tight-money policy.*

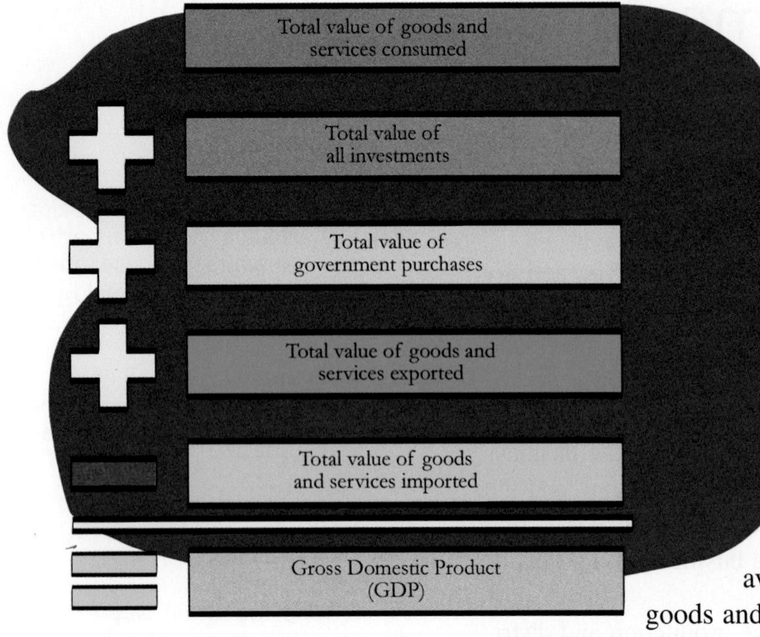

Figure 15.4 Gross domestic product.

The GDP is projected to grow at an annual rate of 3.9 percent from 2004 to 2014. In terms of dollars, it is projected to grow from $10,756,000,000 in 2004 to 14,650,000,000 in 2014. This steady growth in the demand for goods and services is largely due to continually accelerating productivity.

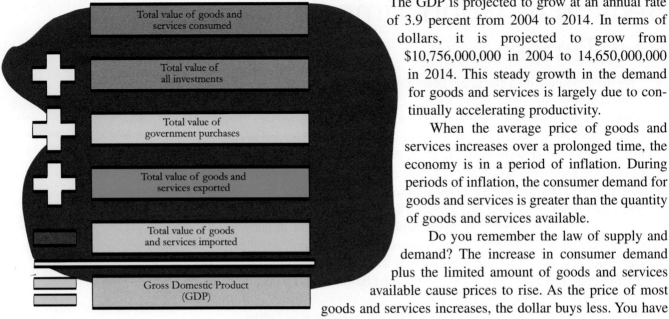

When the average price of goods and services increases over a prolonged time, the economy is in a period of inflation. During periods of inflation, the consumer demand for goods and services is greater than the quantity of goods and services available.

Do you remember the law of supply and demand? The increase in consumer demand plus the limited amount of goods and services available cause prices to rise. As the price of most goods and services increases, the dollar buys less. You have probably heard older people complain that the dollar is not worth as much as it used to be. What they sometimes forget is that their labor is worth more than it used to be. As a result, they have more dollars to buy goods and services.

Statistics that forecast good times and bad times for the economy are *leading economic indicators.* The *index of leading indicators* includes these 11 key statistics:

Enrichment/Cooperative Learning

Divide your class into groups of three or four. Assign an economic indicator from the list to each group. Instruct each group to write answers for the following questions: Why would a change in this particular leading economic indicator signify a change in the economy? What change in this indicator would signify a change toward good times? Toward bad times? Have each group report their conclusions.

- Percentage of firms getting delayed deliveries
- Prices of 500 common stocks
- Average number of hours manufacturing employees work per week
- Consumer expectations of economy's health
- Monthly average of the real money supply
- Weekly claims on unemployment insurance
- Monthly total of building permits issued
- Number of contracts and orders for new plants and equipment
- Orders for manufactured consumer goods and materials
- Change in sensitive materials (commodities) prices
- Change in manufacturers' unfilled orders for durable goods

A recession is indicated when statistics show these factors to be declining. On the other hand, increases in these indicators predict a period of inflation. Modest upward or downward movements in a well-balanced economy indicate good times, whereas sharp, prolonged increases or decreases can spell bad times for the economy.

Career Fact

If a member of your family had invested $100 in Microsoft Corporation in 1986 when it premiered, his or her stock would be worth more than $2.5 million today.

© JIST Works

Section 4: Get Involved

Interview a family member or friend with 10 or more years of work experience. Ask this person the following questions, write down his or her responses on a separate sheet of paper, and be prepared to discuss your findings in class:

1. How were you affected by periods of inflation and recession during the past 10 years?
2. What rate of inflation would you consider acceptable for our economy? Why?

Section 5: Technology and Change

Technology (the science of mechanical and industrial arts) is the foundation of change in today's world of work. It determines the ability of our nation and its workers to compete and prosper in local, regional, and world markets.

The use of technology satisfies an ever-growing demand for goods and services in our country and from our overseas trading partners. Today's technical breakthroughs are tomorrow's routine products. Think about the changes you have witnessed in your lifetime with new or improved tools, transportation, medical treatment, energy resources, fabrics, construction materials, computer applications, and agriculture. Many of those products were very expensive 10 or 20 years ago but are common today.

Technology usually changes in small steps based on past knowledge and scientific breakthroughs. Computer chips, nuclear energy, television, transistors, and semiconductors are examples of scientific breakthroughs. Each of these technical developments eventually opened the door for millions of jobs worldwide.

Discussion Starter

Explain to your students that technology is like a steel ball rolling downhill. Due to its own energy, the further it rolls, the faster it rolls. New technology increases the availability and demand for newer technology. Ask your students: During the past five years, what new technology has made your life less complicated? More complicated? More enjoyable? Less enjoyable? Explain your answers.

Enrichment

Explain to your class that technological advances sponsored by government spending during times of war or national crisis (the space program) frequently result in new services and products for consumers. Send a writer to the chalkboard to make a list of such services and products. Ask your class to identify goods and services for the writer.

Computers: Technical Giants

Computers may be the most profound technology since steam power ignited the Industrial Revolution. Computing power that once cost millions of dollars now costs hundreds. This incredible decrease in cost and increase in computing power is a result of extraordinary advances in the manufacture of microprocessors. Computer technology is altering the form, nature, and future course of the American economy by

- Creating entirely new organizations, products, services, and markets
- Increasing the flow of products to consumers
- Launching an information highway to global product and financial markets
- Increasing worker efficiency
- Changing the *composition* (type of occupations) and geographical distribution of labor

Career Fact

The Internet is changing the economics of transactions, benefiting both consumers and producers. Business-to-business e-commerce and consumers' online spending are surging. E-retail sales account for nearly $200 billion a year. Close to half (47 percent) of all adult Americans have a high-speed Internet connection at home (source: U.S. Department of Commerce, 2007).

Comprehension Check

Instruct your students to close their books. Ask several students: Describe an example of how technology has increased the production of workers in a specific occupation.

As new technology creates changes at a dizzying pace, the skill requirements for jobs become more sophisticated. To produce the maximum number of high-quality products or services, employees will need to maintain and develop the skills necessary to use these new technologies.

Investing in advanced technology; improving current products, processes, and services; and creating entirely new ones are essential for the United States to improve its productivity and competitiveness. Newly automated businesses must deal with worker issues that result from the use of new technology. These issues include employment security, training for new skills, changes in work organization, and a need for teamwork.

Increased Productivity

Discussion Starter

What is another area of production in which advanced technology has increased the quality and quantity of a product or service?

Productivity is the amount of goods or services that a worker produces in a certain time (usually an hour). Improving the technology of tools and machines increases worker productivity. A hundred years ago, thousands of American farmers produced corn. A farmer with a good team of horses could plow about two acres of land each day. Using horses to pull metal plows, disks, and seeders, each farmer could prepare, plant, cultivate, and harvest about 30 acres of land each year, producing about 50 bushels of corn per acre. A single farmer produced far more corn per year than was produced by all of the workers in the earlier Indian village.

Farmers, ranchers, and agricultural managers held about 258,000 jobs in 2006. Most manage crop production activities, while others manage livestock production. The trend continues toward fewer and larger farms.

Today, a much smaller workforce of farmers, equipped with giant air-conditioned tractors, not only produces a much larger harvest of corn than their counterparts of 100 years ago, but in one hour can harvest 900 bushels. The difference in these three periods of corn production results from the technology available to the workers. Which farmer worked the hardest? Which had the least product to show for his or her labor?

Just as consumers expect high-quality goods or services for the dollars they spend, employers expect high-quality production for the dollars they spend on wages. As workers have produced more goods or services per day, employers have reduced the number of hours in the workweek. For example, a 60-hour workweek was common in 1850, but since 1950, a 40-hour week is typical. Still, the average American worker's standard of living, measured in purchasing power, has increased dramatically.

Education and Training/ Cooperative Learning

Divide your class into learning pairs. Allow five minutes for each pair to list changes in the education and training requirements for one specific occupation during the past 100 or more years. Allow time for each pair to report their answer to the class.

© JIST Works

Occupational Specialization

One hundred and fifty years ago, more than 90 percent of the workforce was involved in agriculture. At that time, families were largely independent, producing most of their own food and clothing and frequently building their own homes. There were few specialists in the workforce. Today, less than 2 percent of the workforce is involved in agriculture, and more than 99 percent of U.S. families are interdependent: They produce goods or provide services for others, and they use their earnings to purchase necessities and luxuries. With few exceptions, today's workers are specialists.

Cross-Reference

See the vocabulary term *interdependence* in "Section 1: Having a Positive Attitude," in Chapter 10.

Occupational specialization occurs when a worker focuses on producing one particular item of goods or providing one particular service. It is the foundation of all modern economic systems.

Through specialization, our nation is able to produce a higher volume of goods or services at a lower cost than would otherwise be possible. In turn, specialists use their wages to purchase goods and services from other specialists at a lower cost. The efficiency that results from specialization enables all members of the workforce to have a higher standard of living. Figure 15.5 demonstrates the high degree of interdependence among workers and businesses in the U.S. economy. Notice how money flows in a cycle through our economic system.

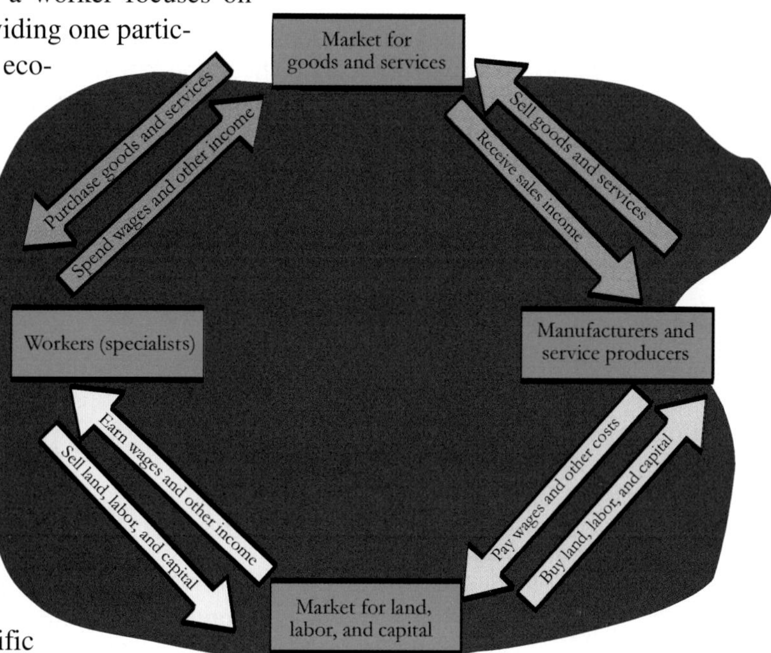

Figure 15.5 The interdependence of workers in a specialized economy.

Specialization may be regional. Regional specialization occurs when producers use specific natural resources in a geographic region. Potatoes from Idaho, wine from California, peaches from Georgia, and cheese from Wisconsin are examples of regional specialization. What specialization takes place in your region of the country? What natural resources or other factors have influenced specialization? What occupations are in demand because of this specialization?

When certain geographic regions or nations are able to produce more of a certain product or provide more of a certain service at a better price than others because of the efficiency they gain from specialization, they have a comparative advantage over competing regions or nations. A **comparative advantage** is the ability of a producer to provide a good or service at a lower opportunity cost than other producers. For example, the nations of Southeast Asia have a comparative advantage over most of the world in their ability to produce natural rubber, largely due to the region's climate. By specializing in a product in which they have a comparative advantage, the nations of Southeast Asia are able to sell natural rubber on the world market. They use the money they receive to purchase other goods and services from other nations.

CLUSTER LINK

Communications and media technology are an important part of every American business. If you are interested in writing articles, designing print materials, or making commercials, you should explore the Arts, A/V Technology, and Communications career cluster. See the appendix for more information.

Another example of comparative advantage is our nation's real manufacturing output as a percentage of real gross national product. Our GDP has been increasing, while manufacturing employment as a percentage of total payroll employment has been declining. This demonstrates that today fewer workers are producing more goods. What effect does this increased output have on employment opportunities in the United States? What effect does it have in your community?

Section 5: Get Involved

Answer the following on a separate sheet of paper, and be prepared to discuss your responses in class.

1. Occupational specialization affects workers worldwide. Workers use money earned from the sale of their specialty products to foreign nations to purchase goods that workers in other nations can produce at lower costs. List imported goods or services used in your region. Make another list of goods or services produced in your region and exported to other nations. Does your region export more than it imports? If so, the balance of trade is in your region's favor. Make another list of specific jobs gained or lost in your region due to the balance of trade with other nations.
2. Television was a major technical development of the twentieth century. How much time have you spent in the past week watching TV? How would you have used this time if television were not available? Without TV, what jobs would be lost in the world of work? What industries would benefit? Ask older friends or relatives about industries that prospered before television.

Discussion Starter

Ask your students: Is it an advantage or disadvantage for American workers to have low-wage, labor-intensive jobs shifted to newly industrialized countries in Latin America, East Asia, and the Caribbean? Explain the reasons for your answer.

TAKE NOTE

The international world of business is tied together by instant information. Money used to purchase goods or build a new business moves globally in a matter of keystrokes. The major countries of Western Europe now use a common currency (the Euro) for international trade. Increasingly, the tendency of the world is to act as one market instead of a series of national ones. The Internet minimizes factors such as communication and distance. This allows small, local businesses to compete globally with large companies.

Section 6: A Global Economy

One of the most significant features of the world of work you are preparing to enter is the growing internationalization of the U.S. economy. Consider these facts:

- Census figures tell us that less than 5 percent of the world's population lives in the United States. This means that about 95 percent of the customers buying goods in the world economy live outside the United States.
- The world's wealth is concentrated in North America, Europe, Japan, Australia, and New Zealand. These countries can afford what the United States has to sell. South of the U.S. border, trading partners from Mexico to Argentina are rapidly growing in importance.
- Nations are removing the political, economic, and social walls that divide them. As a result, goods, services, information, and technology are traded in a global market.
- U.S. companies frequently form partnerships with companies from other nations. The combined technology and resources of these mergers enable both partners to gain a much larger share of the world market.

© JIST Works

- The business of many companies is global. Businesses conduct production or marketing operations in several nations or through branches or subsidiaries in which they have an important interest. When a business either purchases or creates another business in another nation, it is direct investment.
- Offshore businesses developed by Americans vary widely. Many traditional high-volume, standardized production systems and low-wage, labor-intensive production systems have shifted to newly industrialized countries in Latin America, East Asia, and the Caribbean.
- The competitive advantage of U.S. companies is sophisticated, technology-driven, precision-engineered, and custom-tailored commodities or products, manufactured with rapidly changing technology.

Key To Success

Learn as much as possible about America's economic system. The success or failure of American business in the global market will affect your career success.

The global economy is here. The question is no longer "Will the United States be involved in the global economy?" but rather "What must the United States do to be a successful participant in the global economy?"

Government involvement, different monetary systems, and international borders pose problems that nations must negotiate before they become trading partners. Some governments fear losing technology to other countries, and workers fear the loss of jobs to other nations. Inflation, recession, and economic growth are also international concerns because the success or failure of one world trading partner affects all of the others. For example, imagine the economic effect on Japan if the United States had a recession and no one could afford to buy a new car. What would happen to the United States if foreign aircraft technology improved greatly and the world stopped buying U.S. aircraft?

Are you prepared to participate in the global economy?

Trade agreements such as the North American Free Trade Agreement (NAFTA) and the General Agreement of Tariffs and Trade (GATT) help trading partners resolve problems and encourage trade. Although these agreements do not resolve all trade problems, they do provide a framework for negotiation between trading partners.

To better understand this issue, consider the United States' trade relationship with China. Low wages, government subsidies, and questionable trade practices allow China to produce and ship goods to America's shores—sometimes more cheaply than U.S. manufacturers pay for raw materials. Table 15.1 lists facts about U.S. trade with China.

Discussion Starter

Ask your students: Do you know a worker who lost his or her job because of the global economy? Explain the situation.

TAKE NOTE

Auburn University has been using body-scan medical technology to perfect the fit of clothing. Knowing how to fit the U.S. population better should boost sales of the U.S. clothing industry. American textile companies have been losing jobs for several years.

Comprehension Check

Ask several students: In your own words, what are *imports* and *exports*? How do American workers benefit from imports? from exports?

KEY TO SUCCESS

As technology becomes more sophisticated, successful businesses find ways to reinvent themselves. One corporate example in the U.S. economy is the DuPont Corporation. Its products have changed whole industries. For example, DuPont nylon revolutionized the textile industry in 1935. More than once, the company has introduced products and technologies that changed the world. In 1969, the first man on the moon wore a spacesuit made mostly of DuPont materials. And in 2000, DuPont scientists developed Sorona, a biodegradable polyester that can be recycled indefinitely.

Table 15.1 China Trade Facts

U.S. imports from China	$288 billion
U.S. exports to China	$55 billion
U.S. trade deficit	$233 billion
China's share of U.S. imports	16%
China's share of the U.S. trade deficit	38%

Source: U.S. Department of Commerce (data from 2006)

As you prepare to enter the workforce, you need to recognize that competition from abroad is exerting as much influence on the quantity and quality of your job choices as is competition from within the U.S. economy. As a citizen and worker affected by the global economy, you should become familiar with terms commonly used by international trading partners:

- *Direct investment* occurs when a business either purchases or creates a business in another nation.
- *Imports* are goods and services purchased from another nation. The United States imports oil, automobiles, coffee, bananas, tea, silk, natural rubber, and electronic appliances. Many imports are essential to the welfare of a nation's citizens.
- *Exports* are goods and services sold to another nation. The United States exports airplanes, chemicals, paper, scrap iron and steel, and electronic equipment. Shiploads of U.S. wheat and corn cross the oceans. The latest Hollywood movies, Coca-Cola, and McDonald's fast-food restaurants are found around the globe. Exports provide employment opportunities for many workers.
- The *exchange rate* is the price at which a nation's currency can be bought or sold for another nation's currency. (See a recent copy of the *Wall Street Journal* for the current rate of exchange.)
- A *trade quota* is a limit, established by a government, on either the quantity or the value of certain goods that may be imported or exported. Nations sometimes use quotas to protect their industries from foreign competition. This policy is called *protectionism.* In other cases, nations use trade quotas to punish certain other nations for their trade policies, political behaviors, or military actions.
- A *trade surplus* exists when a nation sells more goods and services to other nations than it buys. A nation with a trade surplus has a favorable balance of trade. A trade surplus increases the gross national product.
- A *trade deficit* exists when a nation buys more goods and services from other countries than it sells. A nation with a trade deficit has an unfavorable balance of trade. A trade deficit decreases the gross national product.

© JIST Works

- The *balance of payments* is the difference between the amount of money a nation's economy spends overseas and the money it receives. This difference is sometimes referred to as the *balance of trade.* Workers, businesses, and nations will be ruined financially if they continually spend more money than they receive.

When all is said and done, the capability of individual businesses determines how competitive a nation is in the world market. Likewise, the capability of individual workers determines how competitive a business is in the world market. Making effective use of every employee—from the company's president to its rank-and-file workers—will keep the United States competitive in the world marketplace. This goal requires a workforce with competitive skills and a positive work attitude.

Reteaching

Have students complete the "Descriptive Match" worksheet found in the Chapter 15 file of the *Preparing for Career Success Instructor's CD-ROM, Third Edition.*

Reteaching

Have students complete the "Outlining Economics and Work" worksheet found in the Chapter 15 file of your *Preparing for Career Success Instructor's CD-ROM, Third Edition.*

Section 6: Get Involved

Answer the following on a separate sheet of paper, and be prepared to discuss your responses in class.

1. What are some advantages and disadvantages of selling goods and services overseas?
2. How can communications technology be helpful or troublesome for a business involved in the global economy?
3. Seventy-five years ago, very few U.S. jobs depended on foreign trade. Today, millions of U.S. jobs depend on the global economy. What has caused this change in the world of work, and what changes do you see taking place?

Chapter 15 Review

Reteaching

Have students complete the "Finding the Right Words" and "Checking Your Location" worksheets in Chapter 15 of the *Preparing for Career Success Student Activity Book, Third Edition.*

Enrich Your Vocabulary

On a separate sheet of paper, number from 1 to 18, and complete the following activity. (Do not write in your textbook.) Match each statement with the most appropriate term from the "Enrich Your Vocabulary" list at the beginning of the chapter by writing that term next to the correct statement.

1. The social science concerned with the way a society uses its productive resources to fulfill the needs and wants of each member
2. The U.S. economic system
3. A person or group that buys or uses goods or services to satisfy personal needs or wants
4. The willingness of consumers to buy goods or services at a certain price in the marketplace
5. The willingness of producers to produce and sell goods or services at a certain price in the marketplace
6. The science of mechanical and industrial arts

Enrich Your Vocabulary Answers

1. economics
2. free enterprise system
3. consumer
4. demand
5. supply
6. technology

(continued)

Enrich Your Vocabulary Answers *(continued)*

7. comparative advantage
8. Federal Reserve System
9. limited resources
10. gross national product
11. industrial products
12. opportunity cost
13. profit
14. services
15. market
16. competition
17. economic system
18. scarcity

Check Your Knowledge Answers

1. To provide a process for the production and distribution of goods and services.
2. To intervene and establish protective regulations when matters concerning the public good are at stake. Government regulation reduces fluctuations between good times and bad times; promotes the growth of businesses and the number of jobs; ensures fair competition between businesses; provides programs of importance to all people, such as transportation, national defense, and public education; and takes care of the minimum basic needs of adults and children who are victims of unemployment or other unfortunate circumstances.
3. To satisfy consumers' changing demands for goods and services.
4. Jobs are created for workers, and employers gain the opportunity to earn profits.
5. A production system, a service system, a distribution system, consumers, and a system of exchange.
6. Profit creates new jobs; profit pays for worker training and the cleanup of industrial pollution; profit keeps companies in business. Additional answers may be given.

(continued)

7. The ability of a producer to provide a good or service at a lower opportunity cost than other producers
8. A network of 12 regional banks that regulates banking in the United States
9. Natural resources, labor, capital, and management
10. The total value of goods and services that a nation produces for the marketplace during a specific time period
11. Goods produced for and sold to other producers
12. The resource or benefit that a company gives up to produce a particular product or provide a particular service
13. Money left over after all of the expenses are paid
14. Tasks that other people or machines perform that cannot be physically weighed or measured
15. A group of people or organizations that purchase a particular good or service
16. Striving against others to win something
17. The method a society uses to determine how it will use and distribute available resources
18. The condition that exists when people have limited resources compared to their wants

Check Your Knowledge

On a separate sheet of paper, answer the following questions. (Do not write in your textbook.)

1. What is the major purpose of an economic system?
2. What is the role of government in the economy?
3. What is the goal of economic activity?
4. What are the two major benefits of turning new ideas into products or services and new businesses?
5. What are the five major parts of all economic systems?
6. What are three reasons why profit is necessary in our free enterprise system?

© JIST Works

7. Why has the federal government passed laws to prevent monopolies?
8. What are three safeguards that have been built into our economy to help protect both business owners and workers from large swings in the business cycle?
9. What is the major advantage of specialization?
10. What is a tight-money policy? How does it affect our economy?
11. What are the two major factors that have moved the world toward a global economy?

Develop SCANS Competencies

This activity will give you practice in developing the information and interpersonal skills that successful workers use. Discuss the importance of interest rates with a parent or other adult. Ask how this person's saving, borrowing, and spending decisions might change if interest rates were 2 percent higher or lower. (Do not ask about specific amounts of money.) Write a paragraph that explains the adult's answers and what they show about the importance of interest rates to consumer decisions.

Check Your Knowledge Answers *(continued)*

7. Monopolies destroy competition and eliminate small businesses.
8. Unemployment insurance benefits for workers, corporate policies that attempt to keep dividend payments more stable than corporate profits to protect investors, fiscal and monetary policies of the federal government that regulate the rates of interest paid to businesses or individuals and determine the amount and types of taxes that will be paid or the tax exemptions that will be allowed.
9. Specialists are able to produce a higher volume of goods or services at a lower cost than would otherwise be possible.
10. In a tight-money policy, banks decrease the amount of money in the economy and increase the rate of interest charged for loans. Tight money causes less borrowing, less purchasing of goods and services, fewer jobs, and a move toward recession.
11. Technology and high-tech communications.

Enrichment

Have students complete the Chapter 15 section of the *Preparing for Career Success Student Portfolio, Third Edition.*

© JIST Works

Chapter 16 Resources

Lesson Plans and Preparation

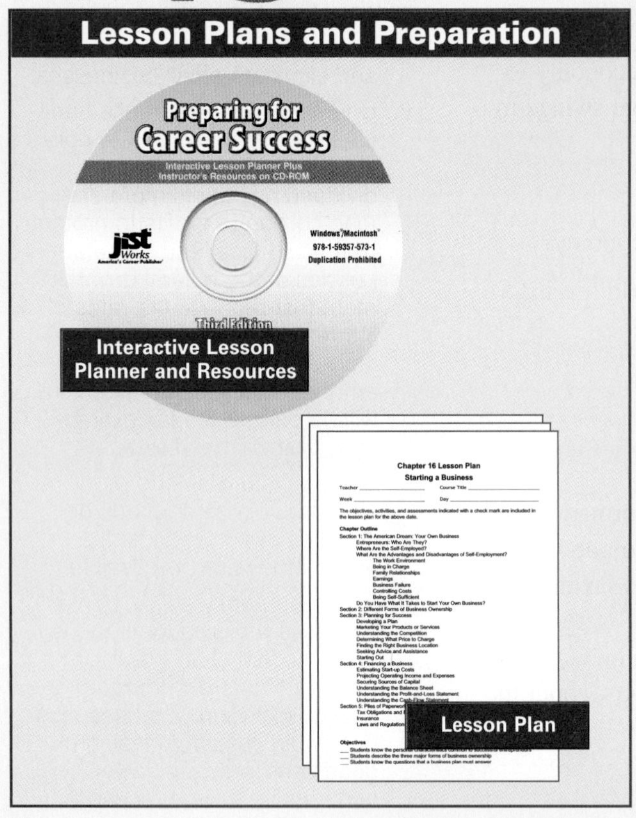

Preparing for Career Success
Interactive Lesson Planner Plus Instructor's Resources on CD-ROM
Windows/Macintosh
978-1-59357-573-1
Duplication Prohibited
Third Edition
Interactive Lesson Planner and Resources
Chapter 16 Lesson Plan
Starting a Business
Lesson Plan

Multimedia

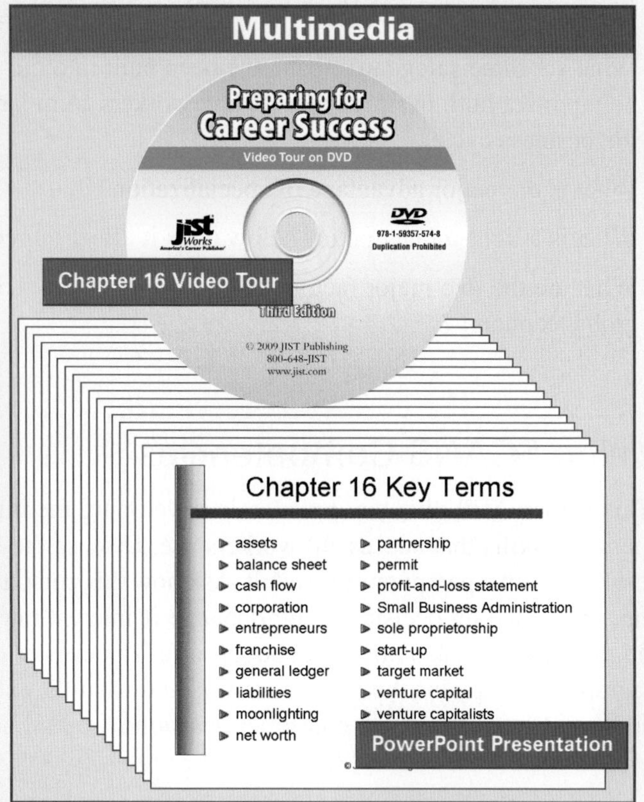

Preparing for Career Success
Video Tour on DVD
978-1-59357-574-8
Duplication Prohibited
Chapter 16 Video Tour
Third Edition
© 2009 JIST Publishing
800-648-JIST
www.jist.com
Chapter 16 Key Terms
assets
balance sheet
cash flow
corporation
entrepreneurs
franchise
general ledger
liabilities
moonlighting
net worth
partnership
permit
profit-and-loss statement
Small Business Administration
sole proprietorship
start-up
target market
venture capital
venture capitalists
PowerPoint Presentation

Activities

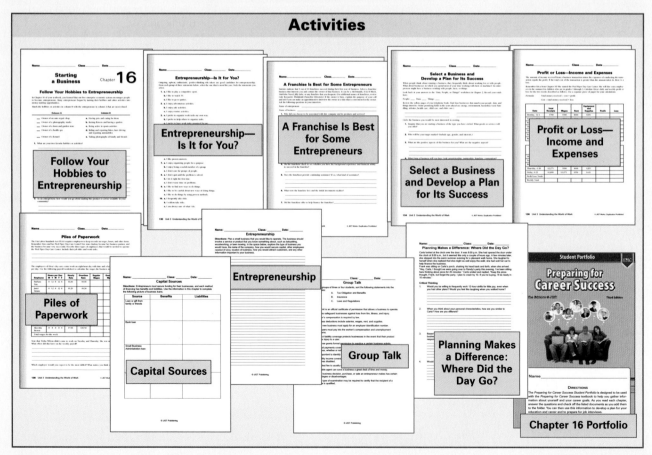

- Follow Your Hobbies to Entrepreneurship
- Entrepreneurship—Is It for You?
- A Franchise Is Best for Some Entrepreneurs
- Select a Business and Develop a Plan for Its Success
- Profit or Loss—Income and Expenses
- Piles of Paperwork
- Capital Sources
- Entrepreneurship
- Group Talk
- Planning Makes a Difference: Where Did the Day Go?
- Chapter 16 Portfolio

© JIST Works

Review and Assessment

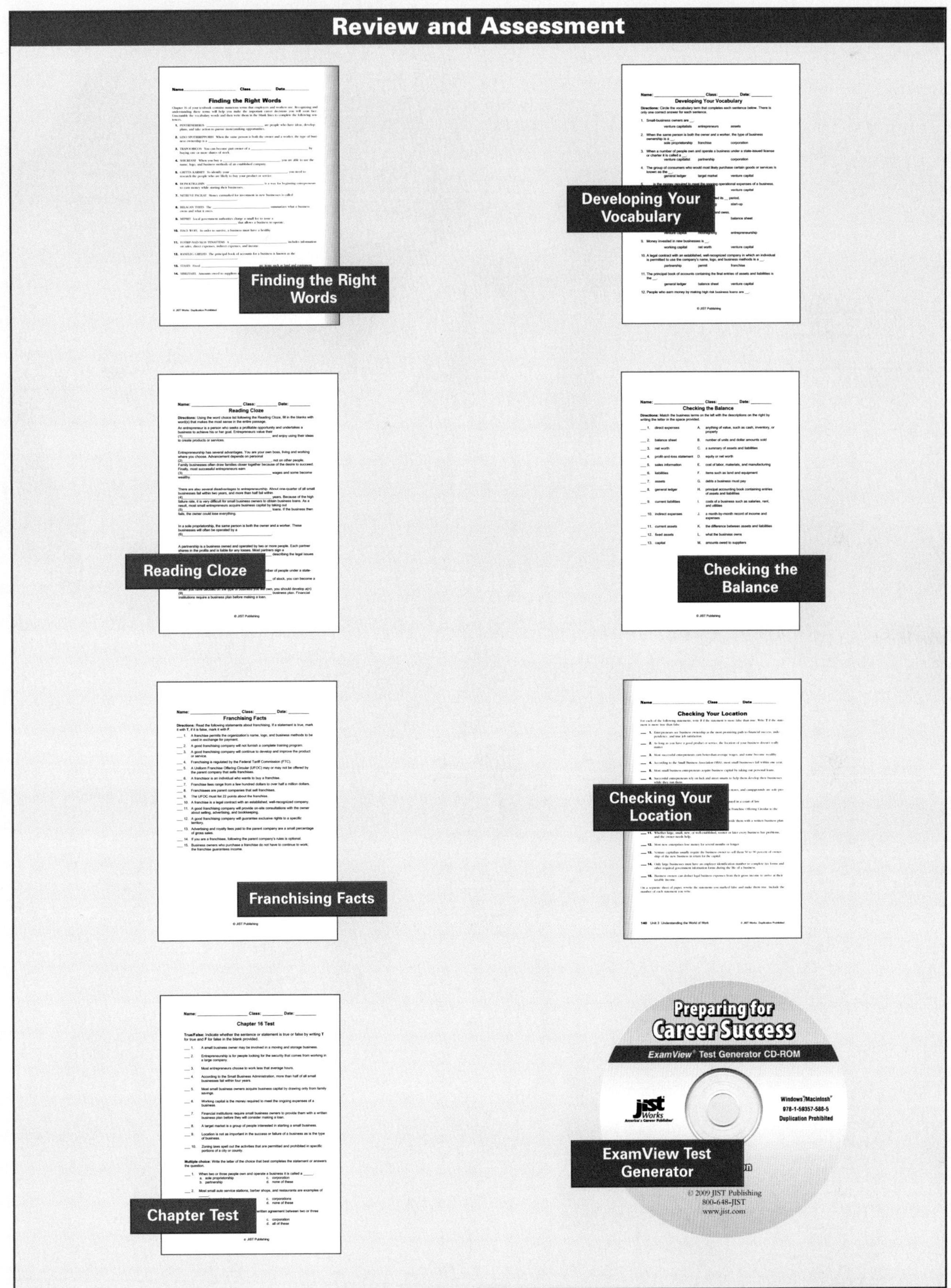

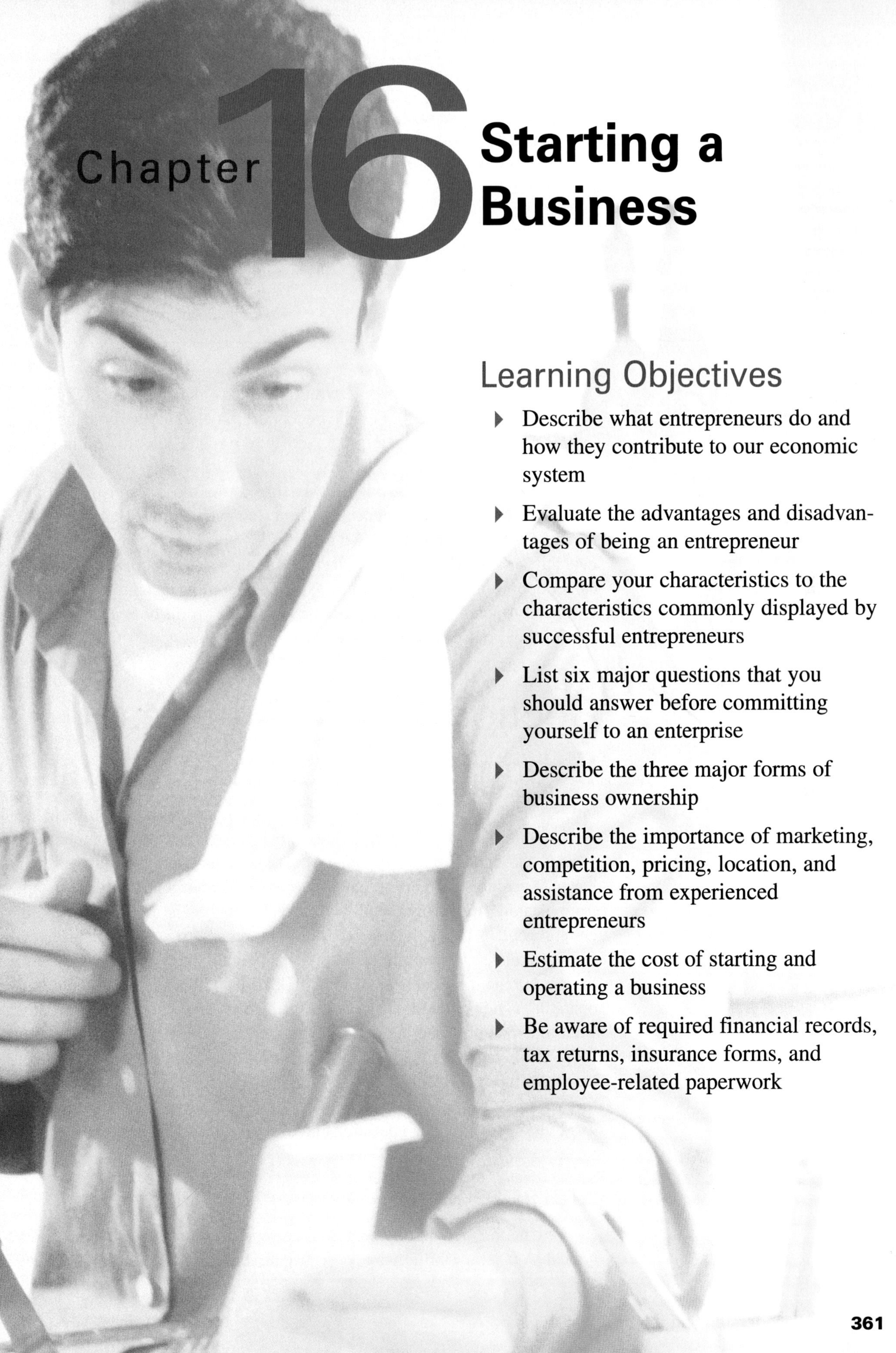

Chapter 16 Starting a Business

Learning Objectives

- Describe what entrepreneurs do and how they contribute to our economic system
- Evaluate the advantages and disadvantages of being an entrepreneur
- Compare your characteristics to the characteristics commonly displayed by successful entrepreneurs
- List six major questions that you should answer before committing yourself to an enterprise
- Describe the three major forms of business ownership
- Describe the importance of marketing, competition, pricing, location, and assistance from experienced entrepreneurs
- Estimate the cost of starting and operating a business
- Be aware of required financial records, tax returns, insurance forms, and employee-related paperwork

Enrich Your Vocabulary

In reading this chapter and doing the exercises, you will learn the following important terms:

assets	general ledger	Small Business Administration
balance sheet	liabilities	sole proprietorship
business plan	moonlighting	start-up
cash flow	net worth	target market
corporation	partnership	venture capital
entrepreneurs	permit	venture capitalists
franchise	profit-and-loss statement	working capital

Vocabulary

You can use the "Developing Your Vocabulary" worksheet in Chapter 16 of the *Preparing for Career Success Instructor's CD-ROM, Third Edition* as a pretest for chapter concepts or as a reteaching worksheet.

Entrepreneurs are people who have ideas, develop plans, and take action to pursue moneymaking opportunities. They assume the risks and manage the enterprise, and they provide jobs for millions of American workers.

Entrepreneurs view business ownership as the most promising path to financial success, independence, and true job satisfaction. Have you ever dreamed about owning your own business? If not, learning about entrepreneurship and small business ownership could open a door to numerous career opportunities. If you have considered becoming an entrepreneur, you will need to learn as much as possible about the world of business before committing your time and money.

The majority of America's colossal fortunes have been made by entering industries in their early stages and developing leadership in them.

—B. C. Forbes

Section 1: The American Dream: Your Own Business

Our free enterprise economic system encourages people to become entrepreneurs. In large cities, small towns, and rural communities throughout the United States, entrepreneurs work at whatever their business requires. When the enterprise is small, they handle every detail, from cleaning to buying supplies to serving customers. In addition, many entrepreneurs perform the necessary accounting and paperwork themselves.

Work tasks and working conditions depend on the type of business and the entrepreneur's goal. For example, Dean Chinrock enjoys owning and operating a flower shop. Dean wants to increase his business but does not want to expand beyond his single location. Mary Chen also owns a flower shop, but her goal is to own a network of flower shops within her state. Dean's thinking reflects that of a typical small business owner, and Mary's, that of an entrepreneur. When Mary acquires three shops, how will her work tasks and working conditions be different from Dean's?

Career Fact

Entrepreneurs often use their own money to get started. Lillian Vernon used $2,000 of wedding-gift money to launch her multimillion-dollar catalog company in 1951. Apple founders Steve Jobs and Stephen Wozniak raised their seed money—$1,300—in 1976 by selling Jobs's car and Wozniak's Hewlett-Packard calculator.

Entrepreneurs: Who Are They?

Few people get rich by accident. Entrepreneurs are no exception. The typical American millionaire is a frugal, hardworking, small business

© JIST Works

Video Tour on DVD

Show students the Chapter 16 segment to introduce them to the content.

Although most small business operations do not grow into a national chain or develop a value of several billion dollars, millions of large American businesses were begun on a small scale.

owner. He or she is a risk-taking, self-sacrificing individualist who never takes financial success for granted. Self-employed people account for an amazing two-thirds of the nation's working millionaires. They seem to view the world more clearly than most and use their vision to anticipate economic trends and customers' needs. These owners of multimillion-dollar businesses started out small.

Cross-Reference

Explain to your students that successful entrepreneurs usually have several characteristics of the persuasive orientation. Instruct students to review "The Persuasive Orientation," Section 2, Chapter 4.

Where Are the Self-Employed?

Both self-employed people and entrepreneurs own their businesses. However, many people pursue self-employment to develop their career expertise into a reliable full-time (business) job. They are satisfied with their business and the lifestyle it provides. On the other hand, entrepreneurs consider their accomplishments as stepping stones to a larger enterprise.

The following are types of businesses that are often owned by the self-employed and entrepreneurs:

- Air conditioning, heating, refrigeration, and plumbing
- Apparel
- Arts, crafts, and hobbies
- Automotive trades
- Barber shops and beauty salons
- Boat building and marinas
- Bookstores
- Building and construction
- Cement and concrete
- Communications and electronics
- E-commerce
- Export and import trade
- Farms and ranches
- Financial firms
- Florists
- Food industries

Comprehension Check

Send three writers to the chalkboard. Explain to the class that the writers will list all of the small businesses the class can think of in a period of three minutes. A student may indicate that he or she has a small business for the list by raising his or her hand. The writers should call on students as fast as they can list the answers. Make sure the class members all understand their assignment, and tell them to begin. At the end of three minutes, tell them to stop.

© JIST Works

Self-Understanding

Which type of business listed here is most related to your planned education and training? Which types relate to the career cluster (see the appendix) you are considering?

Community Resources

Form a committee of students to contact the National Association of Women Business Owners to request information related to businesses owned by women. Have the students inquire whether a member of the association lives in the local area. If so, the committee may wish to invite her to your class as a speaker or visit her at her place of business. Ask the committee to report their information to the class.

Self-Understanding

Instruct your students to review "Personality," in Section 2 of Chapter 2. Give them a time limit to make a list of their personal characteristics before reading "Advantages and Disadvantages of Self-Employment." Instruct them to compare their characteristics to the characteristics of self-employed people described in this section.

TAKE NOTE

Entrepreneurs and small business owners frequently obtain the training to start their businesses while working for someone else.

Community Resources

Form a committee of students to contact the U.S. Small Business Administration (SBA) to obtain additional information about forming a business. Ask the committee to report the information they acquire to the class.

Franchises
Funeral homes
Gift shops
Lumber and forest products
Machine shops
Mail-order
Manufacturing
Medical and health care
Moving and storage
Newspapers and printing
Nurseries and landscaping
Photographic trades
Real estate
Restaurants and catering
Retailing
Sales and consulting
Transportation
Travel agencies

What Are the Advantages and Disadvantages of Self-Employment?

Depending on your personal values and interests, you will form a favorable or unfavorable perception of every occupation. Consider the following characteristics of self-employed people in terms of your personal characteristics.

The Work Environment

Many self-employed workers enjoy the freedom to live and work where they choose. Some choose to work out of their home and avoid the daily commute to a job. This decision saves them time, money, and personal energy. If your business eventually grows to be as large as your dream, you may need to move into a factory, office building, or shopping mall. In the meantime, you will need a lot of self-discipline to "stay with the task," especially on nice days when you would rather be doing something else.

Being in Charge

You will soon discover the true meaning of *being in charge.* You have the freedom to use your own methods. When they work, you get the praise and profit. When they do not work, you get the blame and the bills. You can start your workday as early as you like and continue working as late as you like—the choice is yours. Most beginning entrepreneurs choose to start early and stay late. They soon discover that the *self* in *self-employment* stands for do it your*self.* The business consumes most of the owner's time and energy, especially during the first years of operation. Long workdays are to be expected.

Family Relationships

Starting a small business from scratch frequently draws families closer together because they are working for a common goal—to make the family and the business successful. Family members often consider activities such

© JIST Works

Work-at-Home Schemes

The Federal Trade Commission's Bureau of Consumer Protection (www.ftc.gov) warns consumers to beware of the work-at-home schemes that flood newspapers, magazines, and the Internet. They usually begin with statements like this: "Earn thousands of dollars a month from the comfort of your home." These ads frequently omit the fact that you may have to work many hours without pay, do not disclose all the costs you will have to pay, and may demand that you pay for instruction or "tutorial" software. One classic scheme is medical billing. The reality is that competition in the medical billing market is fierce and revolves around a number of large and well-established firms.

Another scheme is envelope stuffing. For your fee to be an "envelope stuffer," you're likely to receive a letter telling you to place the same "envelope-stuffing" ad in newspapers or magazines or to send the ad to friends and relatives. The only way you will earn money is if other foolish investors respond to your work-at-home ad. Legitimate work-at-home program sponsors should tell you—in writing—what is involved in the program they are selling.

as stuffing and licking envelopes, inputting spreadsheet data, and helping to fill a special order as quality time. Togetherness translates into the efficient production of more goods or services.

Find Out More

For information on businesses owned by women, contact the National Association of Women Business Owners. Using your search engine, key in **National Association of Women Business Owners**, or go online at nawbo-sf.org/.

Earnings

Business owners have the opportunity to earn more money than people who work for someone else. After the business is established, many earn better-than-average wages, and some become wealthy. However, owners usually withdraw the smallest possible salary from a new business. Most workers with similar skills usually earn far more than the owner of a new business does. However, the potential to make a new business grow and prosper can be a great motivator.

Business Failure

The mission of the U.S. **Small Business Administration** (SBA) is to maintain and strengthen the nation's economy by aiding, counseling, and assisting all the interests of small businesses and by helping families and businesses in national disasters.

According to the SBA, about one-quarter of all *small businesses* (those with fewer than 500 employees) fail within two years, and more than half fail within five years. The SBA defines a failed business as one that closes while owing money to one or more creditors. The high rate of small business failures and the lack of collateral make it very difficult for a small business owner to obtain business loans.

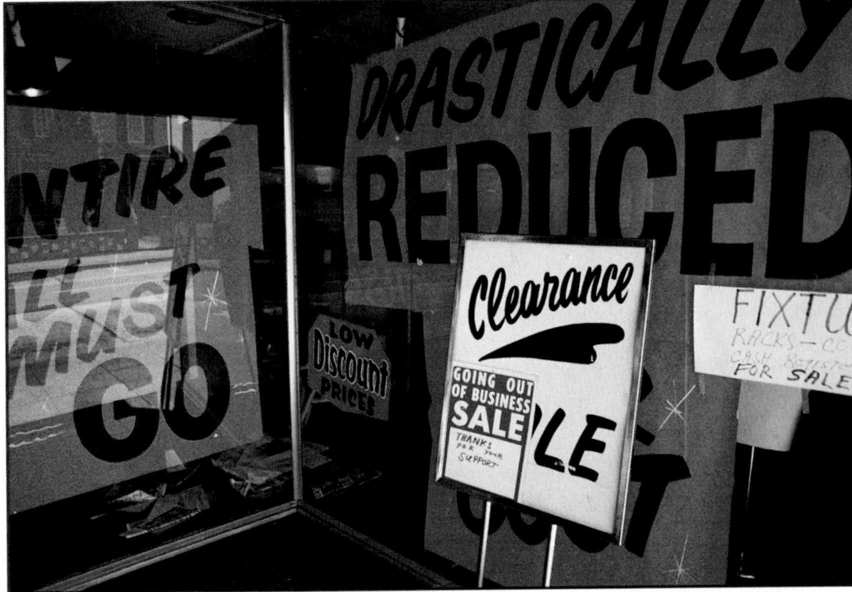

Are you a risk taker? Less than half of small businesses succeed. What can an entrepreneur do to increase his or her likelihood of success?

Comprehension Check

After your students have completed reading "Advantages and Disadvantages of Self-Employment," ask them to close their books. Ask several students: In your own words, what is one disadvantage of owning your own business?

Controlling Costs

Entrepreneurs develop knowledge of business that is not found in a book. It comes from a constant awareness of the enterprise's operating costs and its profits or losses. Operating on a financial shoestring helps the entrepreneur develop a sixth sense about the value of every dollar that flows in and out of the enterprise. Inadequate financing to carry a business through periods of loss or growth is a major cause of business failure.

Self-confidence is the first requisite to great undertakings.

—Samuel Johnson

Being Self-Sufficient

Whether they save $5 by fixing a broken cord on the vacuum cleaner or $5,000 by negotiating a great lease, self-employed people take pride in their accomplishments. They tend to have a deep streak of pride and independence ingrained in their souls.

Do You Have What It Takes to Start Your Own Business?

CAREER FACT

Business owners are not the only people who work long hours for career success. Most managers and professionals work late (no overtime pay) three to five days a week. Of this group, 27 percent work an extra hour, 22 percent work an extra two hours, and 10 percent work an extra 10 hours.

The following personal traits are common in successful entrepreneurs:

- **Optimism:** They know that they will be successful, even when their families and closest friends have lost faith.
- **Uniqueness:** They know that the personal characteristics that make them different also make them special. They learn to use that individuality to their competitive advantage.
- **A strong work ethic:** Most leading businesspeople did not graduate from an Ivy League college or at the top of their class. A surprising number do not have a college degree. However, they work harder—and smarter—than their competitors do.
- **Passion:** They have a passion for the work they do!

Table 16.1 lists further characteristics of entrepreneurs versus other types of workers.

Self-Understanding

Have students complete the "Entrepreneurship—Is It for You?" survey in Chapter 16 of the *Preparing for Career Success Student Activity Book, Third Edition.*

Table 16.1 Two Types of People

Entrepreneurs	Other Workers
Are competitive	Are noncompetitive
Live to work	Work to live
Enjoy taking risks	Prefer security
Tolerate uncertainty	Worry about uncertainty
Enjoy solving problems	Avoid problems
Are impatient	Are patient
Prefer work over hobbies	Prefer hobbies over work

© JIST Works

Section 1: Getting Involved

Review the list of personal characteristics of entrepreneurs and other workers in Table 16.1. Then answer the following on a separate sheet of paper, and be prepared to discuss your responses in class:

1. Which of your characteristics are similar to those of the entrepreneurs? Which ones are similar to those of the other workers?
2. How would each of your entrepreneurial characteristics help you be a successful business owner? How would each of your other worker characteristics hinder you?
3. Are you better suited to be an entrepreneur or to work for an established business? Why?
4. List the specific job skills and human relations skills you possess now or expect to acquire before entering full-time employment. Next, select a small business you could start with the skills on your list. How would you use each of the skills on your list in the business you selected? Be specific. What would you like most about your daily work tasks? What would you dislike most? What would concern you most if you owned the business? What would concern you least?

Section 2: Different Forms of Business Ownership

Erica Millard graduated from a two-year technical college with an associate's degree in child care. After working for two years at a local day-care center, Erica decided to start her own business. She even picked out a name: *The Pied Piper Day-Care Center.*

Erica started her action plan by taking an evening business course at a local college. She learned that before forming a business, would-be entrepreneurs should be able to answer these six questions:

- What licensing is required?
- What are the legal restrictions?
- How much capital will be needed?
- How many workers are needed?
- What liabilities must be assumed?
- What type of business organization is best?

Erica also learned that the type and size of a business are major determinants of the type of ownership and organization needed. She is carefully considering the three major types of business ownership: sole proprietorship, partnership, and corporation.

When the same person is both the owner and a worker, the type of ownership is a **sole proprietorship**. Many small gas stations, barbershops, restaurants, video stores, and campgrounds are sole proprietorships. In some cases, the sole proprietor will employ a few other workers. It is also common for a family to operate this type of business.

Sole proprietorships are easy to form and manage. However, the total financial responsibility rests on the shoulders of the owner. If the business fails, the owner may lose all of his or her personal assets as well as the business.

Cluster Link

Would you be interested in planning, managing, and providing human services including social and related community services? If you are interested in the "helping occupations," review the Human Services career cluster. See the appendix for more information.

Discussion Starter

After your students have finished reading this section, ask the following questions: If you decide to become an entrepreneur, which type of business do you think is best? Why do you think so?

Take Note

Future Business Leaders of America–Phi Beta Lambda (FBLA) is a career and technical student organization that helps students develop their skills in leadership and entrepreneurship. For more information, contact your local chapter or visit the Web site at www.fbla-pbl.org.

© JIST Works

A **partnership** is two or three people owning and operating a business. If you're planning to start this type of business, do not form a partnership with a verbal agreement. Instead, hire an attorney to produce a legal, written agreement (contract) that describes

- The responsibilities of each partner
- The amount of money invested by each partner
- The percentage of profits each partner will receive
- The method used to dispose of each partner's share in the event of his or her death

In a partnership, each partner shares in the profits, and each is liable for any losses. Having two or more people concentrating on the solution to business problems and helping with financing the business is a definite advantage of a partnership.

When a number of people own and operate a business under a state-issued license or charter, it is a **corporation**. A corporation can be owned by several million people (stockholders) or by a few. You can become part owner of a corporation by buying one or more shares of stock.

Take Note

Laws authorize a corporation to transact business and own property as a single entity (as one person). Like any individual person, a corporation must conduct business in a responsible manner. It can sue or be sued in a court of law. Most large firms (and some small firms) choose to operate as a corporation.

Community Resources

Have students interview a franchise owner using the questions from the "A Franchise Is Best for Some Entrepreneurs" worksheet in Chapter 16 of the *Preparing for Career Success Student Activity Book, Third Edition.*

A corporation requires more assistance from lawyers and accountants than other forms of business ownership do. Although stockholders in a large business have very limited liability, this form of ownership will not necessarily protect the small business owner's property or financial assets from lawsuits. The best protection for a business owner is insurance.

Erica has decided that a sole proprietorship would probably be best for starting the Pied Piper Day-Care Center. In addition, she plans to buy liability insurance for protection against possible lawsuits.

Last week, Erica received information about a nationally franchised chain of day-care centers. A **franchise** is a legal contract with an established, well-recognized company. The organization would permit Erica to use its name, logo, and business methods in exchange for payment. Before buying into the franchise, Erica plans to determine all of the costs, the amount of initial investment required, the royalties she would be required to pay, and the amount of financing help she can expect from the franchising company. She is also concerned about any restrictions the organization could place on her future business activities if she decided to sell her franchise.

Erica's Uncle Jerome owns a successful fast-food restaurant franchise with a nationally recognized company. She made an appointment with him to discuss the advantages and disadvantages of buying into a franchise. Jerome told Erica that a good franchising company will

- Furnish a complete training program and assist with the business start-up
- Provide on-site consultations with the owner about selling, advertising, and bookkeeping
- Guarantee exclusive rights to a specific territory

© JIST Works

- Conduct national advertising to create widespread recognition of the company
- Continue to develop and improve the product or service

When you buy a franchised business, you are starting with a well-known name and a record of success. What are the names of some nationally known franchised businesses that are familiar to you?

Uncle Jerome also explained how the Federal Trade Commission (FTC) regulates franchising. The law requires all *franchisers* (parent companies that sell franchises) to provide a Uniform Franchise Offering Circular (UFOC). The UFOC must list 22 points about the franchise, including the names and telephone numbers of *franchisees* (people who have purchased a franchise). In addition, the UFOC must disclose any bankruptcies or lawsuits pending against the parent company.

Erica learned that franchise fees range from a few hundred to several million dollars. In addition, advertising and royalty fees paid to the parent company could amount to half of her gross sales.

Erica likes the idea of starting a franchised day-care business with an organization that already has a record of success. However, she is concerned that she will be required to follow so many of the parent company's rules that she will lose the independence that she is seeking.

That evening at home, Erica was reading the business ads in her newspaper when she discovered a day-care center offered for sale. The next morning, Erica phoned the owner to obtain more information. The owner told her that the 17-year-old business was well known and profitable. The owner wanted to retire and was willing to assist the buyer with financing.

Erica made an appointment to visit the day-care center. She found the building and equipment to be very modern and the two employees to be very competent. The owner's books revealed a business with numerous long-term customers.

Erica wants to make the right decision. She is aware that each form of business ownership and each method of getting started will have several advantages and disadvantages. As she considers the pros and cons of her alternatives, Erica is reviewing her career goals.

Reteaching

Have students complete the "Franchising Facts" worksheet found in the Chapter 16 file of the *Preparing for Career Success Instructor's CD-ROM, Third Edition.*

Comprehension Check/ Vocabulary Builder

After your students have finished reading "Different Forms of Business Ownership," tell them to close their books. Ask several students: In your own words, what is a franchise? After your class understands the term *franchise*, ask several students: What is one advantage or disadvantage of owning a franchise?

Section 2: Get Involved

Answer the following on a separate sheet of paper, and be prepared to discuss your responses in class.

1. If you were Erica, which form of ownership would you select? Why?
2. If you were Erica, would you start your own business, buy a franchise, or buy the established business? Why?
3. What recent technologies will open doors to new types of small business in the next few years? Why do you think so?

© JIST Works

Career Fact

The Internet offers small companies a low-cost process to research their market before investing more dollars in their businesses.

Section 3: Planning for Success

Entrepreneurs translate dreams and ideas into successful business practices by identifying and understanding their markets and developing plans to get through the down cycles. When you are brainstorming for a business idea, think about an existing service or product needed by others, such as entertainment, a business service, or repair work. Consider developing a new product or service, or perhaps market and sell the product(s) or services of other organizations. Your business idea also could be an extension of a personal hobby or interest.

After you formulate an idea, you will need to test its potential against the realities of the business world. This process includes these steps:

1. **Evaluating your product or service:** A good product or service is required to make a good business. People in the business world often measure the potential value of a service or product by its quality, relative value, and convenience for the customer.
2. **Analyzing your competitiveness:** How does the price of your service or product compare to that of your competitors? Successful entrepreneurs find ways to give customers more for their money.
3. **Assessing your human and financial resources:** Consider whether you have the human and financial resources needed to set the business in motion. Do you have or can you hire the personnel with the specific knowledge and skills you will need? How much money will you need to launch the business? Securing bank loans and hiring employees to start a business are formidable tasks for most entrepreneurs.
4. **Determining whether you have the expertise:** Can you produce the product or provide the service?

Key To Success

Never mix personal and business funds. Open a separate bank account for the business. This way, you ensure an accurate record of your income and expenditures.

Developing a Business Plan

After you decide on the form of business you will own, the place where it will be located, and the specific goods or services you will offer, the next step is to develop a plan of action. Successful entrepreneurs develop a written plan to guide them through each step of starting and maintaining a business. A sound **business plan** includes information about the product or service and its potential market. In addition, it describes the marketing strategy, organization of the business, and financial requirements for start-up and operation.

Overall, the business plan should present to the reader a clear picture of the business and its operation. Prospective lenders and investors will use your plan to decide whether your ideas are sound.

Enrichment

Have students complete the "Select a Business and Develop a Plan for Its Success" worksheet in Chapter 16 of the *Preparing for Career Success Student Activity Book, Third Edition.*

© JIST Works

Knowing who your target market is will help you advertise and market your business more effectively.

Marketing Your Products or Services

Research the existing market for your product or service, and identify your target market. A **target market** is the group of consumers who would most likely purchase certain goods or services. Answering the following questions will help you begin exploring the demographics of your target market:

- *Who* are your potential customers, and how old are they? Are they men or women?
- *What* products or services will your company provide? What is the extent of need for your product or service? What are three strategies you will use to make the public aware of your services? What new customers and markets can you reach, and what are their buying habits?
- *Where* are your potential customers generally located, and where are they concentrated?
- *When* are your potential customers available (hours of the day and days of the week)? In terms of holiday seasons or months of the year, when do they buy more? When do they buy less?
- *Why* do your customers purchase your goods or services?

Key To Success

Let customers know their business is wanted and appreciated. Always thank customers, and make certain that everyone in the organization follows this policy.

Planning Makes a Difference: Will Carrie Hit the Target?

Carrie Straight received her high school diploma from a technical career center with a major in cosmetology. After she finished school, she had no difficulty finding a job in a local beauty shop.

After working a year, Carrie decided she would like to own her own beauty shop. She discussed her interest with Mark Ramiro, the owner of the shop where she worked. He suggested that she investigate the two-year associate's degree program in business at a local community college. The course work would help her manage and understand the operation of a business. Within six weeks, Carrie enrolled full-time at Stark Technical College and continued working 20 hours per week for Mark. She quickly discovered that being a business owner involved a great deal more knowledge and

Take Note

Business Professionals of America is a career and technical student organization for students interested in careers related to running a business, such as office administration and information technology. Members test their business skills in competition and develop leadership and teamwork skills by working with other members. For more information, contact your local chapter or connect to www.bpanet.org.

Take Note

The Service Corps of Retired Executives (SCORE) has thousands of volunteer counselors throughout the United States. SCORE began in September 1964 when the Small Business Administration signed up more than 1,100 retired executives to help small businesses learn to achieve greater sales and profits. SCORE members provide advice and counseling to would-be entrepreneurs before they risk entering a tough, competitive marketplace.

Cooperative Learning

After your students finish reading Section 3, divide the class into small groups. Instruct each group to select a small business and then write the name of the product or service they will sell on a separate sheet of paper. Next, have them list the target market(s) for their product or service. Have each group report their answers to the class.

Technology

Being able to use technology wisely is an important part of running a successful business. Although you may need to hire people to help you with the details, you need to have a general idea of how to manage accounting tasks with software, track customer or inventory information in a database, market the business on the Internet, and buy technology that will increase productivity.

work than her regular job did. Now she could understand how her accounting and business management courses would help her succeed when she opened her own business. Carrie also learned that earning an associate's degree required considerable study time in the library and was more difficult than attending high school.

Carrie stayed with the program and graduated with a three-point average. She decided it was time to become an entrepreneur. Mark helped her select a location in a thriving commercial area that was also near a growing residential community. Although one beauty shop was already located in the area, both Carrie and Mark felt the location could easily support another.

A few weeks after Carrie opened her shop, she noticed that the other shop opened at 9:00 a.m. and closed at 6:00 p.m. Carrie decided that to be competitive, she would open her shop at 8:00 a.m. by appointment and close the shop at 8:00 p.m.

Carrie's shop has two chairs and one employee. To accommodate customers who take advantage of the early opening and late closing, Carrie plans to adjust her own hours. She hopes to attract working women with her expanded schedule. This plan will require Carrie to work long hours in the beginning, but she plans to hire more employees as the business grows.

Critical Thinking

Who is Carrie's target market? Will Carrie's plan accommodate her target market? If so, how? If not, why not?

What advice would you offer Carrie as she plans her new business?

Could a Web page help Carrie's business? If so, How? If not, why not?

© JIST Works

Understanding the Competition

As an entrepreneur, you will need to learn all you can about the products or services that your competitors offer. Pinpoint their strengths and weaknesses. For example, how long have they been in business? Being in business a long time is a good indication of stability and profitability. When you are comparing your business with your competition, your target market customers will probably focus on two questions:

1. Are your business prices higher or lower than your competition?
2. What are the benefits of using your product or service instead of your competitors?

Whatever the type of business, always look closely at the firms already in the area you would like to enter. Then try to match the strengths of your competition and identify and develop ways to outperform them on their weak points. Suppose you find out that other firms require a large minimum number of items per order. You could accept smaller orders if you can do so profitably. What else could you try? When competition in the business that interests you is too tough, search for a different business in which you can successfully compete.

TAKE NOTE

Whether you are selling handcrafted baby beds locally or specialty rubber compounds internationally, the Internet may be the answer to some or all of your marketing needs. Customer queries, promotional mailings, and purchase confirmations are instant using electronic mail, without postage or stationery. Your e-mail is sent instantly, and you don't have to pay long-distance phone charges.

The key to your e-business is an appropriate, efficient Web site. Before you begin planning your site, consult with a local Web design specialist. Use your search engine to acquire additional information from The International Academy of Digital Art and Sciences.

Determining What Price to Charge

Maintaining the delicate balance between charging competitive prices, covering the cost of doing business, and allowing for a fair profit is important. You should consider four major questions when determining prices:

1. What are the direct and indirect costs of doing business?
2. What is a reasonable profit?
3. What prices do major competitors charge?
4. What is the market demand for your goods or services?

There is rarely an exact "right" price for goods or services. Instead, there is an acceptable price range. Successful entrepreneurs are just as careful about underpricing as they are about overpricing. Market and pricing information is available from Web sites, newspaper ads, trade magazines, the local chamber of commerce, the county office of economic development, business and professional organizations, and the U.S. Census Bureau.

Discussion Starter

Ask your students: When you make a choice between two businesses, what is most important to you: getting the lowest price, getting a superior product, or getting the best service?

Finding the Right Business Location

A good business location can mean the difference between success and failure. In many cases, you need to choose locations that are convenient for customers and that offer the greatest access to markets. The criteria for selecting a business location are very similar for most businesses, whether

CAREER FACT

Small and family-run businesses employ half of the private workforce in the United States and generate 60 to 80 percent of the new jobs annually. The majority of small businesses begin with less than $10,000 in capital. About 52 percent of small businesses are home-based, and 2 percent are franchises.

© JIST Works

Take Note

In many new Internet-based businesses, location may be less important because the entrepreneur and customer rarely have direct contact.

the enterprise is a neighborhood bakery or a national manufacturing facility. Consider the following:

- **Zoning:** Before you open a new business, thoroughly investigate the zoning laws in the location that you are considering. Zoning laws spell out the activities that are permitted and prohibited in specific portions of a city or county. Obtain a copy of the local zoning laws at the local town hall, zoning office, or library.
- **Business signs:** Will you need to place a sign(s) in front of your business to help your customers and suppliers locate it? Check local laws, and obtain necessary permits before you make a financial commitment to having signs installed.
- **Property improvement:** Whether you are leasing or buying space, negotiate the best terms possible. Make a list of your requirements before considering a property. Never sign a lease until it specifies the total agreement between you and the property owner.
- **Property maintenance:** From fixing leaky faucets to shoveling snow, make certain who is responsible for everyday maintenance chores.

Key To Success

Enlisting the aid of experts, especially of those who have worked with other business owners, can help you analyze your capabilities. That knowledge should reveal any differences between your expectations and the reality of succeeding with a business idea.

Seeking Advice and Assistance

Eventually, every business has problems, and the owner needs specialized help. State economic development agencies, chambers of commerce, local colleges and universities, libraries, manufacturers and suppliers of small business products and services, and small business or industry trade associations offer sources of help for business problems.

The Small Business Administration has programs to assist with every aspect of starting a business—from developing a business plan to obtaining financing, from marketing products and services to managing a company. The SBA's programs and services can guide you through each stage of growing your business. Several associations affiliated with the SBA, such as the Service Corps of Retired Executives (SCORE) and the Women's Network for Entrepreneurial Training, offer business counseling and mentoring at no charge.

Find Out More

For information about small business training, financing, managing, opportunities, and more, key in **Small Business Administration** on your search engine, or go online at www.sba.gov.

Starting Out

Some entrepreneurs ease the financial strain of starting a business by keeping their regular job. **Moonlighting** (working two jobs) has helped many beginning entrepreneurs. They learn to place a new value on time. Efficient, productive use of time is essential for business success. Several entrepreneurs identified the time wasters displayed in Table 16.2 as factors that interfere with productivity.

© JIST Works

Table 16.2 The Top-10 Time Wasters

1. Shifting priorities	6. Ineffective delegation
2. Telephone interruptions	7. Cluttered desk/losing things
3. Lack of direction/objectives	8. Procrastination/lack of self-discipline
4. Attempting too much	9. Inability to say "no"
5. Drop-in visitors	10. Meetings

Source: Get-Organized.com

School-to-Work Transition

Explain to your students that learning to deal with stress at school will help them deal with future career stress. Ask a student to read aloud each of the three guidelines for reducing the stress of business ownership. Make the following changes, and read them again. In the first guideline, substitute the word *schoolwork* for *business.* Read the second one as it appears. In the third guideline, substitute the words *your teachers and classmates* for *people.* Also, substitute the word *school* for *business* and the words *school activities* for *enterprises.*

Demands on time, pressure to complete tasks, financial problems, and personal stress are common for beginning entrepreneurs. Using the following guidelines can reduce stress and increase personal satisfaction:

- Learn to balance the amount of time and energy you spend on your business and your personal life.
- Build a regular fitness program into your daily schedule. Physical fitness increases your mental alertness, productivity, and satisfaction.
- Maintain regular communication with people. Personal contacts help build and maintain your morale, and business contacts are essential for success in all enterprises.

Section 3: Get Involved

Answer the following on a separate sheet of paper, and be prepared to discuss your responses in class.

1. You may have heard that the three major reasons for success in a business are "location, location, and location." A new business could be located at the exit ramp of a large city expressway, the main street of a small town, or at any of numerous other locations. Consider the following businesses: a restaurant, a tool rental shop, an auto repair garage, a small clothing store, a motel, and an apartment building. List a good location in your area for each business. Why do you think these would be good locations? List a poor location for each business. Why would these be poor locations?
2. Do you find any of the time wasters listed in Table 16.2 to have a negative effect on your schoolwork, job, household responsibilities, or personal relationships? Which time wasters have presented the most problems for you? What action could you take to help get these time wasters under control?

Section 4: Financing a Business

Entrepreneurs must carefully consider the financing for a new *venture* (an undertaking of chance) before making a commitment. Entrepreneurs frequently invest all of their personal savings in a venture and still need additional capital. New business owners usually turn to family members, friends, loan institutions, or *investors* (people who put money into an enterprise in the hopes of getting a profitable return).

A new business will find it important to begin with all of the equipment and materials required for daily operations. Being able to do so usually means more-than-normal spending during the **start-up** period (when a

Career Fact

A major reason for the failure of new businesses is a lack of financial planning.

business is beginning). Start-up expenses cause most new enterprises to lose money for several months or longer. To defray these costs, entrepreneurs frequently need to obtain a loan or sell a part of the ownership to operate the business until it begins to earn a profit.

TAKE NOTE

Entrepreneur magazine's 2006 Hot 500 got their start-up capital from the following sources:

- Savings and personal funds (69%)
- Private investors (21%)
- Friends and family (21%)
- Line of credit (18%)
- Bank loan (12%)
- Credit card (10%)

Estimating Start-up Costs

Financial planning begins by estimating start-up costs. These costs include all items that are paid for only once, such as licenses, permits, franchise fees, insurance, telephone deposits, tools, equipment, fixtures, installation costs, furniture, office supplies, remodeling and decorating, promotional advertising, signs, and professional fees (for an attorney, accountant, or computer programmer). In addition, entrepreneurs must consider the expense of renting or leasing space to conduct the business.

Renting a well-located space to conduct your business is important. However, underestimating your start-up costs could put you out of business quickly.

The amount of **working capital** (money required to meet the ongoing expenses of a business) will depend on several factors:

- The amount of money invested in the business
- The time and energy invested by the owner
- The type of business

Some business experts advise that if you expect a new enterprise to earn a profit in 6 months, double that time and be ready to operate without profits for 12 months. This philosophy provides a financial cushion in case of unanticipated expenses or delays.

Comprehension Check

Ask several students: If you were starting a lawn service, what is one start-up cost you would incur?

Projecting Operating Income and Expenses

After you estimate the start-up costs, estimate the *operating expenses* (money needed to keep the business operating for 6 to 12 months). Operating expenses include salaries (including the owner's); expenses for telephone, Internet service, electricity, and heat; office supplies; other supplies or materials; debt interest; advertising fees; maintenance costs; taxes; legal and accounting fees; insurance fees; business membership fees; and special service expenses (such as secretarial, copying, and delivery service).

In addition to business working capital, entrepreneurs must budget money for personal expenses. This estimate should include all normal living expenses for you and your family, such as food, household expenses,

© JIST Works

car payments, rent or mortgage, clothing, medical expenses, entertainment, and taxes.

Comprehension Check

Ask at least three students: In your own words, what is the difference between *operating expenses* and *start-up costs?*

Securing Sources of Capital

Entrepreneurs secure needed capital in a variety of ways. Each method of financing has benefits and liabilities. Consider the following:

Discussion Starter

Borrowing money has ended more than one friendship. Ask your students: Can you think of a time when someone borrowed something from you and did not return it? How did it affect your relationship with that person?

Reteaching

Have students complete the "Capital Sources" worksheet found in the Chapter 16 file of the *Preparing for Career Success Instructor's CD-ROM, Third Edition.*

- *Loans or gifts from family members or friends:* Be certain to make businesslike, written agreements and to disclose fully the potential risk as well as the possible profit.
- *A bank loan:* Banks require a comprehensive statement of the borrower's personal financial condition as well as a business plan. In addition, the loan officer will want written financial projections that include the amount borrowed, the purpose, and the way you will repay the loan.
- *A Small Business Administration loan guarantee:* The SBA is not a bank, but it does extend guarantees and may occasionally participate in a loan when banks are unable or unwilling to provide the entire financing. The SBA loan officer will ask the same questions as bank loan officers and will require the same carefully considered data about your personal finances, start-up costs, and business projections.
- *Venture capital:* **Venture capital** is money invested, or earmarked for investment, in new businesses. For start-up entrepreneurs, some prior managerial or entrepreneurial track record is usually necessary to obtain venture capital. **Venture capitalists** (people who earn money by making high-risk business loans) usually require the business owner to sell them 50 to 90 percent ownership of the new business in return for the capital.

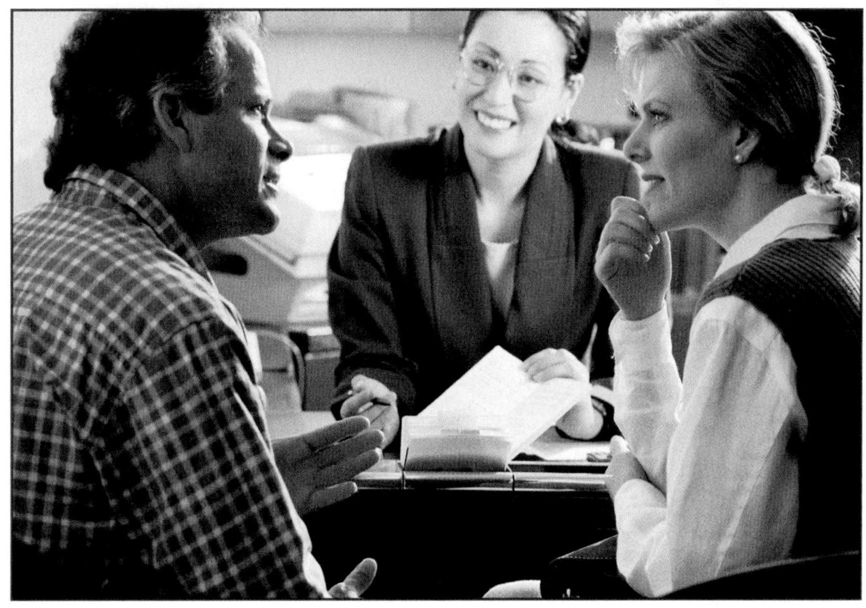

Dan just cosigned a business loan for his friend. If the business fails, Dan will be responsible for the loan. Would you cosign a loan for a friend's business?

Understanding the Balance Sheet

The **balance sheet** is a summary of **assets** (what the business owns), **liabilities** (what the business owes), and **net worth** (the difference between assets and liabilities). Reviewing the balance sheet of a business, along with the profit-and-loss statement and the cash-flow statement, helps owners, investors, and loan institutions make informed financial and business-planning decisions. Figure 16.1 shows a sample balance sheet for Carl's Bookstore.

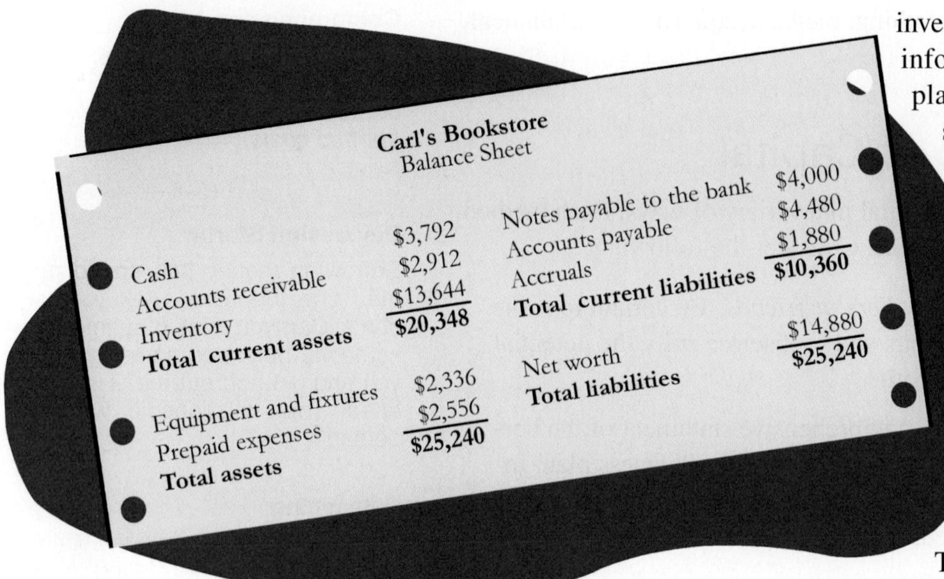

Carl's Bookstore
Balance Sheet

Cash	$3,792	Notes payable to the bank	$4,000
Accounts receivable	$2,912	Accounts payable	$4,480
Inventory	$13,644	Accruals	$1,880
Total current assets	**$20,348**	**Total current liabilities**	**$10,360**
Equipment and fixtures	$2,336	Net worth	$14,880
Prepaid expenses	$2,556	**Total liabilities**	**$25,240**
Total assets	**$25,240**		

Figure 16.1 Sample balance sheet.

A firm's balance sheet is drawn up using totals from the individual accounts kept in the **general ledger** (the principal book of accounts containing the final entries of assets and liabilities). The balance sheet shows the amount left after all creditors are paid. The assets and liabilities sections must balance, resulting in the name *balance sheet.* It is produced quarterly, semiannually, or at the end of each calendar or fiscal year.

Current assets are anything of value (cash, inventory, or property) that the business owner can convert into cash within a year. Fixed assets are items such as land and equipment. Liabilities are debts that the business must pay. Amounts owed to suppliers are considered to be current liabilities. Numerous payments over a long time, such as notes owed to a bank, are long-term liabilities. Capital (also called *equity* or *net worth)* is equal to assets minus liabilities.

Vocabulary Builder/ Cooperative Learning

Write the following terms on the chalkboard: *balance sheet, net worth, assets, liabilities,* and *general ledger.* Divide the class into small groups. Allow 10 minutes for each group to write as few correct sentences as they can using these terms. (Terms may not be used twice.) Score: 1 point for each correct sentence; 1 point for each term used in a grammatically incorrect sentence; 1 point for each unused term. The group with the lowest score wins.

Understanding the Profit-and-Loss Statement

A **profit-and-loss statement** is a detailed, month-by-month record of income obtained from sales and expenses incurred to produce sales. It helps business owners evaluate the effect of business decisions on profit. Business owners use information from profit-and-loss statements to make plans.

Four types of information are included in a profit-and-loss statement:

- Sales information comprises the number of units sold and the dollar amount of sales income.
- Direct expenses are the costs of labor, materials, and *manufacturing overhead* (fixed manufacturing costs).
- Indirect expenses are the costs the business would have if a product was not produced or a service was not provided. They include salaries, rent, utilities, insurance, depreciation, office supplies, taxes, and professional fees.
- Income, or profit, is displayed as pre-tax and after-tax, or net income.

KEY TO SUCCESS

Electronic commerce (e-commerce) not only opens a large potential market to small business owners, but it also eliminates several expenses such as rent and office furniture. Small business owners can use their home, basement, or garage as a production facility or office. Additionally, the space used becomes a legitimate tax deduction.

© JIST Works

A profit-and-loss statement should be prepared at least once a year, and it is a requirement for corporations. The profit-and-loss statement helps the business owner determine the economic health of the business.

Understanding the Cash-Flow Statement

Cash flow is the amount of money available in a business at a specific time. A business must have a healthy cash flow to survive. To keep track of cash flow, entrepreneurs must forecast the funds they expect to receive and pay out over a given time. By predicting a deficiency or surplus of cash, they can plan future business moves.

When it is time to expand the business, hire more employees, or use certain tax breaks, entrepreneurs use the information contained in the balance sheet, profit-and-loss statement, and cash-flow statement to make these and a variety of other managerial decisions.

Education and Training

Send a writer to the chalkboard. Ask the class to give the writer the titles of five occupations. Ask several students to name a business a skilled worker in one of the occupations could logically start. Select one business to write beside each occupation on the list. Ask several students to name a school subject and the reason it would be important for each entrepreneur. Select one school subject to write beside each occupation.

Section 4: Get Involved

Answer the following on a separate sheet of paper, and be prepared to discuss your responses in class.

1. Imagine that a friend asks you to invest your time and money in a business partnership. List the questions you will ask before making your decision.
2. Arrange to interview the manager of the bank where your family has an account, or invite him or her to speak to your class. What is the bank's policy on making business loans? What are the requirements? What are the interest rates? What advice can the bank manager offer to students who are interested in becoming entrepreneurs?

Section 5: Piles of Paperwork

From the moment an owner is legally required to register the name of his or her business with local, state, and federal authorities, he or she has three choices: Sell the business, close the business, or complete piles of paperwork in a precise and timely manner. To perform the nonprofit work and take on the responsibility that goes with paperwork, new business owners must contact each appropriate government agency to acquire the necessary forms and to know when they are due. Always ask for more forms than you need to allow for mistakes and rewriting. When you understand the process, you can find many forms available on government-sponsored Web sites.

Accurate financial records are essential for completing tax returns, making business decisions, and applying for loans. An accountant can help you decide on the best record-keeping system for your business. Your accountant will set up the books for your business, organize and analyze profit-and-loss statements, and provide advice on financial decisions. In addition, an accountant can make budget forecasts, help you prepare a loan application, and handle tax matters. After your accountant sets up a general

FIND OUT MORE

All states provide direct help to new entrepreneurs with *One-Stop Business Permit Centers.* These centers provide detailed information about the permits, licenses, and regulations that are required in your state. Using your favorite search engine, key in ***(your state)* One-Stop Business Permit Center.** To acquire federal forms and information related to everything from hiring employees to paying federal taxes, key in **America's Service Locator.** Next, on the site's home page, click on Business Center.

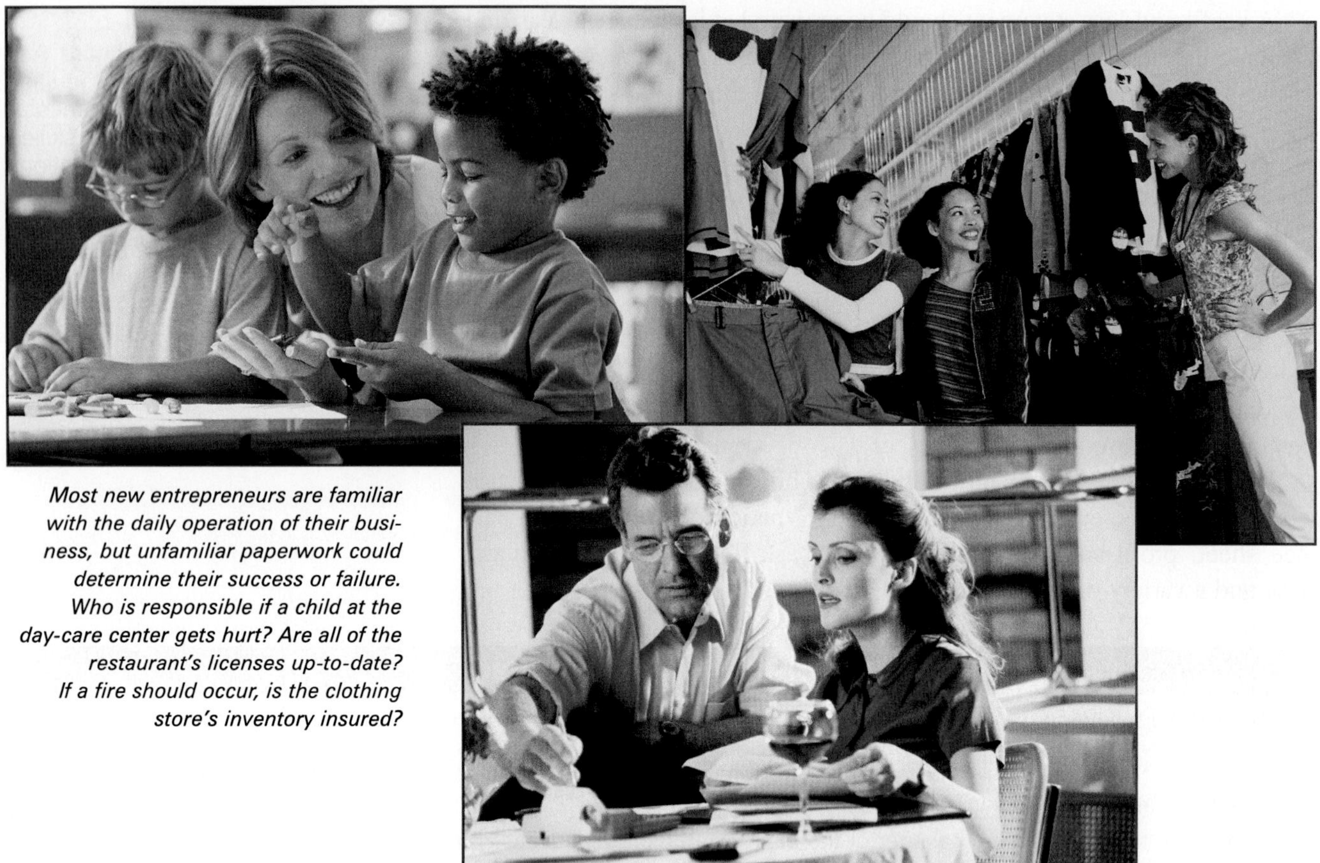

Most new entrepreneurs are familiar with the daily operation of their business, but unfamiliar paperwork could determine their success or failure. Who is responsible if a child at the day-care center gets hurt? Are all of the restaurant's licenses up-to-date? If a fire should occur, is the clothing store's inventory insured?

Comprehension Check

After your class has finished reading "Tax Obligations and Benefits," ask several students: What is a *tax deduction*? After your students understand the meaning of the term, explain that the government doesn't return the entire amount of a deduction. Instead, the tax rate percentage of the deduction is returned. For example, an entrepreneur pays a tax rate of 30 percent of income, and her deduction is $100. In this case, the government returns $30 (30 percent of the $100).

Cooperative Learning

Have students complete the "Group Talk" worksheet in Chapter 16 of the *Preparing for Career Success Instructor's CD-ROM, Third Edition.*

ledger for the business, you can either record the daily transactions yourself or periodically have a bookkeeper post transactions and prepare financial statements.

Tax Obligations and Benefits

The federal government requires every new business to apply for an employer identification number. The necessary application forms are available from the Internal Revenue Service. This number will be used to complete numerous tax forms and other required government information forms during the life of the business.

Each type of business ownership has certain tax advantages, but all businesses must pay taxes. In fact, every business decision, purchase, or sale you make has certain tax advantages or disadvantages.

It is important to identify and declare as many deductions as possible. *Deductions* are business expenses that the government allows business owners to subtract from their gross income in order to arrive at their taxable income. Examples of business deductions include

- Salaries and wages paid to employees
- Rent, supplies used by the business, and utilities
- The purchase or lease of tools, machines, or equipment

© JIST Works

Insurance

The following are some recommended types of business insurance:

- Product liability insurance protects you in the event your product or service causes injury to a user.
- Auto liability and "non-owned" auto liability insurance protects you if you use a vehicle to support the business in any way.
- Medical payments insurance protects you if someone is injured in your place of business, regardless of whether the injury is your fault.
- Worker's compensation provides compensation for workers who are injured or who contract an occupational-related disease on the job; required by law (see the description of workers' compensation laws under the heading "Compensation for Injuries," in Section 3 of Chapter 12).
- Business interruption or earnings insurance protects you if fire or some other cause damages your business and you must totally or partially suspend operation.
- Disability income protection acts as a form of health and accident insurance in case you or an employee becomes disabled.
- Business life insurance provides funds to continue operations if the owner dies.
- Fire insurance protects the business against loss by fire.

CAREER FACT

A reliable insurance agent can save a business a great deal of time and money. Entrepreneurs must select their agents with the same care they exercise in selecting an accountant, attorney, or other professional. Insurance professionals can help entrepreneurs select the right policies for their business needs. In addition, they maintain records and help settle insurance claims.

Enrichment

Have students complete the "Entrepreneurship" worksheet in Chapter 16 of the *Preparing for Career Success Instructor's CD-ROM, Third Edition.*

Community Resources

Have an owner of a small business visit your classroom. Ask him or her to talk about the government agencies that the business must deal with in the course of a year. What licenses or permits are required? What paperwork is required each business quarter and each year? How much time is spent with paperwork? When does the owner normally do the required paperwork? What taxes must be paid? How often are taxes paid?

Laws and Regulations

Most localities have registration and licensing requirements that may apply to your particular business. A license is formal permission to practice a certain business activity. It is issued by the local, state, or federal government. A license may require some type of examination to certify that the recipient is qualified to run a particular business. A **permit** is an official certificate of permission that allows a business to operate. It is issued by local government authorities. A modest fee is usually charged for licenses and permits.

If your business has employees, you are responsible for withholding from their paychecks federal income tax, Social Security tax, and any local or state income taxes that apply. You must also pay into the workers' compensation and unemployment insurance programs. In addition, you must comply with minimum wage, child labor, and employee health laws. If your business operations are *intrastate* (within a state) rather than *interstate* (between states), you will be concerned primarily with state and local, rather than federal, licensing.

TAKE NOTE

Carefully consider the liabilities of operating without proper licenses and registrations. The owner usually pays with embarrassment, time, and money when a business is not properly licensed.

© JIST Works

Section 5: Get Involved

Answer the following on a separate sheet of paper, and be prepared to discuss your responses in class.

1. Phone or visit your local Internal Revenue Service office and ask for a package of government information for starting a new business. After you have an opportunity to review the information packet, answer these questions: How much time would you expect to spend doing the necessary paperwork to start a new business? What additional education or training would help you become an entrepreneur?
2. Review the eight types of business insurance described in this section. Which of the eight types do you consider most important to a new business? Why do you think so? Which of the eight types do you consider least important to a new business? Why do you think so?

Reteaching

Have students complete the "Checking Your Location" worksheet in Chapter 16 of the *Preparing for Career Success Student Activity Book, Third Edition.*

Enrich Your Vocabulary Answers

1. sole proprietorship
2. franchise
3. venture capital
4. target market
5. entrepreneurs
6. partnership
7. venture capitalists
8. assets
9. net worth
10. corporation
11. Small Business Administration
12. moonlighting
13. balance sheet
14. general ledger
15. liabilities

(continued)

Chapter 16 Review

Enrich Your Vocabulary

On a separate sheet of paper, number from 1 to 20, and write the most appropriate term from the "Enrich Your Vocabulary" list at the beginning of the chapter next to the number of the statement it matches.

1. A form of business ownership in which the same person is both the owner and a worker
2. A legal contract with an established, well-recognized company
3. Money invested, or earmarked for investment, in new businesses
4. A group of consumers who would most likely purchase certain goods or services
5. People who have ideas, develop plans, and take action to pursue moneymaking opportunities
6. A form of business ownership in which two or three people own and operate the business
7. People who earn money by making high-risk business loans
8. What the business owns
9. The difference between assets and liabilities
10. A form of business ownership in which a number of people own and operate the business under a state-issued license or charter
11. A government agency that aids, counsels, and assists all the interests of small businesses
12. Working two jobs
13. A summary of assets, liabilities, and net worth
14. The principal book of accounts containing the final entries of assets and liabilities
15. What the business owes

© JIST Works

16. An official certificate of permission that allows a business to operate

17. The period of time when a business is beginning

18. A detailed monthly record of income and expenses

19. The amount of money available in a business at a specific time

20. Money required to meet the ongoing expenses of a business

21. Document that contains information about the product or service that a company sells

Check Your Knowledge

On a separate sheet of paper, complete the following activities.

1. List three personal characteristics that are common to most entrepreneurs.
2. How do the wages and working hours of most entrepreneurs compare to the wages and working hours of most workers?
3. What portion of all small businesses (those with fewer than 500 employees) fail within five years?
4. What six factors should a potential entrepreneur consider before starting a new business?
5. What type of business ownership is used by the owners of most small automobile service stations and video stores?
6. What information should be included in a good business plan?
7. List two of the resources that new entrepreneurs usually turn to for start-up capital.
8. List five records that an entrepreneur must maintain as an essential part of business management.

Develop SCANS Competencies

This activity will give you practice in developing the information and interpersonal skills that successful workers use. Talk with three entrepreneurs (people who have started their own business). Use the traits given in Table 16.1 (the entrepreneur list) to develop a survey for the entrepreneurs to complete. Ask them which of the traits apply to themselves and which trait was most important in helping them to start their own business. Ask them to add any other traits they think are important to entrepreneurs. Compare your results with those of your classmates. Develop a class list of the most important traits the entrepreneurs listed.

Enrich Your Vocabulary Answers *(continued)*

16. permit
17. start-up
18. profit-and-loss statement
19. cash flow
20. working capital
21. business plan

Check Your Knowledge Answers

1. They value their independence, use ideas to create products or services, enjoy the challenge of building and operating a business, have self-confidence, have tenacity, are competitive, tolerate uncertainty, enjoy solving problems, are impatient, and prefer moneymaking work over hobbies.
2. Beginning entrepreneurs earn less money and work longer hours during a start-up. After they are established, most choose to work longer hours but earn better-than-average wages.
3. According to the SBA, more than half fail within five years.
4. Licensing requirements, legal restrictions, the amount of capital needed, the number of workers required, liabilities to be assumed, and the type of business organization that is most suitable.
5. Sole proprietorship
6. Information about the product or service, potential market, marketing strategy, organization of the business, and financial requirements for start-up and operation.
7. Personal savings, family members or friends, loan institutions, and investors.
8. Tax records, a general ledger, profit-and-loss statements, business insurance records, and licenses and permits.

Enrichment

Have students complete the Chapter 16 section of the *Preparing for Career Success Student Portfolio, Third Edition.*

© JIST Works

Unit 4 Living on Your Own

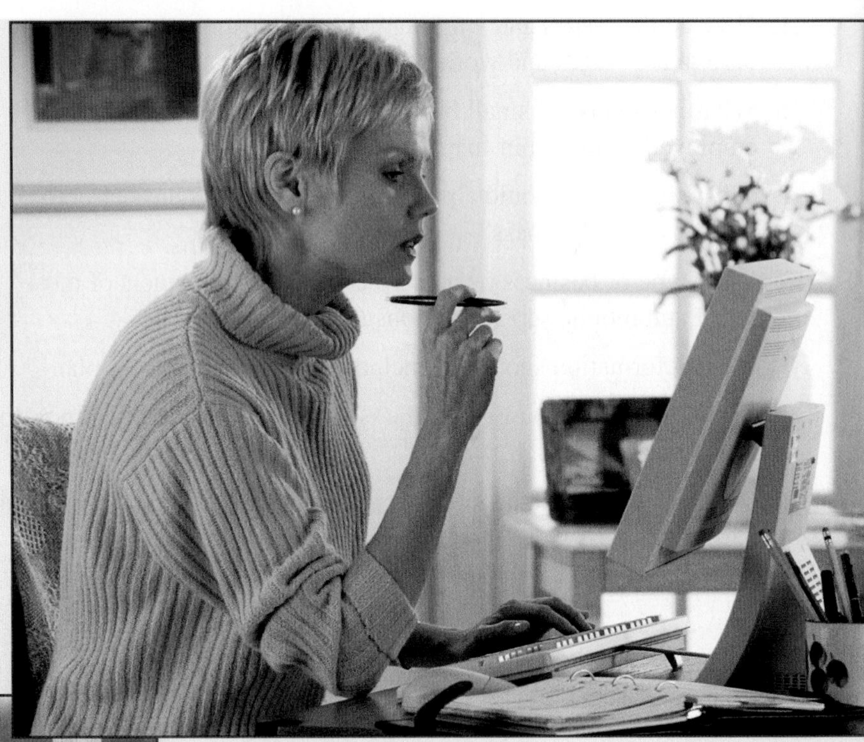

Chapter 17: Managing Your Income

Chapter 18: Being a Wise Consumer

Chapter 19: Achieving Wellness

Chapter 20: Accepting Civic Responsibility

Chapter 21: Balancing Your Career and Your Life

Chapter 17 Resources

Lesson Plans and Preparation

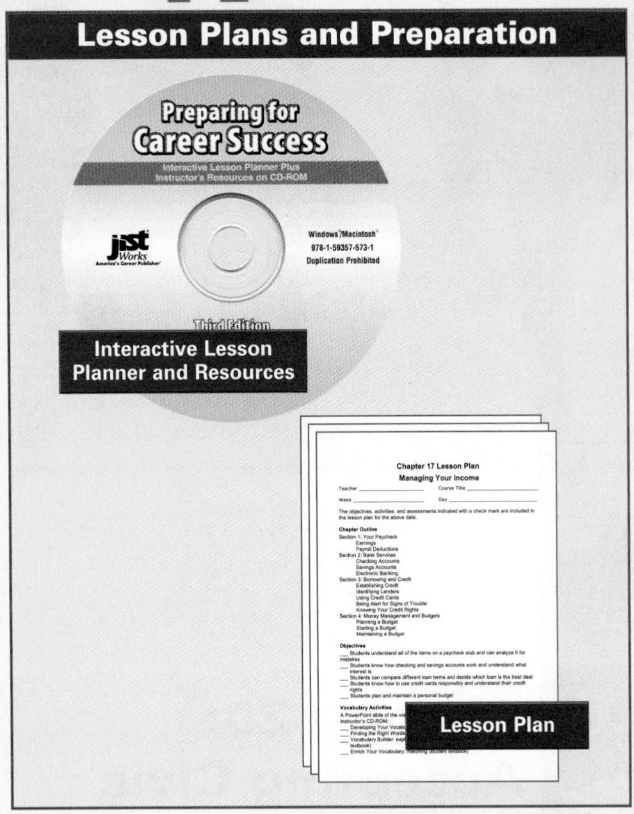

Multimedia

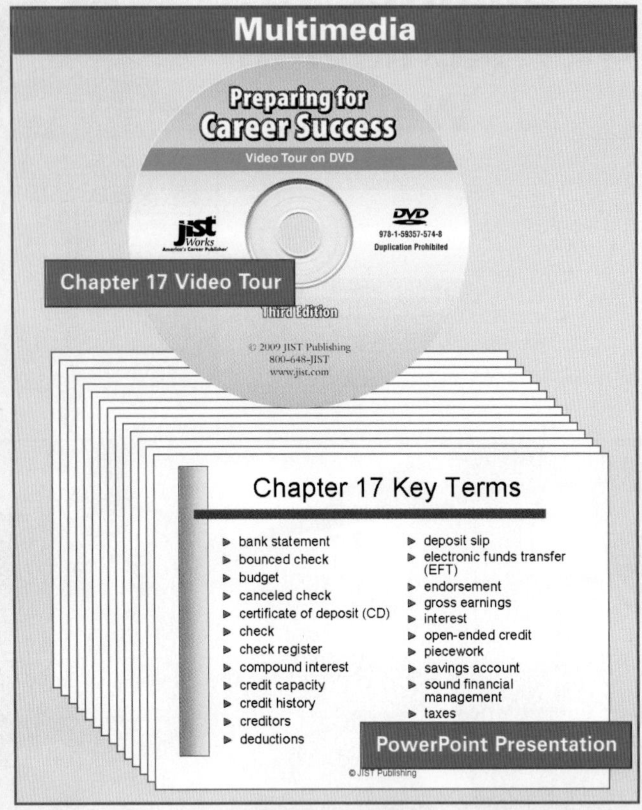

Activities

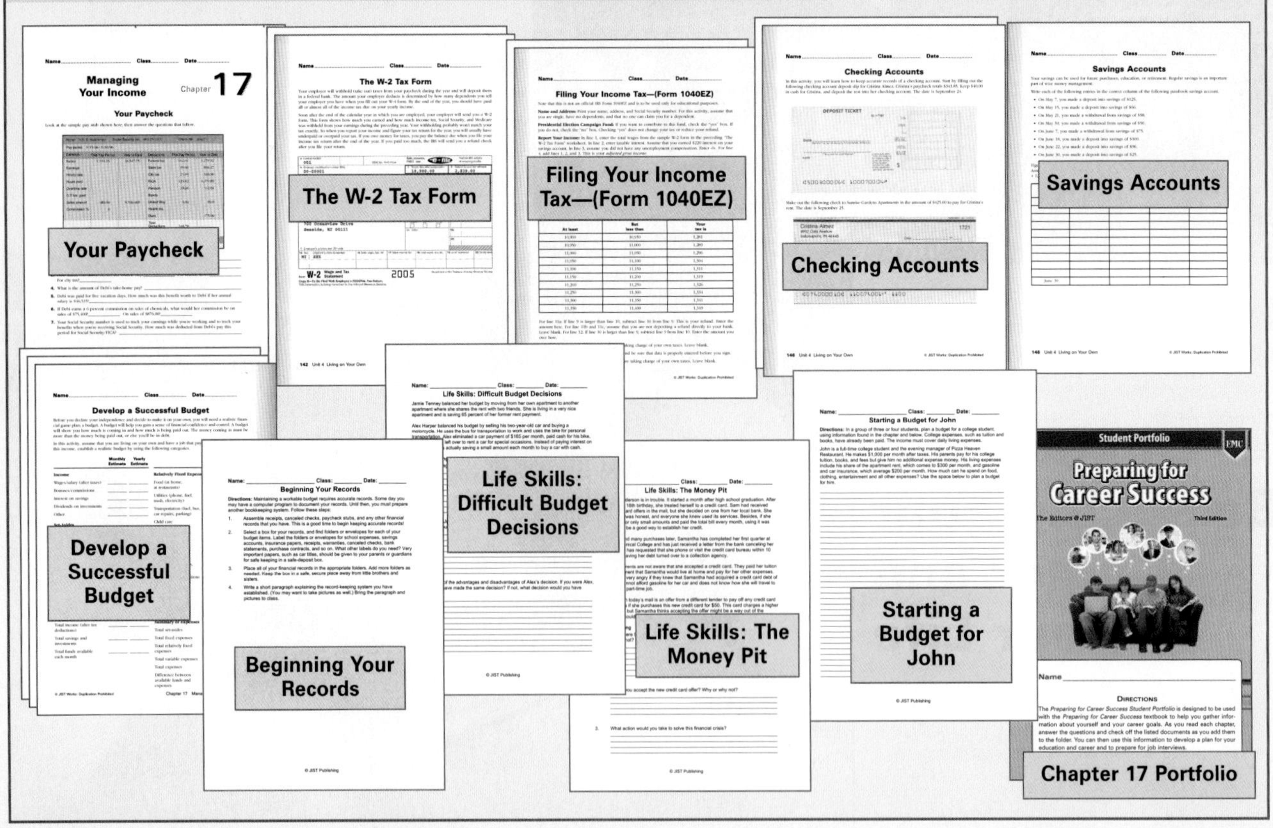

- Your Paycheck
- The W-2 Tax Form
- Filing Your Income Tax—(Form 1040EZ)
- Checking Accounts
- Savings Accounts
- Develop a Successful Budget
- Life Skills: Difficult Budget Decisions
- Beginning Your Records
- Life Skills: The Money Pit
- Starting a Budget for John
- Chapter 17 Portfolio

© JIST Works

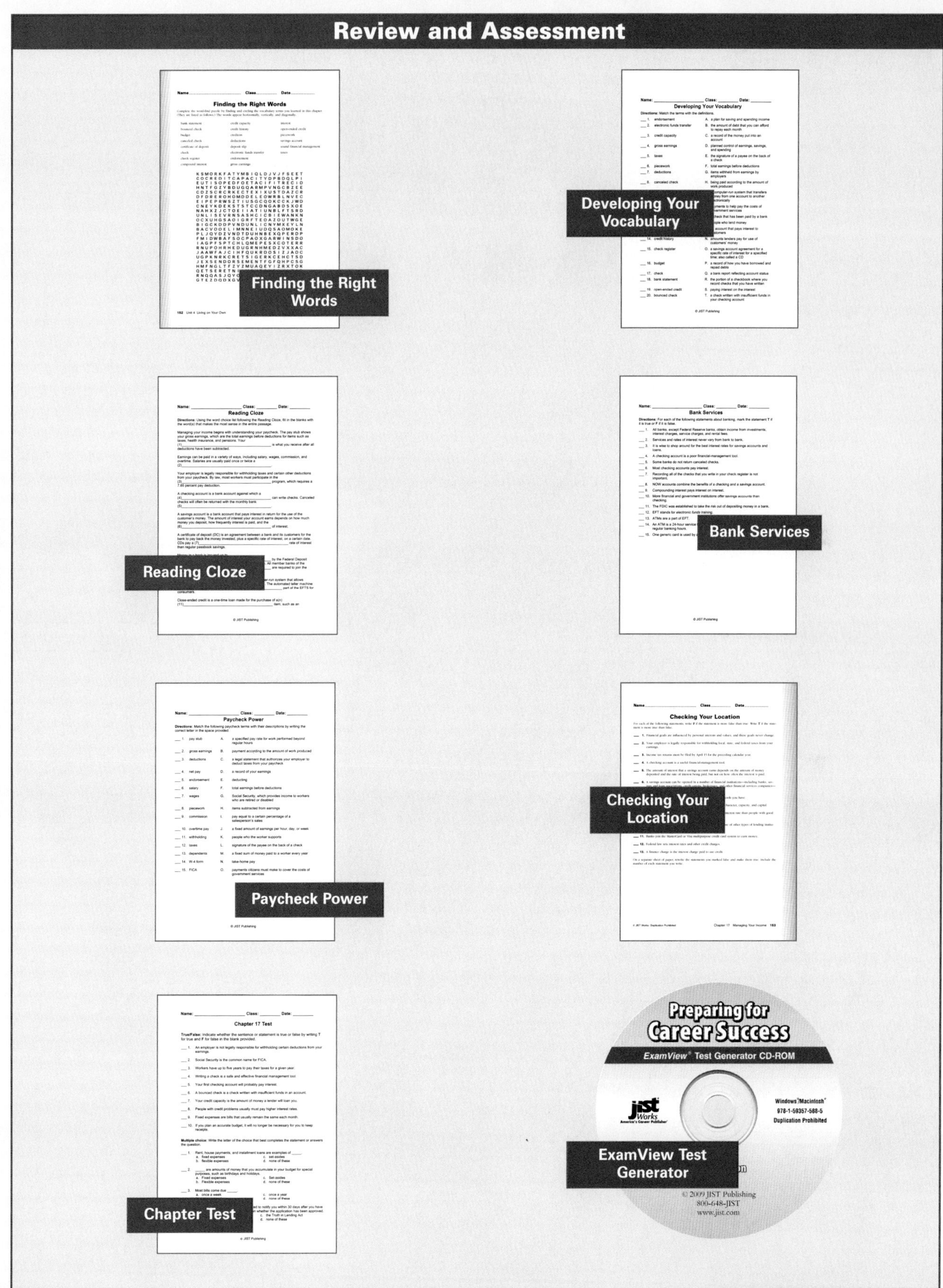
Review and Assessment
Finding the Right Words
Developing Your Vocabulary
Reading Cloze
Bank Services
Paycheck Power
Checking Your Location
Chapter Test
Preparing for Career Success
ExamView® Test Generator CD-ROM
Windows®/Macintosh®
978-1-59357-588-5
Duplication Prohibited
© 2009 JIST Publishing
800-648-JIST
www.jist.com
ExamView Test Generator

Chapter 17 Managing Your Income

Learning Objectives

- Use sound financial management to reach your life goals and meet future financial crises
- Define each category on a pay stub and check it for accuracy
- Open, maintain, and use savings and checking accounts and electronic funds transfer systems
- Select the most advantageous credit terms, and understand the differences between various lending institutions and credit cards
- Understand and use your consumer credit rights
- Write a workable personal or household budget

Financial management is a key to reaching your life goals, and it is a method of handling future financial crises. When you begin earning a paycheck, your income will probably be modest, and your financial life uncomplicated. You therefore may be tempted to ignore long-range financial management. However, your first financial decisions will be a major factor in determining your future career success. To ensure your financial success, you should have a plan for spending your money, set aside a regular amount for savings, and place limits on *credit purchases* (spending your money before you earn it).

Enrich Your Vocabulary

In reading this chapter and doing the exercises, you will learn the following important terms:

bank statement	credit capacity	gross earnings
bounced check	credit history	interest
budget	creditors	open-ended credit
canceled check	deductions	piecework
certificate of deposit (CD)	deposit slip	savings account
check	electronic funds transfer (EFT)	sound financial management
check register	endorsement	taxes
compound interest		

Vocabulary

You can use the "Developing Your Vocabulary" worksheet in Chapter 17 of the *Preparing for Career Success Instructor's CD-ROM, Third Edition* as a pretest or reteaching worksheet.

Vocabulary Builder/ Cooperative Learning

On the chalkboard, write the heading "Financial Management." Have the students brainstorm, and then list things the students expect to pay for and purchase when they begin earning a full-time paycheck. Divide the class into groups of five. Have each group discuss and rank in order of importance each of the things on the chalkboard. List each group's order, and discuss why group opinions differed.

Getting the most for your money through planned control of your earnings, savings, and spending is **sound financial management**. Following these four steps will enable you to become an effective financial manager:

1. Establish your financial goals, and rank them in order of importance.
2. Develop a plan before you spend money.
3. Learn to be a wise consumer.
4. Develop a workable budget.

As you learned in Chapter 3, goals (including financial goals) are influenced by personal interests and values, and they change as your needs and situation change. Your present goal may be to continue your education, buy a car, or take a vacation. Later, you may need a house or a larger apartment in which to raise a family. Managing your income and spending will remain important no matter how your goals change.

Section 1: Your Paycheck

Managing your income begins with understanding your paycheck. When you are paid, you will receive a paycheck and an attached pay stub, which is a record of your earnings. You should keep all of your pay stubs for at least three years. They will enable you to verify your earnings and deductions.

The pay stub shows your **gross earnings** (total earnings before deductions). **Deductions** are those items subtracted from your earnings such as taxes, insurance, pensions, and other miscellaneous items. The amount of pay you receive after subtracting your deductions is your *net pay* (take-home pay). Your gross earnings and your net pay will be very different in size (see Figure 17.1). For example, a beginning worker's gross earnings of $600 per week could amount to a net pay of less than $450 because of deductions.

To cash your paycheck, you must sign the back of the check in ink. This is your **endorsement** (the signature of a payee on the back of a check). Sign your name exactly as it appears on the front of the check.

The tax information printed on your pay stub is forwarded to the appropriate government agencies. Always check your pay stub to make sure that

Take Note

Now nearly all American adults pay income tax, but this tax has gone through many changes through the years. In 1861, Congress imposed a 3 percent federal tax on all incomes above $800 a year (the very rich) to pay for the Civil War, but it repealed this tax in 1872. In 1913, Congress passed the Sixteenth Amendment to the Constitution, which gave Congress the power to collect taxes on all incomes. In 2006, the IRS collected more than $2.2 trillion in taxes and processed 228 million tax returns.

© JIST Works

it is correct. Be sure to keep accurate daily records of the hours you work because mistakes can happen.

Name: Roberta W. O'Day		Social Security No. 123-45-XXXX		Check No. : 0046271	
Pay period: 9/15/XX - 9/30/XX					
Earnings	This Pay Period	Year to Date	Deductions	This Pay Period	Year to Date
Salary	2,308.50	53,095.50	Federal tax	285.22	6,559.84
Earnings			State tax	70.12	1,612.54
Hourly rate			City tax	46.18	1,061.92
Hours paid			FICA	213.54	8,541.60
Overtime rate			Pension		
O.T. hrs. paid			Bonds		
Sales amount			United Way		
Commission %			Health ins.		
			Dues		350.00
			Total Deductions	615.06	
			Net Pay	1,693.44	
Illness Unpaid	Family Illness	Jury Duty	Vacation	Sick Leave Days Accum.	
				15	

Figure 17.1 Sample pay stub.

Earnings

Employers use a variety of methods to pay their employees, including these:

- **Salary:** The employer pays a fixed sum of money to a worker every year. Payment is usually once or twice a month. Wages for a year are calculated and divided into equal pay periods.
- **Wages:** The employer pays a worker a fixed amount of earnings per hour, day, or week.
- **Piecework:** The employer pays a worker according to the amount the worker produces.
- **Commission:** The employer pays a salesperson a certain percentage of his or her sales.
- **Overtime pay:** The employer pays a specified rate for work performed beyond regular hours.

Reteaching

Have students complete the "Paycheck Power" worksheet in Chapter 17 of the *Preparing for Career Success Instructor's CD-ROM, Third Edition.*

Payroll Deductions

Regardless of how workers are paid, their employer is legally responsible for *withholding* (deducting) local, state, and federal **taxes** (payments that all citizens are required by law to make to help pay the costs of government services) from their earnings. Employers withhold tax payments from the workers' base pay and forward them to the appropriate government agencies. Taxes are also withheld on the earnings of corporations.

Workers are required to pay all or a large part of their federal, state, and local income taxes during the year in which they receive the income. The amount withheld depends on each worker's earnings, marital status, number of *dependents* (people who the worker supports), and the percentage of tax determined by law.

The law requires all new workers to complete a W-4 tax form for their employer. The employer uses the information provided on the W-4 to calculate withholdings for each pay period (see Figure 17.2). The W-4 is a legal statement that authorizes your employer to deduct taxes from your paycheck and to pay them to the government for you. If the information on your W-4 is accurate, the amount withheld each year will be close to your annual tax bill.

Find Out More

For online information about tax forms or other tax-related questions, key in **Internal Revenue Service** on your search engine, or go online at www.irs.gov.

Comprehension Check

Have students complete the "Your Paycheck" worksheet in Chapter 17 of the *Preparing for Career Success Student Activity Book, Third Edition.*

Video Tour on DVD

Show students the Chapter 17 segment to introduce them to the content.

Cut here and give Form W-4 to your employer. Keep the top part for your records.

Form **W-4** — **Employee's Withholding Allowance Certificate** — OMB No. 1545-0010

Department of the Treasury
Internal Revenue Service

▶ Your employer must send a copy of this form to the IRS if: (a) you claim more than 10 allowances or (b) you claim "Exempt" and your wages are normally more than $200 per week.

1 Type or print your first name and middle initial | Last name | 2 Your social security number

Home address (number and street or rural route) | 3 ☐ Single ☐ Married ☐ Married, but withhold at higher Single rate.
Note: *If married, but legally separated, or spouse is a nonresident alien, check the "Single" box.*

City or town, state, and ZIP code | 4 **If your last name differs from that shown on your social security card, check here. You must call 1-800-772-1213 for a new card.** ▶ ☐

5 Total number of allowances you are claiming (from line **H** above **or** from the applicable worksheet on page 2) — 5

6 Additional amount, if any, you want withheld from each paycheck . . . . — 6 $

7 I claim exemption from withholding for 2004, and I certify that I meet **both** of the following conditions for exemption:
- Last year I had a right to a refund of **all** Federal income tax withheld because I had **no** tax liability **and**
- This year I expect a refund of **all** Federal income tax withheld because I expect to have **no** tax liability.

If you meet both conditions, write "Exempt" here . . . . ▶ 7

Under penalties of perjury, I certify that I am entitled to the number of withholding allowances claimed on this certificate, or I am entitled to claim exempt status.
Employee's signature
(Form is not valid unless you sign it.) ▶ **Date ▶**

8 Employer's name and address (Employer: Complete lines 8 and 10 only if sending to the IRS.) | 9 Office code (optional) | 10 Employer identification number (EIN)

For Privacy Act and Paperwork Reduction Act Notice, see page 2. Cat. No. 10220Q Form **W-4**

Figure 17.2 Sample W-4 tax form.

Every taxpayer must file an income tax return by April 15 for the preceding calendar year. On the tax return, the taxpayer makes adjustments for any overpayment or underpayment of the total tax due.

Most workers must participate in the *Federal Insurance Contributions Act* (FICA, or Social Security) program. Social Security provides monthly income to workers who are retired or are unable to work because of sickness or injury.

Federal law requires employers to deduct 7.65 percent of each employee's pay for Social Security. How much was deducted from Roberta O'Day's earnings (refer to Figure 17.1) and paid to FICA? The law requires Roberta's employer, the GMF Corporation, to match her contribution.

School-to-Work Transition

Have students estimate how much Roberta O'Day and her employer(s) will pay into FICA over a period of 5, 10, 20, and 30 years. Then have them decide whether this amount with compound interest will provide her with enough pension to live for a period of 20 years after she retires.

Maintaining accurate payroll records and processing the required government forms are expensive and time-consuming processes for employers. Many employees are unaware that employers must consider expenses for their portion of benefits such as Social Security, health insurance, vacations, and sick leave as labor costs.

In some cases, workers may choose whether to have their employers make payroll deductions for health and hospitalization plans, life insurance, company pension plans, savings programs, association or union dues, charitable contributions, or stock-buying plans.

Section 1: Get Involved

Answer the following on a separate sheet of paper, and be prepared to discuss your responses in class.

1. Interview workers paid by salary, hourly wages, piecework, and commission. Ask them about the benefits and liabilities of the way they are paid. Which method do you believe would be best in terms of managing your everyday finances? Which would be best for your long-term finances?
2. Which of the methods of payment listed in this section would you expect if you were a cashier who works for a supermarket? A bricklayer who works for a small, nonunion contractor? A plant manager for a chemical plant? A salesperson for a real estate company?
3. Which method of wage payment would you like most? Why? Which would you like least? Why?
4. What do you suppose would happen if the Social Security number on your pay stub were wrong? What action would you take if the total hours recorded on your pay stub were less than your personal records?

Section 2: Bank Services

The first step toward wise money management is to open a checking account and a savings account. With the exception of the Federal Reserve banks described in Chapter 15, banks are businesses. Privately owned banks obtain income from investments in stocks and

© JIST Works

bonds, interest charges on loans and credit cards, service charges for checking accounts, and rental fees for safe-deposit boxes.

Like all businesses, banks must compete for customers. When you are ready to select the financial institution that you entrust with your money, carefully shop for the best interest rates and lowest fees for your banking accounts.

Life Skills: Careless Habits + Identity Theft = Lost Savings

Antonio Rivers started his working career three years ago. After reviewing his first budget, Antonio decided that a savings plan of $100 per month would leave him with enough money to pay his bills and maintain a reasonable lifestyle. On more than one occasion, he has deposited all or part of his overtime checks. Antonio takes great pride in not owing on a credit card, avoiding debt, and especially in adding to his savings account. Two months ago, his bank statement read $5,200.

Antonio's schedule has been very busy during the past several weeks. He has worked every Saturday to help with an extra large order at the plant. Between his job, bowling league, and friends, Antonio has ignored most of life's little responsibilities. He decided that tonight he would open his pile of mail. When he finished the mail, Antonio wondered why he did not have a bank statement. He checked his file folder and noticed that the last statement came six weeks ago.

The next morning, Antonio phoned the bank, and the manager assured him the statement had been mailed the first day of the month but another would be sent in today's mail. When Antonio opened the new statement, he had a total of $165. This is what the bank manager told Antonio:

"Three weeks ago, you made a withdrawal of $5,000 from savings and opened a checking account, Mr. Rivers. You gave the teller your savings account number and two forms of identification with your picture on each. You did not take any money out at the time. Instead, you transferred the money to your new checking account. According to our records, you have written several checks and have $50 left in your checking account."

The thief stole Antonio's bank statement from his home mailbox, acquiring two important pieces of information in the process: Antonio's account number and Social Security number. Putting together two photo identifications was very easy. After all, the bank teller did not have a photo of Antonio, and the thief did not ask for any money. The bank's position is that it did nothing wrong. Now Antonio must find the thief and prosecute him. Unfortunately, one of the checks on his new account was to an airline for two tickets.

Take Note

Although you probably cannot prevent identity theft entirely, you can help guard against this problem by managing your personal information wisely, cautiously, and with an awareness of the issue. To learn more about this important issue, call the Federal Trade Commission toll free at 1-877-ID-THEFT or visit the Web site www.consumer.gov/idtheft.

Career Fact

All workers are required to have a Social Security number (SSN). Your employer and financial institution will likely need your SSN for wage and tax-reporting purposes. Other private businesses may ask you for your SSN to do a credit check such as when you apply for a car loan. Sometimes, however, they simply want your SSN for general record keeping. You do not have to give businesses your SSN just because they ask for it, but sometimes a business may not provide you with the service or benefit you are seeking if you do not provide your SSN. If someone asks for your SSN, ask the following questions: Why do you want my SSN? How will you use my SSN? What law requires me to give my SSN to you? What will happen if I do not give my SSN to you? Getting answers to these questions will help you decide whether you want to share your SSN with the business.

© JIST Works

TECHNOLOGY

Don't download any files to your home computer unless you know and trust the source, and don't click links in pop-up windows. Doing so may install spyware on your system. Spyware is software that monitors and controls how you use your computer. You can protect your computer from this type of software by installing a firewall, antivirus software, and the most recent versions of the operating system (such as Windows) and Web browser.

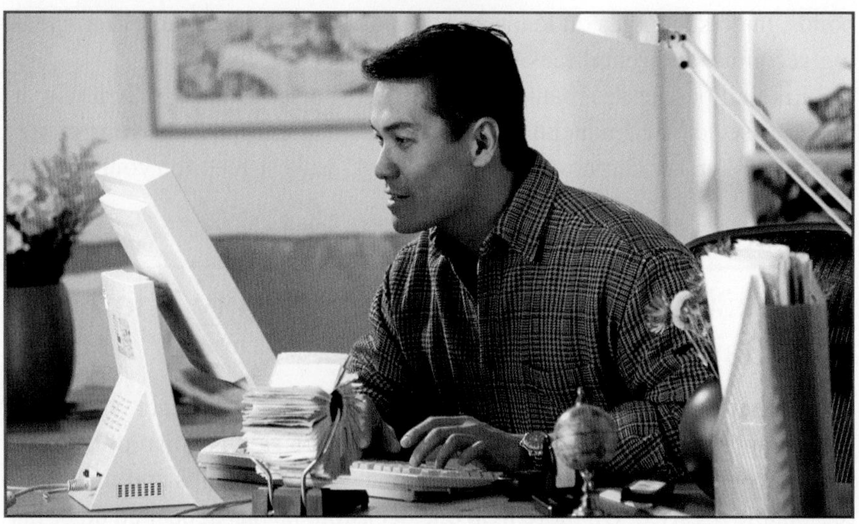

Critical Thinking

Who should be responsible for the money that the identity thief stole from Antonio? Why do you think so?

The thief has stolen Antonio's identity and his hard-earned savings. Do you think the police will catch the thief? If so, why? If not, why not?

If you were Antonio, what would you do next? Why would you choose this course of action?

Enrichment

Assign students to check and compare the following: What is the current rate of interest paid on savings? What service fees are charged for checking accounts? Are deposits insured? What is the rate of interest charged for consumer loans and home mortgages? How convenient is the bank's location and hours of service? Are automatic teller machines available 24 hours a day?

Community Resources

Form a committee of students to invite a bank manager to visit the class to explain bank services. The information in this section will provide the students with specific questions and topics for the banker. Ask a group of students to create a bulletin board about bank services. Banks usually have brochures and colorful literature to illustrate each bank service. Ask the banker to include information about career opportunities in banking.

Reteaching

Have students complete the "Bank Services" worksheet found in the Chapter 17 file of the *Preparing for Career Success Instructor's CD-ROM, Third Edition.*

Checking Accounts

A *checking account* (a bank account against which a depositor can write checks) is a useful financial management tool. Using checks is a convenient way to make payments and provides you with *proof of payment* (a receipt). Checks are a safe way to conduct business because they can be cashed only by the person or business to which the checks are made payable. Writing a check for rent or other payments is convenient. It also eliminates the risk of carrying large sums of cash.

A **check** is an order written by a depositor directing the bank to pay out money (see Figure 17.3). After the bank pays the check, it is entered on your monthly **bank statement** (a bank report that shows the status of the depositor's account). The **canceled check** (a check that has been paid by a bank) is proof of payment. Some banks do not return canceled checks. If you request a copy of a canceled check, the bank will provide it free or for a small charge, or you may be able to view it online.

The **check register** is located in the checkbook; it is the place where you record the checks you write (see Figure 17.4). Keeping an accurate record of your expenditures and deposits is important so that you stay within your budget. The **deposit slip** provides a record of the money put into an account (see Figure 17.5). Be certain to record all checking account deposits in the check register.

© JIST Works

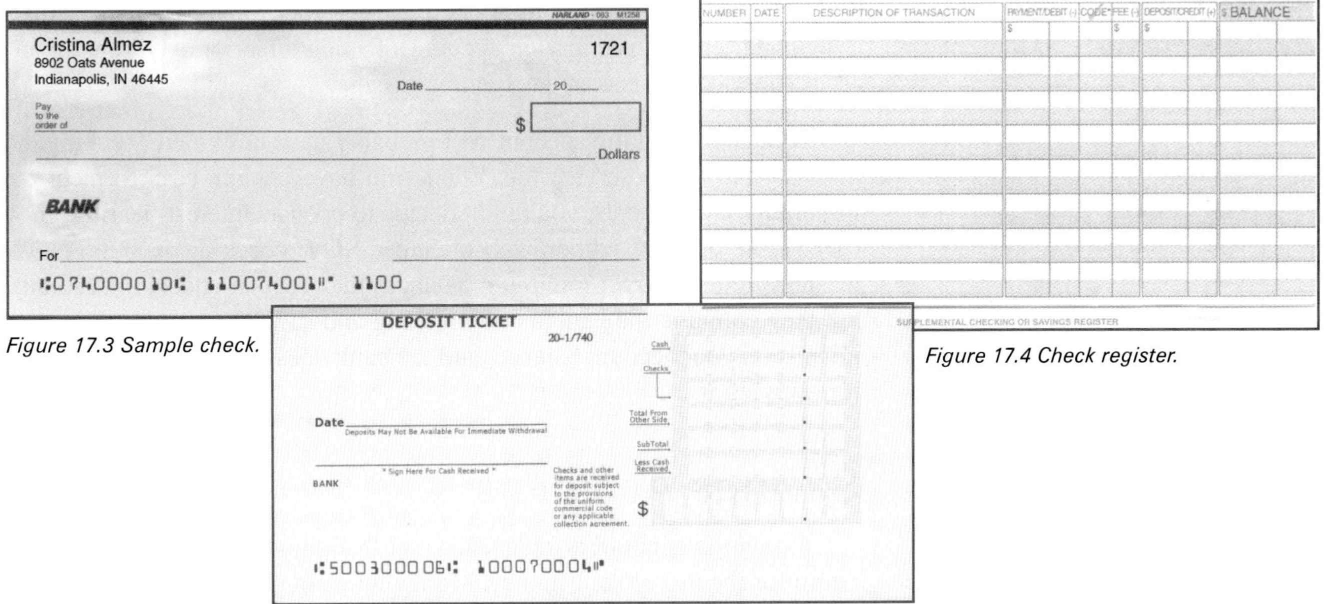

Figure 17.3 Sample check.

Figure 17.4 Check register.

Figure 17.5 Sample bank deposit slip.

Following the journey of a single check should help you understand that part of the banking process. Imagine that you have your car's transmission serviced, and you pay the $59 bill by writing a check on your account at the First Central Bank. In other words, by writing a check, you give instructions to your bank to deduct $59 from your checking account and pay it to Waterloo Transmission.

At the close of the business day, the manager of Waterloo Transmission deposits your check in the Second National Bank (Waterloo's bank). Waterloo's account is credited for $59. However, the Second National Bank does not collect payment directly from the First Central Bank. Paying separately for each of the thousands of checks their customers write every day would be inefficient and costly for them. Instead, the Second National Bank sends your check to a centralized clearinghouse. The clearinghouse totals thousands of checks from several banks every day. Each member bank then makes or receives one daily payment to or from other member banks.

The clearinghouse returns your check to the First Central Bank, and the bank subtracts $59 from your personal checking account. Your check is marked paid and is listed on your bank statement.

Before opening a checking account, estimate how much money you will keep in your account and how many checks you plan to write each month. Because checking accounts differ, you will need to know

- Any fees you pay for writing checks
- Whether free checking is available with a certain minimum balance
- Whether you are eligible for a checking account that pays interest
- What other bank services you will use
- Whether it is more economical to pay a monthly service charge or a per-check fee

Education and Training

Have several students go to the chalkboard. Assign arithmetic problems similar to those they would have in a check register. For example: Your account has a balance of $349.56. Write checks for $33.72, $64.21, and $12.10. Deposit $165.90. The next day, write checks for $43.12. $11.39, and $19.76. What is the balance? See how many at the board get the right/same answer. Discuss the importance of accurate addition and subtraction skills in keeping a check register up-to-date so that checks do not bounce.

Never spend your money before you have it.

—Thomas Jefferson

Vocabulary Builder

Have students illustrate or explain the path a check travels from the time it is written until returned with the balance statement. Tell students to use the terms *deposit slip, check, check register, canceled check,* and *bank statement* in their explanation.

TAKE NOTE

Never endorse a check until you are ready to exchange it for cash or to deposit it in a bank account. Losing a signed check is the same as losing cash.

- The fee charged for a **bounced check** (a check that is written with insufficient funds in your account). Paying a fee for overdrawing on your account is costly and embarrassing.

Your first checking account will probably have unlimited checking, no interest, and a low service fee. When you have enough cash to meet the minimum requirements, you might decide to open an interest-bearing *NOW* (negotiable order of withdrawal) or Super NOW checking account. NOW accounts require larger minimum balances than regular checking accounts, but they combine the benefits of checking and savings accounts. You earn interest on your account balance, and the bank does not charge a service fee for transactions.

Education and Training

Have several students go to the chalkboard. Give them several interest problems to calculate. Use different interest rates for the same amount of money. For example, use 2.3 percent of $1,000, versus 4 percent or 6 percent. Have students figure how much these different interest rates would amount to over a period of 1, 5, and 10 years. Tell your students: If you deposit $100 at an annual interest rate of 7 percent, your account will earn $7 at the end of one year (7 percent of $100 = $7). Your account will begin the second year with an amount of $107 and will earn $7.49 during the second year.

Savings Accounts

A **savings account** is a bank account that pays interest to customers in return for the use of their money. Money may not grow on trees, but it will grow if you deposit it in a savings account that pays **interest** (the amount lenders pay for the use of customers' money). The amount of interest your account earns will depend on the amount of money you deposit, the rate of interest paid, and how often the interest is paid. Some banks **compound interest** (pay interest on the interest) on a daily basis.

Before you open a savings account, make certain the Federal Deposit Insurance Corporation (FDIC) insures it. At one time, depositing money in a bank was risky business. If the bank failed, customers lost part or all of their money. In 1933, the federal government removed this danger by establishing the FDIC. Although the FDIC is a government corporation, member banks provide the money for its operation. The FDIC guarantees *each* account in an insured bank up to $100,000. All member banks of the Federal Reserve System are required to join the FDIC. Always look for a sign posted in the bank stating that it is a member of the Federal Deposit Insurance Corporation.

Enrichment

For extra credit, have students research bank failures before 1933, the savings and loan scandal of the 1980s, and the subprime credit market in 2007. Have the students report their findings to the class. Invite a mortgage banker to visit the class and explain the impact of high-risk borrowers and subprime borrowers on mortgage banks and individual borrowers.

You can open a savings account in a number of financial institutions, including banks, savings and loan associations, credit unions, brokerages, and other financial services companies. The process of opening a savings account is similar to that of opening a checking account. You must complete a signature card, and you will use deposit slips to deposit checks or cash in the account. The savings institution will mail you a monthly or quarterly balance statement and will issue a passbook to record your account transactions. These institutions offer a wide range of savings instruments, interest rates, and security.

Beware of little expenses; a small leak will sink a great ship.

—Benjamin Franklin

A **certificate of deposit (CD)** is a special type of deposit account with a bank or other financial institution that typically offers a higher rate of interest than a regular savings account. CDs feature federal deposit insurance up to $100,000. They usually sell in denominations greater than $1,000, and require that the deposit be for a certain time (six months or more); otherwise, you will pay a penalty for early withdrawal.

© JIST Works

Opening a *traditional passbook savings* account with a small deposit is usually the best choice for first-time savers. If you choose this type, select an account that is insured by the FDIC and provides easy access to your money.

A money market account is a bank account with FDIC protection. This type of account generally offers a greater return than a regular passbook savings account but still allows easy access to your money.

United States saving bonds will repay you on a specified date with a fixed rate of interest. A bond costs as little as $25. Series EE bonds cost half their face value, and the market-based interest rates they earn determine when they reach face value. For example, a bond earning an average of 5 percent interest would reach face value in 14½ years (a $25 bond would be worth $50).

Ask yourself the following questions before you choose a savings plan:

1. How much can I afford to save on a regular basis?
2. How long will I leave my deposits in the account?
3. In case of emergency, how quickly can I obtain my money?

Wise financial planners shop around. As your career progresses, you will have increased and more complex financial responsibilities. Saving a part of your earnings on a regular basis and learning to be a careful spender are giant steps on the road to career success.

KEY TO SUCCESS

Regular savings are an important part of wise money management. You can use your savings for future purchases, such as a vacation, an automobile, or education expenses. Regular deposits will add up, enabling you to pay cash for future purchases and avoid the cost of credit interest.

School-to-Work Transition

The need for thousands of bank tellers was eliminated by the increase in ATM machines and electronic banking even though banks are opening branch offices in more locations and keeping longer hours. Automation and technology will continue to reduce the need for tellers who perform only routine transactions. Brainstorm new jobs created because of ATM machines and electronic banking and list them on the chalkboard. Then discuss the benefits and liabilities of the technology on the labor force.

Electronic Banking

Electronic banking, also known as **electronic funds transfer (EFT)**, uses computer and electronic technology as a substitute for check and other paper transactions. EFTs are initiated through devices such as cards or codes that let you, or those you authorize, access your account. Many financial institutions use ATM or debit cards and a Personal Identification Number (PIN) for this purpose. Some use other forms of debit cards such as those that require, at the most, your signature or a scan. The Federal Electronic Funds Transfer Act (EFT Act) covers some electronic consumer transactions.

Electronic banking involves many different types of transactions:

- *Automated teller machines,* or 24-hour tellers, are electronic terminals that let you bank almost any time. You generally insert an ATM card and enter your PIN. You are entitled to a terminal receipt each time you make an electronic transfer.
- *Direct deposit* lets you authorize specific deposits, such as paychecks and Social Security checks, to your account on a regular basis. You also may preauthorize direct withdrawals so that recurring bills, such as car payments and utility bills, are automatically paid.
- *Pay-by-phone systems* let you call your financial institution with instructions to pay certain bills or to transfer funds between accounts. Be especially careful in telephone transactions because telephone e-checks do not occur face to face.

TAKE NOTE

Imagine that you save $1 a day. That is $365 in one year. If you invest this money at a 4 percent return, computed daily, it will grow like this:

- One year with daily interest equals $372.
- Five years with daily interest equals $2,929.
- Ten years with daily interest equals $4,487.
- Thirty years with daily interest equals $21,169.

© JIST Works

Career Fact

After you report the loss or theft of your ATM or debit card, you are no longer responsible for additional unauthorized transfers occurring after that time. However, the EFT Act does not protect all electronic funds transfers. Stored value cards such as prepaid telephone cards, mass transit passes, and some gift cards are not protected against loss or misuse (Source: Federal Trade Commission, 2007).

- *Personal computer banking* lets you handle many banking transactions via your personal computer. You may use your computer to view your account balance, request transfers between accounts, and pay bills electronically. Most banks use *encryption* to scramble private information and prevent unauthorized access to your account. Never send your PIN in e-mail unless you encrypt it.
- *Point-of-sale transfers* let you pay for purchases with a debit card, which also may be your ATM card. A debit card purchase transfers money from your bank account to the store's account.
- *Electronic check conversion* converts a paper check into an electronic payment at the point of sale or elsewhere, such as when a company receives your check in the mail. When you give your check to a store cashier, for example, the check is processed through an electronic system. After the check is processed, you sign a receipt authorizing the merchant to present the check to your bank electronically and deposit the funds into the merchant's account.

Section 2: Get Involved

Answer the following on a separate sheet of paper, and be prepared to discuss your responses in class.

1. Visit a local bank, and speak with the manager or assistant manager. Obtain the following information, and report it to the class:
   - What causes a bank to fail?
   - What happens to a depositor's money if the bank fails?
   - Is it safe to work in a bank? How does the bank protect employees from robbers?
   - What does being bonded mean?
   - How do electronic banking services help or hinder the operation of the bank?
   - How does the bank attract new customers and keep existing customers?
   - What happens to unclaimed savings accounts?
   - How does your bank work with the Federal Reserve?
   - Is your business a state bank or a national bank?
   - What banking occupations would you recommend to students? What education and training are required for these occupations?
2. Why was the Federal Deposit Insurance Corporation (FDIC) established? Who pays for the insurance protection in FDIC banks?

Discussion Starter

Write the quotation "Neither a borrower nor a lender be" on the chalkboard. This quotation from Shakespeare's *Hamlet* demonstrates how long the use of credit has been a problem for youth. Ask students what this quotation means to them. Then discuss the improbability of someone totally avoiding both borrowing and lending in today's society.

Section 3: Borrowing and Credit

"Buy now, pay later" is the motto of millions of U.S. consumers. They use credit to buy billions of dollars' worth of goods and services each year. Whether they are buying an automobile, house, clothes, gasoline, or a restaurant meal, using credit is a widely accepted method of buying.

© JIST Works

Julie uses her credit card to shop online, but she pays the full amount each month. Luke owes on his credit card, but he is buying CDs. What are your buying and credit habits?

One of the most valuable financial tools you can have is a good credit rating. Credit can help you purchase goods or services you need when money is scarce and in times of a personal emergency. By using credit wisely, you can keep your long-term savings and investments untouched and still obtain the goods and services you want or need.

Establishing Credit

There are two basic types of credit:

- *Closed-ended credit* is a one-time loan made for the purchase of a costly item, such as an automobile or a major appliance. The lender specifies the payment period, number of payments, and payment amounts. Installment loans are closed-ended. A well-planned budget can include a limited amount of closed-ended credit.
- **Open-ended credit** is a loan made on a continuous basis for the purchase of products up to a specific dollar limit. With this type of credit, monthly bills are issued. Credit cards are examples of open-ended credit. Although owning a credit card is convenient, consumers are frequently unaware of the growing finance charges. Borrowing and overspending are both easy with high-interest, open-ended credit.

Creditors (people who lend money) determine whether you are a good credit risk based on the three C's of credit: character, capacity, and capital.

Your *character* predicts how likely you are to pay off your credit in full and make each payment on time. Your past credit history and payment records will influence a lender who is deciding whether to approve credit for you. Missed payments or failure to pay previous debts will reduce your

Career Fact

Credit bureaus begin keeping a credit score as soon as you receive your first credit. The closer you get to 850, the better.

Take Note

Smart cards come with a thumbnail-size computer chip embedded in the plastic. These microprocessors can store thousands of times more information than conventional credit cards backed with magnetic strips. In theory, a single smart card could replace a fistful of credit and debit cards, serve as a driver's license, store a person's medical history, feed a parking meter, and function as a tamper-proof personal ID encoded with an individual's fingerprint.

© JIST Works

Cooperative Learning

Assign or seek volunteer(s) to role-play the borrower and lender in a bank or finance company. Have the borrower create a job, credit history, payment record, present and past residence, record of collateral or capital owned, and the reason for applying for credit. Have the lender develop questions to ask the borrower using the information in this section as a guideline to determine the borrower's capacity for credit. Have students vote on the creditworthiness of the borrower.

chance of obtaining new credit. How long have you been employed at your present job and at your previous jobs? How long have you lived at your present address and at previous addresses? Lenders will use the answers to these questions as indicators of your personal stability.

Your **credit capacity** is the amount of debt that you can afford to repay each month. Lenders weigh your current job position and income level against your living expenses, mortgage or rent payment, car payment, and other debts. Then they determine your ability to repay the credit you are seeking.

Your *collateral* (possessions with cash value) and capital will influence a lender's credit decision. Collateral, such as a home, a car, bank accounts, and investments, provides an added level of assurance that you have means other than personal income to repay your credit obligation.

Your **credit history** (a record of how you've borrowed and repaid debts) will qualify you for the best credit terms. People with previous credit problems are usually charged higher interest rates and approved for a lower purchasing limit. This policy compensates loan companies that deal with high-risk customers.

Identifying Lenders

When you buy on credit, a business trusts you to pay later for the product, service, or money that it loans you today. The business accepts your promise to make regular payments until your debt is paid.

Community Resources

Invite a loan officer at a local bank to speak to your class. Have students make a list of questions they would like to ask. For example, how does the bank collect money from overdue accounts? Is there a minimum age for borrowing money or buying on credit? What is the best way to establish and build a credit record? What becomes of consumer goods that are repossessed?

Banks lend money to borrowers who are likely to repay them when payments are due. Banks' lending requirements are stricter than other types of lending institutions. Banks also handle several other types of financial business. For example, real estate loans are the main business of a *savings and loan bank. Commercial banks* provide full banking services and loan money for education, automobiles, appliances, boats, and other personal needs.

Loaning money is the main way that banks earn money. This enables them to pay interest on various savings accounts and to earn a profit. Although bank loans are usually one of the least expensive means of borrowing, a wise consumer always shops around to obtain the lowest possible interest rate.

Consumer finance companies specialize in making small loans to borrowers with poor or no established credit. They usually lend smaller amounts of money and charge much higher interest rates than banks.

TAKE NOTE

Know your lender's cutoff date for payments, and avoid late payment fees. Lenders consider a payment paid on the day they receive it, not the day you mail it.

Credit unions (see Chapter 12) usually charge a lower interest rate. However, you must be a member of the credit union to borrow money. *Credit cards* usually charge the highest rates of interest and in some cases as much as two or three times the amount you would pay at some credit unions or banks.

Retailers also have revolving charge accounts allowing customers to make a partial payment for the goods purchased each month. There is a limit on the total amount the customer can owe at one time, and the retailer adds an interest charge to the unpaid balance. Interest rates for this type of account are usually very high.

© JIST Works

Using Credit Cards

When you choose to use a credit card, you need to understand that you are getting a loan. Many credit cards are great financial tools, and the loan is free if you pay the full amount every month. If you do not pay off the monthly balance, you will pay a finance charge at a very high rate of interest.

There are two types of credit cards:

- *Single-purpose cards* are issued by a specific business for charge accounts. Oil companies and department stores frequently make cards available to their customers.
- *Multipurpose cards* such as MasterCard and Visa are accepted by most large stores, restaurants, hotels, airlines, and other service companies throughout the United States and most other nations.

Banks can join the MasterCard or Visa system and issue credit cards to earn money. When a business accepts a card for payment, the business must pay the bank that issued the card a fee for each charge made. In turn, the cardholder pays the bank interest on any charges not fully paid each month.

Credit cards are not all the same, and you should comparison shop before you sign up for one. Credit card companies exist to make money, and they want you to increase your debts on their high interest cards. The cost of using a credit card to make purchases is usually greater than the cost of borrowing money from the same bank.

The amount of interest the borrower pays depends on the amount borrowed, the length of time it is borrowed, and the rate of interest charged (see Table 17.1). The Truth in Lending Act requires creditors to explain in writing the finance charge and the annual percentage rate charged before asking borrowers to sign an agreement. Federal law does not set interest rates or other credit charges, but it does require their disclosure so that consumers can compare credit costs.

If you have a credit card or plan to obtain one, be certain to read the literature that accompanies it, especially the credit card agreement. Using the card obligates you to abide by the rules and regulations stated in the agreement. If you are unclear about the agreement, contact the card issuer to ask for an explanation. The box titled "Common Terms in Credit Agreements" defines the words you will find on most credit statements.

Discussion Starter

Explain to students that retailers encourage customers to open charge accounts with them. Charge accounts allow you to charge up to a specific amount at the retailer's store or chain of stores. Regular charge accounts require full payment for goods purchased at the end of each monthly billing period. Discuss responsible use of credit with your students.

Discussion Starter

Ask students to explain why it is to their advantage to have a spotless credit history. Discuss some of the advantages and disadvantages of different lending institutions.

TAKE NOTE

Know where your ATM or debit card is at all times. If you lose a card, report it immediately.

Self-Understanding

Assign students to discuss credit cards and their uses with family members or someone who has at least one credit card. The next day, use the chalkboard to list the types of credit cards and their uses that students learned from the assignment. Assign students to small groups to discuss their opinions on the use and misuse of credit card buying. Have one spokesperson for each group summarize the group's views for the class.

Table 17.1 Sample Credit Agreements

	APR	Length of Loan	Monthly Payment Charge	Total Finance	Total of Payments
Creditor A	14%	three years	$205.07	$1,382.52	$7,382.52
Creditor B	14%	four years	$163.96	$1,870.08	$7,870.08
Creditor C	15%	four years	$166.98	$2,015.04	$8,015.04

Common Terms in Credit Agreements

APR: The annual percentage rate, which is the yearly cost you pay on any outstanding balance.

Credit available: The amount still available after the lender deducts the amount you owe.

Minimum payment: The amount of the balance you must pay; otherwise, you are in arrears. Your minimum could be as low as 2 percent of the unpaid balance.

Variable rate: The interest rate changed by the lender as certain index rates in the economy change.

Tiered rates: Different rates that apply to different levels of your outstanding balance. For example, you may be charged 12 percent interest on balances up to $1,500 and 19 percent on amounts more than $1,500.

Fixed rate: A rate that does not change until the lender gives written notice of a change. Credit card issuers are required to notify you before changing the fixed interest rate.

Average daily balance credit line: The maximum amount you can owe at any time. If you go over your credit line, you may have to pay a fee and a higher interest rate.

Cash advance: Cash amounts you can borrow against your account. The average cash advance rate is more than 19 percent. Avoid using this feature.

Finance charge: The total dollar amount of credit costs, including interest charges, service charges, and credit-related insurance premiums.

Grace period: The time allotted to pay the full amount of your monthly statement before being charged interest (usually 25 days or fewer).

Late-payment charge: A fee charged to your account if the lender receives your payment after the grace period. Lenders may raise the interest rate if you make one or more late payments.

Adjusted balance: The balance you owe after the lender subtracts the previous month's balance.

Previous balance: The amount you owed at the close of the previous billing period. The lender will use this amount to calculate your finance charge.

Enrichment

Read the rules and regulations on the back of a credit card agreement to the class. (They are available at banks and department stores for the asking.) Then explain and discuss the implications of the agreement with the class. Use the interest rates stated in the credit card agreement to figure varying finance charges at the APR stated in the agreement.

Career Fact

Legally, you have 60 days after you receive the statement on which the error first appears to notify the issuer in writing about the nature of the billing error.

Read the monthly statement from the issuer of your credit card promptly and carefully. Incorrect information can be on your credit record if

- An unauthorized person charged items to your credit card.
- The amount on the statement for a purchase does not match your receipt.
- The lender made an error posting a payment you made.

If you find an error on your statement, follow these steps to protect your credit history:

1. Phone the lender's customer service office promptly. Most errors can be resolved efficiently and quickly using this method. Follow up with a letter if the error is not fixed on the next statement.
2. Pay any charges on the statement that you do not challenge.
3. If notified that the charges are correct, pay the bill to maintain your credit rating, and then continue to pursue a correction. In the case of defective goods or services, you may withhold payment if you have made a "good-faith effort" to solve the problem with the merchant, the cost in dispute totals more than $50, and you purchased the item or service in your own state or within 100 miles of your residence.

© JIST Works

Being Alert for Signs of Trouble

Soon after they reach the age of 18, many young adults begin to receive unsolicited credit card applications. These offers of credit require no determination of the person's ability (or desire) to pay back the debt. Accepting these offers starts many young adults down the path of credit card reliance, which easily leads to bankruptcy. This serious delinquent mark stays on a credit report for at least seven years.

Bad debt is borrowing to purchase items or services that do not provide financial benefits or last as long as the loan. Watch out for the following signs of *too much debt*:

- You do not know exactly how much money you owe.
- You are constantly worried about your bills.
- You borrow money to pay off other loans.
- You frequently make late payments.
- You can't afford to pay more than the minimum payment on debts.
- One or more of your credit cards is *maxed out* (at the maximum limit).

Illness, layoffs, and other family emergencies can create serious financial problems. When that happens, seek professional help to solve your credit problem. The Consumer Credit Counseling Service (CCCS) is a nonprofit organization with offices throughout the United States. CCCS counselors will try to arrange a repayment plan that is acceptable to you and your creditors. They will also help you set up a realistic budget.

Comprehension Check

Ask the students to describe warning signs for too much debt.

TAKE NOTE

Just because a lending agency is willing to extend a credit card privilege to you does not mean you can afford it.

FIND OUT MORE

Check the white pages of your telephone directory for the Consumer Credit Counseling Service office nearest you, or use your search engine and key in **Consumer Credit Counseling Service.**

Knowing Your Credit Rights

Understanding your credit rights and knowing when to use them is important. Consumer credit rights are protected by acts of Congress.

The Equal Credit Opportunity Act requires a lender to notify you within 30 days after you have submitted a completed loan application whether the application has been approved. If the application is denied, the notice of denial must be in writing. It must specify why credit was denied or must tell you how to request that information.

The Fair and Accurate Credit Transaction Act entitles you, as a consumer, to a free credit report every year from each of three big credit-reporting bureaus that maintain them. A credit report is a snapshot of a person's financial condition and history (see Figure 17.6). Banks and other lenders both supply the data and use it to evaluate loan applicants. Consumers typically buy a report if they are planning to make a major purchase, such as a house or car, or if they are worried about falling victim to identity theft or fraud. People who spot errors on the reports can call the credit bureaus to correct them, and although most errors are harmless, one survey found that about a quarter of all reports do contain them.

Comprehension Check

Explain to students that an important part of being independent is taking responsibility for knowing and protecting your rights. Discuss the importance of the Equal Credit Opportunity Act and the Fair Credit Reporting Act, the Truth in Lending Act, and the Fair and Accurate Credit Transaction Act to anyone who is denied credit.

CREDIT REPORT DETAIL

SSN: XXX-XX-0000
1234 Oats Avenue
Indianapolis, IN 46216

PERSONAL CREDIT REPORT NUMBER: 8643761

YOUR CREDIT REPORT SHOWS THE FOLLOWING INFORMATION:

TRANSUNION	EXPERIAN	EQUIFAX
Linda Smith SSN: XXX-XX-3636 8902 Oats Avenue Indianapolis IN 46216 1234 Park Boulevard Carmel IN 46000 AKA: SmithEvans, Linda, Carolyn	Linda Smith SSN: XXX-XX-3636 8902 Oats Avenue Indianapolis IN 46216-0000 4321 Orchard Lane Indianapolis IN 46245-1745	Linda Carolyn Smith 8902 Oats Avenue Indianapolis IN 46216-0000 4321 Orchard Lane Indianapolis IN 46245-1745

SUMMARY REPORT

	TRANSUNION	EXPERIAN	EQUIFAX
TRADES			
TOTAL	34	35	33
REVOLVING	16	16	14
INSTALLMENT	13	19	19
MORTGAGE	5	0	0
OTHER	0	0	0
ACTIVITY			
CURRENT ACCTS	33	34	32
DELINQUENT	0	0	0
ACCTS	0	1	0
INQUIRIES 12 MTHS	0	0	0
PUBLIC RECORDS	1	1	1
BALANCES			
TOTAL	194,251	190,998	190,827
REVOLVING	12,746	12,746	12,746
INSTALLMENT	27,340	178,252	178,081
MORTGAGE	154,165	0	0
OTHER	0	0	0
ADDRESS	TRANSUNION PO BOX 1000 CHESTER, PA 19022 800-888-4213	EXPERIAN PO BOX 2104 ALLEN, TX 75013 888-397-3742	EQUIFAX PO BOX 740241 ATLANTA, GA 30374 800-685-1111

Figure 17.6 Sample credit report.

FIND OUT MORE

To get a free credit report, go to the Web site www.Annualcreditreport.com.

Discussion Starter

Begin a class discussion about the categories of information in Figure 17.6. Discuss whether this kind of information is an invasion of one's privacy or merely the right and responsibility of a lender to know the credit history of a borrower.

The Fair Credit Reporting Act requires that a credit agency show you your file if you are refused credit for a specific reason related to your credit report. If errors are found in the report, or if the agency cannot verify certain information, the file must be corrected. If the credit agency refuses to remove an item after the investigation, it is your right to require that your statement, limited to 100 words, be placed in your file.

The Truth in Lending Act limits your liability for credit cards that are lost or stolen to $50 per card if you properly and promptly notify the card issuer of the loss. Keep a record of your credit card numbers and issuer telephone numbers in a safe place.

Section 3: Get Involved

Answer the following on a separate sheet of paper, and be prepared to discuss your responses in class.

1. Imagine you are an appliance store owner. A customer has failed to make his monthly payment on a washing machine for two consecutive months because his hours of employment have been reduced. What will you do? How will your decision help your business? How might it hurt your business?
2. Review the Sample Credit Agreements in Table 17.1, and answer these questions: Which creditor will charge the highest total finance charges? Which will charge the lowest total finance charges? Which creditor will charge the highest monthly payment? Which will charge the lowest? If you were getting a loan, which of these three creditors would you select? Why?

© JIST Works

Section 4: Money Management and Budgets

A **budget** is a plan for saving and spending income. A well-planned budget will let you know where you stand financially and will prevent emergencies from causing a financial strain. By setting clear and realistic goals for the future and including a budget in your money-management plan, you can be confident that you will always be able to meet your expenses and that you will have money put aside for a rainy day.

Enrichment

Form a committee of students to create a bulletin board titled "How to Spend Your Money" or "Maintain a Budget." It could have income going into a budget planner, and the budget planner could be sending out the various categories of a budget such as food, utilities, household expenses, clothing, etc.

Planning a Budget

When you make a budget, you will need to estimate your available income for a specific time and decide how large a portion to set aside for your expenses. Doing this will help you decide what you can and cannot afford, avoid impulse buying, keep track of how you spend your income, make regular savings deposits, and develop financial protection against sickness, unemployment, and accidents.

Your budget can cover any time period (a month, three months, or a year). Most bills come due once a month. However, your bills will not all be due on the same day of the month. You will pay your insurance and taxes *quarterly* (every three months), *semiannually* (twice per year), or *annually* (once per year). Most people also have some *seasonal expenses* (holidays, birthdays, and vacations). Be certain to account for these special occasions in your budget as well.

Whatever time period your budget covers, it must be long enough to include most of your living expenses and income. Planning your first budget for a short trial period might be wise so that you can see what works and what does not. Then continue making improvements until you are satisfied.

Employers normally pay workers every week or every other week. You will be able to pay your bills on time if you use each paycheck to pay your daily expenses and expenses that will be due within the next pay period. Budget a certain amount from each paycheck toward large expenses that will be due later.

Cooperative Learning

Divide the class into family-size groups of two to four students. Then appoint a group leader and recorder. Provide the recorder with several sheets of paper. Tell the groups they will stay together for this section of Chapter 17. Their first task is to establish a family role and age for each member of the group. Their second task is to decide the job(s) titles and income of the family provider(s). Third, they are to discuss why planning a budget is important to the family.

Enrichment

How much will it cost students to live on their own? Ask students to find out how much their families spend for food, utilities, clothing, transportation, recreation, housing, and medical and dental care. Have them keep a detailed record of their family's income and expenses for one month and list the expenses that are fixed and those that are flexible. At the end of the month, they should show their families any ways they have discovered to improve the family budget. What do the families think about the students' budget proposals?

Starting a Budget

On a separate sheet of paper, estimate your income for the time of your budget. Be sure to include in your total all of your sources of income, such as a part-time job, allowance, and gifts. If your earnings are irregular or if overtime pay is involved, it is best to use the lowest likely income for your budget. It is better to underestimate than to overestimate income.

After you have estimated your income for the budget planning period, estimate your expenses. Note that a satisfactory budget allows for unexpected expenses. Group your expenses into three categories.

Cooperative Learning

After students read the section "Starting a Budget," have each family group (which you created in the last Cooperative Learning activity) estimate their family income for a one-month period. Include wages and salary after taxes, bonuses, interest on savings, dividends on investment, alimony, and AFDC payments when applicable.

© JIST Works

Cooperative Learning

Have students complete the "Starting a Budget for John" activity in the Chapter 17 file of the *Preparing for Career Success Instructor's CD-ROM, Third Edition.*

- *Fixed expenses* are bills that usually remain the same each month, such as rent, house payments, and installment loans. Fixed irregular expenses are large payments due once or twice a year, such as insurance premiums or property taxes.
- *Flexible expenses* are bills that usually change from one month to the next, such as the amount spent on food, clothing, utilities, or transportation.
- *Set-asides* are amounts of money that you accumulate in your budget for special purposes, such as birthdays, vacations, emergency funds, and savings.

CLUSTER LINK

Do you have an interest in planning, managing, and providing banking, investment, financial planning, or insurance services? If so, explore the Finance career cluster. See the appendix for more information.

There is an old saying, "If you want to know what's going to happen tomorrow, look at what happened yesterday." This is especially true when making a budget. Use old receipts, bills, and canceled checks to estimate future expenses. Consider which expenses you can reduce and which expenses you will probably need to increase. Carry a pocketsize notebook to record your expenses during a week or a pay period. Total your weekly or pay-period expenses for a month or two. Having an accurate record of your expenses will help you determine your average spending pattern for such things as food, housing, utilities, household operation, clothing, transportation, entertainment, and personal items. Use your spending record to estimate future expenses. In addition, plan for changing conditions that might increase or decrease your expenses.

Total your estimated expenses for a year, and divide by the number of budgeting periods you have *allocated* (assigned). This will help you determine the amount of money to allocate toward each expense during the budgeting period. For example, your total expenses per year divided by 12 equals your monthly budget requirement. To figure out a weekly budget requirement, you would divide the total expenses per year by 52.

Cooperative Learning

Tell the family groups of students that you have established to work out a budget using the income they established for the family on the previous family activity. The family members must discuss and come to an agreement on the amount to allow for each budget category before the recorder writes it down.

On a separate sheet of paper, make a budgetary expense sheet. Group related expenses together in categories. For example, list groceries and restaurant meals in the Food category. Using the information from your expense records, write an estimate for each flexible and fixed budgetary expense in a column next to the list of expenses. Begin with the regular fixed expenses, such as rent. Next, enter those fixed expenses that come due once or twice a year, such as car registration, insurance, or tuition. Many households allocate a specific amount each budget period (each month, for example) toward these expenses. This practice spreads out the cost.

KEY TO SUCCESS

One way to meet major expenses is to include set-aside money in your regular budget. Keep your set-aside funds separate from other funds so you will not be tempted to spend them. If possible, keep them in an account that earns interest.

After you have entered your fixed expenses and your flexible expenses, you are ready to consider your set-asides. Giving yourself a small allowance that is not accounted for provides a sense of freedom and makes budgeting more interesting. You also may want to clear up debts by budgeting extra money for your installment payments. This way, you also reduce the amount you pay for interest charges. Also, consider budgeting a small amount of money for unexpected expenses. Did you ever have a tire go bad, a tooth start to ache, or a television quit working? Decide how much money you need to budget for these unexpected expenses. When your fund reaches

© JIST Works

the amount you have allowed, change your budget, and start saving for something else. Change your budget as your spending needs change.

Next, compare your total expected income with your total planned expenses for the budget period you have established. Do your planned expenses equal your estimated future income? If so, you have a balanced budget. If not, you need to increase your income or decrease your spending.

If your expenses add up to more than your income, review each part of your budget plan. Where can you cut down? Where are you overspending? Next, decide which budget items are most important and which ones can wait. You may be able to trim your flexible expenses. Sometimes you need to reduce large fixed expenses to balance a budget.

If you reduce your expenses as much as seems reasonable and you are still unable to balance your budget, you might consider two options. First, you might acquire more education or training to qualify for a better-paying job. Second, you might need to take a part-time job until you get your budget under control.

Cooperative Learning, continued

Reinforce to students that their family budgets must balance before they conclude this activity. When you are certain budgets are balanced, have each family group designate a spokesperson to explain to the class their family budget and the reasons they allotted the amount to each category.

Enrichment

Have students complete the "Beginning Your Records" worksheet found in the Chapter 17 file of the *Preparing for Career Success Instructor's CD-ROM, Third Edition.*

Maintaining a Budget

Maintaining a workable budget requires accurate records. By keeping track of financial records, receipts, and canceled checks, you will know exactly how much you have spent and how much your lifestyle costs. If you own or have access to a computer, you can purchase a software program to assist in budgeting and record keeping.

Whatever method you use, maintaining a successful personal or household budget requires cooperation from everyone involved. At the end of each budget period, you should enter your receipts in a monthly expense record and store them. It is a good idea to write on the back of each receipt the reason for the purchase, the name of the person who made it, and the date.

Keep a separate file folder or envelope for each of your budget items. Use these folders for filing insurance policies, receipts, warranties, canceled checks, bank statements, purchase contracts, and other important financial papers. Eventually, you may need to rent a safe-deposit box from a bank for storing your most important financial papers, such as a deed, stock certificate, or automobile title.

After obtaining a certain amount of financial success, many people turn to financial planners for assistance with investments. These professionals include stockbrokers, insurance agents, bankers, lawyers, and income tax preparers.

Cooperative Learning/ Self-Understanding

Allow time for the family groups you established in your class to discuss how each of them felt about their role in the family group. Ask various members of each family group to summarize the problems and successes the group experienced in this activity.

KEY TO SUCCESS

Preparing a budget takes planning; following one takes determination. Good record keeping and the ability to refuse temptations to overspend are the keys to a successful day-to-day budget.

Section 4: Get Involved

Answer the following on a separate sheet of paper, and be prepared to discuss your responses in class.

1. Make a list of your short-term financial goals. They may be purchases you want to make, savings goals, or earnings goals. What two goals do you plan to accomplish within the next six weeks? Within the next six months? Within a year?
2. List your long-term financial goals. What two goals do you plan to accomplish within 5 years? Within 10 years?

Reteaching

Have students complete the "Finding the Right Words" and "Checking Your Location" worksheets in Chapter 17 of the *Preparing for Career Success Student Activity Book, Third Edition.*

Enrich Your Vocabulary Answers

1. gross earnings
2. deductions
3. piecework
4. check
5. check register
6. savings account
7. creditors
8. sound financial management
9. endorsement
10. compound interest
11. canceled check
12. deposit slip
13. open-ended credit
14. credit history
15. interest
16. taxes
17. bank statement
18. bounced check
19. electronic funds transfer (EFT)
20. credit capacity
21. budget
22. certificate of deposit (CD)

Chapter 17 Review

Enrich Your Vocabulary

On a separate sheet of paper, number from 1 to 22, and write the term from the "Enrich Your Vocabulary" list at the beginning of the chapter next to the number of the statement it matches.

1. Total earnings before deductions
2. Money subtracted from earnings
3. Earnings paid according to the amount of work produced
4. An order written by a bank depositor directing the bank to pay out money
5. The portion of a checkbook used to record the checks written
6. A bank account that pays interest to customers in return for using their money
7. People who lend money
8. Planning to get the most for your money
9. The signature of a payee on the back of a check
10. Paying interest on the interest
11. A check that has been paid by a bank
12. A record of the money put into an account
13. A limited loan made on a continuous basis for the purchase of products
14. A record of how you've borrowed and repaid debts
15. The amount paid by lenders for using customers' money
16. Payment that citizens are required to make to help pay the costs of government services
17. A bank report that shows the condition of a depositor's account
18. A check that is written with insufficient funds in the account
19. A computer-run system that lets consumers, businesses, and governments transfer money from one account to another
20. The amount of debt that you can afford to repay each month
21. A plan for saving and spending income
22. An agreement between a bank and its customer to pay back money invested at a specific rate on a certain date

© JIST Works

Check Your Knowledge

On a separate sheet of paper, complete the following activities.

1. Give two reasons why financial management is important.
2. List at least three deductions that may be taken from a worker's gross earnings.
3. What is the final date in each calendar year for filing an income tax return?
4. Name four ways that privately owned banks earn their income.
5. Why is it a good idea to have a checking account? Give three reasons.
6. Why is it a good idea to keep money in a bank that is insured by the Federal Deposit Insurance Corporation?
7. List the three C's of creditworthiness.
8. How do the issuers of multipurpose credit cards, such as MasterCard and Visa, earn money?
9. Which federal law limits your liability for lost or stolen credit cards?
10. List five ways that a budget can be an important part of sound money management.

Develop SCANS Competencies

This activity will give you practice in developing the resources and systems skills that successful workers use. Refer to the directions in this chapter in Section 4, "Money Management and Budgets," to make your own budget. Make a simple budget for a period of one week. During this time, keep careful track of your income and spending. Categorize your spending as much as possible. Here are some categories you might use: Food—this category should include all food purchased, even soft drinks and snacks; Transportation—this category will include such things as gas or bus money; Entertainment—Expenses here will include movies, DVD rentals, CD purchases, and so on.

After you complete your budget, analyze it. Determine where you could cut spending so that you might save more money. After you determine where you could cut spending, try the budget for another week to find out whether your new plan works better.

Check Your Knowledge Answers

1. It is a key to reaching your life goals, and it is a method of handling future financial crises.
2. Local, state, and federal taxes; Social Security (FICA); hospitalization plans; life insurance; company pension plans; savings programs; association or union dues; charitable contributions; stock-buying plans.
3. April 15.
4. Investments in stocks and bonds; interest charges on loans and credit cards; service charges for checking accounts; rental fees from safe-deposit boxes.
5. A checking account offers safety and convenience and is a useful financial management tool.
6. It insures each account up to $100,000 in the event that the bank fails.
7. Character, capacity, and capital.
8. When a business accepts a credit card for payment, it must pay the bank that issued the card a fee for each charge made on the card. In turn, the cardholder pays the bank interest on overdue charges and may pay a yearly fee for the use of the card.
9. The Truth in Lending Act.
10. It helps you avoid impulse buying. It helps you decide what you can and cannot afford. It helps you keep track of how you spend your income. It helps you make regular savings deposits. It helps you develop financial protection from sickness, unemployment, and accidents.

Enrichment

Have students complete the Chapter 17 section of the *Preparing for Career Success Student Portfolio, Third Edition.*

Chapter 18 Resources

Lesson Plans and Preparation

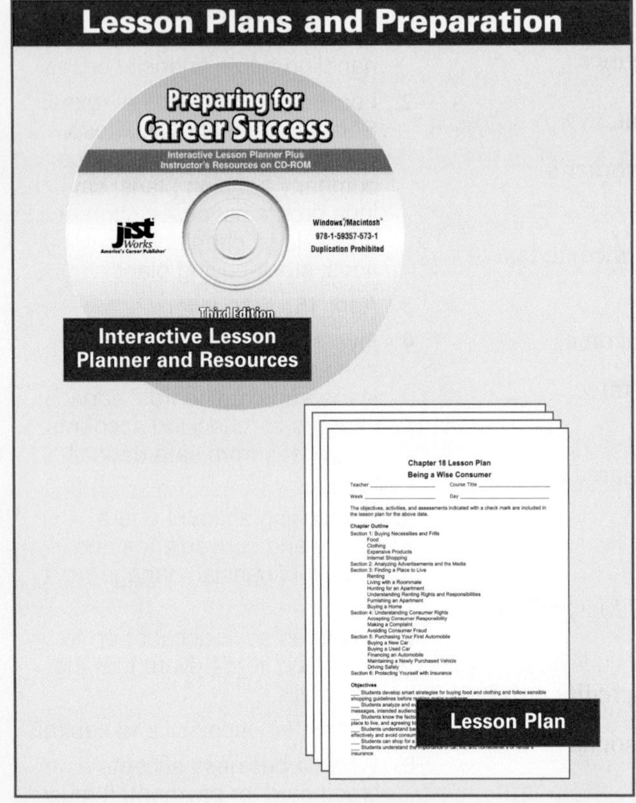

Preparing for Career Success
Interactive Lesson Planner Plus Instructor's Resources on CD-ROM
Windows/Macintosh
978-1-59357-573-1
Duplication Prohibited
Third Edition
Interactive Lesson Planner and Resources
Chapter 18 Lesson Plan
Being a Wise Consumer
Lesson Plan

Multimedia

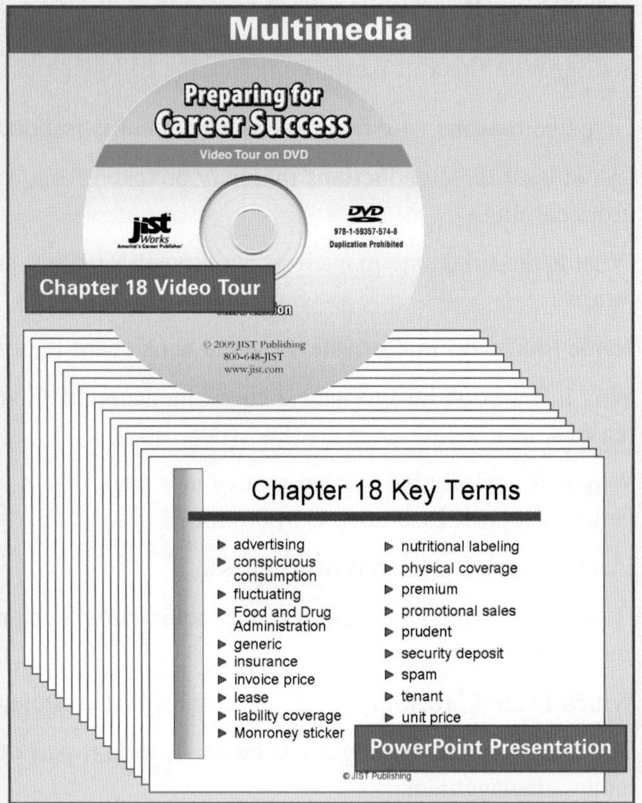

Preparing for Career Success
Video Tour on DVD
978-1-59357-574-8
Duplication Prohibited
Chapter 18 Video Tour
© 2009 JIST Publishing
800-648-JIST
www.jist.com
Chapter 18 Key Terms
advertising
conspicuous consumption
fluctuating
Food and Drug Administration
generic
insurance
invoice price
lease
liability coverage
Monroney sticker
nutritional labeling
physical coverage
premium
promotional sales
prudent
security deposit
spam
tenant
unit price
PowerPoint Presentation
© JIST Publishing

Activities

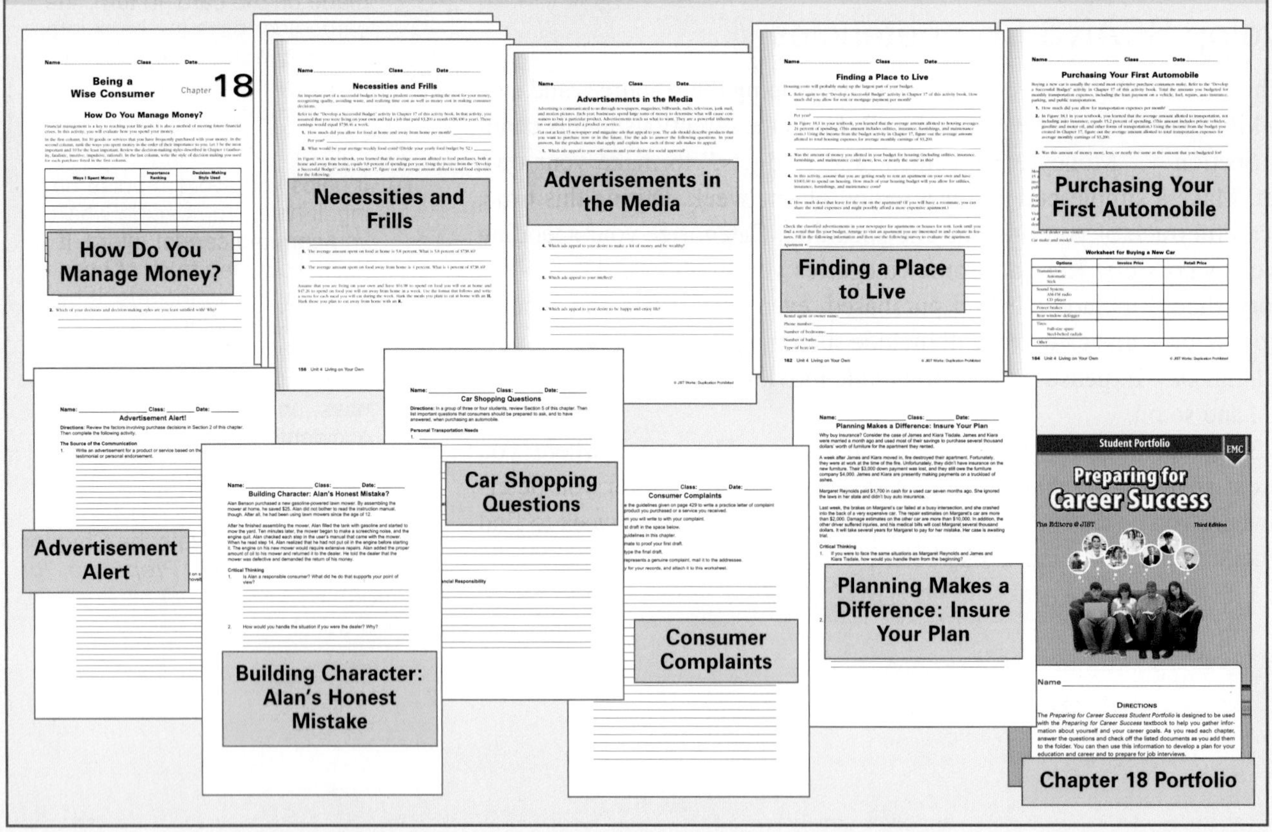

- How Do You Manage Money?
- Necessities and Frills
- Advertisements in the Media
- Finding a Place to Live
- Purchasing Your First Automobile
- Advertisement Alert
- Building Character: Alan's Honest Mistake
- Car Shopping Questions
- Consumer Complaints
- Planning Makes a Difference: Insure Your Plan
- Chapter 18 Portfolio

 © JIST Works

Review and Assessment

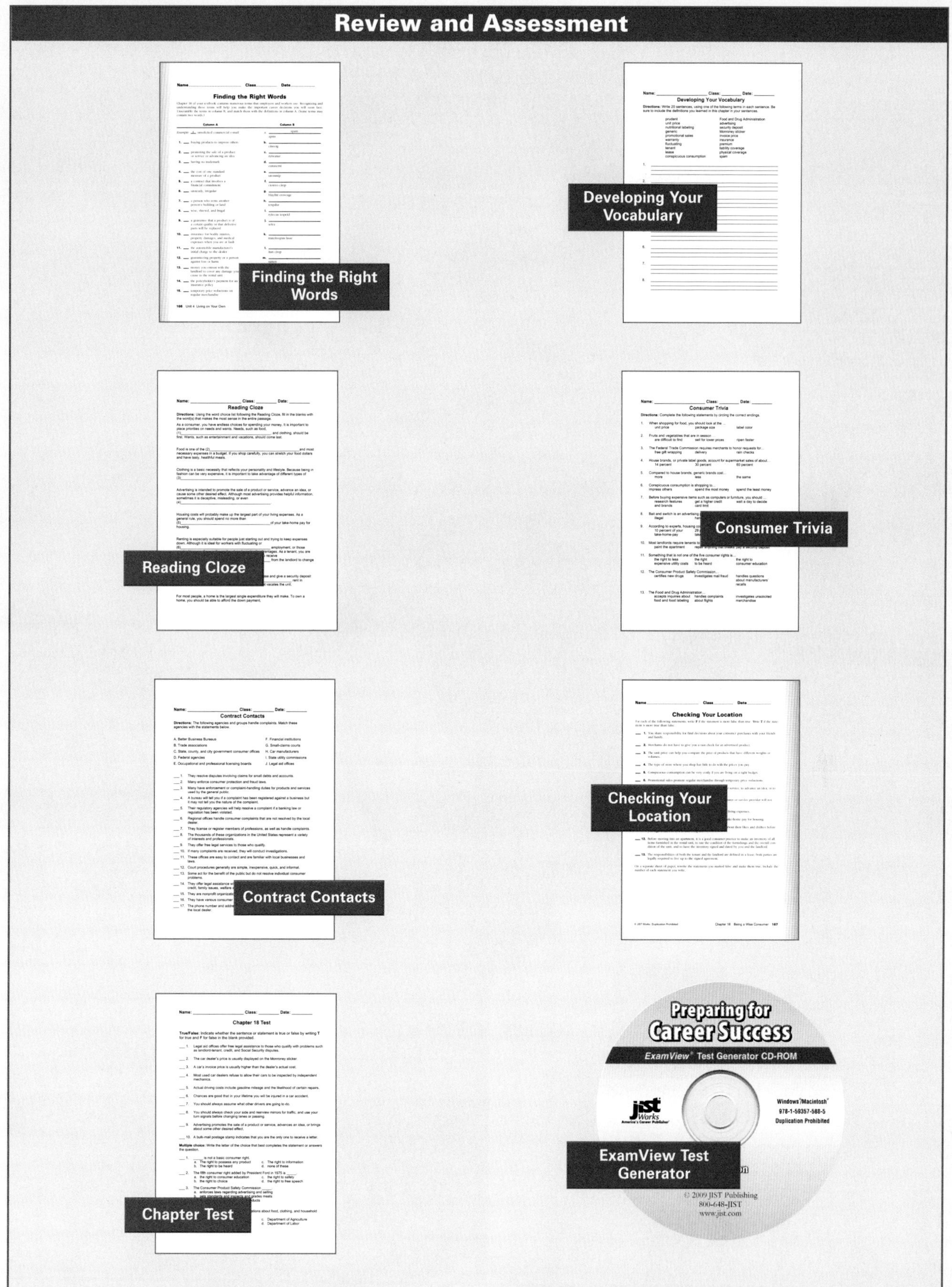

Chapter 18 Being a Wise Consumer

Learning Objectives

- Explain the value of advertising to consumers, and give an example of deceptive, misleading, or illegal advertising
- List specific guidelines for selecting affordable housing, choosing a roommate, signing a lease, and furnishing an apartment or home
- Compare prices, services, variety, and quality on the same or similar items, and decide which is the best choice for you
- Name and explain the purpose of laws and groups that protect consumers
- List specific criteria that will help you make a prudent automobile purchase
- Describe various types of insurance, and explain why it is important to have insurance to protect yourself from certain risks

Enrich Your Vocabulary

In reading this chapter and doing the exercises, you will learn the following important terms:

advertising	lease	prudent
conspicuous consumption	liability coverage	security deposit
fluctuating	Monroney sticker	spam
Food and Drug Administration	nutritional labeling	tenant
generic	physical coverage	unit price
insurance	premium	warranty
invoice price	promotional sales	

Vocabulary

You can use the "Developing Your Vocabulary" worksheet in Chapter 18 of the *Preparing for Career Success Instructor's CD-ROM, Third Edition* as a pretest for chapter concepts or as a reteaching worksheet.

Cross-Reference

Review the decision-making styles, values, and goals in Chapters 3 and 4 with your students. Ask them which decision-making style they use as consumers. What values and goals play an important part in their consumer decisions?

As a consumer, you have almost endless choices and opportunities for spending your money. No matter how successful you become, though, your income will always have limits. Therefore, placing priorities on needs and wants is a crucial part of every spending plan. *Needs,* such as food, housing, clothing, transportation, and medical care, should be first. *Wants,* such as entertainment, a new automobile, or dinner at an expensive restaurant, should come last. Your ability to save money will depend on how you balance your needs with your wants.

Figure 18.1 represents the *mean* (average) American family (a consumer unit of 3.2 persons). This family earns a total of $82,195 before paying any taxes or making purchases. Review the amount this family spends in each of the categories represented. How would you spend this money?

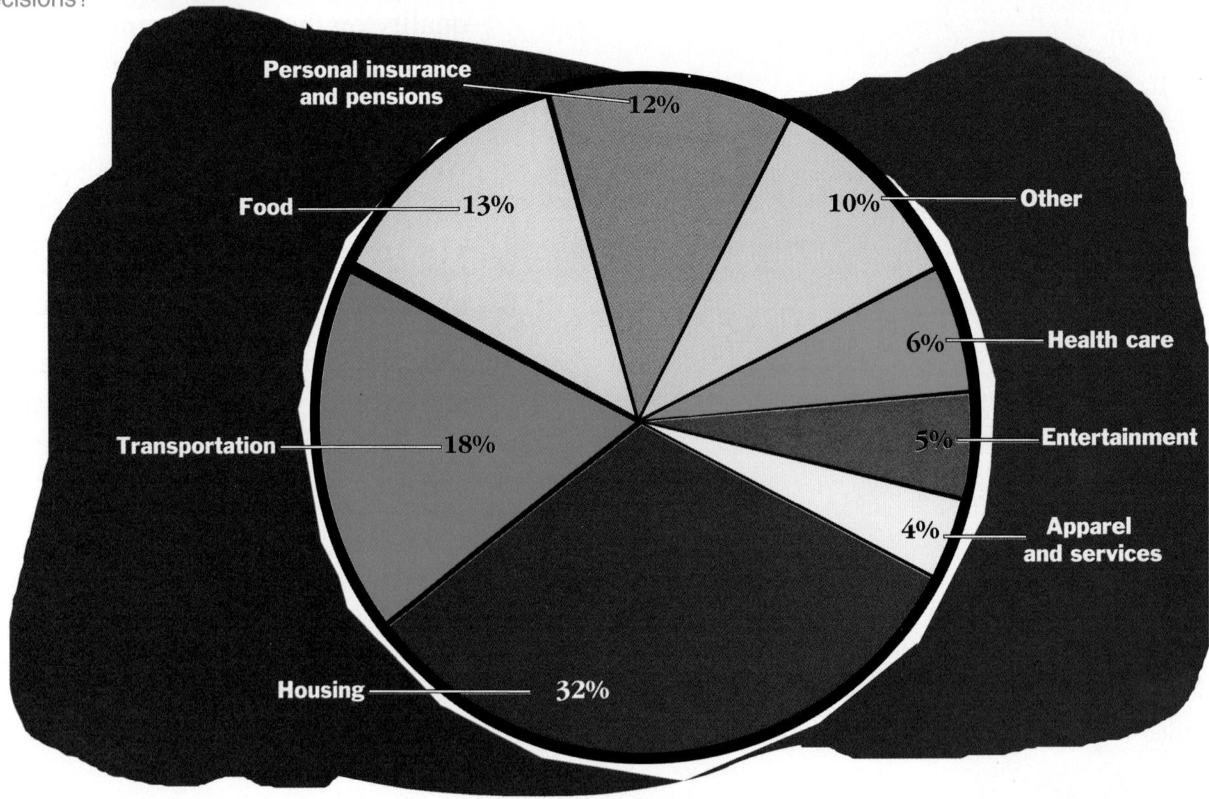

Figure 18.1 Annual expenditures of the mean American family in 2006.
Source: U.S. Department of Labor

© JIST Works

An important part of a successful budget is being a **prudent** (wise, shrewd, frugal) consumer. Before you qualify as a prudent consumer, you must learn to recognize quality, avoid waste, and understand the value of time and travel when making consumer decisions. Media advertisements, friends, and family influence your consumer choices, but you have responsibility for your final decisions.

Section 1: Buying Necessities and Frills

Whatever the item, different sellers offer different prices, services, variety, and quality than their competitors. Learning how to weigh all the different choices is an important skill no matter what your personal spending style is.

Food

Food is one of the largest and most necessary expenses in a budget. How much you spend will depend on how often you eat out, how often you cook at home, how many people you must feed, your personal tastes, and your special nutritional requirements. If you shop carefully, you can stretch your food dollars and have tasty, healthful meals.

While you are still in high school, it is a good idea for you to learn the techniques that prudent shoppers use to purchase groceries. Here are some tips:

1. Plan your meals ahead, and make a shopping list before going to the grocery store. Plan some meals with foods that are inexpensive and provide leftovers. Divide your list into different categories of grocery items, such as fruit and vegetables, meats and fish, canned goods, dairy products, cleaning products, bread and bakery products, and snack foods. Sticking to your list should eliminate impulse buying of unnecessary and non-nutritious items.

The average grocery store stocks its shelves with about 30,000 of the 100,000 branded grocery products available. About 15,000 to 20,000 new products squeeze onto the shelves each year. How many items are you familiar with? Have you compared the taste, quality, and price of specific name-brand and generic-brand products?

Discussion Starter

Explain to your students that the average family consumer group represents the mean for all of the demographics (age, gender, number of children, number of workers, etc.). Have students examine Figure 18.1, and then ask them: Which categories would your family budget a higher percent? Why? A lower percent? Why? You might wish to have students translate the percentages into dollar amounts based on the gross income of $82,195.

Enrichment

Form a committee of students to create a bulletin board titled "So Many Choices—Which Is the Best Buy?" Have students collect photos of the same product at different prices and place them on the bulletin board.

Discussion Starter

Ask students when their emotions rather than their budgets control their spending. Discuss how peer pressure can effect spending. Examine the role of self-control in spending.

Discussion Starter

Discuss the differences between bargain hunting and impulse shopping.

Cooperative Learning

Divide the class into groups of four or five. Have students bring a boxed or canned food product to class. Have each group evaluate the product for appearance, price, and nutritional value. Allow time for a spokesperson from each group to describe the product and explain the reason for the group's evaluation. Have the class vote on whether they believe the product is or is not a good buy.

Reteaching

Have students complete the "Consumer Trivia" worksheet in Chapter 18 of the *Preparing for Career Success Instructor's CD-ROM, Third Edition.*

All life is an experiment. The more experiments you make the better.

—Ralph Waldo Emerson

TAKE NOTE

A recent study by Harris Interactive shows that Generation Y (people born between 1981 and 1995) spends a total $175 billion per year and saves $39 billion per year. Of that total, children (8–12) spend $19.1 billion per year, teens (13–19) spend $94.7 billion per year, and young adults (20–23) spend $61.3 billion per year.

Video Tour on DVD

Show students the Chapter 18 segment to introduce them to the content.

2. Learn when and where supermarkets advertise weekly specials and offer special discount coupons. Note which meats, vegetables, and products are on sale. Most fruits and vegetables are in greater supply and sell for lower prices at certain times during the year. For example, strawberries and asparagus are in season during the spring; tomatoes and beans are in season during the summer.
3. Ask the cashier for a *rain check* (a receipt that allows you to purchase the item at the advertised price by a certain date) when stores are out of an advertised special. The Federal Trade Commission (FTC) requires merchants to honor your request for a rain check.
4. Use manufacturers' coupons. They arrive through the mail and in newspaper supplements. Experienced coupon cutters save between 5 and 10 percent on their bill.
5. Take the time to read the weight and volume of the products you purchase. The size of a can or package can be deceiving. For example, two brands of bacon may look alike, but one package may weigh 12 ounces and another 16 ounces.
6. Compare the **unit price** (the cost of one standard measure of a product) of products that have different weights or volumes. This information is posted on the shelves below food items.
7. Read the label for useful information. The **nutritional labeling** on a product states the number of servings per container and tells how the food is packaged. For example, tuna is packaged in water or oil; pineapple slices are packaged in water or syrup. The label also lists the nutrients in the product. It tells you what percentages of the U.S. Recommended Daily Allowances (U.S. RDA) the product supplies. For products that can spoil, such as milk, cream, and orange juice, the last date for consuming the product is printed on the package. If you want to write to the manufacturer of a food product, you also can find the address on the label.
8. Check out stores' "house" brands that are priced lower than nationally advertised brands. One report showed that private-label goods account for 18.3 percent of all units sold in grocery stores and nearly 14 percent of the total supermarket dollar volume. The same companies that package the nationally advertised brands frequently package house brands for stores.
9. Consider buying **generic** (having no trademark) brands, which cost even less than house brands. They generally have the same or nearly the same nutritional value as the brand-name products but may have inferior quality or taste.

The type of store where you shop influences the prices you pay. Supermarkets operate on a self-service basis and are able to sell food products at a lower margin of profit because of their large volume of business. On the other hand, convenience stores charge higher prices than supermarkets but

© JIST Works

are located in or near residential neighborhoods for the convenience of shoppers. They are often open from early in the morning until late at night. Their lower volume of sales and higher overhead costs require higher prices.

Clothing

Clothing is a necessity that reflects your personality, confidence, and lifestyle. Consider the amount of money you spend on a clothing item in terms of the value you place on the item.

Conspicuous consumption (the practice of buying products and services to impress others) can be very costly if you are living on a tight budget. Being in fashion may be one of your high personal values, but it can create serious financial problems if you consider it more important than necessary expenses.

Before shopping for clothing, select stores that have a range of prices and will allow you to make the most of your clothing budget. Make your money go further by taking advantage of the three major types of sales:

- **Promotional sales** promote regular merchandise through temporary price reductions.
- Clearance sales enable the retailer to reduce specific inventory items.
- Special purchase sales are on goods bought for a special sale rather than marked down from regular merchandise.

Retail stores generally run sales at the same times year after year. For example, they run Presidents' Day sales, January and August white sales, anniversary sales, and end-of-the-month and season clearance sales.

Learn to read clothing labels, recognize quality, and follow care instructions. Knowing about the various qualities of certain fabrics used in the manufacture of clothing can save you considerable money. Labels tell you what fabric the manufacturer used to make the clothing and the care it requires.

As you enter the world of work, your occupation and job tasks will dictate your choices for appropriate clothing. Clothing expenses for employed persons usually exceed those of other family members. Workers who are visible to customers or entertain clients usually need to spend more on clothing than other workers do.

Life Skills: Robert Discovers Comparison Shopping

Robert Long graduated last month, found a good job with the Brice Manufacturing Company, and moved into his first apartment. After he unpacked, he sat down and made a list of the food he needed to buy to stock his kitchen.

Discussion Starter

Present this situation to your students: Tim Parker wants to buy a Nautica jacket. He is the first to admit that it is very expensive and that a certain element of prestige is involved. While shopping, he noticed a similar style and quality of jacket on sale at the same store for half the price. Buying the Nautica brand rather than the unknown brand will consume Tim's total clothing budget for two months, and Tim will need shoes and a couple of new shirts in the next few weeks. He is considering a charge account at the clothing store. What would you do if you were Tim? Why?

Self-Understanding

Ask students to think of four brands of clothing they own. List these brands on the chalkboard. Ask students: What value do your friends place on this brand of clothing? How influenced are you to buy shoes, jackets, or jeans because of name recognition? What makes these products worth more than less-known, lower-priced products? Why is making a "fashion statement" important? What personal values do the clothes you wear express?

Discussion Starter

Ask your students: What are the advantages of postponing the purchase of clothing rather than buying it at the first opportunity? What are the advantages of buying a piece of clothing at the first opportunity?

Key To Success

For considerable savings, shop for clothes at the end of a season. Buy winter clothes in the spring and summer clothes in the fall.

Enrichment

Have students complete the "Necessities and Frills" worksheet in Chapter 18 of the *Preparing for Career Success Student Activity Book, Third Edition.*

During his first visit to the local supermarket, he quickly discovered that the labels on containers could be very confusing. For example, one brand sold a 27-ounce can for $5.35. Another brand sold a 900-gram can of coffee for $5.25. Robert liked both brands, so he based his choice on price. The 900-gram can was slightly smaller than the 27-ounce can. "That's a no-brainer," he thought as he took the 27-ounce can. Pleased with his new wisdom, Robert placed the can in his cart when a silver-haired shopper told him to "put it back."

"You're getting gypped, young man," she said while punching the numbers into her hand-held calculator. "That company uses big cans to fool you. For openers, there are 453.6 grams in a pound, and that is equal to 16 ounces. The 900-gram can is almost 32 ounces, and it is not one-third empty when you open the can. Take this coupon, and give it to the cashier when you check out. You get 25 cents off on the 900-gram can. Now that is a real bargain."

Later, at home, Robert had a good laugh about his experience as he vowed not to laugh at senior coupon cutters. Then he started to search for his hand-held calculator to check the register slip against the contents of his grocery bags. Robert decided to take his calculator along on his next shopping trip to make comparison shopping easier. Robert also planned to check the Sunday paper for coupons. He was on the road to being a wise shopper.

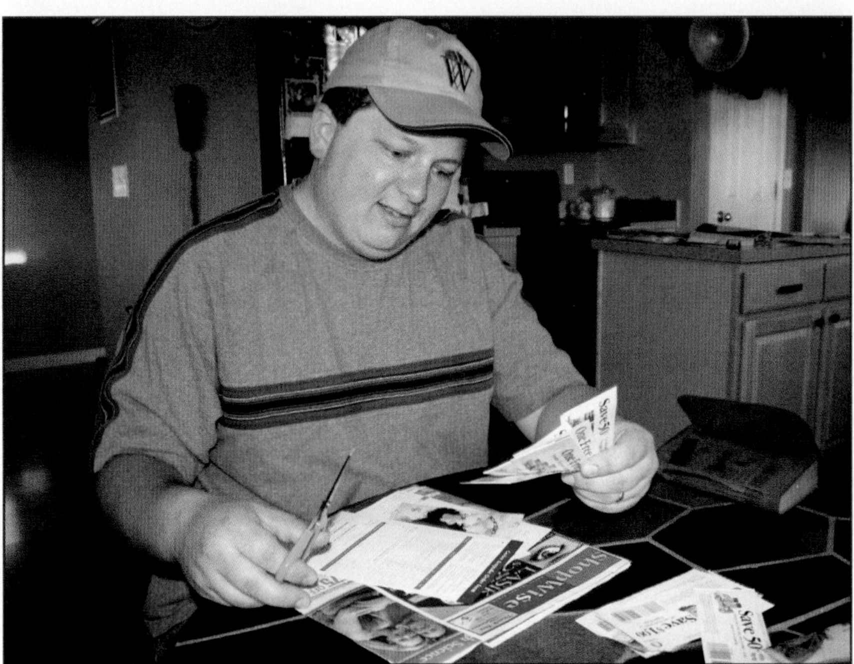

Critical Thinking

What did Robert learn from his conversation in the supermarket?

What did Robert do that indicated he intended to be a prudent shopper even before he met the silver-haired woman?

Would it be worth your while to spend a half hour each week cutting out grocery coupons? Why or why not?

© JIST Works

Expensive Products

When you leave home, will you live in a furnished or unfurnished apartment? If you move into an unfurnished apartment, you will need to purchase some expensive items. Before you make any purchases, decide on certain product features you want; then check *Consumer Reports* magazine, available in libraries, for in-depth product and service information and brand evaluations.

Retailers frequently offer installment options for expensive items such as computer equipment, stereos, and furniture. Although convenient, this purchasing arrangement can be more costly than a bank loan. Before you make a commitment, compare the retailer's interest rate with what you would pay on your credit card, revolving credit line, or a personal bank loan. This kind of shopping effort will pay well for your time and effort.

To make the most of your money and avoid problems related to the quality of your purchase, follow these guidelines before you make a major purchase:

- Decide what you can afford to spend, and identify the features and options you need in the product.
- Ask friends and relatives for personal recommendations, and check your school or public library for consumer magazines, reports, and other publications that compare products and services.
- Narrow your choices to specific *brands* (the name of a product that distinguishes it from another) and model numbers.
- Compare the prices and service of several stores that sell the product. Do not assume that an item is a bargain just because it is advertised as one. Take advantage of sales.
- Check with the Better Business Bureau if you are uncertain about the reputation of the business to see whether consumers have registered complaints against the business and how they were resolved.
- Check for extra charges, such as delivery fees, installation charges, and service costs.
- Ask the salesperson to clarify the service policy and the return or exchange policy. Request a written copy.
- Read and compare contracts and warranties. A **warranty** is a guarantee that the product is of a certain quality or that the defective parts will be replaced. Be sure that you understand what you must do and what the manufacturer must do if you have a problem.
- Carefully examine delivered merchandise before you sign for it to be sure that nothing is missing or damaged.
- Be sure that you read and understand the manufacturer's recommended use and care instructions before attempting to use the product.

Career Fact

If a product costs $15 or more, the law says that the seller must let you examine any warranty before you purchase if you ask to see it. Use your rights to compare the terms and conditions of warranties (or guarantees) on products or services before you buy. Shop for the best warranty and the best product. If you neglect to mail in the owner's registration card, your right to warranty service is unchanged. However, you will need your sales receipt or a canceled check to prove the date of purchase.

Take Note

Whether you can return merchandise for credit or a refund depends entirely on the policy of the company with whom you do business.

Community Resources

Form a committee of students to invite a store manager from an area appliance, computer, or large department store to elaborate on the consumer advice in this section. Ask him or her to also speak on career opportunities in retail sales.

TAKE NOTE

DECA is a career and technical student organization that helps students develop their skills in marketing, management, and entrepreneurship. For more information, contact your local chapter or visit the Web site at www.deca.org.

FIND OUT MORE

For more information about shopping online, visit www.safeshopping.org.

After you make a purchase, follow these guidelines to get the most out of your money:

- Read all instructions and warranty provisions carefully to ensure your safety and to avoid doing anything that may void the warranty. Use the product only for the purposes outlined by the manufacturer's instructions.
- File all sales receipts, warranties, and use and care information for future reference.
- Provide proper maintenance, and follow the use and care recommendations from the manufacturer.
- Report any problems that develop to the merchant or manufacturer as soon as possible. Trying to repair the product yourself could cancel your rights to service under the warranty.

Internet Shopping

The world has become your personal in-home shopping mall. E-business is rapidly becoming a new economic order, one that is remaking the face of global commerce. From Thailand to Iceland, the world is your marketplace. You can start with a keyword search such as **carpets** or **cameras** and step away from your PC in 30 minutes with more information than you might have gathered in a month without a modem. Those who know how to shop online have many advantages over old-fashioned shoppers. Time, price, and convenience are three major benefits.

Online auctions offer an amazing selection of obscure items that you would probably never find anywhere else, but the buyer takes the risk. The auction site acts only as a facilitator to the sale and will not take any responsibility if you are cheated. Many online services offer customized buying guides to their subscribers, making selection much easier.

Be cautious when buying online:

- Do not disclose your personal Internet password.
- Shop only with companies you know and trust. The Better Business Bureau OnLine provides Internet users an easy way to verify the legitimacy of online businesses. Visit www.bbbonline.org for a list of participating companies, program standards, and more.
- Comparison-shop at a variety of online stores.
- Save all transaction details. Print out or make a note of the seller's identification; the item description; and the time, date, and price you paid or bid on the item.
- Never send your credit card number by e-mail unless you are certain of the merchant's honesty and security. Most sites have a toll-free phone number you can use.

© JIST Works

Section 1: Get Involved

Answer the following on a separate sheet of paper, and be prepared to discuss your responses in class.

1. Imagine that you are entertaining a group of four (including yourself) for a special dinner. Use grocery ads to write a menu for your dinner, and determine the cost of each item. Compare the quality and cost of your menu with the menus that your classmates create.
2. Select two big-ticket items, such as a piano, computer, washing machine, bedroom suite, TV set, or stove. Make a list of the quality features you want in each of your two items. Visit several stores to compare brands and prices. Make your selections, and report your findings and decisions to the class.
3. Food, clothing, and entertainment expenses vary from person to person. The amount to budget will depend on family income. How much would you allot for food, clothing, and housing if you used the percentages shown in Figure 18.1 and earned $35,000 a year? What if you earned $55,000 a year?

Section 2: Analyzing Advertisements and the Media

Imagine living in a world with no television, radio, signs, mail, movies, newspapers, or magazines. How would you know what to buy? Who would influence your choices? Media advertising provides the major source of product and service information for most consumers.

Advertising promotes the sale of a product or service, advances an idea, or brings about some other desired effect. Prudent consumers learn to read, view, or listen to advertising carefully and to compare various features of competing products or services. Advertising offers a way to learn how to use products and services, identify their particular features, compare prices, and become aware of special sales.

Discussion Starter

Ask your students: Why do people try to imitate lifestyles they cannot afford? What influence does television have on lifestyle expectations? How close to the reality of the average American's lifestyle are characters on television programs, including sports and entertainment figures?

Your generation, born between 1981 and 1995 and sometimes referred to as Generation Y, Echo Boomers, and the Millennium Generation, is more than 57 million strong. You represent the largest consumer group in United States history and are the future market for most consumer brands. You respond to marketing methods that bring the message to places the Y generation congregates, both offline and online. In addition, your generation is more racially diverse, with one out of three members considering themselves non-Caucasian. One out of every four members lives in a single-parent household, and three in every four

Do you use advertising to compare the special features and prices of competitive products?

Enrichment

Have each student bring in several newspaper and magazine advertisements for restaurants, shampoos, soaps, cereals, movies, weight-loss programs, computers, automobiles, etc. Tape them to the chalkboard. Then write the following headings on the chalkboard: "Wants and Needs," "Visual Appeal," Impressive Information," and "Price." Have students vote on the advertisements according to their appeal in each category, and discuss the results.

Cluster Link

Advertising is big business; the top 500 advertising agencies in the United States earn billions of dollars annually. In 2006, the advertising and public relations services industry employed 458,000 wage and salary workers; an additional 46,800 workers were self-employed. Employment in this industry is expected to increase through the year 2016. If this industry sounds interesting to you, investigate the many careers available in the Retail/Wholesale Sales and Service career cluster. See the appendix for more information.

Comprehension Check

Assign students to observe five television commercials and decide which, if any, forms of deceptive advertising were used. Have them report their findings to the class the next day. Have a class discussion about what was misleading to consumers.

Discussion Starter

Explain to students that ad agencies reach out to certain ethnic and racial groups by reflecting cultural norms. For Asians, for example, family connotes not just parents and children but also grandparents, aunts, and uncles. Consequently, ads created for this population often reflect many generations. Ask your students: How can marketers reach you?

have working mothers. If you were in the advertising industry, how would you market to your generation?

Most advertising provides helpful information. However, as a wise consumer, you must be alert to deceptive, misleading, or illegal advertising. The Better Business Bureau has identified several dishonest or illegal advertising practices:

- **False pricing:** The merchant retickets certain items with a higher price and puts them "on sale" at the regular price.
- **Bait and switch:** The advertisement describes a product or service that is not available when the customer offers to purchase it. The ad is the bait, and the salesperson attempts to switch the customer to a more expensive product or service.
- **Referral plans:** The salesperson describes a special introductory offer. For each customer you refer to the salesperson, he or she will pay you a certain amount of money. In many cases, the salesperson tries to convince you that by making easy referrals of your friends and relatives, you will end up getting the product or service free. Remember the saying, "If it sounds too good to be true, it probably is."
- **High-pressure tactics:** The salesperson refuses to take "no" for an answer. He or she may call in the sales manager or another salesperson. Together, they try to convince you that the price is going up, that this is the last item, or that if you do not buy now, you will never have the opportunity again.
- **Overstated sales claims:** "Our laundry soap will make your clothes twice as clean as any other soap on the market!" "Your skin will look 20 years younger if you use our lotion!" "Your engine will last thousands of miles longer if you use our gasoline!" How many times have you encountered this type of advertising? Will the manufacturer back these claims with a written guarantee? If not, beware of the product or service.

Why do you purchase an advertised product or service? If you are like most consumers, your decision to purchase involves these factors:

- **The source of the communication:** Most consumers are persuaded by people they trust and believe, or they identify with someone's language, gender, religion, age, country of origin, or personality. Testimonials and endorsements are examples of this type of advertisement.
- **The message:** What and how you make a statement influences buying decisions. The purpose of the advertising message is to get the reader's, viewer's, or listener's attention and hold it. The message should then arouse the desire for the product or service. The style, repetition, timing, and novelty of the advertisement affect the choice people make.

© JIST Works

When you decide to buy a certain type of automobile (a product) or use a particular long-distance telephone company (a service), your decision is influenced by a *credible authority* (someone you trust and respect). The advice you receive might be based on what the authority has read in a newspaper or magazine, has heard on the radio, or has seen on television about the relative virtues of the product or service. In this case, the media has influenced your decision indirectly by influencing a person you trust and respect.

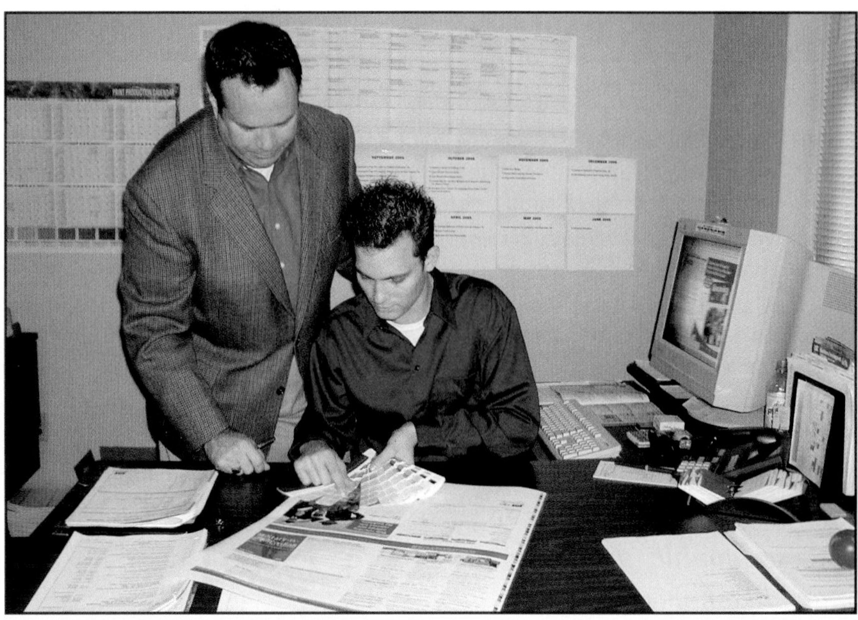
If you are interested in an advertising career, explore information about occupations such as graphic artist, copywriter, and marketing research analyst.

Have you ever received a personally addressed business letter, inviting you to purchase an outstanding product that is available only to a select group of people? Welcome to the world of *direct-mail advertising* (junk mail). Did you notice the bulk-mail postage stamp in place of a regular stamp? This type of postage tells you that a mailing list was used to send thousands of the same letters to potential consumers.

Advertisers send direct-mail advertising to targeted groups, such as people who live in a certain area, are between certain ages, own a particular product, or work in a particular occupation. Direct mail allows an advertiser to send a message with selective appeal. What types of products or services might you purchase that would place you on a direct-mail advertising list? Why?

The newest form of advertising is commercial e-mail. Unsolicited commercial e-mail, commonly know as **spam**, floods the Internet each day. Although many of these messages are from legitimate marketers, many are fraudulent solicitations from con artists who make promises they have no intention of keeping. Internet-e-mail is a cheap and easy way to reach millions of consumers with their messages. Before you respond to commercial e-mail, the Federal Trade Commission suggests that you treat commercial e-mail solicitation the same way you would treat an unsolicited telemarketing sales call. Do not believe promises from strangers.

When was the last time you enjoyed a special program on television, purchased a daily newspaper, or enjoyed a favorite magazine? It is important to remember that producers of products and services buy advertising time on television and radio to provide you with programs you enjoy. In addition, the cost of daily newspapers and magazines is low because of paid advertisements. All of these advertisers are spending a great deal of money to persuade you to buy their products. Therefore, you must analyze the content of the ads carefully before rushing out to buy.

Cooperative Learning

Divide the class into small groups. Assign each group the advertising task of creating a direct-mail letter to a targeted group. When they complete their letters, have a spokesperson from each group read the letter to the class.

Discussion Starter

Ask your students: What group(s) would be a good prospect for information on health care, vacations at the beach, computer equipment, diet food, and new homes?

Discussion Starter

Ask students if they have ever received an e-mail message similar to the following: "You are about to make at least $50,000 in less than 90 days!" The e-mail tells you to send a small amount of money ($5 or $20) to each of several names on a list, replace one of the names on the list with your own, and then forward the revised e-mail to thousands of new names using bulk e-mail. This is a classic chain letter and a scam. Discuss this situation and other scams they may have encountered.

Section 2: Get Involved

Do the following activities on a separate sheet of paper, and be prepared to discuss your responses in class.

1. Newspaper and magazine ads frequently make outrageous claims for certain products. Cut out one ad that you consider untrue. Write to the company that produced the product or to the agency that developed the advertising and ask for verification of the claims made about the product. Enclose the ad with your letter.
2. Pay attention to television commercials for the next week. List the products and specific advertising messages that appeal to your desire to be attractive, important, or wealthy.
3. Make a list of brand-name products that you have purchased. Include clothing, shoes, and big-ticket items such as a bike or sound system. Make a similar list of brand-name food products you have purchased. Why did you decide to buy each of the items rather than a competing brand?

'Mid pleasures and palaces though we may roam, be it ever so humble, there's no place like home.

—John H. Payne

Section 3: Finding a Place to Live

Whether it is an expensive house or a low-budget rental apartment, a well-managed home can provide you with a sense of security and independence. Today's housing market presents choices for every lifestyle and every budget. Housing costs will probably make up the largest part of your living expenses.

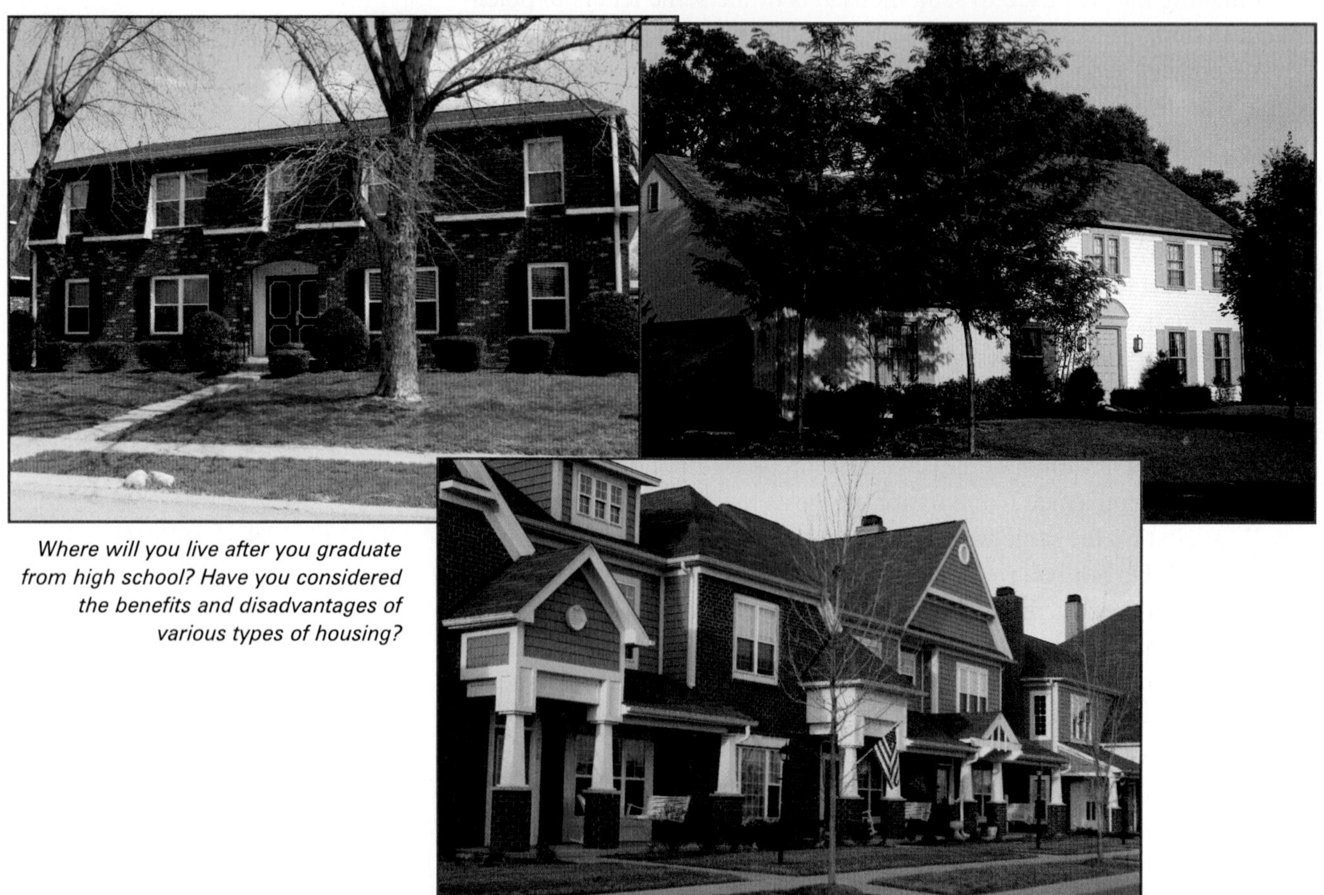

Where will you live after you graduate from high school? Have you considered the benefits and disadvantages of various types of housing?

© JIST Works

Each type of housing has its benefits and disadvantages. If you are seeking a low-maintenance, hassle-free lifestyle, renting an apartment or buying a condominium is probably your best choice. On the other hand, a single-family home provides more privacy and offers the opportunity for a lawn and garden. Whatever your goal, the perfect place may not be available or affordable when you first begin working. Instead, you may need to compromise and develop a savings plan to reach your housing goal.

The housing you choose should fit your budget and your lifestyle. A housing budget includes rent or a mortgage, utilities, homeowner's or renter's insurance, furnishings, decorating, and maintenance. A general rule is to allow no more than 29 percent of your take-home pay for housing. Remember that you must have enough money left in your budget for food, clothing, transportation, and the other essentials you will need to live on your own.

Enrichment

Form a committee of students to create a bulletin board titled "My Dream Home." Have students find pictures of their dream home and place them on the bulletin board with their name under the picture.

KEY TO SUCCESS

After shopping for a place of your own and figuring the total costs, you may decide to continue living at home. Paying your share of the rent, food, and utilities is usually far less than the cost of living alone.

Renting

Renting is usually the most suitable choice for single people or couples who are just starting out and trying to keep expenses down. Renting is also a wise choice for workers who are required to move frequently, have **fluctuating** (irregular, unsteady) or seasonal employment, or prefer to avoid homeownership responsibilities. There are advantages to renting:

- It does not require a large down payment.
- The maximum long-term debt is a one-year lease agreement.
- It is usually less expensive than mortgage payments.
- It is easier to relocate for career opportunities.
- The owner who rents the property is responsible for repairs.
- The failure to make payments will not cause loss of a major investment.
- It allows you to learn about a new community before making an investment.

Renting also presents several disadvantages. As a **tenant** (person paying rent for the temporary use of another person's building or land), you are seldom motivated to improve the property. Carpets and other decor may not be satisfactory. If you want to make changes, you must have permission of the property owner, and any improvements become the property of the owner. However, some owners will agree to reduce your rent for certain improvements you make. These improvements could include interior or exterior painting, replacement of carpets or drapes, or necessary maintenance.

Enrichment

Have students complete the "Finding a Place to Live" worksheet in Chapter 18 of the *Preparing for Career Success Student Activity Book, Third Edition.*

CAREER FACT

If you lived in 1933 and had the money, you would have paid $2,800 for a six-bedroom house in Detroit, $585 for a New Pontiac Coupe, $49.50 for a three-piece bedroom set, $1.69 for a pair of leather shoes, and 29 cents for a pound of sirloin steak.

Living with a Roommate

Sharing an apartment or a house with another person or persons can save on expenses. Rent, utilities, and grocery costs can be divided equally.

© JIST Works

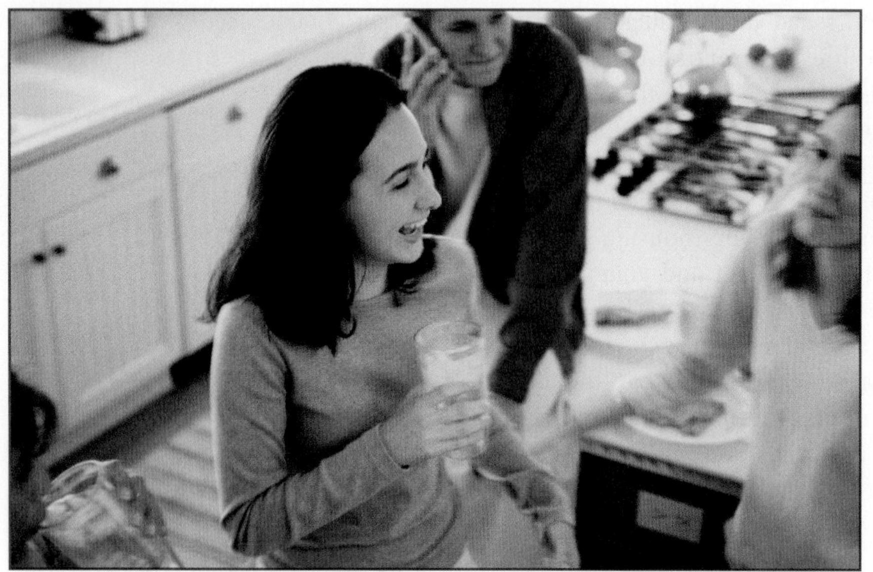

Deciding whether to share an apartment or house with another person is a major decision.

In addition, roommates can help with household tasks, such as cooking and cleaning. Frequently, roommates are friends who share social experiences outside the apartment or house.

Conflicts are bound to arise when two or more people share the same living quarters. What conflicts did you have when you lived at home? You can expect similar problems with your roommate. It is better to avoid conflicts and resolve potential problems before you make a commitment to live with someone. Even good friends should set up some ground rules in writing. Discuss the following points with potential roommates:

Cooperative Learning

Divide the class into groups of four or six. Appoint a group leader and a recorder. Provide the recorder with paper. Then tell the groups they will stay together for this section of Chapter 18. Their first task is to choose someone in the group for a temporary roommate and then answer the 11 questions in "Living with a Roommate"

Cross-Reference

If disagreements occur, have students review "Section 5: Resolving Conflicts" in Chapter 7.

Key To Success

When you start accumulating furnishings, ask an insurance agency to explain the benefits of renter's insurance. It will protect you from loss in case of fire, theft, an accident that happens to a guest in your apartment, or even a broken water pipe that causes water damage to furniture.

1. How much will each of you contribute toward the rent? If one bedroom is larger or nicer than the other, should the person with that room pay more?
2. Will you share utility expenses equally? How will you share the expense of long-distance telephone calls?
3. How will you share cleaning and laundry tasks? What rules can you establish to reduce friction between a poor housekeeper and an extremely neat person?
4. Will grocery shopping and cooking be shared or up to each individual? What if one person eats out or snacks more than the other?
5. What hours of "peace and quiet" does each of you need? How will you handle the problem of noise if one person works the night or evening shift?
6. Does loud music bother either of you? How will you allow for individual preferences in types of music (hip-hop, popular, country, classical) or selection of television programs?
7. Do you want to party on the weekends or get some rest? How many guests are to visit at one time?
8. If either one of you smokes, what rules can you establish to avoid any problems this might cause?
9. How will you meet expenses if one of you loses his or her job? Would you be willing to pay your roommate's share of the expenses for a month or two?
10. Will having a roommate allow you to be as independent as you want to be? How are your responsibilities to a roommate similar to responsibilities of living at home?

© JIST Works

11. If your roommate decides to move, could you find another one in time to pay monthly expenses? A written agreement giving each other at least a 30-day notice would provide added security for each of you.

CAREER FACT

Some property owners do not allow pets. If you have a pet, make certain that your rental agreement or lease grants you permission to keep it.

Hunting for an Apartment

The search for an apartment should be an enjoyable experience. When you're ready to start looking, decide ahead of time the amount you are willing to pay, the size place you want, and the general location that suits you best. The "for-rent" ads in the Sunday newspaper are a good source of information. They will help you determine the cost and availability of rental units in your area. In addition, network with your family, friends, and coworkers for rental leads. Contact building managers and owners of buildings where you would like to live to see whether anything is available. Also, use the yellow pages of the phone book to locate real estate agencies that have listings of rental properties. Keep in mind that rent is usually higher through an agency because the owner must pay a fee for the service. In some instances, the rental fee equals one month's rent.

Cooperative Learning

Have the roommates you established in the previous ·Cooperative Learning use the apartments-for-rent ads in the classified section of the area newspaper to find an apartment they might like to rent.

Talk with other residents in the rental complex about their likes and dislikes before you make a final decision. Ask for their views on whether the owner or caretaker tries to keep the complex in good condition. If neighbors from nearby properties are outside, tell them that you are considering the unit, and ask them what they like or dislike about the area. Compare several rental units before making a decision. Be certain that you are satisfied with the unit before signing any type of rental agreement.

TAKE NOTE

Can someone legally enter your home without your permission? Many rental agreements give the owner permission to enter the unit to make an inspection of the property. Check your rental agreement.

Understanding Renting Rights and Responsibilities

Learn your rights and responsibilities as a tenant as well as those of the owner. The property owner will probably have you fill out an application form if you are interested in a rental unit. He or she will probably request credit references and will want to check your past rental record. Most property owners require a **security deposit** (money you entrust with the landlord to cover any damage you cause to the rental unit) before they accept you as a tenant. In addition, most require a month's rent in advance. These are simply good business practices on the owner's part. They do not suggest that you cannot be trusted.

Community Resources

Invite a rental agent or property owner of an apartment complex to speak to the class about property owner rights, responsibilities, lease agreements, and tenant responsibilities. Have students write a list of questions and concerns to ask the speaker.

The property owner returns the security deposit after a tenant vacates the unit if he or she finds no damage during the moving-out inspection. Some owners place the security deposit in a special bank account, and the earned interest is paid to the tenant after moving out. The advance rental payment is used for the last month's rent or returned with the security deposit.

Before you move in, it is a good consumer practice to make an *inventory* (listing) of all items furnished in the rental unit and to rate the condition of the furnishings and overall condition of the unit. Both you and the

© JIST Works

owner should date and sign the inventory. If an item is in poor condition before you move in, document it so that you are not responsible for it later. An accurate inventory assures a responsible tenant of receiving the full security deposit when leaving and protects the owner from damages caused by irresponsible tenants.

A rental **lease** is a contract that involves a financial commitment for a specific period of time, usually a year. It may be up to several pages in length and may contain numerous details. The responsibilities of both the tenant and owner are defined in the lease. Both parties are legally required to live up to a signed agreement. After the *lessor* (owner) and *lessee* (renter) sign the lease, it is enforceable by law.

The amount of the rent and the due date should be clearly defined. Some leases permit the owner to change the rent for certain reasons. The lease also states how much notice the renter must give before he or she moves out.

All agreements and understandings between a landlord and tenant should be in writing and signed by both parties.

Be sure to read a lease very carefully, and discuss each point with the owner before signing. Make certain that you understand and are willing to meet all of the terms. For example, the property owner usually pays water and trash collection. Utility costs such as gas and electric vary with rental units. The tenant pays telephone installation fees and monthly charges. Charges for painting, cleaning, and repairs vary with property owners.

Ask the owner whether he or she expects you to pay any expenses not covered in the lease. Also ask these questions: What are the tenant's and property owner's rights and responsibilities? What specific rules and regulations must tenants follow? What changes does the owner permit a tenant to make to the property?

Furnishing an Apartment

Cooperative Learning

Have the roommates you established in class look at magazines and then make a list of all the furniture, linens, dishes, and appliances they will need to furnish their apartment. Have them research the cost of each of these items. Allow time for class discussion of how much income they will need to have to make these purchases.

Whether you rent a furnished or unfurnished apartment, the owner will not supply certain items. If this is your first rental home, you will probably need to purchase sheets, blankets, dishes, and towels. You may already have some possessions, such as a radio or television. Determine which furnishings you must have immediately. Then purchase the others as you can afford them.

You can furnish a first apartment with limited funds if you are willing to shop for bargains. Goodwill and Salvation Army thrift stores, garage sales, and classified ads for used furnishings are good sources of

© JIST Works

inexpensive furniture, dishes, lamps, pots and pans, small appliances, and decorative items.

Refinishing used furniture is easier and less expensive than you might think. Your public library is a good source of how-to books of all types. Your local paint or hardware store also can help with the needed materials.

Buying a Home

Although most young workers cannot afford to purchase a home, they frequently establish homeownership as a major life goal. It has been part of the American dream for generations.

Homeownership means having something that is all yours. If you want a yellow kitchen with blue carpet and pink walls, that is your choice. A home is a place where you can express your own personal style. For most people, a home is the largest single expenditure they will make. When you can afford the down payment, closing costs, and mortgage payments, you will be a prime candidate for homeownership.

Before deciding to purchase a home, analyze your financial prospects and employment security. How much you can afford to spend depends on your current net income, expenses, and the amount of savings you have available for a down payment. Financial planners recommend that your mortgage payments not exceed 28 or 29 percent of your *gross income* (monthly income before taxes and other deductions).

How much home will you be able to afford? In Table 18.1, locate your expected annual or monthly gross income. On the same line, locate the maximum amount (29 percent of gross income) that you should spend for your monthly mortgage payment. When you know how much you can afford each month, you will be on your way to finding out how much home you can afford. Keep in mind that the interest rate of your mortgage will make a big difference in your total payment.

Key To Success

Do not commit yourself to larger housing payments than you can afford. Decide whether your income is stable and secure before taking on a large mortgage. A large mortgage with high monthly payments can become a major hardship if you experience prolonged unemployment, illness, disability, or decreased income.

Discussion Starter

Have your students explain what is meant by the saying: "A man's home is his castle."

Cooperative Learning

Form a committee to investigate various types of home financing offered by local banks, savings and loan associations, and credit unions. Report to the class a list of advantages to consider when making decisions about home buying and financing.

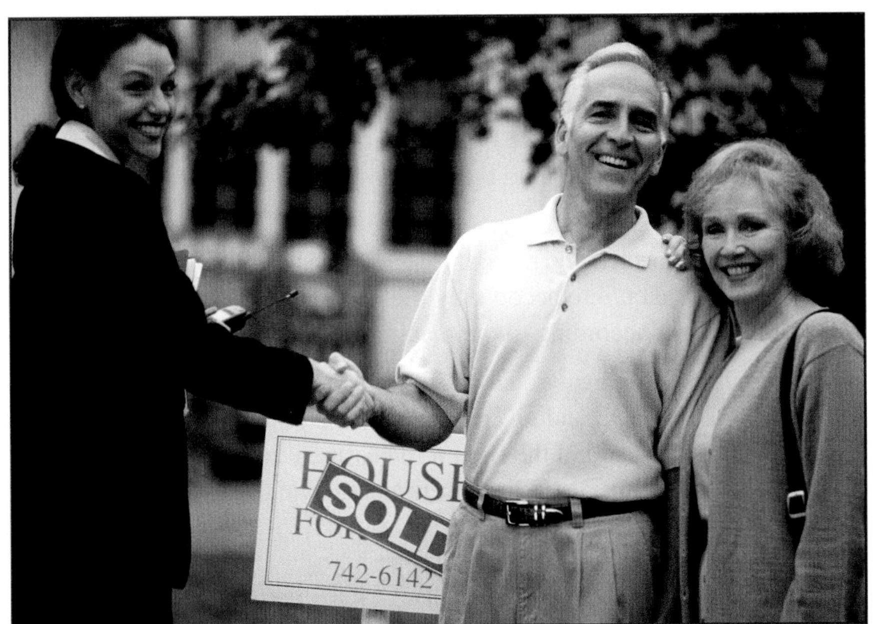

Is home ownership one of your major life goals? Will your earnings from the occupations you are considering enable you to purchase the home of your choice?

Table 18.1 How Much Home Can You Afford?

Annual Gross Income	Monthly Gross Income	29% of Monthly Gross Income
$25,000	$2,083	$604
$30,000	$2,500	$725
$35,000	$2,917	$846
$40,000	$3,333	$967
$45,000	$3,750	$1,088
$50,000	$4,167	$1,208
$55,000	$4,583	$1,329
$65,000	$5,417	$1,571

Section 3: Get Involved

Answer the following on a separate sheet of paper, and be prepared to discuss your responses in class.

1. Check local classified ads to find the cost of renting an apartment in your community. Discuss your findings with the class.
2. Develop a list of your 10 most important criteria for selecting a roommate. Do you know of a friend or relative who meets these criteria? Would you be an "ideal" roommate? Explain your answer.
3. Interview a property owner and inquire about owner and tenant responsibilities and relationships.

Cooperative Learning

Banks and grocery stores usually have free booklets on area homes that are for sale by real estate companies. Bring several of these booklets to class, and have the roommates select a home they expect to be able to afford in six years. Have the roommates you established use Table 18.1 to decide whether they will be able to afford the home they chose with the income from the job they expect to have at that time.

Self-Understanding

Encourage roommates to discuss what they learned about "self" in Section 3.

Section 4: Understanding Consumer Rights

In a message sent to Congress in 1962, President John F. Kennedy declared that every consumer has four basic rights:

- **The right to information:** The right to be given the accurate product information needed to make an informed and free choice and the right to be protected against false or misleading advertising, labeling, or sales practices.
- **The right to choice:** The right to be able to choose from a variety of products and services and the right to be assured of the availability of competitive prices.
- **The right to safety:** The right to expect that the buyer's health and safety are taken into account by the manufacturer and that products will perform according to the manufacturer's claims.
- **The right to be heard:** The right to register dissatisfaction and have a complaint heard and given consideration when a buyer's interests are badly served, and the right to be assured that consumer interests will be fully considered by government lawmakers and enforcement officials.

In 1975, President Ford added a fifth consumer right.

© JIST Works

- **The right to consumer education:** Without this right, consumers cannot maximize their resources, become more effective in the marketplace, or gain the full benefit of the other four rights.

Various government agencies enforce laws enacted and passed by Congress since 1975 that have a direct responsibility to consumers. The federal agencies charged with some aspect of consumer protection include the following:

- The Consumer Product Safety Commission develops safety standards for products to protect the public against unreasonable risk. It also handles complaints and questions about manufacturers' recalls and unsafe products.
- The **Food and Drug Administration** (FDA) enforces laws and regulations concerning the purity, quality, and labeling of food, drugs, and cosmetics. It certifies new drugs and inspects drug- and food-processing plants. The FDA also accepts inquiries about food and drug labeling, diet products, drugs, cosmetics, health, and pesticides.
- The Federal Trade Commission (FTC) enforces laws regarding advertising and selling. Areas of concern to the FTC include deceptive advertising, credit bureau reports and equal credit opportunity, failure to disclose lending and leasing costs, loans, and warranties.
- The Postal Inspection Service investigates mail fraud and misrepresentation, sexually oriented ads, and unsolicited merchandise sent through the mail.
- The Department of Transportation handles complaints involving delayed flights, lost luggage, and problems with *ground packages* (hotel and ground transportation) purchased in conjunction with flights. Individual airlines also handle consumer problems.
- The Department of Agriculture sets standards, inspects, and grades meat, poultry, and canned fruits and vegetables. It follows up on reports concerning the cleanliness of food stores and restaurants and the purity of questionable drugs. It also investigates the use of pesticides, animal health, and weights and measures. The Department of Agriculture provides numerous publications about food, clothing, and household items. These publications are often available through the local office of State Extension Services.

Discussion Starter

Ask your students: Why are there laws to protect consumers? What difference could it make in your life if there were no laws to protect consumers? Name a product that has been recalled in the past three months. What regulations on foods or drugs have been mentioned in the newspaper or on television news programs in the past three months?

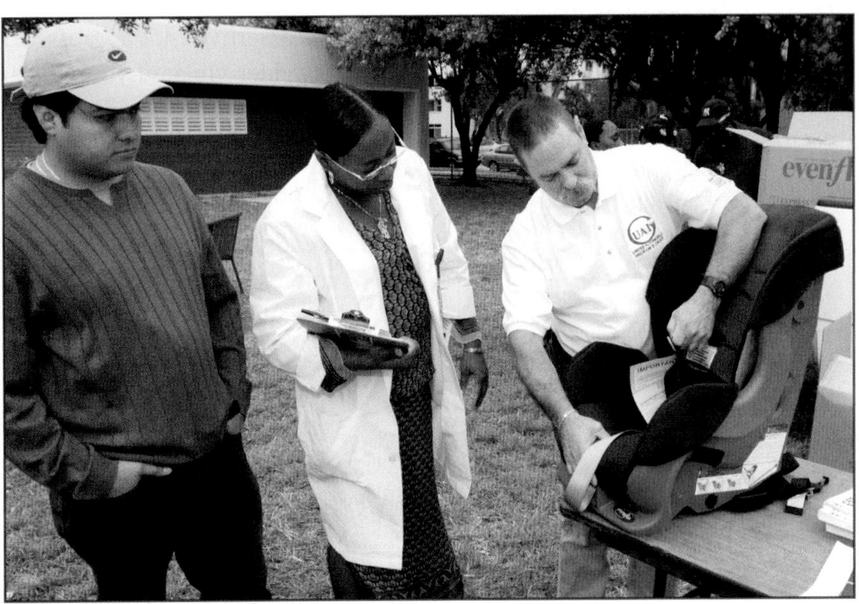

The Consumer Product Safety Commission establishes safety standards for car seats and many other products.

Discussion Starter

Write the title of each of the federal agencies listed in this section on the chalkboard. Ask students how these agencies directly or indirectly affect them. Next, assign or seek volunteers to research the federal agencies listed in this section and to report their findings to the class.

FIND OUT MORE

The Federal Citizen Information Center (FCIC) at www.usa.gov is the official Web portal for the U.S. government, linking citizens to government representatives, services, and information at the federal, state, and local level. These services are also available in Spanish via www.Espanol.gov. In addition to federal agencies, many private groups also serve as a voice for consumer rights. The Direct Marketing Association, the Insurance Information Institute, and the Major Appliance Consumer Action Panel are examples of private consumer-action groups. These organizations provide useful consumer information about various products and services, and all can be located on the Internet.

Accepting Consumer Responsibility

Have you ever heard the warning, "Let the buyer beware"? Basic rights established by law and enforced by numerous government agencies and private consumer groups have altered the meaning of this old saying. In today's economy, it would be more accurate to say, "Let the buyer become aware." As it is with all individual rights, consumer rights accompany responsibilities. As a consumer, you have these responsibilities:

1. Become informed about products or services that you plan to buy by actively seeking and using consumer information.
2. Be an honest consumer by using products and services as the manufacturer or provider intended. Follow the manufacturer's or provider's recommendations.
3. Be assertive (not aggressive) when you think a manufacturer or provider violated your consumer rights. Always report defective goods, and let businesses know when goods or services do not measure up to your expectations.
4. Report unethical business practices to protect other consumers.
5. Read the fine print. For example, some contracts may offer 0 percent interest for one year. Examine the contract; it may state that if you do not start paying interest on the first day after a year, you will owe interest for the entire previous year at a very high rate. These payment traps may add up to more money than you can afford.

Making a Complaint

As a consumer, you have the right to expect quality products and services at fair prices. If something goes wrong, your first step is to try to handle your own complaint. The following actions can help you resolve the problem:

KEY TO SUCCESS

Many companies have toll-free telephone numbers and Internet sites. This information is printed on the product and/or packaging. Keep a list of these numbers and sites in case you need them later.

1. Collect records and start a file about your complaint. Be sure to include copies of sales receipts, repair orders, warranties, canceled checks, and contracts to back up your complaint.
2. Go back to the place where you made the purchase. Contact the person who sold you the item or performed the service. Calmly and accurately explain the problem and state the action you would like. If the salesperson is not helpful, ask to speak to the supervisor or manager, and restate your case.
3. Allow a reasonable amount of time for each person you contact to resolve the problem before you contact someone else.
4. Keep a record of your efforts, and include notes about whom you spoke with and what they said about the problem. Save copies of letters you send or receive.

© JIST Works

5. Do not give up. If you are not satisfied with the response at the local level, phone or write a letter to the person responsible for consumer complaints at the company's headquarters. If you are unable to name the responsible person, send your letter to the consumer office or to the president of the company.
6. Be sure to describe the problem and what you have done to try to resolve it when you complain to a company. Also describe what you think is a fair solution. Do you want your money back? Would you like the product repaired? Do you want the product exchanged?

If speaking with a salesperson or company representative fails to provide a satisfactory solution to a problem, you can write a letter to the company. The federal government suggests that consumers follow these guidelines when writing a letter of complaint:

1. Include your name, address, home and work telephone numbers, and account number (if appropriate).
2. Keep your letter brief and to the point. List all of the important facts about your purchase, including the date and place you made the purchase and any information you can provide about the product, such as the model and serial numbers.
3. If you are writing to complain about a service, describe the service, and give the name of the person who performed it.
4. State exactly what you want done about the problem and how long you are willing to wait for resolution. Be reasonable.
5. Include copies of all documents regarding the problem. Be sure to send copies, not originals.
6. Do not write an angry, sarcastic, or threatening letter. The person reading your letter probably was not responsible for your problem but may be very helpful in resolving it. Type your letter if possible.
7. Keep a copy of all correspondence. If you write a letter to the Better Business Bureau, a government agency, a trade association, or another source of help, include information about what you have done so far to get your complaint resolved. Be sure to keep copies of your letter and all related documents.

Many private and public consumer-aid resources are available. Check your local telephone directory, state consumer office, and Internet sites to locate particular contacts and to gain information. Agencies and groups that handle consumer complaints include the following:

Better Business Bureau (BBB): BBBs are nonprofit organizations, sponsored by private and local businesses. Each BBB has its own policy about reporting information. A bureau will tell you if a complaint has been registered against a business, but it may not tell you the nature of the complaint.

Trade associations: Thousands of trade and professional associations in the United States represent a variety of interests (including banks,

Comprehension Check

Ask the students to think of an experience they had asking for a refund from a sales clerk, manager, or storeowner. Ask them to decide which of the six steps they followed to handle their complaint. Which steps were most effective? Which steps were least effective?

Cooperative Learning

The information in this section lends itself to role-playing the situations students have experienced as consumers. Have students role-play asking for a refund, for example. One student can be the consumer, and another can be the sales clerk, manager, or storeowner.

Enrichment

Have students complete the "Consumer Complaints" worksheet found in the Chapter 18 file of the *Preparing for Career Success Instructor's CD-ROM, Third Edition.*

KEY TO SUCCESS

Whenever you telephone a consumer contact association or agency, have copies of your sales receipts, other sales documents, and all correspondence with the company in front of you.

© JIST Works

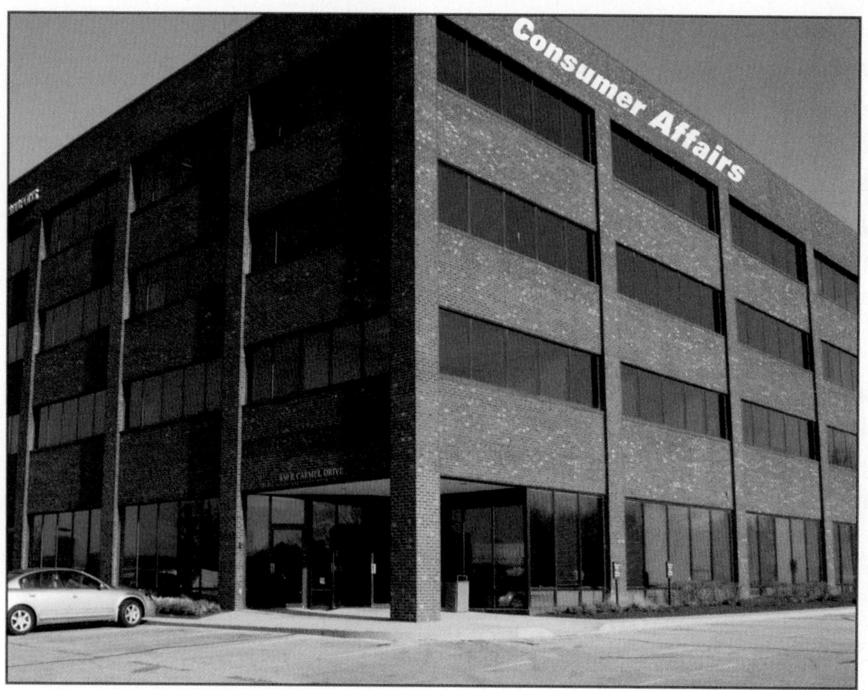

Are you aware of the consumer-aid agencies and groups that are available to handle your consumer complaints?

insurance companies, and clothing manufacturers) and professionals (such as accountants, lawyers, doctors, and therapists). Trade associations have various consumer functions, which the book *National Trade and Professional Associations of the United States* describes. Check your local library for this book and for related sources of help.

State, county, and city government consumer offices: These offices are a good source of information because many of them enforce consumer protection and fraud laws. If no local consumer office is located in your area, contact a state consumer office. Many states also have special commissions and agencies that handle consumer questions and complaints about banks, insurance companies, utilities, vocational and rehabilitation services, and weights and measures.

Federal agencies: Many federal agencies have enforcement or complaint-handling duties for products and services used by the public. Others act for the benefit of the public but do not resolve individual consumer problems. If you need help with your consumer problem, contact the nearest Federal Information Center on the Internet or in the yellow pages of your phone book under "Government."

Occupational and professional licensing boards: Many state agencies license or register members of various professions, including doctors, lawyers, nurses, accountants, pharmacists, funeral directors, plumbers, electricians, cosmetologists, automobile repair shops, employment agencies, and collection agencies.

If you have a consumer complaint and contact a licensing agency, the agency will contact the professional on your behalf. If necessary, the agency may conduct an investigation and take disciplinary action against the professional. Your local telephone directory, state consumer office, and the Internet can help you to locate a particular licensing board.

Regulatory agencies: If you are unable to resolve a complaint against a financial institution directly, you can contact the financial institution's regulatory agency for assistance. The regulatory agencies will be able to help resolve the complaint if the financial institution has violated a banking law or regulation. The Federal Trade Commission can help you contact the appropriate financial agency in your state.

Legal help: Small-claims courts resolve disputes involving claims for small debts and accounts. Court procedures generally are simple, inexpensive, quick, and informal. Check your local telephone directory under the municipal, county, or state government heading for small-claims court offices.

Technology

To protect your valuable personal information while you are online, do not respond to or click links in any e-mail that requests that you update or confirm your bank or credit card account or other personal information, even if the e-mail looks like it's from your bank or credit card company. This scam is called *phishing* because thieves use it to fish for personal information that they can use to steal from you or commit other crimes.

© JIST Works

Car manufacturers: Most foreign and U.S. car manufacturers have regional offices that handle consumer complaints that are not resolved by your local car dealer. Contact the dealer to obtain the phone number and address of the regional office headquarters.

State utility commissions: Your state's utility commission regulates consumer services and rates for gas, electricity, and a variety of other services within your state. If they receive several complaints about the same matter, they will conduct investigations. If you have a question or complaint about a utility matter, write or telephone the utility commission in your state.

Legal aid offices: Legal aid offices offer free legal services to those who qualify. They generally offer legal assistance with problems such as landlord-tenant relations, credit, utilities, family issues (such as divorce and adoption), Social Security, welfare, unemployment, and workers' compensation. Check the telephone directory, or call your local consumer protection office to find the address and telephone number of a legal aid office near you.

Community Resources

Divide the class into committees to learn more about the consumer contacts described in this section. Assign or seek volunteers for each contact. Have each committee report their findings to the class.

Reteaching

Have students complete the "Contract Contacts" worksheet found in the Chapter 18 file of the *Preparing for Career Success Instructor's CD-ROM, Third Edition.*

Avoiding Consumer Fraud

The federal government estimates that **fraud** (intentional misrepresentation of a product or service) costs consumers billions of dollars a year. Unsuspecting citizens become victims. As a consumer, you should watch for the following warning signs when dealing with a *solicitor* (person who seeks trade, business, or donations):

- Sweepstakes that require you to pay an entry fee
- Notices of prizes that require you to call a 900 number
- Mail that looks as though it is from a government agency but isn't
- Classified employment or business opportunity advertisements promising easy money for little work
- Callers who ask for your telephone calling card number or ask you to agree to accept someone else's calls as part of a phone company investigation
- Offers of easy credit despite your past credit history
- Prize awards that require you to give credit card or bank account numbers

Discussion Starter

Ask your students: Have you or someone you know ever been the victim of consumer fraud as described in this section? If so, describe the situation and what happened to the victim and the solicitor.

Discussion Starter

Ask your students: How will you benefit from knowing the warning signs of consumer fraud?

Section 4: Get Involved

Do the following activities, and be prepared to discuss them in class.

1. Using the phone book, list the consumer agencies or organizations that are located in your area. Contact at least two agencies to find out what they do to protect consumers.
2. Locate and read two or more product warranties. List the statements from each warranty that provide specific, clear information. List any statements that you find to be vague or misleading.
3. Interview the manager or owner of a local business about how he or she handles consumer complaints.
4. Write a complaint letter about a product or service that has given you a problem. Use the suggestions for writing a complaint letter in the "Making a Complaint" section.

© JIST Works

Enrichment

Form a committee of students to create a bulletin board titled "Who Wants This Vehicle?" Have students find pictures of the vehicle they would like to own, and place them on the bulletin board with their name under the picture. Ask students to write a paragraph about how the vehicle they chose to place on the bulletin board fits their personal orientation. (Refer students to "Knowing Yourself and Career Decisions," Section 2, Chapter 4 for a review of personal orientations.) Next, ask them to answer these seven questions in terms of purchasing this vehicle.

Cooperative Learning

Have students complete the "Car Shopping Questions" worksheet on the *Preparing for Career Success Instructor's CD-ROM, Third Edition.*

Section 5: Purchasing Your First Automobile

Whether it was 60 days or 60 years ago, most people can still remember the excitement of purchasing their first automobile. For others, it is a rite of passage they anticipate.

Begin by asking yourself these seven questions that apply to the purchase of a car, truck, or motorcycle:

1. What type of transportation do I need?
2. What is my purpose for using this vehicle?
3. Can I afford the cost of maintaining this vehicle?
4. What price am I willing to pay?
5. Who else will drive this vehicle?
6. What must I give up to afford this vehicle?
7. Will owning this vehicle make other economic opportunities available to me?

When you are considering buying a car, it's important to evaluate all the costs of owning a car (see Table 18.2), such as maintenance and repair costs, state and federal taxes, gas, and the insurance rates for various sizes and makes of cars. Comparing all of these costs will help you decide whether a new car or a used car will be the best choice for you.

Whether you decide to purchase a new car or a used one, it is a good idea to determine what makes, models, and options you want and can

Table 18.2 Costs of Owning and Operating Automobiles, Vans, and Light Trucks

Size	Cost (in pennies per mile)	Characteristics
Subcompact	32.2	4 cylinder, Avg. MPG = 32
Compact	42.3	4 cylinder, Avg. MPG = 23
Intermediate	46.9	6 cylinder, Avg. MPG = 20
Full-size auto	51.1	6 cylinder, Avg. MPG = 19
Compact pickup	40.2	4 cylinder, Avg. MPG = 18
Full-size pickup	47.7	8 cylinder, Avg. MPG = 13
Compact utility	45.6	4 cylinder, Avg. MPG = 15
Intermediate utility	51.4	6 cylinder, Avg. MPG = 15
Full-size utility	52.9	8 cylinder, Avg. MPG = 13
Minivan	50.7	6 cylinder, Avg. MPG = 17
Full-size van	52.0	6 cylinder, Avg. MPG = 13

Cost in pennies per mile includes depreciation, financing, insurance, registration fees, taxes, fuel maintenance, and repairs (based on 70,000 miles over five years).

Miles per gallon (MPG) are based on city driving.

Source: U.S. Department of Transportation (2003)

© JIST Works

afford. To help evaluate different makes and models, read magazines such as *Consumer Reports* and *Car and Driver*. You will probably find them in your school or public library. In addition, study newspaper, television, Internet, and magazine advertisements carefully. Test-drive the cars you are considering, and check for comfort and proper handling. Taking this step will help you narrow your choices.

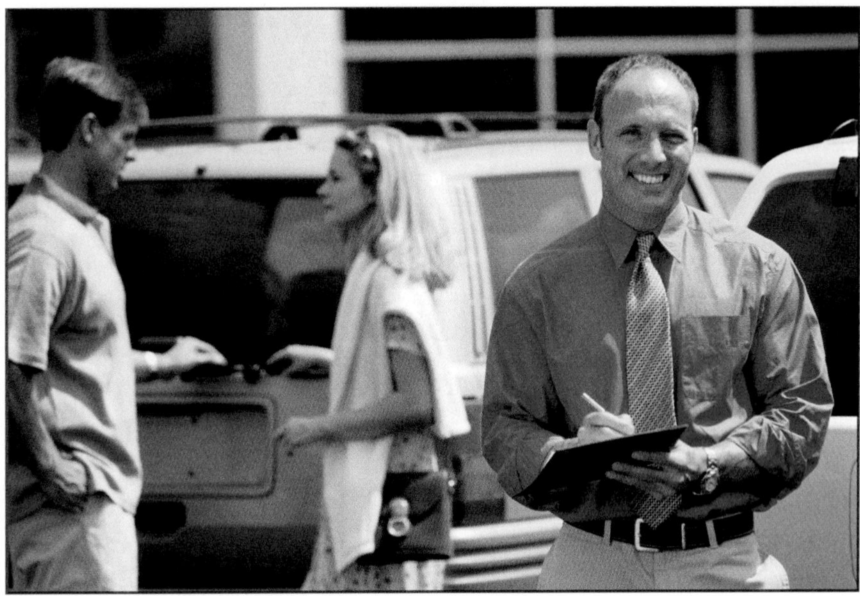

Whether they are 16 or 60, buying an automobile is an exciting experience for most consumers. Have you explored which makes, models, and options you want and can afford?

Buying a New Car

The Federal Trade Commission suggests that consumers comparison-shop for cars by visiting several dealerships. The actual price of a car can vary greatly from dealer to dealer, and wise shopping can result in considerable savings. In new cars, check the official government **Monroney sticker** (see Figure 18.2). Federal law requires that this label be affixed to the window of the car. It shows the base price, the manufacturer's installed options, the manufacturer's suggested retail price, the manufacturer's transportation charge, the fuel economy, and safety ratings. Only the purchaser may remove the label.

The *suggested base price* (cost of the car without options, but including standard equipment, factory warranty, and freight) is printed on the Monroney sticker. The dealer displays the price on a supplemental sticker. It equals the Monroney sticker price plus the suggested retail price of dealer-installed options, additional dealer markup (ADM) or additional dealer profit (ADP), dealer preparation, and undercoating. Dealer preparation charges are paid by the manufacturer or covered by the new car warranty. Check the manufacturer's suggested price, and compare it with the dealer markups.

In most cases, you will need to negotiate a price for the car you want. Dealers are sometimes willing to bargain on their profit margin, which is generally between 15 and 20 percent. This margin is usually the difference between the manufacturer's suggested retail price and the **invoice price** (manufacturer's initial charge to the dealer). The invoice price is usually higher than the dealer's actual cost because dealers often receive rebates, allowances, discounts, and incentive awards from the manufacturer.

If you negotiate a purchase price based on the invoice price (for example, "at invoice," "$100 below invoice," or "2 percent above invoice"), be sure the dealer does not add freight to your sales contract. After you make your selection—but before you give a deposit—determine whether the deposit is refundable. If it is refundable, find out the terms.

Comprehension Check

Have students use Table 18.2 to calculate and compare the driving costs (in dollars) of various sized cars.

Find Out More

The Internet is a great resource for information when it comes to bargaining with a used car sales representative. At car pricing Web sites, you can read expert reviews on older vehicles and then type in a make, model, year, and mileage to receive a professional estimate of a particular car's worth. Kelly Blue Book at www.kbb.com, for example, breaks down prices by method of sale (dealer, retail, or private party) and car condition (poor, fair, good, or excellent).

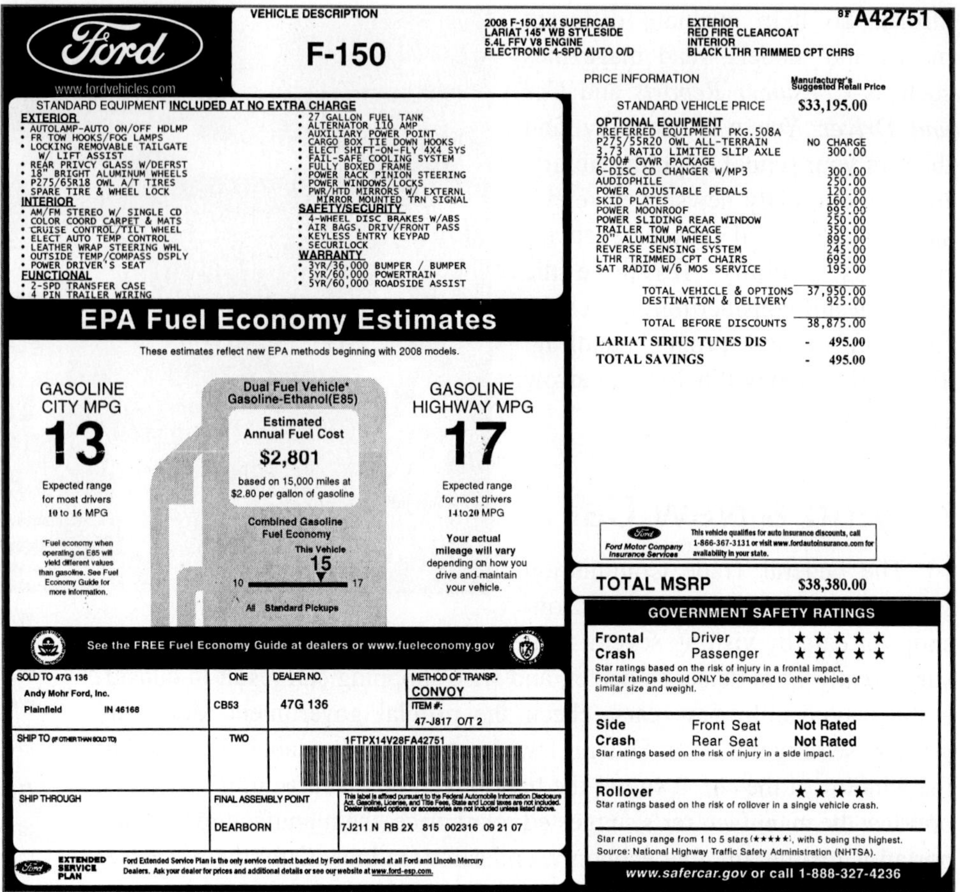

Figure 18.2 Sample Monroney sticker.

Buying a Used Car

Used car shopping can be confusing for someone who is not familiar with the mechanics of automobiles. Doing research ahead of time, asking the advice of a knowledgeable friend, and performing a full road test can be very helpful. Before buying a used car, have it inspected by an independent mechanic or diagnostic center to be sure that there are no hidden problems. Visual concerns include uneven or mismatched paint, excessive or uneven tire wear, leaks, excessive wear on the gas and brake pedals, and nonfunctioning accessories.

Key To Success

Check the history of a used car by asking the dealer for the name and address of the previous owner. Contact the previous owner to discuss the car's mileage, service problems, and accident history. Copies of repair bills may help you verify the mileage and the car's history of mechanical breakdowns or accidents.

Look for a buyer's guide sticker on the window of each car. The buyer's guide, required by the Federal Trade Commission's Used Car Rule, provides the consumer important information and suggestions to consider. It tells you

- Whether the vehicle comes with a warranty and, if so, what specific protection the dealer will provide
- Whether the vehicle comes with no warranty ("as is") or with implied warranties only
- That you should ask to have the car inspected by an independent mechanic before you buy

© JIST Works

- That you should get all promises in writing
- Some of the major problems that may occur with any car

Discussion Starter

Ask your students: Have you or your friends purchased a used vehicle? Did it have a warranty? Have you or they had any major problems with the car? What advice would you give to a first-time buyer of a used car?

Financing an Automobile

If you plan to finance a car, you should follow this advice:

- Check interest rates by shopping around for the best deal. Always compare the annual percentage rates (APRs).
- In addition to the financing offered by the dealer, consider banks, finance companies, and credit unions.
- Read your purchase contract carefully before signing. Make sure you understand everything.
- Check all figures, and draw lines through blank spaces in a contract to indicate no charge.

Career Fact

Buying a new car is usually the second most expensive purchase many people make (the purchase of a home is the first).

Education and Training

Invite an advanced student from an automotive technology class to speak to the class about automotive maintenance. Make certain the invited student has a list of questions and concerns students have about automotive maintenance before he or she speaks to the class. Ask the student to also tell the class about the job opportunities he or she anticipates having after completing the automotive technology program.

Maintaining a Newly Purchased Vehicle

You can help keep the costs of operating your car down by following proper auto maintenance suggestions. New cars are covered by manufacturer warranties assuring they will repair or replace certain parts that prove to be defective in material or workmanship for a specific time or number of miles. If you buy a used car from a dealer, you may have a limited warranty, depending on the dealer's policy. You may get a lower price from an individual, but you will not receive a warranty.

When you enlist the service of an automotive technician, describe the problem and its symptoms. Let the automotive technician determine what needs repaired. For major repairs, get a second opinion, even if the car must be towed to another shop. Before you leave your car for repairs, make certain that you have a written estimate and that the work order describes what you want done. Ask the manager or technician to contact you before making repairs not covered in the work order. Also, keep copies of all work orders and receipts, and get all warranties in writing. Many states have "lemon" laws for new cars with recurring problems. Contact your local or state consumer office to find out if your state has these laws.

In addition to the original purchase price, maintaining a vehicle is a major budget item. Have you compared the reliability of various makes and models?

Take Note

Safe and efficient driving depends on visually searching the traffic scene for dangerous elements and accurately identifying them. According to the American Automobile Association, alcohol consumption affects your visual perception in several ways:

- Your eye focus is distorted.
- The amount of light entering your eye is reduced.
- You may experience double vision.
- Your ability to judge distance is affected.
- Your peripheral vision is reduced.
- Your ability to distinguish colors is impaired.
- Your night vision is reduced.

Discussion Starter

Start a discussion about safe driving by telling students that jumping off a three-story building is similar to the force of a crash at 30 mph. Ask your students: Who has been in an accident? What happened? Who was responsible? How could the accident have been averted?

Driving Safely

With more than 185 million drivers on the road, collisions are the number-one cause of death in the United States for people ages 4 to 33. You can avoid accidents by following these 10 commandments for driving safely:

1. Thou shalt "buckle up" before driving. (Seventy-five percent of car occupants ejected in a car crash died.)
2. Thou shalt check traffic before entering a highway.
3. Thou shalt not assume what other drivers are going to do.
4. Thou shalt practice defensive driving techniques. Remember, the meek shall inherit the earth.
5. Thou shalt always use turn signals and check side and rearview mirrors for traffic before changing lanes or passing.
6. Thou shalt not mix driving with the use of alcohol or drugs nor ride with a driver who does.
7. Thou shalt not allow music to become so loud as to distract or prevent you from hearing sirens, horns, or trains.
8. Thou shalt obey posted speed limits at all times.
9. Thou shalt focus on driving at all times.
10. Thou shalt be responsible for keeping safety equipment (brakes, lights, horn, and muffler) in good working order.

We depend on our cars to operate as the manufacturer claims and to be properly serviced or repaired. If you have an auto-related problem, contact the company that advertised, sold, or repaired the vehicle. If a complaint cannot be resolved directly with the business involved, you may file a complaint with the Attorney General's Consumer Protection staff or attempt to have the problem resolved through the dealer's or manufacturer's arbitration program.

Section 5: Get Involved

Answer the following on a separate sheet of paper, and be prepared to discuss your responses in class.

1. Visit a used car lot, and select a car that you would like to own. What possible problems can you detect by reading the information on the back of the buyer's guide? List three good features of the car you selected. List three possible problems with the car you selected. How did you discover the good features? The problems?
2. Using the classified ads of your local newspaper, determine the average cost of one or more specific models of used cars from 2005 to the present. Use at least five prices to determine the average price for each year.
3. Would it be to your financial advantage to pay cash and save on interest charges or to use credit to buy an automobile? If buying on credit, how much down payment will you be able to afford? How large a monthly payment will comfortably fit into your budget?

© JIST Works

Section 6: Protecting Yourself with Insurance

Insurance is the act, system, or business of guaranteeing property or a person against loss or harm arising in specified occurrences, such as fire, accident, death, or loss of income, in exchange for a payment proportional to the risk involved. All *insurance policies* (the printed documents, issued to the policyholder by the company, that state the terms of the insurance contract) cost a **premium** (the policyholder's payment) that is determined mostly by the amount the insurance company must pay out in claims. Use insurance to transfer your risk from yourself to the insurance company.

Life insurance provides cash to your family after you die. The money your dependents will receive (the death benefit) is an important financial resource. Your dependents can use your insurance benefit to pay the rent or mortgage, operate the household, and pay debts. The suggested amount to purchase is equal to five to seven times your annual gross income. The purpose of life insurance is to protect your survivors.

Homeowner's insurance is purchased to guard against disasters. Homeowner's insurance is often purchased in a package plan and covers personal belongings and the cost of repairing or replacing structures damaged by fire, storms, explosions, vandalism, theft, and snow. Floods, earthquakes, and war are not usually included.

Automobile insurance consists of two basic parts. **Liability coverage** is for bodily injuries, property damages, and medical expenses for others when you are at fault in an automobile accident. **Physical coverage** is for damage to your vehicle caused by collision, fire, or theft. Your automobile's sticker price, average repair costs, overall safety record, and likelihood of theft are used by insurance companies to calculate your premiums. Other considerations include your age and driving record.

Whenever you drive an automobile, you risk having an accident. If you are ever involved in an automobile accident, the damages could be the biggest expense you will have in owning a car. Throughout the United States, state financial responsibility laws require people to prove that they can pay for damages that result in death, injury, or property damage. If you are responsible for an accident involving bodily injury or substantial property damage, you will need to present proof that you can pay damages up to the amounts required by law. Your purchase of automobile insurance will normally meet your financial responsibility requirements.

The cost of automobile insurance varies, and many discounts are available. Check several sources for the best price, and obtain at least three price quotes before buying. Phone local insurance agents and companies, or access them on the Internet.

Community Resources

Invite an insurance agent to visit the class to explain various types of insurance.

Case Study

Have students read the case study "Insure Your Plan" found in the Chapter 18 file of the *Preparing for Career Success Instructor's CD-ROM, Third Edition* and discuss the "Critical Thinking" questions.

TAKE NOTE

Chances are very high that you will eventually be injured in a traffic accident. If you have such an accident, you will have a 1-in-2 chance of suffering a disabling injury. You will have a 1-in-50 chance of dying in the accident.

FIND OUT MORE

Go online for additional information about insurance. Using your search engine, key in **Insurance Information Institute.**

CAREER FACT

Every day, insurance companies pay more than $200 million in claims from policyholders. Those claims result from losses suffered during fires, hurricanes, tornadoes, robberies, auto accidents, dog bites, falls, and a host of other traumatic incidents.

Section 6: Get Involved

Answer the following on a separate sheet of paper, and be prepared to discuss your responses in class.

1. Estimate the amount of life insurance needed by the main wage earner(s) in your household. Consider all monthly expenses and the amount of time that the dependent family members will need to become self-sufficient. Are the wage earners in your household adequately insured or underinsured?
2. A burglar's three worst enemies are light, time, and noise. Using each of these three factors, what can you do to help protect your home or apartment?

Reteaching

Have students complete the "Checking Your Location" worksheet in Chapter 18 of the *Preparing for Career Success Student Activity Book, Third Edition.*

Chapter 18 Review

Enrich Your Vocabulary

On a separate sheet of paper, number from 1 to 20, and write each term from the "Enrich Your Vocabulary" list at the beginning of the chapter next to the number of the statement it matches.

1. Having no trademark
2. Unsteady, irregular
3. A person paying rent for the temporary use of another person's building or land
4. The cost of one standard measure of a product
5. Temporary price reductions on regular merchandise
6. A contract that involves a financial commitment
7. Money you entrust with the landlord to cover any damage you cause to the rental unit
8. A government agency that enforces laws related to food, drugs, and cosmetics
9. Wise, shrewd, and frugal
10. Insurance for bodily injuries, property damages, and medical expenses for others when you are at fault
11. The automobile manufacturer's initial charge to the dealer
12. The policyholder's payment for an insurance policy
13. The act, system, or business of guaranteeing property or a person against loss or harm arising in specified occurrences
14. The label affixed to a new car's window and required by federal law
15. A guarantee that a product is of a certain quality or that defective parts will be replaced
16. Insurance for damage to your vehicle caused by collision, fire, or theft

Enrich Your Vocabulary Answers

1. generic
2. fluctuating
3. tenant
4. unit price
5. promotional sales
6. lease
7. security deposit
8. Food and Drug Administration
9. prudent
10. liability coverage
11. invoice price
12. premium
13. insurance
14. Monroney sticker
15. warranty
16. physical coverage

(continued)

© JIST Works

17. A label that states the various nutrients in a product

18. Unsolicited commercial e-mail

19. Intended to promote the sale of a product or service, advance an idea, or bring about some other effect

20. Buying products and services to impress others

Enrich Your Vocabulary Answers *(continued)*

17. nutritional labeling
18. spam
19. advertising
20. conspicuous consumption

Check Your Knowledge

On a separate sheet of paper, answer the following questions.

1. What is the average income for an American family of 3.2 persons?
2. Food accounts for what percentage of the average American household's spending? What about health care?
3. Why is prudent shopping worth the effort?
4. Why is knowledge of weights and measurements important in being a prudent consumer?
5. What three major types of sales do stores offer to consumers?
6. Of the 10 shopping strategies listed in "Expensive Products" which two are most useful to you? Explain your answer.
7. What are four dishonest or illegal advertising practices described in this chapter?
8. What is the general rule of thumb regarding how much to allow in your budget for housing expenses?
9. President John F. Kennedy declared that every consumer has four basic rights. Which of these rights do you consider to be most important? Why do you think so?
10. What are four responsibilities that you should accept as a consumer?
11. In addition to the make, model, and options, what are four costs you should consider before deciding to buy a specific car?

Check Your Knowledge Answers

1. $82,195
2. Food = 9.8%, Health care = 4.6%
3. Different sellers offer different prices, service, variety, and quality for the same or similar items.
4. Knowledge of weights and measures can point out large price differences between similar products.
5. Promotional sales, clearance sales, and special purchase sales.
6. Answers will vary.
7. (1) False pricing, (2) bait and switch, (3) referral plans, (4) high pressure tactics, (5) overstated sales claims.
8. Not more than 28 to 29 percent of gross monthly income.
9. Answers will vary. (1) The right to information, (2) the right to choice, (3) the right to safety, (4) the right to be heard.
10. (1) Become informed about products or services that you plan to buy. (2) Be an honest consumer. (3) Be assertive when your consumer rights are violated. (4) Report unethical business practices to protect other consumers.
11. (1) Maintenance and repair, (2) state and federal taxes, (3) gas, and (4) insurance rates.

Develop SCANS Competencies

This activity will give you practice in developing the information and technology skills that successful workers use. Go computer shopping! Before you begin, decide what features the computer must have to meet the needs of your family. Shop at several different stores. Record the prices and features for at least five different computers. After you finish shopping, analyze the information you have collected. Decide which computer would be the best buy.

Enrichment

Have students complete the Chapter 18 section of the *Preparing for Career Success Student Portfolio, Third Edition.*

© JIST Works

Chapter 19 Resources

Lesson Plans and Preparation

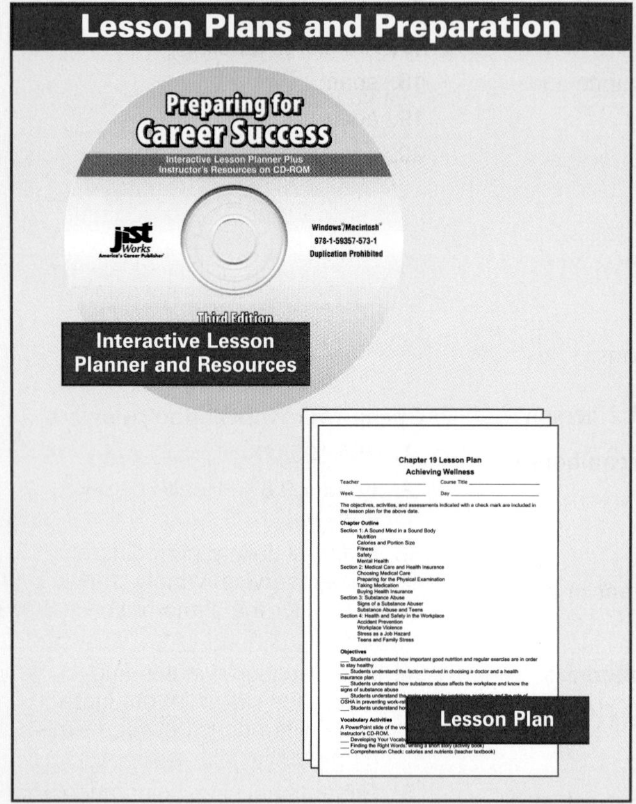

Preparing for Career Success
Interactive Lesson Planner Plus Instructor's Resources on CD-ROM
Windows/Macintosh
978-1-59357-573-1
Duplication Prohibited
Third Edition
Interactive Lesson Planner and Resources
Chapter 19 Lesson Plan
Achieving Wellness
Lesson Plan

Multimedia

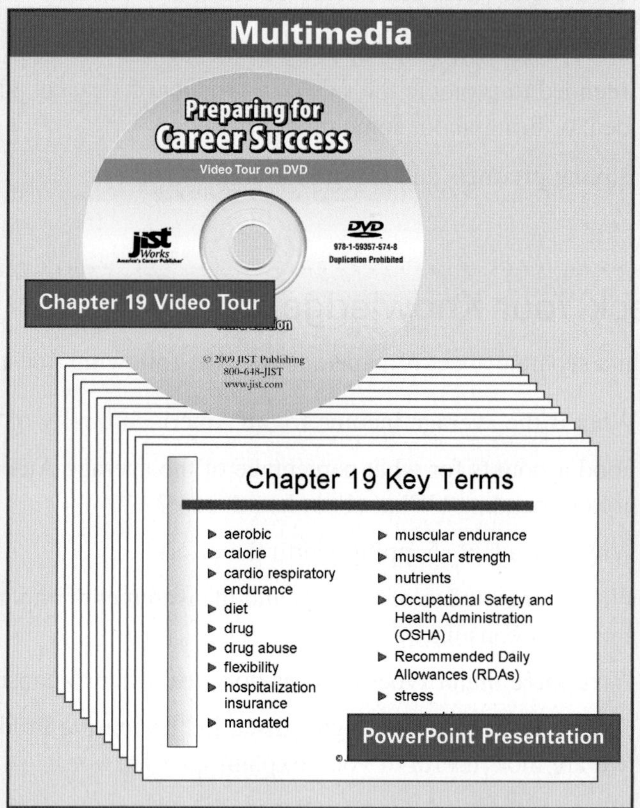

Preparing for Career Success
Video Tour on DVD
DVD
978-1-59357-574-8
Duplication Prohibited
Chapter 19 Video Tour
© 2009 JIST Publishing
800-648-JIST
www.jist.com
Chapter 19 Key Terms
aerobic
calorie
cardio respiratory endurance
diet
drug
drug abuse
flexibility
hospitalization insurance
mandated
muscular endurance
muscular strength
nutrients
Occupational Safety and Health Administration (OSHA)
Recommended Daily Allowances (RDAs)
stress
PowerPoint Presentation

Activities

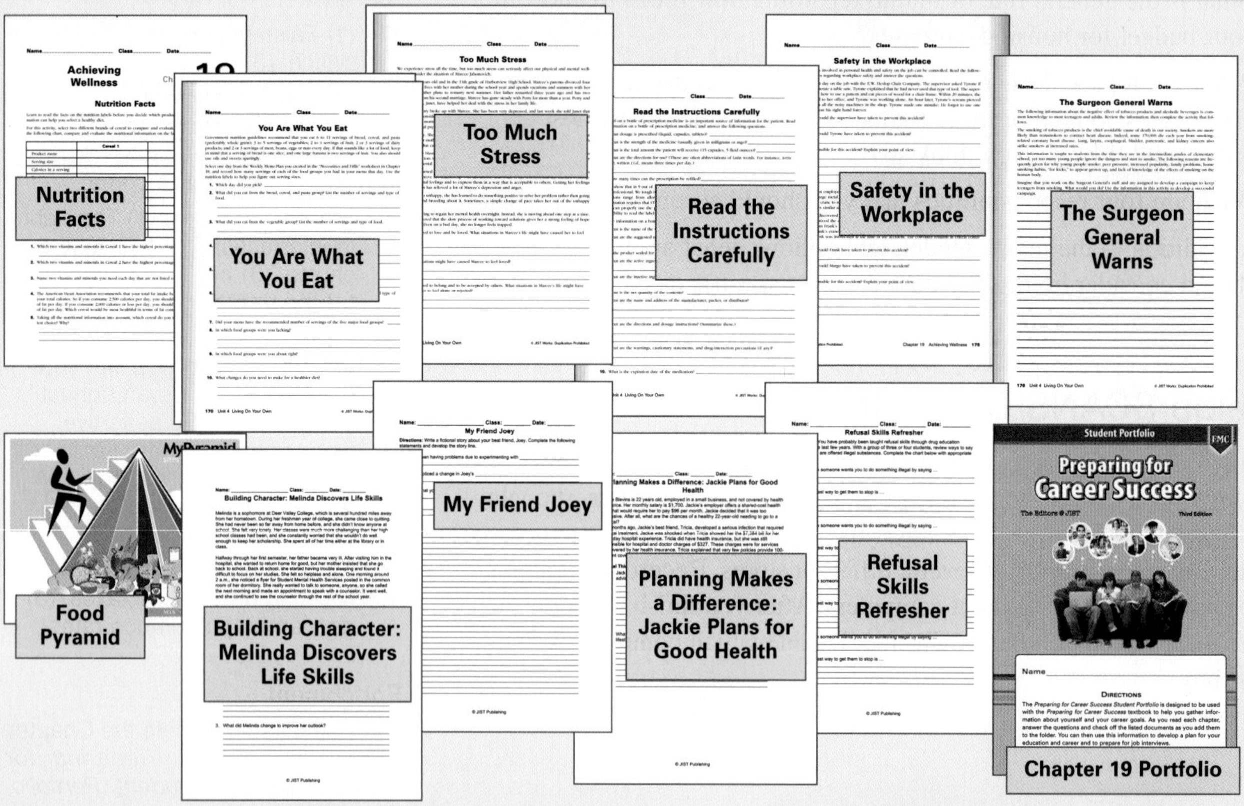

Nutrition Facts

You Are What You Eat

Too Much Stress

Read the Instructions Carefully

Safety in the Workplace

The Surgeon General Warns

Food Pyramid

Building Character: Melinda Discovers Life Skills

My Friend Joey

Planning Makes a Difference: Jackie Plans for Good Health

Refusal Skills Refresher

Chapter 19 Portfolio

© JIST Works

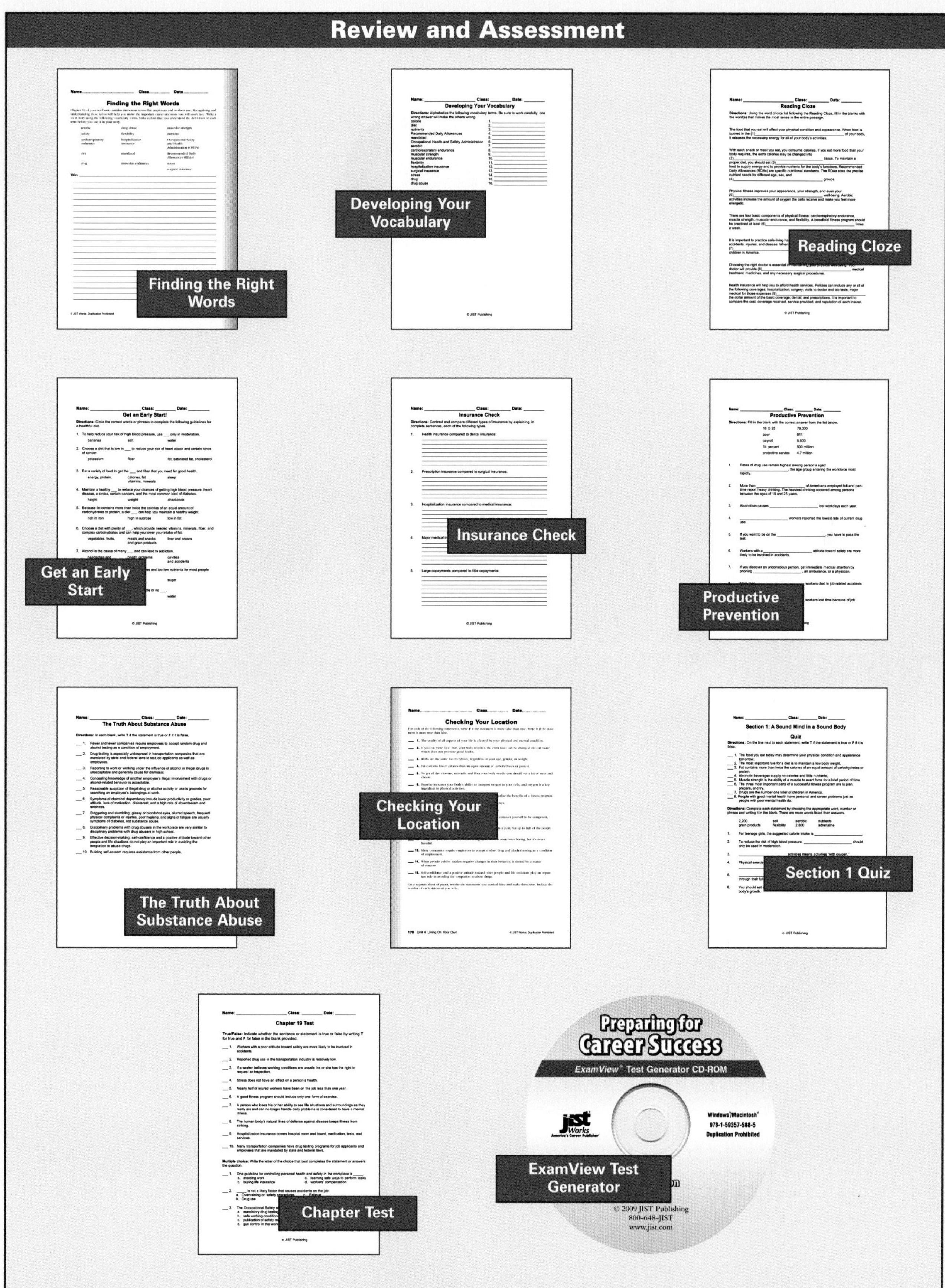

Review and Assessment
Finding the Right Words
Developing Your Vocabulary
Reading Cloze
Get an Early Start
Insurance Check
Productive Prevention
The Truth About Substance Abuse
Checking Your Location
Section 1 Quiz
Chapter Test
Preparing for Career Success
ExamView® Test Generator CD-ROM
Windows/Macintosh
978-1-59357-588-5
Duplication Prohibited
ExamView Test Generator
© 2009 JIST Publishing
800-648-JIST
www.jist.com

Chapter 19 Achieving Wellness

Learning Objectives

- Describe how your physical and mental condition affects the quality of your life
- Explain how what you eat now will affect your physical condition and appearance now and in the future
- Give examples of safe-living practices on the job and away from the job
- List the specific criteria for selecting a personal physician
- Explain the importance of health insurance
- Explain why a workplace that is safe and free from the dangers of drug- or alcohol-induced behavior is good for both employees and employers
- Describe and discuss the major causes of job-related accidents and the procedures for reducing on-the-job health and safety hazards

Your physical and mental condition affects all aspects of your life. Though some of the factors that contribute to good health are beyond your control, most are simply a matter of developing good health habits. What have you done today that has been good or bad for your health?

Enrich Your Vocabulary

In reading this chapter and doing the exercises, you will learn the following important terms:

aerobic
calorie
cardiorespiratory endurance
diet
drug
drug abuse
flexibility
hospitalization insurance
mandated
muscular endurance
muscular strength
nutrients
Occupational Safety and Health Administration (OSHA)
Recommended Daily Allowances (RDAs)
stress
surgical insurance

Cooperative Learning

Divide your class into small groups. Assign each group to decide which three of the "good health habits" they consider most important. List their three selections on a sheet of paper, and write their reasons for each selection. Next, write the nine good health habits on the chalkboard or an overhead transparency. Ask each group to report their three selections and their reasons to the class. Place a mark next to each group's selections to determine the overall opinion of the class.

Video Tour on DVD

Show students the Chapter 19 segment to introduce them to the content.

The first wealth is health.

—Ralph Waldo Emerson

Which of the following good health habits do you consistently practice?

1. Eating well-balanced, nutritious meals
2. Sleeping at least eight hours each night
3. Getting regular checkups from your doctor
4. Thinking about safety and doing things in a safe manner
5. Avoiding the use of tobacco, alcohol, and drugs of abuse
6. Trying to maintain a positive mental attitude toward yourself and others
7. Participating in sports and/or exercising on a regular basis
8. Keeping informed about health risks, such as infectious diseases and environmental hazards
9. Avoiding behaviors, situations, activities, and places that are considered health risks

If you follow all of these good health habits, you are practicing a wellness-oriented lifestyle. If not, take responsibility today for putting yourself on the positive health track. You can take steps to turn your negative responses into positive ones.

Take Note

Excess weight and physical inactivity account for approximately 300,000 premature deaths each year, second only to deaths related to smoking. The National Heart, Lung, and Blood Institute calls obesity a complex chronic disease involving social, behavioral, cultural, physiological, metabolic, and genetic factors.

Section 1: A Sound Mind in a Sound Body

The foods you eat, the quality of the air you breathe, the genetic traits you were born with, the physical activity and mental stresses you experience, the illnesses to which you are exposed—all play a part in determining how healthy you are or will be.

Nutrition

The food you eat today will determine your physical condition and appearance tomorrow. Your body is a remarkable machine with the ability to select needed chemical substances from the food you eat and convert them into flesh and bones and to repair and replace worn-out tissue. The food you

© JIST Works

eat provides the calories needed to stoke the "furnaces" in the cells of your body. When your body burns food, it releases the necessary energy for all of your body's activities. You owe it to yourself to "fuel it well."

With each snack or meal you eat, you consume calories. A **calorie** is the amount of heat needed to raise the temperature of one gram (453.5 grams = 1 pound) of water one degree centigrade. The calories that a portion of food contains are equal to the amount of heat that your body will produce when it burns the food. For example, the suggested calorie intake for most teenage girls is 2,200 calories per day; for teenage boys, it is 2,800 per day. If you eat more of the fuel foods than your body requires, the extra material may change into fat tissue, which does not promote good health.

The most important rule for a **diet** (the food and drink a person customarily consumes) is to eat sufficient food to supply the body's energy needs and to eat a varied diet to supply the **nutrients** (nourishment) needed for the body's growth and functioning. Unfortunately, nature packs some foods full of nutrients and shortchanges others. A food high in one nutrient is likely to have other healthful benefits.

Recommended Daily Allowances (RDAs) are specific nutritional standards that were established by the Food and Nutrition Board of the National Academy of Sciences. The RDAs state nutrient needs, including vitamins and minerals, for different age, gender, and weight groups. For example, teenage males need more protein (59 grams) than teenage females (44 grams) do, but both groups need about the same amount of vitamin C (60 milligrams). Eating a well-balanced diet will help you meet your RDA.

The U.S. Department of Agriculture and the Department of Health and Human Services recommend the following guidelines for a healthful diet:

1. Eat a variety of foods to maintain the level of energy, protein, vitamins, minerals, and fiber you need for good health.
2. Maintain a healthy weight to reduce your chances of developing high blood pressure, heart disease, a stroke, certain cancers, and the most common kind of diabetes.
3. Choose a diet that is low in fat, saturated fat, and cholesterol to reduce your risk of heart attack and certain types of cancer. Because fat contains more than twice the calories of an equal amount of carbohydrates or protein, a diet low in fat can help you maintain a healthy weight.

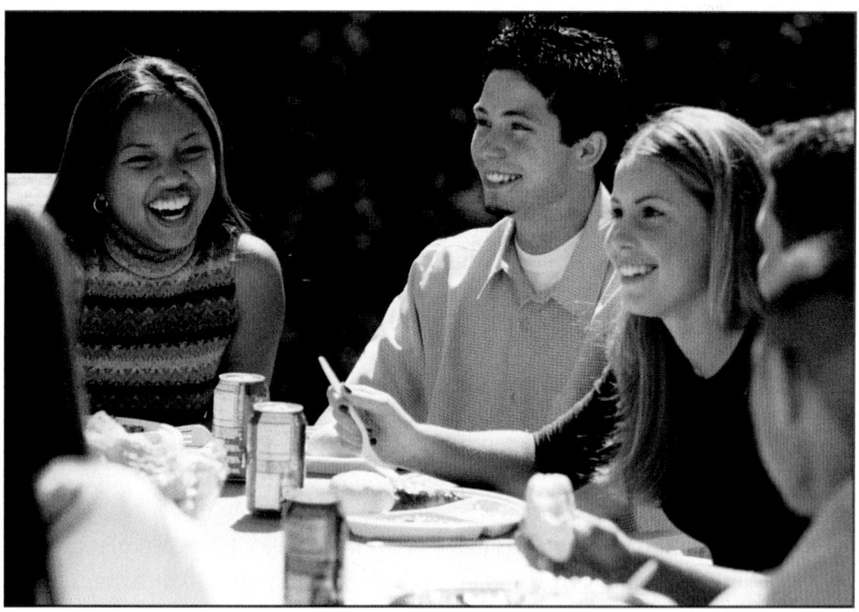

What nutrients are in the typical meals you eat with your friends?

Reteaching

Have students complete the "Get an Early Start!" worksheet in Chapter 19 of the *Preparing for Career Success Instructor's CD-ROM, Third Edition.*

Comprehension Check/Vocabulary Builder

After your students have read this page, have them close their books. Ask several students: Are all nutrients healthful? Why or why not? Are all calories healthful? Why or why not?

Key To Success

A wellness lifestyle is more than a well-balanced diet. Physical fitness improves your appearance, makes you stronger, and increases your emotional energy. Regular exercise through sports or workouts can do wonders for your energy level.

© JIST Works

Self-Understanding

Send a writer to the chalkboard. Ask him or her to write the heading "Guidelines for a Healthful Diet," and number from one to seven under the heading. Next, ask a student to read number one from the text. Then ask your students: Think about your diet during the past 24 hours. How many members of the class could honestly answer yes to this guideline? How many would answer no? Ask the writer to record the number of yes and no answers. Repeat this process for all seven guidelines.

4. Select a diet with adequate vegetables, fruits, and grain products to provide needed vitamins, minerals, fiber, and complex carbohydrates. Doing so will also help you lower your intake of fat.
5. Use sugar in moderation. A diet rich in sugar has too many calories and too few nutrients for most people and can contribute to tooth decay.
6. Use salt in moderation to help reduce your risk of high blood pressure.
7. Avoid drinking alcoholic beverages. They supply calories but little or no nutrients. Alcohol is also the cause of many health problems and accidents and can lead to addiction. Of course, it is illegal for anyone under the age of 21 to drink alcoholic beverages.

KEY TO SUCCESS

If you are trying to lose a few pounds of weight, the goal of losing a pound a week is reasonable. A modest reduction of 500 calories per day will help you achieve this goal. You must burn 3,500 calories to lose one pound of fat. However, if you plan to lose more than 15 to 20 pounds, it is best to have your physician evaluate you before you begin.

Calories and Portion Size

More than 60 percent of Unites States adults are either overweight or obese, according to the Centers for Disease Control and Prevention (CDC). Americans are putting on pounds and sacrificing their health for the sake of supersized portions, extra-large drinks, and two-for-one value meals. Do you agree?

Experts generally agree that the key to losing weight is to "eat less and move more." Successful weight losers follow the USDA-recommended seven guidelines for a healthful diet. They also exercise for about an hour or more a day, *expending* (using up) about 2,900 calories per week on a variety of activities. In addition, successful weight losers eat balanced meals but restrict their portions of food to limit how many calories they are eating throughout the day. After their weight is lost and portion control and exercise habits are a part of their lifestyle, these people find that weight gain is no longer an obstacle.

Food Safety

At the right temperature, bacteria you cannot see, smell, or taste can multiply to the millions in a few short hours. In large numbers, they cause illness. This situation does not need to happen. Estimates are that consumers could avoid 85 percent of food poisoning cases if they handled food properly. The United States Department of Agriculture provides this food-handling advice:

- When you shop, buy cold food last and get it home fast. Do not buy anything you will not use before the use-by date.
- When you store food, keep it safe, refrigerate at 40 degrees, and freeze at 0 degrees.
- When you prepare food, keep all surfaces clean, and thaw foods in the refrigerator or microwave, not on the kitchen counter.
- Cook food thoroughly to kill the harmful bacteria. Cook red meat to 160 degrees, poultry to 180 degrees.
- Microwave safely by using an oven temperature probe or a meat thermometer to check the food.
- When you serve food, never leave perishable food out of the refrigerator more than two hours.
- When you handle leftovers, use small containers for quick cooling.
- Never taste food that looks or smells strange. Discard it.

© JIST Works

Nutrition Facts	Amount/Serving	% Daily Value*	Amount/Serving	% Daily Value*
	Total Fat 15g	23%	**Total Carbohydrate** 74g	25%
	Saturated Fat 4.5g	23%	Dietary Fiber 3g	11%
Serving Size 1 Slice (118g) Servings Per Container 12	**Cholesterol** 20mg	7%	Sugars 51g	
	Sodium 350mg	14%	**Protein** 3g	
Calories 430 Calories from Fat 130	Vitamin A 4% • Vitamin C 0%		• Calcium 4% • Iron 8%	

Nutrition Facts	Amount Per Serving	% Daily Value*	Amount Per Serving	% Daily Value*
Serving Size 10 crackers (30g)	**Total Fat** 4g	6%	**Total Carbohydrate** 22g	7%
Servings Per Container about 10	Saturated Fat 1g	4%	Dietary Fiber less than 1g	3%
Calories 130	**Cholesterol** 0mg	0%	Sugars 8g	
Calories from Fat 35	**Sodium** 125mg	5%	**Protein** 2g	
	Vitamin A 0% • Vitamin C 0%		Calcium 10% • Iron 4%	

Figure 19.1 Which food provides the most beneficial nutrition? Why do you think so?

The food label, found on almost all processed foods, offers complete, useful, and accurate nutrition information. Reading the part of the food label called the Nutrition Facts panel is a good way to make sure you get all the essential nutrients for good health (see Figure 19.1).

The serving size and number of servings per package listed at the top of the Nutrition Facts panel affect all the nutrient amounts listed on the panel. Observe the *amount per serving* section of the Nutrition Facts panel because it shows how many calories are in a serving and whether a food is high in total fat, saturated fat, cholesterol, and sodium.

Fitness

Exercise increases your body's ability to transport oxygen to your cells, and oxygen is a key ingredient in physical activities. That is why activities that burn oxygen are **aerobic** (with oxygen) activities.

Physical exercise also triggers the release of hormonal stimulants, such as adrenaline, into the bloodstream—the same stimulants that make your heart speed up when a car swerves in front of you in fast traffic. The faster heart rate boosts the blood flow to the muscles, brain, and nervous system. When you have good circulation and plenty of oxygen, your body feels energized.

The President's Council on Physical Fitness lists four components that are basic to physical fitness:

1. **Cardiorespiratory endurance:** The ability to deliver oxygen and nutrients to tissues and to remove wastes. The ability to endure a long run or swim is a good method for measuring cardiorespiratory endurance.
2. **Muscular strength:** The ability of a muscle to exert force for a brief time. Various weight-lifting exercises measure upper-body strength.

Take Note

Many people believe the government screens advertising and that all advertised claims about health products must be truthful. This is not the case with most health-care products, except for those drug and medical devices that require pre-market approval by the Food and Drug Administration (FDA). Law enforcement authorities can take action only after the advertisements have appeared. Frequently appearing promotional ads for worthless products and services include the following targets: fitness, weight loss, cancer, hair growth, and arthritis.

Key To Success

Begin an exercise program gradually. Overdoing exercises will cause fatigue and muscle soreness. People who overdo are more likely to quit their exercise program.

Cluster Link

Would you enjoy a career planning, managing, or providing diagnostic, therapeutic, and information services in health care? This is one of the fastest-growing areas of jobs in the U.S. economy. If you are interested in the Health Sciences career cluster, see the appendix for more information.

© JIST Works

Comprehension Check/ Vocabulary Builder

After your students finish reading "Fitness," instruct them to close their books. Ask several students: In your own words, what is cardio respiratory endurance? What examples can you think of to demonstrate the difference between muscular strength and muscular endurance?

3. **Muscular endurance:** The ability of a muscle, or a group of muscles, to sustain repeated contractions or to continue applying force against a fixed object. Push-ups test the endurance of arm and shoulder muscles.
4. **Flexibility:** The ability to move joints and use muscles through their full range of motion. The sit-and-reach exercise is a good measure of flexibility of the lower back and hamstring muscles.

You should practice a beneficial fitness program throughout the year and at least three times a week. Weight-bearing activities such as walking, running, hiking, dancing, tennis, basketball, gymnastics, hockey, and soccer help bones get stronger. Joining a team or group helps many people stick to a schedule. A fitness program can include more than one form of exercise. For example, if you live in a northern climate, you may choose to bicycle during the summer months and swim at an indoor pool during the winter. A fitness program should be enjoyable. For many people, participation in sports becomes a fitness habit that they enjoy throughout their lives.

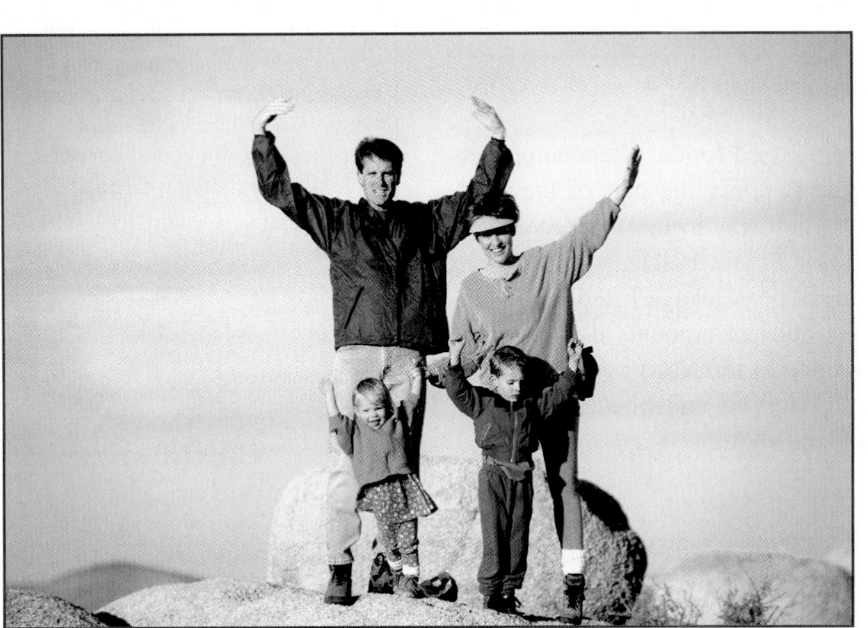

Which of the four components of physical fitness is the Jones family getting during their afternoon of hiking?

If you have not had a physical checkup by your physician for several months, getting one before you begin a strenuous fitness program is a good health practice. If you are really out of shape at the beginning of your fitness program, you will probably need two or three months of regular exercise to realize the benefits of your hard work and determination. The most important part of a successful fitness program is to stick with it. The benefits to your physical health and mental well-being will be worth the effort.

Safety

School-to-Work Transition

Send a writer to the chalkboard. Ask him or her to write the heading "Safety." Then ask the class to provide the writer with safety practices they have learned at school during the past six years. After the class has developed a written list of six or more safety practices, ask them to give examples illustrating how specific safety practices on the list could be used on a specific job.

Remember the old saying "Better safe than sorry"? Being aware of potential hazards and using safe practices can prevent accidents, injuries, and disease. Consider the following facts:

- The most common causes of traumatic brain injury are motor vehicle and bicycle accidents, violence, falls, and sports or recreational accidents.
- Despite the well-publicized menace of HIV and AIDS, teens are endangered by an unprecedented epidemic of sexually transmitted diseases (STDs).

© JIST Works

Mr. Jackson is discussing safe driving with Nancy because accidents are the number-one killer of children in America. What should parents do to make certain their teenage sons or daughters will drive safely?

TAKE NOTE

According to the Centers for Disease Control and the U.S. Department of Health and Human Services, the smoking of tobacco products is the most preventable cause of death in the United States. More adult Americans die from cigarette-related illnesses than from alcohol, car accidents, suicide, AIDS, homicide, and illegal drugs combined. Smokers also are more likely than nonsmokers to develop heart disease, emphysema, and stroke.

- The number of Americans who die from diseases caused by smoking continues to increase.
- Skin cancer strikes more than 1 percent of Americans. Ultraviolet rays from the sun are the chief villain. Tanning salons are another source of ultraviolet rays.

If you believe that safety is something other people should practice, keep in mind that the number-one killer of children in America is not drugs or disease—it is accidents. You can prevent accidents by following safety guidelines such as wearing helmets and other appropriate safety gear when participating in sports. Likewise, you can reduce your risk of getting certain diseases by putting on sunscreen when you spend time outside or not smoking.

Mental Health

Do you consider yourself a competent person? Are you loved and/or well liked by most people? Do you usually get along well with people? If you truthfully answer yes to these questions, you probably have good mental health.

People with good mental health have personal and career problems just as people with poor mental health do. In fact, they probably face more problems because they tend to be more involved in all aspects of life. However, people with good mental health find it easier to handle the everyday changes and challenges of life.

A person needs professional help when family relationships, financial difficulties, substance abuse, or career problems reach the point where they control that person's life in a harmful way. Professionals in the mental health field provide many types of assistance, ranging from personal counseling to treatment with specific drugs.

Case Study

Have students read the case study "Melinda Discovers Life Skills" in Chapter 19 of the *Preparing for Career Success Instructor's CD-ROM, Third Edition,* and discuss the "Critical Thinking" questions. Students can also complete the "Too Much Stress" worksheet in Chapter 19 of the *Preparing for Career Success Student Activity Book, Third Edition.*

Student Evaluation

To evaluate student mastery of concepts, you might want to use the Section 1 quiz found in the Chapter 19 file of the *Preparing for Career Success Instructor's CD-ROM, Third Edition.*

Section 1: Get Involved

Answer the following on a separate sheet of paper, and be prepared to discuss your responses in class.

1. For one week, keep a daily record of the food you eat. Are you eating plenty of fruits, vegetables, and whole grains? How many calories do you eat on a daily basis?
2. Start a personal fitness program by making a list of the physical activities you presently enjoy and those you think you might enjoy. Decide which activities on the list you would most likely continue on a regular basis. Develop a schedule that includes physical activity at least three times a week. Then follow this schedule for at least two months. Be sure to include the four components of physical fitness identified by the President's Council on Physical Fitness.
3. Do you believe that some people are accident prone because of carelessness or because the problem is beyond their control? Explain your answer.

Discussion Starter

Ask your students: How would you determine whether an illness were serious enough to see a doctor? What would you do if your parent or guardian were ill?

Section 2: Medical Care and Health Insurance

Despite the human body's natural lines of defense against disease, illness still strikes. When this happens, you need the care of a physician. Sometimes this care involves multiple office visits, prescriptions, diagnostic work such as blood tests and X rays, and, in serious instances, hospital stays. As a result, health care can become very expensive. That's why you need health insurance.

Key To Success

Employers know that healthy, fit employees are more productive and have better attendance. They also save the company money on medical insurance expenses.

Choosing Medical Care

Choosing the right doctor is one of the most important decisions you will make for your physical well-being. Your doctor is the one who will advise and explain to you options about your medical treatment, medicines you will use, tests you may need, and surgical procedures that may be necessary. A wise doctor realizes his or her limitations and will tell you whether you need to see a specialist.

Take Note

When the patent of a brand-name drug expires, generic versions of the drug are approved for sale. The generic version works like the brand-name drug in dosage, strength, performance, and use, and must meet the same quality and safety standards. When you need a prescription, ask your physician whether a generic drug is available. Generics are less expensive than brand-name drugs.

Good medical care is a partnership between patient and doctor. It is very important to find a doctor whom you feel comfortable talking with about your health problems and who will take the time to explain anything you do not understand. If you are seeking a doctor, good sources of recommendations are family, friends, coworkers, the hospital you prefer, and the local medical society. The hospital or medical society can give you the names of local doctors, their educational backgrounds and training, the number of years they have been in practice, their specialty areas, and their office locations. Your *primary care physician* is usually an *internist* or *family practitioner* who treats a wide range of problems. After you have a list of potential physicians, call the office of those you believe most closely fit your criteria. Questions to ask include

- Will the doctor allow an interview? If so, what is the fee? A face-to-face interview will reveal the physician's personality, medical style, and communication skills.

© JIST Works

- Is the doctor board-certified? If so, the doctor is highly trained in his or her field.
- What are the fees for routine office visits?
- Will the doctor accept your health insurance?
- Is payment due at the time of the visit, or will the office bill your insurer?
- Will the hospital used by the doctor accept your health insurance?

Preparing for the Physical Examination

Some people schedule their yearly physical checkup during the month of their birthday. This type of memory jogger is a good health habit. When you schedule your first appointment with a new physician, do the following:

- Emphasize that you want an annual physical.
- Be prepared to discuss your health history in detail.
- Ask whether the doctor will be doing lab work and whether you should do anything to prepare for the appointment.
- Transfer your medical records from your previous physician before your appointment.
- Bring a list of any prescribed or over-the-counter medications you use.

Some diseases are hereditary. Your checkup will include questions about the medical problems of your relatives, particularly your parents, siblings, and grandparents. This information will provide your physician with necessary information to treat you.

A visit to the doctor's office is not the time to be modest or dishonest about your lifestyle. Information about a drug or alcohol habit, a suspicious physical or mental condition, or safe sex can be critical to your well-being. Allowing your physician to be a fully informed partner in your health care will assure the best possible treatment should you become ill, need surgery, or require the services of a specialist.

Taking Medication

Pharmacists dispense more than two billion prescriptions a year, but up to half of the people do not use them as prescribed. To help prevent medicine misuse, health professionals now voluntarily distribute leaflets that give patients more and better information about their prescription drugs.

Medicine can help you feel better and even save your life. However, how you use a specific medicine makes a big difference in how effective and safe it will be for you. Timing, what you eat and when you eat, proper dosage, and many other factors can cause you to feel better, stay the same, or feel worse. When your doctor prescribes medication, take it correctly;

Key To Success

When your doctor prescribes treatment, follow his or her instructions exactly and use your medicines as directed. If the doctor asks you to phone after a few days or to return within a certain time frame for a checkup, do as requested.

Find Out More

The Medical Information Bureau (MIB) is a database that insurance companies use. Medical information about you is collected from insurers and is available to insurance companies when you apply for individual life, health, or disability insurance. You can obtain a copy of your file by contacting the MIB online. Using your search engine, key in **Medical Information Bureau.**

Community Resources

Identify a small group of students who have been treated in hospitals several times. On a volunteer basis only, ask them to write individual letters, including a signed authorization from their parent or guardian, to request a copy of their Medical Information Bureau (MIB) files. Have the group report their success (or failure) and share any data they receive. You may also wish to obtain a copy of your MIB file. As an adult, you are more likely to be successful.

otherwise, you might put your health and life at risk. The most skillful physician cannot cure a patient who refuses to be a responsible partner in the healing process.

The following rules will help you use medicine in a responsible manner:

- Avoid dangerous drug interactions. If your physician prescribes medication, alert him or her to any prescription or nonprescription drugs that you take on a regular basis.
- Let your doctor know if you are allergic to any medication.
- Report any unexpected symptoms (such as a rash, dizziness, or a headache) to your doctor.
- Never use someone else's prescription medication, and never allow another person to use yours.
- Do not store a drug where children can find it. If you no longer need a drug, flush leftovers down the toilet.

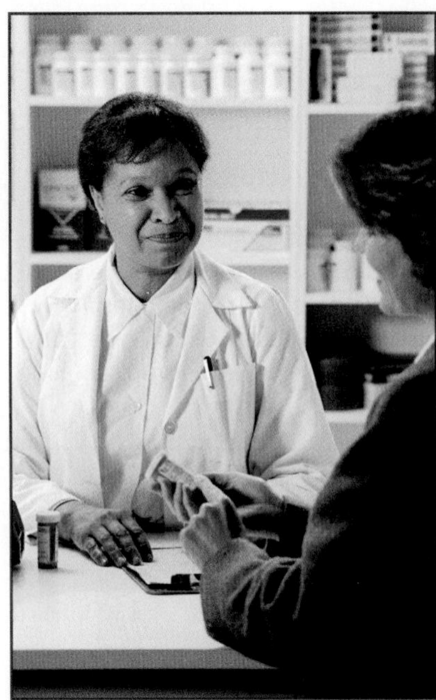

Mrs. Huddleston always discusses the use and purpose of any new medications prescribed to Gloria by her family physician. Why is sharing this information important?

TAKE NOTE

Health Occupations Students of America (HOSA) is a career and technical student organization for students who are interested in medicine, nursing, dentistry, and other health-related careers. This organization focuses on helping students expand their knowledge of health care and develop their leadership, problem-solving, and social skills. Contact your local chapter or the Web site, www.hosa.org, for more information.

Reteaching

Have students complete the "Insurance Check" worksheet in Chapter 19 of the *Preparing for Career Success Instructor's CD-ROM, Third Edition.*

Buying Health Insurance

If you wish to purchase health insurance and a group plan is not available through your job, work out a budget that allows you to self-insure for part of your health care. For example, you may want to self-insure for routine doctor and dental visits by maintaining a special savings account that can earn interest. When you need money to pay for doctor or dental visits, it would come from your savings account instead of from your insurance company. You would save the cost of premiums for routine medical care and buy insurance only against unexpected, high-cost health services. Self-insuring, though, requires a great deal of self-discipline. You need to pay your account a set amount from each paycheck and not use the account for anything other than health care.

You can purchase health insurance to pay expenses for physical examinations and tests, optical and dental work, preventive care, and treatments for physical and mental illnesses. Policies can include any or all of the following coverages (review Chapter 12 regarding medical benefits provided by employers):

1. **Hospitalization insurance** covers hospital room and board, medication, tests, and services.
2. **Surgical insurance** covers specific expenses related to specific operations.
3. *Medical insurance* covers visits to the doctor's office and diagnostic laboratory tests.
4. *Major medical insurance* covers expenses that exceed the dollar limit of the basic coverage.
5. *Comprehensive coverage* includes all of the above.

© JIST Works

6. *Dental insurance* covers most dental expenses.
7. *Prescription coverage* pays for prescribed medication.

Some health insurance policies cover several health services but require large copayments from the policyholder. Others provide less coverage but require little or no copayment. When you shop for health insurance, compare the cost, coverage received, service provided, and business reputation of each insurer.

Do not be pressured to purchase a policy until you have read it carefully and checked out the carrier's financial rating. When you decide on a policy, complete the application carefully. Incomplete applications give the insurer a reason to deny a claim. Be certain that you understand what coverage you will receive before you sign the application. Your policy should arrive within 30 days. If it does not arrive, contact your salesperson for an explanation. If 60 days go by without information, contact your state insurance department.

Cooperative Learning

Divide your class into learning pairs. Allow six minutes for each pair to review the seven types of health insurance, and answer these questions: If you could purchase two of the seven types of health insurance listed, which two would you purchase? Why? Have each learning pair report their answers and reasons to the class.

Discussion Starter

Some people find it difficult or impossible to purchase insurance of any kind because of a chronic, incurable health problem. How might insurance companies or the government help people in this situation?

Section 2: Get Involved

Answer the following on a separate sheet of paper, and be prepared to discuss your responses in class.

1. Imagine that you have moved to a new town and need to visit a doctor. Write a brief medical history of yourself to give to the doctor.
2. Interview parents, aunts, uncles, and grandparents, and list the serious illnesses that they have experienced. Do any of these illnesses tend to run in families? If so, list them to share with your physician. What lifestyle changes could you make to improve your chances of avoiding these illnesses?

Section 3: Substance Abuse

A **drug** is any chemical substance that brings about physical, emotional, or mental changes in people. This same definition applies to the words *medicine* and *medication.* When the use of a drug causes physical, mental, emotional, or social harm to the user or to others, it is considered **drug abuse**.

Consider the following statistics about substance abuse:

- More than 8 percent of the population over 12 years of age have used drugs within the past 30 days. Rates of use remain highest among persons between the ages of 16 and 25—the age group entering the workforce most rapidly.
- More than 14 percent of Americans employed full- and part-time report heavy drinking (five or more drinks on 5 or more days in the past 30 days). The heaviest drinking occurred among persons between the ages of 18 and 25 years.
- Alcoholism causes 500 million lost workdays each year.

Comprehension Check

Ask several students: What is the difference between a drug and a medicine? (All medicines are drugs by definition; however, not all drugs are medicines.) Is alcohol a drug or a medicine when it is used alone as a beverage? Why? When alcohol is in cough syrup, is it a drug or a medicine? Why?

Find Out More

Using your search engine, key in **The National Institute on Drug Abuse**, or go online at www.nida.nih.gov.

© JIST Works

Reteaching

Have students complete the "The Truth About Substance Abuse" worksheet found in the Chapter 19 file of the *Preparing for Career Success Instructor's CD-ROM, Third Edition.*

- Construction workers; sales personnel; food preparers, wait staff, and bartenders; handlers, helpers, and laborers; and machine operators and inspectors reported the highest rates of current illicit drug use. (Protective service workers reported the lowest rate of current drug use.)

Studies reveal that employees who abuse drugs have a tremendously harmful effect on the workplace. They are more likely to have extended absences, show up late, be involved in workplace accidents, and file workers' compensation claims.

Take Note

It is illegal to use, possess, sell, or distribute drugs of abuse at the workplace. In many companies, employees' lockers, desks, files, vehicles, and personal belongings on company property are subject to search, based on management's reasonable suspicion of illegal drug or alcohol activity or use. Some employers also report suspected or known illegal drug activity to the appropriate law enforcement agency.

"If you want to be on the payroll, you have to pass the test" is the position many companies and government agencies have taken with prospective and current employees. Many companies require employees to accept random drug and alcohol testing as a condition of employment. Several large organizations test all prospective hires for drug use. Many transportation companies are **mandated** (required) by state and federal laws to test job applicants as well as employees for drugs.

In most organizations, reporting to work or working under the influence of alcohol or illegal drugs is unacceptable and cause for dismissal. Engaging in off-duty, unlawful involvement with alcohol or drugs is also unacceptable to most employers. In addition, concealing knowledge of another employee's illegal involvement with drugs or alcohol-related behavior is unacceptable.

Most employers believe that employees deserve a workplace that is safe and free from the dangers of drug or alcohol-induced behavior. Most employees feel the same way. Both groups know that chemically dependent employees can affect the morale and safety of other employees.

These facts suggest that workplace substance abuse is an issue all employers need to address. Taking steps to raise awareness among employees about the impact of substance use on workplace performance and offering the appropriate resources and assistance to employees in need will improve worker safety and health. It will also increase workplace productivity and market competitiveness.

Signs of a Substance Abuser

How can you recognize a chemically dependent person? Thousands of employers, supervisors, relatives, and friends face this tough question every day. You may be one of them. Symptoms of chemical dependency at school or work include lower-than-usual productivity or grades, poor attitude, lack of motivation, disinterest, and a high rate of absenteeism and tardiness.

Discussion Starter

Explain to students that parenting and marital problems, financial difficulty, work conflicts, and emotional stress are frequently related to drug and alcohol abuse. Ask your students: What causes a youth to become a drug abuser? What causes a youth to quit abusing drugs?

Physical symptoms may be as obvious as staggering and stumbling, glassy or bloodshot eyes, slurred speech, frequent physical complaints or injuries, poor hygiene, and signs of fatigue, such as sleeping on the job. The most dangerous physical symptom is a state of unconsciousness. If you discover an unconscious person, get immediate medical attention by phoning 911, an ambulance, or a physician.

© JIST Works

Do not jump to conclusions when someone displays the symptoms of drug abuse. Keep in mind that a person suffering from a personal problem, a physical illness, or a reaction to medication might display similar symptoms. However, when people exhibit sudden, negative changes in their behavior, for whatever reason, these changes should be a matter of concern.

Disciplinary problems with drug abusers in the workplace are very similar to disciplinary problems with drug abusers in schools. Offenses include stealing, assaulting coworkers, vandalizing the facility, carrying weapons, being defiant to coworkers and management, breaking rules, failing to perform work tasks, blaming others, using obscene language and gestures, cheating, and lying. In addition, drug abusers commonly obtain money for their habits by selling drugs at work or school.

On the other hand, many drug abusers come to work or school depressed and withdrawn. When privately confronted by an employer, counselor, or principal, the abusers commonly break down into crying spells and describe existing situations and future expectations in an unrealistic manner.

Career Fact

Many firms have employee assistance programs that attempt to identify and provide treatment to workers with drug and alcohol problems before the addiction becomes a hindrance to health, family life, or the job.

Discussion Starter

Ask your students these questions: What can you do when pressured to use drugs of abuse? What are the legal consequences of drug abuse in your state? What are the penalties for driving under the influence of alcohol or drugs? Why is an effective decision-making process so important?

Substance Abuse and Teens

The one source from which virtually all forms of substance abuse among teens arise is the peer subculture. The peer group is especially critical with respect to a teenager's decision to use drugs or alcohol. The use of illicit substances is one means of gaining status and acceptance among peers in schools and neighborhoods. For many, drug experimentation is a way of establishing friends and developing and testing emerging social skills. Drinking and drug use can create illusions of power and competency. Those lacking self-confidence consider substance use as valuable in overcoming inadequacies.

To begin, the teenager must know someone who is a user who will provide the drugs. During the first episodes, the novice learns how to acquire drugs, consume them in correct amounts, and recognize the stages of becoming "high." The user views the drug activity as merely another form of recreation. Refusal to partake is considered cowardice. Thus, peer pressure compels adolescents to become involved in drug and alcohol consumption.

As Gwynn's school counselor, Mrs. Griffin provides her with an opportunity to express her feelings and thoughts without criticism. How does this exchange help Gwynn build the self-confidence needed to avoid substance abuse?

Effective decision making, self-confidence, and a positive attitude toward other people and life situations play an important role in avoiding

© JIST Works

Cooperative Learning/Enrichment

Have students complete the "Refusal Skills Refresher" and the "My Friend Joey" worksheets in Chapter 19 of the *Preparing for Career Success Instructor's CD-ROM, Third Edition.*

TAKE NOTE

According to the National Center on Addiction and Substance Abuse at Columbia University, parents are the single most important influence on their children's decision to smoke, drink, or use drugs.

the temptation to abuse drugs. Unfortunately, some people are unhappy with their lives, are poor decision makers, lack confidence, and display negative attitudes. In other words, they have very low self-esteem. Building self-esteem requires assistance from other people. Here are some ways that you can help another person build self-esteem:

- Be tolerant of mistakes. Provide help and encouragement rather than criticism.
- Provide opportunities for others to express their feelings and thoughts without criticism.
- Be certain that rules and discipline are fair and consistent.
- Offer love, affection, and attention.
- Provide opportunities for successful and exciting experiences.
- Be an honest, moral, thoughtful role model.
- Teach them an effective decision-making process (see Chapter 4).

Section 3: Get Involved

Answer the following on a separate sheet of paper, and be prepared to discuss your responses in class.

1. Using each of the seven tips given in the "Substance Abuse and Teens" section as a guide, explain how parents, friends, relatives, school personnel, employers, and coworkers could help a person build self-esteem.
2. Which of the seven ways to build self-esteem would you consider most important in preventing drug abuse? Why? Which would you consider least important? Why?

CAREER FACT

More than 5,700 workers died in job-related accidents in 2006. More than 4 million lost time because of job-related injuries and illnesses. On average, 65 teenagers die on the job annually, 79,000 receive emergency room treatment, and 140,000 are injured but do not go to a hospital.

Comprehension Check

After your students have finished reading "Accident Prevention," ask them to close their books. Ask your students: Why are workers with a poor attitude toward safety more likely to be involved in accidents? Next, ask your students to draw on their personal experience for an example of any type of accident that was caused by a person's irresponsible behavior or anger.

Section 4: Health and Safety in the Workplace

If you are unable to earn a living because of an accident or a health problem, the outcome will be the same: Your career and your lifestyle will be disrupted. Do you know anyone who has had a job-related accident? What effect did the accident have on his or her career and lifestyle? Many of the factors involved in personal health and safety can be controlled if you understand the potential hazards, learn safe ways to perform tasks, and apply what you know in hazardous situations.

Accident Prevention

Most people are familiar with the old saying "An ounce of prevention is worth a pound of cure." This is certainly true when you consider that the majority of accidents in the workplace are due to human, rather than work-site, causes. In particular, worker experience is involved in more job-related accidents than any other single factor.

© JIST Works

A major study by the Bureau of Labor Statistics reported that 48 percent of injured workers had been on the job less than one year. Another study showed that employees who are injured at work often lack information to protect themselves. In nearly every type of injury studied, the story was the same: Workers often do not receive the safety information they need, even on jobs involving dangerous equipment.

Workers with a poor attitude toward safety are more likely to be involved in accidents. They are usually irresponsible and often quick to anger. Both of these personal characteristics are dangerous in the workplace.

Worker fatigue (exhaustion) can also be a factor in accidents. Fatigue can be caused by not getting enough sleep, working extra long shifts, or suffering from poor health. As stated in the last section, substance abuse by workers also increases the number of accidents in the workplace.

The Occupational Safety and Health Act, passed by Congress in 1970 ensures, as far as possible, safe working conditions for the labor force. This federal law requires every American employer to provide a safe and healthful workplace. To carry out this law, the **Occupational Safety and Health Administration (OSHA)** encourages employers to work with employees to eliminate job safety and health hazards.

With offices throughout the nation, more than 1,100 OSHA inspectors respond to complaints and conduct thousands of random and scheduled workplace inspections annually. When OSHA inspectors find health and safety violations, employers must correct those hazards within fixed time limits and may have to pay fines.

More than 600,000 people a year miss at least one day of work due to injuries from repetitive stretching, bending, or typing. In 2000, OSHA detailed ergonomic standards for everything from how much employees should type or use a mouse in a day to how many pounds they should lift. OSHA has defined repetitive stress as a hazard and ordered employers to take corrective measures. The rules cover workers not employed in agriculture, construction, railroads, or maritime industries. OSHA claims the long-term savings from fewer worker injuries offset the up-front costs employers incur to alter machinery or work practices.

OSHA requires manufacturers to inform their employees about exposure to hazardous chemicals in the workplace. Numerous cities and states have enacted similar laws. The National Labor Relations Board also has ruled that the names of chemicals and other substances in the workplace be given to unions if requested.

Self-Understanding

Send a writer to the chalkboard to list the titles of occupations they are considering for their future careers. Ask various class members to answer this question for each occupation listed: What possible accidents, opportunities for theft, or loss of production to the employer could be caused by a worker in this occupation using drugs or alcohol in the workplace?

Career Fact

Alcohol is the drug most frequently involved in work-related fatalities.

Discussion Starter

Explain that employers frequently criticize OSHA for being overly restrictive and expensive. Ask your students: If you were a member of Congress, would you be in favor of reducing the power of OSHA to enforce laws that ensure safe working conditions? Why or why not?

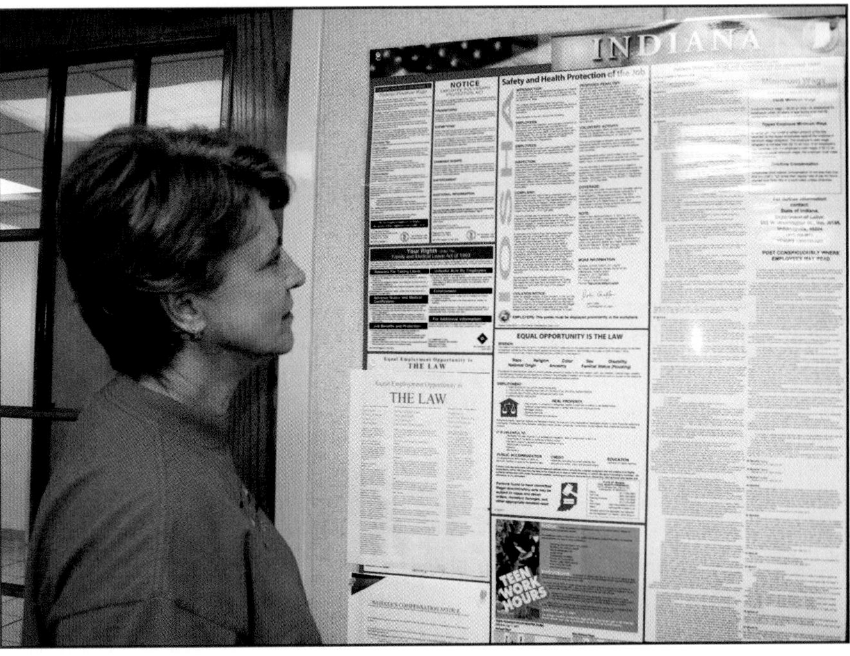

Do you understand the rights and responsibilities of employers and workers? Employers are required to post certain government notices regarding health, safety, and other workplace issues.

Career Fact

Since 1971, OSHA has helped to cut workplace fatalities by more than 62 percent and occupational injury and illness rates by 42 percent. At the same time, the U.S. workforce has more than doubled from 56 million workers at 3.5 million worksites to more than 135 million workers at 8.9 million worksites. The number of injuries and fatalities in the workplace is at its lowest point ever.

Find Out More

If you are concerned about the health effects of exposure to a particular substance or working condition, request a health hazard evaluation of your workplace by the National Institute for Occupational Safety and Health (NIOSH).

Key To Success

Be sure you understand all necessary safety measures before you start a work task. If the explanation is unclear, ask again.

If you believe unsafe or unhealthful conditions exist at your workplace, you have the right to file a complaint. OSHA will withhold the names of complainants on request. If you are discharged or discriminated against for exercising your rights under this law, you may file a discrimination complaint with OSHA within 30 days of the discriminatory action.

Solving the Problem: A Healthy Choice?

John Dent's headache is worse than usual as he steps into the hot shower after his shift. The fumes from the *adhesive* (glue) that he paints on the seam of each piece of fabric passing him on the production line always seem to give him a headache. His employer, Sampson Manufacturing, is a very old company with outdated equipment, but the work is steady and the pay is good. John had mentioned the problem about the fumes to the supervisor before, but the supervisor quickly told him to quit if he did not like his job. His union representative told him that Mr. Sampson had threatened to shut down the plant the last time the workers complained about health and safety conditions.

Many thoughts go through John's mind as he dresses to go home. Should he report the problem to a safety agency like OSHA? The address is on the employee bulletin board. Should he bring up the issue at the next union meeting? Maybe the union representatives will think he is a wimp. Should he look for a new job? He cannot take many more of these headaches.

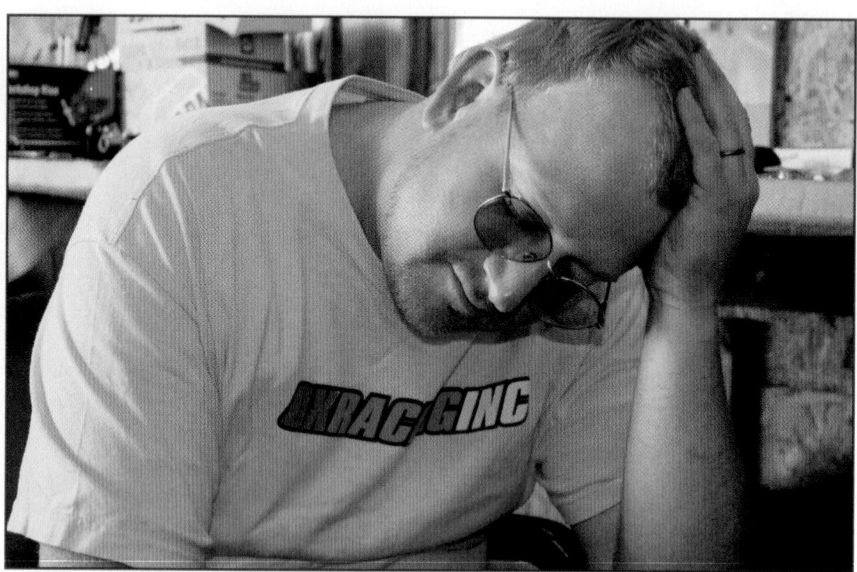

Critical Thinking

How can John be sure that his health and safety are in jeopardy?

If John decides to report the problem, will Mr. Sampson really shut down the plant? Explain your answer.

How would you answer the questions on John's mind?

© JIST Works

Workplace Violence

Every time violence occurs in a workplace, executives want to know how to prevent the same disaster from happening to their organization. The fear of another terrorist attack like that on September 11, 2001, on the World Trade Center or a bioterrorism attack on the workplace has increased anxiety and uncertainty about safety and security. Across the country, crisis management teams have worked to respond effectively to terrorist attacks.

The fear of violence and other criminal behavior such as theft, sabotage, and possible terrorism has caused an increase in workplace security. Most employers currently use surveillance, including video cameras, e-mail monitoring programs, and phone-call tracking systems to alert them to potential problems. To avoid privacy issues, companies notify employees that they might inspect lockers, scan e-mail, monitor Internet use, and listen to telephone conversations.

Workplace homicides totaled 516 in 2006. This total was the lowest ever reported by the fatality census. The high was in 1994, which saw 1,080 workplace homicides. The majority of workplace homicides are robbery-related crimes, with only 9 percent committed by coworkers or former coworkers. Additionally, 76 percent of all workplace homicides are committed with a firearm.

Workers should not try to apprehend criminals or to defend the workplace during a robbery. The safest course of action is to leave this task to professional law enforcement officers. Criminals are often inexperienced and frightened and/or using alcohol or drugs. They are quick to use a knife or gun if they feel threatened by a worker or if they suspect a worker is trying to remember what they look like.

Read the following suggestions. Which would be the most difficult for you to do? Which would be the easiest?

1. Don't maintain direct eye contact with robbers. They will assume that you are trying to form a description of them for the police.
2. Do try to determine the sex, height, weight, race, and any speech accent of the robbers with very short glances and by careful listening.
3. Don't resist the robbers in the name of courage.
4. Do give them what they ask for. Be cooperative.
5. Do not follow the robbers out the door.
6. Do try to identify the type, age, and color of the robbers' car, which way it is parked (which could indicate where they came from), and which way they go—if you can do so without exposing yourself to danger. Any license numbers you see will help.

TAKE NOTE

An important component for preventing workplace violence is early recognition of workers who are contemplating violent acts; indicators are abusive language leading to hostile behavior, concealed weapons, sabotage, and contraband.

Community Relations

Form a committee of students to invite a local law enforcement officer to discuss the subject of violent crime in the workplace. Assign the committee to make a list of questions, and mail them to the speaker before his or her class visit.

CAREER FACT

Every week, 18,000 workers become victims of nonfatal assaults in their workplace. Most nonfatal workplace assaults occur in service settings such as hospitals, nursing homes, and social service agencies. Nonfatal workplace assaults result in nearly a million lost workdays every year.

Stress as a Job Hazard

Stress (mental or physical tension or strain) can cause physical and emotional illness that affects work and home life. Stress puts special negative

Career Fact

The 10 most stressful jobs in the United States are high school teacher (urban), securities/commodities sales agent, police officer, journalist, mine worker, customer service representative, air traffic controller, waiter/waitress, physician intern, and administrative assistant.

School-to-Work Transition

Invite the school counselor or school psychologist to visit your class to discuss specific ways to deal with personal stress. Ask him or her to present information about stress as it relates to students in school, adults at home, and workers on the job.

Discussion Starter

Ask students to review the list of stressful occupations in the sidebar, and have them identify an area of high stress for each occupation. Ask your students: Who would find this area of stress difficult to work with? Who would not find this type of stress difficult?

demands on the body's responses and emotions. Personal stress frequently occurs from wanting the environment we live in to be different but not having the ability to change it. Health problems such as ulcers, emotional exhaustion, high blood pressure, headaches, alcoholism, and even heart disease may result from job stress. Stress is a severe strain on personal endurance and feelings and is unique to each individual. Nearly 66 percent of companies with 750 or more employees have stress-control programs in effect because they realize the seriousness of the problem.

The following working conditions are typical of high-stress jobs:

- Chronic, unrelenting demands, such as an overbearing supervisor
- A rapid pace of work controlled by something other than the workers, such as a machine
- Constant high-risk safety concerns such as working with explosive gases or risking the loss of customers' lives if the product is flawed
- Conflicts with coworkers, such as harassment or opposing views on issues

The effects of job stress frequently spill over into other formerly pleasurable aspects of life, such as family and leisure time. When this happens, it is difficult to escape stress and get relief. Has anything at school ever caused you a great deal of stress? What effect did it have on you emotionally and physically?

Recognizing the early signs of stress and doing something to relieve it can have a dramatic impact on your personal well-being. One of the keys is to identify the situations and events that are causing the stress and then to work on solutions. Stress is so personal that what may be relaxing to one person may be stressful to another.

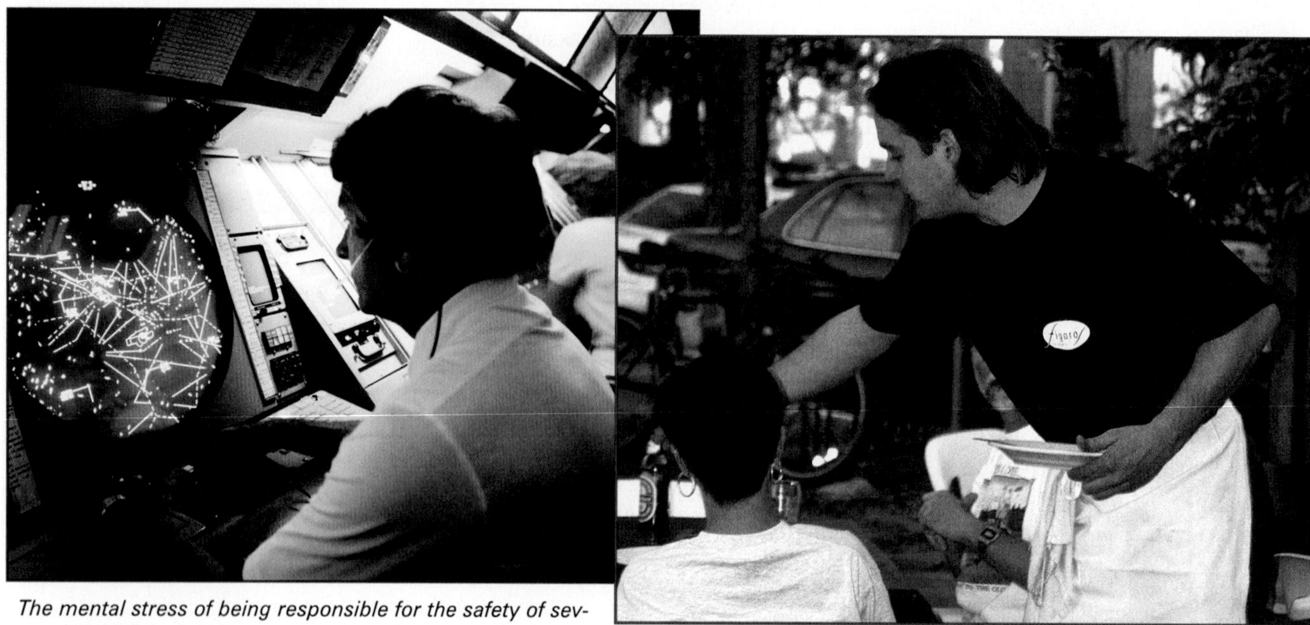

The mental stress of being responsible for the safety of several aircraft and their passengers can be exhausting for an air traffic controller. During busy dining periods, a waiter is under pressure to serve customers quickly and efficiently.

© JIST Works

Stress thrives on feelings and fears that we usually keep to ourselves, so talking about them can be helpful. Sharing stress through communication, knowing your limits, managing time efficiently, being assertive, taking short rest breaks, taking care of yourself through proper diet, and making time for fun relieve stress for most people. How does stress affect you? What do you do to reduce personal stress?

TAKE NOTE

Humor is gaining a reputation as the do-it-yourself wonder drug. Humor has demonstrated its ability to dispel anger and aggression and help people cope with anxiety and stress. Laughter is exercise that increases the heart rate and stimulates circulation, works the diaphragm and abdominal wall, and increases production of hormones that trigger the release of endorphins, the body's natural painkillers. Laughter is like a pressure valve for stress, anger, and emotional pain.

Teens and Family Stress

Your teen years bring new types of stress to you and other family members. The parent-child relationship is rapidly changing to a parent-daughter or parent-son relationship. As a result, all family members see a dramatic change in their roles, rights, and responsibilities. You and your parents or guardians will experience stress through feelings, fears, tensions, and misunderstandings. It is important for all family members to recognize the stress and overcome it together.

To assess your situation, answer the following questions honestly, and ask each member of your family to answer the same questions. Record the number of yes and no answers for each family member.

1. Do you spend less time with your family than you would like? If yes, why?
2. Do you want to see things from your parents' (son's or daughter's) point of view?
3. How do you respond to being criticized, lectured, or uninformed within the family?
4. Do you argue with members of your family?
5. Do you compliment, thank, or say "I love you" to other family members? If so, when was the last occasion? If not, why not?
6. Do you try to understand the stress experienced by other family members from their schoolwork, careers, and other problems?
7. Are you considerate of other family members' financial resources?
8. Do you assist with cleaning, cooking, and other family responsibilities?
9. Are you satisfied with the understanding and appreciation you receive from other family members?
10. Do you demonstrate the understanding and appreciation you feel toward other family members?

KEY TO SUCCESS

Exercise is a very effective way to deal with stress. Physical activity helps bring the body back to a normal hormone balance. It relieves pent-up tensions and stretches tight muscles. Exercise also releases endorphins, which are special hormones that promote a sense of well-being.

© JIST Works

Section 4: Get Involved

Answer the following on a separate sheet of paper, and be prepared to discuss your responses in class:

1. Imagine that you are an employer and that you are starting a "safe-lifting" training program for your employees to prevent back injuries. You plan to include workers from manufacturing, office, cafeteria, and warehouse areas. Employees will vary in their age, gender, body size, state of health, and general physical fitness. Write a paragraph describing the activities you would include in your program.
2. Review your answers to the 10 stress questions on the preceding page. Which of your answers could cause an increase in family stress? Which of your answers could cause a lowering of family stress? Have each family member who answered the questions discuss their responses with each other openly and honestly.

Reteaching

Have students complete the "Finding the Right Words" and "Checking Your Location" worksheets in Chapter 19 of the *Preparing for Career Success Student Activity Book, Third Edition.*

Enrich Your Vocabulary Answers

1. hospitalization insurance
2. surgical insurance
3. mandated
4. Occupational Safety and Health Administration (OSHA)
5. drug
6. calorie
7. Recommended Daily Allowances (RDAs)
8. cardiorespiratory endurance
9. muscular strength
10. flexibility
11. diet
12. stress
13. muscular endurance

(continued)

Chapter 19 Review

Enrich Your Vocabulary

On a separate sheet of paper, number from 1 to 16, and write the term from the "Enrich Your Vocabulary" list at the beginning of the chapter next to the number of the statement it matches.

1. Insurance that covers hospital room and board, medication, tests, and services
2. Insurance that covers specific expenses related to specific operations
3. Required
4. A government agency responsible for safety and health in the workplace
5. Any chemical substance that brings about physical, emotional, or mental changes in people
6. The amount of heat needed to raise the temperature of one gram of water one degree centigrade
7. Nutritional standards for different age, sex, and weight groups
8. The ability to deliver oxygen and nutrients to tissues and to remove wastes
9. The ability of a muscle to exert force for a brief period of time
10. The ability to move joints and use muscles through their full range of motion
11. The food and drink a person customarily consumes
12. Mental or physical tension
13. The ability of a muscle or a group of muscles to sustain repeated contractions or to continue applying force against a fixed object

© JIST Works

14. The use, legal or illegal, of a drug that causes physical, mental, emotional, or social harm to the user or to others
15. Nourishment
16. With oxygen

Check Your Knowledge

On a separate sheet of paper, complete the following activities.

1. List six of the good health habits that are related to a wellness-oriented lifestyle.
2. What are the suggested calorie intakes for most teenage girls and for most teenage boys?
3. What is the most important rule for a diet?
4. State at least two reasons for choosing a diet with plenty of vegetables, fruits, and grain products.
5. List five types of information about local physicians you can obtain from a local hospital or medical association.
6. Review the rules for using medicine responsibly. Select three of these rules, and explain the consequences of breaking each of them.
7. When you shop for health insurance, what four items should you compare?
8. How might you recognize that a person is suffering from mental illness?
9. Why do more and more companies require employees to accept random drug and alcohol testing as a condition of employment?
10. What specific steps have employers taken to improve workplace security?

Develop SCANS Competencies

This activity will give you practice in developing the information, interpersonal, and systems skills that successful workers use. Conduct a safety inspection at your home. Develop a chart that lists all rooms of your home. Then inspect each room for any potential safety hazards. You might look for such things as heavy items a younger brother or sister could pull off a shelf, dangerous chemicals or medicines that are stored where a child might get them, and steps or railings that need to be repaired. After you complete your inspection, try to find possible solutions. Then discuss any unsafe situations with your parents or guardians or possibly with the property owner.

Enrich Your Vocabulary Answers *(continued)*

14. drug abuse
15. nutrients
16. aerobic

Check Your Knowledge Answers

1. The introduction to this chapter lists nine good health habits.
2. For most girls, 2,200 calories; for most boys, 2,800 calories.
3. To eat sufficient food to supply the body's energy needs and to eat a varied diet to supply the necessary nutrients for the body's growth and functioning.
4. They provide needed vitamins, minerals, fiber, and complex carbohydrates and can help you lower your intake of fat.
5. Names of local doctors, their educational backgrounds, years in practice, specialty areas, and office locations.
6. Answers will vary. See Section 2, "Medical Care and Health Insurance."
7. (1) The cost of the policy, (2) the coverage received, (3) the service provided, (4) the insurer's business reputation.
8. When a person loses the ability to view his or her life situations and surroundings as they really are and can no longer handle everyday problems.
9. Because of the problems associated with drug abuse in the workplace.
10. (1) Companies use surveillance, including video cameras, e-mail monitoring programs, and phone-call tracking systems. (2) To avoid privacy issues, companies notify employees that they might inspect lockers, scan e-mail, monitor Internet use, and listen to phone conversations.

Enrichment

Have students complete the Chapter 19 section of the *Preparing for Career Success Student Portfolio, Third Edition.*

Chapter 20 Resources

Lesson Plans and Preparation
Preparing for Career Success
Interactive Lesson Planner Plus Instructor's Resources on CD-ROM
Windows®/Macintosh®
978-1-59357-573-1
Duplication Prohibited
Third Edition
Interactive Lesson Planner and Resources
Chapter 20 Lesson Plan
Accepting Civic Responsibility
Lesson Plan

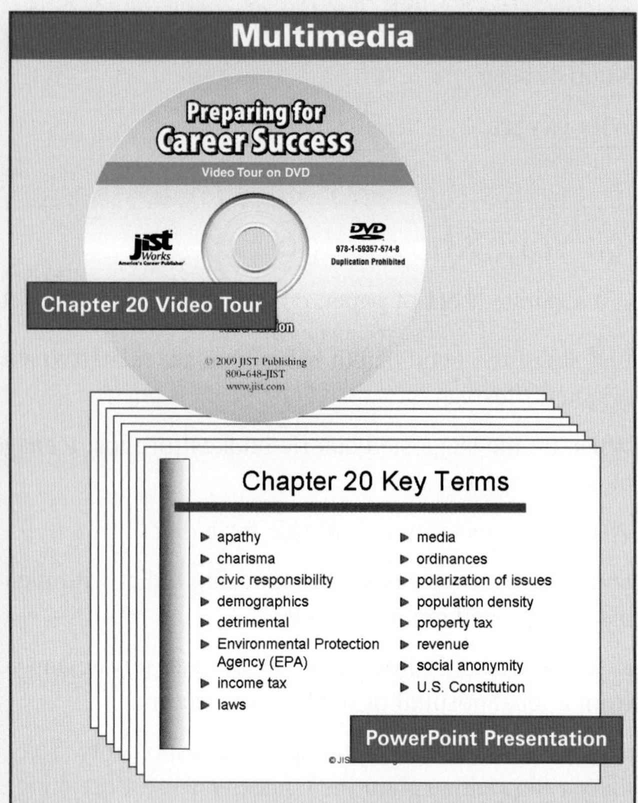

Multimedia
Preparing for Career Success
Video Tour on DVD
DVD
978-1-59357-574-8
Duplication Prohibited
Chapter 20 Video Tour
© 2009 JIST Publishing
800-648-JIST
www.jist.com
Chapter 20 Key Terms
apathy
charisma
civic responsibility
demographics
detrimental
Environmental Protection Agency (EPA)
income tax
laws
media
ordinances
polarization of issues
population density
property tax
revenue
social anonymity
U.S. Constitution
PowerPoint Presentation

Activities

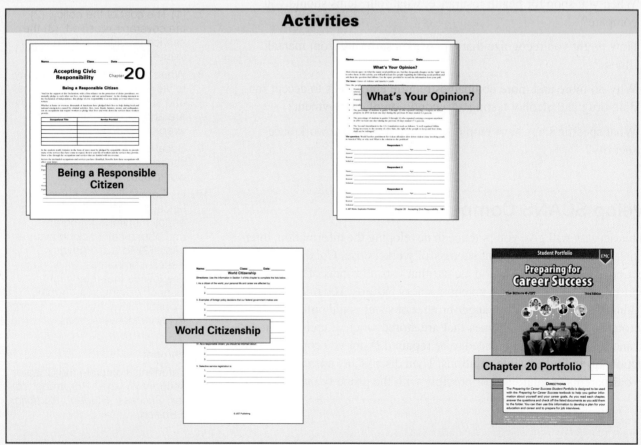

Accepting Civic Responsibility — Chapter 20

Being a Responsible Citizen

What's Your Opinion?

World Citizenship

Student Portfolio — Preparing for Career Success — Third Edition

Chapter 20 Portfolio

© JIST Works

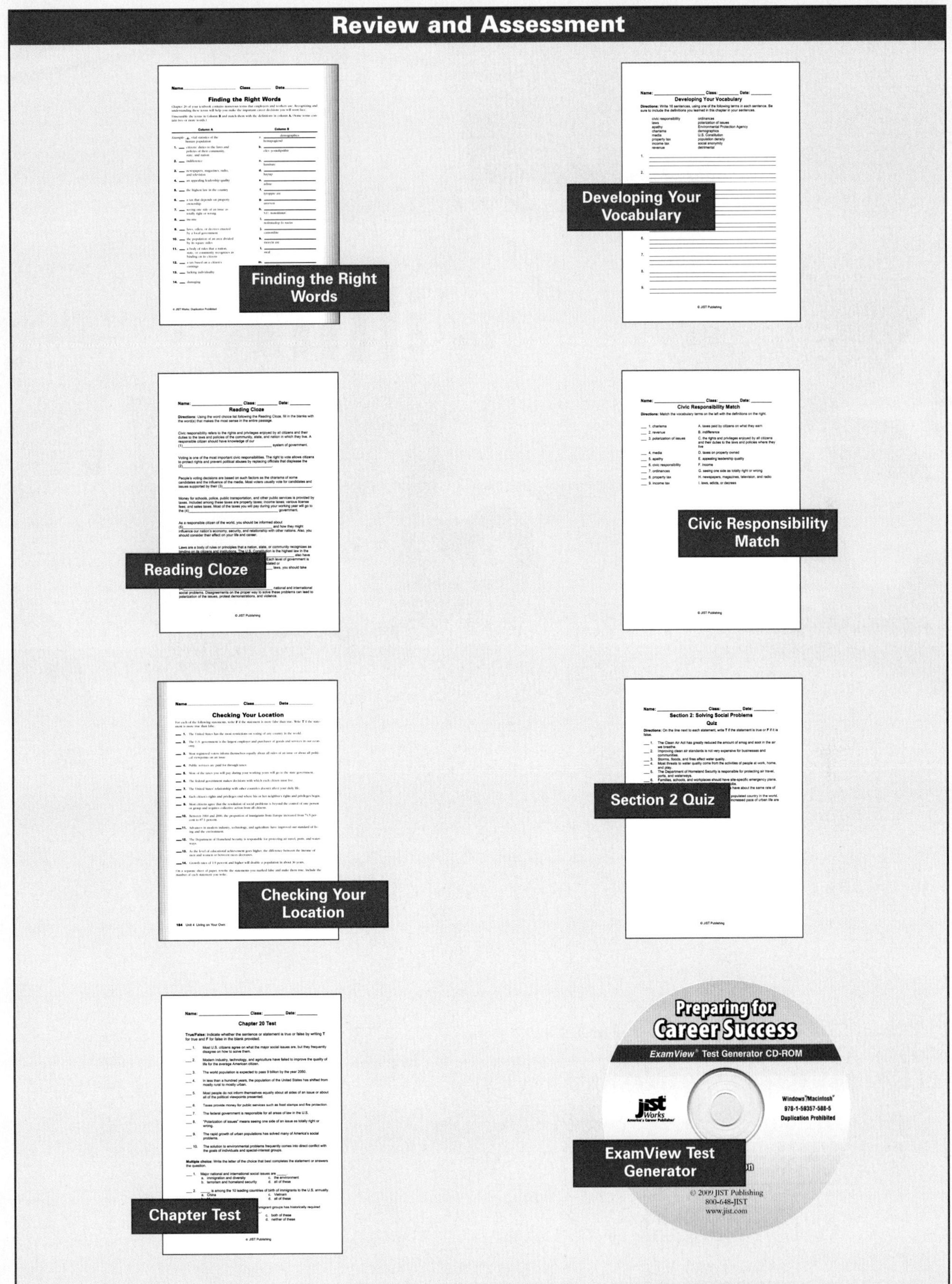

Review and Assessment
Finding the Right Words
Developing Your Vocabulary
Reading Cloze
Civic Responsibility Match
Checking Your Location
Section 2 Quiz
Chapter Test
Preparing for Career Success
ExamView® Test Generator CD-ROM
Windows®/Macintosh®
978-1-59357-588-5
Duplication Prohibited
© 2009 JIST Publishing
800-648-JIST
www.jist.com
ExamView Test Generator

NO TEL

Chapter 20 Accepting Civic Responsibility

Learning Objectives

- Explain why each citizen owes allegiance to the government of the United States and is accountable to local, state, and federal laws
- Explain why responsible citizenship requires a knowledge of the democratic system of government, a commitment of time, and a willingness to become involved in the affairs of government
- Provide examples illustrating how, as a citizen of the world, you are personally affected by the cooperation and conflict that take place between nations
- Identify several of our nation's social problems

"We in this country, in this generation, are—by destiny rather than choice—the watchmen on the walls of world freedom. We ask, therefore, that we may be worthy of our power and responsibility, that we may exercise our strength with wisdom and restraint, and that we may achieve in our time the ancient vision of peace on earth, goodwill toward men. That must always be our goal, and the righteousness of our cause must always underlie our strength. For as was written long ago: 'Except the Lord keep the city, the watchman waketh but in vain.'"

Enrich Your Vocabulary

In reading this chapter and doing the exercises, you will learn the following important terms:

apathy	income tax	population density
charisma	laws	property tax
civic responsibility	media	revenue
demographics	ordinances	social anonymity
detrimental	polarization of issues	U.S. Constitution
Environmental Protection Agency (EPA)		

Enrichment

Have students complete the "Being a Responsible Citizen" worksheet in Chapter 20 of the *Preparing for Career Success Student Activity Book, Third Edition.*

Video Tour on DVD

Show students the Chapter 20 segment to introduce them to the content.

This message from President John F. Kennedy was the final paragraph of the speech he was prepared to deliver in Dallas in 1963—the day he was assassinated. President Kennedy challenged the people of the United States to accept their civic responsibility as both American and world citizens.

Civic responsibility refers to the rights and privileges enjoyed by all citizens and their duties to the laws and policies of the community, state, and nation in which they live. Do you believe that increased civic responsibility by individuals can solve many of our nation's social problems? As you enjoy the rights and privileges of citizenship in your daily life, do you believe you have some responsibility for helping to solve the nation's problems? If citizens are indifferent to national problems and choose not to be involved, what type of person or groups will take over that responsibility? How might this affect the lives of all American citizens?

Career Fact

Suffragettes of the twentieth century fought hard so that women of today could cast their ballot. Until Congress ratified the Nineteenth Amendment to the Constitution on August 26, 1920, only male citizens had the right to vote. The amendment states: "The right of citizens of the United States to vote shall not be denied or abridged by the United States or by any State on account of sex (gender)."

Section 1: Understanding Civic Responsibility

Citizenship is defined in the Fourteenth Amendment to the Constitution of the United States, ratified July 28, 1868; it states in part:

"All persons born or naturalized in the United States, and subject to the jurisdiction thereof, are citizens of the United States and of the State wherein they reside. No State shall make or enforce any law which shall abridge the privileges or immunities of citizens of the United States; nor shall any State deprive any person of life, liberty, or property without due process of law; nor deny to any person within its jurisdiction the equal protection of the laws."

Comprehension Check

After your students finish reading this list, have them close their books and answer this question: Describe a responsible act of citizenship you can perform now. Describe a responsible act you can perform six years from now.

Being a responsible citizen requires knowledge of the democratic system of government, a commitment of time, and a willingness to become involved in the affairs of government. You can perform responsible acts of citizenship by

- Completing a course in American government
- Volunteering to help less fortunate citizens
- Abiding by all federal, state, and local laws

© JIST Works

- Being involved in the election process and casting your vote
- Serving in the armed forces
- Being a productive worker

Discussion Starter

Explain to your students that older people, homeowners, married couples, and people with more education and higher incomes are more likely to vote than those who are younger, are single, and have less education and lower incomes. Ask students why they think there is such a difference in voting patterns between these groups. Ask the class how their generation could increase the percentage of responsible voters.

Voting

The United States has the fewest restrictions on voting of any country in the world, but it has one of the smallest voter turnouts. Even in presidential elections, political **apathy** (indifference) is evident by the large percentage of eligible voters who do not vote. How many of the following excuses have you heard?

- I don't like either of the candidates.
- I'm not interested in politics.
- Why should I bother to vote? My vote won't make any difference.

Community Resources

Form a committee of students to contact the local board of elections. Instruct the committee to make an appointment to visit the board's offices, and obtain information about voter registration and other board responsibilities. Have the committee report their information to the class.

The reason for this apathy is a puzzle. Voter registration in the United States is at an all-time high, but voter participation remains very low. From a world view, the United States ranks 139 out of 172 countries in voter turnout.

Voting is one of the most important civic responsibilities you will have. It is the one indisputable area in which all citizens are, in fact, equal. The right and duty to vote allow you to protect your rights and prevent political abuses. Through elections, citizens can replace officials who displease the majority.

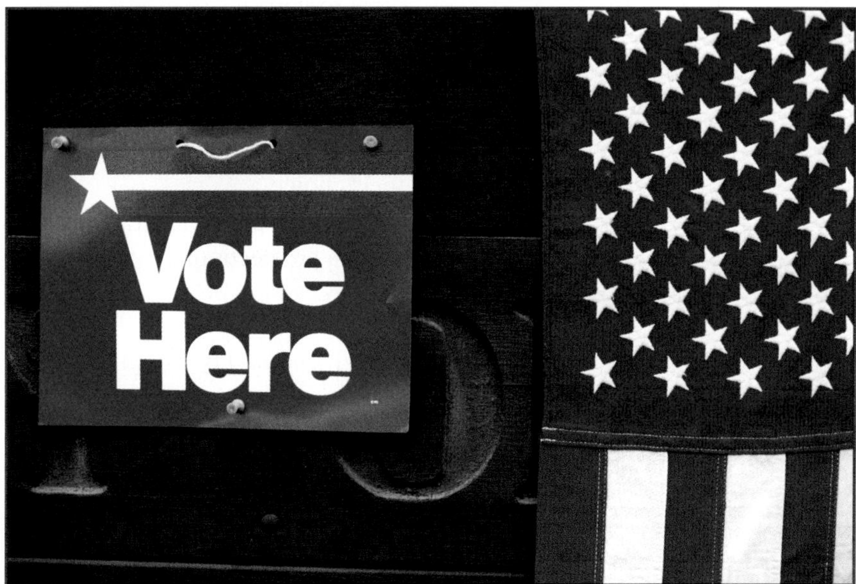

What year will be your first to experience the excitement of voting in a presidential election?

Get involved in the political process. Volunteer to work for the campaign of a political candidate you admire. The men and women you elect to local, state, and federal offices will have the power to speak and act for you as they run all areas of the government. They will pass the laws and regulations that influence your personal life and career opportunities.

The people you elect will appoint thousands of people to government jobs each year. Your local, state, and federal governments employ more workers and purchase more goods and services than any other organization in the United States. Your taxes are used by the people you elect for every paycheck they issue and every item they purchase.

Reteaching

Have students complete the "Civic Responsibility Match" worksheet in Chapter 20 of the *Preparing for Career Success Instructor's CD-ROM, Third Edition.*

How do people decide *how* to vote? The **charisma** (appealing leadership quality) of some candidates frequently sways voters. Can you think of

© JIST Works

The vote you cast on tax issues will influence the quality of public services you receive.

a political candidate who demonstrated a lot of charisma in a local, state, or national election?

The **media** (newspapers, magazines, television, Internet, and radio) also can have a major influence on an election. Can you think of an election in which the media influenced your opinion? If yes, how?

Have you heard the saying "Birds of a feather flock together"? Polls of registered voters indicate that most people do not inform themselves equally about all sides of an issue or about all of the political viewpoints presented. In fact, most people vote for candidates and issues supported by their political party. For example, Democrats tend to listen to speeches presented by Democrats, to read campaign literature and newspaper articles favoring Democrats, and to have friends with similar viewpoints. Republicans behave in the same manner. Which political party appeals most to you?

Discussion Starter

Ask your students: Who sets the sales tax rate? Who regulates the quality of the air you breathe and the food you eat? Who regulates the price you will pay for public utilities or determines whether you can get a driver's license? Discuss the importance of being informed and involved in the political process.

A small group of independent voters frequently provides the margin of victory in elections. Independents are prone to explore all sides of an issue and to consider each candidate based on ability, past performance, and position on important issues. Independents are open to change the candidates of their choice.

As a responsible citizen, follow these guidelines when deciding how to vote in an election:

1. Read information presented by people on both sides of the issues.
2. Listen to all candidates, and read information presented by all political parties.
3. After you gather information, follow the decision-making steps you learned in Chapter 4.
4. Information gathering and decision making have no value until you translate the process into action: Vote!

CAREER FACT

To be able to vote in an election, you must be at least 18 years old by the day of the election, be a citizen of the United States, be a resident of the place where you are voting (residency requirements vary by state), and be registered (unless you live in North Dakota, where registration is not required).

Taxes

Have you ever wondered where the money for food stamps, public schools, roads, parks, police and fire protection, low-income housing, and public transportation comes from? Taxes provide money for these and other public services. The total amount of taxes paid by citizens depends on

- Whether they own property (**property tax**)

© JIST Works

Political Campaigns Throughout History

Trains (1850s): Before trains, presidential candidates did not travel and give speeches. In 1860, Stephen Douglas was one of the first to campaign by train. He lost the election to Abraham Lincoln, who did not campaign at all.

Radio (1920s): Candidates who were effective in person or when their speeches were printed in newspapers often could not make the leap to the new media of radio. In 1932, Al Smith, Governor of New York, was the Democratic presidential candidate. On the radio, his heavy New York accent alienated voters around the country. It helped Herbert Hoover win the election. In the next election, Franklin Roosevelt perfected the use of the radio.

Television (1950s): TV is often said to have decided the 1960 election for John Kennedy. In TV debates, Kennedy appeared youthful and confident. His opponent, Republican Richard Nixon, looked uncomfortable and sweaty under the hot floodlights used in early TV. Nixon learned from the experience, and his use of TV was a major factor in winning the 1968 election.

The Internet (1990s to present): Candidates began to experiment with Internet technology in 1996. By 2004, some candidates used Web sites. *Blogs* (Web sites that contain online personal journals with reflections and comments by the writers) aggressively chronicled campaign developments believed to be under-covered or ignored by traditional media.

- How much they earn (**income tax**)
- Where they live (local and state income tax and sales tax)
- What they own (car, motorcycle, and boat license fees)
- The dollar amount of certain goods and services they buy (sales tax)

Customs duties on imported products and excise taxes on luxury items provide the federal government with additional **revenue** (income).

Although state and local governments use a variety of taxes and license fees to acquire revenue, most of the taxes you will pay during your working years will go to the federal government. As a responsible citizen, you should be knowledgeable about what the government is doing with the money it receives in taxes. Based on your approval or disapproval, you should vote for candidates who support your beliefs about government spending.

Enrichment

Form a committee of students to decorate a bulletin board titled "What You Get for Your Tax Dollar." Ask the class to clip articles from newspapers and magazines concerning taxes and government spending for the committee. Ask the committee to seek tax-based budget information about schools, government agencies, libraries, dams and reservoirs, parks, fire and police protection, schools, and other tax-supported or tax-subsidized organizations.

When there is an income tax, the just man will pay more and the unjust less on the same amount of income.

—Plato

World Citizenship

As a responsible citizen, you need to be informed about foreign affairs and the way they might affect our nation's economy, security, and peace with other nations. The cooperation or conflict that takes place between nations influences the quality of your personal life and career.

Each citizen must accept the outcome of our federal government's foreign policy decisions on issues such as

- Providing aid to famine-ravaged areas of the world (frequently caused by civil wars)
- Aiding nations that suffer from a natural disaster such as the thousands of deaths and billions of dollars in destruction caused by the tsunami that came ashore in Southeast Asia on December 26, 2004
- Defending another nation against armed aggression or our homeland from international terrorism

Reteaching

Have students complete the "World Citizenship" worksheet in Chapter 20 of the *Preparing for Career Success Instructor's CD-ROM, Third Edition.*

© JIST Works

Take Note

All young men must register with the selective service within a month of their 18th birthday. The selective service is a system under which Congress can recruit men for military service. Registration is a required citizenship responsibility for men. Many women have voluntarily served in combat roles in recent wars. Do you believe women should also be required to register for selective service?

- Protecting our national interests abroad and negotiating international trade agreements

Defense budgets and decisions about military conflicts are largely the responsibility of the president with the consent of Congress (a formal declaration of war must come from Congress). How willing would you be to interrupt your education or working career to serve the United States as a member of the armed forces in Iraq, Afghanistan, or a similar situation?

Abiding by the Law

Laws are a body of rules or principles, prescribed by authority or established by custom, that a nation, state, or community recognizes as binding on its citizens and institutions. The **U.S. Constitution** is the highest law in the United States. Individual states also have constitutions. Cities and counties have **ordinances** (laws, edicts, or decrees enacted by a municipal government for local application).

Comprehension Check

After your class finishes reading "Abiding by the Law," have them close their books. Ask your students: In your own words, what is a law? What is the difference between the U.S. Constitution and an ordinance?

Each level of government is responsible for certain areas of law. For example, state governments enforce and make traffic laws, regulate marriage and divorce, operate institutions of higher education, regulate public utility rates (gas, electric, and telephone), maintain state highways, license and regulate liquor dispensers, operate mental institutions, and regulate insurance companies.

Local governments enforce public health laws, operate public elementary and high schools, regulate traffic, control the standards for constructing and remodeling buildings, and grant permits to bury the dead. Many operate water-purification plants and sewage-disposal systems, collect and dispose of garbage and other wastes, provide fire and police protection, and maintain local roads.

Many police officers work as hard to prevent crime as they do to enforce laws.

Whether you are at school, on the job, or enjoying daily life, laws and other established rules protect your rights and provide for your safety. As a responsible citizen, you must obey and respect existing laws.

Taking legitimate action through responsible group activity to change an outdated or unfair law is an act of responsible citizenship. Breaking the law or violating the rights of others to bring about change is irresponsible. When seeking a change in a law, work rule, or school policy, you must remember that each citizen's rights and

© JIST Works

privileges end where his or her neighbor's rights and privileges begin. Can you think of a situation in which one person violated another person's rights in an attempt to bring about change in a law or rule? Can you think of a case in which someone brought about a change without violating the rights of others?

Section 1: Get Involved

For a period of a week, scan one or more newspapers, and cut out articles dealing with political leaders at the local, state, or national levels. Divide the articles into two groups: those praising and those criticizing a certain leader's policies, acts, or opinions. Answer the following for each of the leaders you have selected on a separate sheet of paper and be prepared to discuss your responses in class:

1. What positive or negative effect could the leader's policies, acts, or opinions have on your education, future career, or personal life?
2. What responsible action could you take to influence the leader's policies, acts, or opinions?

Section 2: Solving Social Problems

The United States faces a broad range of unsolved national and international social issues. A short list of the major issues includes immigration and diversity; the environment; terrorism and homeland security; education, poverty, and job opportunities; population growth; and urbanization. What problems would you add to the list?

Most citizens agree on *what* the major social issues are, but they frequently disagree on *how* to solve them. This disagreement can create unfavorable side effects, such as **polarization of issues** (seeing one side as totally right or wrong), large-scale protest demonstrations, and violence. However, most citizens agree that the resolution of social issues is beyond the control of one person or group and requires collective action from all citizens.

Examine the issues presented in this chapter and apply your decision-making skills to find possible solutions. Consider the personal, economic, and career benefits or liabilities that your solutions would have on you, your family, friends, neighborhood, and nation.

Immigration and Diversity

The United States has a diverse population that grows more diverse minute by minute. America is a nation of immigrants and has long embraced newcomers. In so doing, it has been renewed and re-invented in countless ways through the new blood that has crossed its borders. America's changing **demographics** (vital statistics of the human population) in race, gender, religion, disability, ethnicity, and language make diversity a national issue.

Cooperative Learning

List the six issues in this section on the chalkboard. Divide the class into six committees. Then have each committee select one issue to research and prepare a presentation for the class. Have each committee lead a class discussion of the issue it has researched before having the class discuss each issue in terms of the rational decision-making process. See Section 1 in Chapter 4.

Key To Success

According to *Working Mother* magazine, e-learning or Internet-based instruction is a relatively new business-training tool that an estimated 20 percent of large companies now use to educate employees about diversity. E-learning provides access to diversity training courses, legal information, and company policies and is available when employees need it.

Enrichment

Have students research the ethnic background of their family or any immigrant group they wish to know more about. Then have them report their findings to the class.

TAKE NOTE

An estimated 2 million Native Americans are members of approximately 350 federally recognized tribes. They have a unique status with the federal government because of the recognition that they are nations within a nation. Indeed, approximately 250 treaties recognize Native Americans as special entities—sovereign nations. Despite legal agreements with the federal government, Native Americans are underrepresented, underserved, and frequently unrecognized within the United States.

Discussion Starter

Ask students to imagine that they are part of a government committee with responsibility for correcting the social and legal injustices suffered by Native Americans. The committee has a very small budget. How will the committee identify the concerns of Native Americans? What types of action can the committee take with very little money?

Community Resources

Ask for volunteers or assign students to invite a large employer's representative to talk to the students about diversity in the workplace. Also, invite a person or persons from one or more minority groups to explain their cultural background and the ease and difficulties they see that their minority group has had assimilating into American society.

Discussion Starter

Review the section on attitudes in Chapter 3. Ask your students what multicultural diversity means to them. Ask them how American diversity affects our nation's educational, cultural, social, and economic system. What problems do minorities have in these areas? What are some common stereotypes that exist about ethnic groups? Why do these stereotypes exist? Ask them which minority group they consider to be most unjustly treated.

Throughout our nation's history, and for varying reasons, America has continuously remade itself. During the eighteenth and nineteenth centuries, immigrants generally came from two areas of the world, northern Europe and Africa. Asia was a source of immigrants after 1848 when Chinese contract laborers were brought to work both in the gold mines and on the transcontinental railway. By the early 1900s, the majority of newcomers were arriving from southern and eastern Europe.

From 1921 until 1965, immigration quotas were based on an immigrant's nationality or country of origin. In 1965, the quota system was eliminated, leading to a substantial increase in immigration and a change in the geographic origin of immigrants.

Between 1960 and 2000, the proportion of immigrants from Europe dropped from 74.5 to 15.3 percent, and the proportion from Latin America increased from 9.3 percent to 51 percent. Immigration into the United States falls into three major categories. The number of annual admissions listed by the Department of Homeland Security Yearbook of Immigration Statistics (January 2006) is

- 946,142 lawful permanent admissions
- 6,181,822 lawful temporary visa admissions
- 500,000 unlawful admissions (estimated by the U.S. Census Bureau)

The United States is a multicultural nation without precedent anywhere in the world. The large metropolitan areas and states on the East Coast and West Coast, plus Texas and Chicago, Illinois, are the places most immigrants arrive. As a result, the face of America is changing rapidly. Estimates indicate that, by 2025, present-day minorities will constitute a majority or near majority of the population in many states.

Participation in the greater society by immigrant groups has historically required adjustment and assimilation in the labor market and educational system and acceptance of the social customs and values of the "new" country. New arrivals usually look for ethnic communities where they can continue to live in a familiar culture, communicate in their mother language, and share their ethnic cuisine and social network. With each new generation, old traditions blend with the new, and America further expands its multicultural society.

Employers have a responsibility, both legal and ethical, to protect employees against discrimination. Different perspectives, skills, religions, experiences, and opinions cause many citizens to be less tolerant and understanding of newcomers.

1. What can our system of government do to make America a fair and just society for all?
2. What can you do to make America a fair and just society for all?

© JIST Works

The Environment

Modern industry, technology, and agriculture have improved our standard of living and the quality of our lives, but at a high cost to our environment. Many scientists have concluded that many of these improvements threaten humanity's existence. How accurately can you answer the next three questions?

1. What is the weight of the waste created by each American in one day?
2. How much drinking water does one quart of discarded motor oil pollute?
3. What is the total number of glasses of drinking water consumed by Americans each day?

Discussion Starter

Ask your students to answer the three introductory questions under the heading "The Environment." Answers: (1) 4.5 pounds, (2) 250,000 gallons, (3) one billion glasses.

Enrichment

Have students visit the school library or a public library and research the history and purpose of the Environmental Protection Agency. Then have them write a paragraph or two describing the effect the agency has had on the daily lives of citizens.

Cooperative Learning

Stage a class debate (or have a class discussion) on higher standards for clean air, with one side for and one against. At the end of the debate, take a vote. Discuss how much government control is necessary and how much is too much.

The **Environmental Protection Agency (EPA)**, created in 1970, is an independent government agency that is responsible for enforcing federal laws and regulations regarding the environment. This agency has done much to improve the problems facing the environment. However, the solution to environmental problems frequently comes into direct conflict with the goals of individuals and special-interest groups, such as manufacturers, farmers, labor organizations, and construction companies.

Since 1963, the nation's Clean Air Act has dramatically reduced the amounts of smog and soot in the air we breathe. All people agree that they want clean air to breathe and clean water to drink for themselves and their families. The disagreements occur about the government's definition of clean air, clean water, and other pollutants and how the government requires citizens, businesses, and factories to reduce the pollution they create.

Businesses and state governments say the EPA studies on the hazards of smog and soot do not convincingly prove that stricter clean air rules would fix the problem. They also argue that complying with new rules would be too expensive.

Improving clean air standards will cost communities and businesses millions (possibly billions) of dollars. Environmentalists and health officials point to the benefits of cleaner air. They say tens of thousands of people will escape breathing or lung illnesses if higher standards are required.

How do you and your family dispose of old motor oil, paint, or lawn and garden chemicals?

1. What steps could our government take to solve this issue in a fair manner?

Career Fact

If car buyers bought the most efficient cars in each class, they could reduce the nation's carbon dioxide emissions by some 14 million tons and save 1.47 billion gallons of gasoline annually, greatly reducing the United States' growing reliance on foreign oil.

2. Should health issues be more important than the issues of profit and loss for businesses that would be most affected (those that cause the most air pollution)?

Drinking water resources are constantly under siege from multiple threats that affect water quality. These threats include naturally occurring storms, floods, and fires. However, most threats to our water quality come from the activities of people at home, work, and play. For example, each year we apply 67 million pounds of pesticides that contain toxic and harmful chemicals to our lawns. We also produce more than 230 million tons of municipal solid waste that contain bacteria, nitrates, viruses, synthetic detergents, and household chemicals.

Keeping contaminants out of the drinking water source is critical. Water utilities treat nearly 34 billion gallons of water every day. The Safe Drinking Water Act requires utilities to collect and treat water, hire trained and qualified operators, and have an emergency response plan in case of natural disaster or terrorist attack.

Enrichment

Have students complete the "What's Your Opinion?" activity in Chapter 20 of the *Preparing for Career Success Student Activity Book, Third Edition.*

1. What is the source of your local water supply? How does the quality of the water in your community compare to other regions of your state?
2. What are the water contamination threats in your community?
3. How is your water supply protected from sabotage or acts of terrorism?

Being Responsible: Water, Water Everywhere—But Is It Fit to Drink?

Take Note

According to Church World Services, some 1.1 billion people worldwide lack access to safe water, and more than 95 percent of them live in developing nations. Unfortunately, 80 percent of all diseases in the developing world are caused by unsafe water and sanitation-related problems. Upwards of 2.2 million people die annually from water-related diarrhea illnesses. Most of the victims are children under the age of five.

Jamie Miller graduated from high school last June and is presently in her first year of college. The school Jamie attends is about three miles from Lake Pleasant. The lake is the primary source of drinking water for her community and provides recreation in the form of picnicking, canoeing, and fishing.

Last evening, Jamie stopped by the lake to fish for a couple hours on her way home from school. Two guys she recognized from school were sitting on the fishing pier and spoke to her as she sat down to fish and eat a sandwich. One of them had an empty can of motor oil and was about to pitch it into the lake. He noticed Jamie was watching closely and said, "I had to put some oil in my bike, and they don't have a trash can that I can see." Jamie responded, "Give the can to me, and I will put it in my tackle box until I get home." The guy looked at Jamie, laughed, and tossed the can into the lake. The two guys walked down the pier to their motorcycles and rode away.

The *Water Authority* had a large metal sign posted where the boys had been standing on the pier. Throwing trash in the lake was a serious offense and violators could receive a fine up to $500 and/or 30 days in jail. Additionally, a large trash drum was located next to the parked motorcycles.

© JIST Works

Jamie realized that oil was one of the worst pollutants for a lake that provided drinking water and edible fish.

About 10 minutes later, Mr. Wilson, the park security officer, walked by and greeted Jamie. "How's the fishing, Jamie? Is everything O.K. on the pier?"

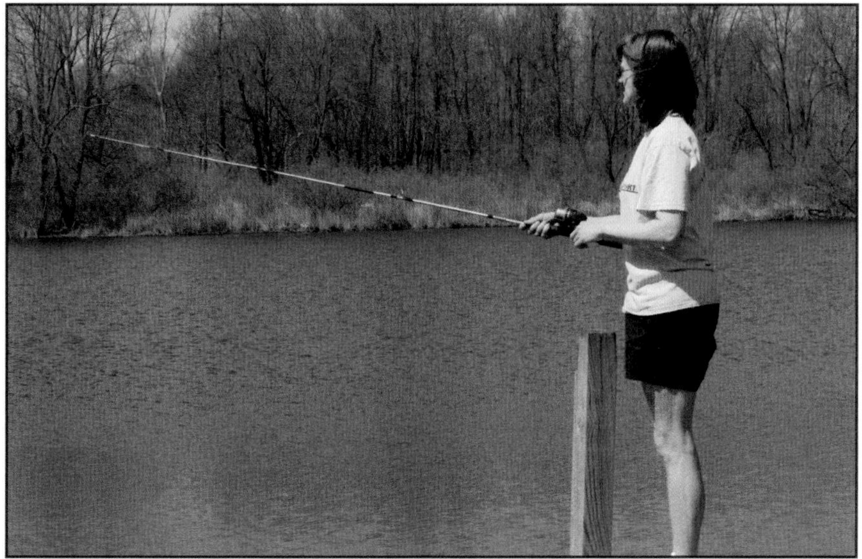

Critical Thinking

If you were Jamie, how would you respond to Mr. Wilson's inquiry? What are the reasons for your response?

Should lakes be used for both drinking water and recreation? Why or why not?

If Jamie tells Mr. Wilson about the boys and the oil can, how would you describe her character? If she does not tell Mr. Wilson, how would you describe her character?

> **TAKE NOTE**
>
> Your brain is about 75 percent water, and your body is 50 to 65 percent water. (Children's bodies are approximately 75 percent water.) On average, a person needs about five gallons of safe water each day to meet his or her drinking, cooking, hygiene, and domestic needs.

> **KEY TO SUCCESS**
>
> The quickest way to get a problem addressed or express a view about an issue is to make a phone call, write a letter, or e-mail a lawmaker's office. In your communication, make sure you identify yourself not only by your name but also by your voting district, city, or county. Keep in mind that the average congressional district has more than 600,000 residents, and a typical member of Congress receives thousands of letters, e-mails, and telephone calls each month. Also note that congressional mail is delayed at least 12 days because of a process the post office uses to destroy anthrax and other deadly agents that could be in envelopes.

Terrorism and Homeland Security

After the attack on the World Trade Center on September 11, 2001, America's view about national safety has changed dramatically. The focus that terrorist groups have placed on the United States has caused Americans to look critically at national security. Four critical areas of national security, which fall under the Department of Homeland Security, are

1. Protecting air travel
2. Protecting ports and waterways
3. Deterring attacks that use weapons of mass destruction, whether nuclear or biological
4. Responding to attacks on the U.S. homeland

Community Resources

Invite a local or state public health agency representative to talk to the students about how public health agencies are prepared to deal with possible biological or chemical attacks and the possible panic that could follow.

Discussion Starter

Ask your students: Did the September 11 terrorist attack influence your thinking? If so, how? Student responses can lead you into a discussion of the three questions at the end of the "Terrorism and Homeland Security" section.

Whatever America hopes to bring to pass in the world must first come to pass in the heart of America.

—Dwight David Eisenhower

Discussion Starter

If your class does not handle committee work effectively, use the questions concerning each issue for class discussions.

CLUSTER LINK

The growth of the world's population provides great challenges and opportunities for workers in the Agriculture and Natural Resources career cluster. If you enjoy the outdoors and have an interest in producing plant or animal products, conserving and developing of land and water resources, or mining and extraction operations, you should investigate the career opportunities within this career cluster. See the appendix for more information.

The Department of Homeland Security suggests that individuals and families, schools, day-care providers, workplaces, neighborhoods, and apartment buildings should all have site-specific emergency plans.

1. What plan does your school have for a terrorist attack? What plan does your community have? How about your family?
2. What additional security measures would you like from the Department of Homeland Security?
3. Terrorists can be anywhere. Can an international organization like the United Nations resolve the problem? If so, how? If not, how can the problem be solved?

Education, Poverty, and Job Opportunities

High poverty rates relate to low levels of educational achievement. Low levels of educational achievement relate to employment in low-wage jobs. Low wages are the basic criteria for poverty. *Low educational achievement*, *low-level jobs*, and *low wages* combine to trap some workers in a cycle of poverty.

Literacy also relates to poverty. Employers find that the level of formal education a worker completes is the best determinant of the worker's literacy.

Not having a high school diploma, a G.E.D., or some form of adult education has also been associated with poverty. Be aware, though, that graduating from high school or college does not guarantee you a high-paying job. However, the level of education you complete is one of the most important factors that will determine your level of economic success. Recent studies reveal that the poverty rate of high school dropouts is three times higher than it is for high school graduates and as the level of educational achievement goes higher, the difference between the income of men and women or between races decreases.

1. Make a list of problems that cause students to drop out of high school. What can society do to help students solve the problems on your list and continue their education and training? How can you help?
2. What reasons might explain the general public's expressed desire to provide youth with high-quality education and training and its continuing opposition to school levies? What can students do to help solve this national problem?

Population Growth

By 2050, the world population is estimated to pass 9 billion. Between 2000 and 2040, nearly 100 percent of population growth will occur in less developed countries in Africa, Asia, and Latin America, whose population growth rates are much higher than those in more developed countries.

© JIST Works

Growth rates of 1.9 percent and higher will double a population in about 36 years.

More highly developed countries in Europe and North America, as well as Japan, Australia, and New Zealand, are growing by less than 1 percent annually. Several European and Asian countries, including Hungary, Ukraine, and Russia, have slowly diminishing populations.

The population of the United States is projected to increase from 282 million in 2000 to 383 million in 2051, an increase of 101 million people. This additional population must be fed, housed, educated, and employed.

With few exceptions, such as changes in national boundaries, a country's available land area remains stable. **Population density** (the number of persons per square mile of land) increases or decreases with the rate of population change. By 2020, Asia is projected to be nearly twice as densely populated as Europe (522 persons per square mile compared with 286). Bangladesh is projected to be the most densely populated country with more than 4,000 persons per square mile. Global population increases are on a collision course with food supplies, fresh water supplies, and other resources necessary to sustain life.

1. In the coming years, what effect do you think population density will have on health, education, social, and employment conditions in nations such as Russia, Ukraine, Japan, and Australia? On Bangladesh? What are the reasons for your answers?
2. As the world population increases, how will people obtain enough safe water, food, medical care, and housing? What effect will a developing nation's success or failure to fill these needs have on its ability to participate in the world economy?
3. In the coming years, what effect do you think population density will have on your health, career, and lifestyle? Why do you think so?
4. Should your government become more involved in problems presented by the population explosion? If so, what should it do? If not, why not?

Urbanization

In less than a hundred years, the population of the United States has shifted from mostly rural to mostly urban. Two major reasons for this shift have been job opportunities and lifestyles. For millions of urban residents, however, the population shift from the country to the city has not helped them fulfill their dreams of economic prosperity and a good life.

The rapid growth of urban populations has created a wide range of social problems. Areas with a high population density have problems with congestion, pollution, housing, traffic, **social anonymity** (lacking individuality), and crime. Many people feel that social anonymity and the increased pace of urban life are **detrimental** (damaging) to good mental health. In addition, many people consider metropolitan city living to be undesirable and unsafe.

Career Fact

According to the International Data Base information compiled by the U.S. Census Bureau, the ten most populous countries in the world (in order) are China, India, United States, Indonesia, Brazil, Pakistan, Bangladesh, Russia, Nigeria, and Japan.

Discussion Starter

Tell students that in 1790 the population of the United States was less than four million. Explain that as our human population increases, there is a rising demand for natural resources. To meet our growing need for food, habitat for wildlife is often lost to deforestation as land is cleared to grow crops. How can humans' needs be balanced with limited natural resources? What might happen to people or wildlife if not enough resources are available? What are some solutions to these problems?

Take Note

Children in many countries of the world spend their childhood working in a factory, stitching clothes, and performing other low-level jobs for pennies an hour. They work long hours in factories that are unsafe, unhealthy, and unpleasant. UNICEF reports that despite international efforts, child trafficking remains a serious problem in West and Central Africa, where aid workers say desperately poor parents give up their children to smuggling rings who promise to educate them and find them jobs. Instead, the children work up to 12 hours a day, are paid little or no money, and are rarely heard from by their parents again. What hazards do children face working in factories? Would you purchase products that you knew were made by children working in sweatshops? Why or why not?

Student Evaluation

To evaluate student mastery of concepts, you might want to use the Section 2 quiz or the chapter test found in the Chapter 20 file of the *Preparing for Career Success Instructor's CD-ROM, Third Edition.*

1. If you were the mayor of a large city, what action would you take to relieve the problems of pollution, crime, homelessness, and unemployment? What groups of people and institutions would you ask for help? What could they do?
2. Many people believe that eliminating social anonymity and developing a sense of community involvement would eliminate many urban problems. What could individual urban citizens do to reduce social anonymity? How could schools, houses of worship, law enforcement agencies, and organized neighborhood groups help? Explain the reasoning for your answers.

Section 2: Get Involved

Answer the following on a separate sheet of paper, and be prepared to discuss your responses in class.

1. Which of the social problems described in this section have the greatest effect on your personal life? What solutions would you offer for these problems? What individuals or groups would probably support your solutions? Why? What individuals or groups would probably oppose your solutions? Why?
2. List the social problems described in this chapter. Name three occupations that are affected by each problem or involved in a possible solution. Describe how each occupation is affected or involved.
3. Have you ever changed your attitude about an issue that you felt very strongly about? Explain your answer.

Reteaching

Have students complete the "Finding the Right Words" and the "Checking Your Location" worksheets in Chapter 20 of the *Preparing for Career Success Student Activity Book, Third Edition.*

Enrich Your Vocabulary Answers

1. civic responsibility
2. property tax
3. revenue
4. U.S. Constitution
5. ordinances
6. demographics
7. population density
8. media
9. laws
10. income tax

(continued)

Chapter 20 Review

Enrich Your Vocabulary

On a separate sheet of paper, number from 1 to 16, and write the most appropriate term from the "Enrich Your Vocabulary" list at the beginning of the chapter next to the number of the statement it matches.

1. The rights and privileges enjoyed by all citizens and their duties to the laws and policies of their community, state, and nation
2. A tax based on property owned
3. Income
4. The highest law in the United States
5. Laws, edicts, or decrees enacted by a municipal government for local application
6. Vital statistics of the human population
7. The population of an area divided by its square miles
8. Newspapers, magazines, television, Internet, and radio
9. A body of rules or principles that a nation, state, or community recognizes as binding on its citizens and institutions
10. A tax based on how much is earned

© JIST Works

11. Seeing one side as totally right or wrong
12. Damaging
13. Lacking individuality
14. Indifference
15. An independent government agency that is responsible for enforcing federal laws and regulations regarding the environment
16. Appealing leadership quality

Enrich Your Vocabulary Answers *(continued)*

11. polarization of issues
12. detrimental
13. social anonymity
14. apathy
15. Environmental Protection Agency
16. charisma

Check Your Knowledge

On a separate sheet of paper, complete the following activities.

1. List at least four ways to demonstrate responsible citizenship.
2. List at least four services supported by tax money.
3. List three factors that combine to trap some workers in a cycle of poverty.
4. Where is most of the world's population growth taking place?
5. List six of the leading countries of birth of immigrants to the United States.
6. List six major social problems associated with the rapid growth of urban populations.

Check Your Knowledge Answers

1. Studying American government, volunteering, following laws, voting, serving in the military, and being a productive worker.
2. Answers will vary. Several are listed in Section 1, under the heading "Taxes": food stamps, public schools, roads, parks, police and fire protection, low-income housing, and public transportation.
3. A low level of educational achievement, low-level jobs, and low-level income.
4. Less developed countries of Africa, Asia, and South America.
5. Mexico, Philippines, India, China, Cuba, El Salvador, South Korea, Vietnam, Canada, and the Dominican Republic.
6. Congestion, pollution, housing, traffic, social anonymity, and crime.

Develop SCANS Competencies

This activity will give you practice in developing the information and interpersonal skills that successful workers have. In a group, decide whether you agree or disagree with the statement: For every right we have as an American citizen, there is also a responsibility.

In your group, assign members to find and list rights we have as American citizens. Some of the rights you may want to list include freedom of speech, freedom of the press, freedom of religion, and right to privacy.

Assign other members to list responsibilities we have as American citizens. Some of those responsibilities are voting, defending civil rights, paying taxes, attending school, and defending the nation.

After all members have completed their lists, combine the lists into one list that shows rights and corresponding responsibilities. For example, you have the right to a trial by an impartial jury, but you also have the responsibility to serve on a jury or as a witness when needed. You may not be able to find a corresponding responsibility for each right.

Enrichment

Have students complete the Chapter 20 section of the *Preparing for Career Success Student Portfolio, Third Edition.*

Chapter 21 Resources

Lesson Plans and Preparation

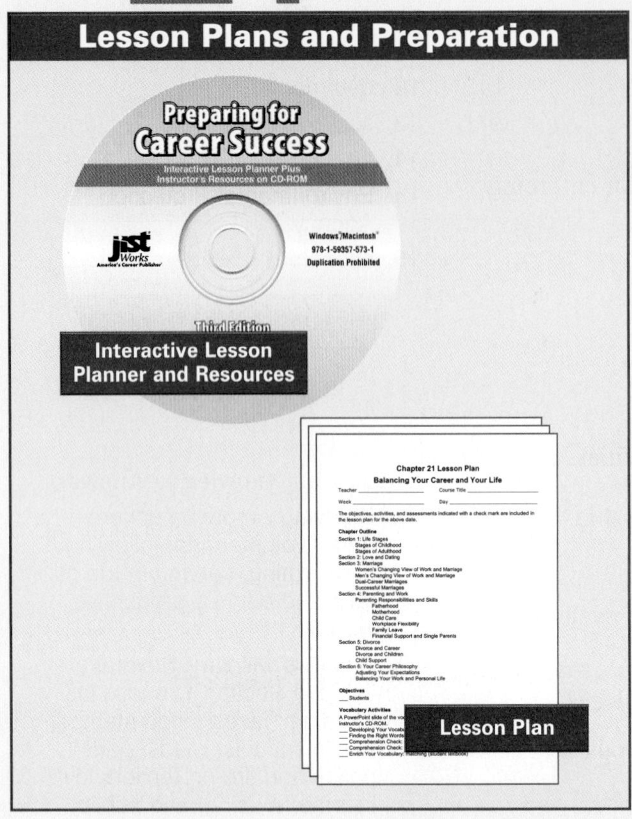

Multimedia

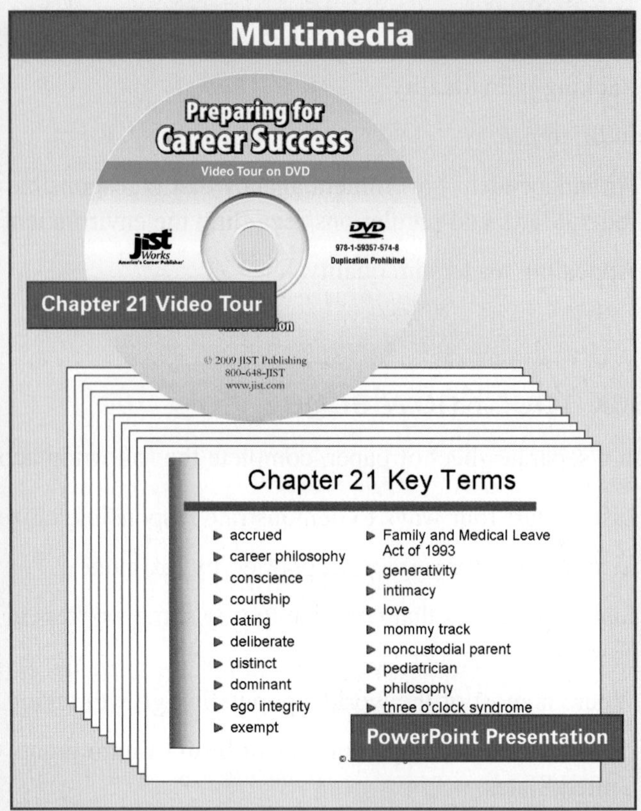

Activities

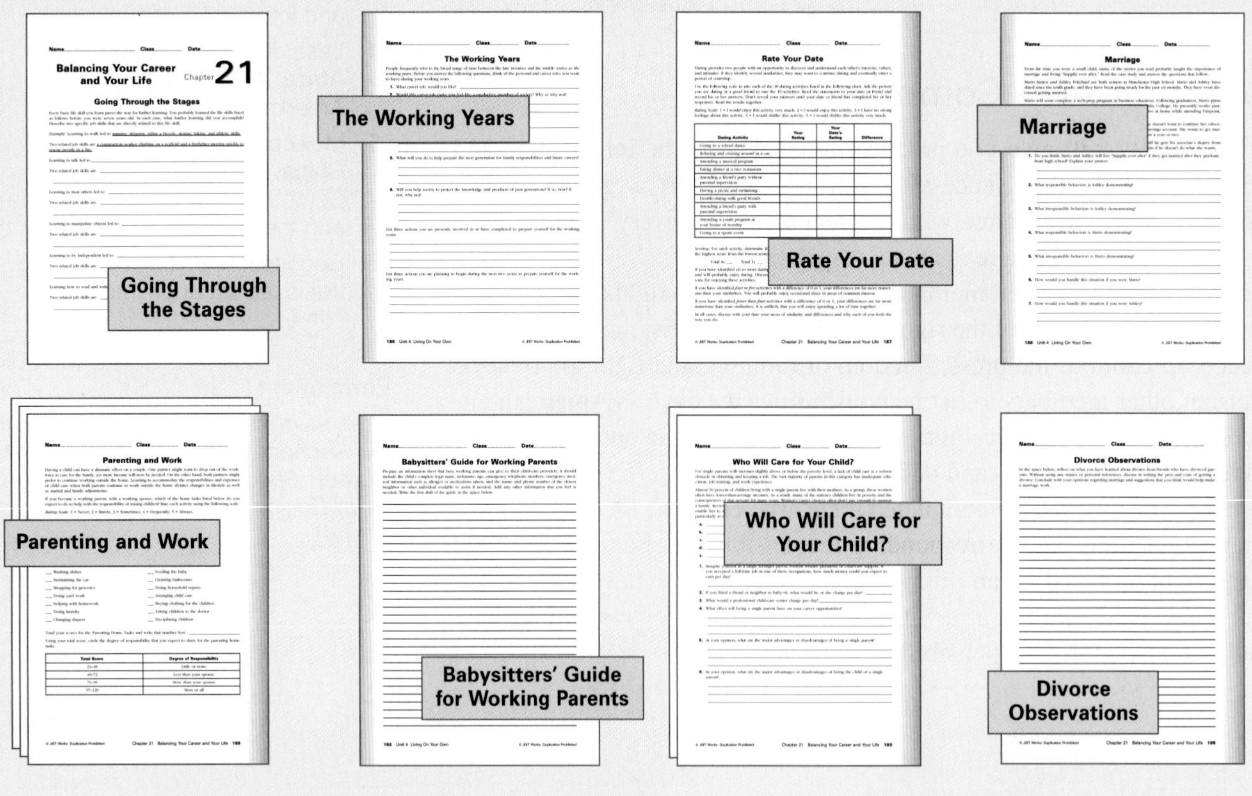

Going Through the Stages

The Working Years

Rate Your Date

Marriage

Parenting and Work

Babysitters' Guide for Working Parents

Who Will Care for Your Child?

Divorce Observations

© JIST Works

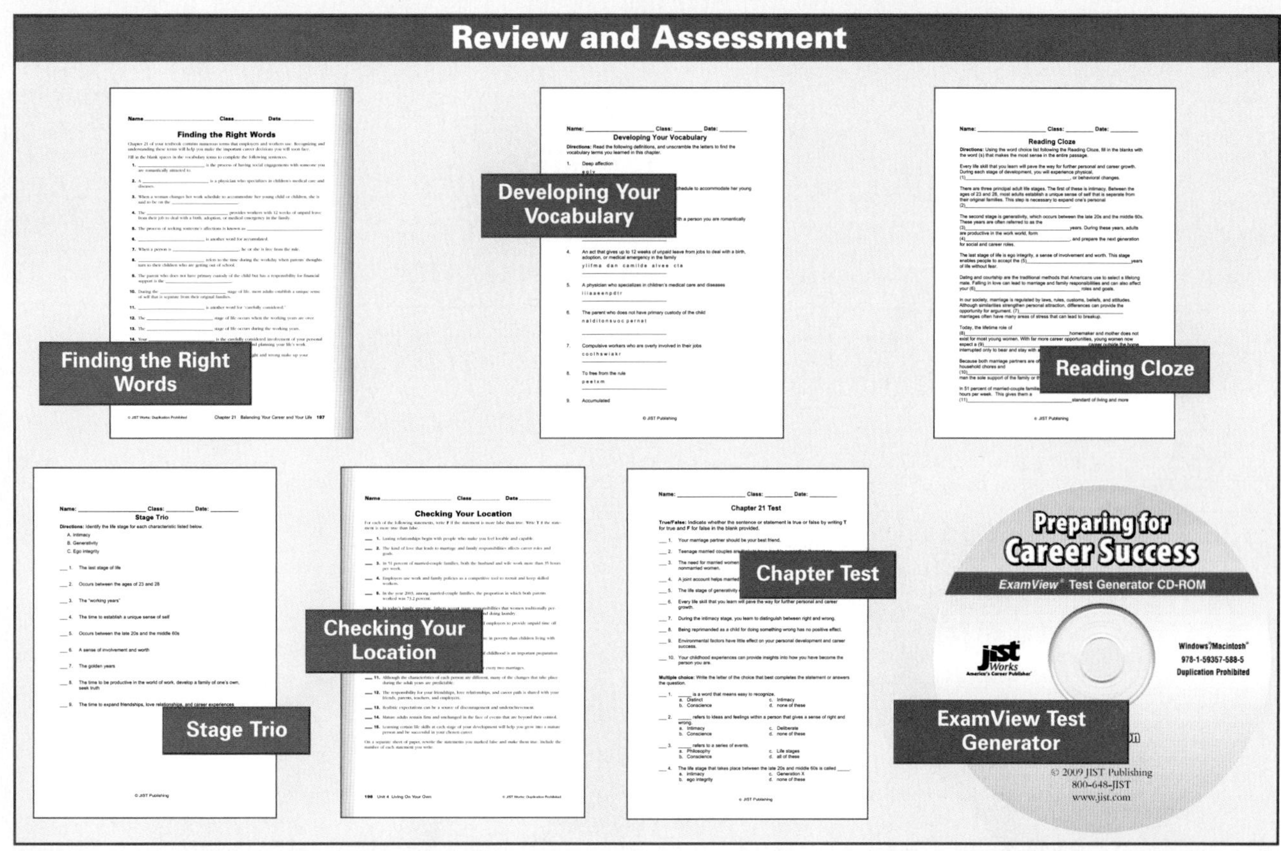

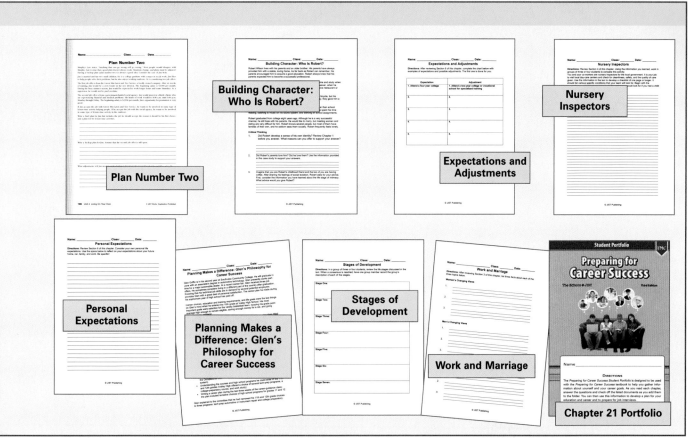

Plan Number Two

Building Character: Who Is Robert?

Expectations and Adjustments

Nursery Inspectors

Personal Expectations

Planning Makes a Difference: Glen's Philosophy for Career Success

Stages of Development

Work and Marriage

Student Portfolio

Preparing for Career Success

Chapter 21 Portfolio

Chapter 21 Balancing Your Career and Your Life

Learning Objectives

- Describe how you have been influenced by the previous stages of your life
- Recognize and understand the new personal and career concerns and priorities that are likely to arise during each stage of life
- Give examples that explain the difficulty of combining family expectations, lifestyles, and household circumstances with the expectations of employers
- List changes in traditional family lifestyles that have caused important changes in employer-employee relationships
- Explain how and why a satisfying marriage eventually becomes the result of meeting the goals of the courtship
- Compare the marriage, work, and family roles and responsibilities of each partner in today's society with those of past generations
- Explain how children's needs affect parents' employment
- Identify realistic career expectations, and make necessary adjustments in your educational plan
- Write your unique career philosophy

Enrich Your Vocabulary

In reading this chapter and doing the exercises, you will learn the following important terms:

accrued	dominant	mommy track
career philosophy	ego integrity	noncustodial parent
conscience	exempt	pediatrician
courtship	Family and Medical Leave Act of 1993	philosophy
dating	generativity	three o'clock syndrome
deliberate	intimacy	workaholics
distinct	love	

Vocabulary

Use the "Developing Your Vocabulary" worksheet found in Chapter 21 of the *Preparing for Career Success Instructor's CD-ROM, Third Edition* as a pretest for chapter concepts or as a reteaching worksheet.

Video Tour on DVD

Show students the Chapter 21 segment to introduce them to the content.

Every individual has a place to fill in the world, and is important in some respect, whether he chooses to be so or not.

—Nathaniel Hawthorne

As you progress through your teens and into your twenties, more of your important decisions will focus on your career, friendships, love relationships, personal values, and lifestyle. Have you thought about whether you might get married someday? If so, have you also considered the type of person you might marry? Have you thought about having your own family? Work, marriage, and caring for a family usually occur within the same life stage. Because they are part of the traditional American way of life, a large part of society expects these behaviors.

More than any time in history, work responsibilities outside the home and family responsibilities within the home must coexist. Relationships between work and family, employers and employees, husbands and wives, and parents and children constantly affect one another. Over the years, the changing expectations, lifestyles, and household circumstances of most families have prompted important changes in employer-employee relationships.

At this point, you have probably thought about your future work and selected some tentative occupations. Now you must find a way to live your dream. You are preparing for career success in a rapidly changing world of work. New technology will create new occupations and eliminate established occupations. Throughout your career, you will need to continually develop new skills that will enable you to take advantage of changing opportunities. During each stage of life, new concerns and priorities will arise. How you respond to these changes will determine the reality of your career dream.

Self-Understanding

Instruct a writer to go to the chalkboard and make two headings, "Positive behaviors" and "Negative behaviors." Ask your students to share one typical positive or negative teenage behavior for the writer's lists. When you are satisfied with the lists, ask the following question for each positive or negative behavior listed: If this behavior continues, how will it affect the teenager's future career? What are the reasons for your answer?

Section 1: Life Stages

Take a moment to think about the many physical and psychological changes you have experienced during your lifetime. Think about the changes in your interests, lifestyle, economic concerns, and physical appearance; then think about the way you deal with social relationships. This process of personal change will continue during your adult years. Being aware of likely changes will help you to prepare for them in a positive way.

© JIST Works

Learning certain life skills at each stage of your development will help you to grow into a mature person and be successful in your chosen career. During each stage of development, certain areas of physical or psychological growth are expected. Human development stages are not always **distinct** (easy to recognize) because they overlap and vary in the ages at which people normally pass from one to another.

Certain parts of each developmental stage will be **dominant** (most influential) at particular periods in your life. Before you can grow into the next stage, you must learn specific behaviors and life skills. With advancing stages of maturity, your behaviors will continue to change in positive ways. Every life skill that you learn will pave the way for further personal and career growth.

Cooperative Learning

Have students complete the "Stages of Development" worksheet in Chapter 21 of the *Preparing for Career Success Instructor's CD-ROM, Third Edition.*

Cooperative Learning/ Self-Understanding

Divide your class into learning pairs. Allow three minutes for each student to tell the other person something he or she accomplished before the age of 10 that made him or her feel proud and competent. Next, ask the students if the accomplishment they shared prepared them for a future success. Ask them to share the accomplishment and the success.

Stages of Childhood

The development of **conscience** (ideas and feelings within a person that give a sense of right and wrong), a personal perception of fair play, and honesty occurs in early childhood. Most children are reprimanded for their misbehaviors by a disapproving adult. Receiving a reprimand instead of approval helps a child learn what is socially, ethically, and morally accepted as right or wrong. The child uses the sense of right and wrong learned in childhood situations as a foundation for his or her personal values.

The child is father to the man.

—Anonymous

Your childhood experiences can provide insights into how you have become the person you are. From birth to age 12, children go through three major life stages.

- **Birth to 3 years: Developing hope for a bright tomorrow.** During this stage, children learn to trust others, communicate, walk and explore immediate surroundings, and manipulate objects.

Who appears to feel independent and confident? Who is unsure?

Enrichment

Have students complete the "Going Through the Stages" worksheet in Chapter 21 of the *Preparing for Career Success Student Activity Book, Third Edition.*

- **3 to 6 years: Developing a sense of personal determination.** During this stage, children learn to play and get along with others and follow instructions. Children also become more independent and create fantasies about future roles at this stage.
- **6 to 12 years: Discovering a reason for personal actions.** For most children, this stage is all about learning reading, writing, and math and feeling competent. It's also a time for developing values and learning how to delay gratification.

KEY TO SUCCESS

Whether it is fair or not, much of your career success will depend on whether others approve of your attitude and behavior.

If you learned these skills, you are probably a happy, self-confident person who is well prepared to move ahead with your career. If you were unsuccessful in getting through certain stages, you are probably not as happy or as self-confident as you could be. Taking time to learn these important life skills will prepare you for the future stages of your life. Can you think of occupations in which it would be important for you to trust others, manipulate objects, or be independent?

Stages of Adulthood

Reteaching

Have students complete the "Stage Trio" worksheet in Chapter 21 of the *Preparing for Career Success Instructor's CD-ROM, Third Edition.*

Have you ever heard an adult describe someone's behavior saying, "It's just a stage she's going through"? Although the characteristics of each person are different, many of the changes that take place during the adult years are predictable.

You have probably noticed that students in your class have different levels of maturity. The reason is that some have mastered more social, physical, and psychological life skills than others have. Although some people develop faster than others do, young and old alike pass through a series of events, called *life stages,* at about the same age.

If you would be loved, love.

—Hecato

Imagine a stranger approaching a Chicago resident and asking, "How long does it take to drive to Chicago?" A likely response would be, "From where?" Every person must continually answer the question "from where?" to be able to understand his or her next stage of life. Like a wall in which each layer of blocks depends on the previous layer for its strength and accuracy, the previous stage influences each stage of life that follows it.

In Chapter 1, you learned about the stage of life you have entered, *the identity stage*. During your adult years, you will travel through three additional stages. All of these life stages were defined and explained by psychologist Erik Erikson in his numerous books on human development.

Discussion Starter

Ask your students: What characteristics of the intimacy stage of life would be essential for successful parenting? Emphasize the themes of "social maturity" and "independence." They are major life skills that characterize this stage of human development.

The first life stage occurring during the adult years is **intimacy**. Between the ages of 23 and 28, most adults establish a unique sense of self that is separate from their original families. This separation is necessary to expand their personal identities through friendships, love relationships, and career experiences.

Recognizing that you are an independent, responsible, productive adult should provide satisfaction for you and your family. It is important for you

© JIST Works

to accept the fact that you will always be a son or daughter, but you will never be a child again. Maintaining a two-way bridge of love and communication provides a sense of security for parents as well as for their sons and daughters. However, each person must accept responsibility for his or her own friendships, love relationships, and career path.

Have you ever heard people refer to the broad range of time between the late 20s and the middle 60s as "the working years"? This is the life stage of **generativity**. During these years, adults who have mastered the life skills of the intimacy stage and the stages preceding it

- Are productive in the world of work
- Have established their own family
- Seek truth by reexamining their personal beliefs and values
- Assume the role of caretaker for the knowledge and products of past generations
- Prepare the next generation for social and career roles

Like a winding brook tumbling through a rapidly changing environment, the mature adult flows through the working years with a sense of caring, purpose, and confidence in the next generation. However, just as a stream of water can be dammed and the remaining water left to stagnate, a person who is unable to find satisfaction during the working years will accept mediocrity, boredom, and self-interest.

When the working years are over, people who were cared for as children, and in turn cared for others, are able to accept the final years of life without fear. This last stage of life is **ego integrity** (a sense of involvement and worth). Learning, growing, and experiencing the previous stages of life bring a wisdom that enables people to accept the cycle of helplessness that comes at the end of life, even as it did in the beginning. The wisdom of ego integrity can make the last years of life the golden years—golden for the younger person who seeks wisdom from the older person, and golden for the older person who feels a sense of worth and involvement.

Unfortunately, many older people complete the working years without learning the important life skills. Suspicious of others; lacking in faith and confidence; without meaningful work, love, or friends, they approach the final years of life with a sense of despair and a fear of death.

Comprehension Check

After your students finish the description of generativity, ask them to close their books. Ask several students: In your own words, what are the life skills that characterize the life stage of "generativity"?

Enrichment

Have students complete the worksheet "The Working Years" in Chapter 21 of the *Preparing for Career Success Student Activity Book, Third Edition.*

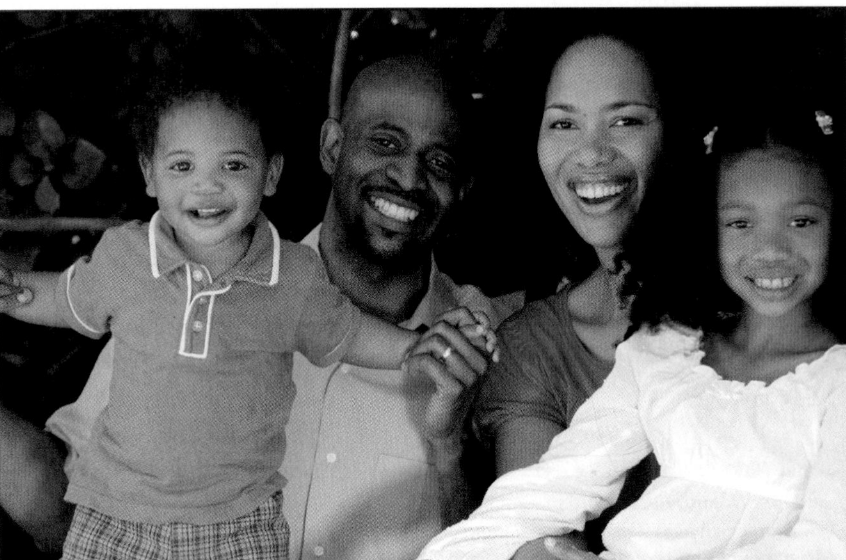

Alex and Wanda were well prepared to become parents. What specific life skills should you learn to prepare for the life stage of generativity?

Community Resources

Form a committee of students to contact the manager of a nursing home. Ask the committee to invite the manager or another staff member to visit your class or request to visit the nursing home and perform some volunteer service. Ask a speaker to discuss the positive and negative characteristics and behaviors of people during old age. If committee members visit the nursing home, have them write about specific behaviors they observe that relate to either ego integrity or despair.

Section 1: Get Involved

Answer the following on a separate sheet of paper, and be prepared to discuss your responses in class.

1. Observe friends and relatives who are in the stages of intimacy, generativity, or ego integrity. What positive or negative characteristics mentioned in this section could you identify in the behaviors of your friends and relatives?
2. Make a list of personal characteristics that you hope to display during the stages of intimacy, generativity, and ego integrity. How will the characteristics on your list be useful in your career and your personal life?

John, Donna, Phil, and Ashley attend Mohican Valley Community College. They enjoy dating and have agreed not to enter a serious relationship.

Section 2: Love and Dating

The act of giving and receiving **love** (deep affection) causes feelings of warm personal attachment and pleasure. Love is a basic need for most people. It takes on different meanings and causes new feelings at different stages in life. Family, special friends, religious faith, even pets can provide an environment for the exchange of love. The love that leads to marriage and family responsibilities affects career roles and goals.

As a child, you learned to love by being loved. Think back to your elementary school days. Did you develop a special caring or loving friendship? Has this friendship lasted into your teenage years? Following the identity stage (the teen years) of life, attraction for a special person frequently becomes romantic love and leads to marriage. For most individuals in our culture, marriage without love would mean no marriage at all. What effect would a love relationship have on your present career goals?

Although the rules of the "mating game" have changed over the years, dating and courtship are still the traditional methods that Americans use to select a lifelong mate. During **courtship** (the process of seeking someone's affections), couples may develop a very close (personal and private) relationship. You will probably experience **dating** (the process of having social engagements with a person you are romantically attracted to) and courtship several times before you develop a special relationship that may eventually lead to a satisfying and happy marriage.

Developing mutual trust, sharing confidences, being open about thoughts and feelings, and having potential for a lasting relationship are characteristics of courtship. Your lifelong mate will also be your best friend. Lasting relationships begin with people who make you feel lovable and capable. They encourage you to be the best person you can be.

Self-Understanding

Ask your students to turn to "The Identity Stage" in Section 1 of Chapter 1. After they reread these few paragraphs, ask them: Which questions and characteristics of the identity stage that will prepare you to be a good wife, husband, mother, or father have you learned? Which tasks and characteristics do you feel you still need to master before entering a serious love relationship?

Enrichment

Offer extra credit to students who research and report to the class on the historic roots of courting and love. Allow for classroom discussion of both the positive and negative aspects of courtship and love in the past and present.

Discussion Starter

Explain to students that a person who has not experienced love and instead has been rejected or abused will have a hard time learning to give and receive love. For this person, learning to love and be loved will require time, determination, and interaction with loving people. Ask your class to suggest experiences that might help this person learn the rewards of giving and receiving love. What will be the most difficult task for this person to overcome? What positive effect can work have on this person? What difficulties will this person probably face in the workplace?

© JIST Works

Section 2: Get Involved

Answer the following on a separate sheet of paper, and be prepared to discuss your responses in class.

1. Think about a person you have dated. What did you learn about him or her? What did you learn about yourself? Think about your best friends now. What personal interests and values do you share with them? What activities do you enjoy together?
2. Make a list of newspaper or magazine articles, movies, television shows, songs, or poems that identify our society's views on the importance of marriage. Write a brief report about your findings. Locate newspaper and magazine pictures that support your position.

Section 3: Marriage

In our society, laws, rules, customs, beliefs, and attitudes that assign rights and responsibilities to each partner regulate marriage. Despite its religious and legal complexities, about 60 percent of all adults are married, and many unmarried adults want to be married in the future.

Entering a marriage relationship during your teens without the education and training needed to enter a rewarding career area adds a burden to the marriage that frequently ends in divorce. Teenage couples are likely to have financial difficulties. Money problems and increased family responsibilities, combined with a loss of personal freedom, create stress. Stress causes disagreements and marriage breakups that in turn create more stress. If you know an adult who has traveled this road, ask his or her opinions on this issue.

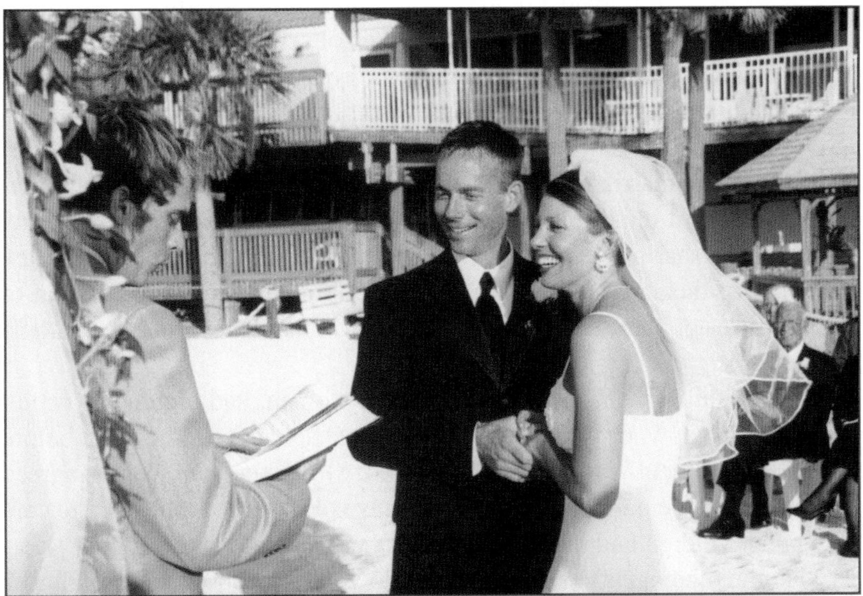

Examine this wedding photo of Albert and Leona. Do you believe they will have a successful marriage? Why or why not?

TAKE NOTE

Most survivors of failed marriages have not rejected the idea of marriage itself. In fact, about 75 percent of all divorced people marry again.

Enrichment

Offer extra credit to students who research and report to the class on the deep roots of wedding traditions. Have them consider traditions such as the wedding party; the veil; the flowers; something old, something new, something borrowed, and something blue; the ring; the cake; and the music.

Case Study

Have students read the case study in the "Marriage" worksheet in Chapter 21 of the *Preparing for Career Success Student Activity Book, Third Edition* and answer the questions.

KEY TO SUCCESS

Two ingredients for a successful marriage are finding the right person and becoming the right person.

Cross-Reference

See "Women in the Workforce," in Section 3 of Chapter 14.

Reteaching

Have students complete the "Work and Marriage" worksheet in Chapter 21 of the *Preparing for Career Success Instructor's CD-ROM, Third Edition.*

Cluster Link

If you have not decided on a specific career and you anticipate a dual-career marriage, consider occupations that are in high demand throughout the nation. Several specific occupations within the following career clusters (see the appendix) have transferable skills and lend themselves to relocation:

- Architecture and Construction
- Education and Training
- Hospitality and Tourism
- Transportation, Distribution, and Logistics
- Retail/Wholesale Sales and Service
- Health Science

What other occupations or career cluster areas could help you avoid relocation problems? In most cases, management-level jobs are the most difficult to relocate without a career penalty.

Women's Changing View of Work and Marriage

Since the 1960s, the changing role of women has altered many of society's attitudes toward marriage, career, and family responsibilities. A lifetime role of full-time homemaker and mother does not exist for most young women today. Most young women expect a lifelong career outside the home, interrupted only to have and/or stay with small children.

Today's young women have career opportunities that did not exist for their mothers and grandmothers. Most parents have raised their daughters to believe that with the appropriate education, training, and determination, they can succeed in any career role.

Increasing occurrences of cohabitation and nonmarital childbearing have also brought about changes in women's roles and attitudes toward marriage, career, and the family. In fact, women in this group have a greater need for employment than married women do.

Yet some women have strong beliefs about a woman's role in the home, and when financially possible, they choose to remain at home. Some well-educated and highly skilled women choose not to work outside the home to avoid a collision of values and attitudes with their husbands.

Men's Changing View of Work and Marriage

As women's roles and attitudes have changed, so have men's. Not many years ago, the "man of the house" was the sole support of the family. His boss was always a man, and his traditional role was as decision maker on almost all issues except routine housework. Rarely did he cook the meals or clean the house; that was not his job.

When both marriage partners are employed, they need to share household chores and child-rearing responsibilities. Some men have difficulty adjusting to sharing responsibility. These men feel threatened and are uncertain of their masculine identity when they interact with a woman of equal or greater status. What problems could this behavior cause at home and at work?

In one study, men, far more often than women, had arguments or felt overburdened at work if they had several household chores the night before or had an argument with their wife or child. More men than women agreed that one marriage partner should take a leave of absence from work to care for young children and that one spouse's career should take a higher priority than the other spouse's career. What do you think about these findings? Which spouse do you think should take the leave of absence, and which should have the higher career priority?

© JIST Works

Dual-Career Marriages

In 51 percent of married-couple families, both the husband and wife work more than 35 hours per week (Source: U.S. Dept. of Labor). These families have a higher standard of living and more lifestyle choices than average single-income families. However, when disagreements arise over how to spend a marriage partner's income, harsh conflicts often result.

To avoid marital problems caused by financial disagreements, marriage partners should reach an early agreement about financial goals and methods to reach them. It is also important to decide who is responsible for paying routine bills, balancing the checking account, and keeping to a budget.

Many couples decide to pool their income into joint checking and savings accounts. They share all financial decisions. Others choose to maintain individual financial identities and build separate credit histories. Which method would you prefer? Should a married couple have joint ownership on everything, including a home and car?

In a dual-career marriage, it is important to divide and share household responsibilities equally or to hire outside help. Discuss this issue before you marry. To begin, list all of the household chores needed to keep the home operating smoothly. Next, determine the preferences of each partner. Perhaps the tasks can be easily divided. For example, some men enjoy cooking meals, and some women enjoy mowing the lawn or washing the car. Consider rotating the chores that neither partner wants and the chores that both prefer. However you divide the household responsibilities, be fair.

Before you enter a dual-career marriage, anticipate potential career conflicts, and devise mutually acceptable solutions with your partner. What rewards do each of you want from a career, and what help do you expect from your partner? Will an increase in future job responsibilities reduce the time you spend together? Will it affect the time each of you spends on household responsibilities or child rearing? Identify possible solutions that will enable you and your partner to both meet your career goals with minimal conflict. Keep in mind that in previous decades, surveys showed that the biggest source of problems of married couples was money; now it is "too little time."

Amy is preparing the family breakfast while her husband, Charles, is getting ready for work. Charles will clean the kitchen and take the children to school. Amy and Charles divide the family responsibilities according to their job schedules. How would you divide family responsibilities in a dual-career marriage?

Cooperative Learning

After your students finish reading "Dual-Career Marriages," divide the class into learning pairs. Allow five minutes for each pair to decide on two major advantages and disadvantages of a dual-career marriage. Ask each pair to report their conclusions to the class.

Self-Understanding

Explain to students that money is a major issue in marriage conflicts. Refer to "Money Management and Budgets," in Section 4 of Chapter 17. Discuss how they believe paychecks should be divided or combined in a marriage, who should pay the bills and maintain the accounts in their marriage, and how they believe new purchases such as a car or appliance should be financed.

Discussion Starter

Ask students: If faced with relocation because of a career opportunity for your spouse, where would you be willing to relocate, and what would you do for a career?

Life Skills: What's a Fair Share?

Joe and Robin Booth have been married for three years. Joe is the manager of a small restaurant and earns $3,100 per month after deductions. Robin is a paralegal with a large law firm, and her take-home pay is $2,600 per month. Their total living expenses (including a car payment) average $4,200 per month.

Joe feels that each marriage partner should do half of the work at home and contribute equally to pay the family bills. From the beginning of their marriage, Joe has reconciled their checkbook and paid the bills. In addition, he usually handles the food shopping and cooking. Robin does the cleaning and laundry chores.

Joe takes $2,100 per month from Robin's check and $2,100 per month from his check to pay the bills. He also takes $350 from each check for their joint savings account. After the bills and savings are covered, Joe keeps his $650 per month, and Robin keeps her $150. Joe earns more, so he keeps more.

Robin would like to spend a large part of their savings on a cruise. She would also like to buy some new clothes for the trip. Joe would rather visit out-of-state relatives this summer and buy a new car for the trip. Joe and Robin had a serious argument over this question last week and have stopped speaking to each other.

Career Fact

The United States is not keeping up with the rest of the world when it comes to maternity leave policies. A study by Columbia University's Institute on Child and Family Policy reveals the following facts about maternity leave in selected countries:

- Canada, 25 weeks, 55 percent paid
- China, 12 weeks, 100 percent paid
- France, 16 weeks, 100 percent paid
- Germany, 14 weeks, 100 percent paid
- Italy, 20 weeks, 80 percent paid
- Norway, 52 weeks, 80 percent paid
- Russia, 28 weeks, 100 percent paid
- United States, 12 weeks, unpaid (although individual companies' policies may vary)

Critical Thinking

Do you approve of the way Joe and Robin handle their money? What do you think of the way they divide their household responsibilities? Explain your point of view.

What advice would you give Joe and Robin to help them resolve their disagreement?

Successful Marriages

Every couple is different, and the success of a relationship depends on how the partners' unique personalities interact. Although there is no list of proven rules for a successful marriage, the following guidelines could be helpful in selecting and getting along with a marriage partner:

1. Take time during the courtship to really understand each other. This way, you can avoid unpleasant surprises after the wedding ceremony.
2. Be aware of the difference between sexual attraction and love.

© JIST Works

Richard and Jessica were married three years ago. Although they have a dual-career marriage, Richard and Jessica plan activities to enjoy and appreciate their time together. Why is their time together important?

3. Avoid getting married for selfish reasons. Getting married to escape an unhappy home life, because you believe you can change your partner, to solve personal problems, or because your friends are doing it is a poor idea.
4. Take time to be certain of your decision. Statistics show a higher failure rate for teenagers who marry than for older adults.

After you are married, following these guidelines will help you have a happy marriage:

1. Accept your partner's shortcomings. Nobody is perfect.
2. Be kind to your partner on a daily basis, and your love will be clear.
3. Discuss your problems. They will not go away with silence or with time; they will only grow.
4. When conflicts arise, listen, respect, and tolerate your partner's viewpoints.
5. Encourage and respect your partner's individuality and uniqueness.
6. Enjoy and appreciate every day you have together. Hold hands.
7. Both of you will change. As change occurs, explore new ways of relating and interacting.

Discussion Starter

Ask several students: Which of the guidelines for selecting a marriage partner is most important for teenagers? Why? Which of the guidelines for selecting a marriage partner is least important for teenagers? Why? After the students discuss their answers, take a vote by a show of hands for 1, 2, 3, and 4. Write the results on the chalkboard.

Enrichment

Assign your students to interview a person who has been married for more than 10 years. Instruct the students to show the married person the guidelines to follow after marriage and ask these questions: Which three guidelines do you consider to be most important? Why do you consider them to be most important? Write the guidelines on the chalkboard, and keep track of the ones your students report as being most important to married people.

CAREER FACT

Men have a more active role in housework and child care than in the past, but women still spend more time than men on these tasks. According to the Department of Labor, 84 percent of men spent some time doing household activities such as cooking and cleaning. On an average day in 2003, 30 percent of men reported doing housework, whereas 55 percent of women did. Men also spent more time doing leisure activities (5.4 hours) than women (4.8 hours). Moreover, working women with children under age six spent 3.3 hours a day on leisure and sports activities, whereas working men with children under age six spent 3.8 hours on leisure and sports.

Section 3: Get Involved

Answer the following on a separate sheet of paper, and be prepared to discuss your responses in class.

1. Entering the workforce has made wives financially less dependent on their husbands. Working women have fewer children. Does this mean that women today are less committed to marriage than in the past? Explain your answer.
2. Make a list of benefits and disadvantages for children of dual-career families. Which two benefits on your list are most important? Why? Which two disadvantages on your list concern you most? Why?
3. Develop a list of questions to ask married couples about how they share household chores. Try to ask at least six couples the questions. Ask two couples who are in their 20s or 30s, two couples who are near your parents' ages, and two couples who are near your grandparents' ages. Compare their answers. How are they similar? How are they different? Why do you think they are different?
4. How do you believe your spouse's income should be spent? What should his or her income pay for in the family budget? Should one marriage partner be in charge of handling all of the income?

Reteaching

Have students complete the "Parenting and Work" worksheet from Chapter 21 of the *Preparing for Career Success Student Activity Book, Third Edition.*

Career Fact

For the first time in 25 years, the percentage of women returning to work after childbirth declined in 2002 (source: U.S. Bureau of Labor Statistics, 2002).

Section 4: Parenting and Work

The makeup of the American family has changed dramatically during the past 50 years. The typical family of the past included a husband supporting a nonworking wife and two children. Mothers rarely worked outside the home until the youngest child entered school or left home. In 1969, only 24 percent of American families had two parents who worked full-time. By 2003, 73.2 percent of American families had two parents who worked full-time, according to the U.S. Bureau of Labor Statistics.

The increasing number of women in the workforce has also altered work life. Family issues, such as the availability and affordability of child care, have become front-burner questions for lawmakers and labor-management negotiators.

Having a child has a dramatic effect on the lifestyle of a working couple. One partner may elect to drop out of the workforce to care for the child. When this happens, the family will need to make major lifestyle and budget changes. On the other hand, neither partner may want to give up his or her career.

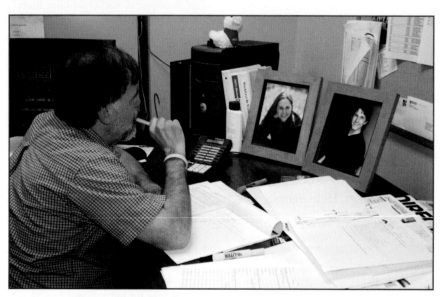

Being a "family man" helps James Preston to be an understanding employer. When pregnancy or childbirth becomes a job issue, James uses a temporary employment agency.

As a working parent, you will need to periodically reevaluate and adjust your work and family life schedule. When you return home from work tired and wanting to relax, parenting responsibilities can become

© JIST Works

exhausting. Pay attention to signs that you are wearing down. When you feel overwhelmed, do not agonize over what you do not complete; instead, praise yourself for what you accomplish.

Work-family choices are personal, and what works for one person may be wrong for another. However, time spent with your children may be the most valuable gift you can give them. When this special time of life is gone, you can never return to it. Will you accept a less orderly home or give up your full-time job for a part-time job? What changes are you willing to make to become the best possible parent(s)?

Cooperative Learning

Divide your class into small groups. Explain that child abuse comes in many forms and at many levels. Ignoring a child's needs when you come home from work is a form of child abuse. Instruct each group to list at least four stress-related forms of child abuse. List one specific source of stress for working parents and some positive ways to eliminate or deal with it. Have each group report their conclusions to the class.

Parenting Responsibilities and Skills

Whether your children are adopted, biological, or living with you because of family circumstances, you will be their parent. You will need to love them, teach them the difference between right and wrong, and help them prepare for their career success.

Preparing yourself for new responsibilities and adjusting to the role of being a parent are not easy. Parenting is a 24-hour-a-day responsibility. You will be expected to provide your child with affection, security, education, social opportunities, and the necessities of food, clothing, shelter, and health care. How prepared are you for these responsibilities? What must you do to become better prepared?

It is not possible to be a perfect parent or raise a perfect child. However, using tried-and-true parenting skills will foster positive physical, mental, and social growth in children. Learning these skills will help you to become a good parent. Make a commitment to learn the skills needed to foster positive development and growth during each stage of your child's life. Teach your child patterns of social behavior and conduct that will encourage positive relationships with family and others. Express your affection regularly. Stay involved by spending time together and learning what is important to them. Laugh and have fun together, and understand the important role you hold in helping your child become a man or woman.

Your family physician or the child's **pediatrician** (a physician who specializes in children's medical care and diseases) can suggest the most current and best-written books on raising children. Ask for literature that describes methods for fostering growth, explains child development, gives advice on discipline, and explains the importance of love and encouragement. Many communities also provide parenting classes that teach these skills. When you have a child of your own, it will be a good idea to keep at least one good book about parenting skills by your bedside.

Helping your child master the developmental needs of childhood is important preparation for the child's future career success. Human-development skills learned in childhood grow into adult employment skills (see Table 21.1). Remember, you are your child's most important teacher.

TAKE NOTE

Any high school student who has taken a child care or other family and consumer sciences class can join the Family, Career, and Community Leaders of America (FCCLA). This career and technical student organization helps students to develop skills in finding a job and working with other people as well as to learn more about careers such as cooking. Contact your local chapter for more information or go to the Web site at www.fcclainc.org.

Enrichment

Have students complete the "Babysitter's Guide for Working Parents" worksheet found in the Chapter 21 file of the *Preparing for Career Success Student Activity Book, Third Edition.*

Community Resources

Form a committee to invite a pediatrician or family physician to speak to the class about the developmental needs of babies and small children, difficulties faced by teenaged parents, and teen pregnancy.

© JIST Works

Table 21.1 The Effect of Childhood Development on Adult Employment Skills

Needs of the Child	If Needs Are Satisfied, the Adult Worker Will...	If Needs Are Not Satisfied, the Adult Worker Will...
To be cared for	Be trusting and feel secure at work	Feel insecure with new work tasks and will have difficulty placing confidence in other workers
To be loved	Feel wanted as a valuable contributing employee	Feel unwanted at work
To have companionship and affection	Feel he or she belongs at work	Feel like an outsider at work
To be taught	Enjoy learning new information and developing new job skills	Have difficulty with education and training
To have positive role models	Exhibit acceptable behaviors	Exhibit some unacceptable behaviors
To be encouraged	Not be afraid to fail and will be open to new methods and constructive criticism	Feel defensive and resist new methods for fear of failure
To play	Be confident of his or her present career role and will attempt new career roles	Dislike or be confused about his or her career role but will resist any change
To socialize	Get along with coworkers and will contribute to team success	Prefer to work alone and will resist teamwork
To develop positive values and attitudes	Be recognized by coworkers as a positive person with a sense of integrity and honor	Be recognized by coworkers as a negative person with questionable ethics
To make choices	Be recognized by coworkers as a good decision maker	Put things off at work to avoid making a decision
To have limits placed on his or her behavior	Follow rules pertaining to work and safety	Complete work tasks as he or she sees fit without following company rules or safety procedures

Community Resources

Arrange for your class to visit a kindergarten or Head Start class. Have each of your students read a short children's book to one of the children and talk to the child about the story. Afterwards, ask the students in your class: Which of the needs listed in Table 21.1 seem to be satisfied or unsatisfied in the child or children to whom you read? What makes you think so?

Fatherhood

Being a father expands a man's role in life and presents him with several new priorities. In most dual-career families, a successful father will need to spend more time with his children and accept more direct responsibilities for their physical care than he would in a traditional single-income household. In today's family structure, fathers accept many responsibilities that women traditionally performed, such as preparing a meal, bathing the baby, changing diapers, and doing the laundry.

Some employers have developed programs to help men deal with family responsibilities and expectations. For example, one organization offers fathers seminars on such topics as pregnancy education and child-care expenses. Others offer support groups for fathers in which they can share the enjoyment and concerns of fatherhood. Why do you suppose these employers invest in parenting education for fathers? Would you enjoy being in a parenting class someday?

© JIST Works

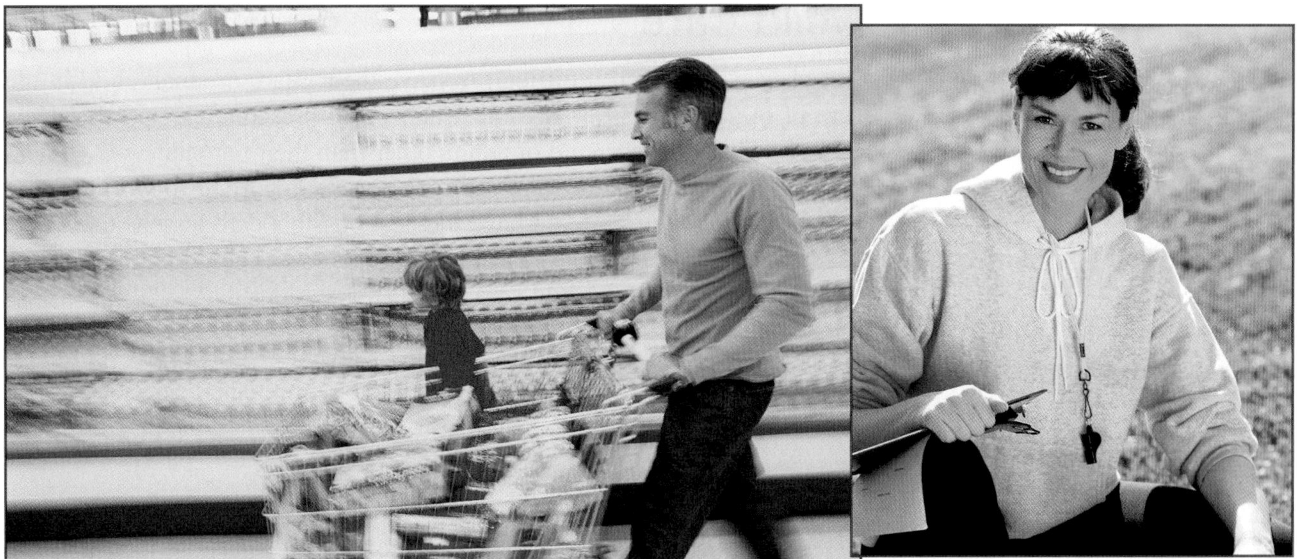

When Mark Evans was a boy, he never dreamed that he would be responsible for caring for his son and shopping for the family's groceries. On the other hand, when Pam Martin was a child, she did not expect to coach her daughter's softball team. What parenting responsibilities do you expect to have in the future?

Motherhood

Motherhood expands a woman's life role and establishes many new priorities. Despite expectations of greater male-female equality in housework, many fathers still do not accept an equal responsibility for the family cooking, dishwashing, house cleaning, shopping, laundry, and child care. For many women, the combination of a career and motherhood requires difficult choices about time management.

The term **mommy track** refers to the time when a woman changes her work schedule to accommodate her young child or children. The mommy track could mean working flexible hours at the same job or the same company, changing career paths to spend more time at home with the baby, or dropping out of the workforce completely for one or many years.

A woman who selects the part-time track usually loses her company-paid health insurance, vacation pay, and opportunities for promotions. However, if she decides to stay employed full-time, the task of balancing her career with motherhood can become overwhelming. Of working couples, 6.8 percent decide that it is better for the mother to continue working and the father to give up his job and stay home with the child. This percentage is increasing every year.

Some women decide to commit themselves to a family in lieu of a career, at least temporarily. When and if you become a mother, which track do you believe you will take, and why? When and if you become a father, which track would you prefer for your wife, and why?

Cross-Reference

Explain to your students that time management is important for students, parents, and workers and that time-management skills can be learned. See "Managing Your Time," in Section 4 of Chapter 11, and the "Section 4: Get Involved" activities.

TAKE NOTE

Taking time off from a job to have a baby is a worry to many working women. They are concerned about being replaced or demoted when they return to work. Despite federal and state laws barring discrimination against pregnant women, this issue remains a valid concern.

KEY TO SUCCESS

Children need time with their parents. Teach your child to eat, talk, play, love, trust, and develop skills. Your parenting style will be a major factor in building your child's self-esteem and future career success.

© JIST Works

Enrichment

Have students complete the "Who Will Care for Your Child?" worksheet in Chapter 21 of the *Preparing for Career Success Student Activity Book, Third Edition.*

Child-care centers can help children of working parents to fill many of their childhood needs. Who helped you to fill these needs? Who could you help?

Cooperative Learning

Have students complete the "Nursery Inspectors" worksheet found in the Chapter 21 file of the *Preparing for Career Success Instructor's CD-ROM, Third Edition.*

CAREER FACT

Most women who have education and training in specific career skills expect to work outside the home, even if they take time off from their careers to have children.

Child Care

Most parents find it difficult to leave their infant or small child in the care of others. Despite this, almost half of all preschoolers spend at least part of their day in the care of adults other than their parents.

Finding reliable child-care services is very important to working parents. Knowing their children have the best possible care lessens the worry of leaving them. Consider the following guidelines when it is time for you to select and evaluate a child-care facility:

1. Check the licensing of the facility. Licensing requirements set minimal standards, such as group size and environmental safety.
2. Inquire about the training of the staff members, especially in child care and development.
3. Ask whether the center provides well-planned activities. Do adults read to the children and ask questions? Does an adult teach skills such as counting or naming shapes? Are age-appropriate toys available?
4. Find out the ratio of staff to children to be certain that supervision is well balanced—for example, one adult per five children, ages birth to 12 months; and one adult per 12 children, ages one to three years.
5. Visit the center for observation more than once before enrolling your child. Note how often the caregiver expresses affection, warmth, or praise. Does the caregiver respond promptly and comfortingly to a child's distress? Does the caregiver listen and respond directly to a child's talk? Do you see positive social behavior among the children?
6. Obtain the name and telephone number of at least two parents whose children attend the facility, and ask them their opinion of the center.
7. Find out what safety precautions the facility practices. Are smoke detectors and fire extinguishers in working order and located where they will do the most good? Are teachers trained to use first aid and CPR?
8. Make certain that workers know who has permission to pick up your child.
9. Observe the cleanliness of the center.
10. Find out the center's policy for sick children.
11. Make certain the center provides safely prepared nutritious meals and snacks.
12. Obtain a written copy of all fees before enrolling your child.
13. Ask the staff and your child (if he or she is old enough to talk) what they did each day.
14. Ask how the center screens child-care professionals before they are hired.

© JIST Works

The care of children by working parents is not limited to small children. By some estimates, 10 million children are alone after school. **Three o'clock syndrome** refers to the time during the workday when parents' thoughts turn to their children who are getting out of school. Some employers report jammed phone lines as children and parents try to make contact. How would you feel about the three o'clock syndrome if you were an employer? Would your view be different if you were a parent?

Have you ever been home alone when an emergency occurred? How did you handle the situation? When you have children, make certain that they know your work telephone number and at least one other number they can call in an emergency. Children at home alone should know how to call the police and fire departments. Instruct your child to keep the doors locked and not to open them to strangers under any circumstances. Ask neighbors you know well to be alert to any problems that might arise.

Child-care arrangements are a major financial investment in a child's future. The availability and affordability of child care are important concerns for working families with children.

Community Resources

Have students call for an appointment to visit a local child-care center and interview a staff member. Ask them to use the 14 recommendations in this section to evaluate the quality of the center during their visit. (If possible, have students visit a center that is operated by an employer for employees' children.) Would the students recommend the child-care center they visited to a working parent? Why or why not?

Discussion Starter

Because of parents' work schedules, millions of older children and teenage youth are unsupervised after school and during the evening hours. What are the positive and negative results of this situation?

Workplace Flexibility

As the number of working mothers increases, the need for family-friendly employer policies and programs has also increased. Though still only a fraction of the total, some organizations are trying to help employees relieve the stress of juggling work and family responsibilities as they balance their career and family lives. For example, *Working Mother* magazine has recognized the following companies for their family-friendly policies:

- At Bristol-Myers Squibb Company, a developer and manufacturer of pharmaceuticals and health-care products, new moms receive 24 weeks of job-guaranteed leave, with 8 weeks fully paid. The company has four on-site child-care centers; backup, in-home, and sick-child care is also available. The company offers flextime, compressed workweeks, telecommuting, and job sharing. College-bound children of Bristol-Myers Squibb employees received scholarships worth $400,000 in 2002.
- Discover Communication Incorporated, a global media and entertainment company, provides 40 hours of paid dependent care for full-time employees (part-timers receive 20 hours). New mothers receive 17 weeks of job-guaranteed leave, with 9 weeks fully paid. Flex options such as variable start times are available for the company's 2,030 staffers.

Of great importance to the growth of family-friendly organizations is the fact that work and family policies are a competitive tool to recruit and keep skilled workers. How far should an employer go in helping resolve employees' conflicts between work and family responsibilities?

Key To Success

If you become a working parent, always have a backup babysitter in case your child becomes ill or the center you rely on cannot provide service.

Discussion Starter

If you were a working parent, would you prefer working for a family-friendly employer? Why or why not? If you did not have children, would you prefer working for a family-friendly employer? Why or why not?

Find Out More

Each year, *Working Mother* magazine publishes a list of the 100 Best Companies for Working Mothers to recognize organizations that successfully implement family-friendly policies. To see the most recent list, go online and key in **Working Mother Magazine 100 Best Companies.**

Cross-Reference

See the introduction to Chapter 16 and "Section 1: The American Dream: Your Own Business."

Should the Family and Medical Leave Act of 1993 be extended to include employers with fewer than 50 workers?

FIND OUT MORE

For a free copy of "The Handbook on Child Support Enforcement," write to Handbook, Department 628 M, Consumer Information Center, Pueblo, CO 81009. This handbook contains information about The Federal Parent Locator Service (FPLS), which is operated by the Office of Child Support Enforcement of the U.S. Department of Health and Human Services. This service assists states in locating "deadbeat" parents to obtain child-support payments. It is also used in cases of parental kidnapping related to custody and visitation disputes. Deadbeat parents nationwide owed their children $92.3 billion in unpaid child support in 2002. For more information, go online and key in **Federal Parent Locator Service.**

To obtain greater workplace flexibility, many women and some men choose to work out of their home. Some start new businesses from their home, and others purchase a franchise from an established firm. If you decide to work out of your home when your children are small, what type of business would you consider?

Family Leave

For parents who are experiencing conflicts between family and work requirements, the **Family and Medical Leave Act of 1993** is a welcome relief. This act gives millions of employees up to 12 weeks of unpaid leave from their jobs to deal with a birth, adoption, or family medical emergency. Although many states already had some form of family leave law and many organizations offered family leave before this act, its passage put the importance of family needs in the national spotlight. Here are some highlights of this act:

- Employers with 50 or more workers within a 75-mile radius must provide unpaid time off for the birth or adoption of a child; the care of a seriously ill child, spouse, or parent; or an employee's own illness.
- The law covers nonprofit and government organizations as well as businesses.
- Employers must continue to offer health-care insurance to employees who take leave.
- Employers guarantee the same or comparable jobs upon the employee's return.
- Employers may substitute an employee's **accrued** (accumulated) paid leave for any part of the 12-week period of family leave.
- Employers may **exempt** (free from the rule) "key" employees. Key employees are the highest-paid 10 percent of the workforce, whose leave would cause economic harm to the employer.
- Employers may exempt employees who have not worked at least one year or who haven't worked at least 1,250 hours, or 25 hours a week, in the previous 12 months.

Although this law does not remove all of a worker's family worries, it signals a change in the way employers and the government view the interaction of work and family. Does this law ask too much of employers? Why or why not?

Financial Support and Single Parents

The number of family households maintained by one adult continues to increase. Most of these households are the result of divorce, separation, or children born out of wedlock.

© JIST Works

Children living with two parents are likely to grow up in circumstances far different from children living with a single parent. Children living with two parents are more likely to be in a home with a better-educated, employed parent with an income well above the poverty level. In contrast, almost 60 percent of children living with just their mother are in poverty or near poverty. However, children living with a divorced single parent (especially the 10 percent who live with their father) often face better circumstances than do those living with a parent who has never married. State and federal governments are trying to improve conditions for children living in poverty with tougher child support laws. (Refer to the heading "Child Support" in the following section for more information.)

Career Fact

According to the National Center for Health Statistics, approximately 33 percent of all births are to unmarried women. However, 41 percent of births to unmarried women are actually babies born to *cohabiting* (unmarried) couples.

Section 4: Get Involved

Answer the following on a separate sheet of paper, and be prepared to discuss your responses in class.

1. Children raised in poverty are less likely to achieve in school, more likely to be involved with the criminal system, and more likely to have out-of-wedlock children of their own. These facts relate to lifetime work patterns. What effect will poverty have on tomorrow's workforce? If you were a lawmaker, what would you do to increase job opportunities for people living in poverty, reduce the number of out-of-wedlock children, and provide a better education for children living in poverty?
2. Single fathers make up one of the fastest-growing groups in the workforce. Juggling work and family roles can be even harder for men than for women because few bosses expect men to take time away from their job duties to care for their children. Is this fair? Explain your answer.
3. The stress of balancing work and parenting can be exhausting. How much involvement should parents have in their children's lives? How much is too much? Should parents get away from their children occasionally? If a parent has somewhere to go alone and the child wants to go along, how should the parent handle the situation?

Section 5: Divorce

The percentage of marriages in the United States that end in divorce continues to be among the highest in the world. In a single year, approximately one divorce occurs for every two marriages.

Comprehension Check

After your students finish reading this section, ask them to close their books. Ask several students: In your own words, what is a workaholic? What causes some divorced people to become workaholics?

Divorce and Career

Divorce creates disruption in the workplace. Parents find it difficult to maintain a balance between personal life and work life and not carry family problems to the job. Some newly divorced people use their work as a place to get away from personal problems. They become **workaholics** (compulsive workers who are overly involved in their jobs) to make up for their feelings of personal failure and injured self-esteem. In the process, they often become fatigued and irritable.

Divorced people who hide from life at the worksite have no place to go if they lose their employment. Because they attach so much importance to their work, they risk greater despair and are more likely to overreact when things do not work out as they had hoped.

Take Note

Divorced people who were married for more than 10 years and have not remarried are eligible to collect Social Security benefits at age 62 based on their spouse's earnings.

Enrichment

Have students complete the "Divorce Observations" worksheet in Chapter 21 of the *Preparing for Career Success Activity Book, Third Edition.*

Discussion Starter

Survey your students to see whether their parents are married, divorced, separated, or if they never knew a parent. Then discuss the problem of choosing between the two when custody or conflicts occur between them. Discuss how they expect their personal experience to affect their position on marriage and family. (It is important to be sensitive and allow students not to participate actively in such activities.)

Other divorced workers are so upset that their job performance declines to an unacceptable level. Talking openly to friends and seeking professional help are important. However, the boss may not be willing to accept low productivity and financial loss while the divorced worker gets his or her life together.

Divorce and Children

Divorce creates pain for parents and children alike. More than a million children watch their fathers and mothers separate every year. These children are divided between the homes of their mother and father, feeling torn between the two. The emotional spin-off affects their schoolwork and social behavior. For some, divorce is a form of motivation to succeed; for others, it creates a sense of guilt or defeat that leads to additional failures.

The pressures of divorced and single-parent homes force parents to spend their time trying to support the family, rather than being home to guide and supervise their children. These children frequently rely on the guidance of peers, the media, or others—often leading to faulty decisions with negative outcomes.

For parents, experiencing divorce and enduring the complications of being a single parent can lower job productivity. Instead of concentrating on work assignments, divorced parents may be distracted with decisions ranging from day care for their children to legal problems with their former spouse.

Children of divorced parents often spend part of their time with each parent. What positive and negative feelings can this situation cause in a child?

Child Support

States are required to make support guidelines available to all people who set child-support amounts. Courts use parents' employment, property, and any other sources of income or assets to establish payment amounts. The court verifies this information before the support order is final. The amount of child support depends on each parent's ability to pay and the needs of the child. Parents can try to have the amount of support changed if their financial situation changes. Even if the **noncustodial parent** (the parent who does not have primary custody of the child but who has a responsibility for financial support) acquires a second family, this does not eliminate his or her financial responsibility to the first family.

Community Resources

Form a committee to obtain "The Handbook on Child Support Enforcement." Ask the committee to prepare a report for the class on child support enforcement.

© JIST Works

Section 5: Get Involved

Answer the following on a separate sheet of paper, and be prepared to discuss your responses in class.

1. Figure a monthly budget for a divorced parent who must pay not only expenses for his or her household but also child support. Assume the parent has a take-home paycheck of $2,500 per month and child support payments of $900 per month. Use the information on creating a budget from Chapter 17.
2. Divorced parents who value their careers must sometimes decide between living close to their children and moving for a career opportunity. If a parent moves, the risk of fading from the children's lives may result. On the other hand, rejecting a career move can cause this parent to sacrifice significant financial and career success. If you were a parent and faced this choice, what would you do and why? If your parent faced this choice, what would you want him or her to do and why?

Section 6: Your Career Philosophy

The word **philosophy** comes from the composite Greek noun *philosophia,* which means "the pursuit of wisdom." Your **career philosophy** is the **deliberate** (carefully considered) involvement of your personal beliefs and behaviors in these areas:

- Choosing an occupation
- Acquiring the necessary education and training for the occupation
- Performing day-to-day work tasks
- Planning a career that might include several occupations

Just as water must be filtered through coffee grounds to produce a unique beverage, your life experiences must be filtered through your inner values, interests, and attitudes to develop your unique career philosophy. At the same time, your career philosophy cannot ignore the outer pressure from the expectations and standards of family, friends, and society.

Self-Understanding

Ask several students: In what ways is your career philosophy similar to the career philosophy of your best friend and your parent(s) or guardian(s)? In what ways is your career philosophy different from the career philosophy of your best friend and your parent(s) or guardian(s)?

Every high school graduate has his or her career philosophy. What is yours?

Adjusting Your Expectations

Everyone has expectations from life. Some people expect a lot, whereas others expect very little. Some have realistic expectations, whereas others fantasize about the future.

Enrichment

Have students complete the "Personal Expectations" worksheet in Chapter 21 of the *Preparing for Career Success Instructor's CD-ROM, Third Edition.*

Case Study

Have students read the case study "Plan Number Two" in Chapter 21 of the *Planning for Career Success Student Activity Book, Third Edition.*

Enrichment

Have students complete the "Expectations and Adjustments" worksheet found in the Chapter 21 file of the *Preparing for Career Success Instructor's CD-ROM, Third Edition.*

Do you know a student who expects to attend college, have a professional career, and earn a large salary but is presently failing high school and not exploring career options? This type of person has high-level, long-term expectations but chooses to ignore the required everyday tasks.

Realistic expectations can be a source of motivation and personal growth. After you achieve a goal (satisfy an expectation), a higher-level expectation usually takes its place. On the other hand, failure to achieve your expectations can lower your self-esteem and lead to a lower level of expectations.

Each year, thousands of students who graduated from high school tech-prep, technical, or work-study programs receive college diplomas. Many of these college graduates were not successful students when they entered high school, however. Establishing a career goal and being successful in their high school programs caused them to adjust the level of their expectations.

It is normal for people to make adjustments and change certain expectations during the span of their working years. Getting married, giving birth, getting laid off from a job, having children leave home and go to college, experiencing the death of a loved one, and retiring from a career force people to adjust their life expectations. Mature adults understand what is attainable, and they adjust to events that are beyond their control.

CAREER FACT

Children are expensive. From the maternity bill to high school graduation, the total price tag for raising the average child is more than $120,000 and going up every year. These costs include housing, food, transportation, clothing, health care, education, child care, and miscellaneous items. As a child ages, the annual cost of raising the child increases.

Balancing Your Work and Personal Life

Balancing your work and personal life is a matter of making the right choices. The objective is to find happiness and satisfaction in both of these areas. Every person will have a different definition of happiness and satisfaction. What is yours? Whether you are at work, at home, or with friends, the following tips can help you learn to increase your level of happiness and satisfaction:

- Do not be afraid to feel deeply and to express your emotions. Loss, anger, joy, fear, love, and other emotions are a part of life's experience. Successful people know when laughing and crying are appropriate, but drinking deep from the cup of experience helps them to understand the meaning of work and life.
- Focus on the present moment. Whether you are reading a textbook, performing a work task, or having a good time with friends, your happiness and success will be increased if you put away thoughts of yesterday and tomorrow and concentrate your energy on the activity at hand.
- Be generous with friends, family, and coworkers. Share your knowledge and skills without expecting anything in return. The size of your gift is not what matters. Your willingness to share with others brings the inner sense of happiness and satisfaction.

© JIST Works

- Be honest in your dealings with friends, family, and coworkers. Unethical and dishonest behaviors destroy feelings of happiness and satisfaction and replace them with guilt, shame, and doubt.

Experiencing periods of time when your life is out of balance is normal. Your boss may assign you to a very important and urgent project, a loved one may become very ill, or you may find yourself in an overwhelming social situation. When emergencies of this type occur, you must adjust your priorities. These changes in the balance of your life should be temporary.

If a situation that takes your life out of balance is frequently repeated, it loses temporary status and becomes permanent. When this happens, it is time for you to review the amount of time you spend at work and with friends and loved ones. Next, take responsibility for your situation, and make decisions that bring your life back into balance. Take time to listen to the messages you are receiving every day from coworkers, loved ones, and friends. This will help you to identify periods of time when your life is slipping out of balance.

Take Note

According to the teachings of Rudolf Dreikurs in the book *Fundamentals of Adlerian Psychology,* the three most important areas of life to bring into balance are your work, love relationships, and friendships.

Section 6: Get Involved

Answer the following on a separate sheet of paper, and be prepared to discuss your responses in class.

1. List any life experiences that have affected you so deeply that you will never forget them. They may be pleasant or unpleasant. How did each of the experiences on your list affect the way you think about your future career?
2. Review what you have learned about preparing for career success, and write your own career philosophy. Be sure to include your views about work, employers, and workers; your important beliefs and the way they relate to work, workers, and worksites; a list of possible occupations on the career path you are considering; the education and training path you are presently considering; contributions you expect to make to your family, friends, or society through your work; and rewards you expect to receive from your family, friends, or society because of your work.
3. List five life expectations that you have already satisfied. Examples include learning to ride a bicycle, getting an A in English, or being selected for the basketball team. Describe any adjustments you made from your original expectations.
4. List the adjustments you have already made with certain expectations because of family problems, economics, race, or gender. Be specific.
5. List your five most important expectations for the next 10 years. Of the five, which is most important to you? If you are unable to achieve your most important expectation, what adjustment will you make?

Chapter 21 Review

Enrich Your Vocabulary

On a separate sheet of paper, number from 1 to 20, and write the most appropriate term from the "Enrich Your Vocabulary" list at the beginning of the chapter next to the number of the statement it matches.

1. A physician who specializes in children's care
2. Free from the rule

Enrich Your Vocabulary Answers

1. pediatrician
2. exempt

(continued)

Enrich Your Vocabulary Answers *(continued)*

3. accrued
4. Family and Medical Leave Act of 1993
5. mommy track
6. noncustodial parent
7. love
8. courtship
9. dating
10. workaholics
11. three o'clock syndrome
12. generativity
13. philosophy
14. intimacy
15. career philosophy
16. ego integrity
17. deliberate
18. dominant
19. conscience
20. distinct

Check Your Knowledge Answers

1. Dating and courtship.
2. (1) Developing mutual trust, (2) sharing confidences, (3) being open about thoughts and feelings, and (4) having potential for a lasting relationship.
3. Approximately 51 percent.
4. About 73 percent.
5. Up to 12 weeks of leave if the employer has 50 or more employees within a 75-mile radius.

(continued)

3. Accumulated
4. A law that gives employees 12 weeks of unpaid leave for family care
5. When a woman changes her work schedule for her child
6. The parent who does not have primary custody of the child
7. Deep affection
8. The process of seeking someone's affections
9. The process of having social engagements with a person you are romantically attracted to
10. Compulsive workers who are overly involved in their jobs
11. When parents' thoughts turn to their children
12. A life stage during which adults are productive in the world of work and develop families of their own
13. A word derived from the Greek noun meaning "the pursuit of wisdom"
14. A life stage during which adults are close and familiar
15. The deliberate involvement of personal beliefs and behaviors in planning, choosing, acquiring, and performing a career
16. A life stage that, when mastered, brings wisdom
17. Carefully considered
18. Most influential
19. Ideas and feelings that give a sense of right and wrong
20. Easy to recognize

Check Your Knowledge

On a separate sheet of paper, complete the following activities.

1. What are the traditional methods Americans use to select a lifelong mate?
2. List four characteristics of courtship.
3. Approximately what percentage of young couples in the United States earn two salaries?
4. What percentage of today's families have two parents with full-time jobs?
5. How many weeks of unpaid leave from their jobs are employees entitled to receive as a result of the Family and Medical Leave Act of 1993?

© JIST Works

6. Why are employers allowed to exempt certain employees from the Family and Medical Leave Act?
7. Why is it important to check for licensing at a child-care facility before enrolling a child?
8. Review Table 21.1. What five childhood needs do you believe are the most important for career success? Explain your answer.
9. Approximately how many children watch their mothers and fathers divorce every year?
10. Many, if not most, workers will need to develop new skills and take advantage of changing opportunities throughout their careers. Why?
11. What is the first life stage that occurs during the adult years?
12. List four tips that can help you to increase your level of happiness and satisfaction.
13. List five tasks of the generativity stage.
14. What four areas does a career philosophy relate to?

Develop SCANS Competencies

This activity will give you practice in developing the resources and information skills that successful workers use. Develop a time line of your life. To begin, categorize at least 20 different events in your life under the following heads: physical development, intellectual development, and social and personality development. These events should show growth on your part. For example, physical development could include learning to walk and, later, learning to ride a bike. After you categorize the events, try to determine your age at the time of the event. You may need to ask your parents or other family members for help.

Finally, transfer the information to a time line of your life. You may add pictures to accompany the information on the time line. Continue the time line into the future. Think about what you plan to be doing in 5, 10, or 15 years. Will you go to college or trade school? If so, where will you go? What type of job would you like to have? Will you be married? Will you have children? Add pictures to this part of the time line, also.

Check Your Knowledge Answers *(continued)*

6. Their leave would cause economic harm to the employer.
7. Licensing requirements set minimal standards, such as class size and environmental safety.
8. Answers will vary. See Table 21.1.
9. More than a million.
10. New technology will create new occupations and will eliminate many established occupations.
11. The stage of intimacy.
12. See the first paragraph of "Balancing Your Work and Personal Life." (1) Do not be afraid to express your deep feelings and emotions. (2) Focus on the present. (3) Be generous. (4) Be honest.
13. (1) Be productive in the world of work. (2) Develop a family of one's own. (3) Seek truth by reviewing personal beliefs and values. (4) Assume the role of caretaker for the knowledge and products of past generations. (5) Prepare the next generation for social and career roles.
14. (1) Choosing an occupation, (2) acquiring the necessary education and training for the occupation, (3) performing day-to-day work tasks, and (4) planning a career that might include several occupations.

Reteaching

To reinforce the ideas in this chapter, have students complete the "Finding the Right Words" and "Checking Your Location" activities for Chapter 21 in the *Preparing for Career Success Student Activity Book, Third Edition.*

Enrichment

Have students complete the Chapter 21 section of the *Preparing for Career Success Student Portfolio, Third Edition.*

The U.S. Department of Education Career Clusters

The following pages include worker characteristics and color-coded listings of occupations related to each of the 16 U.S. Department of Education career clusters. Some occupations may be entered at more than one level of education or training.

- Occupations in green sections may be entered with a high school (tech-prep, technical, or general studies) education.
- Occupations in yellow sections oftentimes require a year or more of a specialty school or apprenticeship training.
- Occupations in orange sections usually require at least a two-year associate degree.
- Occupations in blue sections normally require a four-year college degree or a professional degree.

The numbers in the Employment Data tables are estimates based on information collected by the U.S. Bureau of Labor Statistics in 2006.

Agriculture and Natural Resources Career Cluster

This career cluster includes the following kinds of work:

- Planning, financing, managing, processing, marketing, and distributing food, fiber, and natural resource products and systems
- Providing horticulture and landscaping services
- Mining and extraction operations and related environmental management services

The food processing industry (see the Manufacturing career cluster) and grocery store business (see the Retail/Wholesale Sales and Service career cluster) are also included in this cluster.

Worker Characteristics

Enjoys the outdoors and physical activity

Improves methods of working

Prefers hands-on work

Solves problems

Understands the natural environment

Agricultural and Natural Resources Occupations

Breeder (animal) Earth driller (water/salt) Fisher/deckhand	Operator (agricultural equipment, logging equipment) Roustabout (oil/gas)	Tree trimmer/pruner Worker (extraction, farm, forest, grounds-keeping, nursery)
Breeder (animal) Farmer	Inspector (agricultural) Manager (agricultural)	Rancher
Farmer Manager (agricultural)	Rancher	Technician (food science, forest conservation, geological)
Farmer Forester Geologist (petroleum)	Hydrologist Manager (agricultural) Mineralogist	Rancher Scientist (agricultural) Veterinarian

Employment Data

Occupation	Number of Workers	Occupation	Number of Workers
Agricultural equipment operators	59,000	Fishers and fishing vessel operators	38,000
Agricultural inspectors	16,000	Forest, conservation, and logging workers	88,000
Extraction workers	202,000	Mining machine operators	10,000
Farm workers	710,000	Roustabouts	44,000

Architecture and Construction Career Cluster

This career cluster can include the following kinds of work:

- Designing, building, and maintaining physical structures such as commercial and residential buildings
- Designing, planning, building, and maintaining larger environments such as roadways and bridges

Worker Characteristics

Architect

Consults with clients and develops reports and drawings

Visits construction sites to review the progress of projects

Visualizes objects, distances, sizes, and abstract forms

Construction Worker

Enjoys an outdoor environment

Has skill in using the tools of the trade

Construction Worker Manager

Coordinates and manages people, materials, and equipment

Works with budgets, schedules, and contracts

Oversees the safety of employees and the general public

Architecture and Construction Occupations

Carpenter Fence erector Glazier Installer (carpet/floor, drywall)	Mason (brick, cement, stone) Painter Paperhanger Rigger	Roofer Terrazzo Worker (construction)
Carpenter Construction equipment operator Construction supervisor Drafter Electrician Glazier	Heating/air conditioning/ refrigeration mechanic/installer Installer (carpet/floor, drywall) Mason (brick, cement, stone) Painter Paperhanger	Pipefitter Plasterer Plumber Roofer Technician (mapping, surveying) Worker (construction)
Construction supervisor Drafter	Heating/air conditioning/ refrigeration mechanic/installer	Inspector (building, construction) Technician (civil engineering)
Architect Civil engineer	Construction supervisor Landscape architect	Photogrammetrist Surveyor

Employment Data

Occupation	Number of Workers	Occupation	Number of Workers
Architects	132,000	Surveyors, cartographers, and photogrammetrists	72,000
Landscape architects	28,000		

Arts, A/V Technology, and Communications Career Cluster

This career cluster includes the following kinds of work:

- Designing, writing, and publishing multimedia content, including visual and performing arts and journalism
- Providing entertainment

Worker Characteristics

Entertainer

Demonstrates self-discipline, patience, perseverance, and a devotion to the art

Uses creativity and imagination

Communicates ideas visually and verbally

© JIST Works

Technician

Works with sound, video, or motion pictures

Frequently works with instruments, machines, and tools

Solves problems using technical information and logical thinking

Arts, A/V Technology, and Communications Occupations

Designer (floral) Displayer (merchandise)	Photographer Technician (audio/video equipment)	Trimmer (window)
Actor Announcer (radio/TV) Artist (cartoonist, illustrator) Dancer/choreographer	Designer (floral) Musician Photographer	Technician (audio/video equipment) TV/motion picture camera operator TV/motion picture film editor
Actor Announcer (radio/TV) Art critic Artist (fine, multimedia) Dancer/choreographer	Designer (fashion, graphic) Interpreter/translator Musician Photographer Specialist (public relations)	Technician (audio/video equipment) TV/motion picture camera operator TV/motion picture director Writer/editor
Art critic Artist (fine, multimedia) Dancer/choreographer Designer (fashion, interior) Director (art) Interpreter/translator	Musician News correspondent Photographer Singer Specialist (public relations)	Teacher (art, drama, music) Technician (broadcast) TV/motion picture camera operator TV/motion picture director Writer/editor

Employment Data

Occupation	Number of Workers	Occupation	Number of Workers
Artists	218,000	Public relations specialists	243,000
Floral designers	87,000	Writers, editors, and technical writers	307,000
Graphic designers	261,000		

Business and Administration Career Cluster

This career cluster includes the following kinds of work:

- Planning, managing, and providing administrative support
- Processing accounting information
- Providing human resources management and related management support services

Worker Characteristics

Administrative Support

Deals with the public

Compiles, distributes, and files information and data

Solves problems using traditional, proven procedures

Maintains an established system

Demonstrates honesty, discretion, and trustworthiness in working with confidential information

Manager

Demonstrates good communication skills

Establishes effective relationships with different types of people

Business and Administration Occupations

Clerk (file, mail, office) Customer service representative Data entry worker	Operator (communications equipment, office machine) Secretary	Stock clerk/order filler Word processor
Assistant (administrative) Clerk (accounting)	Desktop publisher Manager (administrative services)	Operator (computer, office machine) Secretary
Assistant (administrative) Clerk (accounting) Computer operator	Cost estimator Desktop publisher Employment specialist	Manager (administrative services, computer/information systems)
Accountant Analyst (budget, management) Auditor	Cost estimator Employment specialist	Manager (administrative services, computer/information systems) Top executive

Employment Data

Occupation	Number of Workers	Occupation	Number of Workers
Administrative services managers	247,000	General office clerks	3,200,000
Customer service representatives	2,202,000		

Education and Training Career Cluster

This career cluster includes the following kinds of work:

- Planning, managing, and providing education and training services and related learning support services, including assessment
- Planning, managing, and providing library and information services

© JIST Works

Worker Characteristics

Administrator

Sets educational standards and goals and establishes the policies and procedures to accomplish them

Educator

Enjoys helping others and working with people

Develops speaking, teaching, empathizing, listening, and conciliating skills

Uses information, computers, and other machines as tools

Training Specialist

Plans, organizes, and directs a wide range of training activities in the private sector

Consults with onsite supervisors regarding available performance improvement services

Conducts orientation sessions

Arranges on-the-job training for new employees

Education and Training Occupations

Nanny	Teacher assistant	
Teacher (assistant, self-enrichment)	Technician (library)	
Teacher (assistant, self-enrichment)	Technician (library, museum)	
Coach (college sports, professional) Dean (college/university) Librarian	Museum archivist or curator President (college/university) School staff (counselor, principal)	Specialist (training) Teacher (adult education, public school, postsecondary) Technician (museum)

Employment Data

Occupation	Number of Workers	Occupation	Number of Workers
Education administrators	413,000	Middle school teachers	658,000
Elementary school teachers	1,540,000	Postsecondary teachers	1,672,000
Kindergarten and preschool teachers	607,000	Secondary school teachers	1,038,000
Librarians	158,000	Training and development specialists	210,000

Finance Career Cluster

This career cluster includes the following kinds of work:

- Planning, managing, and providing banking or insurance services
- Planning, managing, and providing investment and financial planning services

Worker Characteristics

Demonstrates self-confidence and the ability to handle frequent rejections

Works carefully, orderly, and accurately, with attentiveness to details

Demonstrates honesty, discretion, and trustworthiness in working with confidential information

Has exceptional verbal and written communications skills

Finance Occupations

Clerk (financial, insurance claims)	Teller (banks, credit unions)	Worker (data entry)
Broker (real estate) Clerk (financial, insurance claims)	Preparer (tax) Sales agent (insurance, real estate)	Teller (banks, credit unions)
Adjuster (claims) Advisor (personal financial) Analyst (credit) Appraiser	Broker (real estate) Clerk (brokerage, credit, financial) Investigator (insurance) Officer (loan)	Preparer (tax) Sales agent (insurance, real estate, securities/commodities)
Accountant Actuary Adjuster (claims) Advisor (personal financial) Analyst (budget, credit, financial)	Appraiser Auditor Broker (real estate) Economist Investigator (insurance)	Manager (financial) Officer (loan) Sales agent (insurance, securities/commodities) Underwriter (insurance)

Employment Data

Occupation	Number of Workers	Occupation	Number of Workers
Accountants and auditors	1,274,000	Financial managers	506,000
Claims adjusters, examiners, and investigators	305,000	Insurance sales agents	436,000
Financial clerks	4,007,000	Tellers	608,000

Government and Public Administration Career Cluster

This career cluster includes the following kinds of work:

- Planning, managing, and providing government legislative, administrative, and regulatory services at the federal, state, and local levels
- Planning, managing, and providing general-purpose government services at the federal, state, and local levels

 © JIST Works

Worker Characteristics

Federal, state, and local governments employ workers with all types of personal characteristics from more than 400 different occupations.

Government and Public Administration Occupations

Census interviewer Court clerk	Mail (carrier, clerk, processing machine operator, sorter/processor)	
Assistant (social/human service) Controller (air traffic)	Inspector (agricultural) Officer (compliance)	Superintendent (postmaster/mail)
Agent (revenue) Assistant (social/human service) Collector/examiner (tax)	Inspector (agricultural) Superintendent (postmaster/mail)	Technician (occupational health/safety)
Agent (revenue) Anthropologist/archeologist Astronomer Assessor Collector/examiner (tax) Cryptographer Economist	Forester Geographer Hydrologist Manager (natural sciences) Mathematician Physicist Planner (urban/regional)	Scientist (political) Specialist (occupational health/safety) Technician (avionics) Worker (social) Zoologist/wildlife biologist

Employment Data

Federal Government's Percentage Share of Workers in Occupations in the U.S. Workforce

Occupation	Percent	Occupation	Percent
Agricultural inspectors	39	Forest and conservation technicians	76
Air traffic controllers	89	Geographers	61
Anthropologists and archeologists	25	Hydrologists	28
Astronomers	29	Mathematicians	37
Atmospheric and space scientists	37	Natural sciences managers	26
Avionics technicians	14	Physicists	20
Bridge/lock tenders	33	Political scientists	51
Compliance officers, except agriculture/construction/health/safety/transportation	39	Postal service workers	100
Conservation scientists	38	Tax examiners, collectors, and revenue agents	44
Economists	32	Transportation inspectors	17
Explosives workers, blasters, and ordnance handling experts	31	Zoologists and wildlife biologists	25

Health Science Career Cluster

This career cluster includes the following kinds of work:

- Planning, managing, and providing diagnostic, therapeutic, and information services in health care

Worker Characteristics

Carries out a variety of tasks in continually changing situations

Collects and analyzes information about patients

Solves problems

Enjoys helping people

Develops speaking, teaching, empathizing, listening, and conciliating skills

Uses specific tools and instruments

Health Science Occupations

Aide (nursing) Assistant (medical)	Interviewer (admitting) Preparer (medical equipment)	Technician (dental laboratory, dietetic, psychiatric)
Aide (nursing/psychiatric/home health, occupational therapist) Assistant (dental, medical) Diagnostic medical sonographer	Dispensing optician Hygienist (dental) Nurse (licensed practical) Paramedic	Technician (dental laboratory, dietetic, pharmacy) Therapist (massage) Transcriptionist (medical)
Assistant (physician's) Hygienist (dental) Nurse (registered) Repairer (medical equipment)	Sonographer Technician (clinical laboratory, medical records/health information)	Technologist (cardiovascular, nuclear medicine) Therapist (recreation, respiratory) Transcriptionist (medical)
Anesthetist (registered nurse) Assistant (physician's) Audiologist Chiropractor Dentist Dietician/nutritionist Educator (health) Manager (medical/health services)	Midwife (certified nurse) Nurse (practitioner, registered) Optometrist Orthotist/prosthetist Pharmacist Physician/surgeon Podiatrist	Specialist (occupational health/safety) Speech/language pathologist Technologist (clinical laboratory) Therapist (occupational, physical, recreational) Veterinarian

Employment Data

Occupation	Number of Workers	Occupation	Number of Workers
Health diagnosing and treating practitioners	4,460,000	Registered nurses	2,505,000
Medical and health services managers	262,000		

© JIST Works

Hospitality and Tourism Career Cluster

This career cluster includes the following kinds of work:

- Planning, managing, and providing lodging, food, recreation, convention services, and tourism
- Providing related planning and support services such as travel-related services

Worker Characteristics

Pays attention to customers' orders

Recalls faces, names, and preferences of frequent patrons

Has superior communication skills and an outgoing personality

Maintains composure even when dealing with an angry or demanding patron

Is well-groomed

Hospitality and Tourism Occupations

Agent (ticket) Attendant (amusement/recreation) Baggage porter/bellhop Baker Clerk (hotel/motel/resort desk) Concierge	Cook (fast food/short order) Dishwasher Driver (motorcoach) Guide (travel) Host/hostess	Housekeeping/cleaner Server (food/beverage) Supervisor (housekeeping) Usher/ticket taker Worker (kitchen)
Agent (travel) Baker Bartender	Chef/cook Clerk (hotel/motel/resort desk) Concierge	Guide (travel) Supervisor (food preparation) Worker (recreation/fitness)
Agent (travel) Chef/cook	Manager (convention services, food service, hotel/resort, resident)	Planner (convention) Worker (recreation/fitness)
Agent (travel)	Manager (convention services, food service, hotel/resort, resident)	Planner (convention) Worker (recreation/fitness)

Employment Data

Occupation	Number of Workers	Occupation	Number of Workers
Amusement and recreation attendants	247,000	Recreation workers	320,000
Food service managers	350,000	Waiters and waitresses	2,361,000

Human Services Career Cluster

This career cluster includes the following kinds of work:

- Planning, managing, and providing human services, including social and related community services

Worker Characteristics

Works directly with or for others

Is well-groomed, neat, and orderly

Enjoys helping people

Develops communication skills

Gets along with clients and coworkers

Human Services Occupations

Advisor (residential) Attendant (funeral, kennel, locker/ coat/dressing room)	Barber Cosmetologist Hairdresser/hairstylist	Manicurist/pedicurist Worker (animal control, childcare)
Assistant (human services) Barber Cosmetologist	Embalmer Groomer (animal) Hairstylist/hairdresser	Manicurist/pedicurist Trainer (animal) Worker (pest control, childcare)
Assistant (social and human services)	Director (funeral, religious activity/education)	Trainer (animal) Worker (pest control, childcare)
Clergy Counselor (school, marriage)	Director (funeral, education) Sociologist	Trainer (animal) Worker (clinical, school, industrial)

Employment Data

Occupation	Number of Workers	Occupation	Number of Workers
Child care workers	1,388,000	Personal appearance workers	825,000
Clergy	404,000	Social workers	595,000
Counselors	635,000		

Information Technology Career Cluster

This career cluster includes the following kinds of work:

- Designing, developing, managing, and supporting hardware, software, multimedia, and systems-integration services

© JIST Works

Worker Characteristics

Solves problems

Works with data (information), computers, and related hardware and software

May be required to follow a very structured system

May be required to think outside of the box, searching for new alternatives

Information Technology Occupations

Repairer (computer)	Technician (bench)	
Administrator (database) Analyst (computer systems) Designer (Web)	Engineer (computer applications/ software, systems software) Programmer (computer applications)	Repairer (ATM machine, computer) Specialist (telecommunications) Technician (computer service)
Administrator (database) Analyst (computer systems) Designer (Web) Director (project)	Engineer (software, hardware) Manager (computer information systems) Mathematician Officer (chief technology)	Programmer (computer systems) Scientist (computer) Specialist (computer support, telecommunications)

Employment Data

Occupation	Number of Workers	Occupation	Number of Workers
Computer programmers	435,000	Database administrators	119,000
Computer support specialists	552,000	Network and computer systems administrators	309,000
Computer systems analysts	504,000		

Law and Public Safety Career Cluster

This career cluster includes the following kinds of work:

- Planning, managing, and providing judicial, legal, and criminal justice protective services
- Planning, managing, and providing fire protection

Worker Characteristics

Public Safety Worker

Demonstrates mental alertness, self-discipline, courage, mechanical aptitude, endurance, physical strength, and a strong sense of public service

Must be at least 20 or 21 years of age

Must pass civil service examinations or other job-relevant tests, such as tests of hearing and strength

Legal System Worker

Accepts great responsibility

Adheres to a strict code of ethics

Has a strong sense of social justice

Law and Public Safety Occupations

Deputy sheriff/baliff Firefighter	Guard (security) Officer (uniformed police)	Warden (fish/game) Worker (animal control)
Deputy sheriff/baliff Detective (police, private) Firefighter	Guard (security) Inspector (fire)	Officer (compliance, correctional, gaming surveillance) Warden (fish/game)
Assistant (paralegal/legal) Chief (fire department chief/deputy) Deputy sheriff/baliff	Detective (police, private) Firefighter Inspector (fire)	Reporter (court) Technician (forensic science) Warden (fish/game)
Agent (FBI, U.S. border patrol) Assistant (paralegal/legal) Chief (fire department chief/deputy) Clerk (law) Coroner	Detective (police, private) Examiner (financial) Hearing officer/adjudicator Judge Lawyer	Magistrate Officer (probation) Reporter (court) Specialist (correctional treatment, occupational health and safety) Technician (forensic science)

Employment Data

Occupation	Number of Workers	Occupation	Number of Workers
Correctional officers and jailers	442,000	Paralegals and legal assistants	238,000
Judges, magistrate judges, and magistrates	27,000	Security guards	1,040,000
Lawyers	761,000	Uniformed police officers and detectives	654,000
Paid, career firefighters	293,000		

Manufacturing Career Cluster

This career cluster includes the following kinds of work:

- Planning, managing, and performing the processing of materials into intermediate or final products
- Providing related professional and technical support activities such as production planning and control, maintenance, and manufacturing/process engineering

Employment in these jobs will continue to decline due to increasing automation and outsourcing of jobs to countries with lower labor costs.

 © JIST Works

Worker Characteristics

Manufacturing Worker

Uses good eyesight, hand-eye coordination, and manual dexterity

Concentrates on detailed work for long periods of time

Has a year or more of on-the-job work experience

Engineer

Supervises production in factories

Develops human relations skills

Knows scientific principles and mathematics

Manufacturing Occupations

Assembler/fabricator Builder (tire) Cutter/trimmer Inspector/tester/sorter/weigher Installer/repairer (line) Machinist	Mechanic (industrial machinery) Molder/shaper/caster Operator (chemical equipment, cutting/slicing machine, packaging and filling machine, water plant system)	Technician (ophthalmic laboratory) Upholsterer Welding, soldering, and brazing Woodworker (entry-level) Worker (apparel, bookbinder/bindery, food processing)
Assembler/fabricator Carpenter (cabinetmaker/bench) Drafter Engineer (stationary) Etcher/engraver Line installer/repairer	Machinist Mechanic (industrial machinery) Millwright Operator (boiler, chemical plant system, computer control) Repairer (electrical/electronics)	Technician (semiconductor) Tool and die maker Upholsterer Welding, soldering, and brazing Worker (bookbinder/bindery, food processing, precious stones)
Drafter Jeweler	Repairer (electrical/electronics) Technician (chemical, prepress)	Tool and die maker Worker (precious stone/metal)
Designer (industrial)	Engineer (aerospace, chemical, industrial, mechanical)	Manager (industrial production)

Employment Data

Occupation	Number of Workers	Occupation	Number of Workers
Assemblers and fabricators	2,075,000	Industrial production managers	157,000

Retail/Wholesale Sales and Service Career Cluster

This career cluster includes the following kinds of work:

- Planning, managing, and performing wholesaling and retailing services
- Providing related marketing and distribution support services

Worker Characteristics

Has a pleasant appearance, personality, and sense of humor

Communicates well with others

Persuades others to buy the product or service

Has a complete knowledge of and personal interest in the goods or services being sold

Has good planning and decision-making skills and an interest in the total merchandising process

Has computer skills

Performs repetitive tasks accurately

Has basic math skills

Retail/Wholesale Sales and Service Occupations

Agent (advertising sales) Cashier Clerk (counter/rental) Demonstrator/promoter (product)	Installer/repairer (electrical/ electronic, home appliance) Model Salesperson (parts, retail)	Telemarketer Vendor (street) Worker (door-to-door sales, general maintenance)
Agent (real estate) Demonstrator/promoter (product)	Installer/repairer (computer, electrical/electronic, home appliance, office machine) Model	Repairer (watch/clock) Repairer/tuner (musical instrument) Supervisor (sales worker) Technician (bench)
Demonstrator/promoter (product) Installer/repairer	Sales representative Supervisor (sales worker)	Technician (bench)
Agent (purchasing) Buyer (wholesale/retail) Demonstrator/promoter (product)	Engineer (sales) Manager (advertising/marketing, purchasing, sales)	Public relations specialist Sales representative (manufacturing, wholesale)

Employment Data

Occupation	Number of Workers	Occupation	Number of Workers
Cashiers	3,500,000	Wholesale and retail buyers	157,000
Sales and related occupations	15,985,000		

© JIST Works

Scientific Research and Engineering Career Cluster

This career cluster includes the following kinds of work:

- Planning, managing, and providing scientific research and professional and technical services in physical and social science and engineering
- Providing laboratory, testing, research, and development services

Worker Characteristics

Solves problems

Prefers working with information

Prefers independent activities to social situations and leadership roles

Performs well in chemistry, physics, biology, algebra, geometry, trigonometry, and math classes

Scientific Research and Engineering Occupations

Technician (chemical, electrical/electronics)

Drafter

Technician (aerospace engineering, biological, chemical engineering, electrical/electronics engineering, food science, mechanical engineering, nuclear)

Anthropologist
Archeologist
Astronomer
Chemist
Economist
Engineer
Geographer
Geoscientist
Historian
Manager (engineering)
Market/survey researcher
Mathematician
Meteorologist
Physicist
Psychologist (research)
Scientist
Sociologist

Employment Data

Occupation	Number of Workers	Occupation	Number of Workers
Chemists and materials scientists	94,000	Social scientists (economists, psychologists, historians)	530,000
Engineers	1,512,000		

Transportation, Distribution, and Logistics Career Cluster

This career cluster includes the following kinds of work:

- Planning and managing the movement of people, materials, and goods by road, pipeline, air, rail, and water
- Providing related professional and technical support services such as transportation infrastructure planning and management, logistics services, mobile equipment, and facility maintenance

Worker Characteristics

Enjoys physical activity in the outdoors

Can handle stress and mental as well as physical fatigue

Solves practical problems quickly

Transportation, Distribution, and Logistics Occupations

Agent (cargo/freight, ticket) Cleaner (vehicle/equipment) Clerk (shipping/receiving) Collector (refuse) Courier/messenger Dispatcher	Driver (bus, taxi, truck) Engineer/conductor (railroad) Laborer Machine feeder/offbearer Mover (freight/material) Operator (industrial truck/tractor, loading machine, pump)	Repairer (vending machine) Tank/car/truck/ship loader Technician/mechanic (automotive) Weigher/measurer/checker/sampler Worker (postal service, railroad yard)
Agent (cargo/freight) Attendant (flight)	Clerk (shipping/receiving/traffic) Driver (bus, truck)	Repairer (automotive body) Technician/mechanic (diesel)
Attendant (flight) Controller (air traffic)	Engineer (flight) Mechanic (aircraft)	Pilot (aircraft) Technician (avionics)
Attendant (flight) Controller (air traffic) Engineer (civil, flight, logistics)	Mechanic (aircraft) Officer (ship's deck/engineering)	Pilot (aircraft) Technician (avionics)

Employment Data

Occupation	Number of Workers	Occupation	Number of Workers
Material moving occupations	4,825,000	Truck drivers and driver/sales workers	3,356,000
School bus drivers	455,000		

© JIST Works

Bonus Content

Resources for Career Success

By The Editors at JIST

This bonus section expands on the ideas presented in the chapters of this textbook. Use this information to inspire you as you set goals and make plans for your education and career.

Connecting Your Personality with Your Career

Chapter 2, "Knowing Yourself: Interests and Aptitudes," made the point that the first step in choosing a satisfying career is to understand yourself and what makes you unique. The following sections describe some useful theories about personality and explain how you can use these theories to understand yourself better and prepare for a satisfying career.

Intelligence

An important part of your personality is your intelligence. Intelligence is defined in many ways. It can include the ability to reason, plan, adapt to new situations, and learn from experience. How people perceive your intelligence and you perceive your own intelligence affects your educational and employment opportunities. The following sections explain some important ideas about intelligence.

IQ and Intelligence Testing

IQ stands for *intelligence quotient.* It refers to the result of a standardized test that compares a person's ability to correctly answer or complete verbal, mathematic, and other academic questions or tasks to that of other people in the same age group. An IQ of 100 is considered average. The concept of IQ was first developed as a way to predict how well children would perform in school so that they could receive additional training if needed. Since then, intelligence testing has expanded greatly.

For example, the United States military uses an intelligence test called the Armed Forces Qualifying Test to screen out people who will have difficulty with military training. This test includes math, vocabulary, and reading questions and is part of the more comprehensive ASVAB (Armed Forces Vocational Aptitude Battery) that determines eligibility for certain military occupations. College admissions officers use the scores of standardized tests such as the SAT to help them decide whom to accept into their schools.

If you are preparing to take a standardized test, use these tips to help you do your best:

- **Practice.** Go on the Internet or to the library to find practice tests to take. When you score your practice tests, make a note of the areas where you need to improve and review that material.
- **Be comfortable.** Get plenty of sleep the night before the test. On the day of the test, eat a good breakfast, and dress comfortably.

- **Focus.** Read all directions, and make sure you mark your answer in the correct place. Don't let yourself be distracted.
- **Choose wisely.** If you don't know the right answer, try to eliminate one or two wrong answers and then guess. Once you have marked an answer, don't change it unless you are absolutely sure that it's wrong.
- **Manage your time.** Most standardized tests are timed, so wear a watch and check it often to see how much time you have left. Don't get stuck on any one question: Skip the questions that you can't answer right away and come back to them later. Spend the most time on the sections that are worth the most points.

Although intelligence test scores can indicate a student's level of academic ability, they are not a definite predictor of academic achievement and success. Remember that academic success relies heavily on persistence, a willingness to learn, and hard work.

Multiple Intelligences

Dr. Howard Gardner, a professor at Harvard University, developed the concept of multiple intelligences. In his view, intelligence refers to the ability to solve problems, and the different kinds of intelligence refer to the different ways people have of solving problems. Dr. Gardner identifies nine kinds of intelligence:

- **Visual/spatial:** People with this type of intelligence have visual skills and learn best by looking at objects and spaces.
- **Verbal/linguistic:** People with this type of intelligence have language skills and learn best by reading, writing, speaking, and listening.
- **Mathematical/logical:** People with this type of intelligence have math skills and learn best by working with numbers and solving problems.
- **Bodily/kinesthetic:** People with this type of intelligence have physical skills and learn best by doing things and using their bodies.
- **Musical/rhythmic:** People with this type of intelligence have music and rhythm skills and learn best by using musical concepts, songs, patterns, and musical instruments.
- **Intrapersonal:** People with this type of intelligence have self-awareness skills and learn best through their natural understanding of their feelings, values, and ideas.
- **Interpersonal:** People with this type of intelligence have people skills and learn best through their natural ability to understand other people. They learn by working with a group or with a partner.
- **Naturalist:** People with this type of intelligence have outdoor skills and learn best from outdoor activities, animals, and field trips. They appreciate the wonder of nature.
- **Existential:** People with this type of intelligence have mental visualization skills and high ideals. They learn best by looking at the "big picture" of life. They are interested in world issues and in ethical conduct.

You may be intelligent in several or all of these areas. You are probably extra strong in one or two areas. Employers are looking for people who can function and solve problems in several types of situations, and you need to be able to describe and show evidence that you are that kind of person in order to get and keep a job. What classes can you take and what activities can you participate in to develop your multiple intelligences?

© JIST Works

Learning Styles

Learning styles refers to the idea that people prefer to use different methods of understanding and remembering information. There are three main learning styles:

- **Auditory:** This style involves using sound to learn information. Auditory learners prefer to learn from lectures, recordings, music, and verbal repetition.
- **Visual:** This style involves learning through visual information, such as diagrams, charts, and graphs. Visual learners prefer to learn through demonstrations, videos, and presentations.
- **Tactile/kinesthetic:** This style involves using tools or doing some other physical action to learn about something. Tactile/kinesthetic learners prefer to learn from writing notes, conducting experiments, and using computers or other learning tools.

According to this idea, most of us have a certain learning style that works best. Identifying this style and using it may help you to remember information better. Also, using more than one style may involve more of your brain in the learning process and may be able to help you understand information more easily.

The Holland Personality Types

The most widely used personality theory about careers was developed by John L. Holland in the early 1950s. The theory rests on the principle that people tend to be happier and more successful in jobs where they feel comfortable with the work tasks and problems, the physical environment, and the kinds of people who are coworkers. Holland identified six personality types that describe basic aspects of work situations:

- **R (Realistic):** Realistic personalities like work activities that include practical, hands-on problems and solutions. They enjoy dealing with plants, animals, and real-world materials such as wood, tools, and machinery. They enjoy outside work. Often they do not like occupations that mainly involve doing paperwork or working closely with others.
- **I (Investigative):** Investigative personalities like work activities that have to do with ideas and thinking more than with physical activity. They like to search for facts and figure out problems mentally rather than to persuade or lead people.
- **A (Artistic):** Artistic personalities like to express themselves in their work and enjoy work activities that involve artistic components such as forms, designs, and patterns. They prefer settings where they can work without following a clear set of rules.
- **S (Social):** Social personalities like work activities that help people and promote learning and personal development. They prefer communicating with others to working with objects, machines, or data. They like to teach, to give advice, or otherwise to be of service to people.
- **E (Enterprising):** Enterprising personalities like work activities having to do with starting up and carrying out projects, especially business ventures. They like persuading and leading people and making decisions. They like taking risks for profit. These personalities prefer action rather than thought.
- **C (Conventional):** Conventional personalities like work activities that follow set procedures and routines. They prefer working with data and details rather than with ideas. They prefer work in which there are precise standards rather than work in which they have to judge things by themselves. These personalities like working where the lines of authority are clear.

The combination of initials for these personality types, RIASEC, is often used to refer to these six types. Holland argued that most people can be described by one of the RIASEC personality types—the type that dominates—and that likewise each of the various occupations that make up the U.S. economy can be described as having work situations and settings compatible with one of these personality types. Therefore, if you understand your dominant personality type and then identify which jobs are consistent with that type, you will have a clearer idea of which jobs will suit you best.

Holland recognized that many people and jobs also tend toward a second or third personality type. For example, someone might be described primarily as Enterprising and secondarily as Social, and such a person would fit in best working in a job with RIASEC codes beginning with ES. People matching this description should also consider jobs with codes beginning SE, and they may find satisfaction in many jobs with a variety of three-letter RIASEC codes beginning with either E or S.

To find jobs that match the personality codes that best describe you, use the O*NET career database (which was described in Chapter 5). To access this database, use a computer to get on the Internet and follow these steps:

1. Use your Web browser to go to O*NET OnLine at http://online.onetcenter.org.
2. Click on the Find Occupations link.
3. In the O*NET Descriptors section, click on the Interests link.
4. Click on the link for your dominant personality type to see a list of jobs that match that type. You can also enter a second or third personality type to narrow your search.

Developing a Career Portfolio

People use portfolios to collect and document work that relates to a certain topic or area of achievement. For example, students make portfolios for certain classes to show what they have learned, and artists make portfolios to show what kind of work they have created. When you make a career portfolio, the topic is you and your career goals.

Chapter 1, "Preparing for Life's Many Tasks," briefly defined a career portfolio as a collection of materials that show your education and training, skills, and accomplishments. But more than that, a career portfolio is a tool that can help you succeed. The materials in your career portfolio show

- What you have accomplished
- What your skills are
- What experiences you have had
- What you have done to improve yourself
- What your goals and values are
- What you know
- What your school and career preferences are

Think about how your life may change in the future. Remember this: Learning should not end when you graduate from school. You can keep learning throughout your life. In fact, what you are really being taught in high school is how to learn. You are learning the skills you will need to continue to change and grow.

In the past, many people worked at the same company for many years. Today, things are different. You may have several jobs during your life. You will need to be able to

- Find a new job
- Learn new skills
- Find new ways to use the skills you already have

© JIST Works

The world changes rapidly, and changes in other parts of the world affect you. In addition, the American economy and job market are always changing. But you can deal with change if you expect it and know how recognize it. Your portfolio shows how your life has already changed. It helps you make decisions about your education and career. Your portfolio includes specific examples of how you have changed and grown.

A portfolio helps you evaluate yourself and your progress. Portfolios are important because

- Your grades do not show everything about you
- Your grades do not show what you are capable of understanding
- Your grades do not show what you are capable of doing
- Your grades do not show what activities you are involved in when you are not in school

Putting together your portfolio will build your self-confidence. Do you usually overlook what you have accomplished? Do you tend to emphasize the things you aren't good at? If so, you are like most people. Putting together a portfolio lets you see what is good about you. It lets you see how you have grown and what you have done.

As a freshman or sophomore in high school, you can use your portfolio as an important learning tool to get to know yourself better. Also, you can use your portfolio to help your teachers and counselors know you better. Particularly if you go to a big high school with large classes, your teachers and guidance counselors might not know you very well. Yet the more they know about you, the better the advice they will be able to give you. And this advice can be an important part of your success.

In your junior and senior years, you can begin to use your portfolio in interviews. It can help you as you make decisions about your education and career goals. When you finish school, you can use your portfolio as a tool for marketing yourself to potential employers. Or you may use it when you meet with college admissions personnel.

Organizing a Career Portfolio

A portfolio is not put together randomly. It should be organized in a way that clearly shows the steps you have taken to reach your goals. Imagine that you are showing someone your portfolio. You should be able to tell the person what each piece of information represents. You should be able to describe how you have grown as a person, student, and employee.

You do not have to organize your portfolio in date order. For example, you might want to organize it based on your multiple intelligences or the SCANS skills (Chapter 1 discussed these). For an idea of how this type of organization might work, look at the following table. You probably have created many good portfolio items as a result of completing the activities in this textbook.

Using SCANS Skills to Organize a Career Portfolio

SCANS Category	Specific Skill	Portfolio Examples
Basic skills	Writing	A research paper
Thinking skills	Reasoning	A photograph and description of a science fair project
Personal qualities	Being responsible	Attendance records, recommendations from teachers or supervisors
Resources skills	Managing money	A budget spreadsheet
Interpersonal skills	Working with a team	Information relating to a service project you completed as part of a club or organization
Technology skills	Applying technology	Grades or course descriptions for technical classes you have completed

(continued)

(continued)

SCANS Category	Specific Skill	Portfolio Examples
Systems skills	Designing systems	Procedures you have developed for school or extracurricular activities
Information skills	Using computers	Screen shots or a link to a Web site you created

Also, remember that a document can serve more than one purpose. For example, if you win an award in your computer science class, you can use the award to show that you have computer experience and that you value your education. The point is that you can organize your portfolio any way you want, but be sure you can explain why you organized it a certain way.

No matter how you organize your portfolio, there is certain information that every career portfolio should include. First, you should include a table of contents that outlines the major sections of your portfolio. After the table of contents, include a letter of introduction. Although the letter of introduction appears at the beginning of a portfolio, it probably will be the last thing you write. This letter is a short summary of what you discovered about yourself while putting together your career portfolio. Use it to describe your career and education goals and your major interests and special abilities.

As you learned in Chapter 9, your employers will ask you to provide certain documents before you start work. You should include these documents (or copies of them) in your portfolio in a personal information section.

These documents include

- Social Security card
- Birth certificate
- Driver's license, U.S. passport, or other photographic identification
- Health certificate
- Work permit
- Noncitizen status papers

If you developed a personal data sheet, as discussed in Chapter 8, "Conducting the Job Search," include that in this section as well.

Locating and gathering these documents is a critical and often time-consuming part of creating a portfolio. Safeguarding this information is also important. To reduce the potential for identity theft, you should not include these documents in an electronic portfolio. Also, store the original documents in a secured place until you need to present them to an employer or school.

Other items that should be included in a career portfolio are the results of self-assessment activities. For example, you could include your completed *Preparing for Career Success Student Interest Inventory*. Think about what you have learned about yourself while reading and completing the activities in Chapters 1, 2, and 3 of this book. You probably know a lot more about your interests, aptitudes, values, and goals. Show this knowledge in your career portfolio by including information about goals you have achieved and work you have done to support the values that are important to you.

Chapter 6, "Looking Ahead: Education and Training," emphasized how important education and training are to future career success. For this reason, it's important to emphasize information about the skills you have learned through your high school and other life experiences in your career portfolio. This information can include

- Your grades (transcripts)
- Standardized test scores

© JIST Works

- Certificates and diplomas
- Licenses
- Languages you know
- Course descriptions from favorite classes
- School projects
- Things you have taught yourself

You may not have had a paid job yet, but you probably have had some unpaid work experience. Both are important. Unpaid work experience includes unpaid internships, volunteer work, and service learning. Your career portfolio should contain documents relating to your work experience, such as

- Your resume
- A complete description for each job (paid or unpaid)
- The name and address of each organization
- Your supervisors' names
- Your job evaluations

Also, if you can, put some things in your portfolio for the person reviewing it to look at, such as photographs, charts, and designs. Include any kind of visual information you think would reinforce the skills you want to emphasize.

College admissions officers, guidance counselors, and employers love portfolios because they not only provide evidence of what you can do, but they also tell them what other people think about you. For this reason, you should add any kind of positive, written statement about your school, work, or community activities that you receive from teachers, employers, coaches, or community leaders to your career portfolio. Examples of these statements are

- Reference letters
- Certificates of achievement
- School awards
- Newspaper or magazine articles showing what you have done in your community
- Thank-you letters from people you have helped

As you create your first portfolio, you will see that you have more materials than you need. That's good. Get together as much information as you can. Then you can choose the best examples and decide which sections of your portfolio to emphasize. Bits and pieces of information may not say much about you, but when you put everything together, you present a bigger picture of who you are.

Presenting a Career Portfolio

Now that you have collected all the material for your portfolio, you need to consider how you will present it. The key point regarding presentation can be summed up in one word—*professionalism.* No matter how impressive or exciting the content of your portfolio may be, it will not be as effective as it could be if it does not have a professional look and feel. Your ability to present your material professionally can give you an edge in the job search process.

An electronic portfolio is easier to update and distribute than a paper portfolio, and creating an electronic portfolio is a good way to demonstrate your technical skills. The first step in creating an electronic portfolio is to make electronic versions of all your nonelectronic materials. To do this, you will need access to a scanner to make digital copies of paper documents, such as certificates or awards. A digital camera also is useful to take photographs of projects so that you have an image to go along with the descriptions of your achievements.

Make sure you use standard formats for your materials so that they can be viewed on any computer. For example, if you have access to the Adobe Acrobat program, you should convert all your documents to PDF files because these files can be viewed on just about any computer. Most people can view Microsoft Office file types, such as Word, Excel, or PowerPoint, on their computers as well.

To complete the process, you need to create an electronic table of contents or introduction with links to all of your electronic materials to put them in some sort of context. Be sure to include an explanation or description of each item so that it's clear why it is included.

At this point, the portfolio is ready to copy onto CD-ROM. You may want to use a graphics program to create an eye-catching cover and label. At the very least, the label and cover need to display your name, the words *Career Portfolio,* and your contact information. It's a good idea to test the CD on several different computers to make sure everything looks the way you want it to before you present your electronic portfolio to teachers or potential employers.

A more advanced version of the electronic portfolio is the Web-based portfolio. Creating a Web-based career portfolio requires Web publishing software and a Web hosting service. Your school may provide these things, or you can get them from the Internet at little cost.

Follow these guidelines when creating a Web-based portfolio:

- When you are networking for job opportunities, make sure you tell people how they can access your portfolio online. Include this information on your resume as well.
- Limit the amount of personal information you include for your own safety. With newer technology, there are ways to password-protect certain parts of a Web site so that you can control which viewers have access to certain information.
- Keep the layout simple and professional. Avoid hard-to-read fonts, pop-up screens, and excessive graphics.
- Make sure you test your Web-based portfolio before making it available to everyone. Have your friends and family review it.

The increased interactivity of the Web opens up a whole new category of things you can include in a Web-based portfolio, such as blogs and other social networking features. Although other types of portfolios (for a class or another topic of interest, for example) can benefit from letting viewers of the portfolio comment and contribute to it, remember that a career portfolio is about you and your career and educational goals. You should include only the information that fits this purpose.

Even though you have an electronic portfolio, you will need to have a paper-based one as well to take with you to interviews and to store original documents in. Most people use a three-ring binder for their portfolios, but you may want to use a larger, artist-type portfolio case if you have a lot of artwork or large materials.

Follow these guidelines to assemble a professional-looking career portfolio:

- Use original documents whenever possible or clean, clear photocopies.
- Put each document in a transparent plastic cover.
- Use separators and typed labels to divide the sections of your portfolio.
- Make sure your binder or case is the right size for the material you have. You don't want it to look too empty or too stuffed.

© JIST Works

- Include a typed cover sheet on the binder that indicates that this is a portfolio and includes your name, address, e-mail address, and home telephone and cell phone numbers.
- All pictures, graphs, designs, drawings, and other visual aids should be in color, if possible.

Lastly, make sure that you handle your portfolio binder carefully and clean off any smudges or fingerprints.

As you gain more school and work experience, update your portfolio. Reviewing your portfolio on a regular basis provides you with the opportunity to think about whether your plans for your education and career are still right for you or whether you need to consider a different path.

Using a Career Portfolio in Interviews

Creating a positive first impression is important when you are

- Preparing to graduate from high school
- Looking for a job
- Applying for acceptance into college or some other training program

Chapter 9, "Applying and Interviewing for a Job," notes how portfolios can be useful in interviews. When you are talking to an interviewer, that person knows little or nothing about you. You have to paint a picture of yourself that is positive and true.

You know what you have experienced and what you have achieved. You know that you are mature and committed, and you know that these are qualities that interviewers look for. Still, you may have a hard time describing how everything fits together. Your portfolio gives you a way to tell an interviewer about your skills and experiences.

As a full-time student, you probably have limited work experience, so you have to let the interviewer know that you have potential. Many interviewers are more interested in quality people than in people who have years of experience. Each item in your portfolio is evidence of your skills, knowledge, and values. These characteristics define who you are and what kind of student or employee you will be. You can use these and other documents to impress interviewers.

Most interviewers—from college recruiters to restaurant managers—know what type of person they're looking for. They don't have time to hear everything about your life or school activities, but they do want information that helps them make a final decision. During the interview, you need to show them examples from your portfolio that are clear, relevant, and interesting.

In order to do that, you need to look through your portfolio ahead of time and pinpoint items that relate to the interview. If you are applying for a job, learn as much as you can about what your job description would be. Identify materials in your portfolio that show that you have the qualities you would need in that job. For example, if you want a job that involves working on a team, show examples of times when you have worked with other people.

If you are applying for internships, work-study programs, or other educational opportunities, you want to draw attention to materials in your portfolio that show why you are a good candidate for the program you are applying to. For example, you can include a transcript that shows what high grades you have made in relevant courses or include photographs of things you have built to demonstrate your technical knowledge.

After you have figured out what items from your portfolio are relevant to the interview, you need to prepare yourself to talk about them as you show them to an interviewer. Think about how you can describe each item. You can think of these descriptions as short stories. In each story, you should talk about

- One of your skills or accomplishments
- The problem or need you faced

- The action you took to solve that problem or meet that need
- The results of your action

Practice saying each story out loud, and make sure no story is longer than a minute and a half. Remember that you want to convince the interviewer to choose you. Being modest at an interview is not a virtue.

Consider making a copy of your portfolio on CD or DVD that is targeted to one specific job or school by including only the information that relates to that job or school. That way, you can leave a copy with the interviewer that he or she can refer to later or show to others in the organization.

Writing a Business Plan

Chapter 16, "Starting a Business," provided an overview of the issues involved in becoming an entrepreneur. Section 3 in that chapter covered the questions you need to ask yourself while planning a business. (The *Preparing for Career Success Student Activity Book* also has a related worksheet called "Select a Business and Develop a Plan for Its Success.") This section has more details about the format and contents of a written business plan based on information from the Small Business Administration.

A business plan is an essential tool in helping entrepreneurs to manage their businesses and obtain loans and financing from banks and investors. It starts with a short executive summary (no more than four pages) that highlights the most important information in the plan and makes the reader want to know more. This summary should include the following information:

- A brief mission statement that explains what your business is all about
- A history of the business (unless it is brand new), including information about the founders and company growth
- Basic facts about the business, such as location, number of employees, and descriptions of the products or services it provides
- Future plans for the business

If you're just starting a business, you won't have a lot of this information yet. In this case, use the executive summary to explain your experience and background as well as the decisions that led you to start this business. Convince the reader that you have a solid idea and the skills to turn it into a successful business.

After the executive summary, include a table of contents to assist the reader in locating specific sections in your business plan. The first section is the market analysis. This section includes the following information:

- An overview of the industry your business is in
- A summary of the results of any market research you have done
- A detailed description of your target market
- Prices and discounts you will offer
- A competitive analysis of businesses that offer similar products or services, including their strengths and weaknesses
- Lead times, which are the amount of time between when customers place orders and when those orders are delivered
- Details about laws and restrictions that affect the business

© JIST Works

The next section is a company description that explains how all the parts of the business work together. This description identifies the customer need that the business will satisfy. Also, it includes information about business methods and specific customers.

After the company description, you need to include a section on the business's organization and management. This section includes the following information:

- An organizational chart with a description of each major function and who is responsible for it
- Ownership details, including information about forms of ownership, stocks, percentages, names of owners, and company involvement
- Resumes of the company managers and their salary information
- A list of the people on the board of directors (if applicable) and their qualifications

Next, you need to describe your marketing and sales strategies, which are the ways that you will create customers for your business. These strategies can include the following:

- **Growth strategy:** A business can grow in many ways. For example, it can increase its number of employees (an internal strategy), buy another business (an acquisition strategy), spread to other locations (a franchise strategy), or widen its target market (a horizontal strategy).
- **Communication strategy:** This strategy is also known as a marketing strategy, and it answers the question: How are you going to reach your customers? Usually some combination of the following works the best: promotions; advertising; public relations; personal selling; and printed materials such as brochures, catalogs, and flyers.
- **Sales strategy:** How do you plan to sell your product or service? Explain the process behind each sale and attach numbers to each step in the process. For example, how many sales calls should a salesperson make in an hour? What is the average dollar amount for each sale? Also, you need to provide information on how many salespeople you plan to have and how you plan to recruit, train, and pay them.

Describe your business's service or product line in the next section. This description may include the following information:

- A list of all the products or services that your business offers
- An explanation of how customers benefit from your product or service
- Marketing materials
- An analysis of the advantages your product or service has over the competition
- Research and development details, including what stage your product is in (such as idea or prototype) and what new products or services you plan to develop
- Supplier information
- Relevant copyright, patent, trade secret, and legal agreement information

Now that you have your readers excited about your business ideas, it's time to talk about money. The next section of the business plan is the funding request. This request answers two main questions:

- How much money do you need? Be specific. Include the amount you need now and the amounts you will need over the next several years to reach your goals. Also specify whether you are looking for an investment or a loan. If you want a loan, specify the interest rate and loan period you want.

- What will you spend the money on? Are you going to buy equipment? Improve facilities? Create a new product? Outline your financial strategies in this section.

In the financials section, you present the numbers to back up your request for funds. Use graphs when you can to show that your business is growing and would make a good investment. This section includes two main parts:

- **Historical financial data:** If you own an existing business, you need to include balance sheets, cash flow statements, and income statements from the past five years.
- **Prospective financial data:** You must include monthly and quarterly projections for the upcoming year and quarterly and annual projections for up to four years after that. These projections include budgets, cash flow statements, balance sheets, and income statements. These numbers should correspond with the amount of money you are asking for. Also, be sure to explain the assumptions you made to get these numbers.

Lastly, you should compile an appendix of all the documents that support the information in the business plan. Not everyone needs to see this information, but you should have it ready for people who need it in order to make lending decisions. This information can include the following:

- Credit history (personal and business)
- Product pictures
- Letters of reference
- Details of market studies
- Relevant magazine articles or book references
- Licenses, permits, or patents
- Legal documents
- Copies of leases
- Building permits
- Contracts
- List of business consultants, including your attorney and accountant

Make sure you keep track of who has copies of your business plan and update it as needed. For more information about business plans and to look at examples, visit the Small Business Administration at www.sba.gov. Also, joining organizations such as DECA (www.deca.org), Future Business Leaders of America (www.fbla.org), or Junior Achievement (www.ja.org) can help you gain entrepreneurial skills.

Staying Safe on the Job

To protect teenage workers, the federal government has made it illegal for teenagers to do hazardous jobs. The jobs that are considered hazardous vary depending how old you are. Chapter 9 listed the jobs that are prohibited for 14- and 15-year-olds. By law, nonagricultural workers who are 16 or 17 cannot

- Drive a motor vehicle as a regular part of the job or operate a forklift at any time.
- Operate many types of powered equipment such as a circular saw, box crusher, meat slicer, or bakery machine.
- Work in wrecking, demolition, excavation, or roofing.

© JIST Works

- Work in mining, in logging, or at a sawmill.
- Work in meat-packing or slaughtering.
- Work where there is exposure to radiation.
- Work where explosives are manufactured or stored.

Even with these laws in place, thousands of teenage workers are injured on the job every year. In Chapter 19, "Achieving Wellness," you learned about some of the reasons for workplace injuries, including violence, substance abuse, and stress. The best way to be safe on the job is to be aware of potential hazards. This section identifies common hazards for teenage workers according to information from the Department of Labor's Occupational Health and Safety Administration (OSHA). For more information on workplace safety, visit OSHA's Web site at www.osha.gov.

What hazards does a typical teen face at work? Different types of work have different hazards:

- **Agricultural work:** Heavy machinery (tractors), unprotected heights (falls), falling or flying objects, natural hazards, electricity, organic dust, confined spaces, chemicals, noise
- **Restaurant work:** Violent crimes, sharp objects (cuts), hot cooking equipment (burns), slippery floors, electricity, heavy lifting
- **Janitorial/maintenance work:** Hazardous cleaning chemicals, slippery floors, heavy lifting, blood on discarded needles, electricity, vehicles
- **Retail/grocery store work:** Violent crime, heavy lifting, box crushers
- **Industrial work:** Machinery, hot equipment (burns), chemicals, electricity
- **Office/clerical work:** Repetitive trauma (from typing), back and neck strain, stress
- **Construction work:** Machines and tools, confined spaces, falls, electricity
- **Outdoor work:** Sun exposure, extreme temperatures, respiratory hazards

The following sections provide more information on the most common hazards.

Heat and Cold

Doing hard physical work in high temperatures, such as in a kitchen or outside in direct sunlight, can lead to heat-related illnesses such as heat exhaustion or the more serious heat stroke. To avoid these illnesses, follow these precautions:

- Dress in breathable fabrics such as cotton. If you are outdoors, wear a hat and sunscreen.
- Drink plenty of water or other low-sugar, caffeine-free, noncarbonated fluids.
- Tell coworkers if you get a headache or nausea. These can be symptoms of heat-related illness.

Cold can also be a hazard for teen workers who have to spend a long amount of time outdoors. The best way to protect yourself from cold-related injuries is to dress in layers and wear a hat and gloves. Also, take breaks in a heated environment.

Ear and Eye Injuries

Noise is another common job hazard. If you have to shout when you talk to a coworker who is standing next to you, the noise level at your workplace may be hurting your ears. Exposure to loud sounds can cause damage to the sensitive hair cells of the inner ear as well as the hearing nerve. Once these structures are damaged, noise-induced hearing loss occurs and cannot be reversed. Symptoms of hearing loss include ringing or buzzing in the ears, muffled sounds, and difficulty understanding speech. (If you are having symptoms of hearing loss, have your hearing tested by a licensed audiologist or have your ears examined by an ear doctor.) Once you have symptoms, permanent damage may have already occurred.

Sound is measured in decibels (dB). Eight hours of hearing noise at 85 decibels could hurt your hearing. At higher sound levels, you could lose hearing in even less time. The following table lists common jobs for teenagers and their related decibel levels.

Noise Levels for Jobs Employing Teen Workers

Job	Noise Source	Typical Decibel Level
Food server	Restaurant activity	70 dB
Cleaner	Vacuum, factory sounds	80 dB
Landscape worker	Lawn mower	90 dB
Agricultural worker	Farm machinery	110 dB

Workplaces where sound levels are an average of 85 decibels or higher for more than eight hours must have programs to save the hearing of workers. These workplaces also must give free hearing protection devices to workers.

To avoid losing your hearing, follow these guidelines:

- Pay attention to the noises around you and turn down the volume whenever possible.
- Use headphones that contain acoustical limiting devices. Headsets that use acoustical limiting devices are designed to provide sufficient protection to keep the noise level below the level that causes ear damage.
- Avoid the continuous use of MP3 players in noisy conditions. (Listeners tend to turn up their players too high in order to overcome the noisy environment and therefore cause hearing damage).
- Avoid or limit time spent in noisy sports events, rock concerts, and clubs.
- Wear adequate hearing protection, such as foam earplugs or earmuffs, when you must be in a noisy environment or when using loud equipment.

Eye injuries also occur often in the workplace. By law, employers must provide eye protection for you whenever you are exposed to potential eye injuries during your work. For example, if you work in a dusty environment or if you are using chemicals, you may need to wear eye protection. If you are required to use eye protection, your employer must also provide training about its use.

Falls, Strains, Cuts, and Burns

Falls can occur in any workplace. Here are some ways to prevent them from happening in yours:

- Wear appropriate shoes for the job or task. Avoid wearing sandals or open toe shoes, high heels, or shoes made out of canvas. They do not provide protection and high heels may promote slip injuries.
- For wet processes, such as mopping floors, wear nonslip overshoe covers.

© JIST Works

- Clean or wipe up spills from floors as soon as possible.
- Keep walkways free from clutter.

Repetitive tasks, such as typing, reaching, bending, and lifting, can lead to strains. Here are some tips to avoid this type of injury:

- Maintain good back posture while working.
- Shift weight from foot to foot when standing and bending for long periods.
- Stand with feet shoulder-width apart, one foot slightly in front of the other.
- When lifting items, keep a straight back and move down to a squatting position using leg muscles.
- Turn feet and arms to reach for objects rather than twisting your back.
- Take frequent stretch breaks to avoid overusing muscles.
- Get help to lift heavy items (over 35 pounds).

Cuts and burns are common injuries in restaurant work. To avoid this type of injury, follow these guidelines:

- Be properly trained to prepare hot items. Understand how to safely use the equipment you will be required to operate.
- Handle, use, and store knives and other sharp utensils safely.
- Cut in the direction away from your body, and keep your fingers and thumbs out of the way of the cutting line.
- Use any protective clothing provided by your employer, such as steel mesh or Kevlar gloves.

Rights and Responsibilities

As an employee, you have the right to

- Work in a safe and healthful workplace.
- Receive safety and health training (in many cases), including information on chemicals that could be harmful to your health.
- Obtain payment for medical care if you get hurt or sick because of your job. You may also be entitled to lost wages.
- Report safety problems to OSHA without being fired.
- Refuse to work if the job is immediately dangerous to your life or health.

Finally, you need to take responsibility for your own safety in the workplace by following these guidelines:

- Follow your employer's safety and health rules and wear or use all required gear and equipment. Working safely may slow you down, but ignoring safe work procedures is a fast track to injury.
- Ask questions! Ask for workplace training if it is not offered. Ask how to deal with irate customers or how to perform a new task or use a new machine. Don't worry about looking ignorant. Asking questions will help you stay safe.

© JIST Works

- Tell your supervisor, boss, parent, or other adult if you feel threatened or endangered at work. If your employer does not address your concerns, report hazardous conditions to OSHA or your state labor offices.
- Keep work areas clean and neat, and be aware of your environment at all times.
- Know what to do in an emergency.
- Be involved in establishing or improving your worksite safety and health program.
- Trust your instincts. If someone asks you to do something that feels unsafe or makes you uncomfortable, check with your supervisor or safety officer before doing the task. Keeping yourself safe is your first responsibility.

© JIST Works

Glossary

A

ability How well you perform specific work tasks.

absolute earnings The amount of goods and services you can buy with your income.

accredited Meeting the standards established by a recognized agency.

accrued Accumulated.

active vocabulary The words you use in your speech or writing.

adapt Fit into.

advertising Promoting the sale of a product or service.

aerobic Oxygen-burning.

aggressive Unfriendly, insulting, domineering, relentless, and quarrelsome.

Americans with Disabilities Act (ADA) Law protecting qualified individuals with a disability from employment discrimination.

antitrust laws Laws that make monopolies illegal.

apathy Indifference.

apprenticeship On-the-job training with an experienced worker.

aptitude A person's potential for success in performing a certain activity.

arbitrator A third-party expert used by business owners and employee groups to solve labor disputes.

Armed Services Vocational Aptitude Battery (ASVAB) A test that measures potential strengths in job-related activities.

assertive Persistent, understanding, and cooperative.

assets What a business owns.

attitude The way you think about things and act toward others

attributes Qualities or characteristics.

authority style of decision-making Relying on parents and other important people to make decisions for you.

avocation A constructive activity that provides you with personal satisfaction.

B

baccalaureate degree A four-year degree in a specific subject, sometimes called a bachelor's degree or an undergraduate degree.

background check An investigation to verify your former employers, schools attended, and personal references.

balance sheet A summary of assets.

bandwidth The amount of information that can be transmitted each second over a communication channel.

bank statement A report from a financial institution that shows the status of a depositor's account.

base pay The regular salary or wage, excluding bonuses, fringe benefits, overtime pay, and all other extra compensation.

blind ads Job listings that provide only a post office box or e-mail address for sending a response.

bond A type of insurance that pays financial losses if an employee fails to perform his or her duty or is guilty of theft.

bounced check A check that is written with insufficient funds in the account.

budget A plan for saving and spending income.

business letter A written document sent to someone outside an organization.

business plan A document that contains detailed information about what a company sells and how it operates.

C

calorie The amount of heat needed to raise the temperature of one gram of water one degree centigrade.

canceled check A check that has been paid by a bank.

cardiorespiratory endurance The ability to deliver oxygen and nutrients to tissues and to remove wastes.

career The paid and unpaid work you do during your lifetime.

career advancement Moving up in an organization.

career philosophy The deliberate involvement of personal beliefs and behaviors in career choices.

cash flow The amount of money available in a business at a specific time.

certificate of deposit (CD) A special type of deposit account with a bank or other financial institution that typically offers a higher rate of interest than a regular savings account.

character Your sense of morality and the ethical code by which you live.

charisma Appealing leadership quality.

check An order written by a depositor directing the bank to pay out money.

check register The place in the checkbook where you record the checks you write.

chronological resume A history of your career.

civic responsibility The rights and privileges enjoyed by all citizens and their duties to the laws and policies of the community, state, and nation in which they live.

Civil Rights Act of 1964 A law protecting workers against discrimination based on sex, race, color, religion, or national origin.

civil service examinations Preemployment tests developed by the federal government for specific government jobs.

classification systems Systematic divisions into groups.

COBRA The Consolidated Omnibus Budget Reconciliation Act of 1985, which enables certain terminated employees or those who lose insurance coverage because of reduced work to buy group insurance coverage for themselves and their families.

collective bargaining The negotiating process used between labor unions and employers.

college majors Special areas of study.

college work study (CWS) programs Part-time campus jobs awarded to students by the financial aid office.

commissions Percentage of sales paid to a salesperson.

communication Sending and receiving messages.

comparative advantage The ability of a producer to provide a good or service at a lower opportunity cost than other producers.

competence Being capable.

competencies Qualifications.

competition Striving against others to win something.

components Parts.

compound interest Interest on the interest.

compromise Each side gives up some of its demands and meets the other side halfway.

computerized career information systems A method for exploring occupations on an extensive database that is updated periodically.

conciliating Bringing others together, pacifying, winning over.

conscience Ideas and feelings within a person that give a sense of right and wrong.

consequences Resulting advantages and disadvantages.

conspicuous consumption The practice of buying products and services to impress others.

consumer A person or group that buys or uses goods or services to satisfy personal needs and wants.

context Statement or situation in which a word is used.

contingent worker Part-time, temporary, contractual, and leased employees.

contradictory Showing an opposite point of view.

cooperative education plans Students are placed on supervised jobs in the field of work for which they are preparing.

corporate culture The thoughts, feelings, manners, and sense of good taste each business or organization develops.

corporation A form of business ownership in which a number of people own and operate the business under a state-issued license or charter.

correspondence courses Home study.

cost-of-living adjustments (COLAs) Pay increases based on an increase in the cost of living.

courtship The process of seeking someone's affections.

cover letter A letter of introduction to a specific employer regarding your interest in a specific job opening.

coworkers People who are employed by the same organization and rely on each other to complete job tasks.

© JIST Works

creative orientation Reacting to social, school, and work situations by using feelings, imagination, and intuition.

credit capacity The amount of debt that you can afford to repay each month.

credit history A record of how you've borrowed and repaid debts.

credit unions A banking service offered only to employees who choose to become members of the service and make savings contributions through payroll deductions.

creditors People who lend money.

cross-cultural competence An understanding of the international business environment, plus the skills and subject knowledge needed to be effective in new situations.

cultural diversity A society with ethnic, religious, racial, and political differences.

culture The way of life in the society in which a person lives.

D

dating The process of having social engagements with a person you are romantically attracted to.

deductions Those items subtracted from your earnings such as taxes, insurance, pensions, and other miscellaneous items.

delay gratification Postpone the acquisition of certain things or the participation in certain activities.

deliberate Carefully considered or thought about.

demand The willingness of consumers to buy goods or services at a certain price in the marketplace.

demographics Vital statistics of the human population.

deposit slip A record of the money put into an account.

deregulation Removing government controls.

detrimental Damaging.

diet The food and drink a person customarily consumes.

digital resume A virtual or electronic job history.

direct compensation Part of the paycheck that provides you with a source of cash.

discharge Dismissal from employment

distinct Easy to recognize.

dominant Most influential.

downsizing Reducing an organization's size to increase efficiency.

drudgery Dull and tedious labor.

drug Any chemical substance that brings about physical, emotional, or mental changes in people.

drug abuse Use of a drug that causes physical, mental, emotional, or social harm to the user or to others.

E

economic system The method a society uses to determine how it will use and distribute available resources.

economics The name of the social science concerned with the way a society uses its productive resources to fulfill the needs and wants of each member.

ego integrity The last life stage, during which a person should feel a sense of involvement and worth.

electronic funds transfer (EFT) A computer-run system that lets consumers, businesses, and governments transfer money from one account to another, also known as electronic banking.

empathizing Sharing another's thoughts and feelings.

empathy The ability to understand another person's feelings and motives.

employment eligibility verification form Known as Form I-9, this document states that a person is eligible to work in the United States.

employment outlook Present and future employment trends.

employment structure Types of jobs available.

employment service Any assistance that helps a job seeker find a job.

endorsement The signature of a payee on the back of a check.

enhance Strengthen or make better.

entrepreneurs People who have ideas, develop plans, and take action to pursue moneymaking opportunities.

entry level The lowest level of experience for the job.

environment Surroundings.

environmental orientation Enjoying outdoor physical activity and having a practical approach to solving problems.

Environmental Protection Agency (EPA) An independent government agency that is responsible for enforcing federal laws and regulations regarding the environment.

equal pay Being paid as much as coworkers in the same position within an occupation.

Equal Pay Act of 1963 Law requiring employers to pay equal wages to men and women doing equal work.

ethics Unwritten rules governing the code of values of a person, an organization, or a society.

etiquette Manners.

exempt Free from the rule.

F

facilitate To encourage or make something easier to accomplish.

facsimile (FAX) machines Devices that transmit and receive images over regular phone lines.

fair employment program A program in which employers actively seek to hire minorities.

Fair Labor Standards Act (FLSA) A law that protects all workers, including minors.

Family and Medical Leave Act of 1993 A law that gives employees 12 weeks of unpaid leave for family care.

fatalistic style of decision making Believing that your decision doesn't change the consequences.

Federal Reserve System A network of 12 regional banks that regulates banking in the United States.

felony A criminal offense that requires a penalty of one year or more in prison.

financial aid The combination of financial resources you can add to the money that you and your family can pay to meet the cost of your postsecondary education.

flexibility The ability to move joints and use muscles through their full range of motion.

flextime A work schedule in which employees set their own hours of work.

fluctuating Irregular, unsteady.

Food and Drug Administration (FDA) Government agency that enforces laws and regulations concerning the purity, quality, and labeling of food, drugs, and cosmetics.

franchise A business that has a legal contract to operate using an established name and method of production.

fraud Something said or done to deceive.

free enterprise system Economic system in which people can own the means of production, use these means as they see fit, and freely create and operate businesses.

fringe benefits Forms of compensation other than salary or wages.

full potential Highest level of productivity.

full-time job A job that provides you with an opportunity to assume adult responsibilities.

functional resume A resume that highlights qualifications, skills, and accomplishments rather than dates and previous jobs.

G

GED General equivalency diploma.

general ledger The principal book of accounts containing the final entries of assets and liabilities.

generativity An adult life stage during which adults are working productively, raising a family and reexamining personal beliefs.

generic Having no trademark.

glass ceiling An artificial barrier based on attitudinal or organizational bias that prevents qualified individuals from advancing into higher management positions.

goal An aim or objective.

goods-producing sector Portion of the economy that includes mining, construction, manufacturing, agriculture, forestry, and fishing.

grievances Differences of opinion over how contract provisions should be interpreted.

gross domestic product (GDP) Total value of goods and services that a nation produces for the marketplace during a specific period of time.

gross earnings Total earnings before deductions.

Guide for Occupational Exploration (GOE) An occupational reference book compiled by the U.S. Department of Labor dividing occupations into 16 interest areas.

guilds Unions of craftsmen.

H

health certificate Document that may certify that you do not have a specific infectious disease or that you are free of certain drugs.

heredity The transmission of physical or mental characteristics from parent to offspring.

hospitalization insurance Insurance that covers hospital room and board, medication, tests, and services.

human relationships The personal connections people develop with others through their thoughts and behaviors.

human resources department Department responsible for recruiting and hiring new employees, administering employee benefits, and handling employee relations.

© JIST Works

I

identified ads Job listings that provide the name of the employer or employment agency and a person or department to contact.

image consultants People who help others project a desired image.

impulsive style of decision making Rarely considering the consequences of decisions.

incentives Extra financial payments for production above a predetermined standard.

income tax A tax based on how much is earned.

industrial products Goods produced for and sold to other producers.

inflection A change in tone or pitch.

InfoNet A U.S. Department of Labor Internet site containing occupational information.

informational interview A brief meeting between a person who wants to investigate a career and a person working in that career.

initiative Readiness and ability to take the first steps in any undertaking.

insider abuse Using knowledge obtained as a result of your position for personal gain.

insurance The act, system, or business of guaranteeing property or a person against loss or harm arising in specified occurrences.

integrate Combine.

interdependence Relying on one another.

interest The amount lenders pay for the use of customers' money.

interest surveys Tests used to measure interests.

interests Preferences you have for specific topics or activities.

intimacy First life stage occurring during the adult years.

introspective ability Skill to examine one's thoughts and feelings.

intuitive style of decision making Basing choices on personal feelings and values rather than facts.

invoice price The automobile manufacturer's initial charge to the dealer.

J

job applicant A person who applies for employment with a specific company.

job application Form to screen out unqualified applicants.

job banks Listings of available positions.

Job Corps A federally administered employment and training program that serves severely disadvantaged young people aged 16 through 24.

job fair A meeting at which several employers distribute information describing their organizations and briefly discuss career opportunities with interested job seekers.

job interview An opportunity for you to present yourself personally to the employer.

job lead Information about an organization that is hiring new employees and the name of the person who is responsible for hiring.

job market The type and number of jobs available.

job offer A specific offer of employment.

job orientation Meetings and activities to acquaint you with the employer's purpose and organization.

job search The process of seeking employment.

job security Protection against loss of employment and earnings.

journey worker Certified, experienced, skilled craftsperson who has successfully completed an apprenticeship.

L

labor unions Organizations that represent workers in negotiations regarding employee rights.

laws A body of rules that a community recognizes as binding on its citizens.

layoff An involuntary separation of an employee from an employer for a temporary or indefinite period.

lease A contract that involves a financial commitment for a specific period of time.

legitimate absence When an employee misses work for a reason that is acceptable to the employer.

leisure time Time free from your everyday job responsibilities.

liabilities What a business owes.

liability coverage Insurance that pays for bodily injuries, property damages, and medical expenses for others when you are at fault in a car accident.

life experiences significant events in a person's life that affect his or her actions and attitudes.

lifestyle The way you live.

limited resources Natural resources, labor, capital, and management.

line of progression Steps that employees follow from lower- to higher-level positions.

love Deep affection.

M

mandated Required.

market A group of people or organizations that purchase a particular good or service.

materialistic An objective that has monetary worth.

maternity leave A disability leave granted to women as a result of pregnancy and/or childbirth.

mechanical orientation Preferring work involving machines, tools, and logic.

media Newspapers, magazines, television, Internet, and radio.

memorandums Short written communication within a company.

mentor A trusted advisor.

merger The joining together of organizations.

merit increases Increases in a worker's pay rate based on management's performance appraisal.

merit rating A formal, periodic, written evaluation of your job performance.

methodical Systematic, orderly.

minimum wage The lowest hourly payment an employer may pay for certain types of work.

mission statement A broad and specific statement used by many employers as a guideline to define the organization and inspire employees.

mommy track A woman changing her work schedule to accommodate her young child or children.

monitor Check for accuracy.

monopolies Businesses with no competition.

Monroney sticker Label which is affixed to the window of a new car.

moonlighting Working two jobs.

morale Level of enthusiasm.

muscular endurance The ability of a muscle or a group of muscles to sustain repeated contractions or to continue applying force against a fixed object.

muscular strength The ability of a muscle to exert force for a brief time.

N

National Labor Relations Board (NLRB) An independent federal agency established in 1935 to administer the National Labor Relations Act (NLRA), the nation's principal labor relations law.

negative attitudes Complaining and using sarcasm.

negotiation Bargaining by persuasion rather than argument.

net pay The amount an employee receives after deductions.

net worth The difference between assets and liabilities.

networking Using personal contacts to find a job.

noncustodial parent The parent who does not have primary custody of the child but who has a responsibility for financial support.

nonmaterialistic An objective that provides inner satisfaction.

nonprofits Organizations not intending to earn a profit for their members or owners.

nontraditional occupations Those in which women or men comprise 25 percent or less of the workforce.

nonverbal communication Facial expressions and body language.

North American Industrial Classification System (NAICS) A system that standardizes the classification of businesses in Canada, the United States, and Mexico.

nutrients Nourishment.

nutritional labeling Information on a food package, including serving size and vitamins in the food.

O

Occupational Information Network (O*NET) An automated database system for collecting, classifying, and circulating data on U.S. jobs.

Occupational Outlook Handbook (OOH) An easy-to-read reference book updated by the U.S. Department of Labor every two years.

Occupational Safety and Health Administration (OSHA) A government agency responsible for safety and health in the workplace.

offshore Not on the U.S. mainland.

on-the-job training (OJT) A wide range of education provided by employers for their employees.

© JIST Works

open-admissions policy Applicants are accepted without regard to grade point average, test scores, or class rank.

open-ended credit A loan made on a continuous basis for the purchase of products up to a specific dollar amount.

opportunity cost Resources or benefits given up by the business to produce a product.

ordinances Laws, edicts, or decrees enacted by a municipal government for local application.

orientation period The first few weeks and months on a new job.

outplacement programs Programs that provide assistance and training to released employees who are seeking new positions.

outsourcing Employer practice of purchasing parts or finished goods from domestic nonunion shops or from foreign companies.

P

paraphrasing Repeating the speaker's ideas or thoughts in your own words.

parenting leave Time taken off work when a child is born or adopted.

partnership A form of business ownership in which two or three people own and operate the business.

pediatrician A physician who specializes in children's medical care and diseases.

Pell Grant Money given by the federal government for students based on the student's financial needs.

pension plans Plans that provide regular lifetime payments to retired employees.

Perkins Loan A student loan with a low rate of interest that is funded by the federal government.

permit An official certificate of permission that allows a business to operate.

personal appearance The way you look to others.

personal characteristics Qualities that make an individual unique.

personal data sheet A list of information that employers will ask for on a job application.

personal orientation A unique individual direction.

personality The relationship that exists between all of a person's psychological parts.

personality trait A personality characteristic that can be measured.

persuasive orientation Enjoying involvement with people more than information or things and making decisions based on facts and goals.

philosophy The study of the meaning of aspects of life.

physical coverage Car insurance to pay for damage to your vehicle caused by collision, fire, or theft.

piecework Payment based on the amount the worker produces.

pink slip Notice of termination.

polarization of issues Seeing one side as completely right or wrong.

policies and procedures Rules established to serve an organization's unique needs, purpose, and management system.

population density The number of persons per square mile of land.

positive attitudes Expressing interest and enthusiasm.

postsecondary After high school.

preconceived beliefs opinions formed beforehand.

preemployment test A test to determine how well an applicant is likely to perform in a certain area of work.

Pregnancy Discrimination Act of 1978 A law prohibiting companies with 15 or more employees from discrimination because of pregnancy.

prejudice An attitude that refuses to change regardless of new contradictory information or experiences.

premium An insurance policyholder's payment.

premium pay Compensation at greater than regular rates.

preprofessional programs Course of study that satisfies the admissions requirements for a specific professional school as part of the baccalaureate degree.

price fixing Agreements between competitors to establish specific price ranges for their products or services.

probationary period Specific amount of time in which you prove your ability to perform the job.

problem solving The process used to make decisions when you select from two or more possible choices.

production flexibility Ability to respond quickly to production demands.

profit Money that is left over after all of the expenses are paid.

profit sharing A bonus based on a percentage of the organization's profits.

profit-and-loss statement A detailed, month-by-month record of income obtained from sales and expenses incurred to produce sales.

promotional sales Temporary price reductions on regular merchandise.

property tax Taxes paid by citizens.

proprietary school A school that is privately owned and is operated for profit.

prudent Wise, shrewd, frugal.

Q

quality circle Employees from the same department who work as a group to solve product problems.

R

rational style of decision making Considering the feelings and values of the decision maker as well as the facts concerning the situation.

realistic Obtainable.

recognition vocabulary The words you understand when you read them or hear them spoken.

Recommended Daily Allowances (RDAs) Specific nutritional standards established by the Food and Nutrition Board of the National Academy of Sciences.

reference groups People to whom you compare yourself.

references People who have agreed to provide an employer with a statement about your character or ability.

relative earnings The amount of goods and services you can buy with your income compared with what your neighbors can buy with theirs.

resume A written summary of a job seeker's employment objectives, work experience, education and training, proven skills, and personal information.

resume bank A database that job seekers can use to post their digital resume.

revenue Income.

S

salary Pay received by employees.

savings account A bank account that pays interest to customers in return for the use of their money.

scarcity When people have limited resources compared to their wants.

scheduled breaks Rest periods that employers provide so employees can take time out from the workday to relax.

scientific orientation Using intellect to solve problems.

screening interview A preliminary meeting to eliminate unqualified candidates.

security deposit Money you entrust with the landlord to cover any damage you cause to the rental unit.

self That part of your experience that you regard as essentially you

self-concept How a person views his or her own skills, interests, and competence level.

self-esteem Personal evaluation.

self-fulfilling prophesy An act or interpretation of events in a way that causes your beliefs to be reinforced.

seniority Length of time spent with a company.

services Tasks that other people or machines perform that cannot be physically weighed or measured.

services-producing sector The part of the economy that includes health services; transportation; public utilities; wholesale and retail trade; finance, insurance, and real estate; and government.

severance pay A lump-sum payment in exchange for quitting or retiring from a job.

sexual harassment Unwanted sexual attention at work between members of the same or the opposite sex.

Small Business Administration (SBA) A government agency that aids, counsels, and assists all the interests of small businesses.

sociable orientation Focusing on those who need help or counseling and using emotion and concern for others as a basis for decisions.

social anonymity Lacking individuality.

social environment The people you frequently come in contact with.

Social Security Act The federal law established a tax-sponsored pension and disability insurance plan.

social self Your involvement with other people and your view of what they think about you.

sole proprietorship A form of business ownership in which the same person is both the owner and a worker.

sound financial management Getting the most for your money through planned control of your earnings, savings, and spending.

spam Unsolicited commercial e-mail.

© JIST Works

spatial perception Recognizing forms in space and the relationships of plane and solid objects.

staff A group of employees who work for and with someone in charge.

Standard Occupational Classification (SOC) A system that groups occupations according to the type of work performed.

start-up period The time when a business is beginning.

stress Mental or physical tension or strain.

strike A temporary stoppage of work by a group of workers.

structured orientation The direction that describes people who tend to select educational and career goals that are approved by society.

student-faculty ratio The number of professional staff members compared to the number of students.

submissive Apologetic, indifferent, passive, and yielding.

subordinate An employee who follows someone else's orders.

success A favorable result or a hoped-for ending.

superior A person who has the authority to give orders to another person.

supply The willingness of producers to produce and sell goods or services at a certain price in the marketplace.

surgical insurance Insurance that covers specific expenses related to specific operations.

T

tangible Anything you can touch.

target market The group of consumers who would most likely purchase certain goods or services.

taxes Payments that all citizens are required by law to make to help pay the costs of government services.

team adviser A supervisor in a team-oriented management system.

tech-prep program A cooperative program that links high school technical education with two- and four-year college programs.

technical school A school that focuses on training students in fields related to engineering and the physical sciences.

technology The science of mechanical and industrial arts.

telecommuting Working at home for all or part of normally scheduled hours.

temperament refers to the way you usually act, feel, and think in certain situations

temporary employment service An agency that "rents" employees to employers.

tenant Person paying rent for the temporary use of another person's building or land.

tentative Trial or temporary testing to help make a decision.

three o'clock syndrome The time during the workday when parents' thoughts turn to their children who are getting out of school.

time management Planning to make the best use of your time.

timeline Schedule.

training manuals Handbooks detailing the use or repair of equipment or describing procedures to follow on the job.

transcript A record of your academic credits earned, grades, attendance, standardized test scores, and extracurricular activities

U

U.S. Constitution The highest law in the United States.

underemployed Overqualified for the job.

unemployed Without a job and looking for work

unemployment insurance A joint federal-state program under which state-administered funds pay a weekly benefit for a limited time to eligible workers when they are involuntarily unemployed.

unit price The cost of one standard measure of a product.

university The largest type of institution of higher learning.

unprecedented Unheard of, novel.

urban area A community of 2,500 or more.

U.S. Department of Education (USED) career clusters Sixteen broad categories defined by the U.S. Department of Education that encompass virtually all occupations from entry through professional levels.

© JIST Works

V

valid True and supported by facts.

values Cherished ideas and beliefs.

variety A periodic change in the task, the pace, or the location of work.

venture capital Money invested in new businesses.

venture capitalists People who earn money by making high-risk business loans.

videoconferencing and desktop videoconferencing Technology enabling distant participants and coworkers to conduct face-to-face meetings.

volunteer work A contribution of free labor.

W

wages Employee compensation calculated hourly.

warranty A guarantee that the product is of a certain quality or that the defective parts will be replaced.

whistle-blowing Employees reporting wasteful or dishonest company activities to the government.

work environments Settings in which you complete job tasks.

work ethic Belief that through hard work individuals make their own success.

work permit A document that is necessary for employees under 18 in most nonfarm jobs

workaholics Compulsive workers who are overly involved in their jobs.

workers' compensation laws Laws that provide for payments to injured workers.

working capital Money required to meet the ongoing expenses of a business.

working with data Analyzing and using verbal or numerical information.

working with people Job tasks concerned with human relations

working with things Using tools, instruments, or machines.

workshops Short courses that involve a small group of employees.

World Wide Web A multimedia information storage system linking resources around the world.

© JIST Works

Index

© JIST Works

© JIST Works

D

© JIST Works

E

F

© JIST Works

G

H

I

J

© JIST Works

K

L

M

N

© JIST Works

O

P

© JIST Works

Q

R

S

 © JIST Works

T

U

V

© JIST Works

W

X–Z

 © JIST Works